Fodor's Fourth Edition

Europe's Great Cities

The complete guide, thoroughly up-to-date

Packed with details that will make your trip

What to see, what to skip

City strolls all around town

Smart lodging and dining options

Transportation tips and directions

Key contacts, savvy travel tips

Clear, accurate, easy-to-use maps

Excerpted from *Fodor's Europe*

Fodor's Travel Publications • New York, Toronto, London, Sydney, Auckland
www.fodors.com

Fodor's Europe's Great Cities

EDITOR: Nuha Ansari, David Cashion, Sharron Wood

Editorial Contributors: Leslie Adler, Nicola Keegan Behar, Muriel Bolger, Jacqueline Brown, Linda Cabasin, Roland Chambers, Christine Cipriani, Bonnie Dodson, Charles Ferro, Robert Fisher, Aoife Fitzpatrick, Katrin Gygax, Valerie Hamilton, Simon Hewitt, Anto Howard, Rosa Jackson, Raymond Johnston, Nancy Kapstein, Christina Knight, Carla Lionello, Matthew Lombardi, Andrew May, Orna Mulcahy, Lauren Myers, Dan Navid, Heather O'Brian, Tim Perry, Ian Phillips, Patricia Rucidlo, Jürgen Scheunemann, Helayne Schiff, Ted Shoemaker, George Semler, Jonette Stabbert, Melia Tatakis, Julie Tomasz, Alex Wijeratna

Editorial Production: Kristin Milavec

Maps: David Lindroth, *cartographer;* Rebecca Baer and Robert Blake, *map editors*

Design: Fabrizio La Rocca, *creative director;* Guido Caroti, *art director;* Jolie Novak, *senior picture editor;* Melanie Marin, *photo editor*

Cover Design: Pentagram

Production/Manufacturing: Robert B. Shields

Cover Photograph: Tibor Bognar/Corbis Stock Market

Copyright

Fourth Edition

ISBN 0–679–00882–9

ISSN 1074–1216

Important Tip

Although all prices, opening times, and other details in this book are based on information supplied to us at press time, changes occur all the time in the travel world, and Fodor's cannot accept responsibility for facts that become outdated or for inadvertent errors or omissions. So **always confirm information when it matters,** especially if you're making a detour to visit a specific place.

Special Sales

Fodor's Travel Publications are available at special discounts for bulk purchases for sales promotions or premiums. Special editions, including personalized covers, excerpts of existing guides, and corporate imprints, can be created in large quantities for special needs. For more information, contact your local bookseller or write to Special Markets, Fodor's Travel Publications, 280 Park Avenue, New York, NY 10017. Inquiries from Canada should be directed to your local Canadian bookseller or sent to Random House of Canada, Ltd., Marketing Department, 2775 Matheson Boulevard East, Mississauga, Ontario L4W 4P7. Inquiries from the United Kingdom should be sent to Fodor's Travel Publications, 20 Vauxhall Bridge Road, London SW1V 2SA, England.

PRINTED IN THE UNITED STATES OF AMERICA

10 9 8 7 6 5 4 3 2 1

CONTENTS

Italic entries are maps.

On the Road with Fodor's — v
Europe vi–vii

Smart Travel Tips A to Z — viii

1 Amsterdam — 1
Amsterdam 2–3

2 Athens — 21
Athens (Athina) 24–25

3 Barcelona — 44
Barcelona 46–47

4 Berlin — 64
Western Berlin 66–67
Historic Berlin 70

5 Brussels — 81
Brussels (Bruxelles) 84–85

6 Budapest — 97
Budapest 100–101

7 Copenhagen — 117
Copenhagen (København) 118–119

8 Dublin — 134
Dublin 136–137

9 Florence — 154
Florence (Firenze) 156–157

10 London — 171
London 172–173
Greenwich 187

11 Madrid — 207
Madrid 208–209

12 Paris — 227
Paris 230–231

ON THE ROAD WITH FODOR'S

THE MORE YOU KNOW before you go, the better your trip will be. Europe's most fascinating small museum or its most exciting store or wonderful restaurant could be just around the corner from your hotel, but if you don't know it's there, it might as well be on the other side of the globe. That's where this book comes in. It's a great step toward making sure your next trip lives up to your expectations. As you plan, check out the Web as well. Guidebooks have been helping smart travelers find the special places for years; the Web is one more tool. Whatever reference you consult, be savvy about what you read, and always consider the source. Images and language can be massaged to make places appear better than they are. And one traveler's quaint is another's grimy. Here at Fodor's, and at our on-line arm, Fodors.com, our focus is on providing you with information that's not only useful but accurate and on target. Every day Fodor's editors put enormous effort into getting things right, beginning with the search for the right contributors—people who have ob-

jective judgment, broad travel experience, and the writing ability to put their insights into words. There's no substitute for advice from a like-minded friend who has just come back from where you're going, but our writers, having seen all corners of Europe, are the next best thing. They're the kind of people you'd poll for tips yourself if you knew them.

Don't Forget to Write

Your experiences—positive and negative— matter to us. If we have missed or misstated something, we want to hear about it. We follow up on all suggestions. Contact the Europe editor at editors@fodors.com or c/o Fodor's, 280 Park Avenue, New York, New York 10017. And have a fabulous trip!

Karen Cure
Editorial Director

ICELAND
★ Reykjavik

NORWAY
Bergen

SCOTLAND
Edinburgh

North Sea

Skagerrak

NORTHERN IRELAND
Belfast

IRELAND
Irish Sea
Dublin

UNITED KINGDOM

WALES

DENMARK

Hamburg

NETHERLANDS
Amsterdam

The Hague
Rotterdam

GERM

Cardiff

ENGLAND

London

English Channel

Brussels
BELGIUM

Bonn

Frankfurt

ATLANTIC OCEAN

Paris
LUXEMBOURG

F R A N C E

Zürich
Bern
SWITZERLAND

Munich

LIECHTENSTEIN

Lyon

Milan

Venice

Monte Carlo
Nice
MONACO

Marseille

PORTUGAL

Madrid

ANDORRA

Barcelona

Florence

Corsica

Lisbon

S P A I N

Sardinia

Balearic Islands

Tyrrhenia

Seville

Granada

Mediterranean Sea

Gibraltar

MOROCCO

ALGERIA

0 ———— 400 miles

0 ———— 600 km

TUNISIA

ESSENTIAL INFORMATION

AIR TRAVEL

Before booking, **compare different modes of transportation.** Many city pairs are so close together that flying hardly makes sense. For instance, it may take just half an hour to fly between London and Paris, but you must factor in time spent getting to and from the airports, plus check-in time. A 3-hour train ride from city center to city center seems a better alternative. It makes sense to **save air travel for longer distances.**

If you're flying so-called **national carriers,** full-fare tickets often remain the only kind available for one-way trips and restriction-free round-trips, and they are prohibitively expensive for most leisure travelers. On most European flights, your choice is between Business Class (which is what you get when paying full fare) and Economy (coach). Some flights are all Economy. First Class has ceased to exist in Europe. The most reasonable fares have long been nonrefundable and nontransferable round-trips (APEX fares), which require a Saturday night at the destination. But the near-monopoly that used to be enjoyed by these airlines is crumbling, and they have had to start offering less restrictive fares. Check before you fly.

Some national carriers reward transatlantic passengers with fixed-price flight coupons (priced at $100–$120) to destinations from their respective hubs and/or domestic or area air passes. These must be bought before leaving home. If you're young, **ask about youth stand-by fares,** which are available on a number of domestic and some international services.

Over the last few years, a substantial number of local airlines have been created to provide feeder services to major hubs and services between secondary city pairs. Do not, however, expect rock-bottom prices. **Seek advice from local branches of international travel agencies** like American Express or Carlson/Wagonlit.

Low-cost no-frills airlines base their fares on one-way travel, and a return ticket is simply twice the price. Advertised fares are always preceded by the word "from." To get the lowest fare, book two weeks ahead of time; it also helps to be flexible about your date of travel. In general, you have to book directly by calling the airline, credit card in hand. Some also accept reservations by fax. Reservation via Internet is available with companies such as the SABRE-powered Travelocity (www.travelocity.com) and Microsoft's Expedia (www.expedia.com). You can make secure payments via the Net and hunt the cheapest flight deals, as well as reserve hotels. You get a reservation number and pick up your boarding pass at the airport. Note that some flights use relatively distant secondary airports.

ARRIVALS

Passport control has become a perfunctory affair within most of the European Union (EU). The nine signatories to the Schengen Agreement (Austria, Belgium, France, Germany, Italy, Luxembourg, the Netherlands, Portugal, and Spain) have abolished passport controls for travelers between countries in that area, but individual countries can temporarily suspend it.

The most notable exception is Great Britain; when a number of flights from the U.S. arrive at Heathrow or Gatwick close together in the morning, **be prepared for a longish wait** (though rarely as long as Europeans have to wait at JFK in New York).

The Green Channel/Red Channel customs system in operation at most Western European airports and other borders is basically an honor system. If you have nothing to declare, walk through the Green Channel, where there are only spot luggage checks; if in doubt, go through the Red Channel. If you fly between two EU-member countries, go through the new **Blue Channel,** where there are no customs officers except the one who glances at baggage labels to make sure only people off EU flights get through. On average, you need to **count on at least half an hour from deplaning to getting out of the airport.**

BOOKING

When you book, **look for nonstop flights** and **remember that "direct" flights stop at least once.** Try to avoid connecting flights, which require a change of plane. For more booking tips and to check prices and make online flight reservations, log on to www.fodors.com.

CARRIERS

➤ U.S. AIRLINES: **American** (☎ 800/433–7300 in the U.S.; 0345/789–789 in the U.K., WEB www.aa.com). **Continental** (☎ 800/525–0280 in the U.S.; 0800/776–464 in the U.K., WEB www.continental.com). **Delta** (☎ 800/221–1212 in the U.S.; 0800/414–767 in the U.K., WEB www.delta.com). **Northwest** (☎ 800/225–2525 in the U.S.; c/o alliance partner KLM, call 0990/750–9000 in the U.K., WEB www.klm.com). **TWA** (☎ 800/221–2000 in the U.S.; 0845/733–3333 or 020/8814–0707 in the U.K., WEB www.twa.com). **United** (☎ 800/538–2929 in the U.S.; 0845/844–4777 in the U.K., WEB www.unitedairlines.com). **US Airways** (☎ 800/428–4322 in the U.S.; 0800/783–5556 in the U.K., WEB www.usairways.com).

➤ EUROPEAN AIRLINES: Austria: **Austrian Airlines** (☎ 800/843–0002 in the U.S.; 020/7434–7373 in the U.K., WEB www.aua.com). Belgium: **Sabena Belgian World Airlines** (☎ 800/955–2000 in the U.S.; 020/7494–2629 in the U.K., WEB www.sabena-usa.com). The Czech Republic and Slovakia: **Czech Airlines** (CSA, ☎ 212/765–6022 in the U.S.; 020/7255–1898 in the U.K., WEB www.csa.cz). Denmark: **Scandinavian Airlines** (SAS, ☎ 800/221–2350 in the U.S.; 0845/600–7767 in the U.K., WEB www.flysas.com).

France: **Air France** (☎ 800/237–2747 in the U.S.; 0845/084–5111 in the U.K., WEB www.airfrance.com). Germany: **LTU International Airways** (☎ 800/888–0200 in the U.S., www.ltu.com). **Lufthansa** (☎ 800/645–3880 in the U.S.; 0345/737–747 in the U.K., WEB www.lufthansa.com). Great Britain: **British Airways** (☎ 800/247–9297 in the U.S.; 0345/222–111 in the U.K., WEB www.british-airways.com). **Virgin Atlantic** (☎ 800/862–8621 in the U.S.; 0129/3747–747 in the U.K., WEB www.virgin-atlantic.com). Greece: **Olympic Airways** (☎ 800/223–1226 in the U.S.; 0870/606–0460 in the U.K., WEB www.oa-airways.com). Hungary: **Malév Hungarian Airlines** (☎ 212/757–6446; 800/223–6884 outside NY in the U.S., WEB www.baxter.net/malev). Ireland: **Aer Lingus** (☎ 888/474–7424 or 800/223–6537 in the U.S.; 01631/577–5700 in the U.K., WEB www.aerlingus.com). Italy: **Alitalia** (☎ 800/223–5730 in the U.S.; 020/8745–8200 in the U.K., WEB www.alitalia.it). The Netherlands: **KLM Royal Dutch Airlines** (☎ 800/447–4747 in the U.S.; 0990/750–900 in the U.K., WEB www.klm.com). Norway: **SAS** (☎ 800/221–2350 in the U.S.; 0845/600–7767 in the U.K., WEB www.flysas.com). Spain: **Iberia Airlines** (☎ 800/772–4642 in the U.S.; 020/7830–0011 in the U.K., WEB www.iberia.es). Switzerland: **Swissair** (☎ 800/221–4750 in the U.S.; 020/7494–2629 in the U.K., WEB www.swissair.com).

➤ FROM CANADA: **Air Canada** (☎ 888/247–2262, WEB www.aircanada.com). **Air Transat** (☎ 877/872–6728, WEB www.airtransat.com).

➤ FROM THE U.K.: **British Airways** (✉ 156 Regent St., London W1R 5TA, ☎ 0345/222–111, WEB www.britishairways.com). **British Midland** (☎ 0870/607–0555, WEB www.british-midland.com). **EasyJet** (☎ 0870/600–0000, WEB www.easyjet.com). **KLM U.K.** (☎ 0870/507–4074, WEB www.klm.com). **Ryanair** (☎ 0541/569–569, WEB www.ryanair.com). **Virgin Express** (☎ 0800/891–199, WEB www.virgin-express.com).

➤ FROM AUSTRALIA: **Qantas Airways** (☎ 13–12–11 in Australia; 020/

7497–2571 in the U.K., WEB www.
qantas.com).

➤ FROM IRELAND: **Aer Lingus**
(☎ 01/705–3333 in Ireland; 01631/
577–5700 in the U.K., WEB www.
aerlingus.com).

➤ FROM NEW ZEALAND: **Air New
Zealand** (☎ 09/3362–4242 or 0800/
737–000 in New Zealand; 020/8741–
2299 in the U.K., WEB www.
airnewzealand.com).

➤ NO-FRILLS CARRIER RESERVATIONS
WITHIN EUROPE: Belgium: **Virgin
Express** (☎ 2/752–0505; 0800/
891–199 in the U.K., WEB www.
virgin-express.com) from Brussels
to Rome, Madrid, Barcelona,
Copenhagen, and London (Gatwick,
Heathrow, Stansted); from Rome to
Barcelona and Madrid; from London
(Stansted) to Berlin and Shannon.
Ireland: **Ryanair** (☎ 01/609–7800 in
Ireland; 0541/569–569 in the U.K.,
FAX 0541/565–579 in the U.K., WEB
www.ryanair.com) from Dublin to 12
U.K. destinations, to Paris (Beauvais)
and Brussels (Charleroi); from Lon-
don (Stansted, Luton, and Gatwick)
to Dublin; from London (Stansted) to
four other Irish destinations, five
French destinations, four Scandina-
vian destinations, six Italian destina-
tions, and Frankfurt. United
Kingdom: **Buzz** (☎ 0870/240–7070,
WEB www.buzzaway.com) from Lon-
don (Stansted) to Berlin, Paris, and
Vienna. **EasyJet** (☎ 0870/6000–000,
WEB www.easyjet.com) from London
(Luton) to Amsterdam, Barcelona,
Madrid; from London (Luton) to
Athens and Zurich; from Geneva to
Amsterdam, Barcelona, and London
(Luton, Gatwick, and Stansted). **Go**
(☎ 0845/605–4321, WEB www.
go-fly.com) from London (Stansted)
to Copenhagen, Edinburgh, Prague,
Zurich, and four Italian destinations.

CHECK-IN & BOARDING

Always **bring a government-issued
photo I.D. to the airport;** even when
it's not required, a passport is best.

CUTTING COSTS

The least expensive airfares to Europe
must usually be purchased in advance
and are non-refundable. It's smart to
call a number of airlines, and when
you are quoted a good price, **book it
on the spot**—the same fare may not
be available the next day. Always
check different routings and look
into using different airports. Travel
agents, especially low-fare specialists
(☞ Discounts & Deals), are helpful.

Consolidators are another good
source. They buy tickets for scheduled
international flights at reduced rates
from the airlines, then sell them at
prices that beat the best fare available
directly from the airlines, usually
without restrictions. Sometimes you
can even get your money back if you
need to return the ticket. Carefully
read the fine print detailing penalties
for changes and cancellations, and
**confirm your consolidator reservation
with the airline.**

When you **fly as a courier,** you trade
your checked-luggage space for a
ticket deeply subsidized by a courier
service. There are restrictions on
when you can book and how long
you can stay.

**Ask your airline about purchasing
discount passes** for intra-European
flights before you leave the United
States to save significantly on travel
between European cities. If you're
going to be covering a lot of ground,
consider Europebyair.com, which sells
intra-European flights to more than
150 cities for $99 per segment. They
also offer unlimited flight passes good
for 15 or 21 days.

➤ CONSOLIDATORS: **Cheap Tickets**
(☎ 800/377–1000).**Discount Airline
Ticket Service** (☎ 800/576–1600).
Unitravel (☎ 800/325–2222). **Up &
Away Travel** (☎ 212/889–2345).
World Travel Network (☎ 800/409–
6753).

➤ COURIERS: **Air Courier Association**
(✉ 15000 W. 6th Ave., Suite 203,
Golden, CO 80401, ☎ 800/282–
1202, WEB www.aircourier.org).
**International Association of Air
Travel Couriers** (✉ 220 S. Dixie
Hwy. #3, Box 1349, Lake Worth, FL,
33460, ☎ 561/582–8320, FAX 561/
582–1581, WEB www.courier.org).
Now Voyager Travel (✉ 74 Varick
St., Suite 307, New York, NY 10013,
☎ 212/431–1616, FAX 212/219–1753
or 212/334–5243, WEB www.
nowvoyagertravel.com).

➤ DISCOUNT PASSES: **Europebyair.com** (☎ 888/387–2479, WEB www. europebyair.com).

FLYING TIMES

Flights from New York to London take about 6½ hours, to Paris 7½ hours, and to Rome 8½ hours. From Sydney to London, flights take about 23 hours via Bangkok, to Paris 22¾ hours via Singapore, to Frankfurt 22 hours via Singapore, and to Rome 25 hours via Bangkok.

HOW TO COMPLAIN

If your baggage goes astray or your flight goes awry, complain right away. Most carriers require that you **file a claim immediately.**

➤ AIRLINE COMPLAINTS: U.S. Department of Transportation **Aviation Consumer Protection Division** (✉ C-75, Room 4107, Washington, DC 20590, ☎ 202/366–2220, WEB www.dot.gov/airconsumer). **Federal Aviation Administration Consumer Hotline** (☎ 800/322–7873).

RECONFIRMING

Depending on the airline or on whether your ticket was bought through a consolidator, you may have to reconfirm your flights a specified number of hours before departure. **Check with your travel agent or airline** when you buy your ticket.

AIRPORTS

See A to Z sections *in* city chapters.

DUTY-FREE SHOPPING

Duty-free shopping was eliminated for travelers between EU countries as of July 1, 1999. However, duty-free shopping still applies in non-EU countries, and tax-free shopping is available for tourists returning to non-EU countries from the EU. If you're looking for good deals associated with duty-free airport shopping, **check out liquor and beauty products,** although prices vary considerably. The amount of liquor you may buy is restricted, generally to two bottles.

Some airport concourses, notably in Amsterdam, Copenhagen, and Shannon, have practically been transformed into shopping malls, selling everything from electronics and chocolates to fashion and furs. These are tax-free rather than duty-free shops; if this is your last stop before leaving the EU, there's no VAT and you can **avoid the tax-refund rigmarole** (☞ Taxes).

BOAT & FERRY TRAVEL

Ferry routes for passengers and vehicles link the countries surrounding the North Sea, the Irish Sea, and the Baltic Sea; Italy with Greece; and Spain, France, Italy, and Greece with their respective islands in the Mediterranean. Longer ferry routes—between, for instance, Britain and Spain or Scandinavia—can help you **reduce the amount of driving and often save time.** A number of modern ships offer improved comfort and entertainment ranging from one-armed bandits to gourmet dining.

FARES & SCHEDULES

See individual city chapters, or contact operators for specific information on fares and schedules.

➤ BOAT & FERRY INFORMATION: Ferry operators between the British Isles and the Continent include **Brittany Ferries** (✉ Millbay Docks, Plymouth PL1 3EW, ☎ 0870/900–9746, WEB www.brittanyferries.com) from Plymouth to Roscoff (Brittany) and Santander (Spain), from Poole to Cherbourg, and from Portsmouth to Caen and St. Malo; **DFDS Seaways** (✉ Scandinavia House, Parkeston Quay, Harwich, Essex CO12 4QG, ☎ 0990/333–000 or 0125/524–0240; 800/533–3755 in the U.S., WEB www.dfdsseaways.com), from Harwich to Esbjerg (Denmark), Hamburg, and Gothenburg and from Newcastle-upon-Tyne to IJmuiden, 20 mi west of Amsterdam and (summer season) to Gothenburg and Hamburg; **Fjord Line** (✉ International Ferry Terminal, Royal Quays, North Shields NE29 6EE, ☎ 0191/296–1313), from Newcastle to Bergen/Stavanger/Haugesund (Norway); **Hoverspeed** (✉ International Hoverport, Marine Parade, Dover, Kent CT17 9TG, ☎ 0870/240–8070 or 0990/240–241, WEB www.hoverspeed.com), Dover–Calais, Dover–Oostende, Folkestone–Boulogne, and Newhaven–Dieppe;

Irish Ferries (⊠ Reliance House, Water St., Liverpool L2 8TP, ☎ 0990/ 171–717, WEB www.irishferries.ie), Holyhead–Dublin and Pembroke–Rosslare; also Rosslare (Ireland; reservations 01/638–3333) to Cherbourg, and Roscoff; **P&O European Ferries** (⊠ Peninsular House, Wharf Rd., Portsmouth, PO2 8TA, ☎ 0870/ 242–4999, WEB www.poef.com) sails Portsmouth to Cherbourg, Le Havre, and Bilbao (Spain), and Cairnyarn (Scotland)–Larne (Belfast); **P&O North Sea Ferries** (⊠ King George Dock, Hedon Rd., Hull HU9 5QA, ☎ 0148/237–7177, WEB www.ponsf. com), from Hull to Rotterdam and Zeebrugge; **P&O Stena Line** (⊠ Channel House, Channel View Rd., Dover, Kent CT17 9TJ, ☎ 0870/600–0600 or 0130/486–4003, WEB www. posl.com), Dover–Calais; **SeaFrance** (⊠ Eastern Docks, Dover, Kent CT16 1JA, ☎ 0870/571–1711 or 0130/ 421–2696, WEB www.seafrance.co.uk), Dover–Calais; **Stena Line** (⊠ Charter House, Park St., Ashford, Kent TN24 8EX, ☎ 0990/707–070 or 0123/364–7022, WEB www.stenaline.co.uk), Harwich–Hook of Holland, Holyhead–Dun Laoghaire (Dublin), Fishguard–Rosslare, and Stranraer (Scotland)–Belfast; and **Swansea Cork Ferries** (⊠ Harbour Office, Kings Dock, Swansea SA1 1SF, ☎ 01792/ 456–116, WEB www.commerce.ie/cs/ scf), Swansea–Cork (mid-Mar.–early Nov.).

BUS TRAVEL

International bus travel is rapidly expanding in Europe, thanks to changing EU rules and the Channel Tunnel, but it still has some way to go before it achieves the status of a natural choice, except in Britain. In other northern European countries, bus services exist mostly to supplement railroads.

Within several southern European countries—including Greece and parts of Spain—the bus has supplanted the train as the main means of public transportation, and is often quicker and more comfortable, with more frequent service, than the antiquated national rolling stock. Be prepared to discover that the bus is more expensive. Competition among lines is keen, so **ask about air-conditioning and reclining seats before you book.**

Eurolines comprises 30 motor-coach operators of international scheduled services, all no-smoking. They also transport passengers within each country. The 30-nation network serves more than 500 destinations with services ranging from twice weekly to five times daily. Eurolines has its own coach stations in Paris (⊠ 28 av. du Général de Gaulle at Bagnelot; métro: Gallieni), Brussels (80 rue du Progrès, next to the Gare du Nord), and Amsterdam (adjacent to the Amstel Railway Station). In other cities, coaches depart from railway stations or municipal bus terminals.

From the U.K., Eurolines links London with 400 destinations on the European Continent and Ireland, from Stockholm to Rome, from Dublin to Bucharest. All are via Calais, using either ferry services or Le Shuttle/Eurotunnel under the English Channel. Buses leave from Victoria Coach Station (adjoining the railway station). Services link up with the National Express network covering the U.K.

National or regional tourist offices have information about bus services. For reservations on major lines before you go, **contact your travel agent at home.**

CUTTING COSTS

The **Busabout** service can take you to more than 70 cities in Europe with two options: the consecutive pass or the flexipass. If you're planning a whirlwind European tour on a small budget, two weeks of consecutive travel will run you $249; three weeks $359; and one month $479. For a more leisurely pace, the flexipass gives you ten nonconsecutive traveling days in a two-month period for $399 or up to twenty days of nonconsecutive travel in a three-month period for $719. There are also links to London ($45 supplement) and Athens.

There is an on-board guide who not only provides local information but, with notice, can book campsites, bungalows, budget hotels, or hostels.

The **Eurolines Pass** allows unlimited travel between 40 European cities on scheduled bus services. A 30-day summer pass costs $379 ($329 for those under 26 or over 60); a 60-day pass costs $449 ($409). Passes can be bought from Eurolines offices and travel agents in Europe and from the companies listed below.

➤ DISCOUNT PASSES: In the U.S.: Eurolines Passes can be purchased from **DER Travel Services** (✉ 9501 W. Devon Ave., Rosemont, IL 60018, ☎ 847/692–6300 in IL; 800/782–2424), and from most Hostelling International and all STA offices (☞ Students in Europe).

➤ BUS INFORMATION: **Busabout (UK) Ltd.** (✉ Victoria Bus Station, 258 Vauxhall Bridge Rd., London, SW1V 1BF, ☎ 020/7950–1661, FAX 020/7950–1661, WEB www.busabout.com). **Eurolines** (✉ 52 Grosvenor Gardens, London SW1 WOAU, ☎ 0990/143–219 or 020/7730–8235, WEB www.eurolines.com). **Eurolines (UK)** (✉ 4 Cardiff Rd., Luton LU1 1HX, ☎ 01582/404–511, FAX 01582/400–694). For brochures, timetables, and sales agents in the U.S. and Canada, contact the **Eurolines Pass Organization** (✉ Keizersgracht 317, 1016 EE Amsterdam, The Netherlands, ☎ 020/625–3010, FAX 020/420–6904).

CAR RENTAL

The great attraction of renting is obviously that you become independent of public transport. Cost-wise, you should **consider renting a car only if you are with at least one other person;** single travelers pay a tremendous premium. Car rental costs vary from country to country; rates in Scandinavia and Eastern Europe are particularly high. If you're visiting a number of countries with varying rates, it makes sense to **rent a vehicle in the cheapest country.**

Picking up a car at an airport is convenient but often costs extra (up to 10%) as rental companies pass along the fees charged to them by airports.

Sample rates: London, $39 a day and $136 a week for an economy car with air-conditioning, a manual transmission, and unlimited mileage; Paris, $60 a day and $196 a week; Madrid, $37 a day and $132 a week; Rome, $49 a day and $167 a week. These figures do not include tax on car rentals, which ranges from 15% to 21%.

➤ MAJOR AGENCIES: **Alamo** (☎ 800/522–9696; 020/8759–6200 in the U.K., WEB www.alamo.com). **Avis** (☎ 800/331–1084; 800/879–2847 in Canada; 02/9353–9000 in Australia; 09/525–1982 in New Zealand; 0870/606–0100 in the U.K., WEB www.avis.com). **Budget** (☎ 800/527–0700; 0870/156–5656 in the U.K., WEB www.budget.com). **Dollar** (☎ 800/800–6000; 0124/622–0111 in the U.K., where it's affiliated with Sixt; 02/9223–1444 in Australia, WEB www.dollar.com). **Hertz** (☎ 800/654–3001; 800/263–0600 in Canada; 020/8897–2072 in the U.K.; 02/9669–2444 in Australia; 09/256–8690 in New Zealand, WEB www.hertz.com). **National Car Rental** (☎ 800/227–7368; 020/8680–4800 in the U.K., WEB www.nationalcar.com).

CUTTING COSTS

To get the best deal, **book through a travel agent who will shop around.** If you think you'll need a car in Europe but are unsure about when or where, ask your travel agent to check out Kemwel's CarPass. This gives the benefit of pre-paid vouchers with the flexibility of last-minute bookings in Europe. Unused vouchers are refunded. Do **look into wholesalers,** companies that do not own fleets but rent in bulk from those that do and often offer better rates than traditional car-rental operations. Payment must be made before you leave home. Short-term leasing can save money if you need a rental for more than 17 days. Kemwel and Europe by Car are among the wholesalers offering such deals.

➤ WHOLESALERS: **Auto Europe** (☎ 207/842–2000 or 800/223–5555, FAX 207/842–2222, WEB www.autoeurope.com). **Europe by Car** (☎ 212/581–3040 or 800/223–1516, FAX 212/246–1458, WEB www.europebycar.com). **DER Travel Services** (✉ 9501 W. Devon Ave., Rosemont, IL 60018, ☎ 800/782–2424, FAX 800/282–7474 for information; 800/860–9944 for brochures,

WEB www.dertravel.com). **Kemwel Holiday Autos** (☎ 800/678–0678, FAX 914/825–3160, WEB www.kemwel.com).

INSURANCE

When driving a rented car you are generally responsible for any damage to or loss of the vehicle. Before you rent, see what coverage your personal auto-insurance policy and credit cards provide.

Before you buy collision coverage, check your existing policies—you may already be covered. However, collision policies that car-rental companies sell for European rentals usually do not include stolen-vehicle coverage. Note that in Italy, all car-rental companies make you buy theft-protection policies.

REQUIREMENTS & RESTRICTIONS

Your own driver's license is acceptable virtually everywhere. An International Driver's Permit is a good idea, especially if your travel is likely to include Eastern Europe; it's available from the American or Canadian automobile association, and, in the United Kingdom, from the Automobile Association or Royal Automobile Club. These international permits are universally recognized; having one in your wallet may save you a problem with the local authorities.

SURCHARGES

Before you pick up a car in one city and leave it in another, **ask about drop-off charges or one-way service fees,** which can be substantial. Note, too, that some rental agencies charge extra if you return the car before the time specified in your contract. To avoid a hefty refueling fee, **fill the tank just before you turn in the car,** but be aware that gas stations near the rental outlet may overcharge.

CAR TRAVEL

Unless you're in a rush to get from A to B, you will find it rewarding to **avoid the freeways and use alternative routes.**

Motorway tolls can easily add $25 a day to your costs in driving through France, and there are toll roads throughout southern Europe, as well as charges for many tunnels. When crossing borders into Switzerland, you're charged 40 Swiss francs (about $30) for a *vignette* that entitles you to use Swiss freeways for a year. To get a handle on costs, **ask the national tourist office or car rental firm about tolls before you travel.**

If you are driving a rented car, **be sure to carry the necessary papers provided by the rental company.** For U.K. citizens, if the vehicle is your own, you will need proof of ownership, a certificate of roadworthiness (known as a Ministry of Transport, or MOT, road vehicle certificate), up-to-date vehicle registration or tax certificate, and a Green Card proof of insurance, available from your insurance company (fees vary depending on destination and length of stay).

Border controls have been abolished within the EU (except in the U.K., Ireland, Scandinavia, and Greece). The border posts are still standing, but drivers whiz through them without slowing down. Truck traffic is generally routed to separate checkpoints.

Drivers traveling between Great Britain and the Continent can now **consider using the Eurotunnel,** the train carrying cars, buses, motorbikes, and trucks, plus their passengers, through the Channel Tunnel between Folkestone and Calais in 35 minutes. The shuttle trains operate continuously—three to four trains per hour—and reservations are not needed, but to avoid queueing, tickets can be bought in advance from travel agents or by credit card from **Eurotunnel** (☎ 03/2100–6100 in France, 0990/353–535 in the U.K.). Prices vary according to length of stay on the Continent, as well as the season and time of travel. Prices given are for return fares, with the maximum rate applying in the peak July and August holiday period. A short break (less than 5 days) costs £139–£225, and a standard return costs £219–£325. Club Class gives you the right to priority queueing and entry to the Club Class lounge for a premium of 25%–35%. To calculate single fares simply divide by two. Note that you must make advance reservations to benefit from promotional fares and special offers. *See* The Channel Tunnel.

AUTO CLUBS

➤ IN AUSTRALIA: **Australian Automobile Association** (☎ 02/6247–7311).

➤ IN CANADA: **Canadian Automobile Association (CAA,** ☎ 613/820–1890 for membership).

➤ IN NEW ZEALAND: **New Zealand Automobile Association** (☎ 09/377–4660).

➤ IN THE U.K.: **Automobile Association** (AA, ☎ 0990/500–600). **Royal Automobile Club** (RAC, ☎ 0990/722–722 for membership; 0345/121–345 for insurance).

➤ IN THE U.S.: **American Automobile Association** (☎ 800/564–6222).

EMERGENCY SERVICES

You must carry a reflecting red triangle (to be placed 30 meters behind your car in case of breakdown). A first-aid kit and fire extinguisher are strongly recommended.

GASOLINE

Be prepared: gasoline costs three to four times more than in the United States, due to heavy taxes. The better fuel economy of European cars offsets the higher price to some extent.

ROAD CONDITIONS

During peak vacation periods, main routes can be jammed with holiday traffic. In the United Kingdom, **try to avoid driving during any of the long bank-holiday (public holiday) weekends,** when motorways are invariably clogged. The tunnels carrying traffic between Italy and the countries to the north are often overburdened with truck traffic; cross the Alps on a weekend, if you can. In France, Greece, Spain, and Italy, huge numbers of people still take a fixed one-month vacation in August, so **avoid driving** during *le départ,* the first weekend in August, when vast numbers of drivers head south; or *le retour,* when they head back.

RULES OF THE ROAD

Establishing a speed limit for German motorways has proved a tougher nut than any government could crack. On the rest of the Continent, the limit is generally 120 kph (74 mph), but the cruising speed is mostly about 140 kph (about 87 mph). In the United Kingdom, the speed limit is 112 kph (70 mph), but there, too, passing at considerably higher speed is not uncommon. In suburban and urban zones, the speed limit is much lower. For safe driving, **stay in the slower lane unless you want to pass, and make way for faster cars wanting to pass you.**

In the United Kingdom and the Republic of Ireland, cars drive on the left. In other European countries, traffic is on the right. If you're coming off the Eurotunnel's shuttle, or ferries from Britain or Ireland to the Continent (or vice versa), beware the transition.

THE CHANNEL TUNNEL

Short of flying, the "Chunnel" is the fastest way to cross the English Channel: 35 minutes from Folkestone to Calais, 60 minutes from motorway to motorway, or 3 hours from London's Waterloo Station to Paris's Gare du Nord.

➤ CAR TRANSPORT: **Le Shuttle** (☎ 0870/535–3535 in the U.K.).

➤ PASSENGER SERVICE: In the U.K.: **Eurostar** (☎ 0870/518–6186), **Rail Europe** (☎ 0870/584–8848 for credit-card bookings). In the U.S.: **BritRail Travel** (☎ 800/677–8585), **Rail Europe** (☎ 800/942–4866, WEB www.raileurope.com).

CHILDREN IN EUROPE

If you are renting a car, don't forget to **arrange for a car seat** when you reserve. Children under twelve may not travel in the front seat.

For general advice about traveling with children, consult *Fodor's FYI: Travel with Your Baby* (available in bookstores everywhere).

FLYING

If your children are two or older, **ask about children's airfares.** As a general rule, infants under two not occupying a seat fly at greatly reduced fares or even for free. When booking, **confirm carry-on allowances** if you're traveling with infants. In general, for babies charged 10% of the adult fare you are allowed one carry-on bag and a collapsible stroller; if the flight is full, the stroller may have to be checked or you may be limited to less.

Experts agree that it's a good idea to use safety seats aloft for children weighing less than 40 pounds. Airlines set their own policies: U.S. carriers usually require that the child be ticketed, even if he or she is young enough to ride free, since the seats must be strapped into regular seats. Do **check your airline's policy about using safety seats during takeoff and landing.** And since safety seats are not allowed everywhere in the plane, get your seat assignments early.

When reserving, **request children's meals or a freestanding bassinet** if you need them. But note that bulkhead seats, where you must sit to use the bassinet, may lack an overhead bin or storage space on the floor.

LODGING

Most hotels in Europe allow children under a certain age to stay in their parents' room at no extra charge, but others charge for them as extra adults; be sure to **find out the cutoff age for children's discounts.**

SIGHTS & ATTRACTIONS

Places that are especially appealing to children are indicated by a rubber-duckie icon (🐤) in the margin.

CONSUMER PROTECTION

Whenever shopping or buying travel services in Europe, **pay with a major credit card,** if possible, so you can cancel payment or get reimbursed if there's a problem. If you're doing business with a particular company for the first time, **contact your local Better Business Bureau and the attorney general's offices** in your state and (for U.S. businesses) the company's home state as well. Have any complaints been filed? Finally, if you're buying a package or tour, always **consider travel insurance** that includes default coverage.

➤ BBBs: **Council of Better Business Bureaus** (✉ 4200 Wilson Blvd., Suite 800, Arlington, VA 22203, ☎ 703/

276–0100, FAX 703/525–8277, WEB www.bbb.org).

CUSTOMS & DUTIES

When shopping, **keep receipts** for all purchases. Upon reentering the country, **be ready to show customs officials what you've bought.** If you feel a duty is incorrect or object to the way your clearance was handled, note the inspector's badge number and ask to see a supervisor. If the problem isn't resolved, write to the appropriate authorities, beginning with the port director at your point of entry.

IN AUSTRALIA

Australian residents who are 18 or older may bring home $A400 worth of souvenirs and gifts (including jewelry), 250 cigarettes or 250 grams of tobacco, and 1,125 ml of alcohol (including wine, beer, and spirits). Residents under 18 may bring back $A200 worth of goods. Prohibited items include meat products. Seeds, plants, and fruits need to be declared upon arrival.

➤ INFORMATION: **Australian Customs Service** (Regional Director, ✉ Box 8, Sydney, NSW 2001, Australia, ☎ 02/9213–2000, FAX 02/9213–4000, WEB www.customs.gov.au).

IN CANADA

Canadian residents who have been out of Canada for at least seven days may bring home C$750 worth of goods duty-free. If you've been away fewer than seven days but more than 48 hours, the duty-free allowance drops to C$200; if your trip lasts 24–48 hours, the allowance is C$50. You may not pool allowances with family members. Goods claimed under the C$750 exemption may follow you by mail; those claimed under the lesser exemptions must accompany you. Alcohol and tobacco products may be included in the seven-day and 48-hour exemptions but not in the 24-hour exemption. If you meet the age requirements of the province or territory through which you reenter Canada, you may bring in, duty-free, 1.14 liters (40 imperial ounces) of wine or liquor *or* 24 12-ounce cans or bottles of beer or ale. If you are 19 or older you may bring in, duty-free, 200 cigarettes and 50 cigars. Check ahead of time with the Canada Customs Revenue Agency or the Department of Agriculture for policies regarding meat products, seeds, plants, and fruits.

You may send an unlimited number of gifts worth up to C$60 each duty-free to Canada. Label the package UNSOLICITED GIFT—VALUE UNDER $60. Alcohol and tobacco are excluded.

➤ INFORMATION: **Canada Customs Revenue Agency** (✉ 2265 St. Laurent Blvd. S, Ottawa, Ontario K1G 4K3, Canada, ☎ 204/983–3500 or 506/636–5064; 800/461–9999 in Canada, WEB www.ccra-adrc.gc.ca).

IN EUROPE

Since the EU's 1992 agreement on a unified European market, the same customs regulations apply to all 15 member states (Austria, Belgium, Denmark, Finland, France, Germany, Great Britain, Greece, Ireland, Italy, Luxembourg, the Netherlands, Portugal, Spain, and Sweden). If you arrive from another EU country, you do not have to pass through customs.

Duty-free allowances for visitors from outside the EU are the same whatever your nationality (but you have to be over 17): 200 cigarettes or 50 cigars or 100 cigarillos or 250 grams of pipe tobacco; 1 liter of spirits or 2 liters of fortified or sparkling wine or liqueurs; 2 liters of still table wine; 60 milliliters of perfume; 250 milliliters of toilet water (note: 1 U.S. quart equals 0.946 liters); plus $200 worth of other goods, including gifts and souvenirs. Unless otherwise noted in individual country chapters, there are no restrictions on the import or export of currency. These limits remained in force after June 30, 1999, when duty-free shopping for travel within the EU was abolished.

See individual country chapters on non-EU countries for information on their import limits.

IN NEW ZEALAND

Homeward-bound residents 17 or older may bring back $700 worth of souvenirs and gifts. Your duty-free allowance also includes 4.5 liters of wine or beer; one 1,125-ml bottle of spirits; and either 200 cigarettes, 250 grams of tobacco, 50 cigars, or a combination of the three up to 250 grams. Prohibited items include meat products, seeds, plants, and fruits.

➤ INFORMATION: **New Zealand Customs** (Custom House, ✉ 50 Anzac Ave., Box 29, Auckland, New Zealand, ☎ 09/300–5399, FAX 09/359–6730, WEB www.customs.govt.nz).

IN THE U.K.

If you are a U.K. resident and your journey was wholly within the European Union (EU), you won't have to pass through customs when you return to the United Kingdom. If you plan to bring back large quantities of alcohol or tobacco, check EU limits beforehand. From countries outside the European Union, you may bring home, duty-free, 200 cigarettes or 50 cigars; 1 liter of spirits or 2 liters of fortified or sparkling wine or liqueurs; 2 liters of still table wine; 60 ml of perfume; 250 ml of toilet water; plus £145 worth of other goods, including gifts and souvenirs. If returning from outside the EU, prohibited items include meat products, seeds, plants, and fruits.

➤ INFORMATION: **HM Customs and Excise** (✉ St. Christopher House, Southwark, London, SE1 OTE, U.K., ☎ 020/7928–3344, WEB www.hmce.gov.uk).

IN THE U.S.

U.S. residents who have been out of the country for at least 48 hours (and who have not used the $400 allowance or any part of it in the past 30 days) may bring home $400 worth of foreign goods duty-free.

U.S. residents 21 and older may bring back 1 liter of alcohol duty-free. In addition, regardless of your age, you are allowed 200 cigarettes and 100 non-Cuban cigars. Antiques, which the U.S. Customs Service defines as objects more than 100 years old, enter duty-free, as do original works of art done entirely by hand, including paintings, drawings, and sculptures.

You may also mail or ship packages home duty-free: up to $200 worth of goods for personal use, with a limit of one parcel per addressee per day (except alcohol or tobacco products or perfume worth more than $5); label the package PERSONAL USE and attach a list of its contents and their retail value. Do not label the package UNSOLICITED GIFT or your duty-free exemption will drop to $100. Mailed items do not affect your duty-free allowance on your return.

➤ INFORMATION: U.S. Customs Service (✉ 1300 Pennsylvania Ave. NW, Room 6.3D, Washington, DC 20229, WEB www.customs.gov; inquiries ☎ 202/354–1000; complaints c/o 1300 Pennsylvania Ave. NW, Room 5.4D, Washington, DC 20229; registration of equipment c/o Office of Passenger Programs, ☎ 202/927–0530).

DINING

See discussions of dining in individual city chapters. The restaurants we list are the cream of the crop in each price category.

RESERVATIONS & DRESS

Reservations are always a good idea: we mention them only when they're essential or not accepted. We mention dress only when men are required to wear a jacket or a jacket and tie.

DISABILITIES & ACCESSIBILITY

Getting around in many European cities and towns can be difficult if you're using a wheelchair, as cobblestone-paved streets and sidewalks are common in older, historic districts. Generally, newer facilities (including museums, transportation, hotels) provide easier access for people with disabilities.

LODGING

Contact a support organization at home to see whether they have publications with lists of approved accommodation. The U.S.-based Society for the Advancement of Travel for the Handicapped (SATH) is dedicated to promoting access for travelers with disabilities. The British nonprofit Holiday Care Service produces an annual guide, *The Holiday Care Service Guide to Accessible Accommodation and Travel*, which lists more than 1,000 establishments inspected for access by Holiday Care in association with the National Tourist Boards. It has sections on accessible transportation, identifies accessible tourist attractions, and suggests sample itineraries.

➤ SUPPORT ORGANIZATIONS: **Holiday Care Service** (✉ 2nd floor, Imperial Bldgs., Victoria Rd., Horley, Surrey, RH6 7PZ, ☎ 0129/377–4535, FAX 0129/378–4647, WEB www. holidaycare.org.uk). **The Society for the Advancement of Travel for the Handicapped** (SATH; ✉ 347 Fifth Ave., Suite 610, New York, NY 10016, ☎ 212/447–7284, FAX 212/725–8253).

TRAVEL AGENCIES

In the United States, the Americans with Disabilities Act requires that travel firms serve the needs of all travelers. Some agencies specialize in working with people with disabilities.

➤ TRAVELERS WITH MOBILITY PROBLEMS: **Access Adventures** (✉ 206 Chestnut Ridge Rd., Scottsville, NY 14624, ☎ 716/889–9096, dltravel@prodigy.net), run by a former physical-rehabilitation counselor. **CareVacations** (✉ No. 5, 5110–50 Ave., Leduc, Alberta T9E 6V4, Canada, ☎ 780/986–6404 or 877/478–7827, FAX 780/986–8332, WEB www.carevacations.com), for group tours and cruise vacations. **Flying Wheels Travel** (✉ 143 W. Bridge St., Box 382, Owatonna, MN 55060, ☎ 507/451–5005 or 800/535–6790, FAX 507/451–1685, WEB www.flyingwheelstravel.com).

➤ TRAVELERS WITH DEVELOPMENTAL DISABILITIES: **New Directions** (✉ 5276 Hollister Ave., Suite 207, Santa Barbara, CA 93111, ☎ 805/967–2841 or 888/967–2841, FAX 805/964–7344, WEB www.newdirectionstravel.com). **Sprout** (✉ 893 Amsterdam Ave., New York, NY 10025, ☎ 212/222–9575 or 888/222–9575, FAX 212/222–9768, WEB www.gosprout.org).

DISCOUNTS & DEALS

Be a smart shopper and **compare all your options** before making decisions. A plane ticket bought with a promotional coupon from travel clubs, coupon books, and direct-mail offers or on the Internet may not be cheaper than the least expensive fare from a discount ticket agency. And always keep in mind that what you get is just as important as what you save.

DISCOUNT RESERVATIONS

To save money, **look into discount reservations services** with toll-free numbers, which use their buying power to get a better price on hotels, airline tickets, even car rentals. When booking a room, always **call the hotel's local toll-free number** (if one is available) rather than the central reservations number—you'll often get a better price. Always ask about special packages or corporate rates.

When shopping for the best deal on hotels and car rentals, **look for guaranteed exchange rates,** which protect you against a falling dollar. With your rate locked in, you won't pay more, even if the price goes up in the local currency.

➤ AIRLINE TICKETS: ☎ **800/AIR–4LESS.**

➤ HOTEL ROOMS: **Hotel Reservations Network** (☎ 800/964–6835, WEB www.hoteldiscount.com). **International Marketing & Travel Concepts** (☎ 800/790–4682, WEB www.imtc-travel.com). **Players Express Vacations** (☎ 800/458–6161, WEB www.playersexpress.com). **Steigenberger Reservation Service** (☎ 800/223–5652, WEB www.srs-worldhotels.com). **Travel Interlink** (☎ 800/888–5898, WEB www.travelinterlink.com). **Turbotrip.com** (☎ 800/473–7829, WEB www.turbotrip.com).

PACKAGE DEALS

Don't confuse packages and guided tours. When you buy a package, you travel on your own, just as though you had planned the trip yourself. Fly/drive packages, which combine airfare and car rental, are often a good deal. If you **buy a rail/drive pass,** you may save on train tickets and car rentals. All Eurail- and Europass holders get a discount on Eurostar fares through the Channel Tunnel. A German Rail Pass is also good for travel aboard some KD River Steamers and some Deutsche Touring/Europabus routes. Greek Flexipass options may include sightseeing, hotels, and plane tickets.

ELECTRICITY

To use electric-powered equipment purchased in the U.S. or Canada,

bring a converter and adapter. The electrical current in Europe is 220 volts, 50 cycles alternating current (AC); wall outlets in most of Europe take plugs with two round prongs; Great Britain, Malta, and Cyprus use plugs with three oblong prongs and mains current is at 240 volts.

If your appliances are dual-voltage, you'll need only an adapter. Don't use 110-volt outlets marked FOR SHAVERS ONLY for high-wattage appliances such as blow-dryers. Most laptops operate equally well on 110 and 220 volts and so require only an adapter.

LANGUAGE

A phrase book and language-tape set can help get you started. *Fodor's French for Travelers, Fodor's German for Travelers, Fodor's Italian for Travelers,* and *Fodor's Spanish for Travelers* (available at bookstores everywhere) are excellent.

LODGING

For discussions of accommodations in Europe, *see* the Lodging sections in individual country chapters. The lodgings we list are the cream of the crop in each price category. When pricing accommodations, always ask what facilities are included and what costs extra.

APARTMENT & VILLA RENTALS

If you want a home base that's roomy enough for a family and comes with cooking facilities, **consider a furnished rental.** These can save you money, especially if you're traveling with a group. Home-exchange directories sometimes list rentals as well as exchanges.

➤ INTERNATIONAL AGENTS: **At Home Abroad** (⊠ 405 E. 56th St., Suite 6H, New York, NY 10022, ☎ 212/421–9165, FAX 212/752–1591, WEB www.athomeabroadinc.com). **Drawbridge to Europe** (⊠ 98 Granite St., Ashland, OR 97520, ☎ 541/482–7778 or 888/268–1148, FAX 541/482–7779, WEB www.drawbridgetoeurope.com). **Hideaways International** (⊠ 767 Islington St., Portsmouth, NH 03801, ☎ 603/430–4433 or 800/843–4433, FAX 603/430–4444, WEB www.hideaways.com; membership $129). **Hometours International** (⊠ Box

11503, Knoxville, TN 37939, ☎ 865/690-8484 or 800/367-4668, WEB thor.he.net/INSERT TILDEhometour/). **Interhome** (✉ 1990 N.E. 163rd St., Suite 110, N. Miami Beach, FL 33162, ☎ 305/940-2299 or 800/882-6864, FAX 305/940-2911, WEB www.interhome.com). **Vacation Home Rentals Worldwide** (✉ 235 Kensington Ave., Norwood, NJ 07648, ☎ 201/767-9393 or 800/633-3284, FAX 201/767-5510, WEB www.vhrww.com). **Villanet** (✉ 11556 1st Ave. NW, Seattle, WA 98177, ☎ 206/417-3444 or 800/964-1891, FAX 206/417-1832, WEB www.rentavilla.com). **Villas and Apartments Abroad** (✉ 1270 Avenue of the Americas, 15th floor, New York, NY 10020, ☎ 212/897-5045 or 800/433-3020, FAX 212/897-5039, WEB www.ideal-villas.com). **Villas International** (✉ 950 Northgate Dr., Suite 206, San Rafael, CA 94903, ☎ 415/499-9490 or 800/221-2260, FAX 415/499-9491, WEB www.villasintl.com).

HOME EXCHANGES

If you would like to exchange your home for someone else's, **join a home-exchange organization,** which will send you its updated listings of available exchanges for a year and will include your own listing in at least one of them. It's up to you to make specific arrangements.

➤ EXCHANGE CLUBS: **HomeLink International** (✉ Box 47747, Tampa, FL 33647, ☎ 813/975-9825 or 800/638-3841, FAX 813/910-8144, WEB www.homelink.org; $106 per year). **Intervac U.S.** (✉ Box 590504, San Francisco, CA 94159, ☎ 800/756-4663, FAX 415/435-7440, WEB www.intervacus.com; $93 yearly fee includes one catalogue and on-line access).

HOSTELS

No matter what your age, you can **save on lodging costs by staying at hostels.** In some 4,500 locations in more than 70 countries around the world, Hostelling International (HI), the umbrella group for a number of national youth-hostel associations, offers single-sex, dorm-style beds and, at many hostels, rooms for couples and family accommodations. Membership in any HI national hostel association, open to travelers of all ages, allows you to stay in HI-affili-

ated hostels at member rates; one-year membership is about $25 for adults (C$26.75 in Canada, £9.30 in the U.K., $30 in Australia, and $30 in New Zealand); hostels run about $10-$25 per night. Members have priority if the hostel is full; they're also eligible for discounts around the world, even on rail and bus travel in some countries.

➤ ORGANIZATIONS: **Hostelling International—American Youth Hostels** (✉ 733 15th St. NW, Suite 840, Washington, DC 20005, ☎ 202/783-6161, FAX 202/783-6171, WEB www.hiayh.org). **Hostelling International—Canada** (✉ 400-205 Catherine St., Ottawa, Ontario K2P 1C3, Canada, ☎ 613/237-7884; 800/663-5777 in Canada, FAX 613/237-7868, WEB www.hostellingintl.ca). **Youth Hostel Association of England and Wales** (✉ Trevelyan House, 8 St. Stephen's Hill, St. Albans, Hertfordshire AL1 2DY, U.K., ☎ 0870/8708808, FAX 01727/844126, WEB www.yha.org.uk). **Youth Hostel Association Australia** (✉ 10 Mallett St., Camperdown, NSW 2050, Australia, ☎ 02/9565-1699, FAX 02/9565-1325, WEB www.yha.com.au). **Youth Hostels Association of New Zealand** (✉ Level 3, 193 Cashel St., Box 436, Christchurch, New Zealand, ☎ 03/379-9970, FAX 03/365-4476, WEB www.yha.org.nz).

HOTELS

All hotels listed have private bath unless otherwise noted.

RESERVING A ROOM

See individual city chapters for details on last-minute reservation services.

➤ TOLL-FREE NUMBERS: **Best Western** (☎ 800/528-1234, WEB www.bestwestern.com). **Choice** (☎ 800/221-2222, WEB www.hotelchoice.com). **Clarion** (☎ 800/252-7466, WEB www.clarionhotel.com). **Comfort** (☎ 800/228-5150, WEB www.comfortinn.com). **Forte** (☎ 800/225-5843, WEB www.forte-hotels.com). **Hilton** (☎ 800/445-8667, WEB www.hilton.com). **Holiday Inn** (☎ 800/465-4329, WEB www.basshotels.com). **Hyatt Hotels & Resorts** (☎ 800/233-1234, WEB www.hyatt.com). **Inter-Continental** (☎ 800/327-0200, WEB www.interconti.com). **Marriott**

(☏ 800/228–9290, WEB www.marriott.com). **Le Meridien** (☏ 800/543–4300, WEB www.lemeridien-hotels.com). **Nikko Hotels International** (☏ 800/645–5687, WEB www.nikkohotels.com). **Quality Inn** (☏ 800/228–5151, WEB www.qualityinn.com). **Radisson** (☏ 800/333–3333, WEB www.radisson.com). **Ramada** (☏ 800/228–2828, WEB www.ramada.com). **Renaissance Hotels & Resorts** (☏ 800/468–3571, WEB www.renaissancehotels.com/). **Ritz-Carlton** (☏ 800/241–3333, WEB www.ritzcarlton.com). **Sheraton** (☏ 800/325–3535, WEB www.starwoodhotels.com). **Wyndham Hotels & Resorts** (☏ 800/822–4200, WEB www.wyndham.com).

MONEY MATTERS

Admission prices throughout this guide are included for attractions that charge more than $10 or the equivalent. Prices throughout this guide are given for adults. Substantially reduced fees are almost always available for children, students, and senior citizens. For information on taxes, *see* Taxes.

ATMS

ATMs are ubiquitous throughout Europe; you can draw local currency from an ATM in most airports as soon as you deplane.

CREDIT CARDS

Throughout this guide, the following abbreviations are used: **AE,** American Express; **DC,** Diners Club; **MC,** MasterCard; and **V,** Visa.

CURRENCY

On January 1, 2002, the new single European Union (EU) currency, the euro, will finally become the official currency of the 12 countries participating in the European Monetary Union: Austria, Belgium, Finland, France, Germany, Greece, Ireland, Italy, Luxembourg, the Netherlands, Portugal, and Spain. Denmark, Great Britain, and Sweden, although a part of the EU, are not yet part of the monetary union, and therefore will retain the use of their local currencies. At press time (summer 2001), just how graceful this long-awaited physical debut of the much touted euro will be was up for discussion. Those traveling at the beginning of 2002 take note: All banks, businesses, and money machines will be stocked in euros as of January 1, 2002, but there will be a short transition period where the local currencies of the eleven participating countries will co-exist with the euro. Which means that in France, you may buy your morning baguette with your remaining francs and receive euros in return.

Your best bet is to change your old European currency into euros the minute you arrive in Europe (or before you leave), and for once, it doesn't really matter where, because the rate between the monetary union members and the euro was irrevocably fixed in late 1999, thus eliminating any fluctuations in the market and any need for commission.

Although it might take Europeans a little getting used to, the euro will make life for the European traveler much, much easier. Gone are the days when a day trip to Belgium from France meant changing money into yet another currency and paying additional commissions. To make things even easier for travelers from the United States, the euro was created as a direct competitor with the U.S. dollar, which means that their values are quite similar. At press time (summer 2001), one euro was equal to US$.86. It is also equal to 1.30 Canadian dollars, 1.66 Australian dollars, 2.08 New Zealand dollars, and .61 pounds sterling.

In the euro system there are eight coins: 1 and 2 euros, plus 1, 2, 5, 10, 20, and 50 centimes, or cents, of the euro. All coins have one side that has the value of the euro on it and the other side with each country's unique national symbol. There are seven colorful notes: 5, 10, 20, 50, 100, 200, and 500 euros. Notes have the principal architectural styles from antiquity onwards on one side and the map and the flag of Europe on the other and are the same for all countries.

CURRENCY EXCHANGE

For the most favorable rates, **change money through banks.** Although ATM transaction fees may be higher abroad than at home, ATM rates are excellent because they are based on wholesale rates offered only by major banks. You won't do as well at exchange booths in airports or rail and bus stations, in hotels, in restaurants, or in stores. To avoid lines at airport exchange booths, **get a bit of local currency before you leave home.**

➤ EXCHANGE SERVICES: **International Currency Express** (☎ 888/278–6628 for orders, WEB www.foreignmoney. com). **Thomas Cook Currency Services** (☎ 800/287–7362 for telephone orders and retail locations, WEB www. us.thomascook.com).

TRAVELER'S CHECKS

Lost or stolen checks can usually be replaced within 24 hours. To ensure a speedy refund, buy your own traveler's checks—don't let someone else pay for them: irregularities like this can cause delays. The person who bought the checks should make the call to request a refund.

PASSPORTS & VISAS

When traveling internationally, **carry your passport** even if you don't need one (it's always the best form of I.D.) and **make two photocopies of the data page** (one for someone at home and another for you, carried separately from your passport). If you lose your passport, promptly call the nearest embassy or consulate and the local police.

ENTERING EUROPE

Citizens of the United States, Canada, United Kingdom, Ireland, Australia, and New Zealand need passports for travel in Europe. Visas may also be required for visits to or through Hungary and the Czech Republic even for short stays or train trips, and in some cases must be obtained before you'll be allowed to enter. Check with the nearest consulate of the country you'll be visiting for visa requirements and any other applicable information.

PASSPORT OFFICES

The best time to apply for a passport or to renew is in fall and winter. Before any trip, check your passport's expiration date, and, if necessary, renew it as soon as possible.

➤ AUSTRALIAN CITIZENS: **Australian Passport Office** (☎ 131–232, WEB www.dfat.gov.au/passports).

➤ CANADIAN CITIZENS: **Passport Office** (☎ 819/994–3500; 800/567–6868 in Canada, WEB www.dfait-maeci.gc.ca/passport).

➤ NEW ZEALAND CITIZENS: **New Zealand Passport Office** (☎ 04/494–0700, WEB www.passports.govt.nz).

➤ U.K. CITIZENS: **London Passport Office** (☎ 0870/521–0410, WEB www. ukpa.gov.uk) for fees and documentation requirements and to request an emergency passport.

➤ U.S. CITIZENS: **National Passport Information Center** (☎ 900/225–5674; calls are 35¢ per minute for automated service, $1.05 per minute for operator service; WEB www.travel. state.gov/npicinfo.html).

SAFETY

Europe, and Great Britain in particular, has been plagued in recent years by what has now become an agricultural crisis. The first cases of bovine spongiform encephalopathy (BSE), commonly known as "mad cow disease," surfaced in Great Britain in the mid-1980s. BSE is a fatal degenerative disease contracted by cattle. When contaminated beef is eaten by humans, it can result in Creutzfeldt-Jakob Disease (CJD), an extremely rare brain-wasting illness fatal to humans.

Europe reacted swiftly to the threat, placing a ban on all beef exported from Great Britain for a short period and immediately banning all use of feed prepared with animal by-products. People are still wary, but at press time the risk of contracting the disease was considered extremely remote. The Centers for Disease Control and Prevention (www.cdc.gov) reported "The current risk for infection with the BSE agent among travelers to Europe is extremely small, if it exists at all." But, as always, stay informed.

At press time, Great Britain was plagued by yet another crisis, foot and mouth disease. Foot and mouth disease affects animals almost exclusively; human cases are extremely rare, and the United Kingdom Ministry of Agriculture, Fisheries, and

Food considers it harmless to humans. Nevertheless, it has had a catastrophic effect on the British economy due to the fact that all animals suspected of being infected must be slaughtered immediately.

To limit the spread of foot and mouth disease, some hiking routes and coastal footpaths were closed, especially in north and southwestern England, and certain festivities were cancelled. Some rural tourist attractions were also closed due to the crisis, though at press time many had reopened. Also expect stringent border controls, with an enforced ban on carrying English dairy and farm products out of the territory, and you might have to disinfect your luggage and shoes before leaving the country. Again, read the press and stay informed. The Open Britain web site (www.openbritain.gov.uk) has all the latest information, so you can check before you go.

SENIOR-CITIZEN TRAVEL

Radisson SAS Hotels in Europe offer discounts of 25% or more to senior citizens, subject to availability. You need a confirmed reservation.

To qualify for age-related discounts, **mention your senior-citizen status up front** when booking hotel reservations (not when checking out) and before you're seated in restaurants (not when paying the bill). When renting a car, ask about promotional car-rental discounts, which can be cheaper than senior-citizen rates.

➤ EDUCATIONAL PROGRAMS: **Elderhostel** (✉ 11 Ave. de Lafayette, Boston, MA 02111-1746, ☎ 877/426–8056, FAX 877/426–2166, WEB www.elderhostel.org). **Interhostel** (✉ University of New Hampshire, 6 Garrison Ave., Durham, NH 03824, ☎ 603/862–1147 or 800/733–9753, FAX 603/862–1113, WEB www.learn.unh.edu). **Folkways Institute** (✉ 14600 S.E. Aldridge Rd., Portland, OR 97236-6518, ☎ 503/658–6600 or 800/225–4666, FAX 503/658–8672, WEB www.folkwaystravel.com).

STUDENTS IN EUROPE

Students in Europe are entitled to a wide range of discounts on admission and transportation. An **International Student Identity Card,** issued by Council Travel (☞ I.D.s & Services), helps. The globally recognized ISIC card is issued by local student travel organizations that are members of the International Student Travel Confederation, best found by consulting their Web site (www.istc.org).

Many U.S. colleges and universities have study-abroad programs or can connect you with one, and numerous institutions of higher learning in Europe accept foreign students for a semester or year's study. Check with your college administration or contact the CIEE for contacts and brochures.

If you're between 18 and 26, the Ibis hotel chain will let you have a room for $50 or less, provided you show up after 9 PM and they have a room free. You'll be asked for your student I.D. Your chances are best on weekends. There are more than 400 Ibis hotels in Europe, most of them in France.

➤ I.D.s & SERVICES: **Council Travel** (CIEE; ✉ 205 E. 42nd St., 15th floor, New York, NY 10017, ☎ 212/822–2700 or 888/268–6245, FAX 212/822–2699, WEB www.councilexchanges.org) for mail orders only, in the U.S. **Travel Cuts** (✉ 187 College St., Toronto, Ontario M5T 1P7, Canada, ☎ 416/979–2406 or 800/667–2887 in Canada, FAX 416/979–8167, WEB www.travelcuts.com).

TAXES

VALUE-ADDED TAX

Global Refund is a V.A.T. refund service that makes getting your money back hassle-free. The service is available Europe-wide at 130,000 affiliated stores. In participating stores, **ask for the Global Refund refund form** (called a Shopping Cheque). Have it stamped like any customs form by customs officials when you leave the European Union (be ready to show customs officials what you've bought). Then take the form to one of the more than 700 Global Refund counters—conveniently located at every major airport and border crossing—and your money will be refunded on the spot in the form of cash, check, or a refund to your credit-card account (minus a small percentage for processing).

➤ V.A.T. Refunds: **Global Refund**
(✉ 99 Main St., Suite 307, Nyack,
NY 10960, ☎ 800/566–9828,
FAX 845/348–1549, WEB www.
globalrefund.com).

TELEPHONES

Telephone systems in Europe are in
flux; expect new area codes and extra
digits in numbers. Keep in mind that
some countries now rely on phone
cards; it's a good idea to buy one so
you don't have to hunt for a phone
that takes coins. Country codes
appear in the A to Z section at the
beginning of each city chapter. Cellu-
lar telephone companies unfortunately opted for different standards in
the U.S. and Europe, so only the most
sophisticated models with dual or
triple band possibilities will function
on both sides of the Atlantic. Func-
tionality of both cell phones and
pagers will also depend on the kind of
subscription you have with your cell-
phone company.

INTERNATIONAL CALLS

Consult individual chapters for information on dialing international calls.

LONG-DISTANCE SERVICES

AT&T, MCI, and Sprint access codes
make calling long distance relatively
convenient, but you may find the
local access number blocked in many
hotel rooms. First ask the hotel operator to connect you. If the hotel operator balks, ask for an international
operator, or dial the international
operator yourself. One way to im-
prove your odds of getting connected
to your long-distance carrier is to
travel with more than one company's
calling card (a hotel may block Sprint,
for example, but not MCI). If all else
fails, call from a pay phone.

TIME

Most of continental Europe ticks at
Central European Time (CET), one
hour ahead of Greenwich Mean Time
(GMT), which prevails in Great
Britain and Ireland. Eastern European
countries including Greece are two
hours ahead of GMT. In most of
mainland Europe clocks are turned
back one hour during the night of the
last Saturday/Sunday in March and

put forward one hour on the last
Saturday/Sunday night in October.

Europe uses the 24-hour (or "military") clock for everything from
airplane departures to opening arias.
After noon continue counting forward:
13:00 is 1 PM, 14:00 is 2 PM, etc.

TOURS & PACKAGES

Because everything is prearranged on
a prepackaged tour or independent
vacation, you spend less time
planning—and often get it all at
a good price.

BOOKING WITH AN AGENT

Travel agents are excellent resources.
But it's a good idea to collect
brochures from several agencies as
some agents' suggestions may be
influenced by relationships with tour
and package firms that reward them
for volume sales. If you have a special
interest, **find an agent with expertise
in that area**; the American Society of
Travel Agents (ASTA; ☞ Travel
Agencies) has a database of specialists
worldwide.

Make sure your travel agent knows
the accommodations and other services of the place being recommended.
Ask about the hotel's location, room
size, beds, and whether it has a pool,
room service, or programs for children, if you care about these. Has
your agent been there in person or
sent others whom you can contact?

Do some homework on your own,
too: local tourism boards can provide
information about lesser-known and
small-niche operators, some of which
may sell only direct.

BUYER BEWARE

Each year consumers are stranded
or lose their money when tour
operators—even large ones with
excellent reputations—go out of
business. So **check out the operator.**
Ask several travel agents about its
reputation, and try to **book with a
company that has a consumer-protec-
tion program.** (Look for information
in the company's brochure.) In the
United States, members of the
National Tour Association and the
United States Tour Operators Association are required to set aside funds

to cover your payments and travel arrangements in the event that the company defaults. It's also a good idea to choose a company that participates in the American Society of Travel Agents' Tour Operator Program (TOP); ASTA will act as mediator in any disputes between you and your tour operator.

Remember that the more your package or tour includes the better you can predict the ultimate cost of your vacation. Make sure you know exactly what is covered, and **beware of hidden costs.** Are taxes, tips, and transfers included? Entertainment and excursions? These can add up.

➤ TOUR-OPERATOR RECOMMENDATIONS: **American Society of Travel Agents** (☞ Travel Agencies). **National Tour Association** (NTA; ✉ 546 E. Main St., Lexington, KY 40508, ☎ 859/226–4444 or 800/ 682–8886, WEB www.ntaonline.com). **United States Tour Operators Association** (USTOA; ✉ 342 Madison Ave., Suite 1522, New York, NY 10173, ☎ 212/599–6599 or 800/ 468–7862, FAX 212/599–6744, WEB www.ustoa.com).

TRAIN TRAVEL

Some national high-speed train systems have begun to link up to form the nucleus of a pan-European system. On a long journey, you still have to change trains a couple of times, for the national railways are jealously guarding their prerogatives. Deregulation, so far achieved only in Britain and the Netherlands, is vigorously pushed by the European Commission. French TGV (Trains à Grande Vitesse), which serve most major cities in France, have been extended to Geneva, Lausanne, Bern, Zürich, Turin, and Milan. They connect with the latest generation of Italy's tilting Pendolino trains, also called Eurostar Italia. Italy's service extends beyond the country's borders with a service from Turin to Lyon and, in a joint venture with the Swiss Railways, from Milan to Geneva and Zürich. Express Thalys trains operate from Brussels to Paris on high-speed tracks and from Brussels to Amsterdam and Cologne on conventional track. Germany's equally fast ICE trains connect Hamburg and points in between with Basel, and Mannheim with Munich.

High-speed trains travel at speeds of up to 190 mph on dedicated track and over 150 mph on old track, covering the distance from Paris to Marseille in just over 4 hours, Hamburg to Munich in less than 6. They have made both expensive sleeper compartments and budget *couchettes* (seats that convert into bunks) all but obsolete. Their other attraction is the comfort of a super-smooth ride. The flip side is the reservations requirement; rather than just hopping on the next train, you need to **reserve in advance or allow enough time to make a reservation at the station.**

The **Orient Express,** a glamorous recreation of a sumptuous past, takes two days to cover the distance from London to Venice, and if you want to know the price, you can't afford it.

CLASSES

Virtually all European systems, including the high-speed ones, operate a two-class system. First class costs substantially more and is usually a luxury rather than a necessity. Some of the poorer European countries retain a third class, but avoid it unless you're an adventure-minded budget traveler.

CUTTING COSTS

To save money, **look into rail passes.** But be aware that if you don't plan to cover many miles you may come out ahead by buying individual tickets.

Before you invest in a discount pass, compare the cost against the point-to-point fares on your actual itinerary. (Rates given in this section are valid through December 2001, the latest available at press time.) EurailPasses provide unlimited first-class rail travel for the duration of the pass in 17 European countries: Austria, Belgium, Denmark, Finland, France, Germany, Greece, Hungary, the Irish Republic, Italy, Luxembourg, the Netherlands, Norway, Portugal, Spain, Sweden, and Switzerland (but not the United Kingdom). If you plan to rack up miles, get a standard pass. These are available for 15 days ($554, £390), 21 days ($718, £506), one month ($890,

£627), two months ($1,260, £887), and three months ($1,558, £1,097). Note that you will have to pay a supplement for certain high-speed trains—half the fare on Eurostar.

In addition to standard EurailPasses, check out special rail-pass plans. Among these are the Eurail Youthpass (in second class for those under 26, from $388/£273 to $1,089/£767), the Eurail Saverpass (which gives a discount for 2 to 5 people traveling together; a minimum of two people; from $470/£332 to $1,324/£932 per person), and the Eurail Flexipass (which allows 10 or 15 travel days within a two-month period, $654/£461 and $862/£607, respectively). This is also available at a youth rate. If you're going to travel in just one part of Europe, look into a regional pass, such as the East Europe Pass.

If your plans call for only limited train travel, consider Europass, which costs less money than a EurailPass and is available in first class only for adults and second class only for travelers under 26. It has a number of conditions. It is valid only in France, Germany, Italy, Spain, and Switzerland, but "associated countries" can be added at an extra charge. These are Austria/Hungary, the Benelux area, Greece, and Portugal, to a maximum of 2 extensions. You also get from 5 to 15 travel days during a two-month time period. The other side of the coin is that a Europass costs a couple of hundred dollars less than the least expensive EurailPass. A Europass Adult ranges in price from $348/£254 to $728/£603, a Europass Youth from $233/£170 to $513/£431.

It used to be the rule that non-Europeans had to **purchase Eurail passes before leaving** for Europe. This remains the recommended option, but you can now buy a pass in person within six months of your arrival in Europe from Rail Europe (☞ Train Information) in London. Also remember that you need to **book seats ahead even if you are using a rail pass**; seat reservations are required on the cross-Channel Eurostar service and European high-speed trains, and are a good idea on other trains that

may be crowded—particularly around Easter and at the beginning and end of European vacation periods. You will also need to purchase sleeper or couchette (sleeping berth) reservations separately.

European nationals and others who have resided in Europe for at least six months qualify for the **InterRail Pass.** It used to be exclusively for young people but can now also be purchased, at a premium, by older travelers. This entitles you to unlimited second-class travel within up to eight zones you have preselected. One zone for 22 days, for instance, costs £129 for travelers under 26 (£185 for over 26); all zones for one month, £229 (£319). InterRail Passes can be bought only in Europe at main railway stations, or in the United Kingdom from Rail Europe in London (☞ Train Information).

FROM THE U.K.

Sleek, high-speed Eurostar trains use the Channel Tunnel to link London (Waterloo) with Paris (Gare du Nord) in 3 hours and with Brussels (Gare du Midi) in 2 hours, 40 minutes. When the British build their high-speed rail link to London (St. Pancras), probably in 2003, another half hour will be shaved off travel time. There are a minimum of 14 daily services to Paris and 10 to Brussels.

Many of the trains stop at Ashford (Kent), and all at the Lille-Europe station in northern France, where you can change to French TGV trains to Brittany, southwest France, Lyon, the Alps, and the Riviera, eliminating the need to transfer between stations in Paris.

Passengers headed for Germany and the Netherlands can buy through tickets via Brussels to Cologne (5½ hours) and Amsterdam (5 hours, 45 minutes). Eurostar does not accept EurailPasses but allows discounts of 40%–50% to passholders. Check for special prices and deals before you book. Or, if money is no object, you can choose the Premium First Class (to Paris only), complete with limo delivery and pick-up at the stations, improved catering, and greater comfort.

Conventional boat trains from London are timed to dovetail with ferry departures at Channel ports. The ferries connect with onward trains at the main French, Belgian, Dutch and Irish ports. Be sure to ask when making your reservation which London railway station to use.

INDIVIDUAL COUNTRY PASSES

Single-country passes are issued by most national railways, and the majority are sold by Rail Europe (☞ Train Information, and individual country chapters). Great Britain has a number of rail passes, including the Visitor's Travelcard for train and bus discounts and the BritRail Pass and the BritRail Flexi Pass for train discounts. These British passes must be purchased before you leave home from a BritRail agent (☞ Train Information).

FARES & SCHEDULES

A good rail timetable is indispensable if you're doing extensive rail traveling. The Thomas Cook Timetables are updated monthly. There's also an annual summer edition (limited to Britain, France, and the Benelux).

➤ TRAIN INFORMATION: **BritRail Travel International** (☎ 800/677–8585). **CIT Tours Corp.** (✉ 15 W. 44th St., 10th floor, New York, NY 10036, ☎ 800/248–7245 for rail; 800/248–8687 for tours and hotels, rail@cit-rail.com for rail; tour@cittours.com for tours and hotels). **DER Travel Services** (☞ Discount Passes, Eurolines, *in* Bus Travel). **Eurostar** (☎ 800/942–4866; 805/482–8210 in U.S.; 0990/186–186 in the U.K.; 0123/361–7575 to the U.K. from other countries, WEB www.eurostar.com). **Rail Europe** (in the U.S.: ✉ 226–230 Westchester Ave., White Plains, NY 10604, ☎ 800/942–4866, FAX 800/432–1329, info@raileurope.com, WEB www.raileurope.com; in Canada: ✉ 2087 Dundas E., Suite 105, Mississauga, Ontario L4X 1M2, ☎ 905/602–4195; in the U.K.: ✉ 179 Piccadilly, and Victoria Station, London W1V 8BA, ☎ 0990/848–848 in the U.K.; 020/7647–4900 to the U.K. from other countries). **Venice Simplon-**

Orient Express (✉ Sea Containers House, 20 Upper Ground, London SE1 9PF, ☎ 800/524–2420 in the U.S.; 020/7805–5100 in the U.K.; 0870/161–5060 brochures, WEB www.orient-express.com).

TRAVEL AGENCIES

A good travel agent puts your needs first. Look for an agency that has been in business at least five years, emphasizes customer service, and has someone on staff who specializes in your destination. In addition, **make sure the agency belongs to a professional trade organization.** The American Society of Travel Agents (ASTA)—the largest and most influential in the field with more than 26,000 members in some 170 countries—maintains and enforces a strict code of ethics and will step in to help mediate any agent-client disputes if necessary. ASTA (whose motto is "Without a travel agent, youíre on your own") also maintains a Web site that includes a directory of agents.(If a travel agency is also acting as your tour operator, *see* Buyer Beware *in* Tours & Packages.)

➤ LOCAL AGENT REFERRALS: **American Society of Travel Agents** (ASTA; ✉ 1101 King St., Suite 200, Alexandria, VA 22314 ☎ 800/965–2782 24-hr hot line, FAX 703/739–7642, WEB www.astanet.com). **Association of British Travel Agents** (✉ 68–71 Newman St., London W1T 3AH, U.K., ☎ 020/7637–2444, FAX 020/7637–0713, WEB www.abtanet.com). **Association of Canadian Travel Agents** (✉ 130 Albert St., Suite 1705, Ottawa, Ontario K1P 5G4, Canada, ☎ 613/237–3657, FAX 613/237–7052, WEB www.acta.net). **Australian Federation of Travel Agents** (✉ Level 3, 309 Pitt St., Sydney NSW 2000, Australia, ☎ 02/9264–3299, FAX 02/9264–1085, WEB www.afta.com.au). **Travel Agents' Association of New Zealand** (✉ Level 5, Paxus House, 79 Boulcott St., Box 1888, Wellington 10033, New Zealand, ☎ 04/499–0104, FAX 04/499–0827, WEB www.taanz.org.nz).

VISITOR INFORMATION

For general information before you go, contact the national tourism offices.

➤ AUSTRIAN NATIONAL TOURIST OFFICE: **U.S.** (✉ Box 1142, Times Square Station, New York, NY 10108-1142, ☎ 212/944–6880, FAX 212/730–4568, WEB www.austria-tourism.at). **Canada** (✉ 2 Bloor St. E, Suite 3330, Toronto, Ontario M4W 1A8, ☎ 416/967–3381, FAX 416/967–4101). **U.K.** (✉ 14 Cork St., London, W1X 1PF, ☎ 020/7629–0461, FAX 020/7499–6038). **Australia and New Zealand** (✉ 36 Carrington St., 1st floor, Sydney, NSW 2000, ☎ 02/9299–3621, FAX 02/9299–3808). **Ireland** (✉ Merrion Hall, Strand Rd., Sandymount, Box 2506, Dublin 4, ☎ 01/283–0488, FAX 01/283–0531).

➤ BELGIAN NATIONAL TOURIST OFFICE: **U.S.** (✉ 780 Third Ave., Suite 1501, New York, NY 10017, ☎ 212/758–8130, FAX 212/355–7675, WEB www.visitbelgium.com). **Canada** (✉ Box 760, Succursale NDG, Montréal, Québec H4A 3S2, ☎ 514/484–3594, FAX 514/489–8965). **U.K.** (✉ 31 Pepper St., London E14 9RW, ☎ 020/7458–2888, FAX 020/7458–2999).

➤ BRITISH TOURIST AUTHORITY: **U.S.** (✉ 551 Fifth Ave., Suite 701, New York, NY 10176, ☎ 212/986–2200 or 800/462–2748, FAX 212/986–1188; 818/441–8265 24-hour fax information line, WEB www.visitbritain.com; walk-in service only: ✉ 625 N. Michigan Ave., Suite 1510, Chicago, IL 60611). **Canada** (✉ 5915 Airport Rd., Suite 120, Mississauga, Ontario L47V 1T1, ☎ 905/405–1840 or 888/847–4885, FAX 905/405–1835). **U.K.:** Britain Visitors Centre (✉ 1 Regent St., London SW1Y 4PQ, ☎ 0839/123–456; 0891/600–109 for 24-hour brochure line, costs 50p per minute; ✉ Thames Tower, Black's Rd., London, W6 9EL [no information by phone]). **Australia** (✉ Level 16, Gateway, 1 Macquarie Place, Sydney, NSW 2000, ☎ 02/9377–4400, FAX 02/9377–4499). **New Zealand** (✉ Dilworth Bldg., Suite 305, 3rd floor, Corner of Queen & Customs Sts., Auckland 1, ☎ 09/303–1446, FAX 09/377–6965). **Ireland** (✉ 18–19 College Green, Dublin 2, ☎ 01/670–8000, FAX 01/670–8244).

➤ CZECH CENTER: **U.S. and Canada** (✉ 1109 Madison Ave., New York, NY 10028, ☎ 212/288–0830, FAX 212/288–0971, WEB www.czechcenter.com). **Canada** (Czech Tourist Authority, ✉ c/o Czech Airlines, 401 Bay St., Suite 1510 Toronto, Ontario M5H 2Y4, ☎ 416/363–9928, FAX 416/363–0239). **U.K.** (✉ 95 Great Portland St., London W1N 5RA, ☎ 020/7291–9920, FAX 020/7436–1300; Czech and Slovak Tourist Centre, ✉ 16 Frognal Parade, Finchley Rd., London NW3 5HG, ☎ 020/7794–3263, FAX 020/7794–3265).

➤ DANISH TOURIST BOARD: **U.S. and Canada** (✉ 655 Third Ave., 18th floor, New York, NY 10017, ☎ 212/885–9700, FAX 212/885–9726, WEB www.dt.dk). **U.K.** (✉ 55 Sloane St., London SW1X 9SY, ☎ 020/7259–5959; 0900/160–0109 for 24-hour brochure line, costs 50p per minute, FAX 020/7259–5955).

➤ FRENCH GOVERNMENT TOURIST OFFICE: **U.S.** (☎ 900/990–0040 nationwide, 50¢ per minute; ✉ 444 Madison Ave., 16th floor, New York, NY 10022, FAX 212/838–7855, WEB www.francetourism.com; ✉ 676 N. Michigan Ave., Chicago, IL 60611, FAX 312/337–6339; ✉ 9454 Wilshire Blvd., Suite 715, Beverly Hills, CA 90212, FAX 310/276–2835). **Canada** (✉ 1981 Ave. McGill College, Suite 490, Montréal, Québec H3A 2W9, ☎ 514/288–4264, FAX 514/845–4868). **U.K.** (✉ 178 Piccadilly, London W1V OAL, ☎ 0870/556–1434, 50p per minute, FAX 020/7493–6594). **Australia** (✉ 25 Bligh St., Sydney, NSW 2000, ☎ 02/9231–5244, FAX 02/9221–8682). **Ireland** (✉ 35 Lower Abbey St., Dublin 1, ☎ 01/703–4046, FAX 01/874–7324).

➤ GERMAN NATIONAL TOURIST OFFICE: **U.S.** (✉ 122 E. 42nd St., New York, NY 10168, ☎ 212/661–7200, FAX 212/661–7174, WEB www.deutschland-tourismus.de; ✉ 401 N. Michigan Ave., Suite 2525, Chicago, IL 60611, ☎ 312/644–0723, FAX 312/644–0724). **Canada** (✉ 175 Bloor St. E, Suite 604, Toronto, Ontario M4W 3R8, ☎ 416/968–1570, FAX 416/968–1986). **U.K.** (✉ Box 2695, London W1A 3TN, ☎ 020/7317–0908 or 0891/600–100 for brochures, 50p per minute, FAX 020/7495–6129). **Australia** (✉ Box A980, Sydney, NSW 1235, ☎ 02/9267–8148, FAX 02/9267–9035).

➤ GREEK NATIONAL TOURIST ORGANI-
ZATION: U.S. (⊠ 645 Fifth Ave., New
York, NY 10022, ☎ 212/421–5777,
FAX 212/826–6940, WEB www.gnto.gr).
Canada (⊠ 1300 Bay St., Toronto,
Ontario M5R 3K8, ☎ 416/968–
2220, FAX 416/968–6533). U.K.
(⊠ 4 Conduit St., London W1R
0DJ, ☎ 020/7734–5997, FAX 020/
7287–1369). Australia (⊠ 51–57
Pitt St., Sydney, NSW 2000, ☎ 02/
9241–1663, FAX 02/9235–2174).

➤ HUNGARIAN NATIONAL TOURIST
OFFICE: U.S. and Canada (⊠ 150 E.
58th St., 33rd floor, New York, NY
10155, ☎ 212/355–0240, FAX 212/
207–4103, WEB www.hungarytourism.
hu). U.K. (⊠ Embassy of the Republic of Hungary, Commercial Section,
46 Eaton Pl., London SW1X
8AL, ☎ 020/7823–1032,
FAX 020/7823–1459).

➤ IRISH TOURIST BOARD: U.S. (⊠ 345
Park Ave., New York, NY 10154,
☎ 212/418–0800 or 800/223–6470,
FAX 212/371–9052, WEB www.ireland.
travel.ie). Canada (⊠ 160 Bloor St. E,
Suite 1150, Toronto, Ontario M4W
1B9, ☎ 416/487–3335, FAX 416/929–
6783). U.K. (⊠ Ireland House, 150
New Bond St., London W1Y 0AQ,
☎ 020/7493–3201, FAX 020/7493–
9065). Australia (⊠ 36 Carrington
St., 5th floor, Sydney, NSW 2000,
☎ 02/9299–6177, FAX 02/9299–
6323). Ireland (⊠ Baggot Street
Bridge, Dublin 2, ☎ 01/602–4000,
FAX 01/605–7757).

➤ ITALIAN GOVERNMENT TRAVEL
OFFICE (ENIT): U.S. (⊠ 630 Fifth
Ave., Suite 1565, New York, NY
10111, ☎ 212/245–4822, FAX 212/
586–9249, WEB www.italiantourism.
com; ⊠ 500 N. Michigan Ave., Suite
2240, Chicago, IL 60611, ☎ 312/
644–0996, FAX 312/644–3019; ⊠
12400 Wilshire Blvd., Suite 550, Los
Angeles, CA 90025, ☎ 310/820–
1898, FAX 310/820–6357). Canada
(⊠ 1 Pl. Ville Marie, Suite 1914,
Montréal, Québec H3B 3M9, ☎
514/866–7667, FAX 514/392–1429).
U.K. (Italian State Tourist Board,
⊠ 1 Princess St., London W1R 9AY,
☎ 020/7408–1254, FAX 020/7493–
6695). Australia (⊠ c/o Italian
Chamber of Commerce Level 26,
44 Market St., Sydney, NSW 2000,

☎ 02/9262–1666, FAX 02/9262–
1677).

➤ NETHERLANDS BOARD OF TOURISM:
U.S. (⊠ 225 N. Michigan Ave., Suite
1854, Chicago, IL 60601, ☎ 312/
819–1500 or 888/464–6552, FAX 312/
819–1740, WEB www.holland.com).
Canada (⊠ Box 1078, Toronto,
Ontario M5C 2K5, ☎ 888/464–6552
in English; 888/729–7227 in French,
FAX 416/363–1470). U.K. (⊠ 18
Buckingham Gate, London SW1E
6LD, ☎ 020/7828–7900; 0906/871–
7777 for 24-hour brochure line, costs
50p per minute, FAX 020/7828–7941).

➤ TOURIST OFFICE OF SPAIN: U.S. (⊠
666 Fifth Ave., 35th floor, New York,
NY 10103, ☎ 212/265–8822, FAX
212/265–8864, WEB www.okspain.org;
⊠ 845 N. Michigan Ave., Suite 915
E, Chicago, IL 60611, ☎ 312/642–
1992, FAX 312/642–9817; ⊠ 8383
Wilshire Blvd., Suite 956, Los Angeles, CA 90211, ☎ 213/658–7188, FAX
213/658–1061; ⊠ 1221 Brickell Ave.,
Suite 1850, Miami, FL 33131, ☎
305/358–1992, FAX 305/358–8223).
Canada (⊠ 2 Bloor St. W, Suite 3402,
Toronto, Ontario M4W 3E2, ☎ 416/
961–3131, FAX 416/961–1992). U.K.
(⊠ 22–23 Manchester Sq., London
W1M 5AP, ☎ 020/7486–8077 or
0891/669–920, 24-hour brochure
line, costs 50p per minute, FAX 020/
7486–8034).

➤ SWITZERLAND TOURISM: U.S. (⊠
608 Fifth Ave., New York, NY 10020,
☎ 212/757–5944, FAX 212/262–6116,
WEB www.switzerlandtourism.ch; ⊠
222 N. Sepulveda Blvd., Suite 1570,
El Segundo, CA 90245, ☎ 310/335–
5980, FAX 310/335–5982; ⊠ 501 Santa
Monica Blvd., Suite 607, Los Angeles,
CA 90401, ☎ 310/260–2421, FAX 310/
260–2923). Canada (⊠ 926 The East
Mall, Etobicoke Toronto], Ontario
M9B 6KI, ☎ 416/695–2090, FAX 416/
695–2774). U.K. (⊠ Swiss Centre, 1
New Coventry St., London W1V 8EE,
☎ 020/7734–1921, FAX 020/7851–
1720). Australia (⊠ Swissair Building,
33 Pitt St., Level 8, Sydney, NSW
2000, ☎ 02/9231–3744, FAX 02/
9251–6531).

➤ U.S. GOVERNMENT ADVISORIES: U.S.
Department of State (⊠ Overseas
Citizens Services Office, Room 4811
N.S., 2201 C St. NW, Washington,

DC 20520, ☎ 202/647–5225 for interactive hot line, WEB http://travel. state.gov/travel/html); enclose a self-addressed, stamped, business-size envelope.

WEB SITES

Do check out the World Wide Web when planning your trip. You'll find everything from weather forecasts to virtual tours of famous cities. Be sure to **visit Fodors.com** (www.fodors.com), a complete travel-planning site. You can research prices and book plane tickets, hotel rooms, rental cars, vacation packages, and more. In addition, you can post your pressing questions in the Travel Talk section. Other planning tools include a currency converter and weather reports, and there are loads of links to travel resources.

Also check out the European Travel Commission's site, www. visiteurope.com.

WHEN TO GO

➤ FORECASTS: **Weather Channel Connection** (☎ 900/932–8437), 95¢ per minute from a Touch-Tone phone.

1 AMSTERDAM

Amsterdam is a gem of a city for the visitor. Small and densely packed with fine buildings, many dating from the 17th century or earlier, it is easily explored on foot or by bike.

EXPLORING AMSTERDAM

The old heart of the city consists of canals, with narrow streets radiating out like the spokes of a wheel. The hub of this wheel and the most convenient point to begin sightseeing is Centraal Station (Central Station). Across the street, in the same building as the Old Dutch Coffee House, is a tourist information office. The Rokin, once an open canal, is the main route from Central Station via the Dam to the Muntplein. Amsterdam's key points of interest can be covered within two or three days, including visits to one or two of the important museums and galleries. The city center is divided into districts that are easily covered on foot.

Around the Dam

The Dam (Dam Square) is the official center of town. It traces its roots to the 12th century, when wanderers from central Europe came floating in their canoes down the Amstel river and stopped to build a dam. Soon this muddy mound became the focal point of the small city of Amstelledamme and the location of the local weigh house. From these inauspicious beginnings, Amsterdam had developed into one of the richest and most powerful cities in the world by the 17th century.

Numbers in the margin correspond to points of interest on the Amsterdam map.

★ ⑭ **Anne Frankhuis** (Anne Frank House). Immortalized by the poignant diary kept by the young Jewish girl from 1942 to 1944, when she and her family hid here from the German occupying forces, this canal-side house also has an educational exhibition and documents about the Holocaust and civil liberty. ⊠ *Prinsengracht 263,* ☎ *020/5567100,* WEB *www.annefrank.nl.* ⊙ *Apr.–Aug., daily 9–9 (except for May 4, 9–7); Sept.–Mar., daily 9–7 (except Christmas Day and New Year's Day, noon–7). Closed Yom Kippur.*

2

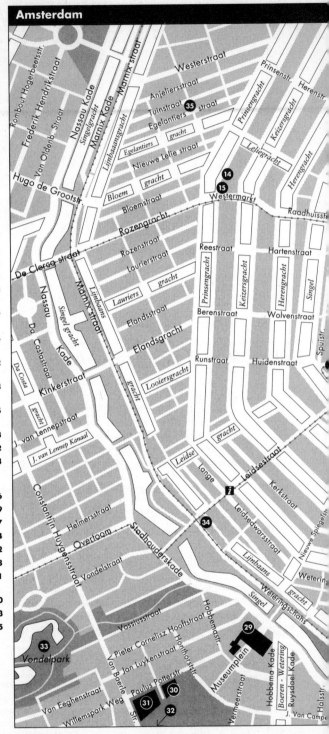

Amsterdam

3

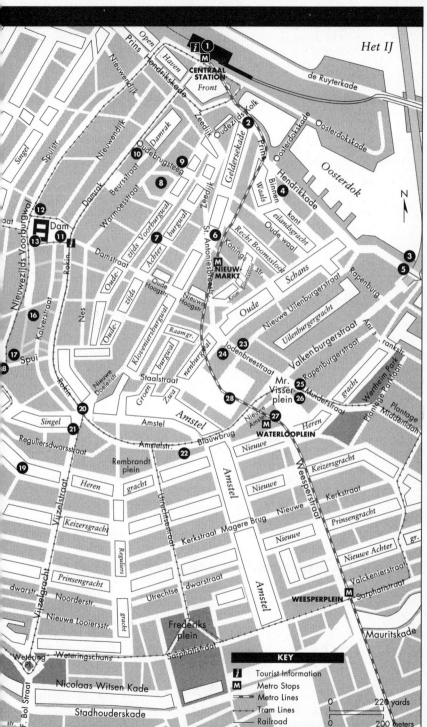

⓾ **Beurs van Berlage** (Berlage's Stock Exchange). This impressive building, completed in 1903, was designed by Hendrik Petrus Berlage (1856–1934), whose principles were to guide modernism. The sculpture and rich decoration of the plain brick interior are among modernism's embryonic masterpieces. It now houses two concert halls, a large exhibition space, and its own museum, which also offers the chance to climb the 138-ft-high tower for its superb views. ⌧ *Beursplein 1,* ☎ *020/5304141.* ⊙ *Museum Tues.–Sun. 10–5.*

❶ **Centraal Station** (Central Station). The flamboyant redbrick and stone portal was designed by P. J. H. Cuijpers (1827–1921) and built in 1884–89. Compare it with Cuijpers's other significant contribution to Amsterdam's architectural heritage—the Rijksmuseum. ⌧ *Stationsplein.*

⓫ **Dam** (Dam Square). This is the broadest square in the old section of the town. Fishermen used to come here to sell their catch. Today it is a busy crossroads, circled with shops and bisected by traffic; it is also a popular spot for outdoor performers. At one side of the square stands a simple monument to Dutch victims of World War II. Eleven urns contain soil from the 11 provinces of the Netherlands, and a 12th contains soil from the former Dutch East Indies, now Indonesia. ⌧ *Junction of Rokin, Damrak, Moses en Aaronstraat, and Paleisstraat.*

❻ **De Waag** (The Weighhouse). Dating from 1488, when it was built as a city gate, this turreted, redbrick monument dominates the Nieuwmarkt (New Market) in the oldest part of Amsterdam. It became a weigh house and was once the headquarters for ancient professional guilds. The magnificently restored **Theatrum Anatomicum**, up the winding stairs, was added in 1691 and set the scene for Rembrandt's painting the *Anatomy Lesson of Dr. Tulp.* The upper floors are now home to the media lab of the Society for Old and New Media, which hosts occasional conferences and exhibitions. Downstairs is a grand café and restaurant. ⌧ *Nieuwmarkt 4,* ☎ *020/5579898,* ⓦⓔⓑ *www.waag.org.*

⓭ **Het Koninklijk Paleis te Amsterdam** (Royal Palace in Amsterdam). The vast, well-proportioned classical structure dominating the Dam was completed in 1655. It is built on 13,659 pilings sunk into the marshy soil. The great pediment sculptures are an allegorical representation of Amsterdam surrounded by Neptune and mythological sea creatures. Filled with opulent 18th- and early 19th-century furnishings, it is the official royal residence but is used only on high state occasions. ⌧ *Dam,* ☎ *020/6248698.* ⊙ *Tues.–Thurs. 1–4; daily 12:30–5 in summer. Occasionally closed for state events.*

❾ **Museum Amstelkring.** The facade carries the inscription *"Ons Lieve Heer Op Solder"* ("Our Lord in the Attic"). In 1578 Amsterdam embraced Protestantism and outlawed the church of Rome. The municipal authorities were so tolerant that secret Catholic chapels were allowed to exist; at one time there were 62 in Amsterdam alone. One such chapel was established in the attics of these three neighboring canal-side houses, built around 1661, and services were held in the attics regularly until 1888, the year the St. Nicolaaskerk was consecrated for Catholic worship. Of interest are the Baroque altar with its revolving tabernacle, the swinging pulpit that can be stowed out of sight, and the upstairs gallery with its displays of religious artifacts. ⌧ *Oudezijds Voorburgwal 40,* ☎ *020/6246604.* ⊙ *Mon.–Sat. 10–5, Sun. 1–5.*

❺ **Nederlands Scheepvaartmuseum** (Netherlands Maritime Museum). This former naval warehouse maintains a collection of restored vessels and a replica of a three-masted trading ship from 1749. The museum explains the history of Dutch shipping, from dugout canoes right through to modern container ships, with maps, paintings, and models. ⌧ *Kat-*

tenburgerplein 1, ☎ *020/5232222.* ⊘ *Tues.–Sun. 10–5, only open Mon. on school holidays.*

⟲ ❸ **NEMO Science & Technology Center.** This interactive museum, formerly called newMetropolis, was designed by Renzo Piano, architect of the Centre Pompidou in Paris. Hands-on exhibits range from elementary physics to the latest technological gadgets. The rooftop terrace offers a panoramic view across the city. ⊠ *Oosterdok 2, Prins Hendrikkade,* ☎ *0900/9191100 costs 75¢ per min,* 🕮 *www. e-NEMO.nl.* ⊘ *Tues.–Sun. 10–5.*

⑫ **Nieuwe Kerk** (New Church). This huge Gothic structure was gradually expanded until 1540, when it reached its present size. Gutted by fire in 1645, it was reconstructed in an imposing Renaissance style, as interpreted by strict Calvinists. The superb oak pulpit, the 14th-century nave, the stained-glass windows, and the great organ (1645) are all shown to great effect on national holidays, when the church is bedecked with flowers. As befits the Netherlands' national church, it is the site of all coronations, most recently that of Queen Beatrix in 1980. In democratic Dutch spirit, the church is also used as a meeting place, has a lively café, and hosts temporary exhibitions and concerts. ⊠ *Dam,* ☎ *020/6386909.* ⊘ *Daily 10–6; Thurs. until 10.*

❽ **Oude Kerk** (Old Church). The city's oldest house of worship dates from the early 14th century, but it was badly damaged by iconoclasts after the Reformation. The church still retains its original bell tower and a few remarkable stained-glass windows. Rembrandt's wife, Saskia, is buried here. ⊠ *Oudekerksplein 23,* ☎ *020/6258284,* 🕮 *www.oudekerk.nl.* ⊘ *Mon.–Sat. 11–5, Sun. 1–5.*

❼ **Rosse Buurt** (Red-Light District). This area is defined by two of the city's oldest canals. In the windows at canal level, women in sheer lingerie slouch, stare, or do their nails. The area can be shocking, but is generally safe, although midnight walks down dark side streets are not advised. If you do explore the area, watch for purse snatchers and pickpockets. ⊠ *Bordered by Oudezijds Voorburgwal and Oudezijds Achterburgwal.*

❹ **Scheepvaartshuis** (Shipping Offices). Designed (1911–16) by J. M. der Mey and the Van Gendt brothers, this office building is the earliest example of the Amsterdam School's unique building style. The fantastical facade is richly decorated in brick and stone, with lead and zinc roofing pouring from on high. ⊠ *Prins Hendrikkade 108–119.*

❷ **Schreierstoren** (Weepers' Tower). Facing the harbor stands a lookout tower, erected in 1480, for women whose men were out at sea. A tablet marks the point from which Henrik (a.k.a. Henry) Hudson set sail on the *Half Moon* on April 4, 1609, on a voyage that eventually took him to what is now New York and the river that bears his name. ⊠ *Prins Hendrikkade 94–95.*

⑮ **Westerkerk** (West Church). The church's 279-ft tower is the city's highest; it also has an outstanding carillon. Rembrandt (1606–69) and his son Titus are buried in the church, which was completed as early as 1631. In summer you can climb to the top of the tower for a fine view over the city. ⊠ *Prinsengracht (corner of Westermarkt),* ☎ *020/ 6247766.* ⊘ *Apr.–Sept., weekdays 11–3; July–Aug., also Sat. 11–3. Tower June–Sept., weekdays 11–3. Closed during private services.*

South of the Dam

From the south of Dam Square to Museumplein lies the artistic heart of Amsterdam, with its wealth of museums and fine architecture. The

Golden Bend, the grandest stretch of canal in town, has some of the finest mansions built by Amsterdam's prosperous merchants.

⑯ Amsterdam Historisch Museum (Amsterdam Historical Museum). The museum traces the city's history from its origins as a fishing village through the 17th-century golden age of material and artistic wealth to the decline of the trading empire during the 18th century. In the courtyard off Kalverstraat a striking Renaissance gate (1581) guards a series of tranquil inner courtyards. In medieval times, this area was an island devoted to piety. Today the bordering canals are filled in. ⊠ *Kalverstraat 92,* ☎ *020/5231822.* ⊙ *Weekdays 10–5, weekends 11–5.*

★ **⑰ Begijnhof** (Beguine Court). This is an enclosed square of almshouses founded in 1346 that is a surprising oasis of peace just a stone's throw from the city's hectic center. The Beguines were women who led a form of convent life, often taking the vow of chastity. The last Beguine died in 1974, and her house, No. 26, has been preserved as she left it. No. 34, dating from the 15th century, is the oldest house and the only one to retain its wooden Gothic facade. A small passageway and courtyard link the Begijnhof to the Amsterdam Historisch Museum. ⊠ *Begijnhof 29,* ☎ *020/6233565.* ⊙ *Daily 9–dusk.*

㉑ Bloemenmarkt (Flower Market). Here floating stalls carry a bright array of freshly cut flowers and foliage, as well as an enviable variety of bulbs and plants. ⊠ *Along Singel Canal, from Muntplein to Koningsplein.* ⊙ *Mon.–Sat. (occasionally Sun.) 8:30–6.*

⑰ Engelse Kerk (English Church). This church was given to Amsterdam's English and Scottish Presbyterians early in the 17th century. On the church wall and in the chancel are tributes to the Pilgrim Fathers, who sailed from Delftshaven (in Rotterdam) to the New World in 1620. Opposite the church is another of the city's secret Catholic chapels, whose exterior looks as though it were two adjoining houses, built in 1671. ⊠ *Begijnhof.*

★ **⑲ Gouden Bocht** (Golden Bend). The Herengracht (Gentlemen's Canal) is the city's most prestigious canal. The stretch of the canal from Leidsestraat to Vijzelstraat is named for the sumptuous patrician houses that line it. Seventeenth-century merchants moved here from the Amstel River to escape the by-products of their wealth: noisy warehouses, unpleasant brewery smells, and the risk of fire in the sugar refineries. The houses display the full range of Amsterdam architectural detailing, from gables in a variety of shapes to elaborate Louis XIV–style cornices and frescoed ceilings. They are best seen from the east side of the canal. ⊠ *Herengracht, Leidsestraat to Vijzelstraat.*

⑳ Munttoren (Mint Tower). Built in 1620 at this busy crossroads, the graceful tower that was later added to this former royal mint has a clock and bells that still seem to mirror the golden age. There are frequent carillon recitals. ⊠ *Muntplein.*

㉒ Museum Willet-Holthuysen. Built in 1690, the elegant residence was bequeathed to the city of Amsterdam on condition that it be retained as a museum. It provides a peek into the lives of the city's well-heeled merchants. ⊠ *Herengracht 605,* ☎ *020/5231870.* ⊙ *Weekdays 10–5, weekends 11–5.*

⑱ Spui (Sluice). In the heart of the university area, the lively square was a center for revolutionary student rallies in 1968. Now you'll find bookstores and bars, including cozy brown cafés. ⊠ *Junction of Nieuwezijds Voorburgwal, Spuistraat, and Singel Canal.*

Jewish Amsterdam

The original settlers in the Jodenbuurt (old Jewish Amsterdam) were wealthy Sephardic Jews from Spain and Portugal, later followed by poorer Ashkenazic refugees from Germany and Poland. At the beginning of the 20th century this was a thriving community of Jewish diamond polishers, dyers, and merchants.

㉓ Jodenbreestraat. During World War II this street marked the southwestern border of the *Joodse wijk* (Jewish neighborhood), then a Nazi-controlled ghetto surrounded by barbed wire. The character of the area was largely destroyed in the name of progress in the guise of highway construction in 1965 and, more recently, by construction of both the Metro and the Muziektheater/Stadhuis complex. However, you can still find a flavor of times past by wandering around the peaceful canals and streets between the Rechtboomsloot and the Oude Schans.

㉗ Joods Historisch Museum (Jewish Historical Museum). This complex of four synagogues, the oldest dating from 1671, opened in 1987 as a unique museum. The succession of synagogues was gradually constructed to accommodate Amsterdam's growing community of Jews, many of whom had fled from oppression and prejudice elsewhere. Before the war, there were about 120,000 Jews here, but only 20,000 of them survived the Nazis and the war. Founded by American and Dutch Jews, the museum displays religious treasures in a clear cultural and historical context. Because the synagogues lost most of their treasures in the war, their architecture and history are more compelling than the exhibits. ⊠ *Jonas Daniël Meijerplein 2–4,* ☎ *020/6269945,* WEB *www.jhm.nl.* ☉ *Daily 11–5. Closed Yom Kippur.*

㉕ Muiderstraat. This pedestrian area east of Waterlooplein retains much of the neighborhood's historic atmosphere. Notice the gateways decorated with pelicans, symbolizing great love; according to legend, the pelican will feed her starving young with her own blood. ⊠ *Muiderstraat/Waterlooplein.*

★ **㉔ Museum het Rembrandthuis** (Rembrandt's House). From 1639 to 1658, Rembrandt lived at Jodenbreestraat 4. For more than 20 years he used the ground floor as living quarters; the sunny upper floor was his studio. The museum has a superb collection of his etchings as well as work by his contemporaries. The modern new wing next door houses a multimedia auditorium, two new exhibition spaces, and a shop. ⊠ *Jodenbreestraat 4–6,* ☎ *020/5200400,* WEB *www.rembrandthuis.nl.* ☉ *Mon.–Sat. 10–5, Sun. 1–5. Closed Jan. 1.*

㉘ Muziektheater/Stadhuis (Music Theater/Town Hall complex). Amsterdammers come to the Town Hall section of the building by day to obtain driver's licenses, pick up welfare payments, and get married. They return by night to the rounded, marble-clad facade overlooking the Amstel River to see opera and ballet performed by the Netherlands' national companies. You can wander into the Town Hall for a look at some interesting sculptures and other displays. A guided tour of the Muziektheater takes you around the dressing rooms, dance studios, backstage, and even to the wig department. ⊠ *Amstel 3,* ☎ *020/5518054.* ☉ *Guided tours Wed. and Sat. at 3.*

★ **㉖ Portugese Israelitische Synagoge** (Portuguese Israelite Synagogue). As one of Amsterdam's five neighboring synagogues, this was part of the largest Jewish religious complex in Europe. The beautiful, austere interior of the 17th-century building is still intact, even if the building itself is marooned on a traffic island. ⊠ *Mr. Visserplein 3,* ☎ *020/*

6245351, WEB *www.esnoga.com.* ☉ *Apr.–Oct., Sun.–Fri. 10–4; Nov.–Mar., Sun.–Thurs. 10–4, Fri. 10–3. Closed Jewish holidays.*

The Museum Quarter

Amsterdam's wealth of art—from Golden Age painters through Van Gogh up to the present day—is concentrated on the area around the grassy Museumplein, which also serves as the transition point between the central canal area and the modern residential sections of the city. The nearby Leidseplein is dotted with cafés and discos and attracts young visitors to the city.

㉜ Concertgebouw (Concert Hall). The sounds of the country's foremost orchestra resonate in this imposing, classical building. The smaller of the two auditoriums is used for chamber music and solo recitals. The main hall hosts world-class concerts. ⊠ *Concertgebouwplein 2–6,* ☎ *020/6718345.*

㉞ Leidseplein. This square is the pulsing heart of the city's nightlife. In summer you can enjoy the entertainment of street performers on the many café terraces. ⊠ *Junction of Leidsestraat, Marnixstraat, and Weteringschans.*

★ **㉙ Rijksmuseum** (State Museum). The museum, the most important of the Dutch museums, was founded in 1808, but the current, rather lavish building dates from 1885 and was designed by the architect of Central Station, P. J. H. Cuijpers. As well as Italian, Flemish, and Spanish paintings, there are also vast collections of furniture, textiles, ceramics, sculpture, and prints. The museum's fame, however, rests on its unrivaled collection of 16th- and 17th-century Dutch masters. Of Rembrandt's masterpieces, the *Night Watch,* concealed during World War II in a cave in Maastricht, was misnamed because of its dull layers of varnish; in reality it depicts the Civil Guard in daylight. Also worth searching out are Frans Hals's family portraits, Jan Steen's drunken scenes, Van Ruysdael's romantic but menacing landscapes, and Vermeer's glimpses of everyday life bathed in his limpid light. The Zuid Vleugel (South Wing) houses a freshly displayed treasure trove of Eastern art. ⊠ *Stadhouderskade 42,* ☎ *020/6747047,* WEB *www.rijksmuseum.nl.* ☉ *Daily 10–5.*

㉛ Stedelijk Museum (Museum of Modern Art). The museum has a stimulating collection of modern art and ever-changing displays of the works of contemporary artists. Before viewing the paintings of Cézanne, Chagall, Kandinsky, and Mondrian, check the list of temporary exhibitions in Room 1. ⊠ *Paulus Potterstraat 13,* ☎ *020/5732911,* WEB *www.stedelijk.nl.* ☉ *Daily 11–5.*

★ **㉚ Van Gogh Museum.** This museum contains the world's largest collection of the artist's works—200 paintings and nearly 500 drawings—as well as works by some 50 of his contemporaries. The main building was designed by Gerrit Rietvelt (1888–1964) and completed in 1972. It was renovated in 1999, and a new wing, designed by Japanese architect Kisho Kurokawa, was added to exhibit van Gogh's prints and accommodate temporary exhibitions, which focus on art from the late 19th and early 20th centuries. ⊠ *Paulus Potterstraat 7,* ☎ *020/5705252,* WEB *www.vangoghmuseum.nl.* ☉ *Daily 10–5:30.*

☾ **㉝ Vondelpark.** Amsterdam's central park is an elongated rectangle of paths, lakes, and pleasant, shady greenery. A monument honors the 17th-century epic poet Joost van den Vondel, after whom the park is named. There are special children's areas with paddling pools and sandboxes. From June through August, the park hosts free outdoor concerts and

plays Wednesday–Sunday. ✉ *Stadhouderskade.* ☎ 020/523–779, <u>WEB</u>
www.openluchttheater.nl.

The Jordaan

⑤ Jordaan. In this old part of Amsterdam the canals and side streets are
named for trees, flowers, and plants. When it was the French quarter
of the city, the area was known as *le jardin* (the garden), a name that
over the years has become Jordaan. The best time to explore the district is on a Sunday morning or in the evening. The Jordaan has attracted many artists and is something of a bohemian quarter, where
run-down buildings are being converted into restaurants, antiques
shops, boutiques, and galleries. ✉ *Bordered by Prinsengracht, Lijnbaansgracht, Brouwersgracht, and Raadhuisstraat.*

DINING

Health-conscious Amsterdammers prefer set menus and early dinners.
For traditionalists the NEDERLANDS DIS soup tureen sign is a promise
of regional recipes and seasonal ingredients.

CATEGORY	COST*
$$$$	over Fl. 100 (€45)
$$$	Fl. 70–Fl. 100 (€32–€45)
$$	Fl. 40–Fl. 70 (€18–€32)
$	under Fl. 40 (€18)

per person for a main course at dinner

$$–$$$ ★ ✕ La Rive. The French cuisine, with an awe-inspiring "truffle menu"
of dishes prepared with exotic (and expensive) ingredients, can be tai-
lored to meet your every whim. Epicureans should inquire about the
"chef's table": with a group of six you can sit at a table alongside the
open kitchen and watch chefs prepare and describe each of your
courses. At this world-class restaurant, you can also enjoy the city's
most elegant view of the river Amstel, and, unusual for this country,
a no-smoking section. ✉ *Amstel Inter-Continental Hotel, Professor Tulpplein 1,* ☎ 020/6226060. *Jacket and tie.* AE, DC, MC, V.

$$–$$$ ✕ Oesterbar. The "Oyster Bar" specializes in seafood, grilled, baked,
or fried. The upstairs dining room is more formal than the downstairs
bistro, but prices don't vary. The sole is prepared in four different ways,
or you can try the local specialties such as halibut and eel; oysters are
a stimulating, if pricey, appetizer. ✉ *Leidseplein 10,* ☎ 020/6232988.
AE, DC, MC, V.

$$–$$$ ★ ✕ 't Swarte Schaep. The "Black Sheep" is named after a proverbial
17th-century sheep that roamed the area. With its creaking boards and
array of copper pots, the interior is reminiscent of a ship's cabin. Classic Dutch dishes include scallops wrapped in bacon for starters and fillet of beef with hazelnuts as a filling main course. ✉ *Korte
Leidsedwarsstraat 24,* ☎ 020/6223021. *Reservations essential. Jacket
and tie.* AE, DC, MC, V.

$–$$$ ★ ✕ Excelsior. The restaurant at the Hôtel de l'Europe offers a varied menu
of French cuisine based on local ingredients. There are no fewer than
15 splendid set menus. Service is discreet and impeccable, and the view
over the Amstel River, to the Muntplein on one side and the Muziek-
theater on the other, is the best in Amsterdam. ✉ *Hôtel de l'Europe,
Nieuwe Doelenstraat 2–8,* ☎ 020/5311705. *Reservations essential.
Jacket and tie.* AE, DC, MC, V. *No lunch Sat.*

$$ ★ ✕ De Silveren Spiegel. In an alarmingly crooked 17th-century house,
you can have an outstanding meal while you enjoy the personal attention
of the owner at one of just a small cluster of tables. Local ingredients

such as Texel lamb and wild rabbit are cooked with subtlety and flair. ✉ *Kattengat 4–6,* ☎ *020/6246589. AE, MC, V. Closed Sun.*

$–$$ ✕ **De Knijp.** Traditional Dutch food and French bistro fare are served here in a traditional Dutch environment. The mezzanine level is especially cozy. Alongside tamer dishes, there are seasonal game specialties including wild boar, ham with red cabbage, and fillet of hare. After-midnight dinner draws concertgoers and performers from the neighboring Concertgebouw. ✉ *Van Baerlestraat 134,* ☎ *020/6714248. Reservations not accepted. AE, DC, MC, V.*

$–$$ ✕ **De Tropen.** The emphasis on the tropics is reflected in the decor, food, and background music in this small, intimate restaurant. Owner/chef Jacob Preyde is somewhat of a sensation on the Amsterdam scene with his innovative Caribbean/Chinese fusion dishes. Pumpkin soup with saffron or parrotfish prepared with exotic herbs and spices are just some of the choices you may find on the ever-changing menu. His homemade cardamom ice cream is a favorite. ✉ *Palmgracht 39,* ☎ *020/4215528. MC, V. Closed Mon.–Tues. No lunch.*

$–$$ ✕ **D' Theeboom.** Just behind the Dam, the ground floor of this historic canal-side warehouse has been converted into a stylish, formal restaurant offering a bargain lunchtime formula. The seasonal menu might include a delicious parcel of vegetables flavored with a selection of mushrooms, followed by carefully prepared red mullet with a saffron sauce. ✉ *Singel 210,* ☎ *020/6238420. AE, DC, MC, V. No lunch weekends.*

$–$$ ✕ **Dynasty.** Surrounded by luxurious Oriental furniture and murals, you can savor dishes from Thailand, Malaysia, and China. Main-course delicacies include mixed seafood in banana leaves and succulent duck and lobster on a bed of watercress. In one of the city's most active nightlife areas, it can get very busy, but service is always impeccable. ✉ *Reguliersdwarsstraat 30,* ☎ *020/6268400. AE, DC, MC, V. Closed Tues. No lunch.*

$–$$ ✕ **In de Waag.** The lofty, beamed interior below the Theatrum Anatomicum has been converted into a grand café and restaurant. The reading table harbors computer terminals for Internet enthusiasts. Dinnertime brings a seasonal selection of hearty cuisine to be savored by candlelight. ✉ *Nieuwmarkt 4,* ☎ *020/4227772. AE, MC, DC, V.*

$–$$ ✕ **Land van Walem.** Elegant breakfast and brunch options are served at this popular, all-day grand café on chic *ciabatta* (a crispy, white Italian bread), while at dinnertime the chefs prepare up-to-the-minute fusion cooking—and ask a higher price tag to go with it. ✉ *Keizersgracht 449,* ☎ *020/6253544. AE, MC, V.*

$–$$ ✕ **L'Indochine.** This is one of the city's first ventures into Vietnamese
★ food, and the chef's skillful preparation of the freshest ingredients, some specially imported, has been an immediate success. Sample the healthy, mint-flavored spring rolls or the meatier seared prawn and beef skewers to start, followed by lightly fried fish with vegetables in a subtly spiced sauce. ✉ *Beulingstraat 9,* ☎ *020/6275755. Reservations essential. AE, MC, V. Closed Mon. No lunch.*

$–$$ ✕ **Lonny's.** Lonny Gerungan's family have been cooks on Bali for gen-
★ erations—even preparing banquets for visiting Dutch royals. His plush restaurant in Amsterdam, draped in silky fabrics, serves the finest authentic Indonesian cuisine. Even the simplest rijsttafel is a feast of more than 15 delicately spiced dishes. ✉ *Rozengracht 46–48,* ☎ *020/ 6238950. Reservations essential. AE, DC, MC, V.*

$–$$ ✕ **Rose's Cantina.** A perennial favorite of the sparkling set, this place offers spicy Tex-Mex food, lethal cocktails, and a high noise level. Weekend reservations are essential. ✉ *Reguliersdwarsstraat 38,* ☎ *020/ 6259797. AE, DC, MC, V.*

$ ✕ **Het Gasthuys.** In this bustling restaurant you'll be served handsome portions of traditional Dutch home cooking—choice cuts of meat with excellent fries and piles of mixed salad. Sit at the bar or take a table high up in the rafters at the back. In summer the enchanting terrace on the canal side opens. ✉ *Grimburgwal 7,* ☎ *020/6248230. No credit cards.*

$ ✕ **Kantjil en de Tijger.** This lively Indonesian restaurant is a favorite with the locals and close to the bars on the Spui. The menu is based on three different rijsttafel, with a profusion of meat and vegetable dishes varying in flavor from coconut-milk sweet to peppery hot. ✉ *Spuistraat 291/293,* ☎ *020/6200994. AE, DC, MC, V. No lunch.*

$ ✕ **Song Kwae.** The traditional offerings in Amsterdam's Chinatown, based around the Nieuwmarkt and Zeedijk, have now been complemented by a surge of Thai restaurants, and this buzzing joint offers speedy service and quality food for a budget price. Alongside the traditional red and green Thai curries and the stir-fry options, there are specialties such as green papaya salad with crab. ✉ *Kloveniersburgwal 14,* ☎ *020/6242568. AE, DC, MC, V.*

$ ✕ **Toscanini.** This cavernous, noisy Italian restaurant has superb cui-
★ sine and an enthusiastic regular clientele. Try a selection of antipasti followed by fresh pasta or the simple fish and meat dishes. ✉ *Lindengracht 75,* ☎ *020/6232813. Reservations essential. AE, DC, MC, V. No lunch.*

LODGING

Accommodations are tight from Easter to summer, so early booking is advised.

CATEGORY	COST*
$$$$	over Fl. 500 (€227)
$$$	Fl. 300–Fl. 500 (€136–€227)
$$	Fl. 200–Fl. 300 (€91–€136)
$	under Fl. 200 (€91)

Prices are for two persons sharing a double room.

$$$$ 🏨 **Amstel Inter-Continental.** Amsterdam's grande dame opened in 1867
★ and was spectacularly renovated in 1992. The spacious rooms have Oriental rugs, brocade upholstery, Delft lamps, and a color scheme inspired by the warm, earthy tones of Makkum pottery. The Amstel is frequented by many of the nation's top businesspeople and sometimes hosts members of the royal family. ✉ *Professor Tulpplein 1, 1018 GX,* ☎ *020/6226060,* FAX *020/6225808,* WEB *www.interconti.com. 55 rooms, 25 suites. Restaurant, indoor pool. AE, DC, MC, V.*

$$$$ 🏨 **Blake's.** British designer Anouska Hempel opened her luxury hotel in 1999 and it became an immediate "in" spot. The beautifully appointed interior has an oriental influence and the entire hotel and courtyard offer serenity in a bustling city. The restaurant is one of Amsterdam's best ($$), with a Thai/French fusion kitchen. ✉ *Keijzersgracht 384, 1016 GB,* ☎ *020/5302010,* FAX *020/5302030,* WEB *www.blakes.site.nl. 15 rooms, 10 suites. Restaurant. AE, DC, MC, V.*

$$$$ 🏨 **Grand Amsterdam.** In 1991 Amsterdam's former city hall was con-
★ verted into a luxury hotel. Parts of this elegant building date from the 16th century, but most of it belongs to the early 20th, when the country's best artists and architects were commissioned to create a building the city could be proud of. Features include a mural by Karel Appel, Jugendstil stained-glass windows, Gobelin tapestries, and palatially luxurious reception areas and rooms. The kitchen of the brasserie-style restaurant, Café Roux, is supervised by the incomparable Albert Roux. ✉ *Oudezijds Voorburgwal 197, 1012 EX,* ☎ *020/5553111,* FAX *020/5553222,* WEB *www.thegrand.nl. 160 rooms, 6 suites, 16 apartments. Restaurant, indoor pool. AE, DC, MC, V.*

$$$$ 🏨 **Hôtel de l'Europe.** Behind the stately facade of this building dating
★   from the end of the 19th century is a full complement of modern facilities, as befits a hotel often ranked among the world's best. Large,
bright rooms overlooking the Amstel are done in pastel colors; others
have warm, rich colors and antiques. Apart from its world-renowned
Excelsior restaurant, the hotel houses a sophisticated leisure complex.
⊠ *Nieuwe Doelenstraat 2–8, 1012 CP,* ☎ *020/5311777,* ⅁AX *020/
5311778,* ⅁EB *www.leurope.nl. 80 rooms, 20 suites. Restaurant, indoor
pool. AE, DC, MC, V.*

$$$$ 🏨 **Pulitzer.** The Pulitzer is one of Europe's most ambitious hotel
★   restorations, using the shells of a block of 24 17th- and 18th-century
merchants' houses. Inside, the refined atmosphere is sustained by the
modern art gallery and the lovingly restored brickwork, oak beams,
and split-level rooms: no two are alike, and many rooms have antique furnishings to match the period architectural features. ⊠ *Prinsengracht 315–331, 1016 GZ,* ☎ *020/5235235,* ⅁AX *020/6276753,*
⅁EB *www.starwood.com. 224 rooms, 3 suites, 4 apartments. Restaurant. AE, DC, MC, V.*

$$$ 🏨 **Ambassade.** With its beautiful canal-side location, its Louis XV–
style decoration, and its Oriental rugs, the Ambassade seems more like
a stately home than a hotel. Service is attentive and room prices in-
clude breakfast in an elegant room overlooking the canal. For other
meals, the neighborhood has a good choice of restaurants. ⊠ *Heren-
gracht 341, 1016 AZ,* ☎ *020/5550222,* ⅁AX *020/5550277,* ⅁EB *www.
ambassade-hotel.nl. 52 rooms, 7 suites, 1 apartment. AE, DC, MC, V.*

$$$ 🏨 **Canal House Hotel.** Get a real sense of sleeping in the 17th century
amid the antique furnishings at this hotel. Spacious rooms overlook
the canal or the atmospheric garden. A hearty Dutch breakfast served
in the breakfast room is included in the price. Children under age 14
are not permitted. ⊠ *Keizersgracht 148, 1015 CX,* ☎ *020/6225182,*
⅁AX *020/6241317,* ⅁EB *www.canalhouse.nl. 26 rooms. AE, DC, MC, V.*

$$–$$$ 🏨 **Golden Tulip Grand Hotel Krasnapolsky.** The fine Old World hotel is
enhanced by the Winter Garden restaurant ($$), which dates from 1818.
The large-scale expansion into neighboring buildings in the '90s has pro-
vided space for extensive conference and business facilities and an amaz-
ing selection of restaurants. The cosmopolitan atmosphere carries through
all the well-equipped rooms, with decor ranging from Victorian to art
deco. ⊠ *Dam 9, 1012 JS,* ☎ *020/5549111,* ⅁AX *020/6228607,* ⅁EB
*www.krasnapolsky.nl. 432 rooms, 1 suite, 36 apartments. 7 restaurants.
AE, DC, MC, V.*

$$–$$$ 🏨 **Hotel Seven Bridges.** Named for the view from its front steps, this
small canal-house hotel has rooms decorated with individual flair.
Oriental rugs warm wooden floors, and there are comfy antique arm-
chairs and marble washstands. The Rembrandtplein is nearby. For a
stunning view, request a canal-side room, but make sure to reserve
months in advance. One of the pleasures here is breakfast in bed.
There are four attic rooms full of character that have shared bath fa-
cilities. ⊠ *Reguliersgracht 31, 1017 LK,* ☎ *020/6231329. 10 rooms,
6 with shower or bath. AE, MC, V.*

$$ 🏨 **Atlas Hotel.** Known for its friendly atmosphere, this small hotel is
in Amsterdam's most prestigious neighborhood, just a block from the
Vondelpark. The moderate-size rooms are decorated in a comfortable, modern style. The main museums are within easy walking distance. ⊠ *Van Eeghenstraat 64, 1071 GK,* ☎ *020/6766336,* ⅁AX *020/
6717633. 23 rooms. Restaurant. AE, DC, MC, V.*

$$ 🏨 **Hotel de Filosoof.** On a quiet street near Vondelpark, the hotel at-
tracts artists, thinkers, and people looking for something a little un-
usual. Each room is decorated in a different philosophical or cultural
motif—such as an Aristotle room and a Goethe room adorned with

texts from *Faust*. A large Dutch breakfast is included in the price. ✉ *Anna van den Vondelstraat 6, 1054 GZ,* ☎ *020/6833013,* FAX *020/ 6853750. 30 rooms. AE, MC, V.*

$–$$ 🏨 **Agora.** The cheerful bustle of the nearby Singel flower market is re-
★   flected in this small hotel in an 18th-century house. Rooms are light and spacious, and some are decorated with vintage furniture; the best overlook the canal or the university. The Agora has a considerate staff, and the neighborhood is relaxed. Book well in advance. ✉ *Singel 462, 1017 AW,* ☎ *020/6272200,* FAX *020/6272202,* WEB *www.hotelagora.nl. 15 rooms, 13 with bath or shower. AE, DC, MC, V.*

$–$$ 🏨 **Hotel Washington.** On a peaceful street, the hotel is just a few blocks from the museum quarter and the Concertgebouw. Many of the world's top musicians find it the ideal place to reside when perform- ing in Amsterdam. Period furniture and attentive service lend this small establishment a homey feel. All except the cheaper upper-floor rooms have bath or shower and toilet. ✉ *Frans van Mierisstraat 10, 1071 RS,* ☎ *020/6796754,* FAX *020/6734435. 24 rooms, 19 with bath or shower. AE, DC, MC, V.*

$ 🏨 **Amstel Botel.** The floating hotel moored near Central Station is an appropriate place to stay in watery Amsterdam. The rooms are small and basic, but the large windows offer fine views across the water to the city. Make sure you don't get a room on the land side of the ves- sel, or you'll end up staring at a postal sorting office. ✉ *Oosterdok- skade 2, 1011 AE,* ☎ *020/6264247,* FAX *020/6391952,* WEB *www. amstelbotel.com. 174 rooms. AE, DC, MC, V.*

NIGHTLIFE AND THE ARTS

The Arts

The arts flourish in cosmopolitan Amsterdam. The best source of in- formation about performances is the monthly English-language *What's On in Amsterdam,* published by the VVV tourist office, where you can also secure tickets for the more popular events. *De Uitkrant* is avail- able in Dutch and covers practically every event. You can also find the latest information and make personal or phone bookings for a small charge at the **Amsterdam Uitburo** (✉ Stadsschouwburg, Leidseplein 26, ☎ 0900/0191, 75¢ per minute, 9–9 daily).

Classical Music

The **Concertgebouw** (✉ Concertgebouwplein 2–6, ☎ 020/6718345) is the home of one of Europe's finest orchestras. A smaller hall in the same building hosts chamber music, recitals, and even jam sessions. While ticket prices for international orchestras are high, most concerts are good value, and Wednesday lunchtime concerts at 12:30 are free.

Film

The greatest concentration of movie theaters is around Leidseplein and near Muntplein. Most foreign films are subtitled rather than dubbed. Conveniently located close to Leidseplein, **City 1–7** (✉ Kleine Gart- manplantsoen 13–25, ☎ 0900/1458, 50¢ per min. for recorded info) has seven screens. **Pathe de Munt** (✉ Vijselstraat 15, ☎ 0900/1458, 50¢ per min for recorded info) is the largest multiplex cinema in Am- sterdam, with thirteen screens.

Opera and Ballet

The Dutch national ballet and opera companies perform in the **Muziek- theater** (✉ Waterlooplein, ☎ 020/6255455). Guest companies from other countries perform here during the Holland Festival in June. The coun- try's smaller regional dance and opera companies usually include performances at the **Stadsschouwburg** (City Municipal Theater; ⊠ Leidseplein 26, ☎ 020/6242311) in their schedules.

Theater

Boom Chicago (⊠ Leidseplein Theater, Leidseplein 12, ☎ 020/5307306, WEB www.boomchicago.nl) offers improvised comedy with a local touch. For experimental theater, contemporary dance, and colorful cabaret in Dutch, catch the shows at **Felix Meritis** (⊠ Keizersgracht 324, ☎ 020/6231311).

Nightlife

Amsterdam has a wide variety of dance clubs, bars, and exotic shows. The more respectable—and expensive—after-dark activities are in and around Leidseplein and Rembrandtsplein; fleshier productions are on Oudezijds Achterburgwal and Thorbeckeplein. Most bars are open Sunday to Thursday to 1 AM and later on weekends, while clubs stay open until 5 AM or later. On weeknights very few clubs charge admission, though the livelier ones sometimes ask for a "club membership" fee of Fl. 20 or more. Watch out around the red-light district, where you many be offered tempting specials for disreputable clubs with floor shows—the experience may turn out to cost more than you bargained for.

Cafés and Bars

Amsterdam, and particularly the Jordaan, is renowned for its brown cafés. There are also grand cafés, with spacious interiors, snappy table service, and well-stocked reading tables. Two other variants of Amsterdam's buzzing bar scene are the *proeflokalen* (tasting houses) and *brouwerijen* (breweries). The Dutch have a relaxed tolerance of the dreaded weed, to be encountered in "coffee shops" with the green leaves of the marijuana plant showing in the window.

Among more fashionable cafés is **Caffe Esprit** (⊠ Spui 10, ☎ 020/6221967), serving delicious burgers and fine lunches; it is often used as a venue for radio and television interviews. The beamed interior of **De Admiraal Proeflokaal en Spijhuis** (⊠ Herengracht 319, ☎ 020/6254334) is an intimate setting in which to enjoy the award-winning jenevers. **De Gijs** (⊠ Lindegracht 249, ☎ 020/6380740) is an atmospheric brown café. **De Jaren** (⊠ Nieuwe Doelenstraat 20, ☎ 020/6255771), a spacious grand café with a canal-side terrace, attracts young businesspeople, arts and media workers, and other trendy types. If Continental lagers no longer tickle your fancy, then the selection of home-brewed beers at **Maximiliaan Amsterdams Brouwhuis** (⊠ Kloveniersburgwal 6, ☎ 020/6266280) is well worth sampling. At the **Rooie Nelis** (⊠ Laurierstraat 101, ☎ 020/6244167), you can spend a rainy afternoon chatting with friendly strangers over homemade meatballs and a beer or apple tart and coffee. **Tweede Kamer** (⊠ Heisteeg 6, just off the Spui, ☎ 020/4222236), named after the Dutch parliament's lower house, offers chess and backgammon in a convivial, civilized atmosphere permeated with the smoke of hemp.

Casino

Holland Casino (⊠ Max Euweplein 62, ☎ 020/6201006), just off Leidseplein, has blackjack, roulette, and slot machines in elegant, canal-side surrounds. You'll need your passport to get in, and although you don't have to wear a tie, sneakers will not get you past the door; the minimum age is 18.

Dance Clubs

Dance clubs tend to fill up after midnight. The cavernous **Escape** (⊠ Rembrandtsplein 11–15, ☎ 020/6221111) has taken on a much hipper mantle. The **iT** (⊠ Amstelstraat 24, ☎ 020/6250111) is gay on Saturday. It's primarily straight on Thursday, Friday, and Sunday—but could never be accused of being straitlaced. **Seymour Likely Lounge** (⊠ Nieuwezijds Voorburgwal 161, ☎ 020/4205663), has a lively, trendy crowd hopping to the latest music.

Gay and Lesbian Nightlife

Amsterdam has a vibrant gay and lesbian community. **Spijker** (⊠ Kerkstraat 4, ☎ 020/6205919) is a popular late-night bar with a sociable pool table and pinball machine. The **Web** (⊠ St. Jacobsstraat 6, ☎ 020/6236758) draws a leather/jeans crowd to its darker environs. **Cockring** (⊠ Warmoestraat 96, ☎ 020/6239604) is a late-night dance bar that features special shows. **Café Rouge** (⊠ Amstel 60, ☎ 020/ 4209881) is home to traditional Dutch oompapa music and frivolity. The **Amstel Taverne** (⊠ Amstel 54, ☎ 020/6234254) is the oldest existing gay bar in Amsterdam and is an early-evening venue. The trendy set prevails at bars along the Reguliersdwarsstraat. A mixed blend of different nationalities and ages meets early in the evening at **April** (⊠ Reguliersdwarsstraat 37, ☎ 020/6259572). **Havana** (⊠ Reguliersdwarsstraat 17, ☎ 020/6206788) sports a relaxed dance club on the first floor. The lesbian community meets at the **Saarein** (⊠ Elandsstraat 119, ☎ 020/6234901), a traditional bar in the Jordaan. The younger set jives at **Vive La Vie** (⊠ Amstelstraat 7, ☎ 020/6240114). There's a popular Saturday night women-only disco in the COC.

The **Gay & Lesbian Switchboard** (☎ 020/6236565) has friendly operators who provide up-to-the-minute information on events in the city, as well as general advice for gay or lesbian visitors. The **COC** (⊠ Rozenstraat 14, ☎ 020/6263087), the Dutch lesbian and gay political organization, operates a coffee shop and weekend discos.

Jazz Clubs

The **Bimhuis** (⊠ Oude Schans 73–77, ☎ 020/6233373) offers the best jazz and improvised music in town. The adjoining BIM café has a magical view across the Oude Schans canal.

Rock Clubs

Melkweg (⊠ Lijnbaansgracht 234, ☎ 020/6241777) is a major rock and pop venue with its large auditorium; it also has a gallery, theater, cinema, and café. The **Paradiso** (⊠ Weteringschans 6, ☎ 020/6264521), converted from a church, is a vibrant venue for rock, New Age, and even contemporary classical music.

SHOPPING

Department Stores

De Bijenkorf (⊠ Dam 1), the city's number one department store, is excellent for contemporary fashions and furnishings. **Maison Bonneterie** (⊠ Rokin 140; Beethovenstraat 32) is gracious, genteel, and understated. The well-stocked departments of **Vroom & Dreesmann** (⊠ Kalverstraat 201) carry all manner of goods.

Gift Ideas

Diamonds

Since the 17th century, "Amsterdam cut" has been synonymous with perfection in the quality of diamonds. At the diamond-cutting houses, the craftsmen explain how a diamond's value depends on the four c's—carat, cut, clarity, and color—before encouraging you to buy. There is a cluster of diamond houses on the Rokin. **Amsterdam Diamond Centre** (⊠ Rokin 1–5, ☎ 020/6245787) is the largest institution on the

Rokin. You can take a free guided diamond factory tour at **Gassan Diamonds** (⌧ Nieuwe Uilenburgerstraat 173–175, ☏ 020/6225333).

Porcelain

The Dutch have been producing Delft, Makkum, and other fine porcelain for centuries. **Focke & Meltzer** (⌧ Gelderlandplein 149, ☏ 020/644429) stores have been selling it since 1823. Pieces range from affordable, hand-painted, modern tiles to expensive Delft blue-and-white pitchers.

Markets

The **Bloemenmarkt** (flower market) on the Singel canal near the Muntplein is world-famous for its bulbs, many certificated for export, and cut flowers. Amsterdam's lively **Waterlooplein flea market,** open Monday–Saturday 9–5, next to the Muziektheater, is the ideal spot to rummage for secondhand clothes, inexpensive antiques, and other curiosities. In summer, you'll find etchings, drawings, and watercolors at the Sunday **art markets** on Thorbeckeplein and the Spui. There are as many English-language books as Dutch ones for browsing at the **book market** on the Spui, every Friday 10–4. A small but choice **stamp market,** open Wednesday and Saturday 1–4, is held on the Nieuwezijds Voorburgwal. **Kunst & Antiekmarkt De Looier** (De Looier Art & Antiques Market; ⌧ Elandsgracht 109, ☏ 020/6249038) is a bustling, warrenlike indoor market, with myriad stalls selling everything from expensive antiques and art to kitschy bric-a-brac; it's open daily 11–5.

Shopping Districts

Leidsestraat, Kalverstraat, Utrechtsestraat, and Nieuwendijk, Amsterdam's chief shopping districts, have largely been turned into **pedestrian-only areas,** but watch out for trams and bikes nevertheless. The imposing **Kalvertoren** shopping mall (⌧ Kalverstraat near Munt) has a rooftop restaurant with magnificent views of the city. **Magna Plaza** shopping center (⌧ Nieuwezijds Voorburgwal 182), built inside the glorious turn-of-the-last-century post office behind the Royal Palace at the Dam, is *the* place for A-to-Z shopping in a huge variety of stores. The **Spiegelkwartier** (⌧ Nieuwe Spiegelstraat and Spiegelgracht), just a stone's throw from the Rijksmuseum, is Amsterdam's antiques center, with galleries for wealthy collectors as well as old curiosity shops. **P. C. Hooftstraat,** and also Van Baerlestraat and Beethovenstraat, are the homes of haute couture and other fine goods. **Rokin** is hectic with traffic and houses a cluster of boutiques and renowned antiques shops selling 18th- and 19th-century furniture, antique jewelry, art deco lamps, and statuettes. The **Jordaan** to the west of the main ring of old canals, and the quaint streets crisscrossing these canals, is a treasure trove of trendy small boutiques and unusual crafts shops. **Schiphol Airport** tax-free shopping center is often lauded as the world's best.

AMSTERDAM A TO Z

To research prices, get advice from other travelers, and book travel arrangements, visit www.fodors.com.

AIRPORTS AND TRANSFERS

Most international flights arrive at Amsterdam's Schiphol Airport. Immigration and customs formalities on arrival are relaxed, with no forms to be completed.

TRANSFERS

The best link is the direct rail line to the central train station, where you can get a taxi or tram to your hotel. The train runs every 10 to 15 minutes throughout the day and takes about a half hour. Make sure you buy a ticket before boarding, or ruthless conductors will impose a fine. Second-class single fare is Fl. 6.25/€3. Taxis from the airport to central hotels cost about Fl. 60/€27.

BIKE TRAVEL

Rental bikes are widely available for around Fl. 12.50/€6 per day with a Fl. 50/€23–Fl. 200/€91 deposit and proof of identity. Several rental companies are close to the central train station; ask at tourist offices for details. Lock your bike whenever you park it, preferably to something immovable. Also, check with the rental company to see what your liability is under their insurance terms. Take-a-Bike is under the main railway station, and you can get cheaper rates if you buy a *huurfietskaart* in combination with a train ticket. MacBike has various rental points around the center.
➤ BIKE RENTALS: **MacBike** (✉ Mr. Visserplein 2, ☎ 020/6200985; ✉ Marnixstraat 220, ☎ 020/6266964). **Take-a-Bike** (✉ Stationsplein 12, ☎ 020/6248391).

BOAT AND FERRY TRAVEL

The Canalbus (Fl. 19.50/€9 for a hop-on, hop-off day card) travels between the central train station and the Rijksmuseum. The Museum Boat (Fl. 22) stops near major museums.

BUS TRAVEL WITHIN AMSTERDAM

See ☞ Transportation Around Amsterdam.

CAR TRAVEL

The city's concentric ring of canals, one-way systems, hordes of cyclists, and lack of parking facilities make driving here unappealing. It's best to put your car in one of the parking lots on the edge of the old center and abandon it for the rest of your stay.

CONSULATES

➤ UNITED KINGDOM: (✉ Koningslaan 44, ☎ 020/6764343).
➤ UNITED STATES: (✉ Museumplein 19, ☎ 020/5755309).

EMERGENCIES

The Central Medical Service supplies names and opening hours of pharmacists and dentists, as well as doctors, outside normal surgery hours.
➤ DOCTORS AND DENTISTS: **Central Medical Service** (☎ 020/5923434).
➤ EMERGENCY SERVICES: **Police, Ambulance, Fire, and Rescue** (☎ 112).

ENGLISH-LANGUAGE MEDIA

➤ BOOKSTORES: **American Book Center** (✉ Kalverstraat 185, ☎ 020/6255537). **Athenaeum Boekhandel** (✉ Spui 14, ☎ 020/6226248). **English Bookshop** (✉ Lauriergracht 71, ☎ 020/6264230). **Waterstone's** (✉ Kalverstraat 152, ☎ 020/6383821).

TAXIS

Taxis are expensive: a 5-km (3-mi) ride costs around Fl. 26/€12. Taxis are not usually hailed on the street but are picked up at stands near stations and other key points, where you will see a yellow column. You can order a taxi by dialing Taxi Centrale (50¢ per minute). Taxi Direkt (22¢ per minute) is a taxi service supplying Amsterdam. Water taxis are more expensive than land taxis: standard-size water taxis—for up to eight people—cost Fl. 150/€68 for a half hour, and Fl. 100/€45 per 15 minutes thereafter. They offer a large range of catering services and are a popular way to enjoy the city or celebrate special occasions.
➤ TAXI COMPANIES: **Taxi Centrale** (☎ 0900/6777777). **Taxi Direkt** (☎ 0900–0724). **Water taxis** (☎ 020/5301090).

TOURS

BICYCLE TOURS

From April through October, guided bike tours are an excellent way to discover Amsterdam. There are also supervised tours to the idyllic countryside and quaint villages just north of the city. The three-hour city tour costs Fl. 32.50/€15, and the 6½-hour countryside tour costs Fl. 45/€20, arranged by Yellow Bike Guided Tours.
➤ FEES AND SCHEDULES: **Yellow Bike Guided Tours** (✉ Nieuwezijds Kolk 29, ☎ 020/6206940).

BOAT TOURS

The most enjoyable way to get to know Amsterdam is on a boat trip along the canals. Departures are frequent from points opposite Central Station, along the Damrak, and along the Rokin and Stadhouderskade (near the Rijksmuseum). For a tour lasting about an hour, the cost is around Fl. 15/€7, but the student guides expect a small tip for their multilingual commentary. A candlelight dinner cruise costs upward of Fl. 47.50/€21. Book trips through the tourist office.

At Canal-Bike, a pedal boat for four costs Fl. 42/€19 per hour. The Museum Boat combines a scenic view of the city with seven stops near 20 museums. Tickets, good for the day and including discounted entry to museums, are Fl. 27.50/€12.
➤ FEES AND SCHEDULES: **Canal-Bike** (✉ corner of Leidsestraat and Keizersgracht; Leidsekade; Stadhouderskade opposite Rijksmuseum; Prinsengracht opposite Westerkerk; ☎ 020/6239886). **Museum Boat** (✉ Stationsplein 8, ☎ 020/5301090).

BUS TOURS

Guided bus tours provide an excellent introduction to Amsterdam. A bus-and-boat tour includes the inevitable trip to a diamond factory. Costing Fl. 25/€11–Fl. 35/€16, the comprehensive, 2½-hour tour can be booked through Key Tours or through Lindbergh.
➤ FEES AND SCHEDULES: **Key Tours** (✉ Dam 19, ☎ 020/6235051). **Lindbergh** (✉ Damrak 26, ☎ 020/6222766).

WALKING TOURS

Amsterdam is a compact city of narrow streets and canals, ideal for exploring on foot. The tourist office issues seven excellent guides in English that detail walking tours around the center.

TRAIN TRAVEL

The city has excellent rail connections with the rest of Europe. Central Station is in the center of town.
➤ TRAIN INFORMATION: **Central Station** (✉ Stationsplein, ☎ 0900/9296 international service information, 50¢ per minute, and sometimes involving a long wait).

TRANSPORTATION AROUND AMSTERDAM

A zonal fare system is used for the public transportation system, which includes metro, tram, and bus. Tickets (starting at Fl. 3) are available from automated dispensers on the Metro or from the drivers on trams and buses; or buy a money-saving strippenkaart. Even simpler is the dagkaart, which covers all city routes for Fl. 11/€5. These discount tickets can be obtained from the main GVB ticket office (open weekdays 7–7 and weekends 8–7), in front of Central Station, and from many newsstands, along with route maps of the public transportation system. The Circle Tram 20 goes both ways around a loop that passes close to most of the main sights and offers a hop-on, hop-off ticket for one to three days.

TRAVEL AGENCIES
➤ LOCAL AGENTS: **American Express** (✉ Damrak 66, ☎ 020/5048787). **Holland International** (✉ Damrak 90, ☎ 020/5550808). **Key Tours** (✉ Dam 19, ☎ 020/6235051).

VISITOR INFORMATION
VVV Amsterdam Tourist Office has offices at Schiphol Airport, at Stationsplein 10, in front of Central Station in the Old Dutch Coffee House, as well as one in the station itself. The information number, listed below, costs Fl. 1.05 per minute, and the electronic queue has a long wait.

The **Museumjaarkaart,** which can be purchased from most museums and all VVV tourist offices, provides a year's free or discounted admission to almost 450 museums throughout the country. It costs Fl. 55, Fl. 25 if you're under 18. A photo and passport are required for purchase. Nearly all museums participate.
➤ TOURIST INFORMATION: **VVV Amsterdam Tourist Office** (✉ Schiphol Airport; ✉ Stationsplein 10, in front of Central Station in the Old Dutch Coffee House; ✉ Spoor 2 [Platform 2] inside the station, ☎ 0900/4004040).

The Netherlands Basics

BUSINESS HOURS
BANKS AND OFFICES
Banks are open weekdays 9–5. Some banks are closed Monday mornings. GWK Border Exchange Offices at major railway stations are generally open Monday–Saturday 8–8, Sunday 10–4. GWK offices at border checkpoints and Schiphol Airport are open 24 hours.

MUSEUMS AND SIGHTS
Museums in Amsterdam are open daily. Elsewhere they close on Monday, but there are exceptions, so check with local tourist offices. In rural areas, some museums close or operate shorter hours in winter. Usual hours are 10–5.

SHOPS
Shops are open weekdays and Saturday 8:30 or 9–5:30 or 6, but outside the cities some close for lunch. Department stores and most shops do not open on Monday until 1 PM. In Amsterdam there is usually late-night shopping until 9 PM on Thursday or Friday. Sunday opening, from noon to 5, varies from city to city.

CUSTOMS AND DUTIES
For details on imports and duty-free limits, *see* Customs and Duties *in* Smart Travel Tips A to Z.

EMBASSIES
All embassies are located in the Hague.
➤ AUSTRALIA: (✉ Carnegielaan 4, ☎ 070/3108200).
➤ CANADA: (✉ Sophialaan 7, ☎ 070/3123456).
➤ IRELAND: (✉ Dr. Kuyperstraat 9, ☎ 070/3630993).
➤ NEW ZEALAND: (✉ Carnegielaan 10, ☎ 070/3469324).
➤ SOUTH AFRICA: (✉ Wassenaarseweg 40, ☎ 070/3924501).
➤ UNITED KINGDOM: (✉ Lange Voorhout 10, ☎ 070/4270427).
➤ UNITED STATES: (✉ Lange Voorhout 102, ☎ 070/3109209).

HOLIDAYS
January 1 (New Year's Day); Easter; April 30 (Queen's Day); May 9 (Ascension); May 19–20 (Pentecost/Whitsunday and Whitmonday); December 25–26 Christmas.

LANGUAGE

Dutch is a difficult language for foreigners, but the Dutch are fine linguists, so almost everyone speaks at least some English, especially in larger cities and tourist centers.

MONEY MATTERS

The Netherlands is prosperous, with a high standard of living, so overall costs are similar to those in other northern European countries. Prices for hotels and services in major cities are 10%–20% higher than those in rural areas. Amsterdam and the Hague are the most expensive. Hotel and restaurant service charges and the 6% value-added tax (VAT) are usually included in the prices quoted. Some sample prices include: half bottle of wine, Fl. 25/€11; glass of beer, Fl. 3.50/€1.50; cup of coffee, Fl. 4/€2; ham and cheese sandwich, Fl. 5/€2.25; 2-km (1-mi) taxi ride, Fl. 14/€6.

CURRENCY

The unit of currency in the Netherlands is the guilder, written as NLG (for Netherlands guilder), Fl., or simply F. (from the centuries-old term for the coinage, florin). Each guilder is divided into 100 cents. Bills are in denominations of 10, 25, 50, 100, 250, and 1,000 guilders. Denominations over Fl. 100 are rarely seen, and many shops refuse to change them. Coins are 1, 2.5, and 5 guilders and 5, 10, and 25 cents. Don't confuse the 1- and 2.5-guilder coins and the 5-guilder and 5-cent coins. The Netherlands is one of 12 countries adopting the euro, the European Union currency. Coins and bills will be issued in January 2002, and in a few months guilders will cease to exist.

At press time (summer 2001), the exchange rate for the guilder was Fl. 2.30 to the U.S. dollar, Fl. 1.60 to the Canadian dollar, Fl. 3.60 to the pound sterling, Fl. 2.80 to the Irish punt, Fl. 1.30 to the Australian dollar, Fl. 1.10 to the New Zealand dollar, and Fl. 0.30 to the South African rand. The euro is equivalent to Fl. 2.20, a fixed rate.

TELEPHONES

COUNTRY AND AREA CODES

The country code for the Netherlands is 31. When dialing a number in the Netherlands from outside the country, drop the initial 0 from the local area code.

INTERNATIONAL CALLS

Direct-dial international calls can be made from any phone booth. To reach an AT&T, MCI (called WorldPhone in the Netherlands), or Sprint operator, dial one of the access codes below.
➤ ACCESS CODES: **AT&T** (☎ 0800/022–9111). **MCI** (☎ 0800/022–9122). **Sprint** (☎ 0800/022–9119).

LOCAL CALLS

All towns and cities have area codes that are used only when you are calling from outside the area. All public phone booths require phone cards, which may be purchased from post offices, railway stations, and newsagents for Fl. 10/€4.50, Fl. 25/€11, or Fl. 50/€23. Pay phones in bars and restaurants take 25¢ or Fl. 1 coins, but rates are often hiked. Dial 0800/0101 for an English-speaking operator.

2 ATHENS

Athens is the point to which all roads lead in Greece and from which many tours take off if for no reason other than that the greatest sight of "the glory that was Greece" is here: the Parthenon and other legendary buildings of the Acropolis. But this perpetual shrine of Western civilization, set high on a rocky bluff, dominates and overlooks a 21st-century boomtown. In 1834, when it became the capital of modern Greece, Athens had a population of fewer than 10,000. Now it houses more than a third of the entire Greek population—around 4.4 million. Needless to say, romantic travelers, nurtured on the truth and beauty of Keats's Grecian urn, are surprised to find that most of Athens has succumbed to that red tubular glare that owes only its name, neon, meaning new, to the Greeks. A modern concrete city has engulfed the old village and sprawls for 388 square km (244 square mi), covering all the surrounding plain from the sea to the encircling mountains. The city has an air-pollution problem, caused mainly by traffic fumes; in an attempt to lessen the congestion, private cars are forbidden in central Athens on alternate workdays. Still, Athens's vibrancy makes it one of the most exciting cities in Europe, and the sprawling cement has failed to overwhelm the astonishing reminders of the fabled ancient metropolis.

Although Athens covers a huge area, the major landmarks of the ancient Greek, Roman, and Byzantine periods are close to the modern city center. You can stroll from the Acropolis to the other sites, taking time to browse in shops and relax in cafés and tavernas along the way. The Acropolis and Filopappou, two craggy hills sitting side by side; the ancient and Roman agoras (marketplaces); and Kerameikos, the first cemetery, form the core of ancient and Roman Athens.

EXPLORING ATHENS

Numbers in the margin correspond to points of interest on the Athens map.

The central district of modern Athens is small, stretching from the Acropolis to Mt. Lycabettus, with its small white church on top. The layout is simple: three parallel streets (Stadiou, Panepistimiou, and Akademias) link two main squares (Syntagma and Omonia). Try to wander off this beaten tourist track: seeing the Athenian butchers in the central market near Monastiraki sleeping on their cold marble slabs during the heat of the afternoon siesta may give you more of a feel for the city than looking at hundreds of fallen pillars. In summer, closing times often depend on the site's available personnel, but throughout the year, arrive at least 45 minutes before the official closing time to ensure that you can buy a ticket. Flash photography is forbidden in museums. The Ministry of Culture's Web site (www.culture.gr) provides a good description of museums and archaeological sites, although the hours are often out-of-date.

❼ Agios Eleftherios (St. Eleftherios). What's fascinating about the city's former cathedral is that the walls of this 12th-century Byzantine church incorporate reliefs—fanciful figures and zodiac signs—from buildings that date back to the classical period. The church is also known as Little Mitropolis and Panagia Gorgoepikoos (Virgin Who Answers Prayers Quickly), based on its 13th-century icon, said to perform miracles. ⊠ *Pl. Mitropolis,* ☎ *no phone.* ☉ *Hrs depend on services, but usually open daily 8–1.*

★ ❶ Akropolis (Acropolis). Even in its bleached and silent state, the Parthenon—the great Panathenic temple that crowns the Acropolis, the tablelike hill that represented the "upper city" of ancient Athens—has the power to stir the heart as few other ancient relics can. Seeing it bathed in the sunlight of the south, or sublimely swathed in moonglow, one marvels at the continuing vitality of this monument of ageless intellect. Well, not completely ageless. The Athenians built this complex during the 5th century BC to honor the goddess Athena, patron of the city. The first ruins you'll see are the **Propylaia,** the monumental gateway that led worshipers from the temporal world into the spiritual world of the sanctuary; now only the columns of Pentelic marble and a fragment of stone ceiling remain. Above, to the right, stands the graceful **Naos Athenas Nikis** or **Apterou Nikis** (Wingless Victory). The temple was mistakenly called the latter because common tradition often confused Athena with the winged goddess Nike. The elegant and architecturally complex **Erechtheion,** most sacred of the shrines of the Acropolis and later turned into a harem by the Turks, has emerged from repair work with dull, heavy copies of the caryatids (draped maidens) supporting the roof. The **Acropolis Museum** houses five of the six originals, their faces much damaged by acid rain. The sixth is in the British Museum in London.

The **Parthenonas** (Parthenon) dominates the Acropolis and indeed the Athens skyline. Designed by Ictinus, with Phidias as master sculptor, it was completed in 438 BC and is the most architecturally sophisticated temple of that period. Even with hordes of tourists wandering around the ruins, it still inspires wonder. The architectural decorations were originally painted vivid red and blue, and the roof was of marble tiles, but time and neglect have given the marble pillars their golden-white shine, and the beauty of the building is all the more stark and striking. The British Museum houses the largest remaining part of the original 532-ft frieze (the Elgin Marbles), but Greece has long been campaigning for its return. The building has 17 fluted columns along each side and eight at the ends; these were cleverly made to lean slightly inward and to bulge, counterbalancing the natural optical distortion. The Parthenon was made into a brothel by the Romans, a church by the Christians, and a mosque by the Turks. The Turks also stored gunpowder in the Propylaia. When this was hit by a Venetian bombardment in 1687, 28 columns of the Parthenon were blown out and a fire raged for two days, leaving the temple in its present condition. Piece by piece, the entire Parthenon complex is now undergoing conservation, as part of an ambitious 20-year rescue plan launched with international support in 1983 by Greek architects. ⊠ *Top of Dionyssiou Areopagitou,* ☎ *01/321–4172 or 01/321–0219.* ⊙ *May–Oct., daily 8–6:30; Nov.–Apr., daily 8:30–2:30.*

❹ **Archaia Agora** (Ancient Agora). Now a sprawling confusion of stones, slabs, and foundations, this was the civic center and focal point of community life in ancient Athens, where Socrates met with his students while merchants haggled over the price of olive oil. It is dominated by the best-preserved Doric temple in Greece, the **Hephaisteion,** built during the 5th century BC. Nearby, the Stoa Attalou (Stoa of Attalos II), reconstructed in the mid-1950s by the American School of Classical Studies in Athens, houses the **Museo tis Agoras** (Museum of Agora Excavations). The museum offers a glimpse of everyday life in ancient Athens, its objects ranging from a child's terra-cotta chamber pot to the shards (*ostraka,* from which the word "ostracism" is derived) used in secret ballots to recommend banishment of Themistocles and other powerful citizens. ⊠ *Three entrances: from Monastiraki, on Adrianou; from Thission, on Apostolos Pavlou; from Acropolis, on descent along Ag. Apostoli,* ☎ *01/321–0185.* ⊙ *Tues.–Sun. 8:30–3.*

❸ **Areios Pagos** (Areopagus). From this rocky outcrop, ancient Athens's supreme court, you can view the Propylaia, the Agora, and the modern city. Legend claims it was here that Orestes was tried for the murder of his mother, and much later St. Paul delivered his Sermon to the Unknown God, so moving that a senator named Dionysius was converted and became the first bishop of Athens. ⊠ *Opposite Acropolis entrance.* ⊙ *Always open.*

★ ⓲ **Ethniko Archaiologiko Museo** (National Archaeological Museum). Among the collection of antiquities are the sensational archaeological finds of Heinrich Schliemann in 1874 at Mycenae; 16th-century BC frescoes from the Akrotiri ruins on Santorini; and the 6½-ft-tall bronze sculpture *Poseidon,* an original work of circa 470 BC that was found in the sea off Cape Artemision. ⊠ *28 Oktovriou (Patission) 44, 10-min walk north of Pl. Omonia,* ☎ *01/821–7717.* ⊙ *May–Oct., Mon. 12:30–7, Tues.–Fri. 8–7; Nov.–Apr., Mon. 10:30–5, Tues.–Sun. 8:30–3.*

★ ⓯ **Goulandri Museo Kikladikis ke Ellinikis Archaias Technis** (Goulandris Museum of Cycladic and Greek Ancient Art). The collection spans 5,000 years, with nearly 100 exhibits of the Cycladic civilization (3000–2000 BC), including many of the marble figurines that so fascinated such artists as Picasso and Modigliani. ⊠ *Neofitou Douka 4 or Irodotou 1,* ☎ *01/722–8321 through 8323,* WEB *www.cycladic-m.gr.* ⊙ *Mon. and Wed.–Fri. 10–4, Sat. 10–3.*

24

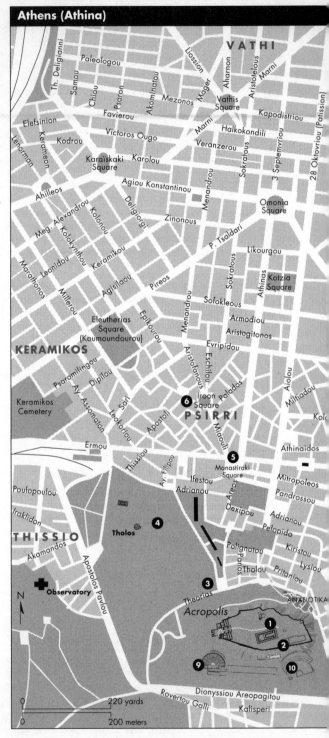

Athens (Athina)

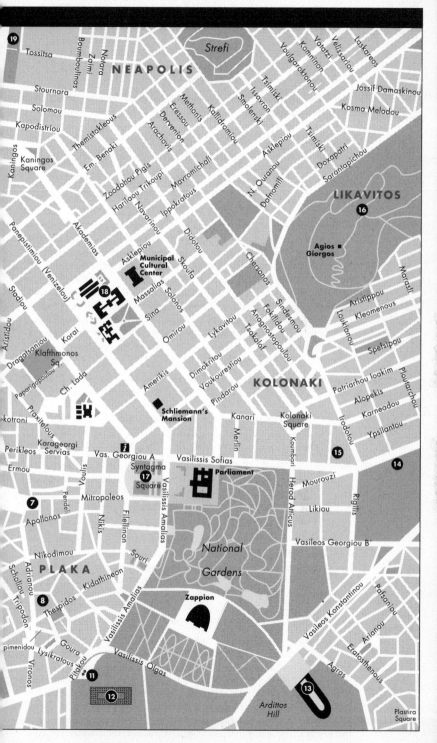

19 Tossitsa

NEAPOLIS

Strefi

LIKAVITOS

16

Agios Giorgos

KOLONAKI

Municipal Cultural Center

18

Schliemann's Mansion

Kolonaki Square

15

14

Klafthmonos Sq.

Vas. Georgiou A

17 Syntagma Square

Vasilissis Sofias

Parliament

7

PLAKA

National Gardens

8

Zappion

11

12

13

Arditos Hill

Plastira Square

⑨ Irodion (Odeon of Herod Atticus). This hauntingly beautiful 2nd-century AD theater was built Greek-style into the hillside but with typical Roman archways in its three-story stage building and barrel-vaulted entrances. Now restored, it hosts Athens Festival performances. ⊠ *Dionyssiou Areopagitou across from Propylaia,* ☎ *01/323–2771.* ☉ *Open only to audiences during performances.*

★ **⑯ Likavitos** (Mt. Lycabettus). Athens's highest hill borders Kolonaki, a residential quarter worth a visit if you enjoy window-shopping and people-watching. A steep funicular climbs to the summit, crowned by whitewashed Agios Giorgios chapel. The view from the top—pollution permitting—is the finest in Athens. ⊠ *Base: 15-min walk northeast of Syntagma; funicular every 10 min from Ploutarchou 1 at Aristippou (take minibus 060 from Kanaris St. or Pl. Kolonaki, except Sun.),* ☎ *01/722–7065.* ☉ *Nov.–Apr., daily 9:15 AM–11:45 PM; May–Oct., daily 9:15 AM–12:45 AM. Closed Nov.*

⑤ Monastiraki. The old Turkish bazaar area takes its name from Panayia Pantanassa Church, commonly called Monastiraki (Little Monastery); it once flourished as a convent, perhaps dating from the 10th century. Near the church stands the Tzistarakis Mosque (1759), exemplifying the East-West paradox that characterizes Athens. But the district's real draw is the Sunday flea market, centered on tiny Abyssinia Square and running along Ifestou and Kynetou streets where Greeks bargain with wildly gesturing hands and dramatic facial expressions. Everything's for sale, from gramophone needles to old matchboxes, from nose rings to lacquered eggs and cool white linens. ⊠ *South of junction Ermou and Athinas Sts.*

★ **❷ Museo Akropoleos** (Acropolis Museum). Tucked into one corner of the Acropolis, this institution contains superb sculptures, including the caryatids and a collection of colored *korai* (statues of women dedicated to Athena, patron of the ancient city). ⊠ *Southeastern corner of Acropolis,* ☎ *01/323–6665.* ☉ *Mid-Apr.–Oct., Mon. 11–6, Tues.–Sun. 8–6; Nov.–mid-Apr., Mon. 10:30–2:30, Tues.–Sun. 8:30–3.*

⑬ Panathinaiko Stadio (Panathenaic Stadium). A reconstruction of the ancient Roman stadium in Athens, this gleaming-white marble structure was built for the first modern Olympic Games in 1896 and seats 80,000 spectators. ⊠ *Near junction Vas. Konstantinou and Vas. Olgas,* ☎ *no phone.* ☉ *Daily 9–2.*

⑪ Pili tou Adrianou (Hadrian's Arch). Built in AD 131–32 by Emperor Hadrian to show where classical Athens ended and his new city, Hadriaopolis, began, the Roman archway with Corinthian pilasters bears an inscription on the side facing the Acropolis that reads, THIS IS ATHENS, THE ANCIENT CITY OF THESEUS. But the side facing the Temple of Olympian Zeus proclaims, THIS IS THE CITY OF HADRIAN AND NOT OF THESEUS. ⊠ *Junction Vas. Amalias and Dionyssiou Areopagitou.*

★ **❽ Plaka.** Stretching east from the Agora, this is almost all that's left of 19th-century Athens, a lovely quarter with winding walkways, neoclassical houses, and such sights as the **Museo Ellinikis Laikis Technis** (Greek Folk Art Museum; ⊠ Kidathineon 17, ☎ 01/322–9031, ☉ Tues.–Sun. 10–2), with a collection dating from 1650, and the Roman Agora's **Aerides** (Tower of the Winds; ⊠ Pelopidas and Aiolou, ☎ 01/324–5220, ☉ Tues.–Sun. 8:30–3), a 1st-century BC water clock. Just down the street from the Tower of the Winds in a neoclassical mansion is the delightful **Museo Ellinikon Laikon Musikon Organon** (Museum of Greek Popular Musical Instruments; ⊠ Diogenous 1–3, ☎ 01/325–0198, ☉ Tues., Thurs.–Sun. 10–2, Wed. noon–6), which gives a crash course in the development of Greek music, with three floors of instruments and headphones so visitors can appreciate recorded sounds made by such unusual organs as goatskin bagpipes and the Cretan lyra. Admission is free. The **Mnimeio Lysikratous** (Monument of Lysikrates; ⊠ Herefondos and Lysikratous Sts.) is one of the few surviving tripods on which stood the award given to the producer of the best play in the Dionyssia festival. Above Plaka, at the northeastern base of the Acropolis, is **Anafiotika,** the closest thing you'll find to a village in Athens. Take time to wander among its white-washed, bougainvillea-framed houses and tiny churches.

❻ Psirri. During the day, little in this former industrial district indicates that at night this rapidly changing quarter becomes a whirl of theaters, clubs, and restaurants, dotted with dramatically lit churches and lively squares. Whether you want to dance on tabletops to live Greek music, sing along with a soulful accordion player, salsa in a Cuban club, or just watch the hoi polloi go by as you snack on trendy or traditional mezedes, this is the place. ⊠ *Off Ermou St., centered on Iroon and Ag. Anargiron Squares.*

⓬ Stiles Olymbiou Dios or Olymbion (Temple of Olympian Zeus). Begun during the 6th century BC, this temple was larger than all other tem-ples in Greece when it was finally completed 700 years later. It was destroyed during the invasion of the Goths in the 4th century; only a few towering, sun-browned columns remain. ⊠ *Vas. Olgas 1,* ☎ *01/ 922–6330.* ⊙ *Tues.–Sun. 8:30–3.*

☙ ⓱ Syntagma (Constitution Square). At the top of the square stands the **Vouli** (Parliament), formerly the royal palace, completed in 1838 for the new monarchy. From the Parliament you can watch the changing of the Evzone honor guard at the **Mnimeio Agnostou Stratiotou** (Tomb of the Unknown Soldier), with its text from Pericles's famous funeral oration and a bas-relief of a dying soldier modeled after a sculpture on the Temple of Aphaia in Aegina. The most elaborate ceremony takes place on Sunday, when the sturdy young guards don their *foustanel-las* (kilts) with 400 pleats, one for each year of the Ottoman occupa-tion. The procession usually arrives in front of Parliament at 11:15 AM. Pop into the gleaming **Stathmo Syntagma** (Syntagma Metro station: ⊠ at upper end of Syntagma Square) to take a look at artifacts from the subway excavations artfully displayed and a vast cross-section of the earth behind glass with the finds in chronological layers, from a skeleton in its ancient grave to traces of the 4th century BC road to Meso-geia, to a Turkish cistern. The Metro station is open daily 5 AM until midnight. On the square's southern side sits the lush **Ethnikos Kipos** (National Garden), its dense foliage, gazebos, and trellised walkways offering a quick escape from the center's bustle. For young visitors, there are two playgrounds, a miniature zoo, duck pond, and refreshments at the stone cottage café. ⊠ *Corner of Vas. Sofias and Vas. Amalias.*

❿ Theatro Dionyssou (Theater of Dionysus). In this theater dating from about 330 BC, the ancient dramas and comedies were performed in con-junction with bacchanalian feasts. The throne in the center was reserved for the priest of Dionysus: it is adorned with regal lions' paws, and the back is carved with reliefs of satyrs and griffins. ⊠ *Dionyssiou Are-opagitou opposite Mitsaion,* ☎ *01/322–4625.* ⊙ *May–Oct., daily 8–6; Nov.–Apr., daily 8:30–2:30.*

⓲ Vivliothiki, Panepistimio, Akademia (Old University complex). These three dramatic buildings belong to the University of Athens, designed by the Hansen brothers in the period after independence and built of white Pentelic marble, with tall columns and decorative friezes. In the center is the Panepistimio, the Senate House of the university; on the right is the Akademia, or Academy, flanked by statues of Athena and

Apollo; and on the left is the Vivliothiki, or National Library. ⊠ *Panepistimiou between Ippokratous and Sina,* ☎ *01/361–4413 Vivliothiki; 01/361–4301 Panepistimio; 01/360–0207 or 01/360–0209 Akademia.* ⊙ *Vivliothiki Sept.–July, Mon.–Thurs. 9–8, Fri.–Sat 9–2. Other buildings weekdays 9–2.*

🄮 **Vizantino Museo** (Byzantine Museum). Housed in an 1848 mansion built by an eccentric French aristocrat, the museum has a unique collection of icons, re-creations of Greek churches throughout the centuries, and a very beautiful 14th-century Byzantine embroidery of the body of Christ, in gold, silver, yellow, and green. Sculptural fragments provide an excellent introduction to Byzantine architecture. ⊠ *Vas. Sofias 22,* ☎ *01/721–1027.* ⊙ *Tues.–Sun. 8:30–3.*

DINING

Search for places with at least a half dozen tables occupied by Athenians—they're discerning customers.

CATEGORY	COST*
$$$$	over 16,000 dr. (€47.06)
$$$	10,000 dr.–16,000 dr. (€29.42–€47.06)
$$	5,500 dr.–10,000 dr. (€16.18–€29.42)
$	under 5,500 dr. (€16.18)

per person for a main course at dinner

$$$$ ✕ **Vardis.** A meal at this French restaurant is worth the ride to the northern suburb of Kifissia. The chef is committed to the classics and to quality ingredients—he brings in sweetwater crayfish from Orhomenos and tracks down rare large shrimp from Thassos island. The clientele may be a little sedate, but the food dazzles. Especially good are the superb crayfish linguine, caramelized lamb cutlets with morel and porcini mushrooms, and salt-crusted duck filled with foie gras and served with a fragrant sherry sauce. The splendid desserts include a soufflé of Grand Marnier and forest berries, crème brûlée, and pear with dark chocolate and espresso sauce. ⊠ *Diligianni 66, in Pentelikon Hotel, Kefalari, Kifissia,* ☎ *01/623–0650 through 0656. Reservations essential. AE, DC, MC, V. Closed Sun. and Aug. No lunch.*

$$$–$$$$ ✕ **Aristera-Dexia.** Chef Chrisanthos Karalomengos enjoyed such a stel-
★ lar reputation from his last hit restaurant (the now-defunct Vitrina) that his latest creation was an instant success. His forte is fusion—exciting, artful combinations such as pheasant sausage with parsnips in Madeira sauce; a tower of *haloumi* (Cypriot cheese) and feta croquettes in a melon-mirin-chili sauce; sardine tempura with black sesame and a vinaigrette with port and dried figs; or the Greek version of sushi, raw squid on a puree of eggplant with anchovies and trout roe. Though located in a less than desirable neighborhood, the restaurant is strikingly designed, with two large partitions dividing the large room (hence, the name "Left-Right") and a glass runway offering a peek at the cellar below, which houses one of the most extensive wine collections in the city. Diners exit through an art gallery. ⊠ *Andronikou 3, Rouf,* ☎ *01/342–2380. Reservations essential. AE, MC, V. Closed Sun. No lunch.*

$$$–$$$$ ✕ **To Varoulko.** Chef Lefteris Lazarou is constantly trying to outdo him-
★ self, with magnificent results. You can sample such appetizers as crab salad studded with mango and grapes, with bits of leek to cut the sweetness; fresh mullet roe from Messolonghi laced with honey and accompanied by cinnamony cauliflower puree; or carpaccio made from *petrobarbouno* (a kind of rockfish). Although the restaurant is most famous for monkfish, it offers a mind-boggling array of other seafood dishes: red mullet marinated in lemon and swirled with fuchsia-

colored beet creme; cockles steamed in Limnos sweet wine; and lobster with wild rice, celery, and champagne sauce. ⊠ *Deligeorgi 14, Piraeus,* ☎ *01/411–2043 or 01/422–1283. Reservations essential. AE, DC, MC, V. Closed Sun. and Aug. No lunch.*

$$$ ✕ **Boschetto.** The restaurant pampers diners with its park setting, expert maître d', and creative nouvelle Italian food. The specialty here is fresh pasta, such as the shrimp cannelloni, green gnocchi with Gorgonzola sauce, or ravioli with duck livers and truffle zabaglione. Entrées may include sea bass with a potato crust, succulent rooster in Riesling, and grilled wild buffalo steak with a sauce of coffee, fig and Mavrodaphne wine. End your meal with the crema cotta followed by the finest espresso in Athens. The tables tend to be close together; reserve near the window or in the courtyard during the summer. ⊠ *Alsos Evangelismos, Hilton area,* ☎ *01/721–0893 or 01/722–7324. Reservations essential. AE, V. Closed Sun. and 2 wks in Aug. No lunch Oct.–Apr.*

$$$ ✕ **Spondi.** This vaulted stone–interior restaurant used to suggest a medieval wine cellar, but now, after redecoration, the ambience is as cool and contemporary as the cuisine. Savor the artichoke terrine with duck confit or black ravioli with honeyed leek and shrimp. Interesting entrées may include a perfectly grilled John Dory with a spirited orange and mustard sauce; lamb tail so tender it falls from the bone, with couscous, raisins and cumin; and chicken with foie gras, truffles, and asparagus in porcini sauce. In good weather, you can sit in the bougainvillea-draped courtyard. ⊠ *Pirronos 5, Pangrati,* ☎ *01/756– 4021 or 01/752–0658. Reservations essential. AE, DC, MC, V. No lunch.*

$$–$$$ ✕ **Azul.** The space may be a bit cramped, but the food is heavenly. Start with mushrooms stuffed with nuts and *anthotiro* cheese (soft, mild, low-fat white cheese made from goat's and sheep's milk), or salmon and trout in pastry with champagne sauce. The spaghetti *à la nona* (godmother's) with chamomile, Gorgonzola, and bacon is an unparalleled combination. Other memorable dishes are beef fillet with raisins and cedar needles, and chicken prepared with lemon leaves. In summer, Azul sets up tables outside. ⊠ *Haritos 43, Kolonaki,* ☎ *01/725–3817. Reservations essential. AE, DC, MC, V. Closed last 2 wks in Aug. and Sun. Oct.–Apr. No lunch.*

$$–$$$ ✕ **Kollias.** Friendly owner Tassos Kollias creates his own dishes, ranging from the humble to the aristocratic: fried whole squid in its ink; sea urchin salad; cuttlefish stew with broccoli and cream; lobster with lemon, balsamic vinegar, and a shot of honey. He's known for bringing in the best-quality catch, whether mullet from Messolonghi or oysters culled by Kalymnos sponge divers, and his prices are usually 25% lower than most fish tavernas. A fitting end to the meal: fresh *loukoumades* (sweet fritters) or *bougatsa* (custard in phyllo). Ask for directions when you call—even locals get lost trying to find this obscure street in the working-class quarter of Piraeus. ⊠ *Stratigou Plastira 3, near junction of Dramas and Kalokairinou, Tabouria,* ☎ *01/ 461–9150 or 01/462–9620. Reservations essential weekends. AE, DC, MC, V. Closed Aug. No lunch Mon.–Sat., no dinner Sun.*

$$–$$$ ✕ **Kouzina-Cine Psirri.** Once a dilapidated wood factory, this chic dining space features lots of stone, golden wood, and a partial glass floor that reveals the wine cellar. The best place to be is the roof terrace with its view of the illuminated Acropolis and the nearby observatory. The talented chef comes up with creative Greek cuisine. Try the appetizer of crab with smoked eggplant puree and fennel root or fish soup accompanied by grilled skate; then move on to such entrées as boar with watermelon chutney, or grilled rooster breast with kumquats. ⊠ *Sarri 40, Psirri,* ☎ *01/321–5534 or 01/321–2476. Reservations essential. MC, V. Closed Mon.*

$$ ✕ **Margaro.** Near Piraeus, next to the Naval Academy, this popular, no-nonsense fish taverna serves just four items, along with excellent barrel wine: fried crayfish, fried red mullet, fried *marida* (a small white fish), and huge Greek salads. Tables on the terrace offer a view of the busy port. If it's crowded, you may be asked to go into the kitchen and prepare your own salad! Try to arrive between 6 and 8 PM, before Greeks eat dinner; reservations are not accepted. ✉ *Hatzikyriakou 126, Piraeus,* ☎ *01/451–4226. No credit cards. Closed 15 days at Greek Easter. No dinner Sun.*

$$ ✕ **Stous 7 Anemous.** The decor is a bit of postmodern pastiche, but the playful food with intense flavors is impressive here. For appetizers sample the fried Dodoni feta wrapped in sesame-enhanced crust and served with marinated tomatoes and walnut sauce, or the tortillas filled with octopus. Main dishes might include lamb ribs with a refreshing kiwi chutney spiked with mint; moist pork fillet with a dense coffee–black currant sauce; and grilled tuna with tomato, thyme, and chamomile. End your meal with the almond pastry (*amigdaloto*) with tsipouro. ✉ *Astiggos 17 (from Ermou 121), Monastiraki,* ☎ *01/324–0386. Reservations essential. AE, DC, MC, V. Closed Aug.*

$$ ✕ **Tade Efi Anna.** Near the end of the Ermou pedestrian zone, this stylish restaurant serves Greek regional cuisine with a modern touch. Try perhaps the best *pita Kaisarias* in Athens (the spicy, cured meat called *pastourmas* with tomato and Kasseri cheese in a crisp phyllo) or *melitzanes amigdalou* (thinly sliced eggplant layered with tomatoes and cheese with a thick topping of crushed almonds). The rabbit is cooked with cinnamony prunes and fresh spinach, and the chicken fillet is first wrapped around Gruyère, then baked in a crust of pistachios. ✉ *Ermou 72, Monastiraki,* ☎ *01/321–3652. V. Closed Mon. and June–Aug.*

$$ ✕ **Vlassis.** Relying on recipes from Thrace, Roumeli, Thessaly, and the
★ islands, the chefs whip up Greek home cooking in generous portions. Musts are the peppery cheese dip called *tirokafteri,* pastitsio (made here with bits of lamb liver), *lahanodolmades* (cabbage rolls), goat with oil and oregano, and octopus *stifado* (stew), tender and sweet with lots of onions. ✉ *Paster 8, Platia Mavili (near American embassy),* ☎ *01/646–3060. Reservations essential. No credit cards. Closed Aug.–mid-Sept. No dinner Sun.*

$ ✕ **Karavitis.** A neighborhood favorite, this taverna near the Olympic Stadium has warm-weather garden seating and a winter dining room decorated with huge wine casks. Classic Greek cuisine is well prepared here, including pungent *tzatziki* (yogurt-garlic dip), *bekri meze* (lamb chunks in a spicy red sauce), and *stamnaki* (beef baked in a clay pot). ✉ *Arktinou 35 and Pausaniou 4, Pangrati,* ☎ *01/721–5155. No credit cards. Closed around Aug. 15 for a week. No lunch.*

$ ✕ **O Platanos.** Set in a picturesque courtyard, this is one of Plaka's old-
★ est yet least touristy tavernas. The waiters are fast but far from ingratiating, and the place is packed with Greeks. Don't miss the oven-baked potatoes, roast lamb, green beans in savory olive oil, and exceptionally cheap but delicious barrel retsina. ✉ *Diogenous 4, Plaka,* ☎ *01/322–0666. No credit cards. Closed Sun.*

$ ✕ **Sigalas–Bairaktaris.** Run by the same family for more than a century, this is one of the best places to eat in Monastiraki. After admiring the painted wine barrels and black-and-white stills of Greek film stars, go to the window case to view the day's *magirefta*—beef *kokkinisto* (stew with red sauce), spicy meat patties seasoned with clove—or sample the gyro platter. Appetizers include tiny cheese pies with sesame seeds, tender mountain greens, and fried zucchini with a garlicky dip. ✉ *Pl. Monastiraki 2, Monastiraki,* ☎ *01/321–3036. AE, MC, V.*

LODGING

It's always advisable to reserve a room. Hotels are clustered around the center of town and along the seacoast toward the airport. Modern hotels are more likely to be air-conditioned and to have double-glazed windows; the center of Athens can be so noisy that it's hard to sleep.

CATEGORY	COST*
$$$$	over 55,000 dr. (€161.77)
$$$	35,000 dr.–55,000 dr. (€102.95–€161.77)
$$	19,000 dr.–35,000 dr. (€55.89–€102.95)
$	under 19,000 dr. (€55.89)

Prices quoted are for a double room in high season, including taxes but not breakfast unless so indicated.

$$$$ ★ **Andromeda Athens Hotel.** On a quiet street near the U.S. embassy and the city's concert hall, this small, luxury hotel prides itself on its business clientele, but the meticulous service and sumptuous decor (Persian carpets, Italian pastels, designer furniture) will be enjoyed by all. For those who need to be plugged in, all rooms have an ISDN digital connection. The restaurant has excellent Polynesian and Chinese cuisine. The hotel also operates a property across the street with security system and 12 executive suites (one- and two-room apartments), which include fully equipped kitchenettes. ✉ *Timoleondos Vassou 22, Pl. Mavili, 11521,* ☎ *01/641–5000,* FAX *01/646–6361,* WEB *www.slh.com. 30 rooms, 5 suites, 4 penthouses. Restaurant. AE, DC, MC, V.*

$$$$ **Athens Hilton.** A 200-year-old olive tree with a Turkish cannonball in its branches adds an earthy touch to the marble lobby. About a 20-minute walk from Syntagma, this is still ranked in the top tier of Athens hotels after nearly 30 years; a shuttle takes guests downtown during the day. The rooms, in muted colors, all have balconies and double-glazed windows, as well as fine views of either the Acropolis or Mt. Ymittos. The Galaxy bar has an outdoor terrace overlooking an enchanting Athens panorama. ✉ *Vas. Sofias 46, 11528,* ☎ *01/728–1000 or 01/728–1100 reservations,* FAX *01/728–1111; 01/725–1919 reservations,* WEB *www.hilton.com. 454 rooms, 19 suites. 4 restaurants, pool, wading pool. AE, DC, MC, V.*

$$$$ ★ **Divani Apollon Palace.** For those who love the sea or need a break from city bustle, this grand modern hotel is the perfect solution. Towering above the posh, residential area of Kavouri, the seaside resort offers a casual ambience but sophisticated service and sparkling facilities. Take a few laps in the indoor pool, spend a hour on the tennis court, dip into the Aegean across the street (lined with a shady stretch of lawn and a few seafood tavernas), arrange to play a round of golf at the Glyfada links 3 km (2 mi) away, or take the hotel shuttle to Glyfada for some serious shopping (the van continues on to downtown Athens). The airy white-and-yellow rooms all have balconies with sea view, satellite-pay TV, and direct-dial phones with voice mail. The suites even have fireplaces. Best, though, are the hotel's large, gleaming public spaces, the outdoor pool with hydromassage, and the comfy Pelagos Bar with its leather sofas. The hotel is 3 km (2 mi) from the airport's international terminal, and limo service is available. ✉ *Ag. Nikolaou 10 and Iliou, Vouliagmeni, 16671,* ☎ *01/891–1100,* FAX *01/965–8010,* WEB *www.divaniapollon.gr. 286 rooms, 7 suites. 2 restaurants, 2 pools, 1 wading pool. AE, DC, MC, V.*

$$$$ **Grande Bretagne.** Built in 1842, the G. B. is an Athens landmark, and its guest list testifies to its colorful history, with such visitors as Edith Piaf, Jackie Kennedy, royalty, and rock stars. A face-lift in 1992 restored the hotel: the lobby has Oriental rugs, tapestries, and ornate chande-

liers, and the coveted Syntagma rooms have large balconies and Acropolis views. There are also "smart" rooms, with desk, printer, fax, photocopier, and a direct telephone line with voice mail, and the third floor is no-smoking. ⊠ *Vas. Georgiou A' 1, Pl. Syntagma, 10564,* ☎ *01/333–0000; 01/331–5555 through 5559 reservations,* FAX *01/322–8034; 01/322–2261; 01/333–0910 reservations,* WEB *www.hotelgrandebretagne-ath.gr. 364 rooms, 23 suites. Restaurant. AE, DC, MC, V.*

$$$$ ⊞ **N. J. V. Athens Plaza.** At an exclusive Syntagma Square address, the fresh, spacious rooms, in gray and burgundy, come equipped with minibar, direct-dial phones with voice mail, satellite and pay TV, and large marble bathrooms with phone extensions. The few rooms in the back are quieter, but even those on the front are quiet, due to double glazing and air-conditioning. Non-smoking rooms are available. The suites on the eighth and ninth floors have sitting areas, breathtaking Acropolis views, and interiors decked out with designer fabrics and furnishings. ⊠ *Vas. Georgiou A' 2, Pl. Syntagma, 10564,* ☎ *01/335–2400,* FAX *01/323–5856. 182 rooms, 15 suites. Restaurant. AE, DC, MC, V.*

$$$–$$$$ ⊞ **Kefalari Suites.** In a turn-of-the-20th-century building among the neoclassical mansions and tree-lined boulevards of the suburb of Kifissia, the hotel offers imaginative themed suites (i.e., Malmaison, Jaipur) at prices lower than those of downtown deluxe hotels. The suites include kitchenettes with utensils, refrigerators, satellite TV, queen-size beds, modem connection, and verandas or balconies; guests share the sundeck, which has a whirlpool tub. Continental deluxe breakfast (cheese, cold cuts, cereal, yogurt, cake) is included in the room rate. ⊠ *Pentelis 1 and Kolokotroni, Kefalari, Kifissia, 14562,* ☎ *01/623–3333,* FAX *01/623–3330,* WEB *www.kefalarisuites.gr. 13 suites. AE, DC, MC, V.*

$$$ ⊞ **Electra Palace.** At the Plaka's edge, this hotel has cozy rooms in warm hues with TV and plenty of storage space, for comparatively low prices in this category. Rooms from the fifth floor up are smaller but have larger balconies and Acropolis views. The renovated roof garden has a bar, a pool and whirlpool tub, barbecue in summer, and stunning Acropolis views. One of the city's best buffet breakfasts (sausage, pancakes, home fries) is included in the price. ⊠ *Nikodimou 18, Plaka, 10557,* ☎ *01/337–0000,* FAX *01/324–1875. 106 rooms, 5 suites. Restaurant, pool. AE, DC, MC, V.*

$$ ⊞ **Acropolis View Hotel.** Major sights are just a stone's throw away from this hotel tucked into a quiet neighborhood below the Acropolis. About half of the agreeable rooms with balconies have Parthenon views. There is a roof garden, staff members in the homey lobby are efficient, and buffet breakfast is included in the price. ⊠ *Webster 10, Acropolis, 11742,* ☎ *01/921–7303, 01/921–7304, or 01/921–7305,* FAX *01/923–0705,* WEB *www.acropolisview.gr. 32 rooms. Air-conditioning. DC, MC, V.*

$$ ⊞ **Athens Cypria Hotel.** A cool oasis in the city center, this hotel is a few minutes from Syntagma Square, offering a reasonably priced alternative for those who want convenience and comfort. Enter the vaguely art deco lobby from the quiet street to find simple and clean air-conditioned guest rooms, done in shades of blue and furnished with satellite TV and standard amenities. Some of the upper floors open out onto a balcony; those on the sixth floor have Acropolis views. American buffet breakfast is included in the price. ⊠ *Diomias 5, Syntagma, 10557,* ☎ *01/323–8034 through 8038,* FAX *01/324–8792. 71 rooms. Bar, air-conditioning. AE, V.*

$$ ⊞ **Hotel Achilleas.** This modern, family-owned hotel is just a few minutes from Syntagma but priced at the low end of its category. It has plain but spacious rooms with TV, direct-dial phones, mini-bar, safe, and air-conditioning. At press time, the hotel was undergoing a major renovation to qualify for a higher government rating, so expect changes for the better. Breakfast is served in an interior courtyard filled with jungly plants and marble-topped blue tables. ✉ *Lekka 21, Syntagma, 10562,* ☎ *01/322–5826, 01/322–8531, or 01/323–3197,* FAX *01/322–2412,* WEB *www.tourhotel.gr/achilleas. 36 rooms. Air-conditioning. AE, DC, MC, V.*

$$ 🏨 **Plaka Hotel.** Close to the ancient sights and the Monastiraki Square Metro, this hotel has a roof garden overlooking the Plaka district's rooftops to the Parthenon. Double-glazed windows cut down the noise; the highest floors are the quietest. All rooms have TV and are simply furnished; those in back from the fifth floor up have the best Acropolis views. ✉ *Kapnikareas 7 and Mitropoleos, Plaka, 10556,* ☎ *01/322–2096 through 2098,* FAX *01/322–2412,* WEB *www.plakahotel.gr. 67 rooms. Air-conditioning. AE, DC, MC, V.*

$–$$ 🏨 **Acropolis House.** Ensconced in a 19th-century Plaka residence, this pension is frequented by artists and academics who appreciate its large rooms, original frescoes, and genteel owners. All rooms have private bathrooms, though about 10 have their bath immediately outside in the hallway. Most rooms have air-conditioning, and a full breakfast is included in the price. ✉ *Kodrou 6–8, Plaka, 10558,* ☎ *01/322–2344 or 01/322–6241,* FAX *01/324–4143. 20 rooms. V.*

$–$$ 🏨 **Adams Hotel.** Favored by young people for its clean rooms and good value, this quiet hotel sits across from Ayia Aikaterini church in Plaka. Most of the rooms have balconies and many, including all on the top floor, enjoy splendid views of the Acropolis. The four rooms that don't have air-conditioning are cooled by ceiling fans. Four cheaper rooms have their private bath outside the room. ✉ *Herefondos 6 at Thalou, Plaka, 10558,* ☎ *01/322–5381 or 01/324–6582,* FAX *01/323–8553,* WEB *www.greektravel.com/adams. 14 rooms. Air-conditioning. MC, V.*

$ 🏨 **Art Gallery Pension.** On a side street not far from the Acropolis, this friendly, handsome house has an old-fashioned look, with family paintings on the muted white walls, comfortable beds, hardwood floors, and ceiling fans. Many rooms have balconies with views of Filopappou or the Acropolis. ✉ *Erecthiou 5, Koukaki, 11742,* ☎ *01/923–8376 or 01/923–1933,* FAX *01/923–3025. 21 rooms, 2 suites. No credit cards. Closed Nov.–Feb.*

$ 🏨 **Attalos Hotel.** Gentlemanly owner Kostas Zissis's personality is reflected in the friendly, helpful atmosphere of this central hotel, just a few minutes from the trendy Psirri district. It has a rooftop garden, and 12 rooms have fine views of the Acropolis or Lycabettus; 37 rooms include balconies. All have direct-dial phone and TV. Try to get a room in the back, where there's less street noise, though it's also reduced by double-glazed windows. ✉ *Athinas 29, Monastiraki, 10554,* ☎ *01/321–2801 through 2803,* FAX *01/324–3124,* WEB *www.attalos.gr. 80 rooms. Air-conditioning. AE, V.*

NIGHTLIFE AND THE ARTS

The English-language newspapers *Athens News* and *Kathemerini*, inserted in the *International Herald Tribune*, list current performances, gallery openings, and films. The free magazine *Now in Athens*, distributed at various hotels and EOT, offers extensive information on culture and entertainment in the capital.

The Arts

The **Athens Festival** (box office; ✉ arcade at Stadiou 4, ☎ 01/322–1459) runs from late June through September with concerts, opera, ballet, folk dancing, and drama. Performances are in various locations, including the theater of Herod Atticus (Irodion; ☎ 01/323–2771 box office) below the Acropolis and Mt. Lycabettus (☎ 01/722–7233 or

01/722–7209). Tickets range in price from 4,000 dr./€11.77 to 20,000 dr./€58.83 and are available a few days before the performance.

The **Krystalleia Festival** stages local and international musical and dance groups from June through July and September in the stately Plakendias mansion (⊠ 16 km/10 mi northeast of Athens on Mt. Pendeli). The concurrent **Pendelis Festival** (end July and Sept.) focuses on classical music, often importing international orchestras to take advantage of the acoustics of the mansion. For information on the festivals, contact EOT. Tickets run from 2,000 dr./€5.89 to 5,000 dr./€14.71 and are usually sold at major record stores in downtown Athens.

Though rather corny, the **sound-and-light shows** (⊠ Pnyx theater box office off Dionyssiou Areopagitou opposite Acropolis, ☎ 01/922–6210 or 01/928–2907), held April–October nightly at 9, display the Acropolis with dramatic lighting and a brief narrated history. The box office opens at 8:20 PM, admission is 1,500 dr./€4.42 and performances are in English.

Concerts and Operas

Greek and world-class international orchestras perform September through June at the **Megaron Athens Concert Hall** (⊠ Vas. Sofias and Kokkali, ☎ 01/728–2333, FAX 01/728–2300; downtown box office, Arcade at Stadiou 4, ☎ 01/322–1459). Information and tickets are available weekdays 10–6 and Saturday 10–4. Prices range from 1,500 dr./€4.42 to 22,000 dr./€64.71; there is a substantial discount for students and those 8–18. Inexpensive and often free classical concerts are held November through May at the **Philippos Nakas Conservatory** (⊠ Ippokratous 41, ☎ 01/363–4000, FAX 01/360–2827). Tickets cost 2,000 dr./€5.89 to 3,000 dr./€8.83.

Dance

The lively **Dora Stratou Troupe** (⊠ Theater, Filopappou Hill, ☎ 01/921–4650; 01/324–4395 troupe's offices, FAX 01/324–6921, WEB users.hol.gr/~grdance) performs Greek and Cypriot folk dances in authentic costumes. Tickets cost 4,000 dr./€11.77. Performances are from the end of May to the end of September, Tuesday–Sunday at 10:15 PM and Wednesday and Sunday at 8:15.

Film

Almost all Athens cinemas now show foreign films; for listings, consult the *Athens News* and the *Kathemerini* insert in the *International Herald-Tribune*. Tickets run about 2,000 dr./€5.89–2,300 dr./€6.77. In summer, films are also shown in open-air cinemas called *therina*.

Nightlife

Athens has an active nightlife; most bars and clubs stay open at least until 3 AM. Drinks are rather steep (about 1,800 dr./€5.29–2,500 dr./€7.35) but generous. Often there is a surcharge on weekends at the most popular clubs, which also have bouncers. Few clubs take credit cards for drinks. In summer many downtown dance clubs move to the seaside. Ask your hotel for recommendations and check ahead for summer closings. For a uniquely Greek evening, visit a club featuring *rembetika* music, a type of blues, or the popular *bouzoukia* (clubs with live bouzouki music). In the larger bouzouki venues, there is usually a per-person minimum or an overpriced, second-rate prix-fixe menu; a bottle of whiskey costs about 42,000 dr./€123.53.

Bars

Balthazar (⊠ Tsoha 27, Ambelokipi, ☎ 01/644–1215 or 01/645–2278), in a neoclassical house, has a lush garden courtyard and sub-

HOW TO USE THIS GUIDE

Great trips begin with great planning, and this guide makes planning easy. It's packed with everything you need—insider advice on hotels and restaurants, cool tools, practical tips, essential maps, and much more.

COOL TOOLS

Fodor's Choice Top picks are marked throughout with a star.

Great Itineraries These tours, planned by Fodor's experts, give you the skinny on what you can see and do in the time you have.

Smart Travel Tips A to Z This special section is packed with important contacts and advice on everything from how to get around to what to pack.

Good Walks You won't miss a thing if you follow the numbered bullets on our maps.

Need a Break? Looking for a quick bite to eat or a spot to rest? These sure bets are along the way.

Off the Beaten Path Some lesser-known sights are worth a detour. We've marked those you should make time for.

POST-IT® FLAGS
Dog-ear no more!

"Post-it" is a registered trademark of 3M.

ICONS AND SYMBOLS

Watch for these symbols throughout:

★	Our special recommendations
✕	Restaurant
⌂	Lodging establishment
✕⌂	Lodging establishment whose restaurant warrants a special trip
☾	Good for kids
☞	Sends you to another section of the guide for more information
✉	Address
☎	Telephone number
FAX	Fax number
WEB	Web site
🎟	Admission price
☾	Opening hours
$-$$$$	Lodging and dining price categories, keyed to strategically sited price charts. Check the index for locations.
① ❶	Numbers in white and black circles on the maps, in the margins, and within tours correspond to one another.

ON THE WEB

Continue your planning with these useful tools found at **www.fodors.com**, the Web's best source for travel information.

"Rich with resources." —*New York Times*

"Navigation is a cinch." —*Forbes* "Best of the Web" list

"Put together by people bursting with know-how."
                                —*Sunday Times* (London)

Create a Miniguide Pinpoint hotels, restaurants, and attractions that have what you want at the price you want to pay.

Rants and Raves Find out what readers say about Fodor's picks—or write your own reviews of hotels and restaurants you've just visited.

Travel Talk Post your questions and get answers from fellow travelers, or share your own experiences.

On-Line Booking Find the best prices on airline tickets, rental cars, cruises, or vacations, and book them on the spot.

About our Books Learn about other Fodor's guides to your destination and many others.

Expert Advice and Trip Ideas From what to tip to how to take great photos, from the national parks to Nepal, Fodors.com has suggestions that'll make your trip a breeze. Log on and get informed and inspired.

Smart Resources Check the weather in your destination or convert your currency. Learn the local language or link to the latest event listings. Or consult hundreds of detailed maps—all in one place.

dued music. **Banana Moon** (⌂ Vas. Olgas 1, Zappio, ☎ 01/321–5414) offers both a lively bar with a glamorous crowd and quieter tables set among the trees of the National Gardens; in winter the bar moves across the street. With low-key music and a romantic park setting, **Parko** (⌂ Eleftherias Park, Ilisia, ☎ 01/722–3784) is another summer favorite. Cinema stars, romancing couples, girlfriends, the local Lotto vendor— all show up at **En Delfois** (⌂ Skoufa 75 on Delfon pedestrian zone, Kolonaki, ☎ 01/360–8269) for its see-and-be-seen atmosphere in a friendly setting with good snacks, eclectic music played at conversational level, and generous drinks. **Folie** (⌂ Eslin 4, Ambelokipi, ☎ 01/646–9852) has a congenial crowd of all ages dancing to reggae, Latin, funk, and ethnic music. Of the bars for the under-40 crowd, mainstream **Privilege** (⌂ Pireos 130 and Alkioneos, Gazi, ☎ 01/347–7388) is especially popular, though tough to get into. **Plus Soda** (⌂ Ermou 161, Thissio, ☎ 01/345–6187), the dance temple of Athens, is very popular and sometimes hard to gain entrance to. Both Privilege and Plus Soda usually move to the seaside in summer. Glitzy **Wild Rose** (⌂ Panepistimiou 10, Syntagma, ☎ 01/364–2160) is an Athens classic, with predominantly house music and some rock. You'll find an artsy, happy crowd enjoying the playlist that runs from cabaret to ethnic to freestyle at the bar-restaurant **Multi-Culti** (⌂ Ag. Theklas 8, Psirri, ☎ 01/324–4643).

Bouzoukia

Apollon Palace (⌂ Syngrou 259, Nea Smyrni, ☎ 01/942–7580 through 7583) is the most popular place with Athenians who want to hear Greece's singing stars, such as Antonis Remos and Stelios Dionyssiou. It's closed Monday–Tuesday. Decadence reigns at the slightly more casual **Iera Odos** (⌂ Iera Odos 18–20, Kerameikos, ☎ 01/342–8272 through 8275) as diners dance the seductive *tsifteteli* to big names like Notis Sfakianakis. It's closed Sunday–Monday.

Live Rock, Jazz, Blues

The laid-back **House of Art** (⌂ Santouri 4 and Sarri, Psirri, ☎ 01/321–7678) hosts small groups. The premier venue for international jazz and blues bands is the sophisticated **Half Note Jazz Club** (⌂ Trivonianou 17, Mets, ☎ 01/921–3310 or 01/923–2460). Lively **Hi-Hat Cafe** (⌂ Dragoumi 28 and Krousovou 1, Hilton, ☎ 01/721–8171) also hosts international artists. Most big names in popular music perform at the informal **Rodon** (⌂ Marni 24, Platia Vathis, ☎ 01/524–7427); in summer, they usually appear at the outdoor Lycabettus amphitheater. Summer also heralds the three-day **Rockwave Festival** in mid-July, usually held somewhere on the Athens coast (Ticket House box office; ⌂ Panepistimiou 42 in arcade, ☎ 01/360–8366 or check with downtown record stores). Past acts have included Patti Smith and Prodigy.

Rembetika Clubs

Rembetika, the blues sung by refugees from Asia Minor who came to Greece in the 1920s, still enthralls Greeks. At **Stathmos** (⌂ Mavromateon 22, Pedion Areos, ☎ 01/883–2393 or 01/822–0883), the band usually starts off slowly but by 1 AM is wailing to a packed dance floor. At **Mnissikleous** (⌂ Mnissikleous 22 and Lyceiou, Plaka, ☎ 01/322–5558 or 01/322–5337), the authentic music of popular *rembetis* Bobis Goles draws audience participation.

SHOPPING

Antiques

Pandrossou Street in Monastiraki is especially rich in shops selling small antiques and icons. Keep in mind that fakes are common and that you must have government permission to export objects from the Classic, Hellenistic, Roman, or Byzantine periods. For serious antiques collecting, including carved dowry chests, head to **Martinos** (⊠ Pandrossou 50, ☎ 01/321–2414). **Motakis** (⊠ Pl. Abyssinia 3 in basement, ☎ 01/321–9005) sells antiques and other beautiful old objects. At **Nasiotis** (⊠ Ifestou 24, ☎ 01/321–2369) you may uncover interesting finds in a basement stacked with engravings, old magazines, and books, including first editions.

Flea Markets

The **Sunday-morning flea market** (⊠ Pandrossou and Ifestou Sts.) sells everything from secondhand guitars to Russian caviar. However little your treasured find costs, you should haggle. On weekdays in **Ifestou**, where coppersmiths have their shops, you can pick up copper wine jugs, candlesticks, and cookware for next to nothing.

Gift Ideas

Better tourist shops sell copies of traditional Greek jewelry; silver filigree; Skyrian pottery; onyx ashtrays and dishes; woven bags; attractive rugs, including flokatis; worry beads in amber or silver; and blue-and-white amulets to ward off the *mati* (evil eye). Reasonably priced natural sponges from Kalymnos also make good gifts. **Goutis** (⊠ Dimokritou 40, Kolonaki, ☎ 01/361–3557) has an eclectic assortment of costumes, embroidery, and old, handcrafted silver items. **Ilias Kokkonis** (⊠ Stoa Arsakeiou 8, Omonia, enter from Panepistimiou or Stadiou, ☎ 01/322–1189 or 01/322–6355) stocks any flag you've hankered after—large or small, from any country. **Mati** (⊠ Voukourestiou 20, Syntagma, ☎ 01/362–6238) has finely designed amulets to battle the evil eye, as well as a collection of monastery lamps and candlesticks. **Mazarakis** (⊠ Voulis 31–33, Syntagma, ☎ 01/323–9428) offers a large selection of flokatis and will ship.

Greeks spend hours heatedly playing *tavli*, or backgammon. To take home a set of your own, look for the hole-in-the-wall, no-name shop affectionately called **Baba** (⊠ Ifestou 30, Monastiraki, ☎ 01/321–9994), which sells boards and pieces in all sizes and designs. For an inexpensive gift pick up some freshly ground Greek coffee and the special coffee pot called *briki* at **Miseyiannis** (⊠ Levendis 7, Kolonaki, ☎ 01/721–0136).

Handicrafts

The **Kentro Ellinikis Paradosis** (Center of Hellenic Tradition; ⊠ Mitropoleos 59, Monastiraki, ☎ 01/321–3023) is an outlet for quality handicrafts. The **Organismos Ethnikos Pronoias** (National Welfare Organization; ⊠ Ipatias 6, and Apollonos, Plaka, ☎ 01/321–8272) displays work by Greek craftspeople—stunning handwoven carpets, flat-weave kilims, hand-embroidered tablecloths, and flokatis.

At **Amorgos** (⊠ Kodrou 3, Plaka, ☎ 01/324–3836) the owners make wooden furniture using motifs from regional Greek designs. They also sell needlework, handwoven fabrics, hanging ceiling lamps, shadow puppets, and other decorative accessories. The Greek cooperative **EOMMEX** (⊠ Mitropoleos 9, Syntagma, ☎ 01/323–0408) operates a showroom with folk and designer rugs made by more than 30 weavers around the country.

Jewelry

Prices for gold and silver are much lower in Greece than in many Western countries, and jewelry is of high quality. Many shops in Plaka carry original-design pieces available at a good price if you bargain hard enough. Great values in gold, often designed by the owners, can be purchased at **Byzantino** (☒ Adrianou 120, Plaka, ☎ 01/324–6605). For more expensive items, the Voukourestiou pedestrian mall off Syntagma Square has a number of the city's leading jewelry shops. The baubles at **J. Vourakis & Fils** (☒ Voukourestiou 8, ☎ 01/331–1087) are both unique modern designs and older, collector's items. **Xanthopoulos** (☒ Voukourestiou 4, ☎ 01/322–6856) carries diamond necklaces, magnificently large gems, and the finest pearls; you can also order custom-made jewelry.

Some of the most original work in gold can be had at **Fanourakis** (☒ Patriarchou Ioakeim 23, Kolonaki, ☎ 01/721–1762; ☒ Evangelistrias 2, Mitropoleos, ☎ 01/324–6642; ☒ Panagitsas 6, Kifissia, ☎ 01/623–2334), where contemporary Athenian artists use gold almost like a fabric—creasing, scoring, and fluting it. **LALAoUNIS** (☒ Panepistimiou 6, Syntagma, ☎ 01/361–1371) showcases pieces by Ilias Lalaounis, who takes his ideas from nature, biology, and ancient Greek pieces.

The **Benaki Museum gift shop** (☒ Koumbari 1, at Vas. Sofias, Kolonaki, ☎ 01/362–7367) has finely rendered copies of classical jewelry. The **Goulandris Cycladic Museum** (☒ Neofitou Douka 4, Kolonaki, ☎ 01/724–9706) carries modern versions of ancient jewelry designs.

Music

CDs of Greek music are much cheaper before they've been exported. One of the biggest selections, along with knowledgeable English-speaking staff, is at the **Virgin Megastore** (☒ Stadiou 7–9, Syntagma, ☎ 01/331–4788 through 4796), where you can listen before you purchase.

ATHENS A TO Z

To research prices, get advice from other travelers, and book travel arrangements, visit www.fodors.com.

AIRPORTS AND TRANSFERS
Ellinikon Airport lies about 10 km (6 mi) from the city center.
➤ AIRPORT INFORMATION: **Ellinikon Airport** (☒ Vas. Georgiou B' 1, ☎ 01/936–3363 through 3366 West Terminal; 01/969–4466 arrivals and departures; 01/969–4531 passenger paging for East Terminal; 01/997–2581 New Charter Terminal).

TRANSFERS
An express bus service connects the East, West, and New Charter terminals; Syntagma Square; Omonia Square; and Piraeus. The express bus (No. E93) runs between the three terminals every 40 minutes around the clock. Between the terminals and Athens, the express bus (No. E91) runs around the clock, about every 30 minutes. You can catch the bus on Syntagma Square between Ermou and Mitropoleos streets or off Omonia Square on Stadiou and Aiolou. From the airport terminals to Piraeus (Pl. Karaiskaki), the express bus (No. E19) leaves about every hour, from 5 AM to midnight. The fare is 250 dr./€.74, 500 dr./€1.48 from 11:30 PM until 5:30 AM (for schedules check with EOT). You can also take the regular city line (No. B2) from Syntagma Square to the West Terminal (for Olympic Airways flights) from about 4:30 AM to 11:50 PM every 15 minutes for most of the day; fare is 120 dr./€.36. It's easier to take taxis: about 2,500 dr./€7.36 to Piraeus; 1,500 dr./€4.42 between terminals; 2,700 dr./€7.95 to the center, more if there is traffic. The price goes up by about two-thirds between midnight and 5 AM.

BOAT AND FERRY TRAVEL

Most ships from the Greek islands dock at Piraeus (port authority), 10 km (6 mi) from the center. EOT distributes boat schedules updated every Wednesday; you can also call a daily Greek recording by dialing 143 for departure times. From the main harbor you can take the nearby Metro right into Omonia Square (150 dr./€.45) or Syntagma Square (change at Omonia, take the line going to Ethniki Aminas, 250 dr./€.74) The trip takes 25–30 minutes. A taxi takes longer because of traffic and costs around 2,500 dr./€7.36. As the driver may wait until he fills the taxi with several passengers headed in the same direction, it's faster to walk to the main street and hail a cab there. If you arrive by hydrofoil in the smaller port of Zea Marina, take Bus 905 or Trolley 20 to the Piraeus Metro. At Rafina port, which serves some of the closer Cyclades and Evia, taxis are hard to find. KTEL buses, which are located slightly uphill from port, leave every 30 minutes from about 5:30 AM until 9:30 PM and cost 500 dr./€1.48.

➤ BOAT AND FERRY INFORMATION: **KTEL** (☎ 01/821–0872). **Piraeus** (☎ 01/451–1311 through 1319). **Rafina Port** (☎ 0294/22–300).

BUS TRAVEL TO AND FROM ATHENS

Greek buses serving parts of northern Greece, including Thessaloniki, and the Peloponnese (Corinth, Olympia, Nauplion, Epidavros, Mycenae) arrive at Terminal A. Those traveling from Evia, most of Thrace, and central Greece, including Delphi, pull in to Terminal B; you must call each region's ticket counter for information. EOT provides a phone list. From Terminal A, take Bus 051 to Omonia Square; from Terminal B, take Bus 24 downtown. To get to the stations, catch Bus 051 at Zinonos and Menandrou off Omonia Square for Terminal A and Bus 024 on Amalias Avenue in front of the National Gardens for Terminal B. International buses drop their passengers off on the street, usually in the Omonia or Syntagma Square area or at Stathmos Peloponnisos.

Most buses to the east Attica coast, including those for Sounion (1,250 dr./€3.67 for inland route and 1,300 dr./€3.83 on coastal road) and Marathon (800 dr./€2.36), leave from the KTEL terminal, which is on the corner Mavromateon and Alexandras near Pedion Areos park.

➤ BUS INFORMATION: **KTEL terminal** (✉ Platia Aigyptiou, ☎ 01/821–3203 for information on bus to Sounion; 01/821–0872 for information on bus to Marathon). **Terminal A** (✉ Kifissou 100, ☎ 01/512–4910). **Terminal B** (✉ Liossion 260, ☎ 01/831–7096 Delphi; 01/831–7173 Livadia [Ossios Loukas via Distomo]; 01/831–1431 Trikala [Meteora]).

BUS TRAVEL WITHIN ATHENS

EOT can provide bus information, as can the Organization for Public Transportation. The office itself is open to visitors weekdays 7:30–3. The fare on buses and trolleys is 120 dr./€.36; monthly passes are sold at the beginning of each month for 5,000 dr./€14.71 (bus and trolley). Purchase tickets at curbside kiosks or from booths at terminals. Validate your ticket in the orange machines when you board to avoid a fine. Buses run from the center to all suburbs and nearby beaches from 5 AM until about midnight. For suburbs north of Kifissia, change at Kifissia's main square, Platia Platanou.

➤ BUS INFORMATION: **Organization for Public Transportation** (✉ Metsovou 15, ☎ 185, 7:30–3 and 7 PM–9 PM).

CAR TRAVEL

You enter Athens by the Ethniki Odos (or National Road, as the main highways going north and south are known) and then follow signs for the center. Leaving Athens, routes to the National Road are marked with signs in English; they usually name Lamia for the north and Corinth or Patras for the southwest.

CONSULATES
➤ NEW ZEALAND: (✉ Kifissias 268, Halandri, ☎ 01/687–4700 or 01/687–4701).

EMERGENCIES
You can call an ambulance in the event of an emergency, but taxis are often faster. Most hotels will call a doctor or dentist for you; you can also contact your embassy for referrals to both. Not all hospitals are open nightly; ask your hotel to check for you, or dial 106 for a Greek listing. The *Athens News* often lists available emergency hospitals, as do most Greek newspapers. Many pharmacies in the center have someone who speaks English, or try Thomas. For late-night pharmacies, call the information line, or check the *Athens News*. For auto accidents, call the city police.
➤ EMERGENCY SERVICES: **Ambulance** (☎ 166). **City Police** (☎ 100). **Coast Guard** (☎ 108). **Fire** (☎ 199). **Tourist police** (✉ Dimitrakopoulou 77, Koukaki, ☎ 171).
➤ 24-HOUR PHARMACIES: **Late-night Pharmacy Information Line** (☎ 107; information in Greek).

ENGLISH-LANGUAGE MEDIA
➤ BOOKSTORES: **Booknest** (✉ Folia tou Bibliou, Panepistimiou 25–29, ☎ 01/322–9560). **Compendium** (✉ Nikis 28, upstairs, ☎ 01/322–1248). **Eleftheroudakis** (✉ Nikis 4, near Syntagma, ☎ 01/322–9388; ✉ Panepistimiou 17, ☎ 01/331–4180). **Pantelides** (✉ Amerikis 11, ☎ 01/362–3673).

SUBWAY TRAVEL
Line 1 runs from Piraeus to Omonia Square and then on to Kifissia, with downtown stops at Thission, Monastiraki, Omonia, and Platia Victorias (near the National Archaeological Museum). Line 2 runs from Sepolia to Syntagma, with a stop at the train stations (Stathmos Larissis) and, as far as Dafne, including a stop for the Acropolis. Line 3 runs from Syntagma to the Greek armed forces' "Pentagon" (Ethnikis Aminas) and includes a stop at Athens's concert hall and the American embassy (Megaron). The fare is 150 dr./€.45 if you stay only on Line 1; otherwise, it's 250 dr./€.74.

TAXIS
Although you can find an empty taxi, it's often faster to call out your destination to one carrying passengers; if the taxi is going in that direction, the driver will pick you up. Most drivers speak basic English. The meter starts at 200 dr./€.59, and even if you join other passengers, you must add this amount to your final charge. The minimum fare is 500 dr./€1.48. The basic charge is 71 dr./€.21 per kilometer (⅔ mi); this increases to 130 dr./€.39 between midnight and 5 AM or if you go outside city limits. There are surcharges for holidays (120 dr./€.36), trips to and from the airport (300 dr./€.89), and rides to, but not from the port, train stations, and bus terminals (150 dr./€.45). There is also a 50 dr./€.14 charge for each suitcase over 10 kilograms (22 pounds), but drivers expect 100 dr./€.29 for each bag they place in the trunk anyway. Waiting time is 2,300 dr./€6.77 per hour. Make sure drivers turn on the meter and use the high tariff ("Tarifa 2") only after midnight; if you encounter trouble, threaten to go to the police. Radio taxis charge an additional 400 dr./€1.18 for the pickup or 600 dr./€1.77 for a later appointment. Some fairly reliable services are Athina 1, Hellas, Kosmos, and Parthenon.

➤ Taxi Companies: **Athina 1** (☎ 01/921–7942). **Hellas** (☎ 01/645–7000 or 01/801–4000). **Kosmos** (☎ 1300). **Parthenon** (☎ 01/532–3300).

TOURS

BUS TOURS

All tour operators offer a four-hour morning bus tour of Athens, including a guided tour of the Acropolis and its museum (10,500 dr./€32.35). Make reservations at your hotel or at a travel agency; many are situated around Filellinon and Nikis streets off Syntagma Square.

PRIVATE GUIDES

All the major tourist agencies can provide English-speaking guides for personally organized tours, or call the Union of Official Guides. Hire only those licensed by the EOT; a four-hour tour including the Acropolis and its museum costs about 28,000 dr./€82.36.
➤ Contacts: **Union of Official Guides** (✉ Apollonas 9A, ☎ 01/322–9705, FAX 01/323–9200).

SINGLE- AND MULTIPLE-DAY TOURS

A one-day tour to Delphi costs 21,500 dr./€63.30 with lunch included, 19,000 dr./€55.89 without lunch; a two-day tour to Mycenae, Nauplion, and Epidauros costs 34,000 dr./€100, including half board in first-class hotels; and a full-day cruise from Piraeus, visiting the islands of Aegina, Poros, and Hydra, costs 20,500 dr./€60.20, including buffet lunch on the ship.

SPECIAL-INTEREST TOURS

For folk dancing take a four-hour evening tour (April–October; 10,000 dr./€29.42) that begins with a sound-and-light show of the Acropolis and goes on to a performance of Greek folk dances in the open-air theater nearby. Another tour offers a dinner show at a taverna in the Plaka area for around 14,000 dr./€41.18. For efficient service, go first to CHAT Tours. For organized adventure travel, contact Trekking Hellas or F-Zein.

TRAIN TRAVEL

Athens has two railway stations, side by side, not far from Omonia Square off Diliyianni street. International trains and those coming from north of Athens use Stathmos Larissis. Take Trolley 1 from the terminal to Omonia Square or the Metro to Omonia and Syntagma squares. Trains from the Peloponnese use the marvelously ornate Stathmos Peloponnisos. To Omonia and Syntagma squares take Bus 057 or the Metro. As the phones are almost always busy, it's easier to get departure times from the main information phone service and call about seat availability or buy tickets at a railway office downtown, open Monday–Saturday 8–2.
➤ Train Information: **Railway offices** (✉ Sina 6, ☎ 01/529–8910; Filellinon 17, ☎ 01/323–6747; ✉ Karolou 1, ☎ 01/529–7006 through 7007). **Stathmos Larissis** (☎ 01/529–8837). **Stathmos Peloponnisos** (☎ 01/529–8735).

TRANSPORTATION AROUND ATHENS

Many of the sights and most of the hotels, cafés, and restaurants are within a fairly small central area. It's easy to walk everywhere, though sidewalks are often obstructed by parked cars. You can buy a monthly pass covering the metro, buses, and trolleys for 10,000 dr./€29.42 at the beginning of each month. Validate your ticket by stamping it in the orange machines at the entrance to the platforms, or you will be fined.

TRAVEL AGENCIES

➤ Local Agents: **American Express** (✉ Ermou 2, ☎ 01/324–4975 through 4975, FAX 01/322–7893). **CHAT Tours** (✉ 4 Stadiou, ☎ 01/

322–2886, FAX 01/323–5270). **Condor Travel** (⊠ Stadiou 43, ☎ 01/
321–2453 or 01/321–6986, FAX 01/321–4296). **F-Zein** (⊠ Syngrou
132, 5th floor, ☎ 01/921–6285, FAX 01/922–9995). **Key Tours** (⊠
Kallirois 4, ☎ 01/923–3166, FAX 01/923–2008). **Travel Plan** (⊠ Chris-
tou Lada 9, ☎ 01/323–8801 through 8804, FAX 01/322–2152). **Trekking
Hellas** (⊠ Fillelinon 7, 3rd floor, ☎ 01/331–0323 through 0326, FAX
01/323–4548).

VISITOR INFORMATION
➤ TOURIST INFORMATION: **EOT** (⊠ Amerikis 2, near Syntagma, ☎ 01/
331–0565 or 01/331–0692; ⊠ Ellinikon Airport, East Terminal [ar-
rivals], ☎ 01/961–2722 or 01/969–4500; ⊠ Piraeus, EOT Building,
1st floor, Zea Marina, ☎ 01/452–2591 or 01/452–2586).

Greece Basics

BUSINESS HOURS
BANKS AND OFFICES
Office and shopping hours vary from season to season. Check with your
hotel for up-to-the-minute information on opening and closing times.
Banks are open weekdays 8–2, except Friday, when they close at 1:30;
they are closed weekends and public holidays. In Athens one branch
of the National Bank of Greece has extended hours for foreign exchange
only, open Monday–Thursday 3:30–6:30, Friday 3–6:30, Saturday 9–
3, Sunday 9–1. Even smaller towns have at least one bank with an ATM.
➤ CONTACTS: **National Bank of Greece** (⊠ Karageorgi Servias 2, Syntagma, ☎ 01/334–0011).

MUSEUMS AND SIGHTS
Museums and archaeological sites are open 8:30–3 off-season, or winter (November–mid-April). Depending on available personnel, sites usually stay open longer mid-April–October, sometimes as late as 7 PM in
July and August. Many museums are closed one day a week, usually
Monday. Archaeological sites and museums are closed January 1,
March 25, Good Friday morning until noon, Easter Sunday, May 1,
and December 25–26; for the reduced visiting hours on other holidays,
check the handout from EOT.

SHOPS
Shops may stay open from 9 AM to 9 PM in summer, though most stores
close Monday, Wednesday, and Saturday afternoons around 3 or 4 PM.
On Tuesday, Thursday, and Friday, many shops close between about
3 and 5 PM. In winter (October–mid-April) hours are slightly reduced,
though this changes every year. Supermarkets are open weekdays until
about 8:30 PM, with reduced hours on Saturday. In tourist areas such
as Athens's Plaka, souvenir shops stay open late.

CUSTOMS AND DUTIES
For details on imports and duty-free limits, *see* Customs & Duties *in*
Smart Travel Tips A to Z.

IN GREECE
You may bring in only one each of such expensive portable items as
camcorders and computers. You should register these with Greek customs upon arrival, to avoid any problems when taking them out of
the country again. Foreign banknotes amounting to more than $2,500
must be declared for re-export, although there are no restrictions on
traveler's checks; foreign visitors may export no more than 100,000
drachma in Greek currency.

EMBASSIES

New Zealand maintains a consular office in Athens (☞ Athens A to Z).

➤ AUSTRALIA: (✉ D. Soutsou 37, Athens, ☎ 01/645–0404).

➤ CANADA: (✉ Gennadiou 4, Athens, ☎ 01/727–3400).

➤ IRELAND: (✉ Vas. Konstantinou 7, Athens, ☎ 01/723–2771).

➤ UNITED KINGDOM: (✉ Ploutarchou 1, Athens, ☎ 01/723–6211 through 6219; 01/727–2600).

➤ UNITED STATES: (✉ Vasilissis Sofias 91, Athens, ☎ 01/721–2951 through 2959).

HOLIDAYS

January 1; January 6 (Epiphany); February 26 (Clean Monday and first day of Lent); March 25 (Independence Day); Good Friday; Greek Easter Sunday; Greek Easter Monday; May 1 (Labor Day); June 3 (Pentecost); August 15 (Assumption); October 28 (Ochi Day); December 25–26.

LANGUAGE

English is widely spoken in hotels and elsewhere, especially by young people, and even in out-of-the-way places someone is always happy to lend a helping word. In this guide names are given in the Roman alphabet according to the Greek pronunciation.

MONEY MATTERS

Fluctuations in currency make it impossible to do accurate budgeting in advance; watch the exchange rates. On the whole, Greece offers good value compared with many other European countries. A modest hotel in a small town will charge only slightly lower rates than a modest hotel in Athens, with the same amenities. The same is true of restaurants. Some sample prices include: cup of coffee, 800 dr./€2.36–1,100 dr./€3.24; bottle of beer, 700 dr./€2.06–900 dr./€2.65; soft drink, 500 dr./€1.48; grilled cheese sandwich, 850 dr./€2.5; 2-km (1-mi) taxi ride, around 500 dr./€1.48. Admission to most museums and archaeological sites is free on Sunday from November through March.

CURRENCY

The Greek monetary unit is the drachma (dr.). Banknotes are in denominations of 100, 200, 500, 1,000, 5,000, and 10,000 dr.; coins, 5, 10, 20, 50, 100, and 500. At press time (summer 2001), there were 355 dr. to the U.S. dollar, 240 dr. to the Canadian dollar, 532 dr. to the pound sterling, 426 dr. to the Irish punt, 212 dr. to the Australian dollar, 168 dr. to the New Zealand dollar, and 51.39 dr. to the South African rand. Daily exchange rates are prominently displayed in banks. Greece is one of the 12 nations adopting the euro, the single European Union currency. Coins and bills will be issued in January 2002, and in a few months the drachma will cease to exist. One euro is equivalent to 340 dr.

TELEPHONES

COUNTRY AND AREA CODES

The country code for Greece is 30. When dialing Greece from outside the country, drop the first zero in the regional telephone code.

DIRECTORY AND OPERATOR ASSISTANCE

For directory information, dial 131; many of the operators speak English. Many places are listed under the owner's name, not the official name, so you must know the name of the establishment's owner, even if it is a taverna or shop. For operator-assisted calls and international directory information in English, dial 161.

INTERNATIONAL CALLS

You can buy phone cards with 100 units (2,500 dr./€7.35), 500 units (5,000dr./€14.71), and 1,000 units (10,000 dr./€29.42) for use at card phones. Kiosks frequently have metered phones for long-distance calls, but their location is often on a bustling street corner. For more privacy, go to the local OTE (Hellenic Telecommunications Organization) office. There is a three-minute minimum charge for operator-assisted station-to-station and person-to-person connections. Numbers for major companies with long-distance operator assistance are listed below.

➤ ACCESS CODES: **AT&T** (☎ 00/800–1311). **Worldphone (MCI)** (☎ 00/800–1211). **Sprint** (☎ 00/800–1411).

LOCAL CALLS

Many kiosks have pay telephones for local calls only. You pay the kiosk owner 20 dr./€.06 per call after you've finished, unless it was a lengthy call, in which case you pay for the number of units you racked up. It's easier to buy a phone card from an OTE office, kiosks, or convenience shops and use it at card phones. The price drops about 50% for long-distance calls daily 10 PM–8 AM; for local calls, Sundays 10 PM–8 AM.

3   BARCELONA

As the capital of Catalunya (Catalonia), 2,000-year-old Barcelona commanded a vast Mediterranean empire when Madrid was still a dusty Moorish outpost on the Spanish steppe. Relegated to second-city status only after Madrid was chosen as site of the royal court in 1561, Barcelona more than rivals Madrid for architecture, culture, and nightlife. Industrious, creative and playful in even parts, the citizens of this thriving metropolis are proud to have and use their own language—street names, museum exhibits, newspapers, radio programs, and movies are all in Catalan. An important milestone here was the city's long-awaited opportunity to host the Olympic Games in summer 1992; the Olympics were of singular importance in Barcelona's modernization. Their legacy includes a vastly improved ring road and several other highways; the cleaning-up of four beaches; and the creation of an entire neighborhood in what used to be the run-down industrial district of Poble Nou. In addition, the promontory of Montjuïc gained a sports stadium, several swimming pools, and an adjoining marina. Few cities can rival the medieval atmosphere of the Gothic Quarter's narrow alleys, the elegance and distinction of the Moderniste (Art Nouveau) Eixample, or the many fruits of Gaudí's whimsical imagination. Extraordinarily endowed with two millenniums of art and architecture, Barcelona remains a world center for design.

EXPLORING BARCELONA

Numbers in the margin correspond to points of interest on the Barcelona map.

It should take you two full days of sightseeing to complete the following tour. The first part covers the Gothic Quarter, the Picasso Museum, and Las Ramblas. The second part takes you to Passeig de Gràcia and the church of the Sagrada Família; and the third, to Montjuïc.

The Barri Gòtic (Gothic Quarter) and The Rambla

Barcelona's Gothic quarter is a jumble of medieval buildings including the cathedral and the Picasso Museum. La Rambla, Barcelona's best-known promenade is a constant and colorful flood of humanity, past flower stalls, bird vendors, mimes, musicians, newspaper kiosks, and outdoor cafés. The whole avenue is referred to as Las Ramblas (Les Rambles in Catalan) or La Rambla, but each section has its own name: Rambla Santa Monica is at the southeastern or port end, Rambla de les Flors in the middle, and Rambla dels Estudis at the top. Beware of pick-pockets in this part of town.

★ ❶ **Catedral de la Seu** (Cathedral). Citizens of Barcelona gather on Sunday morning to dance the *sardana*, a symbol of Catalan identity, on Plaça de la Seu, in front of the cathedral. The elaborate Gothic structure was built between 1298 and 1450, though the spire and Gothic facade were not added until 1892. Inside, highlights are the beautifully carved **choir stalls**; Santa Eulàlia's tomb in the crypt; the battle-scarred crucifix from Don Juan's galley in the naval battle of Lepanto, in the **Capella de Lepanto** (Lepanto Chapel); and the cloisters. ⊠ *Plaça de la Seu,* ☎ *93/315–1554.* ☉ *Daily 7:45–1:30 and 4–7:45.*

⑫ **Gran Teatre del Liceu.** Barcelona's famous opera house was gutted by fire in 1994 but has reopened, a modern replica of its original self. Built between 1845 and 1847, the old Liceu was one of the world's most beautiful opera houses, with ornamental gilt and plush red-velvet fittings. Anna Pavlova danced here in 1930, and Maria Callas sang here in 1959. ⊠ *La Rambla 51–59,* ☎ *93/485–9900.* ☉ *Daily 9:45–10:15.*

❾ **Monument a Colom** (Columbus Monument). You can ride an elevator to the top for a commanding view of the city and port. Columbus faces out to sea, pointing, ironically, east toward Naples. Nearby you can board the cable car to cross the harbor to Barceloneta or catch it in the other direction up Montjuïc. ⊠ *Portal de la Pau s/n,* ☎ *93/302–5224.* ☉ *Weekdays 10–1:30 and 3–6:30, weekends 10–6:30.*

⑮ **Museu d'Art Contemporani de Barcelona** (MACBA; Barcelona Museum of Contemporary Art). Designed by American Richard Meier, the contemporary-art museum is an important addition to Barcelona's treasury of art and architecture. In the once rough-and-tumble Raval district, it and the neighboring **Centre de Cultura Contemporànea** (CCCB; Center for Contemporary Culture) have reclaimed important buildings and spaces as part of the city's renewal of its historic quarters and traditional neighborhoods. ⊠ *Plaça dels Àngels,* ☎ *93/412–0810.* ☉ *Weekdays 11–7, Sat. 10–8, Sun. 10–3.*

❷ **Museu Frederic Marès.** Here you can browse for hours among the miscellany assembled by sculptor-collector Frederic Marès, including everything from polychrome crucifixes to hat pins, pipes, and walking sticks. ⊠ *Plaça Sant Iu 5,* ☎ *93/310–5800.* ☉ *Tues.–Wed. and Fri.–Sat. 10–7, Thurs. 10–5, Sun. 10–3.*

46

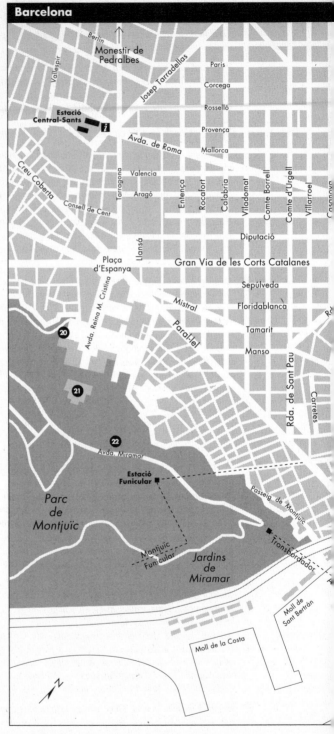

Barcelona

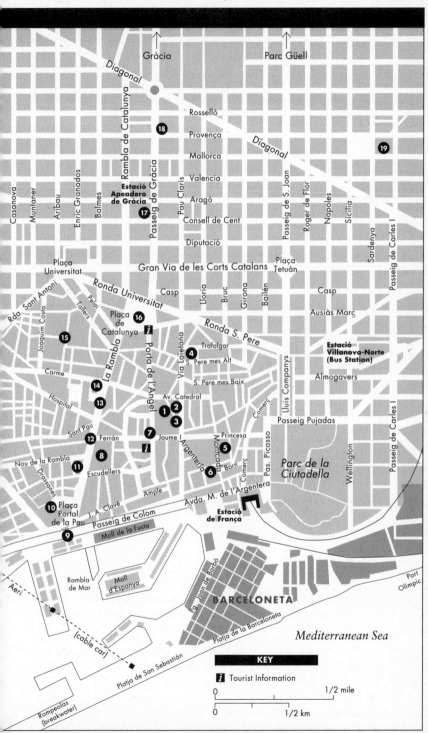

Gràcia

Parc Güell

Diagonal

Rambla de Catalunya

Rosselló

⑱

Provença

Diagonal

Mallorca

⑲

Valencia

Pau Claris

Passeig de Gràcia

Passeig de S. Joan

Roger de Flor

Napoles

Sicilia

Sardenya

Passeig de Carles I

Estació
Apeadero
de Gràcia

⑰

Aragó

Consell de Cent

Casanova

Muntaner

Aribau

Enric Granados

Balmes

Diputació

Plaça
Universitat

Gran Via de les Corts Catalans

Plaça
Tetuán

Ronda Universitat

Casp

Casp

Rda. Sant Antoni

Tallers

Pelai

Plaça
de
Catalunya

⑯

ℹ

Ronda S. Pere

Ausiàs Marc

Joaquim Costa

⑮

Carme

Porta de l'Angel

Via Laietana

Trafalgar

S. Pere mes Alt

Estació
Villanova-Norte
(Bus Station)

Almogavers

La Rambla

S. Pere mes Baix

Lluís Companys

Hospital

⑭

Av. Catedral

⑬

① ②
③

Sant Pau

⑫ Ferràn

⑦

ℹ Jaume I

Princesa

Comerç

Passeig Pujadas

Nou de la Rambla

⑧

Escudellers

Argenteria

Montcada

⑤

Born

Pas. Picasso

Parc de la
Ciutadella

Wellington

Passeig de Carles I

⑪

⑥

Comerç

Drassanes

Ample

Avda. M. de l'Argentera

⑩ Plaça
Portal
de la Pau

J. A. Clavé

Passeig de Colom

Estació
de França

⑨

Moll de la Fusta

Aeri

Rambla
de Mar

Moll
d'Espanya

Fc. Joan de Borbó

BARCELONETA

Port
Olímpic

(cable car)

Platja de la Barceloneta

Mediterranean Sea

KEY

ℹ Tourist Information

Platja de San Sebastián

0   1/2 mile

Rompeolas
(breakwater)

0   1/2 km

⑩ **Museu Marítim** (Maritime Museum). Housed in the 13th-century Drassanes Reiales (Royal Shipyards), this museum is packed with ships, figureheads, and nautical paraphernalia. You can pore over early navigation charts, including a map by Amerigo Vespucci and the 1439 chart of Gabriel de Valseca, the oldest chart in Europe. ⊠ *Plaça Portal de la Pau 1,* ☎ *93/301–1871.* ⊙ *Daily 10–7.*

★ ❺ **Museu Picasso.** Two 15th-century palaces provide a striking setting for these collections of Picasso's early art, donated by Picasso's secretary and then by the artist himself. The works range from childhood sketches to exhibition posters done in Paris shortly before the artist's death. In rare abundance are the Rose Period and Blue Period paintings and the variations on Velázquez's *Las Meninas.* ⊠ *Carrer Montcada 15–19,* ☎ *93/319–6310.* ⊙ *Tues.–Sat. 10–8, Sun. 10–3.*

★ ❹ **Palau de la Música Catalana** (Catalan Music Palace). This flamboyant tour de force designed by Domènech i Muntaner in 1908 is the flagship of Barcelona's Moderniste architecture. Wagnerian cavalry explodes from the right side of the stage while flowery maidens languish on the left; an inverted stained-glass cupola overhead seems to offer the manna of music straight from heaven, and even the stage is dominated by the busts of muselike Art Nouveau instrumentalists. At any important concert the excitement is palpably thick. Tours are conducted daily at 10:30, 2, and 3 (in English) for 700 ptas./€4.21. ⊠ *Ticket office, Sant Francesc de Paula 2 (just off Via Laietana, around a corner from the hall itself),* ☎ *93/295–7200.*

⑭ **Palau de la Virreina.** Built by a onetime Spanish viceroy to Peru in 1778, this building is now a major exhibition center. Check to see what's showing while you're in town. ⊠ *Rambla de les Flors 99,* ☎ *93/301–7775.* ⊙ *Tues.–Sat. 11–8, Sun. 11–2 (last entrance 30 mins before closing).*

★ ⑪ **Palau Güell.** Gaudí built this mansion between 1886 and 1890 for his patron, Count Eusebi de Güell. Gaudí's artful creation of light in the dark Raval neighborhood is one of the highlights in this key visit along the Ruta Modernista. The playful rooftop will remind you of the later Gaudí of Parc Güell. ⊠ *Nou de la Rambla 3–5,* ☎ *93/317–3974.* ⊙ *Weekdays 10–2 and 4–7:30.*

⑯ **Plaça de Catalunya.** This intersection, interesting mainly for its various sculptures and statues, is the transport hub of the modern city. Café Zurich, at the top of Las Ramblas, is Barcelona's most popular meeting point. ⊠ *Top of Las Ramblas.*

❸ **Plaça del Rei.** Several historic buildings surround what is widely considered the most beautiful square in the Gothic Quarter. Following Columbus's first voyage to America, the Catholic Monarchs received him in the **Saló de Tinell,** a magnificent banquet hall built in 1362. Other ancient buildings around the square are the **Palau del Lloctinent** (Lieutenant's Palace); the 14th-century **Capella de Santa Àata** (Chapel of St. Agatha), built right into the Roman city wall; and the **Palau Padellàs** (Padellàs Palace), which houses the **Museu d'Història de la Ciutat** (City History Museum). ⊠ *Plaça del Rei,* ☎ *93/315–1111.* ⊙ *Tues.–Sat. 10–2 and 4–8, Sun. 10–2:30.*

❽ **Plaça Reial.** An elegant and symmetrical 19th-century arcaded square, the Plaça Reial is bordered by elegant ochre facades with balconies overlooking the wrought-iron Fountain of the Three Graces and the lampposts designed by Gaudí in 1879. The place is most colorful on Sunday morning, when crowds gather to sell and trade stamps and coins; at night it's a center of downtown nightlife. **Bar Glaciar,** on the uphill corner toward Las Ramblas, is a booming beer station for young internationals. The **Taxidermist,** across the way, is a hot new restaurant, while **Tarantos** and **Jamboree** are top venues for jazz, flamenco, and rock. ✉ *C. Colom, off Las Ramblas.*

➐ Plaça Sant Jaume. This impressive square in the heart of the Gothic Quarter was built in the 1840s, but the two imposing buildings facing each other across it are much older. The 15th-century **ajuntament** (city hall) has an impressive black-and-gold mural (1928) by Josep María Sert (who also painted the murals in New York's Waldorf-Astoria) and the famous **Saló de Cent,** the first European parliament, from which the Council of One Hundred ruled the city from 1372 to 1714. To visit the interior, check with the protocol office. The **Palau de la Generalitat,** seat of the Autonomous Catalonian Government, is a 15th-century palace open to the public on special days or by arrangement. ✉ *Junction of C. de Ferràn and C. Jaume I.*

➌ Rambla St. Josep. This stretch of the boulevard is one of the most fascinating. The colorful paving stones on the Plaça de la Bouqería were designed by Joan Miró. Glance up at the swirling Moderniste dragon on the **Casa Bruno Quadras** and the Art Nouveau street lamps; then take a look inside the bustling **Boquería market** and the **Antiga Casa Figueras,** a vintage pastry shop on the corner of Petxina, with a splendid mosaic facade. ✉ *Between Plaça de la Boquería and Rambla de les Flors.*

★ ➏ Santa Maria del Mar (St. Mary of the Sea). Simply the best example of Mediterranean Gothic architecture, this church is widely considered Barcelona's loveliest. It was built between 1329 and 1383 in fulfillment of a vow made a century earlier by James I to build a church for the Virgin of the Sailors. The structure's simple beauty is enhanced by a colorful rose window and slender soaring columns. ✉ *Plaça Santa Maria.* ☉ *Weekdays 9–1:30 and 4:30–8.*

Eixample

Above the Plaça de Catalunya you enter modern (post-1860) Barcelona and an elegant area known as the Eixample (literally, "widening"), built in the late 19th century as part of the city's expansion scheme. Much of the building here was done at the height of the Moderniste movement, a Spanish and mainly Catalan version of Art Nouveau, whose leading exponents were the architects Lluís Domènech i Montaner, Josep Puig i Cadafalch, and Antoni Gaudí. The main thoroughfares are the Rambla de Catalunya and the Passeig de Gràcia, both lined with some of the city's most elegant shops and cafés. Moderniste houses are among Barcelona's drawing cards.

★ ⓲ Casa Milà. This Gaudí house is known as **La Pedrera** (stone quarry). Its remarkable curving stone facade, with ornamental balconies, ripples its way around the corner of the block. In the attic of La Pedrera is the superb **Espai Gaudí,** Barcelona's only museum dedicated exclusively to the architect's work. ✉ *Passeig de Gràcia 92,* ☎ *93/484–5995.* ☉ *Daily 10–8; guided visits weekdays 6 PM, weekends 11 AM.*

Casa Montaner i Simó–Fundació Tàpies. This former publishing house exhibits the work of preeminent contemporary Catalan painter Antoni Tàpies, as well as temporary exhibits. On top of the building is a tangle of metal entitled *Núvol i Cadira (Cloud and Chair).* ✉ *Carrer Aragó 255,* ☎ *93/487–0315.* ☉ *Tues.–Sun. 10–8.*

⓱ Mançana de la Discòrdia (Block of Discord). The name is a pun on the Spanish word *manzana,* which means both "block" and "apple." The houses here are quite fantastic: the floral **Casa Lleó Morera** (No. 35) is by Domènech i Montaner, the pseudo-Gothic **Casa Amatller** (No.

41) is by Puig i Cadafalch, and No. 43 is Gaudí's **Casa Batlló.** ⊠ *Passeig de Gràcia, between Consell de Cent and Aragó.*

★ ⑲ **Temple Expiatori de la Sagrada Família** (Expiatory Church of the Holy Family). Barcelona's most eccentric landmark was designed by Gaudí, though only one tower was standing upon his death in 1926. Gaudí's intent was to evangelize with stone, to create an entire history of Christianity on the building's facade. The angular figures on the southwestern Passion Facade by sculptor Joseph Maria Subirach are a stark contrast to Gaudí's Nativity Facade on the opposite lateral facade. With eight towers presently standing, ten more, including the gigantic central tower representing Christ, will complete the project by, according to estimates, the year 2050. Don't miss the museum, with Gaudí's scale models, or the elevator to the top of one of the towers for a magnificent view of the city. Gaudí is buried in the crypt. ⊠ *Plaça de la Sagrada Familia,* ☎ *93/207–3031.* ☉ *Nov.–Mar. and Sept.–Oct., daily 9–6; Apr.–Aug., daily 9–8.*

Montjuïc

The hill of Montjuïc is thought to have been named for the Jewish cemetery once located here. Montjuïc has a fortress, delightful gardens, a model Spanish village, an illuminated fountain, the Mies van der Rohe Pavilion, and a cluster of museums—all of which could keep you busy for several days. The 1992 Olympics were held here.

★ ㉒ **Fundació Miró** (Miró Foundation). A gift from the artist Joan Miró to his native city, this is one of Barcelona's most exciting galleries, with much of its exhibition space devoted to Miró's droll, colorful works. ⊠ *Avda. Miramar 71,* ☎ *93/329–1908.* ☉ *Tues.–Wed. and Fri.–Sat. 10–7, Thurs. 10–9:30, Sun. 10–2:30.*

㉚ **Mies van der Rohe Pavilion.** The reconstructed Mies van der Rohe Pavilion—the German contribution to the 1929 Universal Exhibition, reassembled between 1983 and 1986—is a stunning "less is more" study in interlocking planes of white marble, green onyx, and glass: Barcelona's esthetic antonym for the Moderniste Palau de la Música. ⊠ *Av. Marquès de Comillas s/n,* ☎ *93/423–4016.* ▨ *450 ptas./€2.70.* ☉ *Daily 10–8.*

★ ㉑ **Museu Nacional d'Art de Catalunya** (National Museum of Catalan Art). In the **Palau Nacional** atop a long flight of steps up from the Plaça Espanya, this collection of Romanesque and Gothic art treasures, medieval frescoes, and altarpieces—most from small churches and chapels in the Pyrenees—is simply staggering. The museum's last renovation was directed by architect Gae Aulenti, who also remodeled the Musée d'Orsay, in Paris. ⊠ *Mirador del Palau 6,* ☎ *93/423–7199.* ☉ *Tues.–Wed. and Fri.–Sat. 10–7, Thurs. 10–9, Sun. 10–2:30.*

Elsewhere in Barcelona

Barceloneta. Take a stroll around what was once the fishermen's quarter, built in 1755. There are no-frills fish restaurants on the Passeig Joan de Borbó. Hike out to the end of the *rompeolas* (breakwater), extending 4 km (2½ mi) southeast into the Mediterranean, for a panoramic view of the city and a few breaths of fresh air. The modernized port is home to the Aquarium, one of Europe's best; the Maremagnum shopping center; the IMAX wide-format cinema; the World Trade Center; and numerous bars and restaurants. The 1992 Olympic Village, now a hot tapas and nightlife spot, is up the beach to the north and is easily identifiable by the enormous, gold, Frank Gehry–designed fish sculpture next to the Hotel Arts. ⊠ *East of Estació de França and Ciutadella Park.*

Gràcia. This small, once-independent village within the city is a warren of narrow streets whose names change at every corner. Here you'll find tiny shops that sell everything from old-fashioned tin lanterns to feather dusters. Gaudí's first commission, at Carrer de les Carolines 24–26; Plaça Rius i Taulet, with its clock tower; and the Llibertat and Revolució markets are key sights to seek out. ⊠ *Around C. Gran de Gràcia above Diagonal.*

Monestir de Pedralbes. This is one of Barcelona's best visits, a one-time Clarist convent with a triple-tier cloister and now home of the excellent Thyssen-Bornemisza collection of early paintings. ⊠ *Baixada Monestir 9,* ☎ *93/203–9282.* ☉ *Tues.–Sun. 10–2.*

★ **Parc Güell.** This park in the upper part of town above Gràcia is Gaudí's magical attempt at creating a garden city. ⊠ *C. D'Olot s/n.* ☉ *May–Aug., daily 10–9; Sept.–Apr., daily 10–7.*

Port Vell. The Old Port now includes an extension of the Rambla, the **Rambla de Mar,** which crosses the inner harbor from just below the Columbus Monument. This boardwalk connects the Rambla with the **Moll d'Espanya,** which in turn comprises a shopping mall, restaurants, an aquarium, a cinema, and two yacht clubs. A walk around Port Vell leads past the marina to Passeig Joan de Borbó, both lined with restaurants and their outdoor tables. From here you can go south out to sea along the *rompeolas,* a 3-km (2-mi) excursion, or north (left) down the San Sebastián beach to the Passeig Marítim, which leads to the **Port Olímpic.** Except for the colorful inner streets of Barceloneta, the traditional fishermen's quarter, this new construction is largely devoid of character. Take the Golondrinas boat to the end of the breakwater and walk into Barceloneta for some paella.

Sarrià, originally an outlying village of the Monestir de Pedralbes, retains a distinctive local charm. ⊠ *North of the western end of the Diagonal (best reached by the Sarrià train from Plaça Catalunya to the Reina Elisenda stop).*

BULLFIGHTING

Bullfights are held on Sunday between March and October at the **Monumental** (⊠ Gran Via and Carles I); check the newspaper for details. The **Bullfighting Museum** at the ring is open March–October, daily 10–1 and 5:30–7.

DINING

Spanish restaurants are officially classified from five forks down to one fork, with most places earning two or three forks. In our rating system, prices are for one dinner entrée. Sales tax (IVA) is usually included in the menu price; check the menu for *IVA incluído* or *IVA no incluído.* When it's not included, an additional 7% will be added to your bill. Most restaurants have a prix-fixe menu called a *menú del día*; however, this is often offered only at lunch and at dinner tends to be a reheated version of the same. *Menús* are usually the cheapest way to eat; à la carte dining is more expensive. Service charges are never added to your bill; leave around 10%, less in cheaper (one $) restaurants and bars.

CATEGORY	COST*
$$$$	over 3,000 ptas. (€18.03)
$$$	2,400 ptas.–3,000 ptas. (€14.42–€18.03)
$$	1,500 ptas.–2,400 ptas. (€7.51–€14.42)
$	under 1,500 ptas. (€7.51)

*per person for a main course at dinner

$$$$ ✕ **Botafumeiro.** Barcelona's most exciting seafood restaurant, this
★   Galician spot never fails. Open continuously from 1 PM to 1 AM, Bota-
       fumeiro is always filled with ecstatic people in mid-feeding frenzy. The
       main attraction is the *mariscos Botafumeiro,* a succession of myriad
       plates of shellfish. Costs can mount quickly. Try the half-rations at the
       bar, such as *pulpo a feira* (squid on potato) or *jamón bellota de Gui-
       juelo* (acorn-fed ham from a town near Salamanca). ⊠ *Gran de Grà-
       cia 81,* ☎ *93/218–4230. AE, DC, MC, V. Closed Aug. 5–25.*

$$$–$$$$ ✕ **Jean Luc Figueras.** Every restaurant that Jean Luc Figueras has
       touched has shot straight to the top. This one, installed in an elegant
       Gràcia town house that was once couturier Cristóbal Balenciaga's stu-
       dio, may be the best of all. For an extra $20 or so, the taster's menu
       is the best choice. ⊠ *C. Santa Teresa 10,* ☎ *93/415–2877. Reserva-
       tions essential. AE, DC, MC, V. Closed Sun. No lunch Sat.*

$$$–$$$$ ✕ **El Tragaluz.** This is an excellent choice if you've been prowling the
       Eixample. The roof opens up to the stars in summer, and everything
       from chairs to utensils has been cleverly invented by some playful de-
       signer. There's even good food—modern and light, but hearty. ⊠ *Pas-
       satge de la Concepció 5,* ☎ *93/487–0196. AE, DC, MC, V. Closed Jan.
       5. No lunch Mon.*

$$$–$$$$ ✕ **Tram-Tram.** With chef Isidro Soler at the helm in the kitchen and
★   Reyes Lizán as hostess and pastry chef, Tram-Tram is one of Barcelona's
       culinary highlights. The excursion northwest to the villagelike suburb
       of Sarrià is a delight. Order the taster's menu and let Isidro take care
       of you—you won't regret it. ⊠ *Major de Sarrià 121,* ☎ *93/204–8518.
       AE, MC, V. Closed Sun. and Dec. 24–Jan. 6.*

$$$ ✕ **Can Gaig.** This traditional Barcelona restaurant is well known to
       Catalonian gastronomes. The market-fresh ingredients combine seafood
       with upland products in innovative ways. Try the roast partridge with
       bacon from free-range Iberian pork. ⊠ *Passeig Maragall 402,* ☎ *93/
       429–1017. AE, DC, MC, V. Closed Mon. and Aug. No dinner holi-
       days.*

$$$ ✕ **Can Majó.** On the beach in Barceloneta, Can Majó is one of the pre-
★   mier seafood restaurants in town. The house specialties are *caldera de
       bogavante* (a cross between lobster bouillabaisse and paella) and *suquet*
       (fish stewed in its own juices), but whatever you choose will be excel-
       lent. In summer, the terrace overlooking the Mediterranean is the clos-
       est you can now come to the Barceloneta *chiringuitos* (shanty restaurants)
       that used to line the beach here. ⊠ *Almirall Aixada 23,* ☎ *93/221–5455.
       AE, DC, MC, V. Closed Sun. night–Mon. except holidays.*

$$$ ✕ **Casa Calvet.** This Art Nouveau space in Antoni Gaudí's 1898–
       1900 Casa Calvet is Barcelona's only opportunity to break bread in
       one of the great modernist's creations. The dining room is a graceful
       and spectacular design display, and the cuisine is light and Mediter-
       ranean with more contemporary than traditional fare. ⊠ *Casp 48,* ☎
       93/412–4012. AE, DC, MC, V. Closed Sun. and Aug. 15–31.

$$–$$$ ✕ **El Racó de Can Freixa.** This is one of Barcelona's hottest restaurants,
       with young chef Ramón Freixa taking the work of his father, José María,
       in new directions. The cuisine is innovative and yet traditionally Cata-
       lan; try one of the game specialties in season. One specialty is *peus
       de porc en escabetx de guatlle,* pig's feet with quail in a garlic-and-
       parsley gratin. ⊠ *Sant Elíes 22,* ☎ *93/209–7559. Reservations essen-
       tial. AE, DC, MC, V.*

$$–$$$ ✕ **Los Caracoles.** Just below the Plaça Reial is Barcelona's best-known
       tourist haunt, crawling with Americans having a terrific time. Its walls
       are hung thick with photos of bullfighters and visiting celebrities; its
       specialties are mussels, paella, and of course, *caracoles* (snails). ⊠ *Es-
       cudellers 14,* ☎ *93/309–3185. AE, DC, MC, V.*

$–$$ ✕ **Agut.** Simple, hearty Catalan fare awaits you in this unpretentious restaurant in the lower reaches of the Gothic Quarter. Founded in 1924, Agut has kept its popularity. There's plenty of wine to go with the traditional home cooking, along with a family warmth that always makes the place exciting. ⊠ *Gignàs 16,* ☎ *93/315–1709. AE, MC, V. Closed Mon. and July. No dinner Sun.*

$–$$ ✕ **El Convent.** This small, friendly restaurant hidden behind the Bo-
★ quería market is a real find, known better to locals than to visitors. Its traditional Catalan home cooking, huge desserts, and swift, person-able service all make it a good value. ⊠ *Jerusalem 12,* ☎ *93/301–6208. Reservations not accepted. AE, DC, MC, V. Closed Sun.*

LODGING

Hotels around Las Ramblas and in the Gothic Quarter have generous helpings of Old World charm but are weaker on creature comforts; those in the Eixample are mostly 1950s or '60s buildings, often more recently renovated; and the newest hotels are out along the Diagonal or beyond, with the exception of the Hotel Arts, in the Olympic Port. The Airport and Sants Station have hotel-reservation desks.

CATEGORY	COST*
$$$$	over 28,000 ptas. (€168.28)
$$$	18,000 ptas.–28,000 ptas. (€108.18–€168.28)
$$	11,000 ptas.–18,000 ptas. (€66.11–€108.18)
$	under 11,000 ptas. (€66.11)

Prices are for two people in a double room, not including breakfast.

$$$$ 🏨 **Colón.** This cozy, older hotel has a unique charm and intimacy rem-
★ iniscent of an English country hotel. Rooms are comfortable and taste-ful. The location, right in the heart of the Gothic Quarter, is ideal, and front rooms overlook the cathedral and square. ⊠ *Avda. Catedral 7, 08002,* ☎ *93/301–1404,* FAX *93/317–2915,* WEB *www.hotelcolon.es. 147 rooms. Restaurant. AE, DC, MC, V.*

$$$$ 🏨 **Condes de Barcelona.** The Condes is one of Barcelona's most pop-
★ ular hotels, so rooms must be booked well in advance. The decor is stun-ning, with marble floors and columns, an impressive staircase, and an outstanding bar area. Guest rooms are on the small side. ⊠ *Passeig de Gràcia 75, 08008,* ☎ *93/488–1152,* FAX *93/488–0614,* WEB *www. condesdebarcelona.com. 183 rooms. Restaurant. AE, DC, MC, V.*

$$$$ 🏨 **Hotel Arts.** This luxurious skyscraper, a Ritz-Carlton property, over-looks Barcelona from the Olympic Port, providing unique views of the Mediterranean, the city, and the mountains beyond. A short taxi ride from the city center, it's virtually a world of its own. Rooms are ul-tramodern, with pale wood, CD players, and Frette linens. Three restaurants serve Mediterranean cuisine, Californian cooking, and tapas, such as *gambas al ajillo* (baby shrimp fried in garlic). Barcelona's casino is now directly under the hotel. ⊠ *C. de la Marina 19–21, 08005,* ☎ *93/221–1000,* FAX *93/221–1070,* WEB *www.harts.es. 399 rooms, 56 suites. 3 restaurants, pool. AE, DC, MC, V.*

$$$$ 🏨 **Hotel Claris.** Widely considered Barcelona's best hotel, the Claris is
★ a fascinating mélange of design and tradition; the rooms come in 60 different layouts. Wood and marble furnishings and decorative details are everywhere, and you can dip into a Japanese water garden, a first-rate restaurant, and a rooftop pool—all near the center of Barcelona. ⊠ *Carrer Pau Claris 150, 08009,* ☎ *93/487–6262,* FAX *93/215–7970,* WEB *www.derbyhotels.es. 106 rooms, 18 suites. 2 restaurants, pool. AE, DC, MC, V.*

$$$$ 🏨 **Majestic.** Right in the thick of the Eixample shopping district, sur-rounded by high-style boutiques and within sight of two Gaudí creations, the Majestic is a good choice. The rooms are lovely, painted in soothing pastels and decorated very tastefully. ⊠ *Passeig de Gráia 70, 08008,* ☎ *93/488–1717,* 𝖥𝖠𝖷 *93/488–1880,* 𝖶𝖤𝖡 *www.hotelmajestic.es. 335 rooms. Restaurant, pool. AE, DC, MC, V.*

$$$$ 🏨 **Princesa Sofía.** The most convenient hotel to the airport, the Sofía is removed from the hue and cry of downtown. For business and convenience, it's one of the city's best options. ⊠ *Plaça Pius XII 4, 08028,* ☎ *93/330–7111,* 𝖥𝖠𝖷 *93/411–2106,* 𝖶𝖤𝖡 *www.interconti.com/spain/barcelona/ hotel_barpri.html. 505 rooms. 3 restaurants, 2 pools. AE, DC, MC, V.*

$$$$ 🏨 **Rey Juan Carlos I–Conrad International.** Towering over the western
★   end of Avinguda Diagonal, this skyscraper is as much a commercial complex as a luxury hotel: art, jewelry, furs, caviar, flowers, fashions, and even limousines are for sale or hire on site. The garden has a swan-dappled pond and an Olympic-size pool; Barcelona's finest in-town country club, El Polo, spreads luxuriantly out beyond. There are two restaurants: Chez Vous, with French cuisine, and Café Polo, with a sumptuous buffet and an American bar. ⊠ *Avda. Diagonal 661671, 08028,* ☎ *93/364–4040,* 𝖥𝖠𝖷 *93/448–0607,* 𝖶𝖤𝖡 *www.hrjuancarlos.com. 375 rooms, 40 suites. 2 restaurants, pool. AE, DC, MC, V.*

$$$$ 🏨 **Ritz.** This classic hotel has maintained or even heightened its splen-
★   dor over the past few years. The entrance lobby is awe inspiring; the rooms spacious and furnished with Regency furniture; and the service excellent. ⊠ *Gran Vía 668, 08010,* ☎ *93/318–5200,* 𝖥𝖠𝖷 *93/318–0148,* 𝖶𝖤𝖡 *www.ritzbcn.com. 158 rooms. Restaurant. AE, DC, MC, V.*

$$–$$$ 🏨 **Gran Vía.** Architectural features are the charm of this 19th-century mansion. The original chapel has been preserved, and you can have breakfast in a hall of mirrors, climb a Moderniste staircase, and make calls from elaborate Belle Epoque phone booths. ⊠ *Gran Vía 642, 08007,* ☎ *93/318–1900,* 𝖥𝖠𝖷 *93/318–9997. 53 rooms. AE, DC, MC, V.*

$$–$$$ 🏨 **San Agustín.** Just off Las Ramblas in the leafy square of the same name,
★   this inn has long been a favorite for musicians performing at the nearby Liceu opera house. Rooms are modest in size but charmingly decorated. The staff is helpful and polite. ⊠ *Plaça de Sant Agustí 3, 08001,* ☎ *93/ 318–1708,* 𝖥𝖠𝖷 *93/317–2928. 77 rooms. AE, DC, MC, V.*

$–$$ 🏨 **Continental.** Something of a legend among cost-conscious travelers, this comfortable hostel with canopied balconies stands at the top of Las Ramblas, just below Plaça Catalunya. The rooms are homey and comfortable, the staff is friendly, and the location is ideal. Buffet breakfasts are a plus. ⊠ *Rambla 138, 08002,* ☎ *93/301–2508,* 𝖥𝖠𝖷 *93/302– 7360. 35 rooms. AE, DC, MC, V.*

$–$$ 🏨 **Jardí.** The rooms at this budget hotel are small but have new bathrooms, powerful showers, and, in most cases, views over the charming, traffic-free Plaça del Pi and Plaça Sant Josep Oriol. Noise can be a problem in summer. The quietest rooms are the highest. ⊠ *Plaça Sant Josep Oriol 1, 08002,* ☎ *93/301–5900,* 𝖥𝖠𝖷 *93/318–3664. 40 rooms. AE, DC, MC, V.*

NIGHTLIFE AND THE ARTS

The Arts

To find out what's on, look in the daily papers or the weekly *Guía del Ocio. Actes a la Ciutat* is a weekly list of cultural events published by City Hall and available from its information office on Plaça Sant Jaume, or at the Palau de la Virreina. *El País* lists all events of interest on its *agenda* page.

Concerts

The **Auditori de Barcelona** (✉ Carrer Lepant 150, near Plaça de les Glòries) has a full program of classical music, with occasional jazz and pop thrown in. The **Liceu** (✉ Box office: Rambla de Capuchinos 63, ☎ 93/317–4142), Barcelona's opera house, is alive and thriving. The Art Nouveau **Palau de la Música,** whose ticket office is open weekdays 11–1 and 5–8 and Saturday 5–8, is not to be missed. Sunday-morning concerts (11 AM) are a local tradition. Musical events are also occasionally held in some of Barcelona's finest examples of early architecture, such as the medieval shipyards, **Drassanes,** the church of **Santa Maria del Mar,** or the **Monestir de Pedralbes.**

Dance

El Mercat de les Flors (✉ Lleida 59, ☎ 93/426–1875), not far from Plaça d'Espanya, always has a rich program of modern dance and theater. **L'Espai de Dansa i Mùsica de la Generalitat de Catalunya** (✉ Travessera de Gràcia 63, ☎ 93/414–3133), usually listed simply as "L'Espai" (The Space), is Barcelona's prime venue for ballet and contemporary dance. **Teatre Tivoli** (✉ Casp 8, ☎ 93/412–2063), just above Plaça de Catalunya, hosts major ballet and flamenco troupes.

Film

Many if not most Barcelona theaters show foreign movies in their original languages—indicated by "VO" (*versión original*). **Casablanca** (✉ Passeig de Gràcia 115), just above Passeig de Gràcia, is a favorite for foreign movies. The Olympic Port's 15-screen **Icaria Yelmo** (✉ Salvador Espriu 61, ☎ 93/221–7585), shows everything in VO **Renoir Les Corts** (✉ Eugeni d'Ors 12), near the Corte Inglés Diagonal, has four VO theaters. The Gràcia neighborhood's **Verdi** (✉ Verdi 32, Gràcia, ☎ 93/237–0516) is a standard VO cinema favorite.

Theater

Most plays are in Catalan, but top Spanish productions also open in Barcelona. **El Mercat de les Flors** holds theater and dance performances. The **Teatre Lliure** (✉ Montseny 47, Gràcia, ☎ 93/218–9251) has top theater, dance, and musical events. The **Teatre Nacional de Catalunya** (✉ Plaça de les Arts 1, ☎ 93/900–121133) covers everything from Shakespeare to ballet to avant-garde theater. **Teatre Poliorama** (✉ Rambla Estudios 115, ☎ 93/317–7599), on the upper Rambla, holds excellent theater performances. **Teatre Romea** (✉ Hospital 51, ☎ 93/317–7189) is a traditional haven for dramatic events. **Teatre Tivoli** (✉ Casp 10, ☎ 93/412–2063) stages flamenco, ballet, and plays.

Nightlife

Bars

Champagne Bars. *Xampanyerías,* serving sparkling Catalan *cava,* are a Barcelona specialty. **El Xampanyet** (✉ Montcada 22, ☎ 93/319–7003), near the Picasso Museum, serves cava, cider, and tapas in a lively setting. **La Cava del Palau** (✉ Verdaguer i Callis 10, ☎ 93/310–0938), near the Palau de la Música, has a wide selection of cavas, wines, and cocktails.

Cocktail Bars. The **Passeig del Born,** near the Picasso Museum, is lined with bars. **Dry Martini** (✉ Aribau 162, ☎ 93/217–5072) has more than 80 different gins. **El Copetín** (✉ Passeig del Born 19, ☎ 93/317–7585) has exciting decor and good cocktails. **Miramelindo** (✉ Passeig del Born 15, ☎ 93/319–5376) offers a large selection and often live jazz. **El Paraigua** (✉ Plaça Sant Miquel, behind City Hall, ☎ 93/217–3028) serves cocktails in a stylish setting with classical music.

Tapas Bars. Cal Pep (✉ 8 Plaça de les Olles, ☎ 93/319–6183), near Santa Maria del Mar, is a popular spot, with the best and freshest selection of tapas. **Carrer de la Mercé** is lined with tapas bars, across from the Moll de la Fusta, from Correos (the post office) down to the Iglesia de la Mercé. **Casa Tejada** (⊠ Tenor Viñas, near Plaça Francesc Macià, ☎ 93/200–7341) has some of the finest *cazuelitas* (small hot hors d'oeuvres) in town. **Sagardi** (⊠ Argenteria 62, ☎ 93/319–9993), near Santa Maria del Mar, is one of many, uniformly good, Basque taverns. **El Irati** (⊠ Cardenal Casañas 17, ☎ 93/302–3084), just off Plaça del Pi, is a good, if usually overcrowded, Basque bar. **La Tramoia,** at Rambla de Catalunya and Gran Vía (☎ 93/412–3634), is your best bet on the east side of Passeig de Gràcia, as it is the happy exception to the rest, which generally microwave pre-prepared food. **Ciudad Condal,** across the intersection from La Tramoia (⊠ Rambla de Catalunya 24, ☎ 93/412–9414), has a wide variety of appetizing morsels.

Cabaret

Barcelona City Hall (⊠ Rambla de Catalunya 2–4, access through New Canadian Store, ☎ 93/317–2177) presents sophisticated cabaret in a beautiful music hall.

Cafés

The **Café de l'Opera** (⊠ Rambla 74, ☎ 93/317–7585), across from the Liceu opera house, is a perennial hangout, open daily until 2 AM. **Café Zurich** (⊠ Plaça de Catalunya 1, ☎ 93/302–4140), at the head of Las Ramblas, is Barcelona's number one rendezvous spot. **Carrer Petritxol** (from Portaferrissa to Plaça del Pi) is famous for its *chocolaterías* (serving hot chocolate, tea, coffee, and pastries) and tearooms. Picasso hung out at **Els Quatre Gats** (⊠ Montsió 3, ☎ 93/302–4140), which is a great place to people watch.

Discos and Nightclubs

Costa Breve (⊠ Aribau 230, ☎ 93/414–2778) welcomes all ages, even those over 35. At **Luz de Gas** (⊠ Muntaner 246, ☎ 93/209–7711), live guitar and soul shows are followed by dance music and wild abandon. **Oliver y Hardy** (⊠ Diagonal 593, next to Barcelona Hilton, ☎ 93/419–3181) is popular with over-35s. **Otto Zutz** (⊠ Lincoln 15, below Via Augusta, ☎ 93/238–0722) is a top spot. **Sala Razzmatazze** (⊠ Almogavers 122, ☎ 93/320–8200) offers Friday and Saturday disco madness 'til dawn. Weeknight concerts feature international stars such as Ani diFranco and Enya. **Up and Down** (⊠ Numancia 179, ☎ 93/280–2922), pronounced "pendow," is a lively classic for elegant carousers.

Salsa

Antilla Barcelona (⊠ Aragó, ☎ 93/451–4564) is Cuba-in-Barcelona, with live music, salsa classes and full Caribbean flavor. **Agua de Luna** (⊠ Viladomat 211, ☎ 93/410–0440) is a hot Latin American dance spot.

Flamenco

El Patio Andaluz (⊠ Aribau 242, ☎ 93/209–3378) is a solid option but rather expensive. **Los Tarantos** (⊠ Plaça Reial 17, ☎ 93/318–3067) is the most happening flamenco spot. **El Tablao del Carmen** (⊠ Arcs 9, Poble Espanyol, ☎ 93/325–6895) hosts touring troupes up on Montjüic.

Jazz Clubs

La Cova del Drac (⊠ Vallmajor 33, ☎ 93/200–7032) is Barcelona's most traditional jazz venue. The Gothic Quarter's **Harlem Jazz Club** (⊠ Comtessa Sobradiel 8, ☎ 93/310–0755) is small but sizzling. **Jamboree** (⊠ Plaça Reial 17, ☎ 93/301–7564), downstairs from Los Tarantos, has regular jazz performances featuring top musicians from New York and all over the world.

SHOPPING

Elegant shopping districts are the Passeig de Gràcia, Rambla de Catalunya, and the Diagonal. For more affordable, old-fashioned, and typically Spanish-style shops, explore the area between the Rambla and Via Laietana, especially around Carrer de Ferràn. The area around Plaça del Pi from Boquería to Portaferrisa and Canuda is well stocked with youthful fashion stores and imaginative gift shops.

Barcelona has more shopping plazas every year. **El Triangle** mall in Plaça de Catalunya includes FNAC, Habitat, and the Sephora perfume emporium. **Les Glories** (⊠ Avda. Diagonal 208, Plaça de les Glories, ☎ 93/486–0639) is near the *encants*, Barcelona's flea market. **L'Illa** (⊠ Diagonal 545, between Numancia and Entenza, ☎ 93/444–0000) has everything from FNAC to Decathlon to Marks & Spencer. **Maremagnum** (⊠ Moll d'Espanya s/n, Port Vell, ☎ 93/225–8100) is well stocked with shops. **Carrer Tuset,** north of Diagonal between Aribau and Balmes, has many small boutiques.

Antiques

Carrer de la Palla and Banys Nous, in the Gothic Quarter, are lined with antiques shops. An **antiques market** is held every Thursday in front of the cathedral. The **Centre d'Antiquaris** (⊠ Passeig de Gràcia 57, ☎ 93/215–4499) has some 75 antiques stores. **Gothsland** (⊠ Consell de Cent 331, ☎ 93/488–1922) specializes in Moderniste designs.

Boutiques

Fashionable boutiques line Passeig de Gràcia and Rambla de Catalunya. Others are on Gran Via between Balmes and Pau Claris, and on the Diagonal between Ganduxer and Passeig de Gràcia. **Adolfo Domínguez** (⊠ Passeig de Gràcia 89, Valencia 245, ☎ 93/487–3687) is one of Spain's most popular clothing designers. **Joaquín Berao** (⊠ Rosselló 277, ☎ 93/218–6187) is a top jewelry designer. **La Manual Alpargartera** (⊠ Avinyó 7), just off Carrer Ferran, is a lovely shop specializing in handmade rope-soled sandals and espadrilles.

Loewe (⊠ Passeig de Gràcia 35, Diagonal 570, ☎ 93/216–0400) is Spain's top leather store. Lovers of fine stationery will linger in the Gothic Quarter's **Papirum** (⊠ Baixada de la Llibreria 2), a tiny, medieval-toned shop with exquisite hand-printed papers, marbleized blank books, and writing implements. **Zapata** (⊠ Buenos Aires 64, at Diagonal, ☎ 93/430–4785) is a major jewelry dealer.

Department Stores

With four locations in Barcelona alone, **El Corte Inglés** (⊠ Plaça de Catalunya 14, ☎ 93/302–1212; ⊠ Porta de l'Angel 19–21, ☎ 93/306–3800; ⊠ Avda. Francesc Macià 58, ☎ 93/419–2020; ⊠ Diagonal 617, near María Cristina metro stop, ☎ 93/419–2828) is Spain's great consumer emporium. Both Plaça de Catalunya's Mançana de Oro (a.k.a. El Triangle) and L'Illa include Marks & Spencer and FNAC stores.

Food and Flea Markets

The **Boquería Market** (⊠ Las Ramblas between Carme and Hospital) is an exuberant cornucopia, a colorful display of both food and humanity; it's open every day except Sunday. **Els Encants** (⊠ end of Dos de Maig, on the Plaça Glòries Catalanes), Barcelona's wild-and-woolly flea market, is held every Monday, Wednesday, Friday, and Saturday, 8–7. **Sant Antoni Market** (⊠ end of Ronda Sant Antoni) is an old-fashioned food and clothes market, best on Sunday when there's a **secondhand-book market** with old postcards, press cuttings, lithographs, and prints. There's a **stamp and coin market** (⊠ Plaça Reial) on Sunday morning. An **artists' market** (⊠ Placeta del Pi, off Las Ramblas and Boquería) sets up on Saturday morning.

Gift Ideas

No special handicrafts are associated with Barcelona, but you'll have no trouble finding typical Spanish goods anywhere in town. **Xavier Roca i Coll** (⊠ Sant Pere mes Baix 24, off Via Laietana, ☎ 93/215–1052) specializes in silver models of Barcelona's buildings.

If your friends back home like fashion and jewelry, you're in the right city—Barcelona makes all the headlines on Spain's booming fashion front. Barcelona and Catalonia passed along a playful sense of design even before Antoni Gaudí began creating shock waves more than a century ago. A number of stores and boutiques specialize in design items (jewelry, furnishings, knickknacks). **Bd** (Barcelona Design; ⊠ Mallorca 291293, ☎ 93/458–6909) offers reproduction furniture from many designers. **Dos i Una** (⊠ Rosselló 275, ☎ 93/217–7032) is a good source for clever gifts. **Vinçon** (⊠ Passeig de Gràcia 96, ☎ 93/215–6050) has a huge selection of stylish housewares.

BARCELONA A TO Z

To research prices, get advice from other travelers, and book travel arrangements, visit www.fodors.com.

AIRPORTS AND TRANSFERS

All international and domestic flights arrive at El Prat de Llobregat airport, 14 km (8½ mi) south of Barcelona just off the main highway to Castelldefels and Sitges. For information on arrival and departure times, call the airport or Info-Iberia.

➤ AIRPORT INFORMATION: **El Prat de Llobregat** (☎ 93/478–5000 or 93/478–5032). **Info-Iberia** (☎ 93/412–5667).

TRANSFERS

The airport-to-city train leaves every 30 minutes between 6:30 AM and 11 PM, costs about 400 ptas./€2.40, and reaches the Barcelona Central (Sants) Station in 15 minutes and Plaça de Catalunya, in the heart of the old city (at the head of Las Ramblas), in 20–25 minutes. From there a short taxi ride of 450 ptas./€2.70–550 ptas./€3.31 will take you to most of central Barcelona's hotels. The Aerobus service connects the airport with Plaça de Catalunya every 15 minutes between 6:25 AM and 11 PM; the fare of 475 ptas./€2.85 can be paid with all international credit cards. RENFE also provides a bus service to the Central Station during the night hours. A taxi from the airport to your hotel, including airport and luggage surcharges, will cost about 3,000 ptas./€18.03.

BOAT AND FERRY TRAVEL

Golondrinas (harbor boats) make short trips from the Portal de la Pau, near the Columbus Monument. The fare is 750 ptas./€4.51 for a 30-minute trip. Departures are Holy Week–September, daily 11–7; October–Holy Week, weekends and holidays only 11–5. It's closed December 16–January 2. A one-way ticket lets you off at the end of the breakwater for a 4-km (2½-mi) stroll, surrounded by the Mediterranean, back into Barceloneta.

➤ BOAT AND FERRY INFORMATION: **Golondrinas** (☎ 93/442–3106).

BUS TRAVEL TO AND FROM BARCELONA

Barcelona has no central bus station, but most buses operate either from the old Estació Vilanova, generally known as Estació del Norte. The Estació Autobuses de Sants also dispatches long distance buses. Julià runs buses to Zaragoza and Montserrat. Alsina Graëlls runs to Lérída and Andorra.

➤ Bus Information: **Alsina Graëlls** (⊠ Ronda Universitat 4, ☎ 93/265–6866). **Estació Autobuses de Sants** (⊠ C. Viriato, next to Sants Central train terminal, ☎ 93/490–0202). **Estació del Norte** (⊠ end of Avda. Vilanova, ☎ 93/893–5312). **Julià** (⊠ Ronda Universitat 5, ☎ 93/317–6454).

BUS TRAVEL WITHIN BARCELONA

City buses run from about 5:30 or 6 AM to 10:30 PM, though some stop earlier. There are also night buses to certain destinations. The flat fare is 155 ptas./€0.93. Route plans are displayed at bus stops. You can purchase a tarjeta multiviatge, good for 10 rides, at the transport kiosk on Plaça de Catalunya (895 ptas./€5.38).

CONSULATES

➤ Australia: (⊠ Gran Vía Carles III 98, ☎ 93/330–9496).
➤ Canada: (⊠ Elisenda de Pinos, ☎ 93/204–2700).
➤ New Zealand: (⊠ Travessera de Gràcia 64, ☎ 93/209–0399).
➤ United Kingdom: (⊠ Diagonal 477, ☎ 93/419–9044).
➤ United States: (⊠ Passeig Reina Elisenda 23, ☎ 93/280–2227).

EMERGENCIES

The general emergency number in all EU nations (akin to 911 in the United States) is 112.

➤ Doctors and Dentists: **Medical emergencies** (☎ 061).
➤ Emergency Services: **Police** (☎ 091 National Police; 092 Municipal Police). **Tourist Attention** (⊠ La Rambla 43, ☎ 93/317–7016 24-hr assistance for crime victims).
➤ 24-hour Pharmacies: **Pharmacies** (☎ 010).

ENGLISH-LANGUAGE MEDIA

BOOKS

BCN Books is one of Barcelona's top spots for books in English. Come In is another good option for English books. El Corte Inglés sells English guidebooks and novels, but the selection is limited. For variety, try English Bookshop. The bookstore at the Palau de la Virreina has good books on art, design, and Barcelona.

➤ Bookstores: **BCN Books** (⊠ Aragó 277, ☎ 93/487–3123). **Come In** (⊠ Provença 203, ☎ 93/253–1204). **English Bookshop** (⊠ Entençan 63, ☎ 93/425–4466).

SUBWAY TRAVEL

The metro is the fastest and easiest way to get around. You can pay a flat fare of 170 ptas./€1.02 or buy a *tarjeta multiviatge*, good for 10 rides (890 ptas./€5.35). Maps of the system are available at main metro stations and branches of the Caixa savings bank.

TAXIS

Taxis are black and yellow. When available for hire, they show a LIBRE sign in the daytime and a green light at night. The meter starts at 410 ptas./€2.64 (which lasts for six minutes), and there are supplements for luggage, night travel, Sundays and holidays, rides from a station or to the airport. There are cab stands all over town, and you can also hail cabs on the street. To call a cab, try one of the numbers listed below, 24 hours a day.

➤ Taxi Companies: **24-hr Service** (☎ 93/387–1000, 93/490–2222, or 93/357–7755).

TOURS

BUS TOURS

City sightseeing tours are run by Julià Tours. Pullmantur also has city sightseeing. Tours leave from the terminals listed below, though you may be able to arrange a pickup at your hotel. Both agencies offer the same tours at the same prices. A morning sightseeing tour visits the Gothic Quarter and Montjuïc; an afternoon tour concentrates on Gaudí and the Picasso Museum. You can visit Barcelona's Olympic sites from May through October.

➤ Fees and Schedules: **Julià Tours** (✉ Ronda Universitat 5, ☎ 93/317–6454). **Pullmantur** (✉ Gran Viá de les Corts Catalanes 635, ☎ 93/318–5195).

SINGLE-DAY TOURS

Trips out of town are run by Julià Tours and Pullmantur. The principal attractions are a half-day tour to Montserrat to visit the monastery and shrine of the famous Black Virgin; a full-day trip to the Costa Brava resorts, including a boat cruise to the Medes Isles; and, from June through September, a full-day trip to Andorra for tax-free shopping. If you are not an EU citizen, bring your passport with you.

WALKING TOURS

La Ruta del Modernisme (the Modernism Route), created by Barcelona's *ajuntament* (city hall), connects nine key Art Nouveau sites: Palau Güell, the Palau de la Música, the Fundació Tàpies, Casa Milà (La Pedrera), the Museu Gaudí (in the Parc Güell), the Museu d'Art Modern (in Ciutadella), Gaudí's Sagrada Família church, the Museu de la Música, and the Museo de Zoologia (in Doménech i Muntaner's Castell dels Tres Dragins en la Ciutadella). Guided tours, some in English, are included at Palau Güell and the Palau de la Música. At Casa Milà there is one guided tour daily (6 PM weekdays, 11 AM weekends). At the Sagrada Família the guided tour costs extra. Buy your tickets at Casa Amatller, open Monday through Saturday 10–7, Sunday 10–2. The price, 700 ptas./€4.21, gets you 50% discounts at all nine locations.

The bookstore in the Palau de la Virreina rents cassettes whose walking tours follow footprints painted on sidewalks—different colors for different tours—through Barcelona's most interesting areas. The do-it-yourself method is to pick up the guides produced by the tourist office, *Discovering Romanesque Art* and *Discovering Modernist Art,* which have art itineraries for all of Catalonia. El Consorci Turisme de Barcelona (Barcelona Tourism Cortium) leads walking tours of the Gothic Quarter in English at 10 AM on Saturday. The tour costs 1,000 ptas./€6.01 and includes a visit to the Town Hall.

➤ Fees and Schedules: **Casa Amatller** (✉ Passeig de Gràcia 41, ☎ 93/488–0139). **El Consorci Turisme de Barcelona** (✉ Plaça de Catalunya 17, lower level, ☎ 906/301282). **Palau de la Virreina** (✉ La Rambla 99).

TRAIN TRAVEL

The Sants Central Station at Plaça Països Catalans is Barcelona's main train station, serving international and national destinations as well as suburban areas. The old and elegant Estació de França (Avda. Marquès de l'Argentera) now serves as the main terminal for certain trains to France and some express trains to points in Spain. Inquire at the tourist office to get current travel information and to find out which station you need. Many trains also stop at the Passeig de Gràcia underground station (at C. Aragó); this station is closer to the Plaça de Catalunya and Rambla area than Sants. Tickets and information are

available here, but luggage carts are not. You can also get information on fares and schedules from RENFE with their 24-hour hot line.
➤ TRAIN INFORMATION: **RENFE** (☎ 93/490–0202).

TRAMS AND CABLE CARS
The Montjuïc Funicular is a cog railroad that runs from the junction of Avenida Parallel and Nou de la Rambla to the Miramar Amusement Park on Montjuïc; it's open 10:45 AM–8 PM, except in summer (late June to mid-September), when it runs 11 AM–10 PM. A *teleferico* (cable car) runs from the amusement park up to Montjuïc Castle October–June 21, weekends 11–2:45 and 4–7:30; June 22–September, daily 11:30–9.

The Transbordador Aeri Harbor Cable Car runs from Miramar on Montjuïc to the Torre de Jaume I across the harbor on Barcelona *moll* (quay), and on to the Torre de Sant Sebastià at the end of Passeig Joan de Borbó in Barceloneta. You can board at either stage. Hours are: Oct.–June, weekdays from noon–5:45 and weekends from noon–6:15; and July–Sept., daily from 11–9. A round-trip ticket costs 1,200 ptas./€7.21.

To reach Tibidabo summit, take either Bus 58 or the Ferrocarrils de la Generalitat train from Plaça de Catalunya to Avenida Tibidabo, then the *tramvía blau* (blue tram) to Peu del Funicular, and the *Tibidabo Funicular* from there to the Tibidabo Fairground. The funicular runs every half hour from 7:15 AM to 9:45 PM.
➤ CONTACTS: **El Consorci Turisme de Barcelona** (✉ Plaça de Catalunya 17, lower level, ☎ 906/301282).

TRANSPORTATION AROUND BARCELONA
Modern Barcelona, the Eixample—above the Plaça de Catalunya—is built on a grid system; the Gothic Quarter, from the Plaça de Catalunya to the port, is a warren of narrow streets. Almost all sightseeing can be done on foot, but you may need to use taxis, the metro, or buses to link certain areas, depending on how much time you have. From mid-May to mid-October look for Bus Turistic 100 for low-cost transport between the sights.

El Consorci Turisme de Barcelona (Barcelona Tourism Consortium) sells the very worthwhile Barcelona Card, which costs 2,500 ptas./€15.03 for 24 hours, 3,000 ptas./€18.03 for 48 hours, or 3,500 ptas./€21.04 for 72 hours. Travelers get unlimited travel on all public transport as well as discounts at 27 museums, 10 restaurants, 14 leisure spots, 20 stores, and various other services including walking tours, the airport shuttle, the bus to Tibidabo, and the Tombbus between Barcelona's key shopping areas.

TRAVEL AGENCIES
➤ LOCAL AGENTS: **American Express** (✉ Roselló 257, corner of Passeig de Gràcia, ☎ 93/217–0070). **Bestours** (✉ Diputación 241, ☎ 93/487–8580). **Viajes Iberia** (✉ Rambla 130, ☎ 93/317–9320). **Wagons-Lits Cook** (✉ Passeig de Gràcia 8, ☎ 93/317–5500).

VISITOR INFORMATION
El Prat Airport and Centre d'Informació Turística have general information on Catalonia and Spain. The other offices listed below focus mostly on Barcelona. You can also get general information on the city by dialing 010.
➤ TOURIST INFORMATION: **Ajuntament** (✉ Plaça Sant Jaume, ☎ 93/402–7000 Ext. 433). **Centre d'Informació Turistic de Barcelona** (✉ Plaça de Catalunya 17, lower level, ☎ 906/301282, FAX 93/304–3155). **Centre d'Informació Turística** (✉ Palau Robert, Passeig de Gràcia 107, at Diagonal, ☎ 93/238–4000). **El Prat Airport** (☎ 93/478–4704). **França metro station** (☎ 93/319–5758). **Palau de Congressos** (during special events and conferences; ✉ Avda. María Cristina, ☎ 93/423–3101

Ext. 8356). **Palau de la Virreina** (⌧ Rambla de les Flors 99, ☎ 93/
301–7775). **Sants metro station** (☎ 93/491–4431).

Spain Basics

BUSINESS HOURS

Banks are open Monday–Saturday 8:30 or 9 to 2 or 2:30 from October
through June; in summer they are closed on Saturday. Hours for museums and churches vary; most are open in the morning, but most museums close one day a week, often Monday. Stores are open weekdays from
9 or 10 until 1:30 or 2, then in the afternoon from around 5 to 8. Larger
department stores and supermarkets do not close at midday. In some cities,
especially in summer, stores close on Saturday afternoon.

CUSTOMS AND DUTIES

For details on imports and duty-free limits, *see* Customs and Duties *in*
Smart Travel Tips A to Z.

EMBASSIES

For consulates, *see* Barcelona A to Z.
➤ AUSTRALIA: (⌧ Plaza del Descubridor Diego de Ordás 3, Madrid,
☎ 91/441–9300).
➤ CANADA: (⌧ Núñez de Balboa 35, Madrid, ☎ 91/431–4300).
➤ NEW ZEALAND: (⌧ Plaza de La Lealtad 2, Madrid, ☎ 91/523–0226).
➤ UNITED KINGDOM: (⌧ Fernando el Santo 16, Madrid, ☎ 91/700–8200).
➤ UNITED STATES: (⌧ Serrano 75, Madrid, ☎ 91/577–4000).

HOLIDAYS

New Year's; Epiphany (January 6); Good Friday; Easter; May Day (May
1); St. James's Day (July 25); Assumption (August 15); National Day
(October 12); All Saints' Day (November 1); Constitution (December
6); Immaculate Conception (December 8); Christmas.

LANGUAGE

Spanish (called Castellano, or Castilian) is spoken and understood
throughout Spain. However, the Basques speak Euskera; in Catalonia,
you'll hear Catalan; and in Galicia, Gallego. If you don't speak Spanish, you should have no trouble finding people who speak English in
major cities and coastal resorts, but you won't necessarily be able to
count on the bus driver or the passerby on the street. Fortunately, Spanish is fairly easy to pick up, and your efforts to speak the local tongue
are bound to be graciously received.

MONEY MATTERS

The cost of living in Spain is on a par with that of most other European nations. In recent years, however, currency fluctuations have increased the buying power of those visiting from North America and
the United Kingdom. A cup of coffee costs between 125 ptas./€0.75
and 166 ptas./€1; a glass of wine in a bar, 100 ptas./€0.60–135
ptas./€0.80; a sandwich 300 ptas./€1.80–416 ptas./€2.50; a local
bus or subway ride 125 ptas./€0.75–200 ptas./€1.20; a 2-km (1-mi)
taxi ride, about 500 ptas./€3.

CREDIT CARDS

Most hotels, restaurants, and stores accept credit cards. Visa is the most
widely accepted card, followed by MasterCard (also called EuroCard
in Spain).

CURRENCY

Spain, as one of the euro zone currency countries, will introduce euro
(€) notes and coins on January 1, 2002. The euro and the Spanish peseta (ptas.) will circulate simultaneously through March 2002. Banks

and ATMs will give all money in euros. Shops and restaurants are encouraged to give change in euros whenever possible. Prices are marked in both euros and Spanish pesetas. Pesetas come in bills of 1,000, 2,000, 5,000, and 10,000, and coins of 1, 5, 10, 25, 50, 100, 200, and 500 pesetas. At press time (summer 2001), the exchange rate was 186.52 ptas. to the U.S. dollar, 119.48 ptas. to the Canadian dollar, 268.29 ptas. to the pound sterling, 211.27 ptas. to the Irish punt, 94.87 ptas. to the Australian dollar, 76.08 ptas. to the New Zealand dollar, 23.27 ptas. to the South African rand, and 166.39 ptas. to the euro.

Visitors may take any amount of foreign currency in bills or traveler's checks into Spain, as well as any amount of euros. When leaving Spain you may take out only €3,000 or the equivalent in foreign currency, unless you can prove you declared the excess at customs on entering the country.

CURRENCY EXCHANGE

The word to look for is CAMBIO (exchange). Most Spanish banks take a 1½% commission, though some less scrupulous places charge more; always check, as rates can vary widely. To change money in a bank, you need your passport and plenty of patience, because filling out the forms takes time. Hotels offer rates lower than banks, but they rarely charge a commission, so you may well break even. Restaurants and stores, with the exception of those catering to the tour-bus trade, generally do not accept payment in dollars or traveler's checks. If you have a credit card with a personal identification number, you'll have no trouble drawing cash from automated teller machines.

TELEPHONES

COUNTRY AND AREA CODES

The country code for Spain is 34.

DIRECTORY AND OPERATOR ASSISTANCE

For the operator and directory information for any part of Spain, dial 1003. The international information and assistance operator is at 025 (some operators speak English). If you're in Madrid, dial 1008 to make collect calls to countries in Europe; 1005 for the rest of the world.

INTERNATIONAL CALLS

You can call abroad from any pay phone marked TELÉFONO INTERNACIONAL. Some are coin-operated, but it is best to purchase a *tarjeta telefónica* (telephone card), available at most newsagents and many shops. A few public phones also accept credit cards. Dial 00, then dial 1 for the United States, 0101 for Canada, or 44 for the United Kingdom, followed by the area code and number. For lengthy calls, go to the *telefónica,* a phone office found in all sizable towns: here an operator assigns you a private booth and collects payment at the end of the call. This is the cheapest and by far the easiest way to call overseas, and you can charge calls costing more than €3 to Visa or MasterCard. Private long-distance companies, such as AT&T, MCI, and Sprint, have special access numbers.
➤ ACCESS CODES: **AT&T** (☎ 900/990011). **MCI** (☎ 900/990014). **Sprint** (☎ 900/990013).

LOCAL CALLS

Note that to call anywhere within Spain—even locally—you need to dial the area code first. All provincial codes begin with a 9.

PUBLIC PHONES

Most pay phones have a digital readout, so you can see your money ticking away. You need at least 25 ptas./€0.15 for a local call, 75 ptas./€0.45 to call another province, and at least 100 pts./€0.60 if you are calling a Spanish cell phone. Some pay phones take only phone cards, which can be purchased at any tobacco shop in various denominations.

4 BERLIN

Germany's capital has evolved into a cosmopolitan metropolis. A royal residence during the 15th century, Berlin came into its own under the rule of King Friedrich II (1712–86)—Frederick the Great—whose liberal reforms and artistic patronage led the city's development into a major cultural capital. In the 20th century Hitler and his supporters destroyed Berlin's reputation for tolerance and plunged it headlong into the war that led to its wholesale destruction, and to its eventual division by the infamous Wall. Erected in 1961, the Wall was finally breached in the "Peaceful Revolution" of 1989. Berlin is again on the cutting edge, drawing curious and adventuresome visitors.

EXPLORING BERLIN

Unlike most other large German cities, Berlin is a young and partly planned capital, with streets organized in a unusually clear manner. Yet Berlin is laid out on an epic scale—so allow plenty of time to get around.

Western Berlin

The western districts include Charlottenburg, Tiergarten, Kreuzberg, and Schöneberg, and the entire area is best known for the constant commerce on Kurfürstendamm. The boulevard of shops, art galleries, restaurants, and bars stretches 3 km (2 mi) through the downtown.

Numbers in the margin correspond to points of interest on the Western Berlin map.

★ **⑭** **Ägyptisches Museum** (Egyptian Museum). This small but outstanding museum is home to the portrait bust of Nefertiti known around the world. The 3,300-year-old queen is the centerpiece of a fascinating collection of Egyptian antiquities that includes some of the finest-preserved mummies outside Cairo. ⊠ *Schlosstr. 70,* ☎ *030/3435–7311 or 030/ 3090–5555,* WEB *www.smb.spk-berlin.de.* ☉ *Tues.–Sun. 10–6.*

⑰ Bildungs- und Gedenkstätte Haus der Wannsee-Konferenz (Educational and Memorial Site House of the Wannsee Conference). This elegant Berlin villa hosted the fateful Wannsee-Konferenz held on January 20, 1942, when Nazi leaders planned the systematic deportation and genocide of Europe's Jewish population. This conference and its results are illustrated in an exhibition. From the U-Bahn Wannsee station take Bus 114. ⊠ *Am Grossen Wannsee 56–58,* ☎ *030/805–0010,* WEB *www.ghwk.de.* ☉ *Mon.–Sun. 10–6.*

★ **❼ Brandenburger Tor** (Brandenburg Gate). Berlin's premier landmark was built in 1788 to celebrate the triumphant Prussian armies. The gate was cut off by the Wall, and it became a focal point of celebrations marking the reunification of Berlin and of all Germany. The square behind the gate, **Pariser Platz** (Paris Square), has regained its prewar design. Just a few hundred yards to the south of the gate, Germany's national **Holocaust Mahnmal** (Holocaust Memorial) is being built. ⊠ *Unter den Linden at Pariser Pl.,* WEB *www.brandenburger-tor.de.*

⑱ Dahlemer Museen (Dahlem Museums). This unique complex of four museums includes the **Ethnologisches Museum** (Ethnographic Museum), famous for its artifacts from Africa, Asia, the South Seas, and the Americas. The other museums present early European cultures, ancient Indian culture, and East Asian art. ⊠ *Lansstr. 8, subway line U-2 to Dahlem-Dorf,* ☎ *030/8301–438,* WEB *www.smb.spk-berlin.de.* ☉ *Tues.–Fri. 10–6, weekends 11–6.*

⑯ Grunewald (Green Forest). Together with its Wannsee lakes, this splendid forest is the most popular retreat for Berliners, who come out in force, swimming, sailing their boats, tramping through the woods, and riding horseback. In winter a downhill ski run and ski jump operate on the modest slopes of Teufelsberg hill. Excursion steamers ply the Wannsee, the Havel River, and the Müggelsee. ⊠ *Southwest of downtown western Berlin.*

★ **⑪ Haus am Checkpoint Charlie.** The museum reviews events leading up to the Wall's construction and displays actual tools and equipment, records, and photographs documenting methods used by East Germans to cross over to the West. ⊠ *Friedrichstr. 43–45,* ☎ *030/253–7250,* WEB *www.mauer-museum.com.* ☉ *Daily 9 AM–10 PM.*

⑫ Jüdisches Museum (Jewish Museum). This jagged structure designed by architect Daniel Libeskind has received much acclaim. The history and culture of Germany's Jewish communities are the theme of the exhibits. ⊠ *Lindenstr. 9–14,* ☎ *030/2599–3300,* WEB *www.jmberlin.de.*

★ **❸ Kaiser-Wilhelm-Gedächtniskirche** (Kaiser Wilhelm Memorial Church). This landmark, which once symbolized West Berlin, is a dramatic reminder of the futile destructiveness of war. The shell of the tower is all that remains of the 19th-century church. Adjoining the tower are a new church and bell tower. ⊠ *Breitscheidpl.,* ☎ *030/218–5023,* WEB *www.gedaechtniskirche.com.* ☉ *Old Tower Mon.–Sat. 10–4, Memorial Church daily 9–7.*

★ **❾ Kulturforum** (Cultural Forum). With its unique ensemble of museums, galleries, and libraries, the complex is a cultural jewel. It's also home to the Berlin Philharmonic orchestra. ⊠ *Matthäikirchstr. 1,* ☎ *030/ 2548–8132, 030/2548–8232 or 030/2548–8301,* WEB *www.berlin-philharmonic.com.* ☉ *Box office weekdays 3:30–6, weekends 11–2.*

The **Kunstgewerbemuseum** (Museum of Decorative Arts) displays arts and crafts of Europe from the Middle Ages to the present. ⊠ *Matthäikirchpl. 10,* ☎ *030/266–2902.* ☉ *Tues.–Fri. 10–6, weekends 11–6.*

Western Berlin

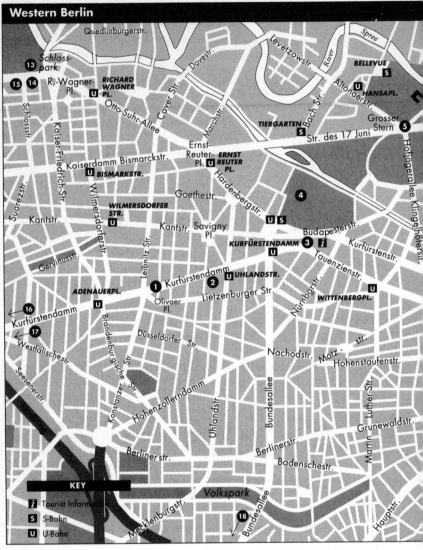

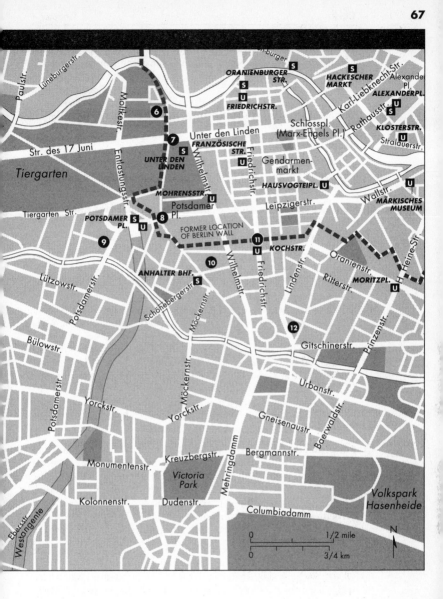

The **Gemäldegalerie** (Painting Gallery) reunites formerly separated collections from eastern and western Berlin. One of Europe's finest art galleries, it has an extensive selection of European paintings from the 13th through 18th centuries, among them works by Dürer, Cranach the Elder, and Holbein, as well as of the Italian masters—Botticelli, Titian, Giotto, Lippi, and Raphael. ⊠ *Matthäikirchpl. 8, ☎ 030/2660; 030/ 2090–5555 for all state museums in Berlin,* WEB *www.smb.spk-berlin.de.* ☼ *Tues.–Wed. 10–6, Thurs. 10–10, Fri.–Sun. 10–6.*

The **Neue Nationalgalerie** (New National Gallery), designed by Mies van der Rohe, exhibits artwork from the 19th and 20th centuries. ⊠ *Potsdamer Str. 50, ☎ 030/266–2662,* WEB *www.smb.spk-berlin.de.* ☼ *Tues.–Fri. 9–6, weekends 10–6.*

★ ➊ **Kurfürstendamm.** Ku'damm, as Berliners call the boulevard, throbs with activity day and night. The **Europa Center,** a shopping center, and the square in front of it are a buzzing, central meeting point.

★ ➑ **Potsdamer Platz.** Sony, Mercedes Benz, Asea Brown Boveri, and others have built their new company headquarters at this entirely reconstructed square, once Europe's busiest plaza before World War II. The **Sony Center** is an architectural marvel designed by German-American architect Helmut Jahn. Within it, the **Filmmuseum Berlin** (⊠ Potsdamer Str. 2, ☎ 030/300–9030, WEB www.filmmuseum-berlin.de; ☼ Tues., Wed., Fri., weekends 10–6, Thurs. 10–8) presents the history of moviemaking and memorabilia of German movie stars, including Marlene Dietrich. Also in the center is the Kaisersaal ("Emperor's Hall"), a café from the prewar Grand Hotel Esplanade that was located on this spot. The **Potsdamer Platz Arkaden** houses 140 upscale shops, a musical theater, a variety stage, cafés, a movie complex, a 3D-IMAX cinema, and even a casino. ⊠ *Arkaden Alte Potsdamer Str. 7, ☎ Arkaden 030/2559– 2766.* ☼ *Arkaden weekdays 9:30–8, Sat. 9:30–4.*

➓ **Prinz-Albrecht-Gelände** (Prince Albrecht Grounds). The buildings that once stood here housed the headquarters of the Gestapo, the secret security police, and other Nazi security organizations. After the war, the buildings were leveled; in 1987, what was left of them was excavated. The exhibit "Topography of Terrors" documents their history and Nazi atrocities. ⊠ *Niederkirchnerstr. 8, ☎ 030/2545–090,* WEB *www. topographie.de.* ☼ *Oct.–Apr., daily 10–6; May.–Sept., daily 10–8.*

★ ➏ **Reichstag** (German Parliament). The monumental building served as Germany's seat of parliament from its completion in 1894 until 1933, when it was gutted by fire under suspicious circumstances. Remodeled under the direction of British architect Sir Norman Foster, the Reichstag is once again hosting the Deutscher Bundestag, Germany's federal parliament. You can view the chambers on a short tour, and get a stunning view of Berlin from underneath the glass cupola. Lines to enter the Reichstag are long. ⊠ *Platz der Republik 1, ☎ 030/2270,* WEB *www.bundestag.de.* ☼ *Daily 8 AM–10 PM.*

★ ⓯ **Sammlung Berggruen** (Berggruen Collection). This small museum focuses on modern art, with work from such artists as Van Gogh, Cézanne, Picasso, Giacometti, and Klee. ⊠ *Schlosstr. 1, ☎ 030/3269– 580,* WEB *www.smb.spk-berlin.de.* ☼ *Tues.–Fri. 10–6, weekends 11–6.*

★ ⓭ **Schloss Charlottenburg.** Built at the end of the 17th century by King Frederick I for his wife, Queen Sophie Charlotte, this grand palace and its magnificent gardens were progressively enlarged for later royal residents and now include museums. ⊠ *Luisenpl., U-7 subway line to Richard-Wagner- Pl. station; from station walk east along Otto-Suhr-Allee, ☎ 030/3209– 1275,* WEB *www.smb.spk-berlin.de.* ☼ *Tues.–Fri. 9–5, weekends 10–5.*

❺ **Siegessäule** (Victory Column). The memorial, erected in 1873, commemorates four Prussian military campaigns. It stands at the center of the 630-acre **Tiergarten** (Animal Park), the former hunting grounds of the Great Elector. After climbing 285 steps to its 213-ft summit, you'll be rewarded with a fine view of Berlin. ⊠ *Am Grossen Stern,* ☎ *030/ 391–2961.* ☉ *Nov.–Mar., daily 9:30–5:30; Apr.–Oct., weekdays 9:30– 7, weekends 9:30–6:30.*

❷ **The Story of Berlin.** An effective mixture of history museum, theme park, and movie theater covers 800 years of Berlin's history. An old nuclear shelter is part of the four-story structure. Many original objects are pieced together in an interactive design in the 26 rooms. ⊠ *Ku'damm Karree, Kurfürstendamm 207–208,* ☎ *030/8872–0100,* WEB *www.story-of-berlin.de.* ☉ *Daily 10–8 (last admission: 6).*

★ ❹ **Zoologischer Garten** (Zoological Gardens). Berlin's enchanting zoo has the world's largest variety of individual types of fauna, along with a fascinating aquarium. ⊠ *Hardenbergpl. 8 and Budapester Str. 34,* ☎ *030/254–010,* WEB *www.zoo-berlin.de.* 🎫 *Combined ticket DM 24/€12.* ☉ *Zoo Jan.–Feb., daily 9–5; Mar.–late Mar., daily 9–5:30; late Mar.– late Sept., daily 9–6:30; Oct., daily 9–6; Nov.–Dec., daily, 9–5. Aquarium daily 9–6.*

Historic Berlin

Most of the really stunning parts of the prewar capital are in the historic eastern part of town, the Mitte district.

Numbers in the margin correspond to points of interest on the Historic Berlin map.

㉔ **Berliner Dom** (Berlin Cathedral). The impressive 19th-century cathedral with its enormous green copper dome is one of the great ecclesiastical buildings in Germany. More than 80 sarcophagi of Prussian royals are in the catacombs. ⊠ *Am Lustgarten,* ☎ *030/2026–9119.* ☉ *Church Mon.–Sat. 9–7, Sun. noon–8. Balcony Mon.–Sat. 9–7, Sun. noon–5. Imperial staircase and crypt Mon.–Sat. 9–8, Sun. noon–7.*

㉗ **Berliner Fernsehturm.** At 1,198 ft high, eastern Berlin's TV tower is 710 ft *taller* than western Berlin's. Its observation deck affords the best view of Berlin; the city's highest café, which revolves, is also up here. ⊠ *Alexanderpl.,* ☎ *030/242–3333,* WEB *www.berlinerfernsehturm.de.* ☉ *Nov.–Apr., daily 10 AM–midnight; May–Oct., daily 9 AM–1 AM (last admission at 11:30 PM).*

㉒ **Deutsches Historisches Museum** (German Historical Museum). The onetime Prussian Zeughaus (arsenal), a magnificent Baroque building constructed in 1695–1730, houses Germany's national history museum. After renovation and the addition of a new, modern wing by I.M. Pei, the museum will reopen in early 2002. ⊠ *Unter den Linden 2.* ☎ *030/ 203–040,* WEB *www.dhm.de.* 🎫 *English-speaking guide DM 60/€31.* ☉ *Thurs.–Tues. 10–6.*

★ ⑲ **Friedrichstrasse** (Frederick Street). Head south on historic Friedrichstrasse from Unter den Linden for chic new shops, including the **Friedrichstadtpassagen,** a gigantic shopping and business complex.

★ ㉚ **Gedenkstätte Berliner Mauer** (Memorial Site Berlin Wall). This is the only original piece of the Berlin Wall left standing. The open-air museum shows a 230-ft-long piece of the whole Wall system, which consisted of two walls and a control path patrolled by border guards. ⊠ *Bernauer Str. 111,* ☎ *030/4641–030.* ☉ *Wed.–Sun. 10–5.*

70

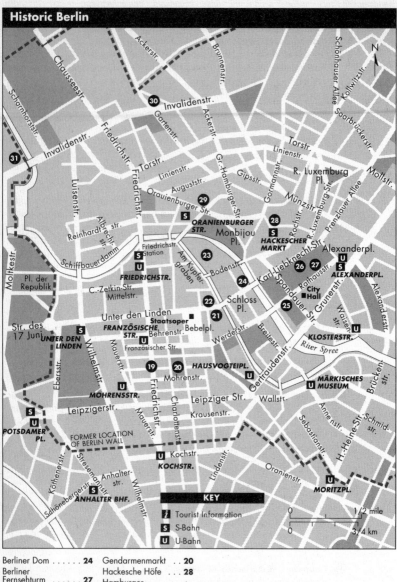

㉕ Gendarmenmarkt. This historic square has the beautiful **Schauspielhaus**—built in 1818 and now one of the city's main concert halls—and twin cathedrals. The **Deutscher Dom** (German cathedral ☎ 030/2273–0431, ☉ Sept.–May, Tues.–Sun. 10–6; June–Aug. Tues.–Sun. 10–7) presents an official exhibit on German history. The **Französischer Dom** (French cathedral; ☎ 030/229–1760, ☉ Tues.–Sat. noon–5, Sun. 11–5) houses a museum displaying the history of Huguenot immigrants in Berlin.

★ **㉘ Hackesche Höfe** (Hackesche Warehouses). Built in 1905–07, the restored Hackesche Höfe are the finest example of art deco industrial architecture in Berlin. Its several bars and theaters are a center of nightlife. ⊠ *Rosenthaler Str. 40–41,* WEB *www.hackeschehoefe.de.*

★ **㉛ Hamburger Bahnhof** (Hamburg Train Station). A remodeled, early 19th-century train station and its huge and spectacular new wing—a stunning interplay of glass, steel, color, and sunlight—display an outstanding collection of contemporary art. German artists Joseph Beuys and Anselm Kiefer have works here, as do Andy Warhol, Cy Twombly, Robert Rauschenberg, and Robert Morris. ⊠ *Invalidenstr. 50–51,* ☎ *030/3978–340,* WEB *www.smb.spk-berlin.de.* ☉ *Tues., Wed., Fri. 10–6, Thurs. 10–10, weekends 11–6.*

㉑ Kronprinzenpalais (Crown Prince's Palace). This magnificent Baroque-style building was constructed in 1732 for Crown Prince Friedrich (who later became Frederick the Great). ⊠ *Unter den Linden 3.*

★ **㉓ Museumsinsel** (Museum Island). This unique complex contains four world-class museums. The **Nationalgalerie** (National Gallery; ⊠ Bodestr.) has 19th- and 20th-century paintings and sculptures, mostly by German artists. The **Altes Museum** (Old Museum; entrance on ⊠ Lustgarten) collections include Roman and Greek sculptures and other antique exhibits as well as German postwar art and works by the Old Masters. The **Pergamonmuseum** (Pergamon Museum; ⊠ Am Kupfergraben), one of Europe's greatest museums, takes its name from its principal exhibit, the Pergamon Altar, a monumental Greek sculpture dating from 180 BC that occupies an entire city block. The museums are free the first Sunday of the month. Due to the continuing reconstruction of the Museumsinsel, the Bodemuseum will be closed in 2002. ⊠ *Museumsinsel (right from Unter den Linden along Spree Canal via Am Zeughaus and Am Kupfergraben),* ☎ *030/2090–5577 or 030/2090–5560 all museums,* WEB *www.smb.spk-berlin.de.* ☉ *All museums Tues.–Sun. 10–6.*

㉙ Neue Synagoge (New Synagogue). Completed in 1866, in Middle Eastern style, this was one of Germany's most beautiful synagogues until it was seriously damaged on Kristallnacht, November 9, 1938, when synagogues and Jewish stores across Germany were vandalized, looted, and burned. Today the outside is perfectly restored, and the interior is connected to the **Centrum Judaicum** (Jewish Center), an institution of culture and learning. ⊠ *Oranienburger Str. 28/30,* ☎ *030/2840–1316,* WEB *www.cjudaiucum.de.* ☉ *Sun.–Thurs. 10–6, Fri. 10–2.*

㉕ Nikolaiviertel (Nikolai Quarter). Berlin's oldest historic quarter is filled with shops, cafés, and restaurants. Nikolaikirchplatz has Berlin's oldest building, the **Nikolaikirche** (St. Nicholas's Church), dating from 1230. ⊠ *Nikolaikirchpl.,* ☎ *030/240–020.* ☉ *Tues.–Sun. 10–6.*

㉖ St. Marienkirche (Church of St. Mary). This medieval church, one of the finest in Berlin, is worth a visit for its late-Gothic fresco *Der Totentanz* (*Dance of Death*). The cross on top of the church tower was an everlasting annoyance to communist rulers, as its golden metal was always mirrored in the windows of the Fernsehturm TV tower, the pride of socialist construction genius. ⊠ *Karl-Liebknecht-Str. 8*, ☎ *030/242–4467.* ⊙ *Mon.–Thurs. 10–4, weekends noon–4. Free tours Mon.–Tues. at 1, Sun. at noon.*

DINING

Typical Berliner meals include *Eisbein mit Sauerkraut* (knuckle of pork with sauerkraut), *Spanferkel* (suckling pig), *Berliner Schüsselsülze* (potted meat in aspic), and *Currywurst* (chubby and very spicy frankfurters sold at wurst stands).

CATEGORY	COST*
$$$$	over DM 50 (€26)
$$$	DM 40–DM 50 (€21–€26)
$$	DM 30–DM 40 (€16–€21)
$	under DM 30 (€16)

per person for a main course at dinner

$$$$ ★ ✕ **First Floor.** Chef Matthias Buchholz's traditional German fare earned him a Michelin star. The menu changes according to the season and his moods, but most of the dishes are new interpretations of German dishes such as *Müritzlammrücken in Olivenkruste mit Bohnenmelange* (Müritz lamb back in olive crust, served with green beans). ⊠ *Hotel Palace, Budapester Str. 42*, ☎ *030/2502–1020. Reservations essential. AE, DC, MC, V. No lunch Sat.*

$$$$ ★ ✕ **VAU.** VAU's excellent German fish and game dishes offer daring combinations such as *Ente mit gezupftem Rotkohl, Quitten und Maronen* (duck with selected red cabbage, quinces, and sweet chestnuts). The VAU's cool interior is all style and modern art. ⊠ *Jägerstr. 54/55*, ☎ *030/202–9730. Reservations essential. AE, DC, MC, V. Closed Sun.*

$$$ ★ ✕ **Borchardt.** At this fashionable meeting place, columns, red plush benches, and an Art Nouveau mosaic create the impression of a 1920s salon. Entrées lean to French preparations. ⊠ *Französische Str. 47*, ☎ *030/2038–7110. Reservations essential. AE, V.*

$$–$$$ ✕ **Paris Bar.** This Charlottenburg restaurant attracts a polyglot clientele of film stars, artists, and executives. The cuisine is creative but medium-quality French. ⊠ *Kantstr. 152*, ☎ *030/313–8052. AE.*

$–$$$ ★ ✕ **Schwarzenraben.** At its white-clothed tables, the rich and beautiful of the new metropolis gather to enjoy their success. The cooking lets you discover new Italian recipes such as Milanese veal hocks. ⊠ *Neue Schönhauser Str. 13*, ☎ *030/2839–1698. Reservations essential. AE, DC, MC, V.*

$–$$ ✕ **Hackescher Hof.** The restaurant is without question one of the most "in" places in town and a great place to experience the upswing in the old East. The food is a mixture of contemporary international cuisine and beefy German cooking—there is also a special dinner menu with more refined dishes. ⊠ *Rosenthaler Str. 40/41*, ☎ *030/2835–293. Reservations essential. AE, MC, V.*

$–$$ ✕ **Reinhard's.** Berliners of all stripes meet here in the Nikolai Quarter to enjoy the carefully prepared entrées and to sample spirits from the amply stocked bar. *Adlon* (honey-glazed breast of duck) is one of the house specialties. Reinhard's has a smaller, more elegant restaurant on the Ku'damm. ⊠ *Poststr. 28*, ☎ *030/242–5295*; ⊠ *Kurfürstendamm 190*, ☎ *030/881–1621. Reservations essential on weekends. AE, DC, MC, V.*

$ ★ ✕ **Café Oren.** This popular Jewish vegetarian eatery is next to the Neue Synagoge. The restaurant buzzes with loud chatter all evening, and the atmosphere and service are friendly. The small backyard is a wonderful spot to enjoy a cool summer evening or a warm autumn afternoon. ⊠ *Oranienburger Str. 28*, ☎ *030/282–8228. AE, V.*

$ ✕ **Grossbeerenkeller.** The cellar restaurant, with its massive, dark-oak
★ furniture and decorative antlers, is one of the most original dining spots
in town. Owner and bartender Ingeborg Zinn-Baier presents such
dishes as *Sülze vom Schweinekopf mit Bratkartoffeln und Remoulade*
(diced pork with home fries and herb sauce). ⊠ *Grossbeerenstr. 90,*
☎ *030/2513–064. No credit cards. Closed Sun.*

$ ✕ **Zur Letzten Instanz.** Established in 1621, Berlin's oldest restaurant
combines the charming atmosphere of Old World Berlin with a limited (but tasty) choice of dishes. The emphasis here is on beer, both in
the recipes and in the mug. Service can be erratic, though engagingly
friendly. ⊠ *Waisenstr. 14–16,* ☎ *030/242–5528. AE, DC, MC, V.*

LODGING

Make reservations well in advance. Prices for rooms can fluctuate
wildly based on season and day of the week. Breakfast is usually, but
not always, included in the room rate.

CATEGORY	COST*
$$$$	over DM 400 (€205)
$$$	DM 300–DM 400 (€153–€205)
$$	DM 200–DM 300 (€102–€153)
$	under DM 200 (€102)

*Prices are for standard double rooms and include tax.

$$$$ 🏨 **Bristol Hotel Kempinski.** This grand hotel in the heart of the city has
the best of Berlin's shopping on its doorstep. All rooms and suites are
luxuriously decorated and equipped, with marble bathrooms, cable TV,
and English-style furnishings. Kids under 12 stay free if they share their
parents' room. ⊠ *Kurfürstendamm 27, D-10719,* ☎ *030/884–340,* FAX
030/883–6075, WEB *www.kempinski-bristol.de. 301 rooms, 52 suites.*
2 restaurants, bar, pool. AE, DC, MC, V.

$$$$ 🏨 **Four Seasons Hotel Berlin.** Smooth and up-to-date services such as
★ portable phones complement turn-of-the-20th-century luxury here.
Thick red carpets, heavy crystal chandeliers, and a romantic restaurant with an open fireplace make for a sophisticated and serene atmosphere. ⊠ *Charlottenstr. 49, D-10117,* ☎ *030/20338,* FAX *030/2033–*
6119, WEB *www.fourseasons.com. 162 rooms, 42 suites. Restaurant.*
AE, DC, MC, V.

$$$$ 🏨 **Grand Hyatt Berlin.** Within reborn Potsdamer Platz, the Grand
★ Hyatt provides large guest rooms with dark cherry-wood furniture, marble bathrooms, and Bauhaus artist photographs. A special attraction
of the first-class hotel is the top-floor gym and swimming pool, which
has a great view of Berlin's skyline. ⊠ *Marlene-Dietrich-Pl. 2, D-10785,*
☎ *030/2553–1234,* FAX *030/2553–1235,* WEB *berlin.hyatt.com. 327*
rooms, 16 suites. Restaurant, bar, pool. AE, DC, MC, V.

$$$$ 🏨 **Hotel Adlon Berlin.** This elegant hotel next to Pariser Platz has man-
★ aged to live up to its almost mythical predecessor, the old Hotel Adlon,
which, until its destruction during World War II, was considered Europe's premier resort. The new Adlon has impeccable service. The
city's priciest guest rooms are furnished in 1920s style with dark-
wood trimmings and bathrooms in black granite and bright marble.
⊠ *Unter den Linden 77, D-10117,* ☎ *030/22610,* FAX *030/2261–2222,*
WEB *www.hotel-adlon.de. 335 rooms, 51 suites. 3 restaurants, pool. AE,*
DC, MC, V.

$$$$ 🏨 **Hotel Palace.** This is probably the most individualized luxury hotel
★ in town and the only one in the heart of western downtown. Each room
has its own design, mostly in dark blues or reds and fitting woods. The
spacious business and corner suites are a good deal. ⊠ *Europa-*
Center, Budapester Str. 26, D-10789, ☎ *030/25020,* FAX *030/2502–1161,*

WEB *www.palace.de. 239 rooms, 43 suites. 3 restaurants, 2 bars. AE, DC, MC, V.*

$$$–$$$$ 🏨 **Heinrich-Heine City-Suites.** This new apartment hotel close to the historic Nikolai Quarter offers junior suites, which are among the best deals in town. All rooms have a full kitchen as well a mini-office. The hotel's extra services include a newspaper and fresh German rolls every morning. ⊠ *Heinrich-Heine-Pl. 11, D-10179,* ☎ *030/278–040,* FAX *030/2780–4780. 38 apartments. AE, DC, MC, V.*

$$–$$$ 🏨 **Hotel Astoria.** This is one of the most traditional, privately owned and run hotels in Berlin and it shows: rooms, service, and the restaurant all have a personal touch. Rooms are spacious, though the 1980s furniture is outdated. The location is good for exploring Kurfürstendamm, yet it's on a quiet street. ⊠ *Fasanenstr. 2, D-10623,* ☎ *030/ 3124–067,* FAX *030/3125–027,* WEB *www.hotelastoria.de. 31 rooms, 1 suite. AE, DC, MC, V.*

$$–$$$ 🏨 **Riehmers Hofgarten.** Surrounded by the bars and restaurants of the
★   colorful Kreuzberg district, this hotel has fast connections to the center of town. The 19th-century building's high-ceiling rooms are stylishly furnished. ⊠ *Yorckstr. 83, D-10965,* ☎ *030/7809–8800,* FAX *030/ 7809–8808,* WEB *www.hotel-riehmers-hofgarten.de. 20 rooms. Restaurant. AE, MC, V.*

$$ 🏨 **Hotel-Pension Dittberner.** The Dittberner, close to Olivaer Platz and
★   Kurfürstendamm, is a family-run hotel in a turn-of-the-20th-century house. Some of the furniture is worn, but the warm atmosphere and the breakfast buffet more than make up for it. ⊠ *Wielandstr. 26, D-10707,* ☎ *030/8846–950,* FAX *030/8854–046. 22 rooms. No credit cards.*

$–$$ 🏨 **Charlottenburger Hof.** A creative flair and a convenient location across from the Charlottenburg S-bahn station make this low-key hotel a great value for no-fuss travelers. The variety of rooms can suit friends, couples, or families. Kurfürstendamm is a 10-minute walk, taxis are easy to catch at the S-bahn station, and the bus to and from Tegel airport stops a block away. ⊠ *Stuttgarter Pl. 14, D-10627,* ☎ *030/32–90– 70,* FAX *030/323–3723,* WEB *www.charlottenburger-hof.de. 46 rooms with bath or shower. AE, MC, V.*

$ 🏨 **Hotel am Scheunenviertel.** This simply furnished but well-kept small hotel offers personal service, a wonderful breakfast buffet, and three restaurants (Mexican, Russian, and German) next door. If you want to indulge in Berlin's hip nightlife, you'll be near the cultural and entertainment hot spots. ⊠ *Oranienburger Str. 38, D-10117,* ☎ *030/282– 2125,* FAX *030/282–1115. 18 rooms with shower. AE, DC, MC, V.*

NIGHTLIFE AND THE ARTS

The Arts

The quality of opera and classical concerts in Berlin is high. One of the centrally located ticket agencies in the western downtown area is **Hekticket office** (⊠ Zoo Palast movie theater, Karl–Liebknecht–Str. 12, ☎ 030/2431–2431). Details about what's going on in Berlin can be found in *Berlin–the magazine,* an English-language monthly magazine published by Berlin's Tourism Board; *Berlin Programm,* a monthly guide to arts, museums, and theaters; and the magazines *prinz, tip,* and *zitty,* which appear every two weeks and provide full arts listings.

Concerts

The Berlin Philharmonic, one of the world's leading orchestras, performs in the **Philharmonie** (⊠ Matthäikirchstr. 1, ☎ 030/2548–8132 or 030/2548–8301). The **Konzerthaus Berlin** (⊠ Gendarmenmarkt, ☎ 030/2030–92101) is an historic concert venue.

Opera and Ballet

The **Deutsche Oper** (German Opera House; ⊠ Bismarckstr. 35, ☎ 030/343–8401), by the U-bahn stop of the same name, is home to both opera and ballet. The grand **Staatsoper Unter den Linden** (German State Opera; ⊠ Unter den Linden 7, ☎ 030/2035–4555) is Berlin's main opera house. **Komische Oper** (Comic Opera House; ⊠ Behrenstr. 55–57, ☎ 030/4799–7400) presents opera and dance performances.

Variety Shows

Variety shows thrive in Berlin. Intimate and intellectually entertaining is the **Bar jeder Vernuft** (⊠ Schaperstr. 24, ☎ 030/8831–582). Hilarious shows that even non-German speakers can appreciate are at the **Chamäleon Varieté** (⊠ Rosenthaler Str. 40/41, ☎ 030/2827–118). The world's largest circus is at the **Friedrichstadtpalast** (⊠ Friedrichstr. 107, ☎ 030/2326–2326). The small but classy **Wintergarten** (⊠ Potsdamer Str. 96, ☎ 030/2308–8230 or 030/2500–8888) pays romantic homage to the '20s. The **Grüner Salon** (⊠ Freie Volksbühne, Rosa-Luxemburg-Pl., ☎ 030/2859–8936) is one of Berlin's hip venues for live music, cabaret, and dancing. The programs change almost daily.

Nightlife

With more than 6,000 *Kneipen* (pubs), bars, and clubs, nightlife in Berlin is no halfhearted affair. The centers of this nocturnal scene are around Savignyplatz in Charlottenburg; Nollendorfplatz and its side streets in Schöneberg; Oranienstrasse and Wienerstrasse in Kreuzberg; Kollwitzplatz in the Prenzlauer Berg district; and Oranienburger Strasse, Rosenthaler Platz, and Hackesche Höfe in Mitte.

Bars and Dance Clubs

A young gay and lesbian crowd frequents the casual, hip **Anderes Ufer** (⊠ Hauptstr. 157, ☎ 030/784–1578). It has a mellow atmosphere and 1950s and '60s music. A Berlin classic, **Bar am Lützowplatz** (⊠ Am Lützowpl. 7, ☎ 030/262–6807) has the longest bar counter in town. Women sip American cocktails while flirting with the handsome bartenders. High-tech **Blu** (⊠ Marlene-Dietrich-Pl. 4, ☎ 030/8261–882), high above the Potsdamer Platz, offers soul and funk music on three floors. The crowd is mixed—teenagers from East Berlin dance next to young managers. The view of the Berlin skyline is magnificent. A clubby gay and hetero crowd mingles within the red-velvet walls of rowdy **Kumpelnest 3000** (⊠ Lützowstr. 23, ☎ 030/261–6918). The historic **Leydicke** (⊠ Mansteinstr. 4, ☎ 030/216–2973) is a must for out-of-towners. The proprietors operate their own distillery and have a superb selection of sweet wines and liqueurs.

Jazz Clubs

Call the tourist office for details on the annual fall international Jazz Fest. Jazz groups from around the world appear throughout the year at the **A-Trane** (⊠ Pestalozzistr. 105, ☎ 030/3132–550). The older and more traditional **Quasimodo** (⊠ Kantstr. 12a, ☎ 030/312–8086) mostly hosts well-known Jazzrock or, at times, country bands.

SHOPPING

The liveliest and most famous shopping area in western Berlin is the Kurfürstendamm and its side streets, especially between Breitscheidplatz and Olivaer Platz. Running east from Breitscheidplatz is Tauentzienstrasse. The Potsdamer Platz Arkaden is the shopping mall on Potsdamer Platz. Eastern Berlin's best shops are along Friedrichstrasse.

Antiques

On weekends from 10 to 5, the colorful and lively antiques and handicrafts fair on **Strasse des 17. Juni** swings into action. Not far from **Wittenbergplatz,** several streets are strong on antiques, including Eisenacher Strasse, Fuggerstrasse, Keithstrasse, Kalckreuthstrasse, Motzstrasse, and Nollendorfstrasse.

Department Stores

Galeries Lafayette (⊠ Französische Str. 23, ☎ 030/209–480), off Friedrichstrasse, carries almost exclusively French products, including designer clothes, perfume, and produce. The small but most luxurious **Department Store Quartier 206** (⊠ Friedrichstr. 71, ☎ 030/2094–6240) offers primarily French designer clothes, perfumes, and home accessories. One of Berlin's classiest department stores is the **Kaufhaus des Westens** (KaDeWe; ⊠ Tauentzienstr. 21, ☎ 030/21210); the food department occupies the whole sixth floor. The main department store in eastern Berlin, **Galleria Kaufhof** (⊠ Alexanderpl. 9, ☎ 030/247–430), is at the north end of Alexanderplatz. **Wertheim** (⊠ Kurfürstendamm 181, ☎ 030/883–8152) has a large selection of fine wares. **Stilwerk** (⊠ Kantstr. 17, ☎ 030/315–150) is an upscale mall with 48 shops and restaurants all catering to design and style.

Gift Ideas

Fine porcelain is still produced at the **Königliche Porzellan Manufaktur** (Royal Prussian Porcelain Factory, or KPM). This delicate, handmade, hand-painted china is sold at KPM's store (⊠ Kurfürstendamm 27, ☎ 030/8867–210) and the factory salesroom (⊠ Wegelystr. 1, ☎ 030/390–090), where seconds are sold at reduced prices. The **Gipsformerei der Staatlichen Museen Preussicher Kulturbesitz** (Plaster Sculpture of the Prussian Cultural Foundation State Museums; ⊠ Sophie-Charlotten-Str. 17, ☎ 030/3267–690) sells plaster casts of the Egyptian queen Nefertiti and other museum treasures.

BERLIN A TO Z

To research prices, get advice from other travelers, and book travel arrangements, visit www.fodors.com.

AIRPORTS AND TRANSFERS

Tegel airport is 7 km (4 mi) from downtown. Tempelhof, even closer to downtown, is used for commuter plane traffic. Schönefeld airport is about 24 km (15 mi) from downtown; it is used primarily for charter flights to Asia and southern and eastern Europe. You can reach all three airports by calling the central service phone number.

➤ AIRPORT INFORMATION: **Central Service** (☎ 0180/500–0186, ⓦⒺⒷ www.berlin-airport.de).

TRANSFERS

Buses 109 and X09 run every 10 minutes between Tegel airport and downtown. The journey takes 30 minutes; the fare is DM 4/€2 and covers all public transportation throughout Berlin. A taxi costs about DM 25/€13. If you're driving from the airport, follow signs for the STADTAUTOBAHN (City Freeway). Tempelhof is right on the U-6 subway line, in the center of the city. A shuttle bus leaves Schönefeld airport every 10–15 minutes for the nearby S-bahn station. S-bahn trains leave every 10 minutes for the Friedrichstrasse and Zoologischer Garten stations. The trip takes about 30 minutes; the fare is DM 4/€2. Taxi fare to your hotel is about DM 40/€20.50–DM 55/€28, and the trip takes about 40 minutes.

BUS TRAVEL TO AND FROM BERLIN

Berlin is linked by bus to 170 European cities. You can reserve seats at the central bus terminal or through DER or other travel agencies.
➤ BUS INFORMATION: **Central bus terminal** (✉ junction Masurenallee 4–6 and Messedamm, ☎ 030/301–8028).

CAR RENTAL

➤ MAJOR AGENCIES: **Avis** (✉ Schönefeld Airport, ☎ 030/6091–5710; ✉ Tegel Airport, ☎ 030/4101–3148; ✉ Budapester Str. 43, at Europa Center, ☎ 030/230–9370; ✉ Holzmarktstr. 15–18, ☎ 030/240–7940, WEB www.avis.de). **Europcar** (✉ Schönefeld Airport, ☎ 030/634–9160; ✉ Tegel Airport, ☎ 030/417–8520; ✉ Kurfürstenstr. 101–104, ☎ 030/235–0640, WEB www.europcar). **Hertz** (✉ Schönefeld Airport, ☎ 030/6091–5730; ✉ Tegel Airport, ☎ 030/4170–4674; ✉ Tempelhof Airport, ☎ 030/6981–9892; ✉ Budapester Str. 39, ☎ 030/261–1053, WEB www.hertz.de). **Sixt** (✉ Schönefeld Airport, ☎ 030/6091–5690; ✉ Tegel Airport, ☎ 030/4101–2886; ✉ Tempelhof Airport, ☎ 030/6951–3816; ✉ Nürnberger Str. 65, ☎ 030/212–9880; ✉ Leipziger Str. 104, ☎ 030/243–9050, WEB www.sixt.de).

CAR TRAVEL

The eight roads linking the western part of Germany with Berlin have been incorporated into the country-wide autobahn network, but be prepared for traffic jams, particularly on weekends. Follow signs for BERLIN–ZENTRUM to reach downtown.

EMERGENCIES

Pharmacies in Berlin offer late-night service on a rotating basis. Every pharmacy displays a notice indicating the location of the nearest shop with evening hours.
➤ DOCTORS AND DENTISTS: **Dentist emergency assistance** (☎ 030/8900–4333).
➤ EMERGENCY SERVICES: **Ambulance** (☎ 030/112). **Emergency poison assistance** (☎ 030/19240). **Police** (☎ 030/110).
➤ HOSPITALS: **Charite** (✉ Schumannstr. 20–21, Mitte, ☎ 030/28020).
➤ HOT LINES: **International Emergency Hotline** (☎ 030/3100–3222 or 030/3100–3243). **American Hotline** (☎ 0177/814–1510).
➤ 24-HOUR PHARMACIES: **Apotheken-Notdienst** (Emergency pharmaceutical assistance; ☎ 01189).

ENGLISH-LANGUAGE MEDIA

➤ BOOKSTORES: **Buchhandlung Kiepert** (✉ Hardenbergstr. 4–5, ☎ 030/311–880). **Dussmann Kulturkaufhaus** (✉ Friedrichstr. 90, ☎ 030/20250). **Hugendubel** (✉ Tauentzienstr. 13, ☎ 030/214060).

TAXIS

The base rate is DM 4/€2, after which prices vary according to a complex tariff system. If your ride will be short, ask in advance for the special Kurzstreckentarif, which is DM 5/€2.60 for rides of less than 2 km (1 mi) or five minutes. Figure on paying around DM 15 for a ride the length of Kurfürstendamm. Hail cabs in the street or at taxi stands, or order one by calling one of the numbers below. U-bahn employees will call a taxi for passengers after 8 PM.
➤ TAXI COMPANIES: ☎ 030/210–101, 030/210–202, 030/443–322, or 030/261–026.

TOURS

BUS TOURS

Bus tours of Berlin are more or less identical, covering Berlin's major sights, as well as day trips to Potsdam. The Berlin tour costs DM

25/€12.80 to DM 47/€24; Potsdam and Sanssouci Palace tour costs DM 65/€33.

➤ FEES AND SCHEDULES: **Berliner Bären Stadtrundfahrt** (BBS; ✉ Seeburgerstr. 19b, ☎ 030/3519–5270). **Berolina Stadtrundfahrten** (✉ Kurfürstendamm 220, corner Meinekestr. 3, ☎ 030/8856–8030, WEB www.berolina-berlin.com). **Bus Verkehr Berlin** (BVB; ✉ Kurfürstendamm 229, ☎ 030/885–9880, WEB www.bvb.net). **Severin & Kühn** (✉ Kurfürstendamm 216, ☎ 030/8804–190).

BOAT TOURS

Tours of downtown Berlin's canals take in sights such as the Charlottenburg Palace and Museum Island. Tours depart from several bridges and piers, such as Hansabrücke in Tiergarten, Kottbusser Bridge in Kreuzberg, Potsdamer Brücke, and Haus der Kulturen der Welt in Tiergarten. Tickets start at DM 8/€4 (one way). For details contact the tourist office.

WALKING TOURS

A walking tour is one of the best ways to familiarize yourself with Berlin's history and sights, and several companies offer native English speakers and thematic tours from which to choose.

➤ FEES AND SCHEDULES: **Berlin Walks** (☎ 030/301–9194, WEB www.berlinwalks.com). **Brewer's Best of Berlin** (☎ 030/2839–1433). **Insider Tours** (☎ 030/692–3149, WEB www.insidertour.de).

TRAIN TRAVEL

Most trains to and from Berlin pass through Bahnhof Zoo. Trains to the north and east usually stop at Lichtenburg station.

TRANSPORTATION AROUND BERLIN

The city has an excellent public transportation system: a combination of U-bahn and S-bahn lines, buses, and streetcars. For DM 4.20/€2.10, you can buy a ticket that covers travel on the entire downtown system (fare zones A and B) for two hours. Buy a *Kurzstreckentarif* for a short trip; it allows you to ride six bus stops or three U-bahn or S-bahn stops for DM 2.50/€1.30. The Day Card, for DM 12/€6.10, is valid until 3 AM of the day of validation.

The BerlinWelcomeCard is the best deal. At DM 32/€16.50 for three days, it entitles one adult and up to three children to unlimited travel as well as free or reduced-fare sightseeing trips and admission to museums, theaters, and other events. If you're caught without a validated ticket, the fine is DM 60/€31. Tickets are available from vending machines at U-bahn and S-bahn stations or from bus drivers. For information call the Berliner Verkehrsbetriebe or go to the information office on Hardenbergplatz, directly in front of the Bahnhof Zoo train station.

➤ CONTACTS: **Berliner Verkehrsbetriebe** (BVG; Berlin Public Transportation; ☎ 030/2561 or 030/19449, WEB www.bvg.de).

TRAVEL AGENCIES

➤ LOCAL AGENTS: **Euroaide** (✉ Hardenbergpl., inside the Zoologischer Garten train station, ☎ 030/2974–9241). **Reiseland American Express Reisebüro** (✉ Wittenbergpl., Bayreuther Str. 37, ☎ 030/2147–6293; ✉ Friedrichstr. 172, ☎ 030/2015–5721).

VISITOR INFORMATION

➤ TOURIST INFORMATION: **Berlin Tourismus Marketing GmbH** (main tourist office: ✉ Europa Center; ✉ Brandenburger Tor; ✉ Tegel Airport; by mail: ✉ Berlin Tourismus Marketing, ✉ Am Karlsbad 11, D-10785 Berlin). **Berlin-Hotline** (☎ 030/250–025 or 0190/754–040, [€1.20 per minute], FAX 030/2500–2424, WEB www.berlin.de).

Germany Basics

BUSINESS HOURS

Banks are usually weekdays from 8:30 or 9 to 3 or 4 (5 or 6 on Thursday). Some close from 12:30 to 1:30. Branches at airports and main train stations open as early as 6:30 AM and close as late as 10:30 PM. Museums are generally open Tuesday through Sunday 10–5. Some close for an hour or more at lunch. Many stay open until 8 or 9 on Wednesday or Thursday. Larger stores open weekdays 9:30–8, Saturday 9:30–4. Smaller shops close around 6:30 PM.

CUSTOMS AND DUTIES

For details on imports and duty-free limits, *see* Customs and Duties *in* Smart Travel Tips A to Z.

EMBASSIES

➤ AUSTRALIA: ⊠ Friedrichstr. 200, Berlin, ☎ 030/880–0880.
➤ CANADA: ⊠ International Trade Center, Friedrichstr. 95, Berlin, ☎ 030/261–1161.
➤ IRELAND: ⊠ Friedrichstr. 200, Berlin, ☎ 030/220–720.
➤ NEW ZEALAND: ⊠ Friedrichstr. 60, Berlin, ☎ 030/260–210.
➤ SOUTH AFRICA: ⊠ Friedrichstr. 60, Berlin, ☎ 030/220–730.
➤ UNITED KINGDOM: ⊠ Wilhelmstr. 70–71, Berlin, ☎ 030/204–570.
➤ UNITED STATES: ⊠ Neustädtische Kirchstr. 4–5, Berlin, ☎ 030/85030.

HOLIDAYS

January 1; January 6 (Epiphany—Bavaria, Baden-Württemberg, and Saxony-Anhalt only); Good Friday; Easter Monday; May 1 (Worker's Day); Ascension, Pentecost Monday, in May; May 30 (Corpus Christi—south Germany only); August 15 (Assumption Day—Bavaria and Saarland only); October 3 (German Unity Day); November 1 (All Saints' Day–Baden Württemberg, Bavaria, North Rhine Westphalia, Rheinland-Pfalz and Saarland only); December 24–26.

LANGUAGE

Among Germany's many dialects, probably the most difficult to comprehend is Bavaria's. Virtually everyone can also speak *Hochdeutsch,* the German equivalent of Oxford English. Many people under age 40 speak some English.

MONEY MATTERS

The most expensive cities are Berlin, Frankfurt, Hamburg, and Munich. Costs are somewhat lower in eastern Germany, but businesses that cater specifically to visitors are increasingly charging western German rates. Some sample prices include: cup of coffee, DM 3.50/€1.80; mug of beer in a beer hall, DM 6/€3; soft drink, DM 3.50/€1.80; ham sandwich, DM 5.50/€2.80; 3-km (2-mi) taxi ride, DM 12/€6.

CREDIT CARDS

All major U.S. credit cards are accepted in Germany. German ATMs accept four-digit PIN numbers.
➤ REPORTING LOST CARDS: **American Express** (☎ 01805/840–840). **Diners Club** (☎ 05921/861–234). **MasterCard** (☎ 0800/819–1040). **Visa** (☎ 08008/149–100).

CURRENCY

The year 2001 marked the final switch from the Deutsche Mark (DM) to the common European euro (€). Both D-marks and euros can be theoretically be used until July 1, 2002, though the transition is likely to be all but complete in March 2002. You may get your change in euros even if you pay in marks during the transition period. The mark is divided into 100 pfennige. There are bills of 5 (rare), 10, 20, 50, 100, 200, 500, and 1,000 marks and coins of 1, 2, 5, 10, and 50 pfennige and 1, 2, and 5 marks. At press time, the mark stood at DM 2.24 to the U.S. dollar, DM 1.39 to the Canadian dollar, DM 3.11 to the pound sterling, DM 2.48 to the Irish punt, DM 1.16 to the Australian dollar, DM.92 to the New Zealand dollar, and DM.27 to the South African rand. The euro is equivalent to DM 1.95, a fixed rate.

TELEPHONES
COUNTRY AND AREA CODES
Germany's country code is 49. When calling Germany from outside the country, drop the initial 0 in the regional code.

INTERNATIONAL CALLS
Calls can be made from just about any telephone booth, most of which are card operated. If you expect to do a lot of calling, international or local, purchase a telephone card. Collect calls can be made by dialing 0180/2001033 (this is also the number to call if you have problems dialing out). You can make international calls from post offices, too, even those in small country towns. Calls to the United States, day or night, cost 48 pf per minute, no matter the length of the call. Pay the clerk at the end of your call, adding a DM 2/€1 service fee.

➤ ACCESS CODES: **AT&T** (☎ 0800–888012). **MCI WorldCom** (☎ 0130–0012). **Sprint** (☎ 0800–888013).

LOCAL CALLS
Card phones have largely replaced coin-operated ones. Cards cost DM 12/€6 or DM 50/€25 (the latter good for DM 60/€30 worth of calls) and are sold at post offices, newsstands, and exchange places. If you need an operator, dial 0180/2001033. Calls made from a public phone cost 20 pfennigs a minute and are much cheaper than those made through a hotel.

5 BRUSSELS

Brussels has become synonymous with the European Union and the project to unite the continent, but while diplomats, politicians, lobbyists, and journalists have flocked to the city, it's far from becoming gray and faceless. Brussels's strength is its diversity. A bilingual city where French- and Dutch-speaking communities are too often divided, Brussels is home to all the cultures of Europe—east and west—as well as Americans, Canadians, Congolese, Rwandans, Vietnamese, Turks, and Moroccans. Art Nouveau flourished in Brussels as nowhere else, and its spirit lives on in gloriously individualistic town houses. Away from the winding alleys of the city center, parks and squares are plentiful, and the Bois de la Cambre, at the end of Avenue Louise, leads straight into a forest as large as the city itself.

EXPLORING BRUSSELS

You need to give yourself at least two days to explore the many riches of Brussels, devoting one day to the lower town (whose cobblestones call for comfortable walking shoes) and the other to the great museums and uptown shopping streets.

Around the Grand'Place

The Grand'Place, whose gilded splendor makes it one of Europe's most impressive squares, serves as an anchor for an area where the ghosts of the past mingle with a lively contemporary scene. Narrow, cobbled streets radiate off the square, with a rich offering of cafés, restaurants, and souvenir shops.

Numbers in the margin correspond to points of interest on the Brussels map.

❾ Cathédrale des Sts-Michel-et-Gudule. The names of the archangel and an obscure 7th-century local saint have been joined for the cathedral of Brussels. Begun in 1226, it combines architectural styles from the Romanesque to full-blown Gothic. The chief treasures are the stained-glass windows inspired by the drawings of Bernard Van Orley, an early 16th-century court painter. The ornately carved pulpit (1699) depicts Adam and Eve being expelled from the Garden of Eden. In the crypt are remnants of the original 11th-century Romanesque church. ✉ *Parvis Ste-Gudule,* ☎ *02/217–8345.* ⊙ *Daily 7:30–6.*

★ ❼ Centre Belge de la Bande Dessinée (Belgian Comic Strip Center). This unique museum celebrates the comic strip, focusing on such famous Belgian graphic artists as Hergé, Tintin's creator; Morris, the progenitor of Lucky Luke; and many others. There are a library, a bookshop, and an airy brasserie. The display is housed in what used to be a draper's wholesale warehouse, designed in 1906 by Art Nouveau pioneer Victor Horta (1861–1947) and restored to its former glory in 1989. ✉ *Rue des Sables 20,* ☎ *02/219–1980,* 𝖂𝖊𝖇 *www.fumetti.org/cbc/cbc.htm.* ⊙ *Tues.–Sun. 10–6.*

❺ Galeries St-Hubert. The oldest covered shopping arcade in western Europe—and still one of its most elegant—was constructed in 1847 and is filled with shops, restaurants, cafés, and theaters. Diffused daylight penetrates the gallery from the glazed vaults high above, and neoclassical gods and heroes look down from their sculpted niches. Midway through, the gallery is traversed by **rue des Bouchers,** which forms the main restaurant area. Caveat: the more lavish the display of food outside, the poorer the cuisine inside. ✉ *Between rue du Marché-aux-Herbes and rue d'Arenberg.*

★ ❶ Grand'Place. The ornate Baroque guild houses here, with their burnished facades, were completed in 1695, just three years after a French bombardment destroyed everything but the Town Hall. The houses are topped by gilded statues of saints and heroes, so vividly rendered that they seem to call out to each other. Thus the end result of Louis XIV's folly is Europe's most sumptuous market square and the heart of the city. On summer nights, music and colored lights flood the entire square. Shops, restaurants, and taverns occupy most ground floors. The Maison des Brasseurs houses the **Brewery Museum** (✉ Grand'Place 10, ☎ 02/511–4987). The Grand'Place comes enchantingly alive during local festivals such as the Ommegang, a magnificent historical pageant re-creating Emperor Charles V's reception in the city (first Tues. and Thurs. in July). ✉ *Rue au Beurre, rue du Chair et du Pain, rue des Harengs, rue de la Colline, rue de l'Étuve, rue de la Tête d'Or.*

❷ Hôtel de Ville (Town Hall). Dominating the Grand'Place, the Town Hall is around 300 years older than the guild houses that line the square. The slender central tower, combining boldness and light, is topped by a statue of the archangel Michael crushing the devil under his feet. The halls are embellished with some of the finest examples of local tapestries from the 16th, 17th, and 18th centuries. ✉ *Grand'Place,* ☎ *02/279–2340.* ⊙ *English-speaking tours Tues. 11:30 and 3:15, Wed. 3:15, Sun. 12:15. No individual visits.*

❸ Maison du Roi (King's House). Despite the name, no king ever lived in this neo-Gothic–style palace facing the Town Hall. It contains the **Musée de la Ville de Bruxelles** (City Museum), whose collections include Gothic sculptures, porcelain, silverware, lace, and paintings such as Brueghel's *The Wedding Procession*. Don't miss the extravagant collection of some 600 costumes for Manneken-Pis. ✉ *Grand'Place,* ☎ *02/279–4350.* ⊙ *Tues.–Fri. 10–5, weekends 10–1.*

❹ Manneken-Pis. The first mention of the "little man" dates from 1377, but the present version, a small bronze statue of a chubby little boy peeing, was made by Jérôme Duquesnoy in 1619. The statue is in fact a copy; the original was kidnapped by 18th-century French soldiers. ⊠ *Corner rue de l'Étuve and rue du Chêne, 3 blocks southwest of Grand'Place.*

Rue Antoine Dansaert. This is the flagship street of Brussels's fashionable quarter, which extends south to the Place St-Géry. Boutiques sell Belgian-designed men's and women's fashions along with other high-fashion names. Slick restaurants, trendy bars, jazz clubs, and cozy cafés rub shoulders with avant-garde galleries and stylish furniture shops. ⊠ *Between rue Van Artevelde at Grand'Place and Porte de Flandre.*

☝ **❻ Théâtre Royal de Toone** (Toone Marionette Theater). Brussels folklore lives on in this tiny, family-run puppet theater, with a cozy adjoining pub and a small museum. The puppeteers irreverently tackle anything from *Hamlet* to *The Three Musketeers* in the broadest of Brussels dialect. There are occasional performances in French, Dutch, and even English. ⊠ *Impasse Schuddeveld 6 off Petite rue des Bouchers 21,* ☎ *02/511–7137 or 02/513–5486.* ✉ *Performances BF400/€10, museum free with ticket for show.* ☉ *Tues.–Sat. 8:30 PM.*

❽ Vismet (Fish Market). The canals around which this lively quay district sprang up have been filled in, but the many seafood restaurants remain, making it a pleasantly animated area, popular with the Bruxellois (residents of Brussels) despite the high prices. When the weather is good, the restaurants all set up tables and chairs on the wide promenade. ⊠ *Quai au Bois-à-Brûler and quai aux Briques.*

Around the Place Royale

The elegantly neoclassical Place Royale is home of Brussels' art museums. The rather austere Palais Royal (Royal Palace) anchors the northern end of the square. The tranquil gardens of the Petit Sablon, just behind the Fine Arts Museum, and the gracious Grand Sablon are lined with tony antique shops.

★ **⓰ Grand Sablon.** A well-to-do, sophisticated square, it's alive with cafés, restaurants, art galleries, and antiques shops. At the upper end of the square stands the church of **Notre-Dame du Sablon,** built in flamboyant Gothic style in 1304 by the crossbowmen who used to train here and is now under restoration. The stained-glass windows are illuminated from within at night, creating a kindly warmth. Weekends, a lively antiques market takes place below the church. Downhill from the Grand Sablon stands the 12th-century church of **Notre-Dame de la Chapelle** (⊠ Pl. de la Chapelle). Its Gothic exterior and surprising Baroque belfry have been splendidly restored. This was the parish church of Pieter Brueghel the Elder (1520–69); he is buried here in a marble tomb.

⓭ Musée d'Art Ancien (Fine Arts Museum). The collection of Old Masters focuses on Flemish and Dutch paintings from the 15th to the 19th century. In the Brueghel Room is one of the world's finest collections of Pieter the Elder's works, including *The Fall of Icarus;* the Rubens Room holds paintings by that master. The museum displays works by Hieronymus Bosch, Memling, Van Dyck, and many others. An underground passage links it with the adjacent Museum of Modern Art. ⊠ *Rue de la Régence 3,* ☎ *02/508–3211,* ⓌⒺⒷ *www.fine-arts-museum.be.* ☉ *Tues.–Sun. 10–5.*

★ **⓫ Musée d'Art Moderne** (Museum of Modern Art). Housed in an exciting feat of modern architecture, the museum descends eight floors

84

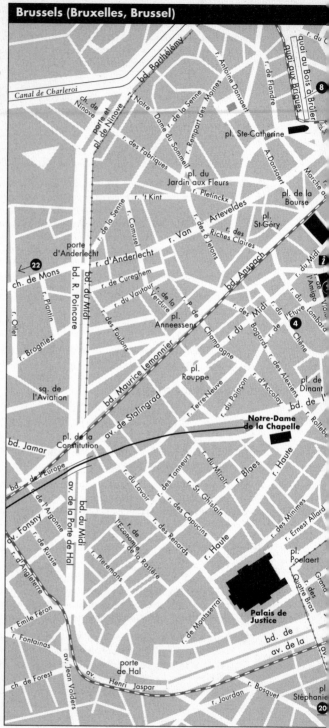

Brussels (Bruxelles, Brussel)

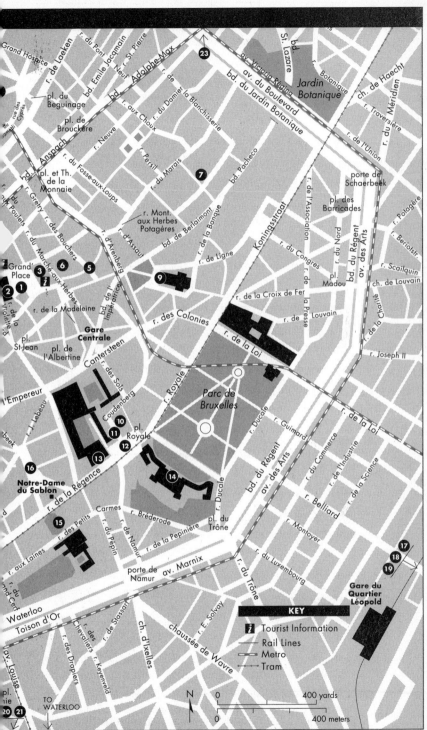

Grand Hospice
r. de Laeken
r. du Pont Neuf
bd. Emile Jacqmain
r. St. Pierre
Adolphe-Max
de
r. aux Choux
r. du Damier la Blanchisserie
av. Victoria Regina
av. du Boulevard
bd. du Jardin Botanique
St. Lazare
bd.
Botanique
Jardin Botanique
ch. de Haecht
r. Traversière
r. du Méridien

23

pl. du Beguinage
rue des Cyprès
pl. de Brouckère
Anspach
r. Neuve
r. Persil
r. du Marais
bd. Pacheco
r. de l'Union
porte de Schaerbeek
pl. des Barricades
r. Potagère
r. Scailquin
r. Bériotstr.

bd. Anspach
r. du Fosse-aux-loups
pl. et Th. de la Monnaie
Grétry
r. des Bouchers
r. Mont. aux Herbes Potagères
bd. de Berlaimont
bd. de la Banque
r. de l'Association
Koningsstraat
r. du Congrès
bd. du Régent
av. des Arts
ch. de Louvain

7

r. Pouers
r. du Marché-aux-Herbes
r. d'Arenberg
r. d'Assaut
r. de Ligne
pl. Madou

Grand' Place
6   5
3
7

9

r. de la Croix de Fer
r. de la Presse
r. de Louvain
r. de la Charité

2 1

r. de la Madeleine
bd. de l'Impératrice
r. des Colonies
r. de la Loi
r. Joseph II

Gare Centrale
pl. St-Jean
pl. de l'Albertine
Cantersteen
r. des Sols
Royale
Parc de Bruxelles
r. Ducale
r. Guimard
r. de la Loi

l'Emperator
r. Lebeau
Coudenberg
10
11
pl. Royale
12
13

14

bd. du Régent
av. des Arts
r. du Commerce
r. de l'Industrie
r. de la Science

16
Notre-Dame du Sablon
r. de la Régence
r. Ducale
r. Belliard

15
r. des Petits Carmes
r. de Namur
r. du Pépin
r. Brédérode
r. de la Pépinière
pl. du Trône
r. Montoyer

r. aux Laines
porte de Namur
av. Marnix
r. du Luxembourg
r. du Trône
Gare du Quartier Léopold

17
18
19

Waterloo
Toison d'Or
r. de Stassart
r. des Chevaliers
r. Keyenveld
ch. d'Ixelles
chaussée de Wavre
r. E. Solvay

av. Louise
pl.

20 21

TO WATERLOO

N

KEY
ℹ️ Tourist Information
— Rail Lines
▯ Metro
┼ Tram

0   400 yards
0   400 meters

into the ground around a central light well. Its strength lies in the quality of Belgian modern art: not only Magritte's luminous fantasies, Delvaux's nudes in surrealist settings, and James Ensor's hallucinatory carnival scenes but also the works of artists such as Léon Spilliaert, Leo Brusselmans, and Rik Wouters from the first half of the century; the post-war COBRA group, including Pierre Alechinsky and Henri Michaux; and on to contemporary works. ⊠ *Pl. Royale 1–2,* ☎ *02/508–3211,* WEB *www.fine-arts-museum.be.* ☉ *Tues.–Sun. 10–5.*

★ ⑩ **Musée Instrumental** (Musical Instruments Museum). Seven thousand instruments, from the Bronze Age to today, make up this extraordinary collection. The saxophone family is well represented, as befits the country of its inventor, Adolphe Sax (1814–94). The museum is housed in the **Old England** building, a glass-and-steel Art Nouveau masterpiece designed by Paul Saintenoy (1862–1952) for the British-owned department store Old England in 1899. ⊠ *Rue Montagne-de-la-Cour 2,* ☎ *02/545–0130,* WEB *www.mim.fgov.be.* ⊡ *BF150/€3.72.* ☉ *Tues., Wed., Fri. 9:30–5, Thurs. 9:30–8, Weekends 10–5. Concerts Thurs. at 8.*

⑭ **Palais Royal** (Royal Palace). The palace facing the Royal Park was rebuilt in 1904 to suit the expansive tastes of Leopold II (1835–1909). The king's architect, Alphonse Balat, achieved his masterpiece with the monumental stairway and the Throne Hall. The Belgian royal family uses this address only on state occasions. When the Belgian flag is flying, you'll know that the king is in Brussels. ⊠ *Pl. des Palais,* ☎ *02/551–2020.* ☉ *July 22–early Sept., Tues.–Sun. 10–4.*

⑮ **Petit Sablon.** Statues of the counts of Egmont and Horne, who were executed by the Spanish in 1568, hold pride of place here. The tranquil square is surrounded by a magnificent wrought-iron fence, topped by 48 small statues representing Brussels's medieval guilds. ⊠ *Rue de la Régence.*

⑫ **Place Royale.** This white, symmetrical square is neoclassical Vienna transposed to Brussels. From here you have a superb view over the lower town. The Coudenberg Palace once stood here. Underneath the square, excavations have revealed the *Aula Magna* (Great Hall), where the Flanders-born king of Spain and Holy Roman emperor Charles V (1500–58) was crowned and where he also announced his abdication two years before his death. The name of the palace lives on in the 18th-century church St-Jacques-sur-Coudenberg. In the center of the square stands the equestrian statue of Godefroid de Bouillon (1060–1100), leader of the First Crusade and ruler of Jerusalem. ⊠ *Jct. rue de la Régence, rue Royale, rue de Namur, and rue Montagne-de-la-Cour.*

Elsewhere in Brussels

⑰ **Autoworld.** This mecca for vintage car aficionados comprises a collection of more than 400 vehicles, all in working order. The surprise star of the show is the Belgian-made Minerva, a luxury car from the early 1930s. ⊠ *Parc du Cinquantenaire 11,* ☎ *02/736–4165,* WEB *www.autoworld.be.* ☉ *Daily: Apr.–Sept. 10–6; Oct.–Mar. 10–5.*

⑱ **European Union Institutions.** The various offices of the European Commission are centered on Rond Point Schuman (Metro: Schuman). The rounded glass summit of the **European Parliament** building (⊠ Rue Wiertz 43) looms behind the Gare de Luxembourg. ⊠ *Rond Point Schuman, rue de la Loi, rue Archimède, bd. Charlemagne, rue Wiertz.*

⑳ **Hôtel Hannon** (Hannon Mansion). The flowering of Art Nouveau produced this handsome, original town house designed by Jules Brunfaut

(1852–1942) in 1903, now a gallery devoted to contemporary photography. In the interior, note the staircase with its romantic fresco, as well as the stained glass. ⊠ *Av. de la Jonction 1,* ☎ *02/538–4220.* ☉ *Aug. 16–July 14, Tues.–Sun. 1–6. Metro: Near Musée Horta; trams 91 and 92 from Place Louise.*

⑲ Koninklijke Museum voor Midden-Afrika (Africa Museum). King Leopold II (1835–1909) was sole owner of the Congo (later Zaire, and now the Republic of Congo)—a colonial adventure that brought great wealth to the exploiters and untold misery to the exploited. He built a museum outside Brussels to house some 250,000 objects emanating from his domain. The museum has since become a leading research center for African studies. ⊠ *Leuvensesteenweg 13, Tervuren,* ☎ *02/769–5211,* WEB *www.africamuseum.be.* ☉ *Tues.–Fri. 10–5, weekends 10–6. Tram 44 from Square Montgomery.*

★ ㉒ Maison d'Erasme (Erasmus House). In the middle of a nondescript neighborhood in Anderlecht, this remarkable redbrick 16th-century house was home to the great humanist Erasmus in 1521. Every detail is authentic, with period furniture, paintings by Holbein and Bosch, prints by Dürer, and first editions of Erasmus's works, including *In Praise of Folly.* ⊠ *Rue du Chapître 31,* ☎ *02/521–1383.* ☉ *Mon., Wed.–Thurs., and weekends 10–noon and 2–5. Metro: St-Guidon.*

☾ ㉓ Mini-Europe. At the foot of the landmark **Atomium,** this popular attraction in a 5-acre park is a collection of 300 models (on a 1:25 scale) of buildings from the 15 EU countries. ⊠ *Brupark,* ☎ *02/478–0550.* ☒ *BF420.* ☉ *Sept.–June, daily 9:30–5; July–Aug., daily 9:30–7, Fri. nights and weekends in July and August until 11. Metro: Heysel.*

☾ Musée des Enfants (Children's Museum). Few kids don't fall in love with this educational center for 2- to 12-year-olds. They get to plunge their arms into sticky goo, dress up in eccentric costumes, walk through a hall of mirrors, and take photographs with an oversize camera. ⊠ *Rue du Bourgmestre 15,* ☎ *02/640–0107.* ☉ *Sept.–July, Wed. and weekends 2:30–5. Trams 93 and 94.*

★ ㉑ Musée Horta (Horta Museum). Victor Horta, the Belgian master of Art Nouveau, designed this building for himself and lived and worked here until 1919. From cellar to attic, every detail of the house displays the exuberant curves of the Art Nouveau style. Horta's aim was to put nature and light back into daily life, and here his floral motifs give a sense of opulence and spaciousness where in fact space is very limited. ⊠ *Rue Américaine 25,* ☎ *02/543–0490.* ☉ *Tues.–Sat. 2–5:30. Tram 91 or 92 from Pl. Louise.*

DINING

Brussels is one of the great dining cities in the world. Three thousand-odd restaurants are supplemented by a multitude of fast-food establishments and snack bars, and most cafés also offer *petite restauration* (light meals). Fixed-price menus, especially in top-dollar restaurants, sometimes cost only half of what you would pay dining à la carte, and the quality of your meal is likely to be just as good. There's less smoking than in the past, but no-smoking areas are rare.

Prices include a whopping 21% value-added tax. Belgian restaurants include a 16% service charge on all bills. Look for fixed-price menus or the daily special (*plat du jour* or *dagschotel*); if you sacrifice choice, you can eat well for less than BF700 in many good restaurants.

CATEGORY	COST*
$$$$	over BF1,200 (€30)
$$$	BF900–BF1,200 (€22–€30)
$$	BF500–BF900 (€12–€22)
$	under BF500 (€12)

*per person for a main course at dinner

$$$$ ✕ **Comme Chez Soi.** Master chef Pierre Wynants runs Brussels's most
★   celebrated restaurant, and the array of toques and stars he has earned
      is well-deserved. One all-time favorite, fillet of sole with a white wine
      mousseline and shrimp, is always on the menu, but the perfectionist
      owner-chef is constantly creating new culinary masterpieces. This stun-
      ning Art Nouveau restaurant is small, so reserve well ahead; you may
      have to wait up to six weeks for a table. ⊠ *Pl. Rouppe 23,* ☎ *02/512–
      2921. Reservations essential. Jacket and tie. AE, DC, MC, V. Closed
      Sun.–Mon., July, and Dec. 25–Jan. 1.*

$$$–$$$$ ✕ **La Truffe Noire.** Luigi Ciciriello's "Black Truffle" is a spacious eatery
★   with cuisine that draws on classic Italian and modern French cooking.
          Carpaccio, prepared at the table, comes with strips of truffle and
          Parmesan, while main courses include pigéon de Vendé with truffles
          and steamed John Dory with truffles and leeks. ⊠ *Bd. de la Cambre
          12,* ☎ *02/640–4422. Reservations essential. Jacket and tie. AE, DC,
          MC, V. Closed Sun., Mon., and last 3 weeks in Aug.*

$$–$$$$ ✕ **Sea Grill.** Gigantic etched-glass murals convey the cool of the Arc-
★   tic fjords that provide inspiration and ingredients for one of Belgium's
         best seafood restaurants. Chef Yves Mattagne's gift for applying meat
         preparations to fish is showcased in dishes like noisettes of tuna Rossini,
         while house classics include whole sea bass baked in salt. ⊠ *Radisson
         SAS, rue du Fossé-aux-Loups 47,* ☎ *02/227–3120. Jacket and tie. AE,
         DC, MC, V. Closed Sun. and 4 wks in July–Aug. No lunch Sat.*

$$$ ✕ **L'Ogenblik.** With green-shaded lamps over marble-topped tables, saw-
★   dust on the floor, and ample servings, l'Ogenblik is a true bistro. The
     long and imaginative menu changes frequently but generally includes
     mille-feuille with lobster and salmon, and saddle of lamb with spring
     vegetables. The kitchen stays open until after midnight, making it a
     favorite for artists and actors after the show. ⊠ *Galerie des Princes 1,*
     ☎ *02/511–6151. AE, DC, MC, V. Closed Sun.*

$$–$$$ ✕ **Aux Armes de Bruxelles.** One of the few restaurants to escape the
        "tourist trap" label on this hectic street, Aux Armes has three rooms
        with a lively atmosphere: The most popular section overlooks the
        street theater outside, but locals prefer the cozy rotunda. It offers the
        classics of Belgian cooking, *waterzooi* (a creamy fish or chicken stew),
        and mussels steamed in white wine. ⊠ *Rue des Bouchers 13,* ☎ *02/
        511–5598. AE, DC, MC, V. Closed Mon. and mid-June–mid-July.*

$–$$$ ✕ **Les Salons de Wittamer.** The elegant upstairs rooms at Brussels's best-
★   known patisserie house a stylish breakfast and lunch restaurant, where
       meals are topped off with the establishment's celebrated pastry or ice-
       cream concoctions. ⊠ *Pl. du Grand Sablon 12–13,* ☎ *02/512–3742.
       AE, DC, MC, V. Closed Mon.*

$$ ✕ **Au Stekerlapatte.** In the shadow of the monstrous Palais de Justice,
    this bustling Marolles bistro is packed nightly with diners craving lib-
    eral portions of Belgian specialties. Try black pudding with caramelized
    apples, sauerkraut, beef fried with shallots, grilled pig's trotters, or
    spareribs. ⊠ *Rue des Prêtres 4,* ☎ *02/512–8681. MC, V. Closed Sun.
    Closed Sun. and Mon. July–Aug. No lunch.*

$$ ✕ **Au Vieux St-Martin.** Belgian specialties dominate the menu here, and
    portions are generous. The restaurant claims to have invented the now
    ubiquitous *filet américain* (the well-seasoned Belgian version of steak
    tartare). The walls are hung with bright contemporary paintings, and

picture windows face the pleasant square. ⊠ *Pl. du Grand Sablon 38,* ☎ *02/512–6476. AE, MC, V.*

$–$$ ✕ **Kasbah.** An Aladdin's den of stained-glass lamps and dark, sumptuous decor, this is one of the best of the capital's many North African restaurants. Steaming portions of couscous and *tajines* (Moroccan casseroles with fish or meat, usually involving fruit, vegetables, and spices) are served in this lively restaurant. ⊠ *Rue Antoine Dansaert 20,* ☎ *02/502–4026. AE, MC, V.*

$–$$ ✕ **Léon.** Critics deride it as McMoules-frites, but this century-old eatery is enormously popular, with franchises across Belgium and even in Paris and Japan. The secret is heaping plates of steaming mussels, specialties such as *anguilles au vert* (eels in green sauce), free children's menus, and great fries. It's loud, brightly lit—and has a charm all its own. ⊠ *Rue des Bouchers 18,* ☎ *02/511–1415. AE, DC, MC, V.*

$–$$ ✕ **Taverne Falstaff.** This huge tavern with an Art Nouveau interior fills
★ up for lunch and keeps going until the wee hours. The ever-changing crowd, from students to pensioners, consumes onion soup, filet mignon, salads, and other brasserie fare. On the heated terrace, a favorite meeting point for groups, the surliness of the waiters is legendary. ⊠ *Rue Henri Maus 17–21,* ☎ *02/511–8987. AE, DC, MC, V.*

$ ✕ **Chez Patrick.** This old-timer next to the Grand'Place has been dishing up good, honest Belgian food for nearly 70 years, in an unpretentious, old-fashioned setting with waitresses in black and white and specials chalked up on the mirrors. Expect large, tasty portions of shrimp croquettes, salmon and endives cooked with beer, and chicken with *kriek* (cherry-flavored beer) and cherries. ⊠ *Rue des Chapeliers 6,* ☎ *02/ 511–9815. AE, DC, MC, V. Closed Mon.*

$ ✕ **Le Pain Quotidien.** These bakeries–cum–snack bars have spread like wildfire all over Brussels (and even to New York and Boston in the U.S.) with the same formula: copious salads, hearty homemade soups, and delicious open sandwiches on farm-style bread, served at a communal table from 7:30 AM to 7 PM. ⊠ *Rue des Sablons 11,* ☎ *02/513–5154;* ⊠ *Rue Antoine Dansaert 16,* ☎ *02/502–2361; and other locations. Reservations not accepted. No credit cards.*

LODGING

The main hotel districts are around the Grand'Place, the Place de Brouckère, and in the avenue Louise shopping area. If you have a problem finding accommodations, go to the TIB tourist office in the Hôtel de Ville at the Grand'Place or telephone BTR (Belgian Tourist Reservations, ☎ 02/513–7484) for their free service. Weekend and summer discounts, often of 50% or more, are available in almost all hotels; be sure to check when you book. Most new hotels have set aside rooms or floors for nonsmokers and offer a limited number of rooms equipped for people with disabilities.

Hotel prices, including sales tax and service charge, are usually posted in each room. All prices listed exclude a 16% service charge and a 14.9% room tax. The tax is slightly lower at suburban hotels.

CATEGORY	COST*
$$$$	over BF9,000 (€223)
$$$	BF6,500–BF9,000 (€161–€223)
$$	BF3,500–BF6,500 (€87–€161)
$	under BF3,500 (€87)

*Prices are for a standard double room, excluding tax and service charge.

$$$$ **Amigo.** Although it was built in the 1950s, this family-owned hotel
★ off the Grand'Place has the charm of an earlier age. Each room is in-

dividually decorated, often in silk, velvet, and brocades. Some 60 rooms, omitted from the most recent refurbishment, are more modestly priced. Ask for a quiet room, away from the main tourist trail. ⊠ *Rue de l'Amigo 1–3, 1000,* ☎ *02/547–4747,* 🗺 *02/513–5277,* 🖦 *www.rfhotels.com. 185 rooms, 7 suites. Restaurant. AE, DC, MC, V.*

$$$$ 🏨 **Brussels Hilton.** The 27-story Hilton was one of the capital's first highrises, dating from the 1960s, and remains a distinctive landmark with great views of the inner town. Corner rooms are the most desirable; there are four floors of executive rooms and superb business facilities. The second-floor Maison du Boeuf restaurant is much appreciated by Brussels gourmets. ⊠ *Bd. de Waterloo 38, 1000,* ☎ *02/504–1111,* 🗺 *02/504–2111. 430 rooms, 39 suites. 2 restaurants. AE, DC, MC, V.*

$$$$ 🏨 **Conrad International.** Opened by the Hilton group in 1993, the Conrad combines the European grand hotel tradition with American tastes and amenities, and has become *the* place to stay for visiting dignitaries. Rooms are spacious, with three telephones, bathrobes, and in-room checkout. The Maison de Maître restaurant maintains the same high standard, and the large bar is pleasantly clublike. ⊠ *Av. Louise 71, 1050,* ☎ *02/542–4242,* 🗺 *02/542–4200,* 🖦 *www.hilton.com. 269 rooms, 15 suites. 2 restaurants. AE, DC, MC, V.*

$$$$ 🏨 **Manos Stéphanie.** This former town house, has a marble lobby, Louis XV furniture, and elegant rooms. Service is friendly, breakfast is included, and children under 12 stay free. ⊠ *Chaussée de Charleroi 28, 1060,* ☎ *02/539–0250,* 🗺 *02/537–5729,* 🖦 *www.manoshotel.com. 55 rooms, 7 suites. Bar. AE, DC, MC, V.*

$$$$ 🏨 **Le Méridien.** Opened in 1995, Le Méridien is Brussels's newest luxury hotel, in a convenient area opposite the Gare Centrale. The marble and gilt-edged lobby recalls palatial Parisian hotels, and the restaurant sets out brightly colored Limoges china. Rooms, in dark blue or green, come with three telephones, large desks, and data ports. ⊠ *Carrefour de l'Europe 3, 1000,* ☎ *02/548–4211,* 🗺 *02/548–4080,* 🖦 *www.meridien.be. 224 rooms, 12 suites. Restaurant. AE, DC, MC, V.*

★

$$$$ 🏨 **Le Metropole.** Built in 1895, this restored Belle Epoque masterpiece is the last trace of elegance in what was once one of Brussels's most charming squares. The lobby has a high coffered ceiling, chandeliers, and Oriental rugs. The theme extends to the restaurant and the café, which opens onto a heated terrace. Most guest rooms are in discreet pastel shades and Art Deco style. ⊠ *Pl. de Brouckère 31, 1000,* ☎ *02/217–2300,* 🗺 *02/218–0220,* 🖦 *www.metropole.be. 400 rooms, 10 suites. 2 restaurants. AE, DC, MC, V.*

$$$$ 🏨 **Radisson SAS.** This excellent 1990 hotel has guest rooms decorated with great panache in four different styles: Scandinavian, Asian, Italian, and Art Deco. A portion of the 12th-century city wall forms part of the atrium. Children under 17 stay free; check weekend rates. ⊠ *Rue du Fossé-aux-Loups 47, 1000,* ☎ *02/219–2828,* 🗺 *02/219–6262. 263 rooms, 18 suites. 3 restaurants. AE, DC, MC, V.*

$$$ 🏨 **Le Dixseptième.** In this stylish 17th-century hotel, originally the residence of the Spanish ambassador, each room is named for a Belgian artist. Suites are up a splendid Louis XV staircase, and the standard rooms surround an interior courtyard. Whitewashed walls, bare floors, exposed beams, and colorful textiles are the style here. Some rooms have kitchenettes; suites have working fireplaces and fax machines. ⊠ *Rue de la Madeleine 25, 1000, 1000,* ☎ *02/539–0250,* 🗺 *02/502–6424. 24 rooms, 12 suites. AE, DC, MC, V.*

$$ 🏨 **Orion.** This residential hotel accepts overnight guests; it's a good choice for families. The exterior is plain, but the location on the Vismet is plum. Rooms have pull-out twin beds; junior suites sleep four. All have kitchenettes. ⊠ *Quai au Bois-à-Brûler 51, 1000,* ☎ *02/221–1411,* 🗺 *02/221–1599. 169 rooms. Breakfast room. AE, DC, MC, V.*

$ 🎦 **Bed & Brussels.** This upscale B&B accommodations service ar-
ranges stays with 100 host families in Brussels or surrounding areas,
most of them with room to spare after children have flown the coop.
Many rooms come with private bath, and breakfast with the hosts is
included. ⊠ *Rue Gustave Biot 2,* ☎ *02/646–0737,* FAX *02/644–0114,*
WEB *www.bnb-brussels.be. MC, V.*

$ 🎦 **Matignon.** Only the Belle Epoque facade of this family-run hotel op-
posite the stock exchange was preserved when it was converted into a
hotel in 1993. The lobby is tiny to make room for the bustling café-
brasserie. Rooms are small but have large beds (and large TVs), and
the duplex suites are good value for families. It's noisy but very central. ⊠ *Rue de la Bourse 10, 1000,* ☎ *02/511–0888,* FAX *02/513–6927.
26 rooms, 9 suites. Restaurant. AE, DC, MC, V.*

$ 🎦 **Welcome Hotel.** This charming hotel, the smallest in Brussels, is owned
★ by Michel and Sophie Smeesters. The rooms, with king- or queen-size
beds, would be a credit to far more expensive establishments; it's essential to book well ahead. There's a charming breakfast room, and
Michel is also chef at the excellent seafood restaurant around the corner, La Truite d'Argent. ⊠ *Rue du Peuplier 5, 1000,* ☎ *02/219–9546,*
FAX *02/217–1887,* WEB *www.hotelwelcome.com. 10 rooms, 3 apartments for stays of at least one month. Restaurant. AE, DC, MC, V.*

NIGHTLIFE AND THE ARTS

The Arts

The best way to find out what's going on in Brussels is to buy a copy
of the English-language weekly the *Bulletin*.

Film

Movies are mainly shown in their original language (indicated as v.o.,
or *version originale*). Complete listings appear in the *Bulletin*. For unusual movies or screen classics, visit the **Musée du Cinéma** (Film Museum; ⊠ Rue Baron Horta 9, ☎ 02/507–8370), where three sound films
and two silents with piano accompaniment are shown every evening.
Unfortunately, those under 16 are not admitted.

Music

Major symphony concerts and recitals are held at the **Palais des Beaux-
Arts** (⊠ Rue Ravenstein 23, ☎ 02/507–8200). Chamber music is best
enjoyed at the intimate **Conservatoire Royal de Musique** (⊠ Rue de la
Régence 30, ☎ 02/511–0427). Free Sunday morning concerts take place
at various churches, including the Cathédrale Sts-Michel-et-Gudule. You
can also experience a Sunday morning concert at the **Église des Minimes** (⊠ Rue des Minimes 62). **Ancienne Belgique** (⊠ Bd. Anspach 110,
☎ 02/548–2424) hosts folk, rock, pop, funk, and jazz concerts.

Opera and Dance

The national opera company, based at the handsome **Théâtre Royal de
la Monnaie** (⊠ Pl. de la Monnaie, ☎ 070/233939), stages productions
of international quality. Touring dance and opera companies often perform at **Cirque Royal** (⊠ Rue de l'Enseignement 81, ☎ 02/218–2015).

Theater

The **Théâtre Royal du Parc** (⊠ Rue de la Loi 3, ☎ 02/505–3030)
stages productions of Molière and other French classics. Avant-garde
theater is performed at **Théâtre Varia** (⊠ Rrue du Sceptre 78, ☎ 02/
640–8258). **Théâtre de Poche** (⊠ Chemin du Gymnase 1a, in the Bois
de la Cambre, ☎ 02/649–1727) presents modern productions.

Nightlife

Bars

There's a café on virtually every corner in Brussels, and all of them serve beer from morning to late at night. If you crave a young crowd, try **Au Soleil** (⊠ Rue Marché au Charbon 86, ☎ 02/513–3430) in the fashionable place St-Gery–rue A. Dansaert part of town. The lively **Beursschouwburg-Café** (⊠ Rue Auguste Orts 22, ☎ 02/513–8290) attracts earnestly trendy young Flemish intellectuals. **Le Cirio** (⊠ Rue de la Bourse 18, ☎ 02/512–1395) is a typical *bruin café* with 1900s-era advertisements and price lists on the mirror-lined walls. Another 1900-style café-bar with a lost-in-time atmosphere is **À La Mort Subite** (⊠ Rue Montagne-aux-Herbes-Potagères 7, ☎ 02/513–1318). On the Grand'-Place, **Le Cerf** (⊠ Grand'Place 20, ☎ 02/511–4791) is particularly pleasant, with atmosphere and furnishings out of the 17th century. Only a 10-minute stroll from the Grand'Place is **La Fleur en Papier Doré** (⊠ Rue des Aléxiens 53, ☎ 02/511–1659), a quaint tavern with a surrealist decor that appeals to an artsy crowd. **Le Greenwich** (⊠ Rue des Chartreux 7, ☎ 02/511–4167), a chess club–cum–café, is where Magritte used to play. **Rick's Café Américain** (⊠ Av. Louise 344, ☎ 02/648–1451) is a favorite with the American and British expat community. Like most other western European cities, Brussels has a sizable number of "Irish" bars. **James Joyce** (⊠ Rue Archimède 34, ☎ 02/230–9894) was the first in Brussels and is the most genuinely Gaelic.

Dance Clubs

In all the clubs the action starts at 10 or after. Electronica fans prefer **Fuse** (⊠ Rue Blaes 208, ☎ 02/511–9789), a bunker-style techno haven with regular gay and lesbian nights. **Griffin's** (⊠ Rue Duquesnoy 5, ☎ 02/505–5555), at the Royal Windsor Hotel, appeals to young adults and business travelers. **Le Mirano Continental** (⊠ Chaussée de Louvain 38, ☎ 02/227–3970) remains the glitzy hangout of choice for the self-styled beautiful people.

Jazz

Most of Brussels's dozen or so jazz haunts present live music only on certain nights; check before you go. **New York Café Jazz Club** (⊠ Chaussée de Charleroi 5, ☎ 02/534–8509) is an American restaurant by day and a modern jazz hangout on Friday and Saturday evenings. **Sounds Jazz Club** (⊠ Rue de la Tulipe 28, ☎ 02/512–9250), a big café, emphasizes jazz-rock, blues, and other modern trends. **Travers** (⊠ Rue Traversière 11, ☎ 02/218–4086), a café–cum–jazz club, is a cramped but outstanding showcase for the country's leading players.

SHOPPING

Gift Ideas

Belgium is where the *praline*—rich chocolate filled with flavored creams, liqueur, or nuts—was invented. Try Corné Toison d'Or, Godiva, Neuhaus, or the lower-priced Leonidas, available at shops throughout the city. **Wittamer** (⊠ Pl. du Grand Sablon 12, ☎ 02/512–3742) is an excellent patisserie with a sideline in superb chocolates. **Pierre Marcolini** (⊠ Pl. du Grand Sablon 39, ☎ 02/514–1206) is the boy wonder of the chocolate world. Exclusive handmade pralines can be bought at **Mary** (⊠ Rue Royale 73, ☎ 02/217–4500), official purveyor of chocolates to the Belgian court.

Only the Val-St-Lambert mark guarantees handblown, hand-carved Belgian lead crystal. Many stores sell crystal tableware and ornaments, including **Art & Selection** (⊠ Rue du Marché-aux-Herbes 83, ☎ 02/511–8448) near the Grand'Place.

When shopping for lace, ask whether it is genuine handmade Belgian or machine-made in East Asia. **Maison F. Rubbrecht** (✉ Grand'Place 23, ☎ 02/512–0218) sells authentic Belgian lace. For a choice of old and modern lace, try **Manufacture Belge de Dentelles** (✉ Galerie de la Reine 6–8, ☎ 02/511–4477).

Markets

On Saturday (9–6) and Sunday (9–2), the upper end of the Place du Grand Sablon becomes an open-air **antiques and book market** with more than 100 stalls. The **Vieux Marché** (✉ Pl. du Jeu de Balle), open daily 7–2, is a flea market worth visiting for the authentic atmosphere of the working-class Marolles district. To make real finds, get here early.

Shopping Districts

The shops in the **Galeries St-Hubert** sell mostly luxury goods or gift items. The **rue Neuve** and the **City 2** mall are good for less expensive boutiques and department stores. Avant-garde clothes are sold in boutiques on **rue Antoine Dansaert,** near the stock exchange.

Uptown, **avenue Louise,** with the arcades Galerie Louise and Espace Louise, counts a large number of boutiques selling expensive clothes and accessories. The **boulevard de Waterloo** is home to the same fashion names as Bond Street and Rodeo Drive. The **Grand Sablon** has more charm; this is the center for antiques and art galleries.

BRUSSELS A TO Z

To research prices, get advice from other travelers, and book travel arrangements, visit www.fodors.com.

AIRPORTS AND TRANSFERS
All international flights arrive at Brussels National Airport at Zaventem (sometimes called simply Zaventem), 15 km (9 mi) northeast of the city center.
➤ AIRPORT INFORMATION: Flight information (☎ 0900–70000).

TRANSFERS
Shuttle trains run between Brussels Airport and all three main railway stations in Brussels: South (Midi), Central (Central), and North (Nord). The Airport City Express runs four times per hour, from about 6 AM to midnight, seven days a week. The journey takes 18 minutes. A one-way ticket costs BF140/€ (1st class) or BF90/€ (2nd class). A taxi to the city center takes about a half hour and costs about BF1,000/€25.

BOAT AND FERRY TRAVEL
Hoverspeed operates a Hovercraft catamaran service between Dover and Calais, carrying cars and foot passengers. Travel time is 35 minutes. Hoverspeed also offers pedestrian-only "SeaCat" service between Dover and Oostende, with travel time just under two hours. Trains at either end connect with London and Brussels. P&O North Sea Ferries operates an overnight ferry service between Hull and Zeebrugge.
➤ BOAT AND FERRY INFORMATION: **Hoverspeed** (☎ 44/870–5240241 in the U.K.). **P&O North Sea Ferries** (☎ 0990/980980 in the U.K.; 050/542222 in Europe).

BUS TRAVEL TO AND FROM BRUSSELS
Eurolines operates up to three daily express services from and to Amsterdam, Berlin, Frankfurt, Paris, and London. The Eurolines Coach Station in Brussels adjoins the Gare du Nord.
➤ BUS INFORMATION: **Eurolines** (✉ Pl. de Brouckère 50, ☎ 02/217–0025). **Eurolines Coach Station** (✉ Rue du Progrès 80, ☎ 02/203–0707).

METRO, TRAM, AND BUS TRAVEL WITHIN BRUSSELS
The Métro (subway), trams (streetcars), and buses are parts of a unified system. All are clean and efficient. A single ticket, valid for one hour's travel, costs BF50/€1.25. The best buy is a 10-trip ticket for BF340/€8.50 or a one-day card costing BF130/€3.25. Tickets are sold in metro stations and at newsstands. Single tickets can be purchased on the bus or tram.

CAR TRAVEL
If you use Le Shuttle under the English Channel or a ferry to Calais, note that the E40 (via Oostende and Brugge) connects with the French highway, cutting driving time from Calais to Brussels to under two hours.

EMERGENCIES
Every pharmacy displays a list of pharmacies on duty outside normal hours.
➤ DOCTORS AND DENTISTS: **Doctor/Pharmacy:** Information about all-night and weekend services: ☎ 02/479–1818. **Dentist** (☎ 02/426–1026).
➤ EMERGENCY SERVICES: **Police** (☎ 101). **Ambulance and Fire Brigade** (☎ 100).
➤ HOT LINES: **Lost/Stolen Bank/Credit Cards** (☎ 070/344344). **24-Hour English-Speaking Info and Crisis Line** (☎ 02/648–4014).

ENGLISH-LANGUAGE MEDIA
➤ BOOKSTORES: **The Reading Room** (✉ Av. Georges Henri 503, ☎ 02/734–7917). **Sterling Books** (✉ Rue du Fossé-aux-Loups 38, ☎ 02/223–6223). **Waterstone's** (✉ Bd. Adolphe Max 71–75, ☎ 02/219–2708).

TOURS
BUS TOURS
Half-day English-language coach tours are organized by ARAU, from March through November, including "Brussels 1900: Art Nouveau" (every Sat.) and "Brussels 1930: Art Deco" (every 3rd Sat.). Admission is BF600/€15. Tours begin in front of Hotel Métropole on Place de Brouckère. Chatterbus tours (early June–Sept.) include visits by minibus or on foot to the main sights. De Boeck Sightseeing Tours operates city tours with multilingual cassette commentary. They also conduct tours of Antwerp, the Ardennes, Brugge, Ghent, Ieper, and Waterloo.
➤ FEES AND SCHEDULES: **ARAU** (✉ Bd. Adolphe Max 55, ☎ 02/219–3345 information and reservations). **Chatterbus** (✉ Rue des Thuyas 12, ☎ 02/673–1835). **De Boeck Sightseeing Tours** (✉ Rue de la Colline 8, Grand'Place, ☎ 02/513–7744).

PRIVATE GUIDES
Qualified guides are available for individual tours from the TIB. Three hours costs BF3,200/€79 for up to 20 people.
➤ FEES AND SCHEDULES: **TIB** (☎ 02/513–8940).

WALKING TOURS
Chatterbus organizes visits (early June–September) on foot or by minibus to the main sights and a walking tour with a visit to a bistro. Walking tours organized by the tourist office depart from the Brussels Tourist Office (TIB) in the Town Hall, May–September, Monday–Saturday.

TAXIS
Cabs don't cruise for fares; call Taxis Verts to have one pick you up. Taxis here are among the most expensive in Europe. The tip is included in the fare.
➤ TAXI COMPANIES: **Taxis Verts** (☎ 02/349–4949).

TRAIN TRAVEL

Ten Eurostar passenger trains a day link Brussels's Gare du Midi with London's Waterloo station via the Channel Tunnel in two hours, 40 minutes. A one-way trip costs BF9,750/€242 in business class and from BF5,000/€124 in economy; rail pass holders qualify for 50% discounts. Reservations are required. Check-in is 20 minutes before departure.

All rail services between Brussels and Paris are on Thalys high-speed trains (1 hr, 25 mins). A one-way trip costs BF3,750/€92 ("Confort 1"), BF2,150/€53 ("Confort 2"). Reservations are required.
➤ TRAIN INFORMATION: **Eurostar** (☎ 0900–10366 information; 0900/10–177 telephone sales). **Thalys** (☎ 070/667788 information; 0900/10366 reservations).

TRAVEL AGENCIES

➤ LOCAL AGENT REFERRALS: **American Express** (✉ Houtweg 24, 1170 Brussels, ☎ 02/245–2250). **Carlson Wagonlit Travel** (✉ Bd. Clovis 53, 1040 Brussels, ☎ 02/287–8811).

VISITOR INFORMATION

At Tourist Information Brussels you can buy a Tourist Passport (BF300/€7)—a one-day public transport card and BF2,000/€50 worth of museum admissions and reductions.
➤ TOURIST INFORMATION: **Tourist Information Brussels** (TIB; ✉ Hôtel de Ville, Grand'Place, ☎ 02/513–8940).

Belgium Basics

BUSINESS HOURS

Banks are usually open weekdays 9 AM–4 or 4:30 PM; some close for an hour at lunch. Currency exchange facilities (*bureaux de change* or *wisselkantoren*) are usually open evenings and weekends, but you'll get a better rate in banks during the week. For instant cash, ATMs are nearly everywhere (but not at railway stations) and accept major credit cards. Museums are generally open 10 AM–5 PM Tuesday through Sunday. Many museums will refuse to admit you after 4:15 PM or so. Large stores are open weekdays and Saturday from 9:30 or 10 AM to 6:30 or 7 PM and generally stay open an hour later on Friday. "Night" shops, for newspapers, tobacco, drinks, and limited grocery items, are open seven days a week from 6 PM until dawn.

CUSTOMS AND DUTIES

For details on imports and duty-free limits for visitors from outside the EU, *see* Customs & Duties *in* Smart Travel Tips A to Z.

EMBASSIES

➤ AUSTRALIA: (✉ Rue Guimard 6, 1040 Brussels, ☎ 02/286–0500).
➤ CANADA: (✉ Av. de Tervuren 2, 1040 Brussels, ☎ 02/741–0611).
➤ IRELAND: (✉ Rue Froissart 81, 1040 Brussels, ☎ 02/230–5337).
➤ NEW ZEALAND: (✉ Sq. de Meeus 1, 7/F, 1000 Brussels, ☎ 02/512–1040).
➤ SOUTH AFRICA: (✉ Wetstraat 26, 1000 Brussels, ☎ 02/285–4400).
➤ UNITED KINGDOM: (✉ Rue d'Arlon 85, 1040 Brussels, ☎ 02/287–6211).
➤ UNITED STATES: (✉ Bd. du Régent 25-27, 1000 Brussels, ☎ 02/508–2111).

HOLIDAYS

January 1; Easter Monday; May 1 (Labor Day); June 1 (Ascension); Pentecost or Whit Monday(last Monday in May); July 21 (Belgian National Day); August 15 (Assumption); November 1 (All Saints' Day); November 11 (Armistice Day); December 25.

LANGUAGE

Language is a sensitive subject and exerts an unhealthy influence on politics at the national and regional levels. There are three official languages in Belgium: French, spoken primarily in the south of the country (Wallonia); Dutch, spoken in the north (Flanders); and German, spoken in a small area in the east near the German border. Brussels is bilingual, with both French and Dutch officially recognized, though the majority of residents are francophones. Many people speak English in Brussels and throughout Flanders; in Wallonia, English-speakers tend to be thin on the ground. Belgian French and Dutch both contain slight differences from the corresponding languages spoken in the neighboring countries to the south and north.

MONEY MATTERS

Costs in Brussels are roughly on a par with those in London and New York. All taxes and service charges (tips) are included in hotel and restaurant bills and taxi fares. Gasoline prices are steep, but highways are toll-free.

Cup of coffee in a café, BF50/€1.25–BF60/€1.50; a glass of draft beer, BF50/€1.25–BF70/€1.75; a glass of wine, about BF120/€2.97. A single bus/metro/tram ride BF50/€1.24.

CURRENCY

Belgium, as one of the euro zone currency countries, will introduce euro (€) notes and coins on January 1, 2002. The euro and the Belgian franc (BF) will circulate simultaneously through February 2002. Banks and ATMs will give all money in euros. Shops and restaurants are encouraged to give change in euros whenever possible. Prices are marked in both euros and Belgian francs. In Belgian francs there are bills of 100, 200, 500, 1,000, 2,000, and 10,000 francs and coins of 1, 5, 20, and 50 francs. At press time (summer 2001), the exchange rate was BF42.66 to the U.S. dollar, BF28.94 to the Canadian dollar, BF64.03 to the pound sterling, BF51.22 to the Irish punt, BF25.57 to the Australian dollar, BF20.20 to the New Zealand dollar, BF6.17 to the South African rand, and BF40.34 to the euro.

TELEPHONES

COUNTRY AND AREA CODES

The country code for Belgium is 32. Under a new dialing procedure, all calls within the country must include the regional telephone code. When dialing Belgium from outside the country, drop the first zero in the regional code.

INTERNATIONAL CALLS

Buy a high-denomination telecard and make a direct call from a phone booth. For credit card and collect calls, dial AT&T, MCI Worldphone, or Sprint Global One.

➤ ACCESS CODES: **AT&T** (☎ 0800–10010). **MCI Worldphone** (☎ 0800–10012). **Sprint Global One** (☎ 0800–10014).

PUBLIC PHONES

Pay phones work mostly with telecards, available at post offices, supermarkets, railway stations, and many newsstands. Cards are sold in denominations of BF200, BF500, and BF1,000. An average local call costs BF20. Coin-operated phones (on the platforms of metro stations) take 5- and 20-franc coins. All telephone numbers must be preceded by their area code prefix, regardless of the location.

BUDAPEST

Budapest, lying on both banks of the Danube, unites the hills of Buda and the wide boulevards of Pest. It was the site of a Roman outpost in the 1st century, and the modern city was not created until 1873, when the towns of Óbuda, Pest, and Buda were joined. The resulting capital is the cultural, political, intellectual, and commercial heart of the nation; for the 20% of the nation's population who live here, anywhere else is just "the country."

Much of the charm of a visit to Budapest consists of unexpected glimpses into shadowy courtyards and long vistas down sunlit cobbled streets. Although some 30,000 buildings were destroyed during World War II and in 1956, the past lingers on in the often crumbling architectural details of the antique structures that remain and in the memories and lifestyles of Budapest's citizens.

EXPLORING BUDAPEST

The principal sights of the city fall roughly into three areas, each of which can be comfortably covered on foot. The Budapest hills are best explored using public transportation. Many street names have been changed since 1989 to purge all reminders of the Communist regime—you can sometimes still see the old name, negated with a victorious red *x*, next to the new. The 22 districts of Budapest are referred to in addresses with Roman numerals, starting with I for the Várhegy (Castle Hill) district; V, VI, and VII indicate the main downtown areas.

Várhegy

Numbers in the margin correspond to points of interest on the Budapest map.

Most of Buda's main sights are on Várhegy (Castle Hill), a long, narrow plateau laced with cobblestone streets, clustered with beautifully preserved Baroque, Gothic, and Renaissance houses and crowned by the stately Royal Palace. Painstaking reconstruction work has been in progress here since the area was nearly leveled during World War II.

❺ Hadtörténeti Múzeum (Museum of Military History). The collection here includes uniforms and regalia, many belonging to the Hungarian generals who took part in the abortive uprising against Austrian rule in 1848. Other exhibits trace the military history of Hungary from the original Magyar conquest in the 9th century up to the middle of the 20th century. English-language tours can be arranged in advance. ⊠ *I, Tóth Árpád sétány 40,* ☎ *1/356–9522,* 🌐 *www.militaria.hu.* ☉ *Apr.– Sept., Tues.–Sun. 10–6; Oct.–Mar., Tues.–Sun. 10–4.*

★ ❸ Halászbástya (Fishermen's Bastion). This wondrous porch overlooking Pest and the Danube was built at the turn of the 20th century as a lookout tower to protect what was once a thriving fishing settlement. Its neo-Romanesque columns and arches frame views over the city and the river. ⊠ *I, behind Mátyás templom.*

★ ❶ Királyi Palota (Royal Palace, also known as Buda Castle). The Nazis made their final stand here and left it a blackened wasteland. Under the rubble archaeologists discovered the medieval foundations of the palace of King Matthias Corvinus, who, in the 15th century, presided over one of the most splendid courts in Europe. The rebuilt palace is now a vast museum complex and cultural center. ⊠ *I, south of Szent György tér.*

In the castle's northern wing, the **Ludwig Múzeum** (Ludwig Museum) houses a collection of more than 200 pieces of Hungarian and contemporary world art, including works by Picasso and Lichtenstein. ⊠ *I, Buda Castle (Wing A), Dísz tér 17,* ☎ *1/375–7533.* ☉ *Tues.–Sun. 10–6.*

The central section of the palace houses the **Magyar Nemzeti Galéria** (Hungarian National Gallery), which exhibits a wide range of Hungarian fine art. Names to look for are Munkácsy, a 19th-century Romantic painter, and Csontváry, an early Surrealist admired by Picasso. Tours for up to five people with an English-speaking guide can be booked in advance. ⊠ *I, Buda Castle (Wing C), Dísz tér 17,* ☎ *1/375–7533; 1/224–3700 Ext. 423 for tours.* ☉ *Mid-Mar.–Nov., Tues.–Sun. 10–6; Dec.–mid-Mar., Tues.–Sun. 10–4.*

The **Budapesti Történeti Múzeum** (Budapest History Museum), the southern block of the palace, displays a permanent exhibit of the city's history from Buda's liberation from the Turks in 1686 through the 1970s. The 19th- and 20th-century photos and videos of the castle, the Chain Bridge, and other Budapest monuments can provide a helpful orientation to the city. Down in the cellars are the original medieval vaults of the palace, a palace chapel, and more royal relics. ⊠ *I, Buda Castle (Wing E), Szt. György tér 2,* ☎ *1/375–7533,* 🌐 *www.btm.hu.* ☉ *Mar.–mid-May and mid-Sept.–Oct., Wed.–Mon. 10–6; mid-May–mid-Sept., daily 10–6; Nov.–Feb., Wed.–Mon. 10–4.*

★ ❷ Mátyás templom (Matthias Church). This venerable church with its distinctive roof of colored, diamond-pattern tiles and skeletal Gothic spire dates from the 13th century. Built as a mosque by the Turks, it was destroyed and reconstructed during the 19th century, only to be bombed during World War II. Only the south porch survives from the original structure. The Habsburg emperors were crowned kings of Hungary here. High mass is held every Sunday at 10 AM with an orchestra and choir, and organ concerts are often held in the summer on Friday at 8 PM. Visitors are asked to remain at the back of the church during services (it's least intrusive to come after 9:30 AM weekdays and between 1 PM and 5 PM Sunday and holidays). ⊠ *I, Szentháromság tér 2,* ☎ *1/355–5657.* ☉ *Church daily 7 AM–8 PM, treasury daily 9:30–5:30.*

❹ **Zenetörténeti Múzeum** (Museum of Music History). The handsome, 18th-century gray-stone palace that once belonged to the noble Erdődy family hosts intimate recitals of classical music and displays rare manuscripts and antique instruments. ✉ *I, Táncsics Mihály u. 7,* ☎ *1/214–6770.* ⊙ *Mid-Mar.–mid-Nov., Tues.–Fri. 10–5, Sat.–Sun. 10–6.*

The Heart of the City

Pest fans out from the Belváros (Inner City), which is bounded by the Kiskörút (Little Ring Road). The Nagykörút (Grand Ring Road) describes a wider semicircle from the Margaret Bridge to the Petőfi Bridge.

⓫ **Belvárosi plébánia templom** (Inner-City Parish Church). The oldest church in Pest dates from the 12th century. It incorporates a succession of Western architectural styles and preserves a Muslim prayer niche from the time when the Turks ruled the country. Liszt, who lived only a few yards away, often played the organ here. ✉ *V, Március 15 tér 2.*

★ **Korzó.** This elegant promenade runs south along the Pest side of the river, providing views of Castle Hill, the Chain Bridge, and Gellért Hill on the other side of the Danube. ✉ *V, from Eötvös tér to Március 15 tér.*

★ ⓱ **Magyar Állami Operaház** (Hungarian State Opera House). Flanked by a pair of marble sphinxes, this 19th-century neo-Renaissance treasure was the crowning achievement of architect Miklós Ybl. It has been restored to its original ornate glory—particularly inside. ✉ *VI, Andrássy út 22,* ☎ *1/331–2550; 1/332–8197 for tours,* 🌐 *www.opera.hu. Foreign-language tours (45 mins) daily at 3 PM and 4 PM; meet at the Sphinx statue in front of opera house on right-hand side.*

⓬ **Magyar Nemzeti Múzeum** (Hungarian National Museum). The stern, classical edifice was built between 1837 and 1847. On its steps, on March 15, 1848, Petőfi Sándor recited his revolutionary poem, "Nemzeti Dal" ("National Song"), declaring "By the God of Magyar,/ Do we swear,/ Do we swear, chains no longer/ Will we wear." This poem, along with the "12 Points," a formal list of political demands by young Hungarians, called upon the people to rise up against the Habsburgs. Celebrations of the national holiday—long banned by the Communist regime—are now held here (and throughout the city) every year on March 15. A host of royal relics can be seen in the domed Hall of Honor. The museum's epic Hungarian history exhibition includes displays chronicling the end of Communism and the much-celebrated exodus of the Russian troops. ✉ *IX, Múzeum körút 14–16,* ☎ *1/338–2122,* 🌐 *www.hnm.hu.* ⊙ *Mid-Mar.–mid-Oct., Tues.–Sun. 10–6; mid-Oct.–mid-Mar., Tues.–Sun. 10–5.*

⓾ **Március 15 tér** (March 15 Square). This square is not particularly picturesque, but it commemorates the 1848 struggle for independence from the Habsburgs with a statue of the poet Petőfi Sándor, who died in a later uprising. On March 15, the national holiday commemorating the revolution, the square is packed with patriotic Hungarians. ✉ *V, end of Apácai Csere János u. just north of Erzsébet Bridge.*

★ ⓭ **Nagy Zsinagóga** (Great Synagogue). Europe's largest synagogue was built between 1844 and 1859 in a Byzantine-Moorish style. Desecrated by German and Hungarian Nazis, it underwent years of massive restorations, completed in the fall of 1996. Liszt and Saint-Saëns are among the great musicians who once played the synagogue's grand organ. ✉ *VII, Dohány u. 2–8,* ☎ *1/342–1335.* ⊙ *Mid-Mar.–Nov., Mon.–Thurs. 10–5, Fri. 10–3, Sun. 10–1. Closed Jewish holidays.*

★ ⓯ **Néprajzi Múzeum** (Museum of Ethnography). Elegant both inside and out, this museum has impressive, exhaustive exhibits—captioned in En-

100

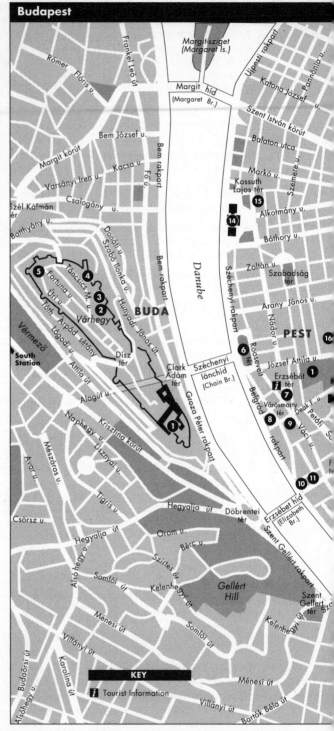

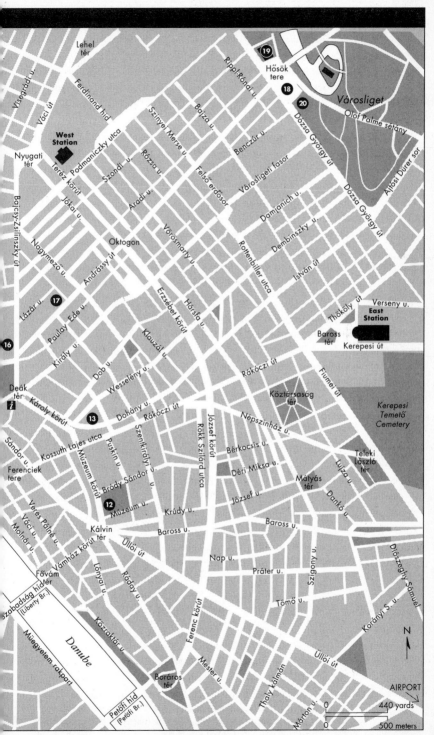

Lehel
tér

Visegrád u.

Váci út

Ferdinánd híd

Rippl-Rónai u.

19

Hősök
tere

18

20

Városliget

Olof Palme sétány

Szinyei Merse u.

Bajza u.

Benczúr u.

Dózsa György út

Dózsa György út

Aitosi Dürer sor

**West
Station**

Podmaniczky utca

Szondi u.

Rózsa u.

Felső erdősor

Városligeti fasor

Nyugati
tér

Teréz körút

Jókai u.

Aradi u.

Damjanich u.

Dembinszky u.

Bajcsy-Zsilinszky út

Nagymező u.

Oktogon

Andrássy út

Vörösmarty u.

Rottenbiller utca

István út

Lázár u.

17

Paulay Ede u.

Erzsébet körút

Hársfa u.

Thököly út

Verseny u.

**East
Station**

16

Király u.

Dob u.

Wesselényi u.

Klauzál u.

Rákóczi út

Fiumei út

Baross
tér

Kerepesi út

Deák
tér

7

Károly körút

13

Dohány u.

Rákóczi út

Köztársaság
tér

Népszínház u.

Kerepesi
Temető
Cemetery

Sándor u.

Kossuth Lajos utca

Múzeum körút

Puskin u.

Szentkirály u.

Rökk Szilárd utca

József körút

Bérkocsis u.

Déri Miksa u.

Mátyás
tér

Luzsa u.

Dankó u.

Teleki
László
tér

Ferenciek
tere

Brody Sándor u.

12

Múzeum u.

Krúdy u.

József u.

Baross u.

Veres Pálné u.

Váci u.

Molnár u.

Kálvin
tér

Vámház körút

Lónyai u.

Üllői út

Baross u.

Nap u.

Práter u.

Szigony u.

Diószeghy Samuel

Korányi S. u.

Fővám
híd

Ráday u.

Ferenc körút

Tömő u.

N

Szabadság híd
(Liberty Br.)

Műegyetem rakpart

Danube

Közraktár u.

Boráros
tér

Mester u.

Thaly Kálmán u.

Üllői út

AIRPORT

Morton u.

Petőfi híd
(Petőfi Br.)

0   440 yards

0   500 meters

glish—of folk costumes and traditions. ⊠ *V, Kossuth Lajos tér 12,* ☎ *1/332–6340,* WEB *www.neprajz.hu.* ⊙ *Mar.–Oct., Tues.–Sun. 10–6; Nov.–Feb., Tues.–Sun. 10–5.*

⑭ Országház (Parliament). The riverfront's most striking landmark is the imposing neo-Gothic Parliament, now minus the red star on top, designed by Imre Steindl. Although it is still a workplace for the nation's legislators, the interior can now be seen during regular guided tours that show off the gilded cathedral ceilings, frescoed walls, intricate glass windows, and majestic stairways (of which there are some 20 km in the building!). The highlight is the nation's Holy Crown, made for Hungary's first king, St. Stephen, 1,000 years ago. The crown, Hungary's national symbol, was relocated from the National Museum and now rests on a velvet pillow flanked by two sword-wielding uniformed guards under Parliament's soaring central cupola. One-hour tours in English are held daily at 10 and 2. Purchase tickets at Gate X, to the right of the main entrance steps. You are advised to arrive at least a half-hour early. ⊠ *V, Kossuth Lajos tér,* ☎ *1/441–4904 or 1/441–4415,* WEB *www.mkogy.hu.* ⊙ *Weekdays 8–6, Sat. 8–4, Sun. 8–2.*

❻ Roosevelt tér (Roosevelt Square). On this picturesque square opening onto the Danube you'll find the 19th-century neoclassical **Magyar Tudományos Akadémia** (Hungarian Academy of Sciences) and the 1907 **Gresham Palota** (Gresham Palace), a crumbling tribute to the age of Art Nouveau currently undergoing massive renovations and eventually to become a Four Seasons hotel. ⊠ *V, at Pest end of Széchenyi lánchíd (Chain Bridge).*

★ Széchenyi lánchíd (Chain Bridge). The most beautiful of the Danube's eight bridges, the Széchenyi lánchíd was built twice: once in the 19th century and again after it was destroyed by the Nazis. ⊠ *Spanning the Danube between I, Clark Ádám tér, and V, Roosevelt tér.*

⑯ Szent István Bazilika (St. Stephen's Basilica). Dark and massive, the 19th-century basilica is one of the landmarks of Pest. It was planned early in the 19th century as a neoclassical building, but by the time it was completed more than 50 years later, it was decidedly neo-Renaissance. The mummified right hand of St. Stephen, Hungary's first king and patron saint, is preserved in the Szent Jobb Chapel; the guard will illuminate it for you for a minimal charge. A climb up to the cupola (or a lift on the elevator) affords a sweeping city view. Restorations are under way, with a target completion date of 2005, so some part of the structure is likely to be under scaffolding when you visit. ⊠ *V, Szt. István tér,* ☎ *1/317–2859.* ⊙ *Church Mon.–Sat. 7–7, Sun 1–7. Szt. Jobb Chapel Apr.–Sept., Mon.–Sat. 9–5; Oct.–Mar., Mon.–Sat. 10–4. Cupola mid-Apr.–Oct., daily 10–5.*

❾ Váci utca (Váci Street). Lined with expensive boutiques and dozens of souvenir shops, this pedestrian-only thoroughfare is Budapest's most upscale shopping street and one of its most kitschy tourist areas. Váci utca stretches south of Kossuth Lajos utca, making the total length extend from Vörösmarty tér to the Szabadság Bridge. ⊠ *V, south from Vörösmarty tér.*

❽ Vigadó tér (Vigadó Square). This square, opening onto a grand Danube view, is named for the **Vigadó concert hall.** The hall was built in an eclectic mix of Byzantine, Moorish, and Romanesque styles; the facade even draws upon the ceremonial knots from the uniforms of the Hungarian hussars. Liszt, Brahms, and Bartók all performed here. Completely destroyed during World War II, it has been faithfully rebuilt. ⊠ *V, off the Korzó, between Vigadó u. and Deák Ferenc u.*

❼ Vörösmarty tér (Vörösmarty Square). In this handsome square in the heart of the Inner City, street musicians and sidewalk cafés combine to make one of the liveliest, albeit sometimes too touristy, atmospheres in Budapest. It's a great spot to sit and relax—but prepare to be approached by caricature artists and money changers. ⊠ *V, at northern end of Váci u.*

Hősök tere and Városliget

Heroes' Square is the gateway to Városliget (City Park): a square km (almost ½ square mi) of recreation, entertainment, nature, and culture.

⑱ Hősök tere (Heroes' Square). Budapest's grandest boulevard, Andrássy út, ends at this sweeping piazza flanked by the Szépművészeti Múzeum and the Műcsarnok. In the center stands the 120-ft bronze **Millenniumi Emlékmű** (Millennium Monument), begun in 1896 to commemorate the 1,000th anniversary of the Magyar Conquest. Statues of Árpád and six other founders of the Magyar nation occupy the base of the monument, while Hungary's greatest rulers and princes stand between the columns on either side. ⊠ *VI, Andrássy út at Dózsa György út.*

⑳ Műcsarnok (Palace of Exhibitions). This striking 1895 structure on Heroes' Square schedules exhibitions of contemporary Hungarian and international art and a rich series of films, plays, and concerts. ⊠ *XIV, Dózsa György út 37,* ☎ *1/343–7401,* WEB *www.mucsarnok.hu.* ☉ *Tues.–Sun. 10–6.*

⑲ Szépművészeti Múzeum (Fine Arts Museum). An entire section of this Heroes' Square museum is devoted to Egyptian, Greek, and Roman artifacts, including many rare Greco-Roman ceramics. The institution's collection of Spanish paintings is among the best of its kind outside Spain. Some wings are undergoing long-term renovation and may be closed when you visit. ⊠ *XIV, Dózsa György út 41,* ☎ *1/343–9759,* WEB *www.szepmuveszeti.hu.* ☉ *Tues.–Sun. 10–5:30.*

★ Városliget (City Park). Just behind Heroes' Square, this park harbors Budapest's zoo, the state circus, an amusement park, and the outdoor swimming pool of the Széchenyi mineral baths. Inside is **Vajdahunyad Vár** (Vajdahunyad Castle), an art historian's Disneyland, created for the millennial celebration in 1896 and incorporating architectural elements typical of various periods of Hungary's history all in one complex. ⊠ *XIV, between Dózsa György út and Hungária körút, and Vágány u. and Ajtósi Dürer sor.*

Elsewhere in the City

Aquincum. The reconstructed remains of the capital of the Roman province of Pannonia, dating from the 1st century AD, lie in northern Budapest's Óbuda district. A varied selection of artifacts and mosaics has been unearthed, giving a tantalizing inkling of what life was like on the northern fringes of the Roman empire. The on-site **Aquincum Museum** displays the dig's most notable finds. ⊠ *III, Szentendrei út 139,* ☎ *1/250–1650.* ☉ *Mid-Apr.–late Apr. and Oct., Tues.–Sun. 10– 5; May–Sept., Tues.–Sun. 10–6. Grounds open at 9.*

Jánoshegy (János Hill). A *libegő* (chairlift) will take you to the summit, the highest point in Budapest, where you can climb a lookout tower for the best view of the city. ⊠ *Take Bus 158 from Moszkva tér to last stop, Zugligeti út,* ☎ *1/200–9993 or 1/394–3764.* ☉ *Mid-May–mid-Sept., daily 9–5; mid-Sept.–mid-May (depending on weather), daily 9:30– 4. Closed alternate Mon.*

Szobor Park (Statue Park). For a look at Budapest's too-recent Iron Curtain past, make the 30-minute drive out to this open-air exhibit clev-

erly nicknamed "Tons of Socialism." Forty-two Communist statues and
memorials that once dominated the city have been exiled here since
the political changes in 1989. You can wander among mammoth figures of Lenin and Marx while listening to songs from the Hungarian
and Russian workers' movement blaring from loudspeakers. To get here
by public transport, take the yellow Volánbus from stall 6 at Kosztolányi
Dezső tér. ⊠ *XXII, Balatoni út, corner of Szabadkai út,* ☎ FAX *1/227–
7446,* WEB *www.szoborpark.hu.* ⊙ *Daily 10–dusk.*

DINING

Private restaurateurs are breathing excitement into the Budapest dining scene. You can choose from Chinese, Mexican, Italian, French, Indian, or various other cuisines—there are even vegetarian restaurants.
Or you can stick to solid, traditional Hungarian fare. Be sure to check
out the less expensive spots favored by locals. If you get a craving for
sushi or tortellini, consult the restaurant listings in the *Budapest Sun,
Where Budapest* magazine, and *Budapest in Your Pocket.*

Prices in Budapest tend to be a good 30% higher than elsewhere in
Hungary.

CATEGORY	COST*
$$$$	over 3,500 Ft.
$$$	2,500 Ft.–3,500 Ft.
$$	1,500 Ft.–2,500 Ft.
$	under 1,500 Ft.

per person for a main course at dinner

$$$$ ✕ **Gundel.** George Lang, Hungary's best-known restaurateur, show-
★   cases his country's cuisine at this turn-of-the-20th-century palazzo in
City Park. Dark-wood paneling, rich navy-blue and pink fabrics, and
tables set with Zsolnay porcelain make the oversize dining room plush
and handsome. Violinist György Lakatos, of the Lakatos Gypsy mu-
sician dynasty, strolls from table to table playing folk music. Waiters
in black tie serve traditional favorites such as tender beef tournedos
topped with goose liver and forest mushroom sauce or excellent fish
specialties. ⊠ *XIV, Állatkerti út 2,* ☎ *1/321–3550. Reservations essential. AE, DC, MC, V. Closed daily 4–6:30.*

$$$$ ✕ **Vadrózsa.** This restaurant in a romantic old villa in Buda's exclusive Rózsadomb district is elegant to the last detail—even the service
is white glove—and the garden is delightful in summer. Kitchen fortes
include venison and a variety of grilled fish; the house specialty is grilled
goose liver. ⊠ *II, Pentelei Molnár u. 15,* ☎ *1/326–5817. Reservations
essential. AE, DC, MC, V. Closed daily 3–7.*

$$$–$$$$ ✕ **Múzeum.** Named for its location just steps from the National Mu-
seum, this elegant salon with mirrors, mosaics, and swift waiters serves
authentic Hungarian cuisine with a lighter touch. The salads are fresh,
the Hungarian wines excellent, and the chef dares to be creative. ⊠
VIII, Múzeum körút 12, ☎ *1/267–0375. DC, MC, V. Closed Sun.*

$$–$$$$ ✕ **Kacsa.** Hungarian and international dishes with a focus on duck are
done with a light touch, with quiet chamber music in the background,
in this small, celebrated restaurant just a few steps from the river. Try the
crisp wild duck stuffed with plums. ⊠ *II, Fő u. 75,* ☎ *1/201–9992. Reservations essential. AE, DC, MC, V. Closed daily 3–6. No lunch weekends.*

$$–$$$ ✕ **Lou Lou.** Since it opened in 1995, this convivial bistro tucked onto
★   a side street near the Danube has been the hottest restaurant in Budapest. Framed prints, low lighting, and candles conjure a tasteful, elegantly romantic atmosphere. Blending local and Continental cuisines,
the menu includes excellent rack of lamb and succulent fresh salmon

with lemongrass. ⊠ *V, Vigyázó Ferenc u. 4,* ☎ *1/312–4505. Reservations essential. AE. Closed daily 3–6:30 and Sun. No lunch Sat.*

$$–$$$ ✕ **Művészinas.** This bustling, bistrolike restaurant in the heart of Pest has a romantic, old-world ambience. Dozens of Hungarian specialties fill the long menu, from sirloin "Budapest style" (smothered in a goose liver, mushrooms, and sweet-pepper ragout) to spinach-stuffed turkey breast in fragrant garlic sauce. Crepes with a seasonal fruit sauce are a sublime dessert. ⊠ *VI, Bajcsy-Zsilinszky út 9,* ☎ *1/268–1439. Reservations essential. AE, MC, V.*

$$ ✕ **Bagolyvár.** George Lang opened this restaurant next door to his gastronomic palace, Gundel, in 1993. The immaculate dining room with soaring beamed ceilings has a familial yet professional atmosphere, and the kitchen produces first-rate daily menus of home-style Hungarian specialties. Soups are particularly good. Musicians entertain with cimbalom (gypsy dulcimer) music nightly from 7 PM. In warm weather there is outdoor dining on a roomy back patio. ⊠ *VI, Állatkerti körút 2,* ☎ *1/343–0217. AE, DC, MC, V.*

$$ ✕ **Kisbuda Gyöngye.** This Budapest favorite, hidden away on a small street in Óbuda, is filled with mixed antique furniture, and its walls are covered with a patchwork of antique carved wooden cupboard doors. Try the fresh trout smothered in cream sauce with mushrooms and capers. ⊠ *III, Kenyeres u. 34,* ☎ *1/368–6402 or 1/368–9246. Reservations essential. AE, DC, MC, V. Closed Sun.*

$–$$ ✕ **Café Kör.** Vaulted ceilings, low lighting, and wood floors with
★ Oriental-style rugs render a warm and classy atmosphere. Service is excellent. The kitchen has won tremendous popularity for its lighter touch on Hungarian and Continental meat dishes and ample salads. The Kör appetizer platter, generously piled with pâtés, Brie, vegetables, goose liver, salmon, and more, is perfect for sharing. Avoid the tables by the bathroom doors and immediately at the entrance. ⊠ *V, Sas u. 17,* ☎ *1/311–0053. Reservations essential. No credit cards. Closed Sun.*

$–$$ ✕ **Náncsi Néni.** "Aunt Nancy's" out-of-the-way restaurant is irre-
★ sistibly cozy. The dining room feels like a country kitchen: chains of paprikas and garlic dangle from the low wooden ceiling, and shelves along the walls are crammed with jars of home-pickled vegetables. On the Hungarian menu (large portions!), turkey dishes are given a creative flair, such as breast fillets stuffed with apples, peaches, mushrooms, cheese, and sour cream. Special touches include an outdoor garden in summer and free champagne for all couples in love. Reservations are recommended. ⊠ *II, Ördögárok út 80,* ☎ *1/397–2742. MC, V.*

$ ✕ **Tüköry Söröző.** At this traditional Hungarian spot, carnivores can sample the beefsteak tartare, topped with a raw egg; many say it's the best in town. ⊠ *V, Hold u. 15,* ☎ *1/269–5027. AE, MC, V. Closed weekends.*

LODGING

Some 30 million tourists come to Hungary every year, and the boom has encouraged hotel building; several major new luxury properties are currently under construction in Budapest's best locales. If you arrive in Budapest without a reservation, go to the 24-hour Tribus Hotel Service or to one of the tourist offices at any of the train stations or at the airport.

The following price categories are for a double room with bath, including VAT but not breakfast, during the peak season; rates are markedly lower off-season and in the countryside, sometimes under $20 for two. For single rooms with bath, count on about 80% of the double-room rate. As most large hotels require payment in hard currency, rates are given in dollars below.

During the peak season (June–August), full board may be compulsory at some of the Lake Balaton hotels, although this is increasingly rare. During the off-season (in Budapest, September–March; at Lake Balaton and the Danube Bend, May and September), rates can be considerably lower than those given above and are frequently negotiable.

CATEGORY	COST*
$$$$	over $200
$$$	$140–$200
$$	$80–$140
$	under $80

Prices are for two persons sharing a double room, including VAT.

$$$$ ⊡ **Budapest Hilton.** Built in 1977 around a 13th-century monastery ad-
★ jacent to the Matthias Church, this perfectly integrated architectural wonder overlooks the Danube from the best site on Castle Hill. Every ample
room has a remarkable view. Service is of the highest caliber. ⊠ *I, Hess
András tér 1–3, H-1014,* ☎ *1/488–6600; 800/445–8667 in U.S. and
Canada,* 𝔽𝔸𝕏 *1/488–6688,* 𝚆𝙴𝙱 *www.danubiusgroup.com/hilton. 295
rooms, 27 suites. 3 restaurants, air-conditioning. AE, DC, MC, V.*

$$$$ ⊡ **Hotel Inter-Continental Budapest.** Formerly the Forum Hotel, this
★ boxy, modern riverside hotel consistently wins applause for its superior business facilities, friendly service, and gorgeous views across the
Danube to Castle Hill. Sixty percent of the rooms face the river (and
are slightly more expensive than those that don't). The hotel café, Bécsi
Kávéház, is locally renowned for its pastries—and the fitness facilities are similarly excellent. ⊠ *V, Apáczai Csere János u. 12–14,
H-1368,* ☎ *1/327–6333 or 800/327–0200 (in the U.S.),* 𝔽𝔸𝕏 *1/327–
6357,* 𝚆𝙴𝙱 *www.interconti.com. 382 rooms, 16 suites. 2 restaurants,
air-conditioning, pool. AE, DC, MC, V.*

$$$$ ⊡ **Kempinski Hotel Corvinus Budapest.** Afternoon chamber music sets
★ the tone at this sleek luxury hotel. Rooms are spacious, with elegant contemporary decor accented by geometric blond-and-black Swedish inlaid
woods. The large, sparkling bathrooms are the best in Budapest. ⊠ *V,
Erzsébet tér 7–8, H-1051,* ☎ *1/429–3777; 800/426–3135 in the U.S.
and Canada,* 𝔽𝔸𝕏 *1/429–4777,* 𝚆𝙴𝙱 *www.kempinski-budapest.com. 340
rooms, 29 suites. 4 restaurants, air-conditioning, pool. AE, DC, MC, V.*

$$$$ ⊡ **Le Meridien Budapest.** From Persian carpets and heavy silk draperies
★ in the hushed lobby to polished walnut surfaces and twinkling chandeliers in the guest rooms, refined Old World elegance is everywhere.
In a 1913 historic landmark building in the heart of downtown Pest,
this five-star hotel is well situated for business as well as sightseeing.
Breakfast and afternoon high tea are served under the lobby's soaring stained-glass cupola. ⊠ *V, Erzsébet tér 9–10, H-1051,* ☎ *1/429–
5500; 800/225–5843 in the U.S. and Canada,* 𝔽𝔸𝕏 *1/429–5555,* 𝚆𝙴𝙱
*www.lemeridien-hotels.com. 192 rooms, 26 suites. Restaurant, air-
conditioning, pool. AE, DC, MC, V.*

$$$ ⊡ **art'otel.** A short walk up the Danube from the Chain Bridge, this
hip new boutique hotel is the first of its kind in Budapest. Like its sib-
ling properties in Berlin and Dresden, the hotel-cum-gallery is completely
dedicated to the work of a single artist—in this case, American Don-
ald Sultan. From the carpets to the paintings, the teacups to the
bathrobes, the entire hotel is decorated with Sultan's designs. Inter-
connecting a new building and four 18th-century Baroque houses on
the Buda riverfront, the art'otel adroitly blends old and new. Sleek con-
temporary furniture contrasts elegantly with restored original mold-
ings and doorframes in the older buildings' rooms. Rates include
breakfast. ⊠ *I, Bem rakpart 16–19, H-1011,* ☎ *1/487–9487,* 𝔽𝔸𝕏 *1/
487–9488,* 𝚆𝙴𝙱 *www.parkplazaww.com. 156 rooms, 9 suites. Restau-
rant, air-conditioning. AE, DC, MC, V.*

$$$ ⊞ **Budapest Marriott.** At this sophisticated yet friendly hotel near downtown Pest, every detail sparkles, including the marble floors and dark-wood paneling in the lobby. Stunning vistas open from every guest room, the ballroom, and even the outstanding fitness room. Most rooms have a balcony. ⊠ *V, Apáczai Csere János u. 4, H-1052,* ☎ *1/266–7000; 800/228–9290 in U.S. and Canada,* FAX *1/266–5000,* WEB *www.marriotthotels.com/BUDHU. 351 rooms, 11 suites. 3 restaurants, air-conditioning. AE, DC, MC, V.*

$$$ ⊞ **Danubius Grand Hotel.** Set on a car-free island in the Danube and connected to a bubbling thermal spa (free for guests), the Danubius (formerly Ramada) Grand feels removed from the city but is still only a short taxi or bus ride away. This venerable hotel, built in 1873, has been completely modernized, yet retains its period look, with high ceilings and Old World furnishings. Room prices include breakfast. ⊠ *XIII, Margit-sziget, H-1138,* ☎ *1/452–6200; 1/452–6251 reservations,* FAX *1/452–6262,* WEB *www.danubiusgroup.com/grand. 154 rooms, 10 suites. Restaurant, pool. AE, DC, MC, V.*

$$$ ⊞ **Danubius Hotel Gellért.** Built in 1918 in the Jugendstil (Art Nouveau style), this grand old lady with its double-deck rotunda sits regally at the foot of Gellért Hill. One of Hungary's most prized spa hotels, it also houses ornate thermal baths—free to guests. Rooms range from palatial suites to tiny spaces and have either early 20th-century furnishings or newer, more basic contemporary decor. Rooms that face the building's inner core are drastically less expensive but cramped and viewless. The Gellért has begun an ambitious overhaul, adding air-conditioning and refurnishing all rooms in the mood of the building's original style. Inquire about completed rooms when you reserve. Breakfast is included in the room rates. ⊠ *XI, Gellért tér 1, H-1111,* ☎ *1/385–2200,* FAX *1/466–6631,* WEB *www.danubiusgroup.com/gellert. 220 rooms, 13 suites. Restaurant, 2 pools. AE, DC, MC, V.*

$$ ⊞ **Astoria.** Revolutionaries and intellectuals once gathered in the marble-and-gilt Art Deco lobby here. Rooms are Empire-style and renovations have not obscured their charm. In fact, the addition of soundproofing was essential, as the Astoria stands at a busy downtown intersection. Breakfast is included. ⊠ *V, Kossuth Lajos u. 19–21, H-1053,* ☎ *1/317–3411,* FAX *1/318–6798,* WEB *www.danubiusgroup.com/astoria. 124 rooms, 5 suites. Restaurant. AE, DC, MC, V.*

$$ ⊞ **Carlton Budapest.** Tucked into an alleyway at the foot of Castle Hill, this spotless, modern hotel (formerly the Alba Hotel) is a short walk via the Chain Bridge from business and shopping districts. Rooms are snug and quiet, with white and pale-gray contemporary decor and quintessentially Budapestian views over rooftops and chimneys. A buffet breakfast is included in the room price. ⊠ *I, Apor Péter u. 3, H-1011,* ☎ *1/224–0999,* FAX *1/224–0990. 50 rooms with bath, 45 with shower. Air-conditioning. AE, DC, MC, V.*

$$ ⊞ **Victoria.** The stately Parliament building is visible from every room ★ of this intimate establishment right on the Danube. The absence of conventioneers is a plus, and the location—an easy walk from Castle Hill and downtown Pest—couldn't be better. Room rates include breakfast. ⊠ *I, Bem rakpart 11, H-1011,* ☎ *1/457–8080,* FAX *1/457–8088,* WEB *www.victoria.hu. 27 rooms, 1 suite. AE, DC, MC, V.*

$ ⊞ **Kulturinnov.** One wing of a magnificent 1902 neo-Baroque castle ★ now houses basic budget accommodations. Rooms come with two or three beds and are clean and peaceful; breakfast is included in the rates. The neighborhood—one of Budapest's most famous squares in the luxurious castle district—is magical. ⊠ *I, Szentháromság tér 6, H-1014,* ☎ *1/355–0122,* FAX *1/375–1886. 16 rooms. AE, DC, MC, V.*

$ ⊞ **Molnár Panzió.** Fresh air, peace, and quiet reign at this immaculate guest house high above Buda on Széchenyi Hill. Rooms in the octagonal main house are polyhedral, clean, and bright; most have distant views of Castle Hill and Gellért Hill, and some have balconies. Twelve rooms in a building next door are more private and have superior bathrooms. Service is friendly and professional, and the restaurant is first rate. A Finnish sauna and garden setting add to the pension's appeal. ⊠ *XII, Fodor u. 143, H-1124,* ☎ *1/395–1873 or 1/395–1874,* ☎ FAX *1/395–1872,* WEB *www.hotel-molnar.hu. 23 rooms. Restaurant. AE, DC, MC, V.*

NIGHTLIFE AND THE ARTS

The Arts

The English-language *Budapest Sun* lists some of the week's entertainment and cultural events. *Where Budapest,* free in most hotels, is a slightly richer source. Hotels and tourist offices distribute the monthly *Programme,* which contains details of all cultural events in the city. Buy tickets at venue box offices, your hotel desk, many tourist offices, or ticket agencies. For music in Budapest, try the **National Philharmonic Ticket Office** (⊠ V, Mérleg u. 10, ☎ 1/318–0281). For various cultural events in Budapest, contact the **Vigadó Ticket Office** (⊠ V, Vörösmarty tér 1, ☎ 1/327–4322).

Arts festivals begin to fill the calendar in early spring. The season's first and biggest, the **Budapest Spring Festival** (early to mid-March), showcases Hungary's best opera, music, theater, fine arts, and dance, as well as visiting foreign artists. The weeklong **BudaFest** opera and ballet festival (mid-August) takes place at the Opera House. Information and tickets are available from ticket agencies.

Concerts and Musicals

Several excellent orchestras, such as the Budapest Festival Orchestra, are based in Budapest. Concerts frequently include works by Hungarian composers Bartók, Kodály, and Liszt. **Liszt Ferenc Zeneakadémia** (Franz Liszt Academy of Music; ⊠ VI, Liszt Ferenc tér 8, ☎ 1/342–0179 or 1/341–4788) is Budapest's premier classical concert venue; orchestra and chamber music performances take place in its splendid main hall. Classical concerts are also held at the **Pesti Vigadó** (Pest Concert Hall; ⊠ V, Vigadó tér 2, ☎ 1/327–4322). The **Régi Zeneakadémia** (Old Academy of Music; ⊠ VI, Vörösmarty u. 35, ☎ 1/322–9804) is a smaller venue for chamber music. The 1896 **Vígszínház** (Comedy Theater; ⊠ XIII, Pannónia út 1, ☎ 1/329–2340) presents mostly musicals. Operettas and Hungarian renditions of popular Broadway musicals are staged at the **Operett Színház** (Operetta Theater; ⊠ VI, Nagymező u. 19, ☎ 1/269–3870).

Opera and Dance

Budapest has two opera houses, one of which is the gorgeous neo-Renaissance **Magyar Állami Operaház** (Hungarian State Opera House; ⊠ VI, Andrássy út 22, ☎ 1/353–0170), also the city's main venue for classical ballet. There's also the plainer **Erkel Színház** (Erkel Theater; ⊠ VIII, Köztársaság tér, ☎ 1/333–0540).

The young **Trafó Kortárs Művészetek Háza** (Trafo House of Contemporary Arts; ⊠ IX, Liliom u. 41, ☎ 1/456–2044) has become the hub of Budapest's modern and avant-garde dance and music productions. From May through September, displays of Hungarian folk dancing take place at the **Folklór Centrum** (Folklore Center; ⊠ XI, Fehérvári út 47, ☎ 1/203–3868). The Hungarian State Folk Ensemble performs regularly at the **Budai Vigadó** (⊠ I, Corvin tér 8, ☎ 1/225–1012). There are regular participatory folk-dance evenings—with instructions for beginners—at district cultural centers; consult the entertainment listings of *Where Budapest* and *Programme* for schedules and locations, or check with a hotel concierge.

Nightlife

Budapest is a lively city by night. Establishments stay open well past midnight, and Western European–style bars and British-style pubs have sprung up all over the city. For quiet conversation, hotel bars are a good choice, but beware of the inflated prices. Expect to pay cash for your night on the town. The city also has its share of seedy go-go clubs and "cabarets," some of which have been shut down for scandalously excessive billing and physical intimidation and assault. Avoid places where women lingering nearby "invite" you in, and never order without first seeing the price.

Bars

The most popular of Budapest's Irish pubs and a favorite expat watering hole is **Becketts** (⊠ V, Bajcsy-Zsilinszky út 72, ☎ 1/311–1035, ⊙ Mon.–Fri. 5 PM–1 or 2 AM, Sat.–Sun. noon–1 or 2 AM), where Guinness flows amid polished-wood and brass decor. A hip, low-key crowd mingles at the stylish **Café Incognito** (⊠ VI, Liszt Ferenc tér 3, ☎ 1/342–1471, ⊙ Mon.–Fri. 10 AM–midnight, Sat.–Sun. noon–midnight), with low lighting and funky music kept at a conversation-friendly volume by savvy DJs. **Café Pierrot** (⊠ I, Fortuna u. 14, ☎ 1/375–6971) is an elegant café and piano bar on a small street on Castle Hill. The stylish, new **Vörös és Fehér** (VI, Andrássy út 41, ☎ 1/413–1545) wine bar, opened by the Budapest Wine Society, is the perfect place to taste Hungary's exceptional (and inexpensive) wines by the glass.

Casinos

Most casinos are open daily from 2 PM until 4 or 5 AM and offer gambling in hard currency—usually dollars—only. You must be 18 to enter a casino in Hungary. The popular **Las Vegas Casino** (⊠ V, Roosevelt tér 2, ☎ 1/317–6022) is centrally located in the Atrium Hyatt Hotel. In an 1879 building designed by the architect Miklós Ybl, who also designed the Hungarian State Opera House, the **Várkert Casino** (⊠ I, Miklós Ybl tér 9, ☎ 1/202–4244) is the most attractive in the city.

Jazz and Dance Clubs

Established Hungarian headliners and young up-and-comers perform nightly at the **Jazz Garden** (⊠ V, Veres Pálné u. 44/a, ☎ 1/266–7364). Shows start at 8:30 PM; there is a 500-Ft. cover charge.

With wrought-iron and maroon-velvet decor, the stylish but unpretentious **Fél 10 Jazz Club** (⊠ VIII, Baross u. 30, ☎ 06/60–318–467) has a dance floor and two bars on three open levels. A welcoming, gay-friendly crowd flocks to late-night hot spot **Café Capella** (⊠ V, Belgrád rakpart 23, ☎ 1/318–6231) for glittery drag shows (held nightly) and DJ'd club music. It's open Sun.–Thurs. 9 PM to 4 AM, and Fri.–Sat. until 5 AM. There's a 500-Ft. drink minimum every night, plus a cover charge (500 Ft. Wed.–Thurs. and Sun., 1,000 Ft. Fri.–Sat.; Mon.–Tues. no cover).

SHOPPING

You'll find plenty of expensive boutiques, folk art and souvenir shops, and classical record shops on or around **Váci utca**, Budapest's pedestrian-only promenade. Browsing among some of the smaller, less touristy, more typically Hungarian shops in Pest—on the **Kiskörút** (Small Ring Boulevard) and **Nagykörút** (Great Ring Boulevard)—may prove more interesting and less pricey. Artsy boutiques are springing up in the section of district V south of Ferenciek tere toward the Danube and around Kálvin tér. **Falk Miksa utca,** north of Parliament, is home to some of the city's best antiques stores. You'll also encounter Transylvanian women dressed in colorful folk costume standing on busy sidewalks selling their own handmade embroideries and ceramics at rock-bottom prices. Look for them at **Moszkva tér, Jászai Mari tér,** outside the **Kossuth tér Metro,** and around **Váci utca.**

For a Hungarian take on a most American concept, you can visit one of the many mega-malls springing up around the city. **Mammut** (✉ II, Lövőház u. 2–6, ☎ 1/345–8020) is in central Buda. It's open Monday–Saturday 10 AM–9 PM, Sunday 10–6. The **West End** (✉ Váci út 1–3, ☎ 1/238–7777), behind Nyugati train station in downtown Pest, comes complete with a waterfall and a T.G.I. Friday's restaurant. Hours are Sunday–Thursday 8 AM–1 AM, Friday–Saturday 8 AM–2 AM.

A good place for special gifts, **Holló Műhely** (✉ V, Vitkovics Mihály u. 12, ☎ 1/317–8103) sells the work of László Holló, a master wood craftsman who has resurrected traditional motifs and styles of earlier centuries. There are lovely hope chests, chairs, jewelry boxes, candlesticks, and more, all hand-carved and hand-painted with cheery folk motifs—a predominance of birds and flowers in reds, blues, and greens.

Stores specializing in Hungary's excellent wines have become a trend in Budapest. Among the best of them is the store run by the **Budapest Bortársaság** (Budapest Wine Society; ✉ I, Batthyány u. 59, ☎ 1/212–0262). The cellar shop, at the base of Castle Hill, always has an excellent selection of Hungary's finest wines, chosen by the wine society's discerning staff, who will happily help you with your purchases. Tastings are held Saturday afternoons from 2 to 5.

Markets

The magnificent, cavernous, three-story **Vásárcsarnok** (Central Market Hall; ✉ IX, Vámház körút 1–3) teems with shoppers browsing among stalls packed with salamis, red paprika chains, and other enticements. Upstairs you can buy folk embroideries and souvenirs.

A good way to find bargains (and adventure) is to make an early morning trip out to **Ecseri Piac** (✉ IX, Nagykőrösi út; take Bus 54 from Boráros tér), a vast, colorful, chaotic flea market on the outskirts of Budapest. Try to go Saturday morning, when the most vendors are out. Foreigners are a favorite target for overcharging, so be tough when bargaining.

BUDAPEST A TO Z

To research prices, get advice from other travelers, and book travel arrangements, visit www.fodors.com.

AIR TRAVEL TO AND FROM BUDAPEST
The only nonstop service between Budapest and the United States is aboard Malév.
➤ AIRLINES AND CONTACTS: **Malév** (☎ 06/40–212–121 toll free; 1/235–3804 sales and information).

AIRPORTS AND TRANSFERS
Hungary's international airport, Ferihegy is about 22 km (14 mi) southeast of the city. All Malév flights operate from Terminal 2a; other airlines use the new Terminal 2b. For same-day flight information call the airport authority, where automated information is available in English.

Minibuses marked LRI CENTRUM-AIRPORT-CENTRUM leave every half hour from 5:30 AM to 9:30 PM for Erzsébet tér (in front of the Kempinski Hotel) in downtown Budapest. The trip takes 30–40 minutes and costs around 900 Ft. The modern minivans of the reliable LRI Airport Shuttle take you to any destination in Budapest, door to door, for around 2,000 Ft., even less than the least expensive taxi—and most employees speak English. At the airport buy tickets at the LRI counter in the arrivals hall near baggage claim; for your return trip call ahead for a pick-up. There are also approved Airport Taxi stands outside both terminals, with fixed rates based on which district you are going to. The cost to the central districts is about 4,800 Ft. Going to the airport, the cost is 3,000 Ft. from Pest, 3,500 Ft. from Buda; call one day ahead to arrange for a pick-up.

➤ AIRPORT INFORMATION: **Airport Taxi** (☎ 1/341–0000). **Ferihegy** (☎ 1/296–9696; airport authority ☎ 1/296–7155). **LRI Airport Shuttle** (☎ 1/296–8555 or 1/296–6283).

BIKE TRAVEL

On Margaret Island in Budapest, Bringóvár rents four-wheeled pedaled contraptions called *Bringóhintós,* as well as traditional two-wheelers; mountain bikes cost about 850 Ft. per hour, 2,500 Ft. for 24 hours. One-speeders cost less. For more information about renting in Budapest, contact Tourism Office of Budapest.

➤ BIKE RENTALS: **Bringóvár** (✉ Hajós Alfréd sétány 1, across from the Thermal Hotel, ☎ 1/329–2746). **Tourism Office of Budapest** (✉ VI, Liszt Ferenc tér 11, ☎ 1/322–4098 or 1/342–9390).

BUS TRAVEL TO AND FROM BUDAPEST

Most buses to Budapest from the western region of Hungary and from Vienna arrive at Erzsébet tér station downtown. The station is likely to be relocated some time in 2002; check with Tourinform for details.

➤ BUS INFORMATION: **Erzsébet tér station** (✉ V, Erzsébet tér, ☎ 1/317–2966).

CAR TRAVEL

The main routes into Budapest are the M1 from Vienna (via Győr), the M5 from Kecskemét, the M3 from near Gyöngyös, and the M7 from the Balaton region.

EMERGENCIES

➤ DOCTORS AND DENTISTS: **R-Klinika** (☎ 1/325–9999 private English-speaking).

➤ EMERGENCY SERVICES: **Ambulance** (☎ 104; 1/200–0100 private English-speaking). **Police** (☎ 107).

➤ 24-HOUR PHARMACIES: **Gyógyszertár** (☎ 1/311–4439 in Pest; 1/355–4691 in Buda).

ENGLISH-LANGUAGE MEDIA

➤ BOOKSTORES: **Bestsellers** (✉ V, Október 6 u. 11, ☎ 1/312–1295). **Central European University Academic Bookshop** (✉ V, Nádor u. 9, ☎ 1/327–3096).

TAXIS

Taxis are plentiful and are a good value, but be careful to avoid the also plentiful rogue cabbies. The city of Budapest recently established a tariff ceiling for taxi drivers. For a hassle-free ride, avoid unmarked "freelance" taxis; stick with those affiliated with an established company. Rather than hailing a taxi in the street, your safest bet is to order one by phone; a car will arrive in about 5 to 10 minutes. The average initial charge for taxis ordered by phone is 250 Ft., to which is added

about 200 Ft. per kilometer (½ mi) plus 50 Ft. per minute of waiting
time. The best rates are offered by Citytaxi and Főtaxi.
➤ Taxi Companies: **Citytaxi** (☎ 1/211–1111; English spoken). **Főtaxi**
(☎ 1/222–2222).

TOURS
IBUSZ Travel, Cityrama, and Budapest Tourist organize a number of unusual tours, including horseback riding, bicycling, and angling, as well
as visits to the National Gallery. These companies provide personal guides
on request. Also check at your hotel's reception desk. The Chosen Tours
offers an excellent three-hour combination bus and walking tour (about
$17, hotel pick-up and drop-off included), Budapest Through Jewish Eyes,
highlighting the sights and cultural life of the city's Jewish community.
➤ Fees and Schedules: **Chosen Tours** (☎ FAX 1/355–2202).

BOAT TOURS
From April through October, boats leave from the quay at Vigadó tér
on 1½-hour cruises between the railroad bridges north and south of the
Árpád and Petőfi bridges, respectively. The trip, organized by MAHART
Tours, runs only on weekends and holidays until late April, then once
or twice a day, depending on the season; the trip costs around 900 Ft.
➤ Fees and Schedules: **MAHART Tours** (☎ 1/318–1704).

BUS TOURS
Cityrama offers a three-hour city bus tour (about 6,000 Ft. per person). Year-round, IBUSZ Travel sponsors three-hour bus tours of the
city that cost about 6,000 Ft; starting from Erzsébet tér, they take in
parts of both Buda and Pest. Specify whether you prefer live or recorded
commentary.
➤ Fees and Schedules: **Cityrama** (✉ V, Báthori u. 22, ☎ 1/302–4382
or 1/331–0043).

SINGLE-DAY TOURS
Excursions farther afield include daylong trips to the Puszta (Great Plain),
the Danube Bend, the Eger wine region, and Lake Balaton. IBUSZ Travel
offers trips to the Buda Hills and stays in many of Hungary's historic
castles and mansions.

TRAIN TRAVEL
Call the MÁV Passenger Service for train information. Call one of the
three main train stations in Budapest for information during off-hours
(8 PM–6 AM): Déli, Keleti, and Nyugati. Trains for Vienna usually depart from Keleti station, those for Lake Balaton from Déli.
➤ Train Information: **Déli** (Southern; ✉ XII, Alkotás u., ☎ 1/375–
6293). **Keleti** (Eastern; ✉ VII, Rákóczi út, ☎ 1/313–6835). **Nyugati**
(Western; ✉ V, Nyugati tér, ☎ 1/349–0115).

TRANSPORTATION AROUND BUDAPEST
Budapest is best explored on foot. The maps provided by tourist offices are not very detailed, so arm yourself with one from any of the
bookshops in Váci utca or from a stationery shop or newsstand.

Roman-numeral prefixes in Budapest street addresses refer to one of
the city's 22 districts. Full postal addresses do not cite a Roman numeral, as the district is indicated by the zip code. Getting around is
easier if you learn a few basic terms: *utca* (abbreviated *u.*) and *út*, which
mean "street" and "road" or "avenue," respectively; *tér* or *tere* (square);
and *körút* (ring road).

The Budapest Transportation Authority (BKV) runs the public transportation system—the Metro (subway) with three lines, buses, streetcars, and trolleybuses—and it's cheap, efficient, and simple to use. Most

of it closes down around 11:30 PM, but certain trams and buses run on a limited schedule all night. A *napijegy* (day ticket) costs about 800 Ft. (a *turista-jegy,* or three-day tourist ticket, costs around 1,600 Ft.) and allows unlimited travel on all services within the city limits. Metro stations or newsstands sell single-ride tickets for about 100 Ft. You can travel on all trams, buses, and on the subway with this ticket, but you can't change lines or direction.

Bus, streetcar, and trolleybus tickets must be canceled on board—watch how other passengers do it. Metro tickets are canceled at station entrances. Plainclothes agents wearing red armbands spot check frequently, often targeting tourists, and you can be fined 1,500 Ft. if you don't have a canceled ticket.

TRAVEL AGENCIES

➤ LOCAL AGENTS: **American Express** (✉ V, Déak Ferenc u. 10, ☎ 1/235–4330). **Getz International** (✉ V, Falk Miksa u. 5, ☎ 1/312–0649 or 1/269–3728). **Vista Travel Center** (✉ VI, Andrássy út 1, ☎ 1/269–6032 air tickets; 1/328–4030 train, bus, boat tickets and youth, student travel, WEB www.vista.hu/english).

VISITOR INFORMATION

Vista Visitor Center/Café has created a uniquely welcoming environment for visitors seeking information about Budapest and Hungary. You can linger over lunch in the popular café, browse through brochures, and get information about (and make bookings for) tours, events, accommodations, and more from the young, English-speaking staff. Computer terminals are rented by the hour for Internet surfing and E-mailing; storage lockers are also available, as are international telephone stations with good rates.

The monthly *Where Budapest* magazine and the *Budapest in Your Pocket* guide are good sources. The English-language weekly the *Budapest Sun* covers news, business, and culture.

The Tourism Office of Budapest has developed the Budapest Card, which entitles holders to unlimited travel on public transportation; free admission to many museums and sights; and discounts on various purchases, entertainment events, tours, meals, and services from participating businesses. The cost is 3,400 Ft. for two days, 4,000 Ft. for three days; one card is valid for an adult plus a child under 14. Budapest Cards are sold at main metro ticket windows, tourist information offices, and hotels.

➤ TOURIST INFORMATION: **IBUSZ Travel** (main branch, ✉ V, Ferenciek tere 10, ☎ 1/485–2762, 06/20–944–9091, or 1/317–7767 tours and programs; one central branch, ✉ V, Vörösmarty tér 6, ☎ 1/317–0532). **Tourinform** (✉ Vörösmarty tér, at Vigadó u., H-1052 Budapest, ☎ 1/438–8080; 06/80–660–044 automated telephone service, ⊙ 24 hours; ✉ Sütő u. 2, H-1052 Budapest, ☎ 1/317–9800, ⊙ daily 8–8, www.hungarytourism.hu; WEB www.tourinform.hu). **Tourism Office of Budapest** (✉ VI, Liszt Ferenc tér 11, ☎ 1/322–4098 or 1/342–9390, FAX 1/342–2541; ✉ VII, Király u. 93, ☎ 1/352–1433; ✉ XIII, Nyugati pályaudvar, ☎ 1/302–8580; ✉ I, Tárnok u. 9–11, ☎ 1/488–0453). **Tribus Hotel Service** (✉ V, Apáczai Csere János u. 1, ☎ 1/318–5776 or 1/266–8042). **Vista Visitor Center/Café** (✉ VI, Paulay Ede u. 7, ☎ 1/267–8603).

Hungary Basics

BUSINESS HOURS

BANKS AND OFFICES

Banks are generally open weekdays 8–2 or 3, often with a one-hour lunch break around noon; most close at 1 on Friday.

Museums are generally open 10–6 Tuesday–Sunday; many stop selling admission 30 minutes before closing. Note that some museums change their opening and closing times by an hour or so at the beginning and end of peak seasons based on visitor traffic; it's prudent to double-check hours. Many have free admission one day a week.

Department stores are open weekdays 10–5 or 6, Saturday until 1. Grocery stores are generally open weekdays 7–6 or 7, Saturday until 1; "nonstops" or *éjjeli-nappali* (24-hour convenience stores) are (theoretically) open 24 hours.

CUSTOMS AND DUTIES

Objects for personal use may be imported freely. If you are over 16, you may also bring in 250 cigarettes or 50 cigars or 250 grams of tobacco, plus 2 liters of wine, 1 liter of spirits, 5 liters of beer, and 0.25 liters of perfume. A customs charge is made on gifts valued in Hungary at more than 27,000 Ft.

Keep receipts of any purchases from Konsumtourist, Intertourist, or Képcsarnok Vállalat. A special permit is needed for works of art, antiques, or objects of museum value. You are entitled to a VAT refund on new goods (i.e., not works of art, antiques, or objects of museum value) valued at more than 50,000 Ft.

For further customs information, inquire at the Hungarian Customs Office. If you can't speak Hungarian, ask the English-speaking staff at Tourinform for help.
➤ INFORMATION: **Hungarian Customs Office** (✉ IX, Mester u. 7, Budapest, ☎ 1/456–9500 or 1/470–4121).

EMBASSIES

➤ AUSTRALIA: (✉ XII, Királyhágó tér 8–9, Budapest 1126, ☎ 1/457–9777).
➤ CANADA: (✉ Mailing address: XII, Budakeszi út 32, Budapest 1121; ✉ Street address: XII, Zugligeti út 51–53, Budapest 1121, ☎ 1/275–1200).
➤ UNITED KINGDOM: (✉ V, Harmincad u. 6, Budapest 1051, ☎ 1/266–2888).
➤ UNITED STATES: (✉ V, Szabadság tér 12, Budapest 1054, ☎ 1/475–4400).

HOLIDAYS

January 1; March 15 (Anniversary of 1848 Revolution); Easter and Easter Monday; May 1 (Labor Day); Pentecost; August 20 (St. Stephen's and Constitution Day); October 23 (1956 Revolution Day); December 24–26.

LANGUAGE

Hungarian (Magyar) tends to look and sound intimidating to English-speakers. Generally, older people speak some German, and many younger people speak at least rudimentary English, which has become the most popular language to learn. It's a safe bet that anyone in the tourist trade will speak at least one of the two languages.

MONEY MATTERS

The forint was significantly devalued over the past few years and continues its decline, but inflation has dramatically decreased to around 9% from an annual rate of more than 25%. Although you receive more forints for your dollar, prices have risen to keep up with inflation. Nevertheless, even with inflation and the 25% value-added tax (VAT) in the service industry, enjoyable vacations with all the trimmings remain less expensive than in nearby Western European cities such as Vienna.

Sample prices include: cup of espresso, 200 Ft.; bottle of beer at a bar or restaurant, 300 Ft.–400 Ft.; soft drinks, 200 Ft.; 2-km (1-mi) taxi ride, 600 Ft.; museum admission 300 Ft.–600 Ft.

ATMS

Hundreds of ATMs have appeared throughout the capital and in other major towns. Some accept Plus network bank cards and Visa credit cards, others Cirrus and MasterCard. You can withdraw forints only (automatically converted at the bank's official exchange rate) directly from your account; most levy a 1% or $3 service charge. Many cash-exchange machines, into which you feed paper currency for forints, have also sprung up.

CURRENCY

The unit of currency is the forint (Ft.). There are bills of 200, 500, 1,000, 2,000, 5,000, 10,000, and 20,000 forints and coins of 1, 2, 5, 10, 20, 50, and 100 forints. At press time (summer 2001), the exchange rate was 274 Ft. to the U.S. dollar, 186 Ft. to the Canadian dollar, 411 Ft. to the pound sterling, 329 Ft. to the Irish punt, 165 Ft. to the Australian dollar, 130 Ft. to the New Zealand dollar, and 39 Ft. to the South African rand.

There is still a black market in hard currency, but changing money on the street is risky and illegal, and the bank rate almost always comes close. Stick with banks and official exchange offices.

TRAVELER'S CHECKS

Eurocheque holders can cash personal checks in all banks and in most hotels. Many banks now also cash American Express and Visa traveler's checks. American Express has a full-service office in Budapest, and a smaller branch on Castle Hill—in the Sisi Restaurant, closed January–mid-March—offers only currency exchange. Hungary's first Citibank offers full services to account holders, including a 24-hour ATM.

➤ CONTACTS: **American Express** (✉ V, Deák Ferenc u. 10, Budapest, ☎ 1/235–4330 travel service; 1/235–4349 cardmember services, FAX 1/235–4303; ✉ In Sisi Restaurant, ☎ 1/224–0118). **Citibank** (✉ V, Vörösmarty tér 4, Budapest).

PASSPORTS AND VISAS

U.S., British, and Canadian citizens must carry a valid passport.

TELEPHONES

COUNTRY AND AREA CODES

The country code for Hungary is 36.

DIRECTORY AND OPERATOR ASSISTANCE

For operator-assisted calls within Hungary, dial ☎ 191. Dial ☎ 198 for directory assistance throughout the country. Operators are unlikely to speak English. A safer bet is to consult *The Phone Book,* an English-language yellow pages–style telephone directory that also has cultural and tourist information; it's free in most major hotels, at many restaurants, and at English-language bookstores.

INTERNATIONAL CALLS

Direct calls to foreign countries can be made from Budapest and all major provincial towns by dialing 00 and waiting for the international dialing tone; on pay phones the initial charge is 60 Ft. Operator-assisted international calls can be made by dialing 190. To reach a long-distance operator, call AT&T, MCI, or Sprint.

➤ ACCESS CODES: **AT&T** (☎ 06–800–01111). **MCI** (☎ 06–800–01411). **Sprint** (☎ 06–800–01877).

LOCAL CALLS

The cost of a three-minute local call is 20 Ft. Pay phones use 10, 20, 50, and 100 Ft. coins. Most towns in Hungary can be dialed direct—dial 06 and wait for the buzzing tone, then dial the local number. It is unnecessary to use the city code, 1, when dialing within Budapest.

While Hungary's telephone system continues to be modernized, phone numbers are subject to change—usually without forewarning and sometimes several times. A recording in Hungarian and English may provide the new number. If you're having trouble getting through, ask your concierge to check the number.

PUBLIC PHONES

Gray card-operated telephones are common in Budapest and the Balaton region. The cards—available at post offices, newsstands, and kiosks—come in units of 60 (800 Ft.) and 90 (1,800 Ft.) calls.

7 COPENHAGEN

When you arrive in Copenhagen Airport on the isle of Amager, as you taxi into the city you are met with no startling skyline, no seething metropolis. Instead, elegant spires and central cobbled streets characterize Scandinavia's most populous capital and one of its oldest towns. It is not divided like most other cities into single-purpose districts; instead it is a rich, multi-layered capital where people work, play, shop, and live throughout its central core. Surrounded by water, be it sea or canal, and connected by bridges and drawbridges, it has a maritime atmosphere that is indelible.

EXPLORING COPENHAGEN

Numbers in the margin correspond to points of interest on the Copenhagen map.

When Denmark ruled Norway and Sweden during the 15th century, Copenhagen was the capital of all three countries. Today it is still a lively northern capital, with about 1 million inhabitants. It's a city meant for walking, the first in Europe to recognize the value of pedestrian streets in fostering community spirit. As you stroll through the cobbled streets and squares, you'll find that Copenhagen combines the excitement and variety of big-city life with a small-town atmosphere. If there's such a thing as a cozy metropolis, this is it.

In Copenhagen you're never far from water, whether sea or canal. The original city itself is built upon two main islands, Slotsholmen and Christianshavn, connected by drawbridges. The ancient heart of the city is intersected by two heavily peopled walking streets—part of the five such streets known collectively as Strøget—and around them curls a maze of cobbled streets packed with tiny boutiques, cafés, and restaurants—all best explored on foot. In summer, when Copenhagen moves outside, the most engaging views of city life are from sidewalk cafés in

118

Copenhagen (København)

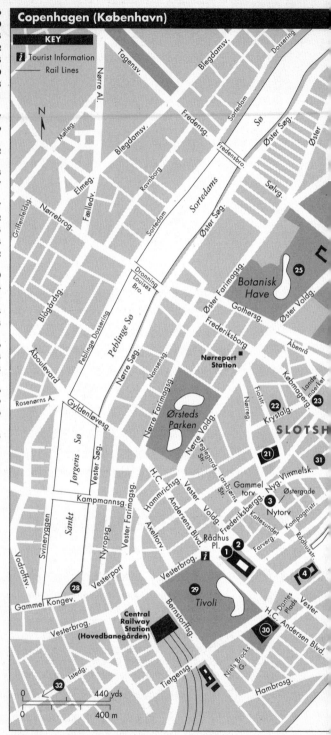

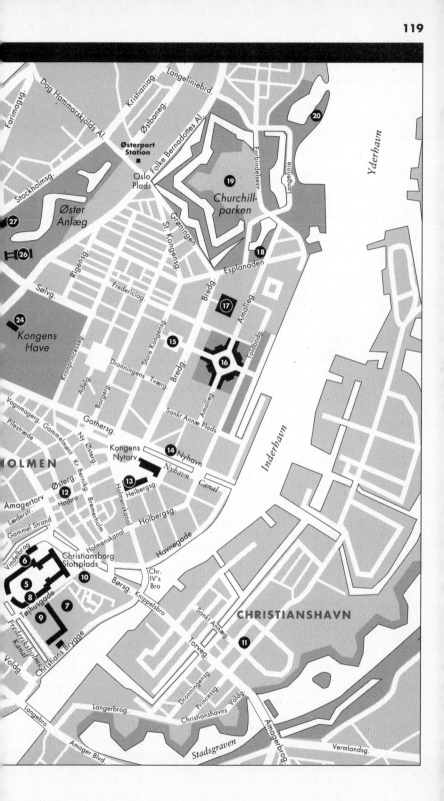

the sunny squares. Walk down Nyhavn Canal, once the haunt of a salty crew of sailors, now gentrified and filled with chic restaurants.

🔟 **Amalienborg** (Amalia's Castle). During the fall and winter, when members of the royal family return to their principal residence as they have since 1784, the Royal Guard and band march through the city at noon to change the palace guard. Amalienborg's other main attraction is the second division of the Royal Collection (the first is at Rosenborg), housed inside the **Amalienborg Museum.** Among the collection's offerings are the study of King Christian IX (1818–1906) and the drawing room of his wife, Queen Louise. Also included are a set of rococo banquet silver, highlighted by a bombastic Viking ship centerpiece, and a small costume exhibit. Afterward, you can view visiting yachts along the castle's harbor, as well as the modern sculptures and manicured flower beds of **Amalienhaven** (Amalia's Gardens). ⊠ *Amalienborg Pl.,* ☎ *33/40–10–10.* ⊘ *May–late Oct., daily 11–4; late Oct.– Apr., Tues.–Sun. 11–4.*

🔟 **Børsen** (Stock Exchange). This edifice is believed to be the oldest such structure still in use, though it functions only on special occasions. It was built by the 16th-century monarch King Christian IV, a scholar, warrior, and the architect of much of the city. With its steep roofs, tiny windows, and gables, the building is one of Copenhagen's treasures. ⊠ *Christiansborg Slotspl. Not open to public.*

㉕ **Botanisk Have** (Botanical Garden). Copenhagen's 25-acre botanical garden, with a spectacular Palm House containing tropical and subtropical plants, upstages the palatial gardens of **Rosenborg Slot** (Rosenborg Castle). Also on the grounds are an observatory, geological museum, and cactus and orchid house. ⊠ *Gothersg. 128,* ☎ *35/32–22–40.* ▨ *Free.* ⊘ *Grounds May–Aug., daily 8:30–6; Sept.–Apr., daily 8:30–4. Palm House daily 10–3. Cactus House Wed. and Sun. 1–3.*

㉜ **Carlsberg Bryggeri** (Carlsberg Brewery). Granite elephants guard the entrance to the first Carlsberg brewery, opened in 1847; inside you can visit the draft-horse stalls and **Carlsberg Visitors' Centre,** and taste the local product. ⊠ *Gl. Carlsbergvej 11,* ☎ *33/27–13–14,* 🕸 *www. carlsberg.dk.* ⊘ *Tues.–Sun. 10–4; groups book in advance.*

★ ⑤ **Christiansborg Slot** (Christiansborg Castle). This massive gray complex contains the Folketinget (Parliament House) and the Royal Reception Chambers. It is on the site of the city's first fortress, built by Bishop Absalon in 1167. While the castle was being built at the beginning of the 20th century, the National Museum excavated the ruins beneath the site. ⊠ *Christiansborg,* ☎ *33/92–64–92 Christiansborg ruins; 33/ 37–55–00 Folketinget; 33/92–64–92 reception chambers.* ⊘ *Christiansborg ruins: Jan.–Sept. 30, Mon.–Sun. 9:30–3:30; Oct. 1–Dec. 31, Tues., Thurs., Sat.–Sun. 9:30–3:30. Folketinget: tour times vary; call ahead. Reception chambers: June 5–Sept., daily; guided tours only, 11, 1, 3; Oct.–Dec. 31, Tues., Thurs., weekends, guided tours 11, 3.*

㉚ **Den Lille Havfrue** (The Little Mermaid). In 1913 this statue was erected to commemorate Hans Christian Andersen's lovelorn creation. It's now the subject of hundreds of travel posters. On Sunday, **Langelinie,** the spit of land you follow to reach the famed nymph, is thronged with promenading Danes and tourists—the pack of whom are often much more absorbing to watch than the somewhat overrated sculpture. The mermaid has been mysteriously decapitated a couple of times since she was set on her perch; the most recent incident took place in early 1998, and though her head was returned within a week, she gained much more publicity without it. ⊠ *Langelinie promenade.*

⑱ **Frihedsmuseet** (Liberty Museum). Evocative displays commemorate the heroic World War II Danish resistance movement, which saved 7,000 Jews from the Nazis by hiding them and then smuggling them across to Sweden. ⊠ *Churchillparken,* ☎ *33/13–77–14.* ◷ *Tues.–Sat. 10–4, Sun. 10–5.*

㉛ **Heligånds Kirken** (Church of the Holy Ghost). This church on Strøget contains a marble font by the sculptor Bertel Thovaldsen (1770–1844) in its 18th-century choir. ⊠ *Niels Hemmingsensg. 5, Amagertorv section of Strøget,* ☎ *33/12–95–55.* ◷ *Weekdays 9–1, Sat. 10–noon.*

㉗ **Hirschsprungske Samling** (Hirschsprung Collection). This cozy museum displays works from Denmark's golden age of painting, the mid-19th-century school of Naturalism pioneered by C. W. Eckersberg, whose pictures contain a remarkable wealth of detail and technical skill combined with limpid, cool, luminescent color. Other prominent painters of the trend include Christian Købke and Julius Exner. The Hirschsprungske also has a collection of paintings by the late-19th-century artists of the Danish Skagen school, as well as interiors with furnishings from the artists' homes. ⊠ *Stockholmsg. 20,* ☎ *35/42–03–36,* WEB *www.dhs.dk.* ◷ *Thurs.–Mon. 11–4, Wed. 11–9.*

⑲ **Kastellet** (Citadel). Once surrounded by two rings of moats, this building was the city's main fortress during the 17th century, but, in a grim reversal during World War II, the Germans used it as one of their headquarters during their occupation of Denmark. The lovely green area around it, **Churchillparken,** cut throughout with walking paths, is a favorite among the Danes, who flock here on weekends. If you have time, walk past the spired **St. Alban's,** an Anglican church that stands at the park's entrance. ⊠ *Churchillparken.* ◷ *Grounds daily 6 AM–sunset.*

㉒ **Københavns Synagoge** (Copenhagen Synagogue). This synagogue was designed by the contemporary architect Gustav Friedrich Hetsch, who borrowed from the Doric and Egyptian styles in creating the arklike structure. ⊠ *Krystalg. 12.* ◷ *Daily services 4:15.*

⑬ **Kongelig Teater** (Royal Theater). The home of Danish opera and ballet as well as theater occupies the southeast side of Kongens Nytorv. The Danish Royal Ballet remains one of the world's great companies, with a repertoire ranging from classical to modern. On the western side of the square you'll see the stately facade of the **D'Angleterre,** the grandest of Copenhagen's hotels. ⊠ *Tordenskjoldsg. 3,* ☎ *33/69–69–69,* WEB *www.kgl-teater.dk. Not open for tours.*

❼ **Kongelige Bibliotek** (Royal Library). This library houses the country's largest collection of books, newspapers, and manuscripts. Look for early records of the Viking journeys to America and Greenland and the statue of the philosopher Søren Kierkegaard in the garden. A dark marble annex next door, known as the Black Diamond, has reading rooms, a ground-floor performance space, and a bookstore. ⊠ *Søren Kierkegaards Pl. 1,* ☎ *33/47–47–47,* WEB *www.kb.dk.* ◷ *Mon.–Sat. 10–7.*

⑰ **Kunstindustrimuseet** (Museum of Decorative Art). The highlights of this museum's collection are a large assortment of European and Asian handicrafts, as well as ceramics, silver, and tapestries. The quiet library full of design tomes and magazines doubles as a primer for Danish functionalism with its Le Klint paper lamp shades and wooden desks. ⊠ *Bredg. 68,* ☎ *33/18–56–56,* WEB *www.kunstindustrimuseet.dk.* ◷ *Special exhibits Tues.–Fri. 10–4, weekends noon–4; permanent exhibition Tues.–Fri. 1–4, weekends noon–4.*

❷ **Lurblæserne** (Lur Blower Column). Topped by two Vikings blowing an ancient trumpet called a *lur,* this column erected in 1914 displays a good deal of artistic license—the lur dates from the Bronze Age, 1500 BC, whereas the Vikings lived a mere 1,000 years ago. The monument is a starting point for sightseeing tours of the city. ⊠ *East side of Rådhus Pl.*

⑮ Marmorkirken (Marble Church). The ponderous Frederikskirke, commonly called the Marmorkirken, is a Baroque church that was begun in 1749 in high-priced Norwegian marble and stood unfinished (because of budget constraints) from 1770 to 1874. It was finally completed and consecrated in 1894. Perched around the exterior are 16 statues of various religious leaders from Moses to Luther, and below them stand sculptures of outstanding Danish ministers and bishops. ⊠ *Frederiksgade 4,* ☎ *33/15–01–44.* ☉ *Mon.–Tues. and Thurs.–Sat. 10–6, Sun. noon–5, with service at 10:30.*

⊛ ④ Nationalmuseet (National Museum). This museum has extensive collections chronicling Danish cultural history to modern times and displays of Egyptian, Greek, and Roman antiquities. You can see Viking runic stones in the Danish cultural history section. The children's museum is an excellent place to ease kids into the joys of history; though the original relics are secured behind glass, there is plenty of stuff, including clothing and a school, to play in and with. ⊠ *Ny Vesterg. 10,* ☎ *33/13–44–11,* WEB *www.natmus.dk.* ☉ *Tues.–Sun. 10–5.*

⑫ Nikolaj Kirken (St. Nicholas Church). In Østergade, the easternmost of the streets that make up Strøget, you cannot miss the green spire of this building. The present structure was built in the 20th century; the previous one, dating from the 13th century, was destroyed by fire in 1728. Today the building is no longer a church but an art gallery and exhibition center. ⊠ *Nikolaipl.,* ☎ *33/93–16–26.* ☉ *Daily noon–5.*

★ ㉚ Ny Carlsberg Glyptotek (New Carlsberg Sculpture Museum). This elaborate neoclassical building houses one of Europe's greatest collections of Greek and Roman antiquities and sculpture. A modern wing houses an impressive pre-Impressionist collection including works from the Barbizon school; Impressionist paintings, with works by Monet, Sisley, and Pissarro; and a post-Impressionist section, with 50 Gauguin paintings plus 12 of his very rare sculptures. ⊠ *Dantes Pl. 7,* ☎ *33/41–81–41,* WEB *www.glyptoteket.dk.* ☉ *Tues.–Sun. 10–4.*

★ ⑭ Nyhavn (New Harbor). You can relax with a beer in one of the most gentrified parts of the city, a longtime haunt of sailors. Now restaurants and cafés outnumber tattoo shops. The name refers to both the street and the canal leading southeast out of Kongens Nytorv. The area still gets rowdy on long, hot summer nights, with Scandinavians reveling against the backdrop of a fleet of old-time sailing ships and well-preserved 18th-century buildings. Hans Christian Andersen lived at numbers 18 and 20. Nearer to the harbor are old shipping warehouses, including two—Nyhavn 71 and the Admiral—that have been converted into comfortable hotels. ⊠ *East of Kongens Nytorv.*

★ ① Rådhus Pladsen (City Hall Square). This hub of Copenhagen's commercial district is the best place to start a stroll. The Renaissance-style building dominating it is the **Rådhuset** (Town Hall), completed in 1905. A statue of Copenhagen's 12th-century founder, Bishop Absalon, sits atop the main entrance. Inside, you can see the first World Clock, an astrological timepiece invented and built by Jens Olsen and set in motion in 1955. You can take a guided tour partway up the 350-ft **tower** for a panoramic view. ⊠ *Square in Strøget at eastern end of Vesterbrog. and western end of Frederiksbergg.,* ☎ *33/66–25–82.* ☉ *Rådhus Mon.–Wed. and Fri. 9:30–3, Thurs. 9:30–4, Sat. 9:30–1. Tours in English weekdays at 3, Sat. at 10 and 11. Tower tours Oct.–May, Mon.–Sat. at noon; June–Sept., Mon.–Sat. at 10, noon, and 2. Call to confirm hrs.*

★ ㉔ **Rosenborg Slot** (Rosenborg Castle). This Renaissance palace—built by jack-of-all-trades Christian IV—houses the Crown Jewels, as well as a collection of costumes and royal memorabilia. Don't miss Christian IV's pearl-studded saddle. ⊠ *Øster Voldg. 4A,* ☎ *33/15–32–86.* ☉ *Nov.– Dec. 17 and Jan.–Apr., Tues.–Sun. 11–2; May–Sept., daily 10–4; Oct., daily 11–3.*

㉓ **Rundetårn** (Round Tower). It is said that Peter the Great of Russia drove a horse and carriage up the 600 ft of the inner staircase of this round tower, built as an observatory in 1642 by Christian IV. It's a formidable walk, but the view is worth it, and there is sometimes an astronomer available to answer questions. At the base of the tower is the university church, Trinitas; halfway up the tower you can take a break at the tower's art gallery. ⊠ *Købmagerg. 52A,* ☎ *33/73–03–73.* ☉ *Tower: Sept.–May, Mon.–Sat. 10–5, Sun. noon–5; June–Aug., Mon.–Sat. 10– 8, Sun. noon–8. Observatory and telescope: mid-Oct.–mid-Mar., Tues.– Wed. 7–10 PM; June 20–Aug. 10, Sun. 1–4.*

☝ ㉖ **Statens Museum for Kunst** (National Art Gallery). The original 100-year-old building and a new, modern structure house works of Danish art from the golden age (early 19th century) to the present, as well as paintings by Rubens, Dürer, the Impressionists, and other European masters—but the space also includes a children's museum, an amphitheater, a documentation center and study room, a bookstore, and a restaurant. ⊠ *Sølvg. 48–50,* ☎ *33/74–84–94,* WEB *www.smk.dk.* ☉ *Tues., Thurs.–Sun. 10–5, Wed. 10–8.*

❸ **Strøget.** Frederiksberggade is the first of the five pedestrian streets that make up Strøget, Copenhagen's shopping district and promenade area. Walk past the cafés and trendy boutiques to the double square of **Gammeltorv** and **Nytorv,** where, farther along, the street is paved with mosaic tiles. Outside the posh displays of the fur and porcelain shops the sidewalks have the festive aura of a street fair. **Kongens Nytorv** (King's New Market) is the square marking the end of Strøget.

❽ **Teatermuseum** (Theater Museum). Built in 1767 in the Royal Court, this museum is devoted to exhibits on theater and ballet history. You can wander around the boxes, stage, and dressing rooms to see where it all happened. ⊠ *Christiansborg Ridebane 18,* ☎ *33/11–51–76.* ☉ *Wed. 2–4, weekends noon–4.*

★ ❻ **Thorvaldsen Museum.** The 19th-century Danish sculptor Bertel Thorvaldsen, whose tomb stands in the center of the museum, was greatly influenced by the statues and reliefs of classical antiquity. In addition to his own works, the collection includes drawings and paintings by others that illustrate the influence of Italy on the artists of Denmark's golden age. ⊠ *Porthusg. 2,* ☎ *33/32–15–32,* WEB *www. thorvaldsensmuseum.dk.* ☉ *Tues.–Sun. 10–5.*

★ ☝ ㉙ **Tivoli.** In the 1840s the Danish architect Georg Carstensen convinced King Christian VIII that an amusement park would be the perfect opiate for the masses, arguing that "when people amuse themselves, they forget politics." In the season from May through September, about 4 million people come through the gates. Tivoli is more sophisticated than a mere fun fair: it offers a pantomime theater and an open-air stage, elegant restaurants, and frequent classical, jazz, and rock concerts in addition to a museum chronicling its own history. On weekends there are elaborate fireworks displays. Try to see Tivoli at least once by night, when the trees are illuminated along with the Chinese Pagoda and the main fountain. In recent years Tivoli has also been opened a month before Christmas with a gift and decorations market and children's rides. Most of the restaurants are also open, but there are plenty of less expensive food stalls serving everything from Asian specialties to mulled wine. ⊠ *Vesterbrog. 3,* ☎ *33/15–10–01,* WEB *www.tivoli.dk.* ☉ *May–mid-Sept., and at Christmas time, daily 11 AM–midnight, Fri.–Sat. until 1 AM.*

⑨ Tøjhusmuseet (Royal Armory). The Renaissance structure was built by King Christian IV. It houses impressive displays of uniforms, weapons, and armor in an arched hall 200 yards long. ⊠ *Tøjhusg. 3,* ☎ *33/11–60–37,* WEB *www.thm.dk.* ☉ *Tues.–Sun. noon–4.*

㉘ Tycho Brahe Planetarium. This modern, cylindrical building has astronomy exhibits and an Omnimax theater that takes visitors on a simulated journey up into space and down into the depths of the seas (reservations are advised for the theater). Because these films can be disorienting, planetarium officials do not recommend them for children under seven. ⊠ *Gammel Kongevej 10,* ☎ *33/12–12–24,* WEB *www.tycho.dk.* 🎫 *Exhibition and theater DKr70.* ☉ *Daily 10:30–9.*

⑪ Vor Frelsers Kirken (Our Savior's Church). Legend has it that the staircase encircling the fantastic green-and-gold spire of this 1696 Gothic structure was built curling the wrong way around, and that when its architect reached the top and saw what he had done, he jumped. ⊠ *Skt. Annæg. 9,* ☎ *31/57–63–25.* ☉ *Weekdays 9–1. Closed during services and special functions; call ahead.*

㉑ Vor Frue Kirken (Church of Our Lady). This has been Copenhagen's cathedral since 1924, but the site itself has been a place of worship since the 13th century, when Bishop Absalon built a chapel here. The spare, neoclassical facade is a 19th-century innovation repairing damage suffered during Nelson's bombing of the city in 1801. If the church is open, you can see Thorvaldsen's marble sculptures of Christ and the Apostles. Afterward, if you're on your way to the Nørreport train station, you'll pass the stoic, columned **Københavns Universitet** (Copenhagen University; ⊠ Nørregade 10). It was built in the 19th century on the site of the medieval bishops' palace. ⊠ *Pilestræde 67,* ☎ *33/14–41–28.* ☉ *Weekdays 8:30–5.*

DINING

Food is one of the great pleasures in Copenhagen, a city with more than 2,000 restaurants. Traditional Danish fare spans all the price categories: you can order a light lunch of smørrebrød, snack from a store kolde bord, or dine on lobster and Limfjord oysters. You can also enjoy fast food Danish style, in the form of *pølser* (hot dogs) sold from trailers on the street. Team any of this with some pastry from a bakery (the shops displaying an upside-down gold pretzel), and you've got yourself a meal on the go. Many restaurants close for Christmas, roughly from December 24 through December 31.

Meal prices vary little between town and country.

CATEGORY	COST*
$$$$	over DKr200
$$$	DKr120–DKr200
$$	DKr80–DKr120
$	under DKr80

*per person for a main course at dinner

$$$$ ✕ Kommandanten. The 300-year-old building, once the apartment of
★ the Commander of Copenhagen, houses Scandinavia's most celebrated restaurant. The ever-varying set-course menu follows what's freshest at the market, including sliced breast of guinea fowl with quail eggs

or wild duck with confit. Expect adventurous French cooking of the highest caliber and service attuned to the lift of an eyebrow. If possible, book before your trip—this epicurean favorite seats only 50. ✉ *Ny Adelgade 7,* ☎ *33/12–09–90,* WEB *www.kommandanten.dk. AE, DC, MC, V. Closed Sun.*

$$$$ ✕ **Kong Hans Kaelder.** In this hushed cloister with medieval vaulted
★ ceilings you'll find one of the city's outstanding restaurants. The menu is classic French, with a focus on the creative use of local ingredients, including mushrooms brought by bicycle from nearby forests. You haven't tasted salmon like this before, prepped for 36 hours in the restaurant's own cold smoker. Save room for the outstanding selection of gourmet cheeses, many homemade. ✉ *Vingårdstr. 6,* ☎ *33/11–68–68,* WEB *www.konghans.dk. AE, DC, MC, V. Closed Sun.–Mon. June–mid-July and Aug.; mid–late July; and Easter wk. No lunch.*

$$$$ ✕ **Krogs.** Fish is to Denmark what wine is to France, and the reigning champion among Copenhagen seafood restaurants remains venerable Krogs, equal to the best in food and tops in local charm and history. Gilded mirrors, high ceilings, and 19th-century paintings are a study in old-fashioned opulence, as is a menu including grilled lobster with vanilla polenta, poached fish in Parmesan bouillon, and the locally famous bouillabaisse. ✉ *Gammel Strand 38,* ☎ *33/15–89–15,* WEB *www.krogs.dk. Reservations essential. AE, DC, MC, V. Closed Sun., and around Christmas, Easter.*

$$$ ✕ **Els.** Said to be a favorite of the queen, Els is a piece of Danish his-
★ tory, largely unchanged since it first catered to the theater crowd in 1853. The flip side of the restaurant's proud past is an occasionally supercilious attitude toward foreigners, but a touch of stiffness seems in keeping with the 19th-century tiles, Renaissance-style painted muses, and antique samovar greeting you at the bar. Enjoy fine French cooking with a focus on fish, and wild game and fowl. ✉ *Store Strandstr. 3,* ☎ *33/14–13–41. Reservations essential. AE, DC, MC, V.*

$$$ ✕ **L'Alsace.** In the cobbled courtyard of Pistolstraede and hung with paintings by Danish surrealist Wilhelm Freddie, this restaurant is peaceful and quiet. The menu includes a hearty *choucroute* (sauerkraut) with sausage and pork, plus fruit tarts and cakes for dessert. ✉ *Ny Østerg. 9,* ☎ *33/14–57–43. AE, DC, MC, V. Closed Sun.*

$$$ ✕ **Le Sommelier.** Classic French country cooking is served here with a dazzling selection of wines by the glass. Enjoy the popular steamed mussels, homemade foie gras, or pigeon breast with mushrooms and glazed beets. Take a break from worrying about secondhand smoke and give in to the European ambience: patrons can select from 30 brands of cigarettes to go with any of 12 varieties of coffee. ✉ *Bredg. 63,* ☎ *33/11–45–15,* WEB *www.lesommelier.dk. AE, DC, MC, V. Closed between lunch and dinner sittings, approx. 4–6. Closed Christmas–New Year.*

$$$ ✕ **Schiøtt's.** The city's newest modern French hit, this cozy cellar restaurant offers superb creative fare in the Provençal style, including flavorful shoulder of lamb with peppers, eggplant, and olives. It offers an elegant experience at the price. The walk along the Christianhavn Canal adds to the pleasure on warm summer nights. ✉ *Overgaden neden vandet 17,* ☎ *32/54–54–08,* WEB *www.schoetts.dk. AE, DC, MC, V. Closed around Christmas and Easter.*

$$$ ✕ **Victor.** This French-style corner café has great people-watching and bistro fare. It's best during weekend lunches, when Danes gather for such specialties as rib roast, homemade pâté, smoked salmon, and cheese platters. Careful ordering here can get you an inexpensive meal. ✉ *Ny Østerg. 8,* ☎ *33/13–36–13,* WEB *www.cafevictor.dk. AE, DC, MC, V.*

$$ ✕ **El Meson.** Ceiling-hung pottery, knowledgeable waiters, and a top-notch menu make this Copenhagen's best Spanish restaurant. Choose carefully for a moderately priced meal, which might include beef spiced with spearmint, lamb with honey sauce, or paella for two. ⊠ *Hauser Pl. 12,* ☎ *33/11–91–31. AE, DC, MC, V. Closed Sun. No lunch.*

$$ ✕ **Havfruen.** A full-size wooden mermaid swings decorously from the ceiling in this small, rustic fish restaurant in Nyhavn. Natives love the maritime-bistro ambience and the daily-evolving French and Danish menu. ⊠ *Nyhavn 39,* ☎ *33/11–11–38. DC, MC, V. Closed Sun.*

$$ ✕ **Ida Davidsen.** Five generations old (counting Ida's children, Oscar
★ and Ida Maria), this world-renowned lunch spot has become synonymous with smørrebrød. Choose from these creative open-face sandwiches, piled high with such ingredients as pâté, bacon, and steak tartare, or even kangaroo, or opt for smoked duck served with a beet salad and potatoes. ⊠ *St. Kongensg. 70,* ☎ *33/91–36–55. Reservations essential. AE, DC, MC, V. Closed weekends and July. No dinner.*

$$ ✕ **Olsen's.** Urban-modern in appearance, this popular spot prides itself on its *husmandskost*—old-fashioned Danish food, carefully prepared and served with gusto. For a truly local experience order the *flæskesteg* (roast pork) and enjoy the fat and rind, as Danes do. ⊠ *St. Kongensg. 66,* ☎ *33/93–91–95,* Ⓦ *www.olsen.dk. AE, DC, MC, V. May be closed for part of July.*

$ ✕ **Lai Hoo.** Denmark's Princess Alexandra, a native of Hong Kong, is a fan of this Chinese restaurant near the city's main square. The lunch specialty is an inspired variety of steamed dumplings (dim sum), and for dinner the best bet is the fixed menu—try the salt-baked prawns in pepper or the luscious lemon duck. ⊠ *St. Kongensg. 18,* ☎ *33/93–93–19. DC, MC, V.*

$ ✕ **Quattro Fontane.** On a corner west of the lakes, one of Copenhagen's busiest Italian restaurants is a noisy, two-story affair packed tight with marble-top tables and a steady flow of young Danes. Chatty Italian waiters serve cheese or beef ravioli, cannelloni, linguine with clam sauce, and thick pizzas. Reservations are essential on weekends. ⊠ *Guldbersg. 3,* ☎ *35/39–39–31. No credit cards.*

$ ✕ **Riz Raz.** On a corner off Strøget, this Middle Eastern restaurant packs
★ in young and old, families, and singles every night and on weekends. The very inexpensive all-you-can-eat buffet is heaped with healthy dishes, including lentils, falafel, bean salads, and occasionally pizza. Reservations are essential on weekends. ⊠ *Kompagnistr. 20,* ☎ *33/15–05–75,* Ⓦ *www.rizraz.dk. DC, MC, V.*

LODGING

Copenhagen is well served by a wide range of hotels, which are almost always clean, comfortable, and well run. Most but not all Danish hotels include a substantial breakfast in the room rate. Summertime reservations are a good idea, but if you should arrive without one, try the hotel booking service at the Danish Tourist Board. They can also give you a "same-day, last-minute price," which is about DKr400–DKr500 for a double hotel room. This service will also locate rooms in private homes, with rates starting at about DKr300 for a double. Try the **Ungdoms Information** lodging service (⊠ Rådhusstr. 13, ☎ 33/73–06–50) for budget accommodations.

CATEGORY	COST*
$$$$	over DKr1,700
$$$	DKr1,400–DKr1,700
$$	DKr900–DKr1,400
$	under DKr900

All prices are for a standard double room, excluding service charges and 14.9% room tax.

$$$$ ⬛ **D'Angleterre.** The grande dame of Copenhagen hotels underwent
★ major changes during the 20th century, but the hotel still retains its
Old World, old-money aura. The rooms are done in pinks and blues,
with overstuffed chairs and antique escritoires and armoires. Bathrooms
sparkle with brass, mahogany, and marble. If you are a light sleeper,
choose a back room; some guests complain of noise from the nearby
bars, as well as early morning deliveries. ✉ *Kongens Nytorv 34, DK
1051 KBH K,* ☎ *33/12–00–95,* FAX *33/12–11–18,* WEB *www.remmen.
dk/hda.htm. 110 rooms, 20 suites. 2 restaurants, pool. AE, DC, MC, V.*

$$$$ ⬛ **Radisson SAS Scandinavia.** Near the airport, this is one of northern Europe's largest hotels and Copenhagen's token skyscraper. An immense lobby, with cool, recessed lighting and streamlined furniture, gives
access to the city's first (and only) casino. Guest rooms are large and
somewhat institutional but offer every modern convenience. Breakfast
is not included in the rates. ✉ *Amager Blvd. 70, DK 2300 KBH S,* ☎
33/96–50–00, FAX *33/96–55–00,* WEB *www.radissonsas.com. 542 rooms,
52 suites. 4 restaurants, pool. AE, DC, MC, V.*

$$$ ⬛ **Kong Frederik.** West of Rådhus Pladsen, near Strøget, this intimate
hotel is a cozy version of its big sister, D'Angleterre. The sunny Queen's
Garden restaurant serves a breakfast buffet (not included in the rate);
rooms are elegant with Oriental vases, mauve carpets, and all modern
amenities. ✉ *Vester Voldg. 25, DK 1552 KBH K,* ☎ *33/12–59–02,*
FAX *33/93–59–01,* WEB *www.remmen.dk/hkf.htm. 110 rooms, 17 suites.
Restaurant. AE, DC, MC, V.*

$$$ ⬛ **Neptun.** The centrally sited Neptun has been in business for nearly
150 years and shows no signs of flagging. Guest rooms decorated with
blond wood are favored by Americans. Though charming, this Best Western hotel can become very busy with tour groups. Moreover, because
it is housed in a old building, room sizes vary greatly, and so does the
noise from the street. Ask for details when booking a room. ✉ *Skt.
Annæ Pl. 18, DK 1250 KBH K,* ☎ *33/13–89–00,* FAX *33/14–12–50.
123 rooms, 14 suites. Restaurant. AE, DC, MC, V.*

$$$ ⬛ **Nyhavn 71.** In a 200-year-old warehouse overlooking the old ships
of Nyhavn, this quiet hotel is a good choice for privacy-seekers. The
maritime interiors have been preserved with their original plaster walls
and exposed brick. Rooms are tiny but cozy, with warm woolen
spreads, dark woods, soft leather furniture, and exposed timbers. ✉
Nyhavn 71, DK 1051 KBH K, ☎ *33/11–85–85,* FAX *33/93–15–85,* WEB
www.nyhavnhotel.dk. 84 rooms. Restaurant. AE, DC, MC, V.

$$$ ⬛ **The Phoenix.** This luxury hotel welcomes guests with crystal chan-
deliers and gilt touches everywhere. The staff switch languages as they
register business and cruise guests. Suites and executive-class rooms
have Biedermeier-style furniture and 18-karat-gold-plated bathroom
fixtures, but the standard rooms are very small, at barely 9 by 15 ft.
If you're a light sleeper, ask for a room above the second floor to avoid
street noise. ✉ *Bredg. 37, DK 1260 KBH K,* ☎ *33/95–95–00,* FAX *33/
33–98–33,* WEB *www.phoenix.dk. 208 rooms, 7 suites. Restaurant.
AE, DC, MC, V.*

$$ ⬛ **Ascot.** A charming old building downtown, this family-owned hotel
has a classically columned entrance and an excellent breakfast buffet.
Rooms have colorful geometric-pattern bedspreads and cozy bath-
rooms. A few have kitchenettes. Repeat guests often ask for their reg-
ular rooms. Be warned: in recent years, a nearby late-night disco has
disturbed some guests. Be sure to ask for a room as far away from it
as possible. The restaurant serves breakfast only. ✉ *Studiestr. 61, DK
1554 KBH K,* ☎ *33/12–60–00,* FAX *33/14–60–40. 161 rooms, 4 suites.
Restaurant. AE, DC, MC, V.*

$$ ⬛ **Copenhagen Admiral.** Overlooking old Copenhagen and Amalienborg, the monolithic Admiral, once a grain warehouse, now offers his-

toric but airy accommodations. With massive stone walls broken by rows of tiny windows, it's one of the less expensive top hotels, though in recent years it's been upping both frills and prices. Guest rooms are spare, with jutting beams and modern prints. ✉ *Toldbodg. 24–28, DK 1253 KBH K,* ☎ *33/11–82–82,* FAX *33/32–55–42,* WEB *www.admiralhotel.dk. 365 rooms. Restaurant. AE, DC, MC, V.*

$ 🖭 **Cab-Inn Scandinavia.** Winter business travelers and budget-minded summer backpackers and families alike flock to Copenhagen's answer to Japanese-style hotel minirooms. More cozy than futuristic, shiplike "berths" are brightly decorated, all with standard furnishings, including a small wall-hung desk with chair. Around the corner, at Danasvej 32, is a sister hotel, the Cab-Inn Copenhagen, with 86 rooms. ✉ *Vodroffsvej 55, DK 1900 FR C,* ☎ *35/36–11–11,* FAX *35/36–11–14,* WEB *www.cab-inn.dk. 201 rooms with shower. AE, DC, MC, V.*

$ 🖭 **Missionhotellet Nebo.** This budget hotel is between the main train station and Istedgade's seediest porn shops. Nonetheless, it's a prim hotel, comfortable and well maintained by a friendly staff. The dormlike guest rooms are furnished with industrial carpeting, polished pine furniture, and soft duvet covers. Baths, showers, and toilets are clustered at the center of each hallway, and the breakfast restaurant downstairs has a tiny courtyard. ✉ *Istedg. 6, DK 1650 KBH V,* ☎ *31/21–12–17,* FAX *31/23–47–74,* WEB *www.nebo.dk. 88 rooms, 40 with bath. AE, DC, MC, V.*

$ 🖭 **Triton.** Despite seedy surroundings, this streamlined hotel attracts a cosmopolitan clientele thanks to a central location in Vesterbro. The large rooms, in blond wood and warm tones, have new bathrooms and state-of-the-art fixtures. The buffet breakfast included in the price is exceptionally generous, and the staff is friendly. There are also family rooms, each with a separate bedroom and fold-out couch. The restaurant serves breakfast only. ✉ *Helgolandsg. 7–11, DK 1653 KBH K,* ☎ *31/31–32–66,* FAX *31/31–69–70,* WEB *www.accorhotel.dk. 123 rooms. Restaurant. AE, DC, MC, V.*

NIGHTLIFE AND THE ARTS

English-language *Copenhagen This Week* has good information on musical and theatrical happenings, as well as on special events and exhibitions. An excellent Web site for learning about shopping, dining, accommodations, and entertainment, in fact everything about Copenhagen (which is what AOK stands for) is WEB www.aok.dk. It also features similar information about other Danish cities. Concert and festival information is available from the **Dansk Musik Information Center** (DMIC; ✉ Gråbrødretorv 16, ☎ 33/11–20–66, WEB www.mic.dk. Copenhagen's main theater and concert season runs from September through May, and tickets can be obtained either directly from theaters and concert halls or from ticket agencies; ask your hotel concierge for advice. **Billetnet** (☎ 70/15–65–65, WEB www.billetnet.dk), a box-office service available at all large post offices, has tickets for most major events. Keep in mind that same-day purchases at the box office at **Tivoli** (✉ Vesterbrogade 3, ☎ 33/15–10–12) are half price if you pick them up after noon.

The Arts

Music
Tivoli Concert Hall (✉ Tietensg. 20, ☎ 33/15–10–12) offers more than 150 concerts each summer, presenting a host of Danish and foreign soloists, conductors, and orchestras.

Theater

The **Royal Theater** (✉ Kongens Nytorv, ☎ 33/14–10–02, WEB www.kgl-teater.dk) regularly holds theater, ballet, and opera performances. For English-language theater, try to catch a performance of the professional **London Toast Theatre** (☎ 33/22–86–86, WEB www.londontoast.dk).

Nightlife

Many of the city's restaurants, cafés, bars, and clubs stay open after midnight, some as late as 5 AM. Copenhagen is famous for jazz, but you'll find nightspots catering to musical tastes ranging from bop to ballroom music. In the inner city most discos open at 11 PM, have a cover charge (about DKr40), and pile on steep drink prices. A few streets behind the railway station is Copenhagen's red-light district, where sex shops share space with grocers. Although the area is fairly well lighted and lively, women may feel uncomfortable here alone at night.

Jazz

The upscale **Copenhagen Jazz House** (✉ Niels Hemmingsensg. 10, ☎ 33/15–26–00, WEB www.jazzhouse.dk) attracts European and some international talent to its chic, modern barlike ambience. **La Fontaine** (✉ Kompagnistr. 11, ☎ 33/11–60–98) is Copenhagen's quintessential jazz dive, with sagging curtains, impenetrable smoke, crusty lounge lizards, and the random barmaid nymph; for jazz lovers, the bordello mood and Scandinavian jazz talent make this a must. **Tivoli Jazzhouse Mantra** (✉ Vesterbrog. 3, ☎ 33/11–11–13), Tivoli's jazz club, lures some of the biggest names in the world.

Nightclubs and Dancing

The young set gets down on the disco floor in the fashionable **Park Café** (✉ Østerbrog. 79, ☎ 35/26–63–42). Mellower folks come for brunch when the place transforms back to its Old World roots, or to check out the movie theater next door. **Rosie McGees** (✉ Vesterbrog. 2A, ☎ 33/32–19–23) is a very popular English-style pub with Mexican food and dancing. **Sabor Latino** (✉ Vester Voldg. 85, ☎ 33/11–97–66) is the U.N. of discos, with an international crowd dancing to salsa and other Latin beats. Among the most enduring clubs is **Woodstock** (✉ Vesterg. 12, ☎ 33/11–20–71), where a mixed audience grooves to 1960s classics.

SHOPPING

Strøget's pedestrian streets are synonymous with shopping.

Specialty Shops

Just off Østergade is **Pistolstræde,** a typical old courtyard filled with intriguing boutiques. Farther down the street toward the town-hall square is a compound that includes several important stores: **Georg Jensen** (✉ Amagertorv 4, ☎ 33/11–40–80), one of the world's finest silversmiths, gleams with a wide array of silver patterns and jewelry. Don't miss the **Georg Jensen Museum** (✉ Amagertorv 6, ☎ 33/14–02–29), which showcases glass and silver creations ranging from tiny, twisted-glass shot glasses to an $85,000 silver fish dish. **Royal Copenhagen Porcelain** (✉ Amagertorv 6, ☎ 33/13–71–81) carries both old and new china, plus porcelain patterns and figurines.

Bang & Olufsen (✉ Østerg. 3–5, ☎ 33/15–04–22) offers reasonable prices for radios, TVs, and stereo equipment in its own upscale shop. Along Strøget, at furrier **Birger Christensen** (✉ Østerg. 38, ☎ 33/11–

55–55), you can peruse designer clothes and chic furs. **FONA** (⊠ Østerg. 47, ☎ 33/15–90–55) carries stereo equipment, including the superior design and sound of Bang & Olufsen. **Illum** (⊠ Østerg. 52, ☎ 33/14–40–02) is a department store that has a fine basement grocery and eating arcade. Don't confuse Illum with **Illums Bolighus** (⊠ Amagertorv 10, ☎ 33/14–19–41), where designer furnishings, porcelain, quality clothing, and gifts are displayed in near-gallery surroundings. **Magasin** (⊠ Kongens Nytorv 13, ☎ 33/11–44–33), one of the largest department stores in Scandinavia, offers all kinds of clothing and gifts, as well as an excellent grocery department.

COPENHAGEN A TO Z

To research prices, get advice from other travelers, and book travel arrangements, visit www.fodors.com.

AIRPORTS AND TRANSFERS
The main airport for both international and domestic flights is Copenhagen Airport, 10 km (6 mi) southeast of town.

TRANSFERS

Trains from the airport's sleek new subterranean train station take less than 10 minutes to zip into Copenhagen's main station. Buy a ticket upstairs in the airport train station (DKr18); three trains an hour go into Copenhagen, while a fourth travels farther to Roskilde. Bus service to the city is frequent. The airport bus to the central station leaves every 15 minutes: the trip takes about 25 minutes, with a fare of about DKr50 (pay on the bus). Public buses cost about DKr18 and run as often but take longer. Bus 250S takes you to Rådhus Pladsen, the city-hall square. A taxi ride takes 15 minutes and costs about DKr150, though slightly more after 4 PM and weekends.

BIKE TRAVEL
More than half the 5 million Danes are said to ride bikes, which visitors use as well. Bike rental costs DKr50–DKr200 a day, though weekly rates are available, with a deposit of DKr300–DKr1,000. Contact Københavns Cykler or Østerport Cykler.
➤ BIKE RENTAL: **Københavns Cykler** (⊠ Central Station, ☎ 33/33–86–13). **Østerport Cykler** (⊠ Oslo Plads, ☎ 33/33–85–13).

BUS TRAVEL WITHIN COPENHAGEN
Buses and suburban trains operate on the same ticket system and divide Copenhagen and environs into three zones. Tickets are validated on the time system: on the basic ticket, which costs DKr11 for an hour, you can travel anywhere in the zone in which you started. You can buy a discount *klip kort* (clip card), equivalent to 10 basic tickets, for DKr85. Call the 24-hour information service for zone information. Buses and S-trains run from 5 AM (6 AM on Sunday) to 12:30 AM. A reduced network of buses drives through the night.
➤ BUS INFORMATION: **Information service** (☎ 36/45–45–45 buses; 70/13–14–15 S-trains; wait for the Danish message to end and an operator will answer).

CAR TRAVEL
Copenhagen is a city for walkers, not drivers. The charm of its pedestrian streets is paid for by a complicated one-way road system and difficult parking. Leave your car in the garage: attractions are relatively close together, and public transportation is excellent.

EMERGENCIES

If you use the dental emergency service listed below, expect to pay cash. Emergency doctor fees are also payable in cash only, and nighttime visits include a DKr350 surcharge.

➤ DOCTORS AND DENTISTS: **Dental Emergency Service** (✉ Tandlægevagten 14, Oslo Pl., near Østerport station, ☎ 35/38–02–51). **Doctor** (☎ 33/93–63–00 weekdays 8–4; 38/88–60–41 daily after 4 PM).
➤ EMERGENCY SERVICES: **Auto Rescue/Falck** (☎ 70/10–20–30). **Police, fire, ambulance** (☎ 112).
➤ 24-HOUR PHARMACIES: **Steno Apotek** (✉ Vesterbrog. 6C, ☎ 33/14–82–66). **Sønderbro Apotek** (✉ Amagerbrog. 158, Amager area, ☎ 32/58–01–40).

ENGLISH-LANGUAGE MEDIA

➤ BOOKSTORES: **Arnold Busck** (✉ Købmagerg. 49, ☎ 33/73–35–00). **Boghallen** (✉ Rådhus Pl. 37, ☎ 33/47–25–60).

TAXIS

The computer-metered Mercedeses and Volvos are not cheap. The base charge is DKr22, plus DKr10–DKr13 per kilometer (½ mi). A cab is available when it displays the green sign FRI (free); you can either hail a cab (though this can be difficult outside the center), pick one up at a taxi stand, or call the number listed below.
➤ TAXI COMPANIES: (☎ 35/35–35–35).

TOURS

BOAT TOURS

The Harbor and Canal Tour by boat leaves from Gammel Strand and the east side of Kongens Nytorv; it runs from April through mid-October, daily every half hour from 10 to 5.

BUS TOURS

Several bus tours, conducted by Copenhagen Excursions, leave from the Lur Blowers Column in Rådhus Pladsen, late March–September.
➤ FEES AND SCHEDULES: **Copenhagen Excursions** (☎ 32/54–06–06).

PRIVATE GUIDES

The Danish Tourist Board can recommend multilingual guides for individual needs; travel agents have details on hiring a limousine and guide.

SINGLE-DAY TOURS

The Danish Tourist Board has full details relating to excursions outside the city, including visits to castles (such as Hamlet's castle) and the Viking Ship Museum.

WALKING TOURS

The Danish Tourist Board supplies maps and brochures and can recommend a walking tour.

TRAIN TRAVEL

Copenhagen's clean and convenient central station, Hovedbanegården, is the hub of the country's train network. Intercity express trains leave hourly, on the hour, from 6 AM to 10 PM for principal towns in Fyn and Jylland. Find out more from DSB Information at the central station. You can make reservations at the central station as well as most other stations, and through travel agents.
➤ TRAIN INFORMATION: **DSB Information** (☎ 70/13–14–15). **Hovedbanegården** (✉ just south of Vesterbrog, ☎ 33/14–88–00).

TRANSPORTATION AROUND COPENHAGEN

The best bet for visitors is the Copenhagen Card, affording unlimited travel on buses and suburban trains (S-trains), admission to some 60 museums and sights around metropolitan Copenhagen and Malmö, Sweden, and a reduction on the ferry crossing to Sweden. Buy the card, which costs about DKr155 (24 hours), DKr255 (48 hours), or DKr320 (72 hours)—half price for children ages 5 to 11—at bus/train stations, tourist offices, and hotels or from travel agents.

TRAVEL AGENCIES
➤ LOCAL AGENTS: **Carlson Wagonlit Travel** (⊠ Ved Vesterport 6, ☎ 33/63–78–78). **DSB Rejsebureau Terminus** (⊠ Central Station, ☎ 33/14–11–26). **Spies** (⊠ Nyropsg. 41, ☎ 70/10–42–00).

Denmark Basics

BUSINESS HOURS
BANKS AND OFFICES
Banks in Copenhagen are open weekdays 9:30–4 and Thursday until 6. Several bureaux de change, including those at Copenhagen's central station and airport, stay open until 10 PM. Outside Copenhagen, banking hours vary.

MUSEUMS AND SIGHTS
Museums are generally open 10–3 or 11–4 and closed Monday. In winter, opening hours are shorter, and some museums close for the season. Check the local papers or ask at tourist offices.

SHOPS
Small shops and boutiques are open weekdays 10–5:30; most stay open Friday until 7 or 8 and close on Saturday at 1 or 2. On the first and last Saturday of every month, most shops stay open until 4 or 5. Call to double-check weekend opening hours for specific stores to avoid disappointment.

CUSTOMS AND DUTIES
For details on imports and duty-free limits, *see* Customs and Duties *in* Smart Travel Tips A to Z.

EMBASSIES
All embassies are in Copenhagen.
➤ CANADA: (⊠ Kristen Bernikowsg. 1, 1105 KBH , ☎ 33/48–32–00).
➤ IRELAND: (⊠ Østbanegade 21, 2100 KBH, Ø, ☎ 35/42–32–33).
➤ SOUTH AFRICA: (⊠ Gammel Vartov Vej 8, DK-2900 Hellerup, ☎ 39/18–01–55).
➤ UNITED KINGDOM: (⊠ Kastelsvej 40, 2100 KBH Ø, ☎ 35/44–52–00).
➤ UNITED STATES: (⊠ Dag Hammarskjölds Allé 24, 2100 KBH Ø, ☎ 35/55–31–44).

HOLIDAYS
January 1; Easter (Thursday–Monday); Common Prayer (May); Ascension (40 days after Easter); June 5 (Constitution Day; shops close at noon); Whitsun/Pentecost (10 days after Ascension); December 24–26 (Christmas).

LANGUAGE
Danish is a difficult tongue for foreigners—except those from Norway and Sweden—to understand, let alone speak. Danes are good linguists, however, and almost everyone, except perhaps elderly people in rural areas, speaks English well in addition to a third language, usually French or German.

MONEY MATTERS
Denmark's economy is stable, and inflation remains reasonably low. The standard and the cost of living are high, especially for such luxu-

ries as alcohol and cigarettes. Prices are highest in Copenhagen; the least expensive areas are Fyn and Jylland.

Sample prices include: cup of coffee, DKr14–DKr25; bottle of beer, DKr20–DKr35; soda, DKr10–DKr15; ham sandwich, DKr22–DKr40; 1½-km (1-mi) taxi ride, DKr50.

CURRENCY

The monetary unit in Denmark is the krone (kr., DKr, or DKK), which is divided into 100 øre. At press time (summer 2001), the krone stood at DKr8.20 to the U.S. dollar, DKr5.27 to the Canadian dollar, DKr11.71 to the pound sterling, DKr9.46 to the Irish punt, DKr4.50 to the Australian dollar, DKr3.49 to the New Zealand dollar, and DKr1.05 to the South African rand. Most well-known credit cards are accepted in Denmark, though it would be wise to inquire about American Express and Diners Club beforehand. Traveler's checks can be cashed in banks and in many hotels, restaurants, and shops.

TELEPHONES

COUNTRY AND AREA CODES

The country code for Denmark is 45.

DIRECTORY AND OPERATOR ASSISTANCE

To ask an operator, most of whom speak English, for local assistance, dial 118; for an international operator, dial 113.

INTERNATIONAL CALLS

Dial 00, then the country code, area code, and the desired number. You can reach AT&T, MCI, and Sprint by dialing one of the access codes below.

➤ ACCESS CODES: **AT&T** (☎ 800/10010). **MCI WorldCom** (☎ 800/10022). **Sprint** (☎ 800/10877).

LOCAL CALLS

Pay phones take DKr1, DKr2, DKr5, and DKr10 coins. You must use area codes even when dialing a local number. Calling cards, which are sold at Danish State Railways stations, post offices, and some kiosks, cost DKr30, DKr50, DKr75, or DKr150 and are increasingly necessary as pay phones that accept coins become a thing of the past.

8 DUBLIN

Europe's most intimate capital has become a boom-town—the soul of the Republic of Ireland is in the throes of what may be the nation's most dramatic period of transformation since the Georgian era. Dublin is riding the back of its "Celtic Tiger" economy, and massive construction cranes are hovering over both shiny new hotels and old Georgian houses. Irish culture is hot: in recent years, Patriot Michael Collins became a Hollywood box-office star, Frank McCourt's *Angela's Ashes* conquered best-seller lists in the United States and was made into a movie, and *Riverdance* became a worldwide old-Irish mass jig. Because of these and other attractions, travelers are coming to Dublin in ever-greater numbers, so don't be surprised if you stop to consult your map in Temple Bar—the city's most happening neighborhood—and are swept away by the ceaseless flow of bustling crowds. Dublin has become a colossally entertaining, engaging city—all the more astonishing considering its gentle size. The quiet pubs and little empty backstreets might be harder to find now that Dublin has been "discovered," but a bit of effort and research can still unearth the old "Dear Dirty Dumpling," a city that Joyce was so fond of.

EXPLORING DUBLIN

Numbers in the margin correspond to points of interest on the Dublin map.

Originally a Viking settlement, Dublin sits on the banks of the River Liffey, which divides the city north and south. The liveliest round-the-clock spots, including Temple Bar and Grafton Street, are on the south side, although a variety of construction projects on the north side are helping to reinvigorate these areas. The majority of the city's most notable buildings date from the 18th century—the Georgian era—and, although many of its finer Georgian buildings disappeared in the redevelopment of the 1970s, enough remain to recall the elegant Dublin of centuries past. Dublin is small as capital cities go, with a compact downtown area, and the best way to soak in the full flavor of the city is on foot. Literary Dublin can still be recaptured by following the footsteps of Leopold Bloom's progress, as described in James Joyce's *Ulysses*. Trinity College, alma mater of Oliver Goldsmith, Jonathan Swift, and Samuel Beckett, among others, is a green, Georgian oasis, alive with students.

South of the Liffey

South of the Liffey are graceful squares and fashionable terraces from Dublin's elegant heyday, and, interspersed with some of the city's leading sights, this area is perfect for an introductory city tour. You might begin at O'Connell Bridge—as Dublin has no central focal point, most natives regard it as the city's Piccadilly Circus or Times Square—then head south down Westmoreland Street to Parliament House. Continue on to Trinity College—the Book of Kells, Ireland's greatest artistic treasure, is on view here—then eastward to Merrion Square and the National Gallery; south to St. Stephen's Green and Fitzwilliam Square; west to Dublin's two beautiful cathedrals, Christ Church and St. Patrick's; and end with dinner in a Temple Bar restaurant overlooking the Liffey.

② **Bank of Ireland.** With a grand facade of marble columns, the Bank of Ireland is one of Dublin's most striking buildings. Across the street from the front entrance to Trinity College, the Georgian structure was once the home of the Irish Parliament. Built in 1729, it was bought by the Bank of Ireland in 1803. Hurricane-shape rosettes adorn the coffered ceiling in the pastel-hued, colonnaded, clerestoried main banking hall, once the Court of Requests, where citizens' petitions were heard. Just down the hall is the original House of Lords, with tapestries, an oak-panel nave, and a 1,233-piece Waterford glass chandelier; ask a guard to show you in. Visitors are welcome during normal banking hours; a brief guided tour is given every Tuesday at 10:30, 11:30, and 1:45. ⊠ *2 College Green,* ☎ *01/677–6801.* ⊙ *Mon.–Wed. and Fri. 10–4, Thurs. 10–5.*

⑰ **Christ Church Cathedral.** You'd never know from the outside that the first Christianized Danish king built a wooden church at this site in 1038; thanks to the extensive 19th-century renovation of its stonework and trim, the cathedral looks more Victorian than Anglo-Norman. Stone construction was begun in 1172 by Strongbow, a Norman baron and conqueror of Dublin for the English crown. The vast, sturdy **crypt,** with its 12th- and 13th-century vaults, is Dublin's oldest surviving structure and the building's most notable feature. At 6 PM on Wednesdays and Thursdays you can enjoy a choral evensong. ⊠ *Christ Church Pl. and Winetavern St.,* ☎ *01/677–8099.* ⊙ *Daily 9:45–5.*

⑯ **City Hall.** Facing the Liffey from the top of Parliament Street, this grand Georgian municipal building (1769–79), once the Royal Exchange,

136

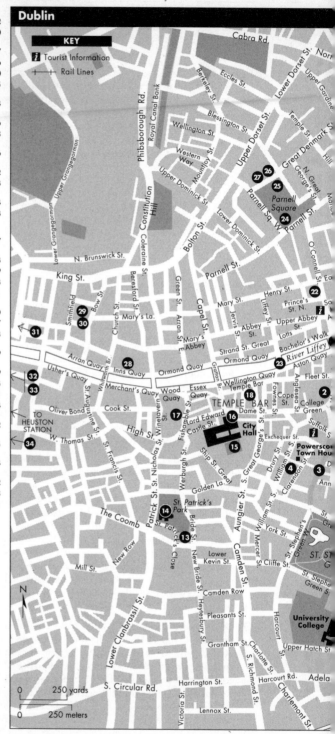

Dublin

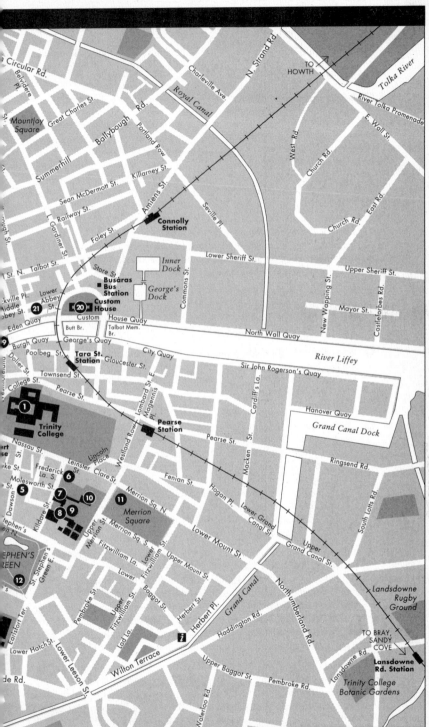

was designed by Thomas Cooley. It has a central rotunda encircled by 12 columns, a fine mosaic floor, and 12 frescoes depicting Dublin legends and ancient Irish historical scenes. The building is now home to an exhibition tracing the evolution of Ireland's 1,000-year-old capital. ⊠ *Dame Street,* ☎ *01/672–2204,* WEB *www.dublincorp.ie.* ⊙ *Mon.– Sat. 10–5:15, Sun. 2–5.*

⑮ Dublin Castle. The film *Michael Collins* captures this structure's near-indomitable status in the city. Just off Dame Street behind City Hall, the grounds of the castle encompass a number of buildings, including the **Record Tower,** a remnant of the original 13th-century Norman castle that was the seat of English power in Ireland for almost 7½ centuries, as well as various 18th- and 19th-century additions. The lavishly furnished **state apartments** are now used to entertain visiting heads of state. Guided tours run every half hour, but the rooms are closed when in official use, so call first. The **Castle Vaults** now hold an elegant little patisserie and bistro. The castle is also the home of the **Chester Beatty Library.** Among the library's exhibits are clay tablets from Babylon dating from 2700 BC, Japanese color wood-block prints, Chinese jade books, and Turkish and Persian paintings. ⊠ *Castle St.,* ☎ *01/677–7129,* WEB *www.dublincastle.ie.* ⊙ *Weekdays 10–5, weekends 2–5.*

④ Dublin Civic Museum. Built in 1765–71 as an assembly house for the Society of Artists, the museum displays drawings, models, maps of Dublin, and other civic memorabilia. ⊠ *58 S. William St.,* ☎ *01/679– 4260.* ⊙ *Tues.–Sat. 10–6, Sun. 11–2.*

⑥ Genealogical Office. The reference library here is a good place to begin ancestor tracing. It also houses the **Heraldic Museum,** where displays of flags, coins, stamps, silver, and family crests highlight the uses and development of heraldry in Ireland. ⊠ *2 Kildare St.,* ☎ *01/661–8811,* WEB *www.nli.ie.* ⊙ *Weekdays 10–4:30, Sat. 10–12:30.*

★ **③ Grafton Street.** Open only to pedestrians, brick-lined Grafton Street is one of Dublin's vital spines: the most direct route between the front door of Trinity College and Stephen's Green; the city's premier shopping street, off which radiate smaller streets housing stylish shops and pubs; and home to many of the city's street musicians and flower sellers. Browse through the designer clothing and housewares at **Brown Thomas,** Ireland's most elegant department store. The **Powerscourt Town House** is a shopping arcade installed in the covered courtyard of one of Dublin's most famous Georgian mansions.

⑨ Leinster House. When it was built in 1745 it was the largest private residence in Dublin. Today it is the seat of Dáil Eireann (pronounced "Dawl Erin"), the Irish House of Parliament. The building has two facades: the one facing Merrion Square is designed in the style of a country house; the other, on Kildare Street, is in the style of a town house. ⊠ *Kildare St.,* ☎ *01/618–3000,* WEB *www.irlgov.ie.* ⊙ *Tours Mon. and Fri. by prior arrangement (when Parliament is not in session). Dáil visitors' gallery access with an introduction from a member of Parliament.*

⑬ Marsh's Library. A short walk west from Stephen's Green and accessed through a tiny but charming cottage garden lies a gem of old Dublin: the city's—and Ireland's—first public library, opened in 1701 to "All Graduates and Gentlemen." Its interior has been left practically unchanged since it was built—it still contains "cages" into which scholars who wanted to peruse rare books were locked. (The cages were to discourage students who, often impecunious, may have been tempted to make the books their own.) ⊠ *St. Patrick's Close,* ☎ *01/454–3511,* WEB *www.kst.dit.ie.* ⊙ *Mon. and Wed.–Fri. 10–12:45 and 2–5, Sat. 10:30–12:45.*

★ **⑪** **Merrion Square.** Created between 1762 and 1764, this tranquil Georgian square is lined on three sides by some of Dublin's best-preserved Georgian town houses. Even when the flower gardens are not in bloom, the vibrant green grounds, dotted with sculpture and threaded with meandering paths, are worth a walk. **No. 1,** at the northwest corner, was the home of Sir William and Speranza Wilde, Oscar's parents. ✉ *East end of Nassau St.* ☉ *Daily sunrise–sunset.*

★ **⑩** **National Gallery of Ireland.** On the west side of Merrion Square, this 1854 building contains the country's finest collection of Old Masters—treasures include Vermeer's *Woman Writing a Letter* (twice stolen from Sir Alfred Beit and now safe at last), Gainsborough's *Cottage Girl,* and Caravaggio's *The Arrest of Christ.* The gallery's restaurant is one of the city's best spots for an inexpensive, top-rate lunch. Free guided tours are available on Saturday at 3 PM and on Sunday at 2:15, 3, and 4. ✉ *Merrion Sq. W,* ☎ *01/661–5133,* WEB *www.nationalgallery.ie.* ☉ *Mon.–Wed. and Fri.–Sat. 10–5:30, Thurs. 10–8:30, Sun. 2–5.*

❼ **National Library.** The collections here include first editions of every major Irish writer. Temporary exhibits are held in the entrance hall, off the colonnaded rotunda. The main reading room, opened in 1890, has a dramatic dome ceiling. ✉ *Kildare St.,* ☎ *01/661–8811,* WEB *www.nli.ie.* ☉ *Mon.–Wed. 10–9, Thurs.–Fri. 10–5, Sat. 10–1.*

❽ **National Museum.** On the other side of Leinster House from the National Library, the museum is most famous for its spectacular collection of Irish artifacts from 7000 BC to the present, including the Tara Brooch, the Ardagh Chalice, the Cross of Cong, and a fabled hoard of Celtic gold jewelry. Upstairs, Viking Age Ireland is a permanent exhibit on the Norsemen, featuring a full-size Viking skeleton, swords, leather works recovered in Dublin and surrounding areas, and a replica of a small Viking boat. ✉ *Kildare St.,* ☎ *01/660–1117,* WEB *www. museum.ie.* ☉ *Tues.–Sat. 10–5, Sun. 2–5.*

⑲ **O'Connell Bridge.** Strange but true: the main bridge spanning the Liffey is wider than it is long. The north side of the bridge is dominated by an elaborate memorial to Daniel O'Connell, "The Liberator," erected as a tribute to the great 19th-century orator's achievement in securing Catholic Emancipation in 1829. Today **O'Connell Street,** one of the widest in Europe, is less a street to loiter in than to pass through on your way to elsewhere. **Henry Street,** to the left just beyond the General Post Office, is, like a downscale Grafton Street, a busy pedestrian thoroughfare where you'll find throngs of Dubliners out doing their shopping. A few steps down Henry Street off to the right is the colorful **Moore Street Market,** where street vendors recall their most famous ancestor, Molly Malone, by singing their wares—mainly flowers and fruit—in the traditional Dublin style.

❺ **Royal Irish Academy.** The country's leading learned society houses important manuscripts in its 18th-century library. Just below the academy is the **Mansion House,** the official residence of the Lord Mayor of Dublin. Its Round Room, the site of the first assembly of Dáil Eireann in January 1919, is now used mainly for exhibitions. ✉ *19 Dawson St.,* ☎ *01/676–2570,* WEB *www.ria.ie.* ☉ *Weekdays 9:30–5.*

⑭ **St. Patrick's Cathedral.** Legend has it that St. Patrick baptized many converts at a well on the site of the cathedral in the 5th century. The building dates from 1190 and is mainly early English Gothic in style. At 305 ft, it is the longest church in the country. In the 17th century Oliver Cromwell, dour ruler of England and no friend of the Irish, had his troops stable their horses in the cathedral. It wasn't until the 19th century that restoration work to repair the damage was begun. St.

Patrick's is the national cathedral of the Anglican Church in Ireland and has had many illustrious deans. The most famous was Jonathan Swift, author of *Gulliver's Travels,* who held office from 1713 to 1745. Swift's tomb is in the south aisle. Memorials to many other celebrated figures from Ireland's past line the walls. "Living Stones" is the cathedral's permanent exhibition celebrating Saint Patrick's place in the life of the city. Matins (9:45 AM) and evensong (5:35 PM) are still sung on most days, a real treat for the music lover. ⊠ *Patrick St.,* ☎ *01/453–9472,* WEB *www.stpatrickscathedral.ie.* ◷ *May and Sept.–Oct., weekdays 9–6, Sat. 9–5, Sun. 10–11 and 12:30–3; June–Aug., weekdays 9–6, Sat. 9–4, Sun. 9:30–3 and 4:15–5:15; Nov.–Apr., weekdays 9–6, Sat. 9–4, Sun. 10–11 and 12:45–3.*

⑫ **St. Stephen's Green.** Dubliners call it simply Stephen's Green; green it is—strikingly so, year-round (you can even spot a palm tree or two). Among the park's many statues are a memorial to Yeats and another to Joyce by Henry Moore. The north side is dominated by the magnificent **Shelbourne Méridien Hotel.** A drink in one of its two bars, or afternoon tea in the elegant Lord Mayor's Room is the most financially painless way to soak in the old-fashioned luxury.

★ ⑱ **Temple Bar.** Dublin's hippest neighborhood—bordered by Dame Street to the south, the Liffey to the north, Fishamble Street to the west, and Westmoreland Street to the east—is the city's version of the Latin Quarter, the playing ground of "young Dublin." Representative of the improved fortunes of the area, with its narrow, winding pedestrian-only cobblestone streets, is the **Clarence** (⊠ 6–8 Wellington Quay, ☎ 01/670–9000), a favorite old Dublin hotel now owned by Bono and the Edge of U2. The area is chock-full of small hip stores, art galleries, and inexpensive restaurants and pubs. The **Irish Film Centre** (⊠ 6 Eustace St., ☎ 01/679–5744) is emblematic of the area's vibrant mix of high and alternative culture.

★ ❶ **Trinity College.** Ireland's oldest and most famous college is the heart of college-town Dublin. Trinity College, Dublin (officially titled Dublin University but familiarly known as Trinity), was founded by Elizabeth I in 1592 and offered a free education to Catholics—providing they accepted the Protestant faith. As a legacy of this condition, until 1966 Catholics who wished to study at Trinity had to obtain a dispensation from their bishop or face excommunication. Today more than 70% of Trinity's students are Catholics, an indication of how far away those days seem now.

The pedimented, neoclassical Georgian facade, built between 1755 and 1759, consists of a magnificent portico with Corinthian columns. The design is repeated on the interior, so the view from outside the gates and from the quadrangle inside is the same. On the quad's lawn are statues of two of the university's illustrious alumni—statesman Edmund Burke and poet Oliver Goldsmith. Other famous students include the philosopher George Berkeley (who gave his name to the northern California city), Jonathan Swift, Thomas Moore, Oscar Wilde, John Millington Synge, Bram Stoker, Edward Carson, and Samuel Beckett. The 18th-century building on the left, just inside the entrance, is the **chapel.** There's an identical building opposite, the **Examination Hall.** The oldest buildings are the library in the far right-hand corner, completed in 1712, and a 1690 row of redbrick buildings known as the **Rubrics,** which contains student apartments.

Ireland's largest collection of books and manuscripts is housed in **Trinity College Library,** entered through the library shop. Its principal treasure is the Book of Kells, generally considered the most striking manuscript ever produced in the Anglo-Saxon world. Only a few pages from the 682-page, 9th-century gospel are displayed at a time, but an informative exhibit has reproductions of many of them. At peak hours you may have to wait in line to enter the library; it's less busy early in the day. Don't miss the grand and glorious Long Room, an impressive 213 ft long and 42 ft wide, which houses 200,000 volumes in its 21 alcoves. ☎ 01/677–2941, WEB *www.bookofkells.ie.* ☉ *Mon.–Sat. 9:30–4:45, Sun. noon–4:30.*

In the Thomas Davis Theatre in the Arts Building, **"Dublin Experience"** is an audiovisual presentation devoted to the history of the city over the last 1,000 years. ☎ *01/677–2941.* ☉ *Late-May–Oct., daily 10–5; shows every hr on the hr.*

North of the Liffey

The Northside city center is a mix of densely thronged shopping streets and slightly run-down sections of once-genteel homes, which are now being bought up and renovated. There are some classic sights in the area, including gorgeous Georgian monuments—the Custom House, the General Post Office, Parnell Square, and the Hugh Lane Gallery—and two landmarks of literary Dublin, the Dublin Writers Museum and the James Joyce Cultural Center, hub of Bloomsday celebrations. A good way to begin is by heading up O'Connell Street to Parnell Square and the heart of James Joyce Country.

㉑ Abbey Theatre. Ireland's national theater was founded by W. B. Yeats and Lady Gregory in 1904. Works by Yeats, Synge, O'Casey, Kavanagh, and Friel have premiered here. The original building was destroyed in a fire in 1951; the present, rather austere theater was built in 1966. It has some noteworthy portraits and mementos in the foyer. Seats are usually available for about IR£12/€15.25; all tickets are IR£8/€10.15 for Monday performances. ⊠ *Lower Abbey St.,* ☎ *01/ 878–7222,* WEB *www.abbeytheatre.ie.*

㉒ Custom House. Extending 375 ft on the north side of the Liffey, this is the city's most spectacular Georgian building (1781–91), the work of James Gandon, an English architect. The central portico is linked by arcades to the pavilions at each end. A statue of Commerce tops the graceful copper dome; additional allegorical statues adorn the main facade. Republicans set the building on fire in 1921, but it was completely restored; it now houses government offices and a visitor center tracing the building's history and significance, and the life of Gandon. ⊠ *Custom House Quay,* ☎ *01/876–7660.* ☉ *Mid-Mar.–Oct, weekdays 10–5:30, weekends 2–5:30; Nov–mid-Mar., Wed.–Fri. 10–5, Sun. 2–5:30.*

★ **㉖ Dublin Writers Museum.** Two restored 18th-century town houses on the north side of Parnell Square, an area rich in literary associations, lodge one of Dublin's finest cultural sights. Rare manuscripts, diaries, posters, letters, limited and first editions, photographs, and other mementos commemorate the lives and works of the nation's greatest writers, including Joyce, Shaw, Wilde, Yeats, and Beckett. The bookshop and café make this an ideal place to spend a rainy afternoon. ⊠ *18–19 Parnell Sq. N,* ☎ *01/872–2077,* WEB *www.visitdublin.com.* ☉ *June–Aug., Mon.–Sat. 10–6, Sun. 11–5; Sept.–May, Mon.–Sat. 10–5, Sun. 11–5.*

㉒ General Post Office. The GPO (1818), still a working post office, is one of the great civic buildings of Dublin's Georgian era, but its fame derives from the role it played during the Easter Rising. Here, on Easter Monday, 1916, the Republican forces stormed the building and issued the Proclamation of the Irish Republic. After a week of shelling, the GPO lay in ruins; 13 rebels were ultimately executed. Most of the original building was destroyed; only the facade—you can still see the scars of bullets on its pillars—remained. ⊠ *O'Connell St.,* ☎ *01/872–8888,* WEB *www.anpost.ie.* ⊘ *Mon.–Sat. 8–8, Sun. 10:30–6:30.*

㉓ Ha'penny Bridge. This heavily trafficked footbridge crosses the Liffey at a prime spot: Temple Bar is on the south side, and the bridge provides the fastest route to the thriving Mary and Henry Street shopping areas to the north. Until early in this century, a half-penny toll was charged to cross it. Yeats was one among many Dubliners who found this too high a price to pay—more a matter of principle than of finance—and so made the detour via O'Connell Bridge.

★ **㉗ Hugh Lane Municipal Gallery of Modern Art.** The imposing Palladian facade of this town house, once the home of the Earl of Charlemont, dominates the north side of Parnell Square. Sir Hugh Lane, a nephew of Lady Gregory (Yeats's patron), collected Impressionist paintings and 19th-century Irish and Anglo-Irish works. Among them are canvases by Jack Yeats (W. B.'s brother) and Paul Henry. The late Francis Bacon's partner donated the entire contents of the artist's studio to the Hugh Lane Gallery, where it has been reconstructed. ⊠ *Parnell Sq.,* ☎ *01/874–1903,* WEB *www.hughlane.ie.* ⊘ *Tues.–Thurs. 9:30–6, Fri.–Sat. 9:30–5, Sun. 11–5.*

㉕ Parnell Square. This is the Northside's most notable Georgian square and one of Dublin's oldest. Because fashionable hostesses liked passersby to be able to peer into the first-floor reception rooms of the elegant brick-face town houses and admire the distinguished guests, their windows are much larger than the others.

㉔ Rotunda Hospital. Founded in 1745 as the first maternity hospital in Ireland or Britain, the Rotunda is now most worth a visit for its **chapel,** with elaborate plasterwork, appropriately honoring motherhood. The **Gate Theatre,** housed in an extension, attracts large crowds with its fine repertoire of classic Irish and European drama. ⊠ *Parnell St.,* ☎ *01/873–0700.*

Dublin West

If you're not an enthusiastic walker, hop a bus or find a cab to take you to these sights in westernmost Dublin.

★ 🖐 **㉚ Ceol.** "Ceol" is the Irish word for music, and this museum tells the ancient story of Celtic music in a thoroughly modern fashion. Computerized exhibits allow you to customize your learning, and touch screens give access to recordings of the masters of the genre plus hundreds of film clips of them performing. The Stories Room contains a priceless oral history of musicians and storytellers from the early part of the 20th century. A children's area includes an ingenious game of musical twister, allowing kids to play along with a tune using parts of their body to play the notes. *Smithfield Village,* ☎ *01/817–3820,* WEB *www.ceol.ie.* ⊘ *Mon.–Sat. 10–6, Sun. 12–6.*

㉘ Four Courts. Today the seat of the High Court of Justice of Ireland, the Four Courts are James Gandon's second Dublin masterpiece, built between 1786 and 1802. The courts were destroyed during the Troubles of the 1920s and restored by 1932. Its distinctive copper-covered dome atop a colonnaded rotunda makes this one of Dublin's most recognizable buildings. You are allowed to listen in on court proceedings, which can often be interesting, educational, even scandalous. ⊠ *Inns Quay,* ☎ *01/872–5555,* WEB *www.courts.ie.* ⊘ *Daily 10:30–1 and 2:15–4.*

★ **㉞ Guinness Brewery and Storehouse.** Founded by Arthur Guinness in 1759, Ireland's all-dominating brewery is on a 60-acre spread west of

Christ Church Cathedral; it is the most popular tourist destination in town. The brewery itself is closed to the public, but the Storehouse is a spectacular tourist attraction with a high-tech exhibition about the brewing process of the "dark stuff." Located in a cast-iron and brick warehouse, it covers six floors built around a huge central glass atrium. But without doubt the star attraction is the top floor **Gravity Bar,** with it's 360°, floor-to-ceiling glass walls and a stunning view over the city. ✉ *St. James's Gate,* ☎ *01/408–4800,* WEB *www.guinness.com.* ⊙ *April–Sept., Mon.–Sat. 9:30–7, Sun. 11–5; Oct.–Mar., daily 9:30–5.*

㉝ **Kilmainham Gaol.** This grim, forbidding structure was where leaders of the 1916 Easter Rising, including Pádrig Pearse and James Connolly, were held before being executed. A guided tour and a 30-minute audiovisual presentation relate a graphic account of Ireland's political history over the past 200 years from a Nationalist viewpoint. ✉ *Inchicore Rd.,* ☎ *01/453–5984,* WEB *www.heritageireland.ie.* ⊙ *Apr.–Sept., daily 9:30–5; Oct.–Mar., weekdays 9:30–4, Sun. 10–5.*

㉙ **Old Jameson Distillery.** The birthplace of one of Ireland's best whiskeys has been fully restored and offers a fascinating insight into the making of *uisce batha,* or "holy water," as whiskey is known in Irish. There is a 40-minute guided tour of the old distillery, a 20-minute audiovisual tour, and a complimentary tasting. ✉ *Bow St.,* ☎ *01/807–2355,* WEB *www.irish-whiskey-trail.com.* ⊙ *Daily 9:30–5:30; tours every ½ hr.*

★ ㉛ **Phoenix Park.** Europe's largest public park encompasses 1,752 acres of verdant lawns, woods, lakes, playing fields, a zoo, a flower garden, and two residences—those of the president of Ireland and the ambassador for the United States. A 210-ft-tall obelisk, built in 1817, commemorates the Duke of Wellington's defeat of Napoléon. It is a runner's paradise, but Sunday is the best time to visit, when all kinds of games are likely to be in progress.

★ ㉜ **Royal Hospital Kilmainham.** A short ride by taxi or bus from the city center, this structure is regarded as the most important 17th-century building in Ireland. Completed in 1684 as a hospice for soldiers, it survived into the 1920s as a hospital. The ceiling of the Baroque chapel is extraordinary. It now houses the **Irish Museum of Modern Art,** which displays works by such non-Irish greats as Picasso and Miró but concentrates on the work of Irish artists. ✉ *Kilmainham La.,* ☎ *01/612–9900,* WEB *www.modernart.ie.* ⊙ *Tues.–Sat. 10–5:30, Sun. noon–5:30; Royal Hospital tours every ½ hr; museum tours Wed. and Fri. at 2:30, Sat. at 11:30.*

DINING

Beyond the restaurants recommended here, the area between Grafton Street and South Great George's Street has many to offer, as does Temple Bar, just across Dame Street. It's also worth checking out suburban villages like Ranelagh, Blackrock, and Sandycove for good local restaurants.

Sales tax is included in the price. Many places add a 10%–15% service charge—if not, a 10% tip is fine.

CATEGORY	COST*
$$$$	over IR£23 (€29)
$$$	IR£17–IR£23 (€21–€29)
$$	IR£10–IR£16 (€13–€20)
$	under IR£10 (€13)

*per person for a main course at dinner

$$$$ ✕ **The Commons Restaurant.** This restaurant is in a large, elegant room with French windows in the basement of Newman House, where James Joyce was a student in the original premises of University College Dublin. The seasonal menu encompasses a light treatment of classic themes. ✉ *85–86 St. Stephen's Green,* ☎ *01/478–0530. AE, DC, MC, V. Closed weekends.*

$$$$ ✕ **Le Coq Hardi.** John Howard has been running one of the best restaurants in Dublin in this Georgian house for many years. One of his signature dishes—a little old-fashioned, perhaps, but still popular—is Coq Hardi chicken stuffed with potatoes and mushrooms, wrapped in bacon before going into the oven, and finished off with a dash of Irish whiskey. ✉ *35 Pembroke Rd., Ballsbridge,* ☎ *01/668–9070. Reservations essential. AE, DC, MC, V. Closed Sun.*

$$$$ ✕ **Patrick Guilbaud.** Everything is French here, including the eponymous owner, his chef, and the maître d'. The cooking is a fluent expression of modern French cuisine—not particularly flamboyant, but coolly professional. ✉ *Hotel Merrion, Merrion St.,* ☎ *01/676–4192. AE, DC, MC, V. Closed Sun.–Mon. and late Dec.–mid-Jan.*
★

$$$$ ✕ **Thornton's.** Owner Kevin Thornton is one of the finest chefs in Ireland, and a visit to his town-house restaurant on the north bank of the Grand Canal is a must for serious foodies. The space is elegantly understated, the service is formal, and the French cuisine is exquisite, if expensive. ✉ *1 Portobello Rd.,* ☎ *01/454–9067. Reservations essential. AE, DC, MC, V. Closed Sun.–Mon. No lunch Sat.–Thurs.*
★

$$$ ✕ **Chapter One.** In the vaulted, stone-walled basement of the Dublin Writers Museum, this is one of the most notable restaurants in Northside Dublin. Dishes include pressed duck and black pudding terrine with a pear chutney, and grilled black sole with ravioli stuffed with salmon mousse. ✉ *18–19 Parnell Sq.,* ☎ *01/873–2266. AE, DC, MC, V. Closed Sun.–Mon. No lunch Sat.*

$$$ ✕ **Cooke's Café.** Johnny Cooke has turned this central, Californian-Mediterranean-style bistro into a cool spot. It's busy and service can be slow; the outdoor seating on nice summer days is a consolation. ✉ *14 S. William St.,* ☎ *01/679–0536. AE, DC, MC, V.*

$$–$$$ ✕ **Brownes Brasserie.** In this elegant restaurant, huge mirrors reflect the light from crystal chandeliers, glowing on jewel-colored walls and upholstery. The food is rich and heartwarming, with such classics as Irish smoked salmon and confit of duck with lentils. ✉ *22 St. Stephen's Green,* ☎ *01/638–3939. AE, DC, MC, V. No lunch Sat.*

$$–$$$ ✕ **Bruno's.** At this French–Mediterranean bistro on one of the busiest corners in Temple Bar, enjoy simple but stylish dishes ranging from starters of fresh crab claws with chilies, lemongrass, and tomato concassé to main dishes of char-grilled chicken with raisins, dried prunes, Moroccan semolina, and walnut dressing. ✉ *30 Essex St. E,* ☎ *01/ 670–6767. AE, DC, MC, V. Closed Sun.*

$$–$$$ ✕ **La Stampa.** One of the most dramatic dining rooms in Dublin, La Stampa has huge gilt mirrors and elaborate candelabra that are gloriously over the top. The menu changes frequently to reflect an eclectic, international style. For a main course you may get rack of organic lamb with braised beans, tomatoes, and rosemary jus, or roast scallops with artichoke mash and a tomato vinaigrette. ✉ *35 Dawson St.,* ☎ *01/ 677–8611. AE, DC, MC, V. No lunch.*
★

$$ ✕ **Caviston's.** The Cavistons have been dispensing recipes for years from their fish counter and delicatessen in Sandycove, just south of the ferry port of Dun Laoghaire, 30 minutes by taxi or DART train south of Dublin. The fish restaurant next door is a lively and intimate spot for lunch, but you should book in advance. ✉ *59 Glasthule Rd., Dun Laoghaire,* ☎ *01/280–9120. MC, V. Closed Sun.–Mon. and late Dec.– early Jan. No dinner.*

$$ ✗ **Eden.** This popular brasserie-style restaurant overlooking one of Temple Bar's main squares turns out good contemporary cuisine, such as vegetarian buckwheat pancake filled with garlic, spinach, and cheddar, and duck leg confit with lentils. Try to go when there are open-air movies in the square. ⊠ *Meeting House Sq.,* ☎ *01/670–5372. Reservations essential. AE, MC, V.*

$$ ✗ **The Lord Edward.** Creaking floorboards and an old fireplace give the impression of being in someone's drawing room at this restaurant, one of the oldest in the city. Start with classic fish dishes such as prawn cocktail or smoked salmon, followed by fresh and simply cooked Dover sole, salmon, or lobster. ⊠ *23 Christ Church Pl.,* ☎ *01/454–2420. AE, DC, MC, V. No lunch Sat. Closed Sun.*

$ ✗ **Milano.** In a well-designed dining room with lots of brio, choose from a tempting array of inventive, thin-crust pizzas. ⊠ *38 Dawson St.,* ☎ *01/670–7744; 18 Essex St. E, Temple Bar;* ☎ *01/670–3384. AE, DC, MC, V.*

Pub Food

Most pubs serve food at lunchtime, some throughout the day. Food ranges from hearty soups and stews to chicken curries, smoked salmon salads, and sandwiches. Expect to pay IR£4/€5.10–IR£6/€7.60 for a main course. Larger pubs tend to take credit cards.

✗ **Davy Byrne's.** James Joyce immortalized Davy Byrne's in *Ulysses.* Nowadays it's more akin to a cocktail bar than a Dublin pub, but it's good for fresh and smoked salmon, salads, and a hot daily special. ⊠ *21 Duke St.,* ☎ *01/671–1298.*

✗ **Old Stand.** Conveniently close to Grafton Street, the Old Stand serves grilled food, including steaks. ⊠ *37 Exchequer St.,* ☎ *01/677-7220.*

✗ **Porterhouse.** Ireland's first brewpub has an open kitchen and a dazzling range of beers—from pale ales to dark stouts. ⊠ *16–18 Parliament St.,* ☎ *01/679-8847.*

✗ **Stag's Head.** The Stag's Head is a favorite of Trinity students and businesspeople, who come for one of the best pub lunches in the city. ⊠ *1 Dame Ct.,* ☎ *01/679–3701.*

✗ **Zanzibar.** This is a spectacular and cavernous bar that looks as though it might be more at home in downtown Marakesh. While away an afternoon on one of its wicker chairs. ⊠ *34–35 Lower Ormond Quay,* ☎ *01/878-7212.*

Cafés

Though Dublin has nowhere near as many cafés as pubs, it's easier than ever to find a good cup of coffee at most hours of the day or night.

✗ **Bewley's Coffee House.** The granddaddy of the capital's cafés, Bewley's has been supplying Dubliners with coffee and buns for more than a century. ⊠ *78 Grafton St.; 12 Westmoreland St.; all* ☎ *01/677–6761.*

✗ **Kaffe Moka.** One of Dublin's hottest haunts for the caffeine-addicted, this spot has three hyperstylish floors and a central location in the heart of the city center. ⊠ *39 S. William St.,* ☎ *01/679-8475.*

✗ **Thomas Read's.** By day it's a café, by night a pub. Its large windows overlooking a busy corner in Temple Bar make it a great spot for people watching. ⊠ *1 Parliament St.,* ☎ *01/671-7283.*

LODGING

On the lodging front Dublin is in the midst of a major hotel boom. For value stay in a guest house or a B&B; both tend to be in suburban areas—

generally a 10-minute bus ride from the center of the city. **Bord Fáilte** can usually help find you a place to stay if you don't have reservations.

CATEGORY	COST*
$$$$	over IR£180 (€229)
$$$	IR£140–IR£180 (€178–€229)
$$	IR£100–IR£140 (€127–€178)
$	under IR£100 (€127)

Prices are for two people in a double room, based on high-season (June–mid-September) rates, including value-added tax (VAT) and service charges.

$$$$ 🏨 **Conrad Dublin International.** A subsidiary of Hilton Hotels, the Conrad is aimed at the international business executive. The seven-story redbrick and smoked-glass building is just off Stephen's Green. The spacious rooms are done in light brown and pastel greens. Alfie Byrne's, the main bar, attempts to re-create a traditional Irish pub atmosphere. ⊠ *Earlsfort Terr., Dublin 2,* ☎ *01/676–5555,* FAX *01/676–5424,* WEB *www.conrad-international.ie. 182 rooms, 9 suites. 2 restaurants, bar. AE, DC, MC, V.*

$$$$ 🏨 **Jurys and the Towers.** These adjacent seven-story hotels, a short cab ride from the center of town, are popular with businesspeople and vacationers. Both have more atmosphere than most comparable modern hotels, though the Towers has an edge over Jurys, its less expensive companion. ⊠ *Pemroke Rd., Ballsbridge, Dublin 4,* ☎ *01/660–5000,* FAX *01/660–5540,* WEB *www.jurys.com. Jurys: 288 rooms, 5 suites; the Towers: 100 rooms, 5 suites. 3 restaurants, pool. AE, DC, MC, V.*

$$$$ 🏨 **Merrion.** Four restored Georgian town houses make up part of this
★   luxurious hotel. The stately rooms have been richly appointed in classic Georgian style down to the last detail. Leading Dublin restaurateur Patrick Guilbaud's eponymous restaurant is here. ⊠ *Upper Merrion St., Dublin 2,* ☎ *01/603–0600,* FAX *01/603–0700,* WEB *www.merrionhotel.com. 127 rooms, 18 suites. 2 restaurants, 2 bars. AE, DC, MC, V.*

$$$$ 🏨 **Shelbourne Méridien Hotel.** Old-fashioned luxury prevails at this
★   magnificent showplace, which has presided over Stephen's Green since 1824. Each room has its own fine, carefully selected furnishings. Those in front overlook the green; rooms in the back are quieter. The restaurant, 27 The Green, is one of the most elegant rooms in Dublin; Lord Mayor's Room, off the lobby, serves a lovely afternoon tea. ⊠ *27 Stephen's Green, Dublin 2,* ☎ *01/663–4500; 800/543–4300 in the U.S.,* FAX *01/661–6006,* WEB *www.shelbourne.ie. 194 rooms, 9 suites. 2 restaurants, 2 bars. AE, DC, MC, V.*

$$$$ 🏨 **Westbury.** This comfortable, modern hotel is right off the city's shopping mecca, Grafton Street. The spacious main lobby, where you can have afternoon tea, is furnished with antiques and large sofas. Rooms are rather utilitarian; the suites, which combine European decor with Japanese prints and screens, are more inviting. The flowery Russell Room serves formal lunches and dinners. ⊠ *Grafton St., Dublin 2,* ☎ *01/ 679–1122,* FAX *01/679–7078,* WEB *www.jurys.com. 203 rooms, 8 suites. 2 restaurants, bar. AE, DC, MC, V.*

$$$–$$$$ 🏨 **Chief O'Neill's.** Next door to the traditional music museum Ceol, this modern hotel has a huge lobby-bar area looking out onto a cobbled courtyard. Smallish, high-tech rooms all have chrome fixtures and minimalist furnishings. Top-floor suites have delightful rooftop gardens with views of the city on both sides of the Liffey. ⊠ *Smithfield Village, Dublin 7,* ☎ *01/817–3838,* FAX *01/817–3839,* WEB *www. chiefoneills.com. 69 rooms, 4 suites. Restaurant, bar. AE, DC, MC, V.*

$$$–$$$$ 🏨 **Hibernian.** An early 20th-century Edwardian nurses' home was converted into this hotel, retaining the distinctive red-and-amber brick facade. Every room is a different shape, though all are done in light pastels with deep-pile carpets. Public rooms are slightly small but are

attractive in cheerful chintz and stripes. ⊠ *Eastmoreland Pl., off Upper Baggot St., Dublin 4,* ☎ *01/668–7666,* 𝖥𝖠𝖷 *01/660–2655,* 𝖶𝖤𝖡 *hibernian hotel.com. 40 rooms. Restaurant, bar. AE, DC, MC, V.*

$$–$$$ 🏨 **Central Hotel.** Established in 1887, this grand, old-style redbrick hotel is in the heart of the city. Rooms are small but have high ceilings and tasteful furnishings. The Library Bar on the second floor is one of the best spots in the city for a quiet pint. ⊠ *1–5 Exchequer St., Dublin 2,* ☎ *01/679–7302,* 𝖥𝖠𝖷 *01/679–7303,* 𝖶𝖤𝖡 *www.centralhotel.ie. 67 rooms, 3 suites. Restaurant, 2 bars. AE, DC, MC, V.*

$$ 🏨 **Number 31.** Two renovated Georgian mews are connected via a small
★ garden to the grand town house they once served; together they form a marvelous guest house a short walk from Stephen's Green. Owners Deirdre and Noel Comer offer gracious hospitality and made-to-order breakfasts. ⊠ *31 Leeson Close, Dublin 2,* ☎ *01/676–5011,* 𝖥𝖠𝖷 *01/676–2929,* 𝖶𝖤𝖡 *www.number31.ie. 18 rooms. AE, MC, V.*

$$ 🏨 **Paramount.** On the corner of Parliament Street and Essex Gate at the heart of Temple Bar, this medium-size hotel has kept its classy Victorian facade. The bedrooms are all dark woods and subtle colors, very 1930s; you just know if Bogart and Bacall ever come to Dublin they'll have to stay here. If your fond of a tipple try the hotel's art-deco Turks Head Bar and Chop House. ⊠ *Parliament Street and Essex Gate, Dublin 2,* ☎ *01/417–9900,* 𝖥𝖠𝖷 *01/417–9904,* 𝖶𝖤𝖡 *www.paramounthotel.ie. 70 rooms. Restaurant, bar. AE, DC, MC, V.*

$–$$ 🏨 **Mount Herbert Hotel.** Close to the luxury hotels in the tree-lined inner suburb of Ballsbridge, a 10-minute DART ride from Dublin's center, the Loughran family's sprawling accommodation is popular with budget-minded visitors. Rooms are small, but all have 10-channel TVs and hair dryers. There's no bar on the premises, but there are plenty to choose from nearby. ⊠ *7 Herbert Rd., Ballsbridge, Dublin 4,* ☎ *01/668–4321,* 𝖥𝖠𝖷 *01/660–7077,* 𝖶𝖤𝖡 *www.mountherberthotel.ie. 200 rooms. Restaurant. AE, DC, MC, V.*

$ 🏨 **Ariel Guest House.** Dublin's leading guest house is in a tree-lined
★ suburb, a 10-minute walk from Stephen's Green, and close to a DART stop. Rooms in the main house are lovingly filled with antiques; those at the back of the house are more spartan; all are immaculate. Owner Michael O'Brien is a helpful and gracious host. ⊠ *52 Lansdowne Rd., Dublin 4,* ☎ *01/668–5512,* 𝖥𝖠𝖷 *01/668–5845,* 𝖶𝖤𝖡 *www.ariel-house.com. 40 rooms. Breakfast room, wine bar. MC, V.*

$ 🏨 **Avalon House.** Many young, independent travelers rate this cleverly restored, Victorian redbrick building the most appealing of Dublin's hostels. A 2-minute walk from Grafton Street and 5–10 minutes from some of the city's best music venues, it has a mix of dormitories, rooms without bath, and rooms with bath. The Avalon Café serves food until 10 PM, but is open as a common room after hours. ⊠ *55 Aungier St., Dublin 2,* ☎ *01/475–0001,* 𝖥𝖠𝖷 *01/475–0303,* 𝖶𝖤𝖡 *www.avalon-house.ie. 312 beds. Bar, café. AE, MC, V.*

$ 🏨 **Jurys Christchurch Inn.** Expect few frills at this functional budget hotel (part of an otherwise upscale hotel chain), where there's a fixed room rate for up to three adults or two adults and two children. The biggest plus: the pleasant location, facing Christ Church Cathedral and within walking distance of most city-center attractions. Rooms are in pastel colors. The bar serves a pub lunch, and the restaurant, breakfast and dinner. ⊠ *Christchurch Pl., Dublin 8,* ☎ *01/454–0000,* 𝖥𝖠𝖷 *01/454–0012,* 𝖶𝖤𝖡 *www.jurys.com. 182 rooms. Restaurant, bar. AE, DC, MC, V.*

NIGHTLIFE AND THE ARTS

The weekly magazines *In Dublin* and the *Big Issue* (at newsstands) contain comprehensive details of upcoming events, including ticket availability. *The Event Guide* also lists events and is free at many pubs and cafés. In peak season, consult the free Bord Fáilte leaflet "Events of the Week."

Cabarets

The following all have cabaret shows, with dancing, music, and traditional Irish song; they are open only in peak season (roughly May–October; call to confirm): **Abbey Tavern** (✉ Howth, Co. Dublin, ☎ 01/839–0307). **Clontarf Castle** (✉ Castle Ave., Clontarf, ☎ 01/833–2321). **Doyle Burlington Hotel** (✉ Upper Leeson St., ☎01/660–5222). **Jurys Hotel** (✉ Pembroke Rd., Ballsbridge, ☎ 01/660–5000).

Classical Music

The **National Concert Hall** (✉ Earlsfort Terr., ☎ 01/475–1666), just off Stephen's Green, is home to the National Symphony Orchestra of Ireland and is Dublin's main theater for classical music of all kinds. **St. Stephen's Church** (✉ Merrion Sq., ☎ 01/288–0663) has a regular program of choral and orchestral events.

Nightclubs

The **Kitchen** (✉ Essex St., ☎ 01/677–6635) is part-owned by U2 and attracts a young, vibrant clientele. The **POD** (✉ Harcourt St., ☎ 01/478–0166) is the city's hippest spot for twenty-somethings. **Rí Ra** (✉ Dame Court, ☎ 01/677–4835) means "uproar" in Irish, and on most nights the place does go a little wild; it's one of the best spots for fun, no-frills dancing in Dublin.

Pubs

Check advertisements in evening papers for folk, ballad, Irish traditional, or jazz music performances. The pubs listed below generally have some form of musical entertainment. The **Brazen Head** (✉ 20 Lower Bridge St., ☎ 01/677–9549)—Dublin's oldest pub, dating from 1688—has music every night. **Chief O'Neill's** (✉ Smithfield Village, ☎ 01/817–3838) has an open, airy bar-café. The **Cobblestone** (✉ N. King St., ☎ 01/872–1799) is a glorious house of ale in the best Dublin tradition. **Doheny & Nesbitt's** (✉ 5 Lower Baggot St., ☎ 01/676–2945) is frequented by local businesspeople, politicians, and legal eagles. In the **Horseshoe Bar** (✉ Shelbourne Méridien Hotel, St. Stephen's Green, ☎ 01/676–6471) you can eavesdrop on Dublin's social elite. **Kehoe's** (✉ 9 S. Anne St., ☎ 01/677–8312) is popular with students, artists, and writers. Locals and tourists bask in the theatrical atmosphere of **Neary's** (✉ 1 Chatham St., ☎ 01/676–2807). **O'Donoghue's** (✉ 15 Merrion Row, ☎ 01/661–4303) features some form of musical entertainment on most nights. The **Palace Bar** (✉ 21 Fleet St., ☎ 01/677–9290) is a journalists' haunt.

Theaters

Ireland has a rich theatrical tradition. The **Abbey Theatre** (✉ Marlborough St., ☎ 01/878–7222) is the home of Ireland's national theater company, its name forever associated with J. M. Synge, W. B. Yeats, and Sean O'Casey. The **Peacock Theatre** is the Abbey's more experimental small stage. The **Gaiety Theatre** (✉ S. King St., ☎ 01/677–1717) features musical comedy, opera, drama, and revues. The **Gate Theatre** (✉ Cavendish Row, Parnell Sq., ☎ 01/874–4045) is an intimate spot for modern drama and plays by Irish writers. The **Olympia Theatre** (✉ Dame St., ☎ 01/677–7744) has comedy, vaudeville, and

ballet performances. The **Project Arts Centre** (⊠ 39 E. Essex St., ☎ 01/
679–6622) is an established fringe theater.

SHOPPING

The rest of the country is well supplied with crafts shops, but Dublin
is the place to seek out more specialized items—antiques, haute couture, designer ceramics, books and prints, silverware and jewelry, and
designer hand-knit items.

Shopping Centers and Department Stores

The shops north of the river—many of them chain stores and lackluster
department stores—tend to be less expensive and less design-
conscious. The one exception is the **Jervis Shopping Center** (⊠ Jervis
St. at Mary St., ☎ 01/878–1323), a major shopping center with chain
stores as well as smaller boutiques. **Arnotts** (⊠ Henry St., ☎ 01/805–
0400) is Dublin's largest department store and carries a good range
of cut crystal. **Brown Thomas** (⊠ Grafton St., ☎ 01/605–6666) is
Dublin's most elegant department store. **St. Stephen's Green Center** (⊠
St. Stephen's Green, ☎ 01/478–0888) contains 70 stores in a vast
Moorish-style glass-roof building.

Shopping Districts

Grafton Street is the most sophisticated shopping area in Dublin's city
center. **Francis Street** and **Dawson Street** are the places to browse for
antiques. **Nassau Street** and **Dawson Street** are for books; the smaller
side streets are good for jewelry, art galleries, and old prints. The
pedestrianized **Temple Bar** area, with its young, offbeat ambience, has
a number of small art galleries, specialty shops (music and books), and
inexpensive, trendy clothing shops. The area is further enlivened by
buskers (street musicians) and street artists.

Bookstores

Fred Hanna's (⊠ 29 Nassau St., ☎ 01/677–1255) sells old and new
books, with a good choice of books on travel and Ireland. **Hodges Fig-
gis** (⊠ 56–58 Dawson St., ☎ 01/677–4754) is Dublin's leading independent, with a café on the first floor. **Waterstone's** (⊠ 7 Dawson St.,
☎ 01/679–1415) is the Dublin branch of the renowned British chain.
Hughes & Hughes (⊠ St. Stephen's Green Centre, ☎ 01/478–3060)
has strong travel and Irish-interest sections. There is also a store at Dublin
Airport.

Gift Items

Blarney Woollen Mills (⊠ Nassau St., ☎ 01/671–0068) has a good selection of tweed, linen, and woolen sweaters. **Dublin Woolen Mills** (⊠
Metal Bridge Corner, 41 Lower Ormond Quay, ☎ 01/677–5014), at
Ha'penny Bridge, sells hand-knit and other woolen sweaters at com-
petitive prices. **Kevin & Howlin** (⊠ Nassau St., ☎ 01/677–0257) carries tweeds for men. **Kilkenny Shop** (⊠ Nassau St., ☎ 01/677–7066)
is good for contemporary Irish-made ceramics, pottery, and silver jewelry. **McDowell** (⊠ 3 Upper O'Connell St., ☎ 01/874–4961), in business for more than 100 years, is a popular jewelry shop. **Tierneys** (⊠
St. Stephen's Green Centre, ☎ 01/478–2873) carries a good selection
of crystal, china, claddagh rings, pendants, and brooches.

Outdoor Markets

Moore Street (⊠ Henry St.), a large mall behind the Ilac Center, is open from Monday to Saturday 9–6; stalls lining both sides of the street sell fruits and vegetables. A variety of bric-a-brac is sold at the **Liberty Market** on the north end of Meath Street, open on Friday and Saturday 10–6, Sunday noon–5:30. The indoor **Mother Redcap's Market,** opposite Christ Church, is open Friday, Saturday, and Sunday 10–5; come here for antiques and other finds.

DUBLIN A TO Z

To research prices, get advice from other travelers, and book travel arrangements, visit www.fodors.com.

AIRPORTS AND TRANSFERS
All flights arrive at Dublin Airport, 10 km (6 mi) north of town.
➤ AIRPORT INFORMATION: (☎ 01/814–1111).

TRANSFERS
Express buses leave every 20 minutes from outside the Arrivals door for the central bus station in downtown Dublin. The ride takes about 30 minutes, depending on the traffic, and the fare is IR£3/€3.80. If you have time, take a regular bus for IR£1.15/€1.45. A taxi ride into town will cost from IR£12/€15.25 to IR£14/€17.80, depending on your destination. Be sure to ask in advance if the cab has no meter.

BOAT AND FERRY TRAVEL
Irish Ferries has a regular car and passenger service directly into Dublin port from Holyhead in Wales. Stena Sealink docks in Dublin port (3½-hour service to Holyhead) and in Dun Laoghaire (High Speed Service, known as "HSS," which takes 99 minutes). Prices and departure times vary according to season, so call to confirm. In summer, reservations are strongly recommended. Dozens of taxis wait to take you into town from both ports, or you can take DART or a bus to the city center.
➤ BOAT AND FERRY INFORMATION: **Irish Ferries** (⊠ Merrion Row, ☎ 01/661–0511). **Stena Sealink** (⊠ Ferryport, Dun Laoghaire, ☎ 01/204–7777).

BUS TRAVEL TO AND FROM DUBLIN
The central bus station is Busaras; some buses also terminate near O'-Connell Bridge. Bus Éireann provides express and provincial service.
➤ BUS INFORMATION: **Busaras** (⊠ Store St. near the Custom House). **Bus Éireann** (☎ 01/836–6111).

BUS TRAVEL WITHIN DUBLIN
Dublin Bus provides city service, including transport to and from the airport. Most city buses originate in or pass through the area of O'-Connell Street and O'Connell Bridge. If the destination board indicates AN LÁR, that means that the bus is going to the city center. Timetables (IR£2.50/€3.20) are available from Dublin Bus; the minimum fare is 55p/€.70.
➤ BUS INFORMATION: **Dublin Bus** (⊠ 59 Upper O'Connell St., ☎ 01/873–4222).

CAR TRAVEL
The main access route from the north is N1; from the west, N4; from the south and southwest, N7; from the east coast, N11. All routes have clearly marked signs indicating the center of the city: AN LÁR. The M50 motorway encircles the city from Dublin Airport in the north to Tallaght in the south.

The number of cars in Ireland has grown exponentially in the last few years, and nowhere has their impact been felt more than in Dublin, where the city's complicated one-way streets are often congested. Avoid driving a car in the city except to get you into and out of it, and ask your hotel or guest house for clear directions when you leave.

EMERGENCIES
➤ DOCTORS AND DENTISTS: **Dentist: Dublin Dental Hospital** (☎ 01/662–0766). **Doctor: Eastern Help Board** (☎ 01/679–0700).
➤ EMERGENCY SERVICES: **Ambulance** (☎ 999). **Police** (☎ 999).
➤ PHARMACIES: **Hamilton Long** (☎ 01/874–8456).

TAXIS
Official licensed taxis, metered and designated by roof signs, do not cruise; they can be found beside the central bus station, at train stations, at O'Connell Bridge, Stephen's Green, College Green, and near major hotels. The initial charge is IR£1.80/€2.30, with an additional charge of about IR£1.60/€2.05 per 2 km (1 mi) thereafter (make sure the meter is on). Hackney cabs, which also operate in the city, have neither roof signs nor meters and will sometimes respond to hotels' requests for a cab. Negotiate the fare before your journey begins.

TOURS
BUS TOURS
Bus Éireann runs day trips to all the major sights around the capital. Gray Line Tours organizes bus tours of Dublin and its major sights; they also have daylong tours into the surrounding countryside and longer tours elsewhere (the price for excursion tours includes accommodations, breakfast, and admission). Dublin Bus runs a continuous guided open-top bus tour (IR£5/€6.35) that allows you to hop on and off the bus as often as you wish and visit some 15 sights along its route.
➤ FEES AND SCHEDULES: **Bus Éireann** (☎ 01/836–6111). **Dublin Bus** (☎ 01/873–0000). **Gray Line Tours** (☎ 01/670–8822).

SPECIAL INTEREST TOURS
Elegant Ireland arranges tours for groups interested in architecture and the fine arts; these include visits with the owners of some of Ireland's stately homes and castles.
➤ FEES AND SCHEDULES: **Elegant Ireland** (☎ 01/475–1665).

WALKING TOURS
The tourist office has leaflets giving information on a selection of walking tours, including "Literary Dublin," "Georgian Dublin," and "Pub Tours." Bord Fáilte has a "Tourist Trail" walk, which takes in the main sites of central Dublin and can be completed in about three hours, and a "Rock 'n Stroll" tour, which covers the city's major pop and rock music sites.

TRAIN TRAVEL
Irish Rail provides train service throughout the country. Dublin has three main stations. Connolly Station is the departure point for Belfast, the east coast, and the west. Heuston Station is the departure point for the south and southwest. Pearse Station is for Bray and connections via Dun Laoghaire to the Liverpool-Holyhead ferries.

An electric train commuter service, DART, serves the suburbs out to Howth, on the north side of the city, and to Bray, County Wicklow, on the south side. Fares are about the same as for buses. Street-direction signs to DART stations read STAISIUN/STATION.

➤ TRAIN INFORMATION: **Connolly Station** (✉ at Amiens St.). **Heuston Station** (✉ at Kingsbridge). **Irish Rail** (✉ 35 Lower Abbey St., ☎ 01/836–6222 information). **Pearse Station** (✉ on Westland Row).

TRAVEL AGENCIES

➤ LOCAL AGENTS: **American Express** (✉ 116 Grafton St., ☎ 01/677–2874). **Thomas Cook** (✉ 118 Grafton St., ☎ 01/677–1721).

VISITOR INFORMATION

In addition to the visitor information offices in the entrance hall of the headquarters of Bord Fáilte, Dublin Tourism has visitor information at the airport (Arrivals level), open daily 8 AM–10 PM; and at the Ferryport, Dun Laoghaire, open daily 10 AM–9 PM.

Ireland Basics

BUSINESS HOURS

Banks are open weekdays 10–4 and until 5 on Thursday. In small towns they may close for lunch from 12:30 to 1:30. Museums are usually closed on Mondays but open Tuesday–Saturday 10–5, and Sunday 2–5. Always make a point of checking, however, as hours can change unexpectedly. Shops are open Monday–Saturday 9–5:30, closing earlier on Wednesday, Thursday, or Saturday, depending on the locality. Most shops, however, remain open until 9 PM on Thursday.

CUSTOMS AND DUTIES

For details on imports and duty-free limits, *see* Customs and Duties *in* Smart Travel Tips A to Z.

EMBASSIES

➤ AUSTRALIA: (✉ Fitzwilton House, Fitzwilton Terr., Dublin 2, ☎ 01/676–1517).
➤ CANADA: (✉ 65 St. Stephen's Green, Dublin 2, ☎ 01/478–1988).
➤ SOUTH AFRICA: (✉ Alexandra House, 2nd floor, Earlsfort Terrace, Dublin 2, ☎ 01/661–5553).
➤ UNITED KINGDOM: (✉ 31 Merrion Rd., Dublin 2, ☎ 01/205–3700).
➤ UNITED STATES: (✉ 42 Elgin Rd., Ballsbridge, Dublin 4, ☎ 01/668–8777).

HOLIDAYS

January 1; St. Patrick's Day; Good Friday; Easter Monday; May 6 (May Holiday); Whitmonday; August 5 (August Holiday); October 28 (October Holiday); and December 25–26 (Christmas and St. Stephen's Day).

LANGUAGE

Officially, Irish (Gaelic) is the first language of the Republic, but the everyday language of the vast majority of Irish people is English. Except for isolated parts of the northwest and Connemara, where many signs are not translated, most signs in the country are written in English, with an Irish translation. There is one important exception to this rule, with which you should familiarize yourself: FIR (pronounced "fear") and MNÁ (pronounced "muh-*naw*") translate, respectively, into "men" and "women." The Gaeltacht (pronounced "*gale*-tocked")—areas in which Irish *is* the everyday language of most people—comprises only 6% of the land, and all its inhabitants are, in any case, bilingual.

MONEY MATTERS

Dublin is expensive—an unfortunate state of affairs that manifests itself most obviously in hotel rates and restaurant menus. You can generally keep costs lower if you visit Ireland on a package tour. Alternatively, consider staying in a guest house or a B&B; they provide an economical and atmospheric option. That the Irish themselves complain bitterly about the high cost of living is partly attributable to the rate of value-added tax (VAT)—a stinging 21% on "luxury" goods and 12½% on hotel accommodations.

Sample prices include: cup of coffee, IR£1/€1.30; pint of beer, IR£2.30/€3; Coca-Cola, 95p/€1.20; a sandwich, IR£1.80/€2.30; 2-km (1-mi) taxi ride, IR£4/€5.10.

The unit of currency in Ireland is the pound, or punt (pronounced "poont"), written as IR£ to avoid confusion with the pound sterling (£). The currency is divided into the same denominations as in Britain, with IR£1 divided into 100 pence (written *p*). Although the Irish pound is the only legal tender in the Republic, U.S. dollars and British currency are often accepted in large hotels and shops licensed as bureaux de change. Banks give the best rate of exchange. Change U.K. pounds at a bank when you get to Ireland (pound coins not accepted); change Irish pounds before you leave. Ireland is a member of the European Monetary Union (EMU) and since January 1, 1999, all prices have been quoted in pounds and euros. January 2002 is to see the introduction of the euro coins and notes and the gradual withdrawal of the local currency. The rate of exchange at press time (summer 2001) was 82p/€1.05 to the U.S. dollar, 55p/€.71 to the Canadian dollar, IR£1.25/€1.60 to the pound sterling, 47p/€.60 to the Australian dollar, 39p/€.50 to the New Zealand dollar, and 12p/€.15 to the South African rand.

TELEPHONES
COUNTRY AND AREA CODES
The country code for the Republic of Ireland is 353.

INTERNATIONAL CALLS
Calls to the United States and Canada can be made by dialing 001 followed by the area code. For calls to the United Kingdom, dial 0044 followed by the number, dropping the beginning zero. For long-distance operators, call one of the service providers below.
➤ ACCESS CODES: **AT&T** (☎ 800/550–000). **MCI** (☎ 800/551–001). **Sprint** (☎ 800/552–001).

LOCAL CALLS
Pay phones can be found in all post offices and most hotels and bars, as well as in street booths. Local calls cost 20p/€.25 for three minutes, calls within Ireland cost about 80p/€1.00 for three minutes, and calls to Britain cost about IR£2/€2.50 for three minutes. Telephone cards are available at post offices and most newsagents. Prices range from IR£2/€2.50 for 10 units to IR£8/€10.15 for 50 units. Card booths are as common as coin booths. Rates go down by about a third after 6 PM and all day Saturday and Sunday.

The birthplace of the Renaissance and one of Europe's preeminent treasures, Florence draws visitors from all over the world. Lining the narrow streets of the historic center are 15th-century palazzi whose plain and sober facades often give way to delightful courtyards. The classical dignity of the High Renaissance and the exuberant invention of the Baroque are mostly absent in Florentine buildings; here, the typical exterior gives nothing away of the treasures contained within.

EXPLORING FLORENCE

Numbers in the margin correspond to points of interest on the Florence map.

Founded by Julius Caesar, Florence was built in the familiar grid pattern common to all Roman colonies. Except for the major monuments, which are appropriately imposing, the buildings are low and unpretentious and the streets are narrow. At times Florence can be a nightmare of mass tourism. Plan, if you can, to visit the city in late fall, early spring, or even in winter to avoid the crowds. A special museum ticket valid for three days on the Michelangelo Trail includes the Galleria dell'Accademia, Cappelle Medicee, and the Museo del Bargello; it costs 25,000 lire/€12.90.

Piazza del Duomo and Piazza della Signoria

The area between Piazza del Duomo and Piazza della Signoria comprises the core of the centro storico. Piazza del Duomo has been the center of Florence's religious life for centuries; work began on the Duomo in 1296, and the structure that sprang from the site is testament to religious fervor and a wealthy populace. Via Calzaiouli links this piazza to Piazza della Signoria, the center of Florentine government since the end of the 13th century. The piazza is lined with Renaissance sculpture (some originals, some copies). The Galleria degli Uffizi, next to

Palazzo Vecchio, houses one of the most important collections of Renaissance painting in the world.

★ ❸ **Battistero** (Baptistery). In front of the Duomo is the octagonal baptistery, one of the city's oldest (modern excavations suggest its foundations date from the 4th to 5th and the 8th to 9th centuries) and most beloved buildings. The interior dome mosaics are famous but cannot outshine the building's renowned gilded bronze east·doors (facing the Duomo), the work of Lorenzo Ghiberti (1378–1455). The ones you see at the Baptistery, however, are copies; the originals are preserved in the Museo dell'Opera del Duomo. ⊠ *Piazza del Duomo,* ☎ *055/2302885,* WEB *www.operaduomo.firenze.it.* ⊙ *Mon.–Sat. 12:30–6:30, Sun. 8:30–1:30.*

❷ **Campanile** (Bell tower). This early 14th-century bell tower, designed by Giotto (1266–1337), is richly decorated with colored marble and sculpture reproductions; the originals are in the Museo dell'Opera del Duomo. The 414-step climb to the top is less strenuous than that to the cupola on the Duomo. ⊠ *Piazza del Duomo,* ☎ *055/2302885,* WEB *www.operaduomo.firenze.it.* ⊙ *Apr.–Oct., daily 9–7:30; Nov.–Mar., daily 9–6:50.*

★ ❶ **Duomo.** The Cattedrale di Santa Maria del Fiore is dominated by a cupola representing a landmark in the history of architecture. Work began on the cathedral itself in 1296 under the supervision of master sculptor and architect Arnolfo di Cambio, and its construction took 140 years to complete. Gothic architecture predominates; the facade was added in the 1870s but is based on Tuscan Gothic models. Inside, the church is cool and austere, a fine example of the architecture of the period. Take a good look at the frescoes of equestrian figures on the left wall of the nave: the one on the right is by Paolo Uccello (1397–1475), the one on the left by Andrea del Castagno (circa 1419–57). The dome frescoes by Vasari take second place to the dome itself, Brunelleschi's (1377–1446) greatest architectural and technical achievement. The dome was also the inspiration behind the one Michelangelo designed for St. Peter's in Rome and even for the dome of the Capitol in Washington. You can visit early medieval and ancient Roman remains of previous constructions excavated under the cathedral. And you can climb to the top of the dome, 463 exhausting steps up between the two layers of the double dome for a fine view. ⊠ *Piazza del Duomo,* ☎ *055/2302885,* WEB *www. operaduomo.firenze.it.* ⊙ *Mon.–Wed., Fri.–Sat. 10–5, Thurs. and 1st Sat. of every month 10–3:20, other Sat. 8:30–5, Sun. 1–5. Crypt Mon.– Sat. 10–5. Dome Mon.–Sat. 8:30–6:20 (1st Sat. of month 8:30–3:20).*

★ ❾ **Galleria degli Uffizi** (Uffizi Gallery). The Uffizi was built to house the administrative offices of the Medici, onetime rulers of the city. Later their fabulous art collection was arranged in a gallery on the top floor, which was opened to the public in the 17th century—making this the world's first modern public gallery. It comprises Italy's most important collection of paintings, with the emphasis on Italian art from the 13th to 16th centuries. Make sure you see the *Ognissanti Madonna* by Giotto (1266–1337), and look for Botticelli's (1445–1510) *Birth of Venus* and *Primavera* in Rooms X–XIV, Michelangelo's *Holy Family* in Room XXV, and works by Raphael next door in Room XXVI. In addition to its art treasures, the gallery offers a magnificent close-up view of the Palazzo Vecchio tower from the coffee bar. Avoid long lines at the ticket booths by purchasing tickets in advance from Consorzio ITA. ⊠ *Piazzale degli Uffizi 6,* ☎ *055/23885. Advance tickets:* ⊠ *Consorzio ITA, Piazza Pitti 1, 50121,* ☎ *055/294883,* WEB *www. uffizi.firenze.it.* 🎟 *12,000 lire/€6.20.* ⊙ *Apr.–Oct., Tues.–Sat. 8:30– 10, Sun. 8:30–6; Nov.–Mar., Tues.–Sat. 8:30–6:50, Sun. 8:30–7.*

156

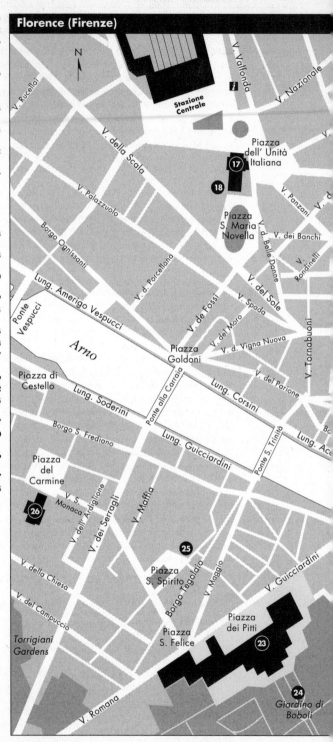

Florence (Firenze)

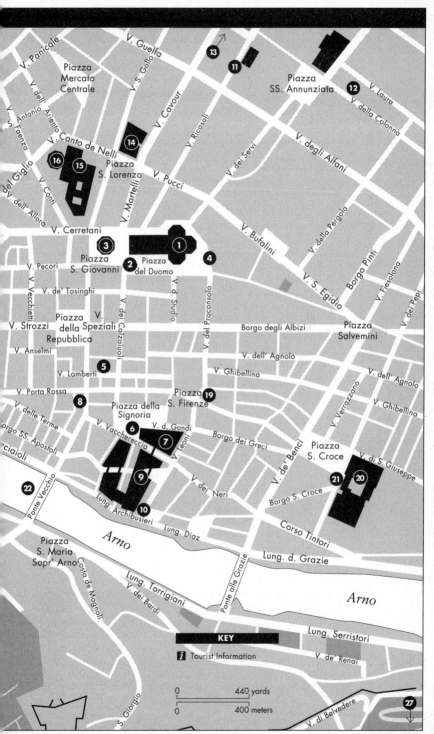

V. Panicale

V. Guelfa

13

11

Piazza
Mercato
Centrale

V. de' Ariento

V. S. Gallo

V. Cavour

Piazza
SS. Annunziata

12

V. Laura

V. della Colonna

V. S. Antonio

V. Faenza

Canto de Nelli

V. Ricasoli

V. dei Servi

V. degli Alfani

del Giglio

16 **15**

V. Conti

Piazza
S. Lorenzo

14

V. Martelli

V. Pucci

V. della Pergola

V. dell' Alloro

V. Cerretani

3 **1** **4**

V. Bufalini

Piazza
S. Giovanni

2 Piazza
del Duomo

V. Pecori

V. d. Studio

V. S. Egidio

Piazza
Salvemini

Borgo Pinti

V. Flesolana

V. de' Pepi

V. de' Tosinghi

V. Vecchietti

V. Strozzi

Piazza
della
Repubblica

V.
Speziali

V. dei Calzaiuoli

V. del Proconsolo

Borgo degli Albizi

V. Anselmi

V. dell' Agnolo

V. dell' Agnolo

V. Lamberti

5

V. Ghibellina

V. Ghibellina

V. Porta Rossa

8

Piazza
S. Firenze

19

V. delle Terme

Piazza della
Signoria

6

V. d. Gondi

V. Vaccchereccia

7

V. Leoni

Borgo dei Greci

V. Verrazzano

orgo SS. Apostoli

ciaioli

9

V. dei Neri

V. de' Benci

Piazza
S. Croce

V. di S. Giuseppe

22

10

21 **20**

Ponte Vecchio

Lung. Archibusieri

Lung. Diaz

Borgo S. Croce

Corso Tintori

Arno

Piazza
S. Maria
Sopr' Arno

Costa de Magnoli

Lung. Torrigiani

V. dei Bardi

Ponte alle Grazie

Lung. d. Grazie

Arno

Lung. Serristori

KEY

🛈 Tourist Information

V. de' Renai

S. Giorgio

0 —————— 440 yards

0 —————— 400 meters

V. di Belvedere

27

❽ Mercato Nuovo (New Market). This open-air loggia was completed in 1551. Beyond the slew of souvenir stands, its main attraction is a copy of Pietro Tacca's bronze *Porcellino* (though it means *Little Pig*, it's actually a wild boar) on the south side, dating from around 1612 and copied from an earlier Roman work now in the Uffizi. The Porcellino is Florence's equivalent of the Trevi Fountain: put a coin in his mouth, and if it lands properly, it means that one day you'll return to Florence. ⊠ *Via Por San Maria at Via Porta Rossa.* ☉ *Market Tues.–Sat. 8–7, Mon. 1–7.*

★ **❹ Museo dell'Opera del Duomo** (Cathedral Museum). The museum contains some superb sculptures by Donatello (circa 1386–1466) and Luca della Robbia (1400–82)—especially their *cantorie*, or singers' galleries—and an unfinished *Pietà* by Michelangelo that was intended for his own tomb. ⊠ *Piazza del Duomo 9,* ☎ *055/2302885,* 🌐 *www.operaduomo.firenze.it.* ☉ *Mon.–Sat. 9:30–6:30, Sun. 8–2.*

❿ Museo di Storia della Scienza (Museum of the History of Science). You don't have to know a lot about science to appreciate the antique scientific instruments presented here in informative, eye-catching exhibits. From astrolabes and armillary spheres to some of Galileo's own instruments, the collection is one of Florence's lesser-known treasures. ⊠ *Piazza dei Giudici 1,* ☎ *055/2398876,* 🌐 *www.imss.fi.it.* ☉ *Museum: Mon.–Sat. 9:30–6:30, Sun. 8–2. Planetarium: Mon., Wed.–Sat. 9:30–5, Tues. 9:30–1; open 10–1 2nd Sun. of the month; closed Dec. 25–26, Jan. 1 and 6, Easter and Easter Mon.*

❺ Orsanmichele (Garden of St. Michael). For centuries this was an odd combination of first-floor church and second-floor granary. Today it serves as a museum, and the statues in the niches on the exterior (many of which are now copies) constitute an anthology of the work of eminent Renaissance sculptors, including Donatello, Ghiberti, and Verrocchio (1435–88). The tabernacle inside is an extraordinary piece by Andrea Orcagna (1308–68). Many of the original statues can be seen in the Museo di Orsanmichele contained within. ⊠ *Via dei Calzaiuoli; museum entrance at via Arte della Lana,* ☎ *055/284944.* ☉ *Guided visits Mon.–Fri. at 9, 10, and 11; non-guided opening hrs Sat.–Sun. 9–1 and 4–6. Closed 1st and last Mon. of month.*

❼ Palazzo Vecchio (Old Palace). Also called Palazzo della Signoria, this massive, fortresslike city hall was begun in 1299 and was taken over, along with the rest of Florence, by the Medici. Inside, the impressive, frescoed salons and the *studiolo* (little study) of Francesco I are the main attractions. ⊠ *Piazza della Signoria,* ☎ *055/2768465.* ☉ *Mon.–Wed., Fri.–Sat. 9–7, Thurs., Sun. 9–2.*

❻ Piazza della Signoria. This is the heart of Florence and the city's largest square. In the pavement in the center of the square a plaque marks the spot where Savonarola, the reformist Dominican friar who urged Florentines to burn their pictures, books, musical instruments, and other worldly objects, was hanged and then burned at the stake as a heretic in 1498. The square, the Fontana di Nettuno (Neptune Fountain) by Ammanati (1511–92), and the surrounding cafés are popular gathering places for Florentines and for tourists who come to admire the Palazzo della Signoria, the copy of Michelangelo's *David* standing in front of it, and the sculptures in the 14th-century Loggia dei Lanzi.

San Marco, San Lorenzo, Santa Maria Novella, Santa Croce

San Marco is the old neighborhood of the Medici, and their imprint is still very much in evidence today. Visual reminders of their power can be seen in the Cappelle Medicee and in San Lorenzo, which was the church that the Medici viewed as their very own. This area is teeming with churches filled with great works of art, and two must-see museums. The Accademia is home to Michelangelo's David, arguably the most famous sculpture in the world, and the Bargello boasts a collection of Renaissance sculpture that is unparalleled.

★ ⑯ **Cappelle Medicee** (Medici Chapels). These extraordinary chapels, part of the church of San Lorenzo complex, contain the tombs of practically every member of the Medici family, which guided Florence's destiny from the 15th century to 1737. Cosimo I (1519–74), a Medici whose acumen made him the richest man in Europe, is buried in the crypt beneath the **Cappella dei Principi** (Chapel of the Princes), and Donatello's tomb is next to that of his patron, Cosimo il Vecchio (1389–1464). Upstairs is a dazzling array of colored marble panels. Michelangelo's **Sagrestia Nuova** (New Sacristy) tombs of Giuliano and Lorenzo de' Medici are adorned with the justly famed sculptures of *Dawn* and *Dusk, Night* and *Day.* ✉ *Piazza di Madonna degli Aldobrandini,* ☎ *Reservations: 055/ 294 883,* WEB *www.sanlorenzo.com.* 💰 *11,000 lire/€5.70* ⊙ *Daily 8:15–5; closed 1st, 3rd, and 5th Mon. and 2nd and 4th Sun. of month.*

★ ⑪ **Galleria dell'Accademia** (Accademia Gallery). Michelangelo's *David* is a tour de force of artistic conception and technical ability, for he was using a piece of stone that had already been worked on by a lesser sculptor. Take time to see the forceful *Slaves,* also by Michelangelo; their rough-hewn, unfinished surfaces contrast dramatically with the highly polished, meticulously carved *David.* Michelangelo left the *Slaves* "unfinished," it is often claimed, to accentuate the figures' struggle to escape the bondage of stone. Actually, he simply abandoned them because his patron changed his mind about the tomb monument for which they were planned. Try to be first in line at opening time or go shortly before closing time so you can get the full impact without having to fight your way through the crowds. ✉ *Via Ricasoli 60,* ☎ *Reservations: 055/ 294 883; Galleria: 055/2388609,* WEB *www.mega.it.* 💰 *15,000 lire/€7.75* ⊙ *Apr.–Oct., Tues.–Sat. 8:30–10, Sun. 8:30–6; Nov.–Mar., Tues.–Sat. 8:30–6:50, Sun. 8:30–7.*

⑫ **Museo Archeologico** (Archaeological Museum). Fine Etruscan and Roman antiquities and a pretty garden are the draw here. ✉ *Via della Colonna 38,* ☎ *055/23575,* WEB *www.mega.it.* ⊙ *Mon. 2–7, Tues., Thurs. 8:30–7, Wed., Fri.–Sun. 8:30–2.*

㉑ **Museo dell'Opera di Santa Croce e Cappella dei Pazzi** (Museum of Santa Croce and Pazzi Chapel). From the cloister of the convent adjacent to Santa Croce you can visit the small museum and see what remains of the Cimbaue crucifix that was irreparably damaged by a flood in 1966, when water rose to 16 ft in parts of the church. The **Cappella dei Pazzi** in the cloister is an architectural gem by Brunelleschi. The interior is a lesson in spatial equilibrium and harmony. ✉ *Piazza Santa Croce,* ☎ *055/244619.* ⊙ *Mar.–Oct., Thurs.–Tues. 10–7; Nov.–Feb., Thurs.–Tues. 10–6.*

⑬ **Museo di San Marco.** A former Dominican convent houses this museum, which contains many works by Fra Angelico (1400–55). Within the same walls where the unfortunate Savonarola, the reformist friar, later contemplated the sins of the Florentines, Fra Angelico went humbly about his work, decorating many of the otherwise austere cells and corridors with brilliantly colored frescoes on religious subjects. Look for his masterpiece, the *Annunciation.* Together with many of his paintings arranged on the ground floor, just off the little cloister, they form a fascinating collection. ✉ *Piazza San Marco 1,* ☎ *055/2388608.*

🕐 *Mon.–Fri. 8:30–1:50, Sat. 8:30–6:50, Sun. 8:30–7. Closed 2nd and 4th Mon. of month.*

⑱ Museo di Santa Maria Novella. Adjacent to the church, this museum is worth a visit for its serene atmosphere and the faded Paolo Uccello frescoes from Genesis, as well as the **Cappellone degli Spagnoli** (Spanish Chapel), with frescoes by Andrea di Buonaiuto. ⊠ *Piazza Santa Maria Novella 19,* ☎ *055/282187.* 🕐 *Wed.–Mon. 9–2.*

★ **⑲ Museo Nazionale del Bargello.** This grim, fortresslike palace served in medieval times as a residence of Florence's chief magistrate and later as a prison. It is now a treasure trove of Italian Renaissance sculpture. In this historic setting you can see masterpieces by Donatello, Verrocchio, Michelangelo, and other major sculptors amid an eclectic array of arms and ceramics. For Renaissance enthusiasts this museum is on a par with the Uffizi. ⊠ *Via del Proconsolo 4,* ☎ *055/2388606,* 🕸 *www.arca.net/db/musei/bargello.htm.* 🕐 *Daily 8:30–1:50. Closed 2nd and 4th Mon. of month and 1st, 3rd, and 5th Sun. of month.*

⑭ Palazzo Medici-Riccardi. Few tourists know about Benozzo Gozzoli's (1420–97) glorious frescoes in the tiny second-floor chapel of this palace, built in 1444 for Cosimo de' Medici (Il Vecchio, 1389–1464). Glimmering with gold, they represent the journey of the Magi as a spectacular cavalcade with cameo portraits of various Medici and the artist himself. ⊠ *Via Cavour 1,* ☎ *055/2760340.* 🕐 *Thurs.–Tues. 9–7.*

⑮ San Lorenzo. The facade of this church was never finished, but the Brunelleschi interior is elegantly austere. Stand in the middle of the nave at the entrance, on the line that stretches to the high altar, and you'll see what Brunelleschi achieved with the grid of inlaid marble in the pavement. Every architectural element in the church is placed to create a dramatic effect of single-point perspective. The **Sagrestia Vecchia** (Old Sacristy), decorated with stuccoes by Donatello, is attributed to Brunelleschi. ⊠ *Piazza San Lorenzo,* ☎ *055/216634.* 🕐 *Church: Mon.–Sat. 7–12 and 3:30–5:30, Sun. 3:30–5. Old Sacristy: Mon.–Sat. 8–noon and 3:30–5:30, Sun. 3:30–5:30. Closed Dec. and Jan.*

★ **⑳ Santa Croce.** The mighty church of Santa Croce was begun in 1294 and has become a pantheon for Florentine greats; monumental tombs of Michelangelo, Galileo (1564–1642), Machiavelli (1469–1527), and other Renaissance luminaries line the walls. Inside are two chapels frescoed by Giotto and another painted by Taddeo Gaddi (1300–66), as well as an *Annunciation* and crucifix by Donatello. But it is the scale of this grandiose church that proclaims the power and ambition of medieval Florence. ⊠ *Piazza Santa Croce 16,* ☎ *055/244619.* 🕐 *Nov.–Mar., Mon.–Sat. 9:30–12:15 and 3–5:30, Sun. 3–5:30; Apr.–Oct., Mon.–Sat. 9:30–5:30 and Sun. 3–5:30.*

⑰ Santa Maria Novella. A Tuscan interpretation of the Gothic style, this handsome church should be seen from the opposite end of Piazza Santa Maria Novella for the best view of its facade. Inside are some famous paintings, especially Masaccio's (1401–28) *Trinity*, a Giotto crucifix in the sacristy, and Ghirlandaio's frescoes in the **Capella Maggiore** (Main Chapel). ⊠ *Piazza Santa Maria Novella,* ☎ *055/210113.* 🕐 *Mon.–Sat. 7–noon and 3–6, Sun. 3–5.*

The Oltrarno

The Oltrarno, which means "beyond the Arno," is on the south side of the Arno. It's a neighborhood filled with artisans' workshops, and in that respect, it has changed little since the Renaissance. The gargantuan Palazzo Pitti stands as a sweeping reminder of the power of the Medici family, and there some lovely Renaissance churches, terrific restaurants, and first-rate shoe stores—all reason enough to cross over and explore.

㉔ Giardini Boboli (Boboli Gardens). The main entrance to this garden on a landscaped hillside is in the right wing of Palazzo Pitti. The garden was laid out in 1549 for Cosimo I's wife, Eleanora da Toledo, who made the Palazzo her home, and was further developed by later Medici dukes. ⊠ *Enter through Palazzo Pitti,* ☎ *055/2651816.* ☺ *Apr.–Oct., daily 8:15–5:30; Nov.–Mar., daily 8:15–4:30. Closed 1st and last Mon. of each month.*

㉓ Palazzo Pitti. This enormous palace is a 16th-century extravaganza the Medici acquired from the Pitti family after the latter had gone deeply into debt to build the central portion. The Medici enlarged the building, extending its facade along the immense piazza. Solid and severe, it looks like a Roman aqueduct turned into a palace. The palace houses several museums: the **Museo degli Argenti** (Silver Museum) displays the fabulous Medici collection of objects in silver and gold; another has the collections of the **Galleria d'Arte Moderna** (Gallery of Modern Art). The most famous museum, though, is the **Galleria Palatina** (Palatine Gallery), with an extraordinary collection of paintings, many hung frame-to-frame in a clear case of artistic overkill. Some are high up in dark corners, so try to go on a bright day. ⊠ *Piazza Pitti,* ☎ *055/ 210323,* 𝚆𝙴𝙱 *www.thais.it.* ☺ *Museo degli Argenti Nov.–Mar., daily 8:30– 1:50. Closed 2nd and 4th Sun. and 1st, 3rd, and 5th Mon. of month. Galleria Palatina Nov.–Mar., Tues.–Sat. 8:30–6:50, Sun. 8:30–8; Apr.– Oct., Tues.–Sat. 8:30 AM–10 PM, Sun. 8:30–7.*

★ **㉒ Ponte Vecchio** (Old Bridge). Florence's oldest bridge appears to be just another street lined with goldsmiths' shops until you get to the middle and catch a glimpse of the Arno below. Spared during World War II by the retreating Germans (who blew up every other bridge in the city), it also survived the 1966 flood. It leads into the **Oltrarno,** where the atmosphere of working-class Florence is preserved amid fascinating artisans' workshops. ⊠ *East of Ponte Santa Trinita and west of Ponte alle Grazie.*

㉗ San Miniato al Monte. One of Florence's oldest churches, this charming green-and-white marble Romanesque edifice is full of artistic riches, among them the gorgeous Renaissance chapel where a Portuguese cardinal was laid to rest in 1459 under a ceiling by Luca della Robbia. ⊠ *Viale Michelangelo, or take stairs from Piazzale Michelangelo,* ☎ *055/ 2342731.* ☺ *Mon.–Sat. 8–12:30 and 2–6, Sun. 8–6.*

㉖ Santa Maria del Carmine. The church is of little architectural interest but of immense significance in the history of Renaissance art. It contains the celebrated frescoes painted by Masaccio in the **Cappella Brancacci.** The chapel was a classroom for such artistic giants as Botticelli, Leonardo da Vinci (1452–1519), Michelangelo, and Raphael, since they all came to study Masaccio's realistic use of light and perspective and his creation of space and depth. ⊠ *Piazza del Carmine,* ☎ *055/2382195.* ☺ *Mon., Wed.–Sat. 10–5, Sun. 1–5.*

㉕ Santo Spirito. Its plain, unfinished facade is less than impressive, but this church is important because it is one of Brunelleschi's finest architectural creations. It contains some superb paintings, including a *Madonna* by Filippo Lippi. Santo Spirito is the hub of a colorful, trendy neighborhood of artisans and intellectuals. An outdoor market enlivens the square every morning except Sunday; in the afternoon, pigeons, pet owners, and pensioners take over. ⊠ *Piazza Santo Spirito,* ☎ *055/210030.* ☺ *Church: Thurs.–Tues. 9–noon and 4–6, Wed. 9– 12. Cenacolo: Tues.–Sun. 10–2.*

DINING

Mealtimes in Florence are from 12:30 to 2:30 and 7:30 to 9 or later. Reservations are always advisable; to find a table at inexpensive places, get there early.

CATEGORY	COST*
$$$$	over 45,000 lire (€23)
$$$	35,000 lire–45,000 lire (€18–€23)
$$	25,000 lire–35,000 lire (€13–€18)
$	under 25,000 lire (€13)

per person for a main course at dinner

$$$$ ✕ **Cibrèo.** The food at this classic Florentine trattoria is fantastic, from
★ the first bite of seamless, creamy *crostini di fegatini* (savory Tuscan chicken liver spread on grilled bread) to the last bite of one of the melt-in-your-mouth-good desserts. If you thought you'd never try tripe, let alone like it, this is the place to lay any doubts to rest: the cold tripe salad with parsley and garlic is an epiphany. ⊠ *Via dei Macci 118/r,* ☎ *055/2341100. Reservations essential. AE, DC, MC, V. Closed Sun.–Mon., July 25–Sept. 5, and Dec. 31–Jan. 7.*

$$$$ ✕ **Enoteca Pinchiorri.** A sumptuous Renaissance palace with high, frescoed ceilings and bouquets in silver vases provides the setting for this restaurant, one of the most expensive in Italy. Some consider it one of the best, and others consider it an expensive, non-Italian ripoff. Prices are high and portions are small. A variety of fish, game, and meat dishes are always on the menu, along with pasta combinations such as the *ignudi*—ricotta and cheese dumplings with a lobster and coxcomb fricassee. ⊠ *Via Ghibellina 87,* ☎ *055/242777. Reservations essential. AE, MC, V. Closed Sun. and Aug. No lunch Mon.*

$$$ ✕ **Alle Murate.** This sophisticated restaurant features creative versions of classic Tuscan dishes. The main dining room has a rich, uncluttered look, with warm wood floors and paneling and soft lights. In a smaller adjacent room called the *vineria* (wine bar or bistro), you get the same splendid service and substantially reduced prices. Be warned that there's no middle ground with the wine list—only a smattering of inexpensive offerings before it soars to exalted heights. ⊠ *Via Ghibellina 52/r,* ☎ *055/240618. AE, DC, MC, V. Closed Mon. No lunch.*

$$$ ✕ **Beccofino.** Written on the menu is *"esercizi di cucina italiana"* (Ital-
★ ian cooking exercises), which is a disarmingly modest way to alert the diner that something wonderfully different is going on here. The interior has a pale-wood serpentine bar separating the ochre-walled wine bar from the green-walled restaurant. Chef Francesco Berardinelli has paid some dues in the United States, and it shows in the inventiveness of his food, which ends up tasting wholly and wonderfully Italian. The wine bar offers a shorter and less expensive menu; in the summer, you can enjoy this food on an outdoor terrace facing the Arno. ⊠ *Piazza degli Scarlatti 1/r (Lungarno Guicciardini),* ☎ *055/290076. Reservations essential. MC, V. Closed Mon. Nov.–Mar.*

$$–$$$ ✕ **La Giostra.** La Giostra, which means "carousel" in Italian, is owned
★ and run by Prince Dimitri Kunz d'Asburgo Lorena. It has a clubby feel, with white walls and tablecloths and dim lighting accented with a few tiny blue lights twinkling on the ceiling. Try the unusually good pastas, maybe the *carbonara di tartufo,* decadently rich spaghetti with eggs and white truffles. Leave room for dessert: this might be the only show in town with a sublime tiramisu and a wonderfully gooey Sacher torte. ⊠ *Borgo Pinti 12/r,* ☎ *055/241341. AE, DC, MC, V.*

$$ ✕ **Pallottino.** With its tile floor, photograph-filled walls, and wooden tables, Pallottino is the quintessential Tuscan trattoria, with such hearty, heartwarming classics as *pappa al pomodoro* (tomato and

When you pack your MCI Calling Card, it's like packing your loved ones along too.

Your MCI Calling Card is the easy way to stay in touch when you travel. Use it to call to and from over 125 countries. Plus, every time you call, you can earn frequent flier miles. So wherever your travels take you, call home with your MCI Calling Card. It's even easy to get one. Just visit **www.mci.com/worldphone.**

EASY TO CALL WORLDWIDE

1. Just enter the WorldPhone® access number of the country you're calling from.
2. Enter or give the operator your MCI Calling Card number.
3. Enter or give the number you're calling.

Austria ◆	0800-200-235
Belgium ◆	0800-10012
Czech Republic ◆	00-42-000112
Denmark ◆	8001-0022
Estonia ★	0800-800-1122
Finland ◆	08001-102-80
France ◆	0-800-99-0019
Germany ◆	0800-888-8000
Greece ◆	00-800-1211
Hungary ◆	06▼-800-01411
Ireland	1-800-55-1001
Italy ◆	172-1022
Luxembourg	8002-0112
Netherlands ◆	0800-022-91-22
Norway ◆	800-19912
Poland ÷	00-800-111-21-22
Portugal ÷	800-800-123
Romania ÷	01-800-1800
Russia ◆ ÷	747-3322
Spain	900-99-0014
Sweden ◆	020-795-922
Switzerland ◆	0800-89-0222
Ukraine ÷	8▼10-013
United Kingdom	0800-89-0222
Vatican City	172-1022

◆ Public phones may require deposit of coin or phone card for dial tone. ★ Not available from public pay phones.
▼ Wait for second dial tone. ÷ Limited availability.

EARN FREQUENT FLIER MILES

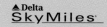

MCI®

SEE THE WORLD
IN FULL COLOR

Fodor's Exploring Guides bring all the great sights vividly to life with hundreds of photographs, fascinating historical background, and colorful anecdotes. Detailed maps and practical information keep you headed in the right direction.

Pair a **Fodor's** Exploring Guide with your trusted Gold Guide for a complete planning package.

Fodor's EXPLORING GUIDES

At bookstores everywhere.

bread soup) and *peposo alla toscana* (beef stew laced with black pepper). The lunch special—*primo and secondo* (first and second courses)—could be, at 10,000 lire/€5, the best bargain in town. ⊠ *Via Isola delle Stinche 1/r*, ☎ *055/289573. AE, DC, MC, V (no credit cards at lunch). Closed Mon. and Aug. 1–20.*

$–$$ ✕ **Baldovino.** This lively, brightly hued spot down the street from the church of Santa Croce is the brainchild of David and Catherine Gardner, expat Scots. From its humble beginnings as a pizzeria, it has evolved into something more. Happily, pizza is still on the menu, but now it shares billing with sophisticated primi and secondi. The menu changes monthly and offers such treats as *filetto di manzo alla Bernaise* (filet mignon with a light Béarnaise sauce). ⊠ *Via San Giuseppe 22/r*, ☎ *055/241773. MC, V. Closed Mon. Nov.–Mar.*

$–$$ ✕ **Il Latini.** This may be the noisiest, most crowded trattoria in Florence. It's also a fun place to go precisely because it is so lively. Four big rooms are lined with bottles of wine and prints, and somehow they manage to feel cozy—perhaps because there are always a lot of happy Florentines tucking into their *salsicce e fagioli* (sausage and beans) or, in season, *agnello fritto* (fried lamb). Portions are big—you'll think you won't be able to eat it all, but you will. Reservations are advised. ⊠ *Via dei Palchetti 6/r*, ☎ *055/210916. AE, DC, MC, V. Closed Mon. and 15 days over Christmas.*

$ ✕ **La Casalinga.** "Casalinga" means housewife, and this place has all the charm of a 1950s kitchen with Tuscan comfort food to match. There's not much interior decor beyond mediocre paintings cluttering the semi-paneled walls. Tables are set close together and the place is usually jammed, and with good reason. The menu is long, portions are plentiful, and service is prompt and friendly. If you eat ribollita anywhere in Florence, eat it here—the setting couldn't be more authentic. ⊠ *Via Michelozzi 9/r*, ☎ *055/218624. AE, DC, MC, V. Closed Sun., 1 wk at Christmas, 3 wks in Aug. No lunch in July.*

LODGING

Hotel rooms are at a premium in Florence for most of the year. Reserve well in advance. If you arrive without a reservation, the **Consorzio ITA** office in the train station (⊠ Stazione Centrale di Santa Maria Novella), open 8:20 AM–9 PM, can help you, but there may be a long line (take a number and wait). Now that much traffic is banned in the centro storico, many central hotel rooms are quieter. Local traffic and motorcycles can still be bothersome, however, so check the decibel level before you settle in. From November through March, ask for special low winter rates.

CATEGORY	COST*
$$$$	over 500,000 lire (€258)
$$$	350,000 lire–500,000 lire (€180–€258)
$$	200,000 lire–350,000 lire (€103–€180)
$	under 200,000 lire (€103)

Price categories are determined by the cost of two people in a double room.

$$$$ 🏨 **Brunelleschi.** Architects united a Byzantine tower, a medieval church, ★ and a later building in a stunning structure in the very heart of the centro storico to make this unique hotel. Medieval stone walls and brick arches contrast pleasantly with the plush, contemporary decor. The comfortable, soundproof rooms are done in coordinated patterns and soft colors. ⊠ *Piazza Sant'Elisabetta 3/r (off Via dei Calzaiuoli), 50122*, ☎ *055/27370,* ℻ *055/219653,* 🌐 *www.hotelbrunelleschi.it. 96 rooms, 7 junior suites. Restaurant, bar. AE, DC, MC, V.*

$$$$ ⊞ **Excelsior.** Florentine hotels do not get much more exquisite or ex-
★   pensive than this. Rooms are decorated in Empire style but still feel
up-to-date. High ceilings, dramatic views of the Arno, patterned rugs,
and tasteful prints lend the rooms a sense of extravagant well-being.
Public rooms have stained glass and acres of Oriental carpets strewn
over marble floors. The opulence of 19th-century Florentine antiques
is set off by charming old prints of the city and long mirrors. ⊠ *Piazza Ognissanti 3, 50123,* ☎ *055/264201,* FAX *055/210278,* WEB
www.luxurycollection.com. 168 rooms. Restaurant. AE, DC, MC, V.

$$$$ ⊞ **Grand.** This Florentine classic provides all the luxuries. Rooms are
decorated in either Renaissance or Empire style; the former have deep,
richly hued damask brocades and canopied beds, the latter a lovely pro-
fusion of crisp prints and patterned fabric offsetting white walls. The
overall effect is sumptuous, as is the view of either the Arno or a small
courtyard lined with potted orange trees. Avoid the piano bar, which
is high-priced karaoke. ⊠ *Piazza Ognissanti 1, 50123,* ☎ *055/288781,*
FAX *055/217400,* WEB *www.luxurycollection.com. 107 rooms. Restaurant, bar. AE, DC, MC, V.*

$$$$ ⊞ **Hotel Savoy.** From the outside, it looks very much like the turn-of-
the-19th-century building that it is. But step inside where sleek mini-
malism prevails at this hotel in the heart of the centro storico. Sitting
rooms have a funky edge with their cream-colored walls dotted with
contemporary prints and photographs. Many of the rooms, decorated
in muted colors, with clean lines and soaring ceilings, overlook Piazza
Repubblica and have views of the Duomo's cupola. ⊠ *Piazza della
Repubblica 7, 50123,* ☎ *055/27351,* FAX *055/2735888,* WEB *www.
rfhotels.com. 98 rooms, 9 suites. Restaurant, bar. AE, DC, MC, V.*

$$$$ ⊞ **Lungarno.** Rooms and suites in this hotel across the Arno from the
Palazzo Vecchio and the Duomo have private terraces jutting out over
the river. The chic decor approximates a breezily elegant home, with
lots of crisp white fabrics trimmed in blue. Four suites in a 13th-cen-
tury tower preserve exposed stone walls and old archways. More than
100 paintings and drawings—from Picassos to Cocteaus—hang in
hallways and bedrooms. ⊠ *Borgo San Jacopo 14, 50125,* ☎ *055/27261,*
FAX *055/268437,* WEB *www.lungarnohotels.com. 60 rooms, 11 suites.
Restaurant, bar. AE, DC, MC, V.*

$$$ ⊞ **Hermitage.** This place is centrally located and, given the price, a great
★   bargain. All rooms are hung with lively wallpaper; some have views
of the Palazzo Vecchio and others of the Arno. The rooftop terrace,
where you can breakfast or enjoy a cocktail, is decked with flowers.
The lobby feels like a friendly living room, with warm yellow walls.
⊠ *Vicolo Marzio 1 (Piazza del Pesce, Ponte Vecchio), 50122,* ☎ *055/
287216,* FAX *055/212208,* WEB *www.hermitagehotel.com. 27 rooms, 1
suite. MC, V.*

$$$ ⊞ **Loggiato dei Serviti.** Occupying a 16th-century former monastery,
★   this attractively spare Renaissance building was originally a refuge for
traveling priests. Vaulted ceilings, tasteful furnishings (some antique),
canopied beds, and rich fabrics give you the feel of Old Florence while
you enjoy modern creature comforts. ⊠ *Piazza Santissima Annunziata 3, 50122,* ☎ *055/289592,* FAX *055/289595,* WEB *www.venere.it. 29
rooms. AE, DC, MC, V.*

$$$ ⊞ **Monna Lisa.** Housed in a 15th-century palazzo, parts of which date
★   from the 13th century, this hotel retains some of its original wood cof-
fered ceilings from the 1500s, as well as its original marble staircase.
The rooms are on the small side, but they are tastefully decorated. The
public rooms retain a 19th-century aura. ⊠ *Borgo Pinti 27, 50121,*
☎ *055/2479751,* FAX *055/2479755,* WEB *www.monnalisa.it. 30 rooms.
Bar. AE, DC, MC, V.*

$$$ 🏨 **Porta Faenza.** A hospitable Italian-Canadian couple owns and manages this conveniently positioned hotel near the station. Spacious rooms in Florentine style and sparkling bathrooms that, though compact, have such amenities as hair dryers make this a good value. The staff is helpful and attentive to your needs. ⊠ *Via Faenza 77, 50123,* ☎ *055/284119,* FAX *055/210101,* WEB *www.hotelportafaenza.it. 25 rooms. AE, DC, MC, V.*

$$ 🏨 **Alessandra.** The location, a block from the Ponte Vecchio, and clean, ample rooms make this a good choice for basic accommodations at reasonable rates. The English-speaking staff makes sure guests are happy. ⊠ *Borgo Santi Apostoli 17, 50123,* ☎ *055/283438,* FAX *055/ 210619,* WEB *www.hotelalessandra.com. 25 rooms, 9 without bath. AE, MC, V. Closed Dec. 10–26.*

$$ 🏨 **Hotel Ritz.** Set amid a row of buildings facing the Arno, this family-managed hotel makes you feel as if you are a guest in a pretty, 19th-century Florentine home with 21st-century amenities. Most rooms have lovely views of either the Arno or the domed, red-roofed "skyline" of Florence. ⊠ *Lungarno Zecca Vecchia 24, 50122,* ☎ *055/ 2340650,* FAX *055/240863,* WEB *www.florenceitaly.net. 30 rooms. AE, DC, MC, V.*

$$ 🏨 **Morandi alla Crocetta.** This charming and distinguished residence
★ near Piazza Santissima Annunziata was once a monastery, and access is up a flight of stairs. It is furnished in the classic style of a Florentine home, and guests feel like privileged friends of the family. Small and exceptional, it is also a good value and must be booked well in advance. ⊠ *Via Laura 50, 50121,* ☎ *055/2344747,* FAX *055/2480954,* WEB *www.hotelmorandi.it. 9 rooms. AE, DC, MC, V.*

$$ 🏨 **Pendini.** The atmosphere of an old-fashioned Florentine pensione is intact here; bedrooms have floral wallpaper, pastel carpeting, and modern baths. Public rooms have a Belle Epoque look, with some antiques. It's central, and off-season rates here are a real bargain. ⊠ *Via Strozzi 2, 50123,* ☎ *055/211170,* FAX *055/281807,* WEB *www.florence-italy.net. 42 rooms. AE, DC, MC, V.*

$$ 🏨 **Villa Azalee.** A five-minute walk from the train station and a short distance from the Fortezza da Basso (site of the Pitti fashion shows), this 19th-century villa deftly recalls its previous incarnation as a private residence. Some rooms have private terraces, many have views of the hotel's flower-filled garden. ⊠ *Viale Fratelli Rosselli 44, 50123,* ☎ *055/214242,* FAX *055/268264,* WEB *www.villaazalee.it. 25 rooms. AE, DC, MC, V.*

$ 🏨 **Bellettini.** This small, central hotel occupies two floors of an old but
★ well-kept building near San Lorenzo, in an area with many inexpensive restaurants. Rooms are ample, with Venetian or Tuscan decor, and bathrooms are modern. The management is friendly and helpful. ⊠ *Via dei Conti 7, 50123,* ☎ *055/213561,* FAX *055/283551,* WEB *www.firenze.net. 27 rooms, 4 without bath. AE, DC, MC, V.*

$ 🏨 **Nuova Italia.** Near the main train station and within walking distance of the sights, this homey hotel in a dignified palazzo is run by a genial English-speaking family. Rooms are clean and simply furnished, and the triple-glazed windows ensure restful nights. ⊠ *Via Faenza 26, 50123,* ☎ *055/268430,* FAX *055/210941. 20 rooms. AE, MC, V.*

NIGHTLIFE AND THE ARTS

The Arts

Film

You can find movie listings in *La Nazione*, the daily Florence newspaper. English-language films are shown Tuesday–Sunday evenings at the **Cinema Astro** (⊠ Piazza San Simone, near Santa Croce). Every Monday, first-run English language films are shown at the **Odeon** (⊠ Piazza Strozzi). The **Goldoni** (⊠ Via dei Serragli) offers first-run English-language films every Wednesday.

Music

Most major musical events are staged at the **Teatro Comunale** (⊠ Corso Italia 16, ☎ 055/2779236). The box office (closed Sunday and Monday) is open from 9 to 1 and a half hour before performances. It's best to order your tickets by mail, however, as they're difficult to come by at the last minute. Amici della Musica (Friends of Music) puts on a series of concerts at the **Teatro della Pergola** (box office; ⊠ Via della Pergola 10a/r, ☎ 055/2479651). For information contact the **Amici della Musica** (⊠ Via Alamanni 39, ☎ 055/2479651) directly.

Nightlife

Bars

Rex (⊠ Via Fiesolana 23–25/r, Santa Croce, ☎ 055/2480331) has a trendy atmosphere and an arty clientele. The oh-so-cool vibe at **La Dolce Vita** (⊠ Piazza del Carmine 6/r, ☎ 055/284595) attracts Florentines and occasionally the visiting American movie star.

Nightclubs

Central Park (⊠ Via del Fosso Macinante 2, ☎ 055/353505) is a great spot if you want to put on your dancing shoes. **Maracaná** (⊠ Via Faenza 4, ☎ 055/210298) serves as a restaurant and pizzeria featuring Brazilian specialties; at 11 PM, it transforms itself into a cabaret floor show and then into a disco until 4 AM. Remember to book a table if you want to eat. Young up-to-the-minute Florentines drink and dance 'til the wee hours at **Maramao** (⊠ Via dei Macci 79/r, ☎ 055/244341), which opens at 11 PM and doesn't really get going until much before 2. **Space Electronic** (⊠ Via Palazzuolo 37, ☎ 055/293082) has two floors, with karaoke upstairs and an enormous disco downstairs. **Yab** (⊠ Via Sassetti 5/r, ☎ 055/215160) is one of the largest clubs in Florence, with a young clientele. Popular especially on Tuesday and Thursday nights, it packs in locals and foreigners.

SHOPPING

Markets

Don't miss the indoor, two-story **Mercato Centrale** (⊠ Piazza del Mercato Centrale), near San Lorenzo, open in the morning Monday–Saturday. The **Mercato di San Lorenzo** (⊠ Piazza San Lorenzo and Via dell'Ariento) is a fine place to browse for buys in leather goods and souvenirs; it's open Tuesday–Saturday 8–7 (June–September, Sunday 8–7).

Shopping Districts

Via Tornabuoni is the high-end shopping street. **Via della Vigna Nuova** is just as fashionable. Goldsmiths and jewelry shops can be found on and around the **Ponte Vecchio** and in the **Santa Croce** area, where there is also a high concentration of leather shops and inconspicuous shops selling gold and silver jewelry at prices much lower than those of the elegant jewelers near Ponte Vecchio. The convent of **Santa Croce** (⊠ Via San Giuseppe 5/r; ⊠ Piazza Santa Croce 16) houses a leather-working school and showroom. Antiques dealers can be found in and around the center but are concentrated on **Via Maggio** in the Oltrarno area. **Borgo Ognissanti** also has shops selling period decorative objects.

FLORENCE A TO Z

To research prices, get advice from other travelers, and book travel arrangements, visit www.fodors.com.

ADDRESSES
It is easy to find your way around in Florence: major sights can be explored on foot, as they are packed into a relatively small area. Wear comfortable shoes. The system of street addresses is unusual, with commercial addresses (those with an *r* in them, meaning *rosso*, or red) and residential addresses numbered separately (32/r might be next to or a block away from plain 32).

AIRPORTS AND TRANSFERS
The airport that handles most arrivals is Aeroporto Galileo Galilei, more commonly known as Aeroporto Pisa-Galilei. Some domestic and European flights use Florence's Aeroporto Vespucci.
➤ AIRPORT INFORMATION: **Aeroporto Galileo Galilei** (✉ Pisa, ☎ 050/ 500707, WEB www.pisa-airport.com). **Aeroporto Vespucci** (✉ Peretola, ☎ 055/373498, WEB www.safnet.it).

TRANSFERS
Pisa-Galilei Airport offers direct train service to the Stazione Centrale di Santa Maria Novella. There are hourly departures throughout the day, and the trip takes about 60 minutes. When departing, you can buy train tickets for the airport and check in for all flights leaving from Aeroporto Pisa-Galilei at the Florence Air Terminal at Track 5 of Santa Maria Novella. Aeroporto Vespucci is connected to downtown Florence by SITA bus.

BIKE AND MOPED TRAVEL
➤ BIKE AND MOPED RENTALS: **Alinari** (✉ Via Guelfa 85/r, ☎ 055/ 280500).

BUS TRAVEL TO AND FROM FLORENCE
For excursions outside Florence, to Siena, for instance, you take SITA near the Stazione Centrale di Santa Maria Novella. The CAP bus terminal is also near the train station.
➤ BUS INFORMATION: **CAP** (✉ Via Nazionale 13). **SITA** (bus terminal, ✉ Via Santa Caterina da Siena 17).

BUS TRAVEL WITHIN FLORENCE
Bus maps and timetables are available for a small fee at the Azienda Transporti Autolinee Fiorentine city bus information booths. The same maps may be free at visitor information offices. ATAF city buses run from about 5:15 AM to 1 AM. Buy tickets before you board the bus; they are sold at many tobacco shops and newsstands. The cost is 1,500 lire/€.75 for a ticket good for one hour, 2,500 lire/€1.30 for two hours, and 5,800 lire/€3 for four one-hour tickets, called a *multiplo*. A 24-hour tourist ticket (*turistico*) costs 6,000 lire/€3.10.
➤ BUS INFORMATION: **Azienda Transporti Autolinee Fiorentine** (ATAF; ✉ near Stazione Centrale di Santa Maria Novella; Piazza del Duomo 57/r).

CAR TRAVEL
The north–south access route to Florence is the Autostrada del Sole (A1) from Milan or Rome. The Florence–Mare autostrada (A11) links Florence with the Tyrrhenian coast, Pisa, and the A12 coastal autostrada. Parking in Florence is severely restricted.

CONSULATES

➤ UNITED KINGDOM: (✉ Lungarno Corsini 2, ☎ 055/284133).
➤ UNITED STATES: (✉ Lungarno Vespucci 38, ☎ 055/2398276).

EMERGENCIES

Pharmacies are open Sunday and holidays by rotation. Signs posted outside pharmacies list those open all night and on weekends. The pharmacy at Santa Maria Novella train station is always open.

➤ DOCTORS AND DENTISTS: **Tourist Medical Service** (✉ Via Lorenzo il Magnifico 59, ☎ 055/475411).
➤ EMERGENCY SERVICES: **Ambulance** (☎ 118). **Police** (☎ 113).

ENGLISH-LANGUAGE MEDIA

➤ BOOKSTORES: **BM Bookshop** (✉ Borgo Ognissanti 4/r, ☎ 055/294575). **Paperback Exchange** (✉ Via Fiesolana 31/r, ☎ 055/2478154). **Seeber** (✉ Via Tornabuoni 70/r, ☎ 055/215697).

TAXIS

Taxis wait at stands throughout the centro storico; you can also telephone them. Hailing them from the street is not done here. Use only authorized cabs, which are white with a yellow stripe or rectangle on the door. The meter starts at 4,500 lire/€2.30, with extra charges for nights, holidays, or radio dispatch.

➤ TAXI COMPANIES: (☎ 055/4798 or 055/4390).

TOURS

BUS TOURS

A bus consortium (through hotels and travel agents) offers tours in air-conditioned buses covering the important sights in Florence with a trip to Fiesole. The cost is about 48,000 lire/€24.80 for a three-hour tour, including entrance fees, and bookings can be made through travel agents.

Operators offer a half-day excursion to Pisa, usually in the afternoon, costing about 48,000 lire/€24.80, and a full-day excursion to Siena and San Gimignano, costing about 68,000 lire/€35. Pick up a timetable at ATAF information offices near the train station, at SITA. Also enquire at the APT tourist office.

SPECIAL INTEREST TOURS

Inquire at travel agents or at Turismo Verde for visits and stays at farm estates. The APT tourist office has information on garden tours in and around Florence.

➤ FEES AND SCHEDULES: **Turismo Verde** (✉ Via Verdi 5, ☎ 055/2344925).

TRAIN TRAVEL

The main station is Stazione Centrale di Santa Maria Novella. Florence is on the main north–south route between Rome, Bologna, Milan, and Venice. High-speed Eurostar trains reach Rome in less than two hours and Milan in less than three.

➤ TRAIN INFORMATION: **Stazione Centrale di Santa Maria Novella** (☎ 8488/88088 toll-free).

TRAVEL AGENCIES

➤ LOCAL AGENTS: **American Express** (✉ Via Dante Alighieri 22/r, ☎ 055/50981). **CIT Italia** (✉ Piazza Stazione 51/r, ☎ 055/284145). **Micos Travel Box** (✉ Via dell'Oriuolo 50–52/r, ☎ 055/2340228).

VISITOR INFORMATION

➤ TOURIST INFORMATION: **Azienda Promozione Turistica** (APT; ✉ Via Cavour 1/r, 50100, ☎ 055/290832).

Italy Basics

BUSINESS HOURS

Banks are open weekdays 8:30–1:30 and 2:45–3:45. Churches are usually open from early morning to noon or 12:30, when they close for about two hours or more, opening again in the afternoon until about 7 PM. National museums (*musei statali*) are usually open from 9 AM until 2 and are often closed on Monday, but there are many exceptions, especially at major museums. Non-national museums have entirely different hours, which may vary according to season. Most major archaeological sites are open every day from early morning to dusk, except some holidays. At all museums and sites, ticket offices close an hour or so before official closing time. Always check with the local tourist office for current hours and holiday closings. Shops are open, with individual variations, from 9 to 1 and from 3:30 or 4 to 7:30 or 8. They are open Monday–Saturday but close for a half day during the week; for example, in Rome most shops are closed on Monday morning, although food shops close on Thursday afternoon in fall–spring. All shops, including food shops, close Saturday afternoon in July and August, though a 1995 ordinance allows greater freedom. Some tourist-oriented shops and department stores—in downtown Rome, Florence, and Venice—are open all day, every day.

CUSTOMS AND DUTIES

For details on imports and duty-free limits in Italy, *see* Customs and Duties *in* Smart Travel Tips A to Z.

HOLIDAYS

January 1; January 6 (Epiphany); Easter Sunday and Monday; April 25 (Liberation Day); May 1 (May Day); August 15 (Assumption, known as Ferragosto); November 1 (All Saints' Day); December 8 (Immaculate Conception); December 25–26.

The feast days of patron saints are observed locally. Many businesses and shops may be closed in Florence, Genoa, and Turin on June 24 (St. John the Baptist); in Rome on June 29 (Sts. Peter and Paul); in Palermo on July 15 (Santa Rosalia); in Naples on September 19 (San Gennaro); in Bologna on October 4 (San Petronio); in Trieste on November 3 (San Giusto); and in Milan on December 7 (St. Ambrose). Venice's feast of St. Mark is April 25, the same as Liberation Day, and the city also celebrates November 21 (Madonna della Salute).

LANGUAGE

Italy is accustomed to English-speaking tourists, and in major cities you will find that many people speak at least a little English. In smaller hotels and restaurants and on public transportation, knowing a few phrases of Italian comes in handy.

MONEY MATTERS

Venice, Milan, Florence, and Rome are the more expensive Italian cities to visit. Taxes are usually included in hotel bills; there is a 20% tax on car rentals, usually included in the rates.

A cup of espresso enjoyed while standing at a bar costs from 1,000 lire/€.50 to 1,500 lire/€.75, the same cup served at a table, triple that. At a bar, beer costs from 4,000 lire/€2.05 to 6,000 lire/€3.10, a soft drink about 3,000 lire/€1.55. A *tramezzino* (small sandwich) costs about 2,500 lire/€1.30, a more substantial one about 3,500 lire/€1.80–5,000 lire/€2.60. You will pay about 15,000 lire/€7.75 for a short taxi ride. Admission to a major museum is about 12,000 lire/€6.20.

CREDIT CARDS

Credit cards are generally accepted in shops and hotels but may not always be welcome in restaurants. When you wish to leave a tip beyond the 15% service charge that is usually included with your bill, leave it in cash rather than adding it to the credit card slip.

CURRENCY

The unit of currency in Italy is the lira (plural, lire). There are bills of 1,000, 2,000, 5,000, 10,000, 50,000, 100,000, and 500,000 lire (impossible to change, except in banks); coins are worth 50, 100, 200, 500, and 1,000 lire. In 1999 the new single currency of the European Union, the euro, was introduced as a banking currency. Euro coins and notes will be issued in January 2002, and in a few months lire will be withdrawn from circulation. At press time (summer 2001) the exchange rate was 2,171 lire/€1.12 to the U.S. dollar, 1,376 lire/€.71 to the Canadian dollar, 3,108 lire/€1.60 to the pound sterling, 2,458 lire/€1.27 to the Irish punt, 1,054 lire/€.54 to the Australian dollar, 876 lire/€.45 to the New Zealand dollar, and 267 lire/€.14 to the South African rand.

When your purchases run into hundreds of thousands of lire, beware of being shortchanged, a dodge that is practiced at ticket windows, toll booths, and cashiers' desks, as well as in shops and even in banks. *Always count your change before you leave the counter.* Always carry some smaller-denomination bills for sundry purchases.

TELEPHONES

COUNTRY AND AREA CODES

The country code for Italy is 39. Do not drop the 0 in the regional code when calling Italy.

INTERNATIONAL CALLS

To place an international call, insert a phone card, dial 00, then the country code, area code, and phone number. The cheaper and easier option, however, is to use your AT&T, MCI, or Sprint calling card. To make collect calls, dial the AT&T USADirect number below. For information and operators in Europe and the Mediterranean area, dial 15; for intercontinental service, dial 170.

➤ ACCESS CODES: **AT&T USADirect** (☎ 172–1011). **MCI Call USA** (☎ 172–1022). **Sprint Express** (☎ 172–1877).

LOCAL CALLS

For all local calls, you must dial the regional area codes, even in cities. Most local calls cost 200 lire/€.10 for two minutes. Pay phones take either 100-, 200-, or 500-lire coins or *schede telefoniche* (phone cards), purchased in bars, tobacconists, and post offices in either 5,000-10,000-, or 15,000-lire denominations. The phone card called Time Europa (50,000 lire/€25.80) is a good-value card for calling Europe and the United States, at only 540 lire/€.30 per minute. For directory information in Italy, dial 12.

10 LONDON

If London contained only its famous landmarks—Buckingham Palace, Big Ben, Parliament, the Tower of London—it would still rank as one of the world's great destinations. A city that loves to be explored, London beckons with great museums, royal pageantry, and houses that are steeped in history. Marvel at the Duke of Wellington's house, track Jack the Ripper's shadow in Whitechapel, then get Beatle-ized at Abbey Road. From the East End to the West End, you'll find London is a dickens of a place.

EXPLORING LONDON

Traditionally London has been divided between the City, to the east, where its banking and commercial interests lie, and Westminster, to the west, the seat of the royal court and of government. It is in these two areas that you will find most of the grand buildings that have played a central role in British history: the Tower of London and St. Paul's Cathedral, Westminster Abbey and the Houses of Parliament, Buckingham Palace, and the older royal palace of St. James's.

Visitors who restrict their sightseeing to the well-known tourist areas miss much of the best the city has to offer. Within a few minutes' walk of Buckingham Palace, for instance, lie St. James's and Mayfair, two neighboring quarters of elegant town houses built for the nobility during the 17th and early 18th centuries and now notable for the shopping opportunities they house. The same lesson applies to the City, where, tucked away in quiet corners, stand many of the churches Christopher Wren built to replace those destroyed during the Great Fire of 1666.

Other parts of London worth exploring include Covent Garden, a former fruit and flower market converted into a lively shopping and entertainment center where you can wander for hours enjoying the friendly bustle of the streets. Hyde Park and Kensington Gardens, by contrast, offer a great swath of green parkland across the city center, preserved by past kings and queens for their own hunting and relax-

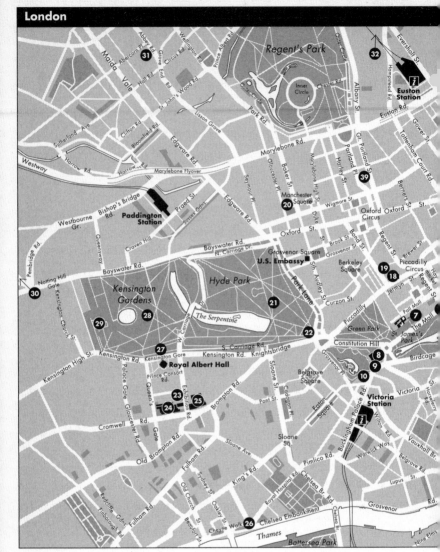

King's Cross Station

St. Pancras Station

Pentonville Rd.

King's Cross Rd.

Gray's Inn Rd.

Goswell Rd.

City Rd.

Hackney Rd.

Bethnal Green Rd.

Coram's Fields

Guilford St.

Theobald's Rd.

Clerkenwell Rd.

Rosebery Ave.

Farringdon Rd.

St. John's St.

Aldersgate

Bunhill Row

City Rd.

Old St.

Gr. Eastern St.

Hoxton St.

Curtain Rd.

Kingsland Rd.

East Road

Wilson St.

Appold St.

Shoreditch High St.

Commercial St.

Fournier St.

Whitechapel Rd.

Commercial Rd.

Cable St.

The Highway

Woburn Pl.

Southampton Row

Clerkenwell Rd.

Greville St.

Charterhouse St.

West Smithfield

Holborn Viaduct

Beech St.

Golden Ln.

Whitecross St.

London Wall

Gresham St.

Broad St. Station

Liverpool St. Station

Eldon St.

Moorgate

Bishopsgate

Houndsditch

Bevis Marks

Madison St.

40

New Oxford St.

High Holborn

Kingsway

Drury Ln.

Chancery Ln.

41

Old Bailey

Newgate St.

Fleet St.

Cheapside

42 45

Cornhill

Leadenhall St.

Fenchurch St.

Minories

Mansell St.

Leman St.

Shaftesbury Ave.

Charing Cross Rd.

38

34 36

35

37

Strand

Aldwych

Law Courts

Victoria Embankment

Queen Victoria St.

Upper Thames St.

Cannon St.

Lower Thames St.

Tower Hill

Blackfriars Station

Cannon St. Station

Blackfriars Br.

48

2
3
4
1

Charing Cross Stn.

5

17 16

13

12

Whitehall

15

14

Westminster Br.

South Bank Arts Complex

Waterloo Station

Upper Ground

Stamford St.

46 47

Southwark St.

Union St.

Thames

Tooley St.

London Bridge Station

TO MILLENNIUM DOME →

Jamaica Rd.

Waterloo Rd.

Blackfriars Rd.

The Cut

Suffolk St.

Borough High St.

Snowsfields

St. Thomas St.

Long Lane

Bermondsey St.

Tower Bridge Rd.

Grange Rd.

Abbey St.

Willow Walk

Walk

Westminster Br. Rd.

Lambeth Palace Rd.

Lambeth Rd.

Kennington Rd.

Imperial War Museum

Brook Dr.

New Kent Rd.

Borough Rd.

London Rd.

Great Dover St.

Tabard St.

Harper Rd.

Walworth Rd.

Old Kent Rd.

Horseferry Rd.

Lambeth Br.

Marsham St.

Millbank

Albert Embankment

Kennington Ln.

Kennington Park Rd.

11

Rd.

Vauxhall Br.

Vauxhall Station

Kennington Oval

N

KEY

ℹ Tourist Information

0 _____ 1 mile

0 _____ 1 km

ation. A walk across Hyde Park will bring you to the museum district of South Kensington, with three major national collections: the Natural History Museum, the Science Museum, and the Victoria & Albert Museum, which specializes in the fine and applied arts.

The south side of the River Thames has its treats as well. A short stroll across Waterloo Bridge brings you to the South Bank Arts Complex, which includes the Royal National Theatre, the Royal Festival Hall, the Hayward Gallery (with changing exhibitions of international art), and the National Film Theatre. Here also are the exciting reconstruction of Shakespeare's Globe theater and its sister museum, and the new home, at Bankside Power Station, of the Tate Gallery of Modern Art—and now called simply Tate Modern. The London Eye observation wheel gives the most stunning views—to the west are the Houses of Parliament and Big Ben; to the east the dome of St. Paul's looks smaller on London's changing modern architectural skyline. The Millennium Bridge leaps across the Thames like a so-called steel "blaze of light" joining Tate Modern to St. Paul's in the city. London, although not simple of layout, is a rewarding walking city, and this remains the best way to get to know its nooks and crannies. The infamous weather may not be on your side, but there's plenty of indoor entertainment to keep you amused if you forget the umbrella.

Westminster

Numbers in the margin correspond to points of interest on the London map.

Westminster is the royal backyard—the traditional center of the royal court and of government. Here, within 1 km (½ mi) or so of one another, are nearly all of London's most celebrated buildings, and there is a strong feeling of history all around you. Generations of kings and queens have lived here since the end of the 11th century—including the current monarch.

16 Banqueting House. On the right side of the grand processional avenue known as Whitehall—site of many important government offices—stands this famous monument of the English Renaissance period. Designed by Inigo Jones in 1625 for court entertainments, it is the only part of Whitehall Palace, the monarch's principal residence during the 16th and 17th centuries, that did not burn down in 1698. It has a magnificent ceiling by Rubens, and outside is an inscription that marks the window through which King Charles I stepped to his execution. ⊠ *Whitehall, SW1,* ☎ *020/7930–4179,* WEB *www.hrp.org.uk.* ☞ *£3.60, includes free audio guide.* ☉ *Mon.–Sat. 10–5 (closed on short notice for banquets, so call first). Tube: Westminster, Embankment, Charing Cross.*

8 Buckingham Palace. Supreme among the symbols of London, indeed of Britain generally, and of the royal family, Buckingham Palace tops many must-see lists—although the building itself is no masterpiece and has housed the monarch only since Victoria moved here from Kensington Palace at her accession in 1837. Located at the end of the Mall, the palace is the London home of the queen and the administrative hub of the entire royal family. When the queen is in residence (normally on weekdays except in January, August, September, and part of June), the royal standard flies over the east front. Inside are dozens of ornate 19th-century-style state rooms used on formal occasions. The private apartments of Queen Elizabeth and Prince Philip are in the north wing. Parts of Buckingham Palace are open to the public during August and September; during the entire year, the former chapel, bombed during World War II and rebuilt in 1961, is the site of the **Queen's Gallery,**

which shows treasures from the vast royal art collections. The ceremony of the **Changing of the Guard** takes place in front of the palace at 11:30 daily, April–July, and on alternate days during the rest of the year. Arrive early, as people are invariably stacked several deep along the railings, whatever the weather. ⊠ *Buckingham Palace Rd., SW1,* ☎ *020/7839–1377; 020/7799–2331 24-hr information; 020/7321–2233 credit-card reservations (50p booking charge),* WEB *www.royal.gov.uk.* ⊠ *£11.* ☼ *Early Aug.–early Oct. (confirm dates, which are subject to queen's mandate), daily 9:30–4:15. Tube: St. James's Park, Victoria.*

⑫ Cabinet War Rooms. It was from this small maze of 17 bomb-proof underground rooms—in back of the hulking Foreign Office—that Britain's World War II fortunes were directed. During air raids the Cabinet met here—the Cabinet Room is still arranged as if a meeting were about to convene. Visit the Prime Minister's Room, from which Winston Churchill made many of his inspiring wartime broadcasts, and the Transatlantic Telephone Room, from which he spoke directly to President Roosevelt in the White House. ⊠ *Clive Steps, King Charles St., SW1,* ☎ *020/7930–6961,* WEB *www.iwm.org.uk.* ⊠ *£4.80.* ☼ *Apr.–Sept., daily 9:30–5:15; Oct.–Mar., daily 10–5:15. Tube: Westminster.*

⑥ Carlton House Terrace. This Regency-era showpiece on the Mall was built in 1827–32 by John Nash in imposing white stucco and with massive Corinthian columns. It is home to the Institute of Contemporary Arts. ⊠ *The Mall, W1,* ☎ *020/7930–3647,* WEB *www.ica.org.uk.* ☼ *Daily noon–9:30, later for some events. Tube: Charing Cross.*

⑰ Horse Guards Parade. The former tiltyard of Whitehall Palace is the site of the annual ceremony of Trooping the Colour, when the queen takes the salute in the great military parade that marks her official birthday on the second Saturday in June (her real one is on April 21). Demand for tickets is great, and tickets are available for the ceremony, as well as the queenless rehearsals on the preceding two Saturdays (for information, call ☎ *020/7414–2479*). There is also a daily guard-changing ceremony outside the guard house, on Whitehall, at 11 AM (10 on Sunday)—one of London's best photo-ops. ⊠ *Whitehall, opposite Downing St., SW1. Tube: Westminster.*

⑭ Houses of Parliament. The Houses of Parliament are among the city's most famous and photogenic sights. The Clock Tower keeps watch on Parliament Square, in which stand statues of everyone from Richard the Lionhearted to Abraham Lincoln, and, across the way, Westminster Abbey. Also known as the **Palace of Westminster**, this was the site of the monarch's main residence from the 11th century until 1512; the court then moved to the newly built Whitehall Palace. The only parts of the original building to have survived are the **Jewel Tower,** which was built in 1365 as a treasure-house for Edward III, and **Westminster Hall,** which has a fine hammer-beam roof. The rest of the structure was destroyed in a disastrous fire in 1834 and was rebuilt in the newly popular mock-medieval Gothic style. The architect, Augustus Pugin, designed the entire place, right down to the Gothic umbrella stands. This newer part of the palace contains the debating chambers and committee rooms of the two Houses of Parliament—the Commons (whose members are elected) and the Lords (whose members are appointed or inherit their seats). There are no tours of the palace, but the public is admitted to the Public Gallery of each House; expect to wait in line for several hours (the line for the Lords is generally much shorter than that for the Commons). The most famous features of the palace are its towers. At the south end is the 336-ft **Victoria Tower.** At the other end is **St. Stephen's Tower,** or the Clock Tower, better known, but inaccurately so, as **Big Ben;** that name properly belongs to the 13-

ton bell in the tower on which the hours are struck. Big Ben himself was probably Sir Benjamin Hall, commissioner of works when the bell was installed in the 1850s. A light shines from the top of the tower during a night sitting of Parliament. Be sure to have your name placed on the waiting list for the twice-weekly tours of the private residence of the Lord Chancellor within the Palace of Westminster. You can also apply in advance for the special "line of route" tour—open only to overseas visitors—by writing to the **Parliamentary Education Unit** (✉ House of Commons Information Office, House of Commons, London, SW1A 2TT) at least a month in advance of your visit. ✉ *St. Stephen's Entrance, St. Margaret St., SW1,* ☎ *020/7219–3000; 020/7219–4272 Commons information; 020/7219–3107 Lords information; 020/7219–2184 Lord Chancellor's Residence,* WEB *www.parliament.uk.* ⊙ *Commons Nov.–June, Mon.–Thurs. 2:30–10, Fri. 9:30–3 (although not every Fri.); Lords Nov.–June, Mon.–Thurs. 2:30–10; Lord Chancellor's Residence Tues. and Thurs. Closed Easter wk and 3 wks at Christmas. Tube: Westminster. Jewel Tower, Abingdon St.,* ☎ *020/7222–2219.* ⊙ *Apr.–Sept., daily 10–6; Oct., daily 10–5; Nov.–Mar., daily 10–4.*

❺ The Mall. The splendid **Admiralty Arch** guards the entrance to The Mall, the noted ceremonial way that leads alongside **St. James's Park** to Buckingham Palace. The Mall takes its name from a game called *palle maille,* a version of croquet that James I imported from France and Charles II popularized during the late 1600s. The park was developed by successive monarchs, most recently by George IV in the 1820s, having originally been used for hunting by Henry VIII. Join office workers relaxing with a lunchtime sandwich, or stroll here on a summer's evening when the illuminated fountains play and Westminster Abbey and the Houses of Parliament are floodlit. Toward Buckingham Palace, along the Mall, you'll pass the foot of the imposing **Carlton House Terrace.** *The Mall, Cockspur St., Trafalgar Sq., SW1. Tube: Charing Cross.*

★ **❷ National Gallery.** Generally ranked right after the Louvre, the National Gallery is one of the world's greatest museums. Occupying the long neoclassical building on the north side of Trafalgar Square, it contains works by virtually every famous artist and school from the 14th through the 19th centuries. Its galleries overflow with masterpieces, including Jan van Eyck's *Arnolfini Marriage,* Leonardo da Vinci's *Burlington Virgin and Child,* Velásquez's *The Toilet of Venus* (known as "The Rokeby Venus"), and Constable's *Hay Wain.* The collection is especially strong on Flemish and Dutch masters, Rubens and Rembrandt among them, and on Italian Renaissance works. The museum's Brasserie is an excellent spot for lunch. ✉ *Trafalgar Sq., WC2,* ☎ *020/ 7747–2885,* WEB *www.nationalgallery.org.uk.* ⊙ *Daily 10–6, Wed. until 9 (special exhibition in Sainsbury Wing, Wed. until 10); 1-hr free guided tour of whole gallery starts at Sainsbury Wing daily at 11:30 and 2:30; and 6.30 Wed. Tube: Charing Cross, Leicester Sq.*

❸ National Portrait Gallery. This fascinating collection contains portraits of well-known (and not-so-well-known) Britons, including monarchs, statesmen, and writers. It provides a separate research center for the study of British portraiture, a bookstore, a café, and a top-floor restaurant with viewing area across to the river. Don't miss the Victorian and early 20th-century galleries. ✉ *2 St. Martin's Pl., at foot of Charing Cross Rd., WC2,* ☎ *020/7312–2463 recorded information,* WEB *www.npg.org.uk.* ⊙ *Mon.–Wed., Sat.–Sun. 10–6, Thurs.–Fri. 10–9. Tube: Charing Cross, Leicester Sq.*

❾ Queen's Gallery. This former chapel at the south side of Buckingham Palace is due to re-open in February 2002, to coincide with the queen's Golden Jubilee, after a complete renovation, expansion, and technological update. A Standing Gallery displays a selection of paintings, and the Graphic Art Gallery exhibits drawings and watercolors, while the original main gallery shows changing exhibitions including fine furniture, porcelain and decorative arts. In the micro gallery you can view other works in Her Majesty's vast art collection, not on display but on screen. ✉ *Buckingham Palace Rd., SW1,* ☎ *020/7799–2331,* WEB *www.royal.gov.uk.* ☉ *Opening hours and prices not available at press time. Tube: St. James's Park, Victoria.*

⑩ Royal Mews. Unmissable children's entertainment, this museum is the home of Her Majesty's Coronation Coach. Some of the queen's horses are stabled here and the elaborately gilded state coaches are on view. ✉ *Buckingham Palace Rd.,* ☎ *020/7799–2331,* WEB *www.royal.gov.uk.* 🎟 *£4.60.* ☉ *Aug. 2–Sept., Mon.–Thurs. 10:30–4:30; Oct.–Aug. 1, Mon.–Thurs. noon–4. Tube: St. James's Park, Victoria.*

❹ St. Martin-in-the-Fields. Soaring above Trafalgar Square, this landmark church may seem familiar to many Americans because James Gibbs's classical-temple-with-spire design became a pattern for churches in early Colonial America. Built in about 1730, the distinctive neoclassical church is the site for regular lunchtime music recitals (tickets for free lunchtime concerts and evening concerts are available from the Box Office in the crypt). The crypt is a hive of lively activity, with a café, bookshop, plus the **London Brass-Rubbing Centre,** where you can make your own souvenir knight, lady, or monarch from replica tomb brasses for about £5. ✉ *Trafalgar Sq., WC2,* ☎ *020/7930–0089; 020/7839–8362 credit-card bookings for evening concerts,* WEB *www.stmartin-in-the-fields.org.* ☉ *Church daily 8–8; crypt Mon.–Sat. 10–8, Sun. noon–6. Tube: Charing Cross, Leicester Sq.*

⑪ Tate Britain. By the river to the north of Chelsea, on traffic-laden Millbank, the Tate—now renamed Tate Britain, after the opening of the new Tate Modern south of the river, is the most important collection of modern British art. "Modern" is slightly misleading, as the gallery's collection consists of British art from 1545 to the present, including works by Thomas Gainsborough, Sir Joshua Reynolds, and George Stubbs from the 18th century; and by John Constable, William Blake, and the Pre-Raphaelite painters from the 19th century (don't miss Sir John Everett Millais's unforgettable *Ophelia*). Also on display is one of the highlights of the Tate's collections, the incredible Turner Bequest, consisting of the personal collection of England's greatest romantic painter, J. M. W. Turner. ✉ *Millbank, SW1,* ☎ *020/7887–8000; 020/7887–8008 recorded information,* WEB *www.tate.org.uk.* ☉ *Daily 10–5:50. Tube: Pimlico.*

⑬ Ten Downing Street. As you walk along Whitehall, past government offices, you'll note, on the north side of the street, the entrance to Downing Street, a row of unassuming 18th-century houses. The prime minister's official office is at No. 10, with a private apartment on the top floor (although Tony Blair and his family don't use this as their main address). The chancellor of the exchequer, the finance minister, occupies No. 11. The street is gated off from the main thoroughfare. Nearby, in the middle of Whitehall, is the **Cenotaph,** a stone national memorial to the dead of both world wars. At 11 AM on the Sunday closest to the 11th day of the 11th month, the queen and other dignitaries lay flowers in tribute here. ✉ *Whitehall, SW1. Tube: Westminster.*

❶ Trafalgar Square. This is the center of London, by dint of a plaque on the corner of the Strand and Charing Cross Road from which distances on U.K. signposts are measured. It is the home of the **National Gallery** and of one of London's most distinctive landmarks, **Nelson's Column,**

a tribute to one of England's favorite heroes, Admiral Lord Horatio Nelson, who routed the French at the Battle of Trafalgar in 1805. Constantly alive with Londoners and tourists alike, roaring traffic, and pigeons, it remains London's "living room"—great events, such as New Year's, royal weddings, elections, and sporting triumphs, will always see the crowds gathering in the city's most famous square. ⊠ *Trafalgar Sq., SW1. Tube: Charing Cross.*

★ ⓯ **Westminster Abbey.** The most ancient and important of London's great churches, it is here that Britain's monarchs are crowned. Most of the abbey dates from the 13th and 14th centuries. The main nave is packed with atmosphere and memories, as it has witnessed many splendid coronation ceremonies, royal weddings, and funerals. It is also packed with crowds—so many, in fact, that there is an admission fee to the main nave (always free, of course, for participants in religious services). **Henry VII's Chapel,** an exquisite example of the heavily decorated late-Gothic style, was not built until the early 1600s, and the twin towers over the west entrance are an 18th-century addition. There is much to see inside, including the tomb of the Unknown Warrior, a nameless World War I soldier buried, in memory of the war's victims, in earth brought with his corpse from France; and the famous Poets' Corner, where England's great writers—Milton, Chaucer, Shakespeare, et al.—are memorialized and some are actually buried. Behind the high altar are the royal tombs, including those of Queen Elizabeth I; Mary, Queen of Scots; and Henry V. In the Chapel of Edward the Confessor stands the Coronation Chair.

It is all too easy to forget, swamped by the crowds trying to see the abbey's sights, that this is a place of worship. Early morning is a good moment to catch something of the building's atmosphere. Better still, take time to attend a service. Photography is not permitted. ⊠ *Broad Sanctuary, SW1,* ☎ *020/7222–5152.* 🎟 *£5; Undercroft, Pyx Chamber, Chapter House, and Treasury £2.50 (£1 if you bought ticket to abbey).* ☉ *Mon.– Sat. 9–3:45 (last admission Sat. 1:45). Undercroft, Pyx Chamber treasury, and Chapter House, Apr.–Oct., daily 10:30–5:30; Nov.–Mar., daily 10:30–4. Abbey closed weekdays and Sun. to visitors during services.*

St. James's and Mayfair

These are two of London's most exclusive neighborhoods, where the homes are fashionable and the shopping is world class. You can start by walking west from Piccadilly Circus along Piccadilly, a busy street lined with some very English shops (including Hatchards, the booksellers; Swaine, Adeney Brigg, the equestrian outfitters; and Fortnum & Mason, the department store that supplies the queen's groceries).

㉒ **Apsley House.** Once known, quite simply, as No. 1, London, this was long celebrated as the best address in town. Built by Robert Adam in the 1770s, this was where the Duke of Wellington lived from the 1820s until his death in 1852. It has been kept as the Iron Duke liked it, his uniforms and weapons, his porcelain and plate, and his extensive art collection displayed in opulent 19th-century rooms. Unmissable, in every sense, is the gigantic Canova statue of a nude (but fig-leafed) Napoléon Bonaparte, Wellington's archenemy. ⊠ *149 Piccadilly, SW1,* ☎ *020/7499–5676,* 🖳 *www.vam.ac.uk.* 🎟 *£4.50; includes free sound guides.* ☉ *Tues.–Sun. 11–4:30. Tube: Hyde Park Corner.*

㊴ **BBC Experience.** To celebrate its 75th anniversary, the BBC opened the doors of its own in-house museum in 1997. Included are an audiovisual show, an interactive section, and, of course, a massive gift shop. Admission is on a prebooked and timed system. ⊠ *Broadcasting*

House, Portland Pl., W1, ☎ *0870/603–0304,* WEB *www.bbc.co.uk.* ✉
£7.50. ☉ *Daily 9:30–5:30. Tube: Oxford Circus.*

⑲ Burlington Arcade. This perfectly picturesque covered walkway dates
from 1819. Here, shops sell cashmere sweaters, silk scarves, handmade
chocolates, and leather-bound books. If not the choice shopping spot
it once was, it still makes a great photo-op, particularly if you can snap
the uniformed beadle (he ensures that no one runs, whistles, or sings
here) on duty. ✉ *Off Piccadilly, W1. Tube: Piccadilly Circus.*

⑱ Royal Academy of Arts. On the north side of Piccadilly, the grand marble pile of **Burlington House** contains the offices of many learned so-
cieties and the headquarters of the Royal Academy. The RA, as it is
generally known, stages major visiting art exhibitions. Once most famous for its Summer Exhibition (May–August)—a chaotic hodgepodge of works by living and mostly conservative British artists—the
RA has now adopted an impressive schedule of exhibitions that ranks
among the most prestigious and cutting-edge in the country. ✉ *Burlington House, Piccadilly, W1,* ☎ *020/7300–8000; 020/7300–5760 recorded
information,* WEB *www.royalacademy.org.uk.* ☉ *Sat.–Thurs. 10–6, Fri.
10–8:30. Tube: Piccadilly Circus, Green Park.*

❼ St. James's Palace. This historic royal palace is the current residence of
the Prince of Wales. Although the earliest parts of the lovely brick building date from the 1530s, it had a relatively short career as the center of
royal affairs—from the destruction of Whitehall Palace in 1698 until 1837,
when Victoria became queen and moved the royal household down the
road to Buckingham Palace. Today, the palace is closed to the public,
but your viewfinder will love the picturesque exterior and regimental guard
on duty. ✉ *Friary Court, Pall Mall, SW1. Tube: Green Park.*

⑳ Wallace Collection. A palatial town-house museum, the Wallace is important, exciting, undervisited—and free. As at the Frick Collection in
New York, the setting here, Hertford House, is part of the show—built
for the Duke of Manchester and now stuffed with armor, exquisite furniture, and great paintings, including Bouchers, Watteaus, Fragonard's
The Swing, and Frans Hals's *Laughing Cavalier.* The modernized basement floor is used for educational activities, and has a Watercolour
Gallery. The museum courtyard provides yet more exhibition space and
an upscale restaurant. ✉ *Hertford House, Manchester Sq., W1,* ☎ *020/
7935–0687,* WEB *www.the-wallace-collection.org.uk.* ☉ *Mon.–Sat. 10–
5, Sun. noon–5. Tube: Bond Street.*

Hyde Park, Kensington, and Beyond

When in need of elbow room, Londoners head for Hyde Park and Kensington Gardens. Viewed by natives as their own private backyards, they
form an open swath across central London, and in and around them
are some of London's most noted museums and monuments.

㉗ Albert Memorial. Magnificently restored in 1998 to its original gilded
glory, this florid monument of the 19th century commemorates Queen
Victoria's much-loved husband, Prince Albert, who died in 1861 at the
age of 42. The monument, itself the epitome of high Victorian pomp
and circumstance, commemorates the many socially uplifting projects
of the prince, among them the Great Exhibition of 1851, whose cata-
log he is holding. The memorial is directly opposite the Royal Albert
Hall. ✉ *Kensington Gore. Tube: Knightsbridge.*

㉖ Cheyne Walk. The most beautiful spot in Chelsea—one of London's
most arty (and expensive) residential districts—this Thameside street
is adorned with Queen Anne houses and legendary addresses. Author

George Eliot died at No. 4 in 1880; Pre-Raphaelite artist Dante Gabriel Rossetti lived at No. 16. Two other resident artists were James McNeill Whistler and J. M. W. Turner.

㉑ Hyde Park. Along with the smaller St. James's and Green parks to the east, Hyde Park started as Henry VIII's hunting grounds. Nowadays, it remains a tranquil oasis from urban London—tranquil, that is, except for Sunday morning, when soapbox orators take over **Speakers' Corner,** near the northeast corner of the park (feel free to get up and holler if you fancy spreading your message to the masses). Not far away, along the south side of the park, is **Rotten Row,** which was Henry VIII's royal path to the hunt—*la route du roi*—hence the name. It's still used by the Household Cavalry, the queen's guard. You can see them leave on horseback, in full regalia, at around 10:30 or await their exhausted return at about noon. ⊠ *Bounded by the Ring, Bayswater Rd., Park La., and Knightsbridge,* ☎ *020/7298–2100,* ⲱᴇʙ *www.royalparks.co.uk.* ☉ *Daily 5–midnight. Tube: Hyde Park Corner, Lancaster Gate, Marble Arch, Knightsbridge.*

㉘ Kensington Gardens. More formal than neighboring Hyde Park, Kensington Gardens was first laid out as palace grounds and adjoins Kensington Palace. George Frampton's 1912 **Peter Pan,** a bronze of the boy who lived on an island in the Serpentine and never grew up, overlooks the Long Water. His creator, J. M. Barrie, lived at 100 Bayswater Road, not 500 yards from here. At the **Round Pond,** you can feed the swans. Nearby is boating and swimming in the **Serpentine,** an S-shape lake. Refreshments can be had at the lakeside tearooms. The **Serpentine Gallery** (☎ 020/7402–6075) holds noteworthy exhibitions of modern art. ⊠ *Bounded by the Broad Walk, Bayswater Rd., the Ring, and Kensington Rd.,* ⲱᴇʙ *www.royalparks.co.uk.* ☉ *Daily dawn–dusk. Tube: Lancaster Gate or Queensway.*

㉙ Kensington Palace. This has been a royal home since the late 17th century. From the outside it looks less like a palace than a country house, which it was until William III bought it in 1689. Queen Victoria spent a less-than-happy childhood at Kensington Palace and Princess Diana a less-than-happy marriage. Called the "royal ghetto," the palace is home to many Windsors (they live in a distant section cordoned off from the public). Kensington Palace's state apartments have been restored to how they appeared in Princess Victoria's day. Drop in on the Orangery here for a very elegant cup of tea. ⊠ *The Broad Walk, Kensington Gardens, W8,* ☎ *020/7937–9561,* ⲱᴇʙ *www.hrg.org.uk.* ⊠ *£9.50, including admission to the Dress Collection.* ☉ *Daily 10–5. Tube: High Street Kensington.*

㉔ Natural History Museum. Housed in an ornate late-Victorian building with striking modern additions, this museum features displays on such topics as human biology and evolution. ⊠ *Cromwell Rd., SW7,* ☎ *020/7942–5000,* ⲱᴇʙ *www.nhm.ac.uk.* ☉ *Mon.–Sat. 10–5:50, Sun. 11–5:50. Tube: South Kensington.*

㉚ Portobello Road. North of Kensington Gardens is the lively **Notting Hill** district, full of stylish restaurants and cafés where some of London's trend-setters gather. The best-known attraction in this area is Portobello Road, where a lively antiques and bric-a-brac market is held each Saturday (arrive at 6 AM for the best finds); the southern end is focused on antiques, the northern end on food, flowers, and second-hand clothes. The street is also full of regular antiques shops that are open most weekdays.

㉓ Science Museum. The leading national collection of science and technology, this museum has extensive hands-on exhibits on outer space, astronomy, and hundreds of other subjects. The dramatic Wellcome Wing, a £45 million modern addition to the museum, is devoted to contemporary science, medicine, and technology. It also includes a 450-seat IMAX cinema. ⊠ *Exhibition Rd., SW7,* ☎ *020/7942–4000,* WEB *www.sciencemuseum.org.uk.* ⊙ *Daily 10–6. Tube: South Kensington.*

★ ㉕ **Victoria & Albert Museum.** The V&A, as it is commonly known, originated during the 19th century as a museum of the decorative arts and has extensive collections of costumes, paintings, jewelry, and crafts from every part of the globe. Don't miss the sculpture court, the vintage couture collections, and the great Raphael Room. The provocative architectural addition of *The Spiral* is scheduled to open in 2005, but for now visitors will have to content themselves with the impressive British Galleries chronicling the last 400 years of British history, design, and life. ⊠ *Cromwell Rd., SW7,* ☎ *020/7942–2000,* WEB *www.vam.ac.uk.* ⊙ *Daily 10–5:45, Wed. Late View Wed. 6:30–9:30, last Fri. of the month 6–10. Tube: South Kensington.*

Covent Garden

The Covent Garden district—which lies just to the east of Soho—has gone from a down-at-the-heels area to one of the busiest, most raffishly enjoyable parts of the city. Continental-style open-air cafés create a very un-English atmosphere, with vintage fashion boutiques, art galleries, and street buskers attracting crowds.

㉞ **Covent Garden.** You could easily spend several hours exploring the block of streets north of the Strand known as Covent Garden. The heart of the area is a former wholesale fruit and vegetable market—made famous as one of Eliza Doolittle's haunts in *My Fair Lady*—established in 1656. The **Piazza,** the Victorian Market Building, is now a vibrant shopping center, with numerous boutiques, crafts shops, and cafés. On the south side of the market building is the **Jubilee market,** with crafts and clothing stalls. The section is anchored by **St. Paul's Church** and the **Royal Opera House.** For interesting specialty shops, head north of the Market Building. Shops on **Long Acre** sell maps, art books and materials, and clothing; shops on **Neal Street** sell clothes, pottery, jewelry, tea, housewares, and goods from East Asia. ⊠ *Bounded by the Strand, Charing Cross Rd., Long Acre, and Drury La., WC2. Tube: Charing Cross, Covent Garden, Leicester Sq.*

㊳ **Royal Opera House.** This is the fabled home of the Royal Ballet and Britain's finest opera company. The glass-and-steel Floral Hall is the most wonderful feature, and visitors can wander in during the day and enjoy the Piazza concourse and the Amphitheatre Bar, which gives a splendid panorama across the city, or listen to a free lunchtime chamber concert. ⊠ *Bow St., WC2,* ☎ *020/7240–1200 or 020/7304–4000,* WEB *www.royaloperahouse.org. Tube: Covent Garden.*

㉟ **St. Paul's Church.** A landmark of the Covent Garden market area, this 1633 church, designed by Inigo Jones, is known as the Actors' Church. Inside are numerous memorials to theater people. Look for the open-air entertainers performing under the church's portico. ⊠ *Bedford St., WC2. Tube: Covent Garden.*

㊲ **Somerset House.** A royal palace once stood on the site, but was replaced in the 18th century with a classic structure by William Chambers. For the first time in over one hundred years, it is open to visitors who can view the 18th-century chambers, including the Seamen's Waiting Hall, the Nelson Stair, and Navy Commissioners' Barge. Lighting up the vaults is London's latest museum of intricate works of silver, gold snuff boxes and Italian mosaics, **The Gilbert Collection. The Hermitage Rooms** also house objects with foreign origins; they are the new permanent home for some of the treasures from Russia's eponymous premier museum. The **Courtauld Institute of Art** occupies the north building of Somerset House. Here, London's finest Impressionist and Postimpressionist collection spans from Bonnard to Van Gogh (Manet's *Bar at the Folies-Bergère* is the star), with bonus post-Renaissance works. Arts events are held in the Italianate courtyard between the Courtauld and the rest of Somerset House. Cafés and a river terrace complete the clutch of cultural delights that visitors can reach directly by walkway from Waterloo Bridge. ✉ *The Strand, WC2* ☎ *020/7845–4600, 020/7240–4080 Gilbert Collection, 020/7845–4630 Hermitage,* WEB *www.somerset-house.org.uk.* ⏲ *Courtauld Mon.–Sat. 10–6, Sun. noon–6 (last admission 5:15).* 🎫 *Somerset House, free; Gilbert Collection £4 (combined ticket to Gilbert and Courtauld Institute of Art £7, free admission to both Mon. 10–2); Hermitage Rooms £6.* ⏲ *Mon.–Sat. 10–6, Sun. noon–6 (last admission 5:15).*

36 **Theatre Museum.** A comprehensive collection of material on the history of the English theater, this museum traces the history not merely of the classic drama but also of opera, music hall, pantomime, and musical comedy. A highlight is the re-creation of a dressing room filled with memorabilia of former stars. ✉ *Russell St., WC2,* ☎ *020/7836–7891,* WEB *www.theatremuseum.org.* 🎫 *£4.50.* ⏲ *Tues.–Sun. 10–6. Tube: Covent Garden.*

Bloomsbury

Bloomsbury is a semiresidential district to the north of Covent Garden that contains some spacious and elegant 17th- and 18th-century squares. It could be called the intellectual center of London, as both the British Museum and the University of London are here. The area also gave its name to the Bloomsbury Group, a clique of writers and painters who thrived here in the early 20th century.

33 **British Library.** Since it opened in 1759, the British Library had always been housed in the British Museum on Gordon Square—but space ran out long ago, necessitating this grand new edifice, a few blocks north of the British Museum. The library's treasures: the Magna Carta, Gutenberg Bible, Jane Austen's writings, Shakespeare's First Folio, and music manuscripts by Handel are on view to the general public in the John Ritblat Gallery. The library's Piazza hosts a series of free concerts. ✉ *96 Euston Rd., NW1,* ☎ *020/7412–7332,* WEB *www.bl.uk.* ⏲ *Mon. and Wed.–Fri. 9:30–6, Tues. 9:30–8, Sat. 9:30–5, Sun. 11–5. Tube: Euston, King's Cross.*

★ 40 **British Museum.** The focal point in this fabled collection of antiquities is the unmissable techno-classical Great Court, where beneath a vast glass roof lies the museum's inner courtyard. The space also gives room for new galleries, an I.T. center for viewing the collection on screen, cafés, and shops. But back to the stuff of the museum—the priceless collection of treasures, including Egyptian, Greek, and Roman antiquities; Renaissance jewelry; pottery; coins; glass; and drawings from virtually every European school since the 15th century. Some of the highlights are the **Elgin Marbles,** sculptures that formerly decorated the Parthenon in Athens; the **Rosetta Stone,** which helped archaeologists to interpret Egyptian hieroglyphs; and the Chase Manhattan Gallery of **North America,** which has one of the largest collections of native culture outside the American Continent. The revered gold and blue Reading Room is open to the public and has banks of computers. It's best to pick one section that particularly interests you—to try to see everything would be an overwhelming and exhausting task. ✉

Great Russell St., WC1, ☎ 020/7636–1555, WEB www.thebritishmuseum. ac.uk. ☺ Mon.–Sat. 10–5, Sun. noon–6. Tube: Tottenham Court Rd., Holborn, Russell Sq.

★ ④ **Sir John Soane's Museum.** On the border of London's legal district, this museum, stuffed with antique busts and myriad decorative delights, is an eccentric, smile-inducing 19th-century collection of art and artifacts in the former home of the architect of the Bank of England. ⊠ *13 Lincoln's Inn Fields, WC2, ☎ 020/7405–2107, WEB www.soane.org. ☺ Tues.– Sat. 10–5, also 6–9 PM 1st Tues. of every month. Tube: Holborn.*

The City and South Bank

The City, the commercial center of London, was once the site of the great Roman city of Londinium. Since those days, the City has been rebuilt innumerable times, and today, ancient and modern jostle each other elbow to elbow. Several of London's most famous attractions are here, along with the adjacent area across the Thames commonly called the South Bank. Here, Shakespeare's Globe Theatre, the new Tate Museum of Modern Art, and the British Airways London Eye—the world's largest Ferris-type wheel—are drawing both natives and visitors in droves.

④ **Barbican Centre.** A vast arts center built by the City of London, the Barbican takes its name from the watchtower that stood here during the Middle Ages. It contains a concert hall (where the London Symphony Orchestra is based), two theaters, an art gallery, a cinema, and several restaurants. The theaters are the London home of the **Royal Shakespeare Company.** ☎ *020/7638–8891; 020/7628–3351 RSC backstage tour, WEB www.barbican.org.uk. ☺ Barbican Centre Mon.–Sat. 9 AM–11 PM, Sun. noon–11; gallery Mon.–Sat. 10–7:30, Sun. noon– 7:30; conservatory weekends noon–5:30 when not in use for private function (call first). Tube: Moorgate, Barbican.*

④ **Museum of London.** At **London Wall,** so called because it follows the line of the wall that surrounded the Roman settlement, the Museum of London enables you to come to grips with a great deal of the city's history. Oliver Cromwell's death mask, Queen Victoria's crinolined gowns, Selfridge's Art Deco elevators, and the Lord Mayor's Coach are just some of the goodies here. ⊠ *London Wall, EC2, ☎ 020/7600– 0807. ☒ £5 (free 4:30–5:50; tickets are good for one year). ☺ Mon.– Sat. 10–5:50, Sun. noon–5:50. Tube: Barbican.*

④ **St. Mary-le-Bow.** This church, a landmark of the Cheapside district, was rebuilt by Christopher Wren after the Great Fire; it was built again after being bombed during World War II. It is said that to be a true Cockney, you must be born within the sound of Bow bells. This was the marketplace of medieval London (the word *ceap* is Old English for "to barter"), as the street names hereabouts indicate: Milk Street, Ironmonger Lane, and so on. Despite rebuilding, many of the streets still run on the medieval pattern. ⊠ *Cheapside, EC2. ☺ Mon.– Thurs. 6:30–5:45, Fri. 6:30–4, weekends special services only. Tube: Mansion House.*

★ ④ **St. Paul's Cathedral.** London's symbolic heart, St. Paul's is Sir Christopher Wren's masterpiece. Its dome—the world's third largest—can be seen from many an angle in other parts of the city. The cathedral was completed in 1710 following the Great Fire. Wren was the architect who was also responsible for designing 50 City parish churches to replace those lost in that disaster. Fittingly, he is buried in the crypt under a simple Latin epitaph, composed by his son, which translates as: "Reader, if you seek his monument, look around you." The cathedral has been the site of many famous state occasions, including the funeral of Winston Churchill in 1965 and the ill-fated marriage of the Prince and Princess of Wales in 1981. In the ambulatory (the area behind the high altar) is the American Chapel, a memorial to the 28,000 U.S. servicemen and -women stationed in Britain during World War II who lost their lives while on active service. The greatest architectural glory of the cathedral is the dome. This consists of three distinct elements: an outer, timber-frame dome covered with lead; an interior dome built of brick and decorated with frescoes of the life of St. Paul by the 18th-century artist Sir James Thornhill; and, in between, a brick cone that supports and strengthens both. There is a good view of the church from the **Whispering Gallery,** high up in the inner dome. The gallery is so called because of its remarkable acoustics, whereby words spoken on one side can be clearly heard on the other, 107 ft away. Above this gallery are two others, both external, from which there are fine views over the City and beyond. ⊠ *St. Paul's Churchyard, Paternoster Sq., Ludgate Hill, EC4,* ☎ *020/7236–4128,* WEB *www.stpauls.co.uk.* ⊡ *Cathedral, crypt, ambulatory, and gallery £5.* ⊙ *Cathedral Mon.–Sat. 8:30–4; ambulatory, crypt, and galleries Mon.–Sat. 9:30–4:15. Tube: St. Paul's.*

★ ④⑦ **Shakespeare's Globe Theatre.** This spectacular theater is a replica of Shakespeare's open-roof Globe Playhouse (built in 1599, incinerated in 1613), where most of the playwright's great plays premiered. It stands 200 yards from the original, overlooking the Thames. It was built with the use of authentic Elizabethan materials, down to the first thatch roof in London since the Great Fire. Plays are presented in natural light (and sometimes rain), to 1,000 people on wooden benches in the "bays," plus 500 "groundlings," standing on a carpet of filbert shells and clinker, just as they did nearly four centuries ago. The main theater season runs from June through September, but throughout the year you can tour the Globe through admission to the **New Shakespeare's Globe Exhibition,** which opened in September 1999 and is the largest ever to focus on the Bard. In addition, productions are now scheduled throughout the year in a second, indoor theater, built to a design by the 17th-century architect Inigo Jones. Call for performance schedule. ⊠ *New Globe Walk, Bankside (South Bank),* ☎ *020/7902–1500,* WEB *www.shakespeares-globe.org.* ⊙ *Daily 10–5.*

④⑥ **Tate Modern.** Opposite St. Paul's Cathedral on the Thames in South Bank, this is the new branch of the museum formerly known as the Tate Gallery of Modern British Art, now boldly renamed the Tate Britain. The £100 million state-of-the-art transformation of the former Bankside Power Station by Swiss architects Herzog and de Meuron opened in May 2000 and firmly establishes this gallery as one of the great world-class modern art museums, continuing the picture—where the National Gallery finishes—from the 19th century on. ⊠ *25 Summer St., SE1,* ☎ *020/7887–8000,* WEB *www.tate.org.uk.* ⊙ *Sun.–Thurs. 10–6, Fri.–Sat 10–10. Tube: Blackfriars or Southwark.*

★ ④⑧ **Tower of London.** A guaranteed spine-chiller, this is one of London's most famous sights and one of its most crowded, too. Come as early in the day as possible and head for the Crown Jewels so you can see them before the crowds arrive. The tower served the monarchs of medieval England as both fortress and palace. Every British sovereign from William the Conqueror in the 11th century to Henry VIII in the 16th lived here, and it remains a royal palace, in name at least. The **White Tower** is the oldest and also the most conspicuous building in the entire complex. Inside, the **Royal Armouries,** England's national collection of arms and armor, occupy the ground floor. On the first floor, the **Chapel of St. John** is one of the few unaltered parts of the tower, and its simple, original architectural features makes it one of the most distinctive church interiors of its time in England.

The group of buildings which make up the old **Medieval Palace** is best entered by Water Lane, beside **Traitors' Gate.** There are three towers to explore: **St. Thomas's Tower,** which contains the monarch's rooms and lobby with waterside entrance (now known as Traitors' Gate); the Wakefield Tower; and Lanthorn Tower, both of which have more royal accommodations joined by a walkway along the battlements. In the furnished rooms of the **Wakefield Tower,** costumed actors describe daily life in the Medieval Palace and its evolution over the centuries. Henry VI is alleged to have been murdered in the Wakefield Tower in 1471, during England's medieval civil war, the Wars of the Roses. Among other buildings worth seeing is the **Bloody Tower.** The little princes in the tower—the uncrowned boy-king Edward V and his brother Richard, duke of York, supposedly murdered on the orders of the duke of Gloucester, later crowned Richard III—certainly lived in the Bloody Tower and may well have died here, too. It was a rare honor to be beheaded in private inside the tower on the Scaffold Site of Tower Green; most people were executed outside, on **Tower Hill,** where the crowds could get a much better view. The church of **St. Peter ad Vincula** has the burial places of the unfortunate queens and bishops who upset the Tudor monarchy and can be seen as part of a Yeoman's Tour.

The **Crown Jewels,** a breathtaking collection of regalia, precious stones, gold, and silver, used for the coronation of the present sovereign, are housed in the **Jewel House, Waterloo Barracks.** An exhibition illustrating their history precedes the gems themselves. The Royal Scepter contains the largest cut diamond in the world. The Imperial State Crown, made for the 1838 coronation of Queen Victoria, contains some 3,000 precious stones, largely diamonds and pearls. The jewels used to be housed in the **Martin Tower** (in less secure circumstances, when a daring Thomas Blood made an attempt to steal them in 1671), where an exhibit—Crowns and Diamonds—shows the making of the royal regalia and displays some state crowns made for earlier kings and queens. Look for the ravens—Hardey, George, Mumin, Cedric, Odin, Thor (who talks), and Gwylem—near the Wakefield Tower. Their presence at the Tower is traditional, and it is said that if they leave, the Tower will fall and England will lose her greatness. ☒ *Tower Hill, EC3N,* ☎ *020/7709–0765; 020/7680–9004 recorded information,* WEB *www.hrp.org.uk.* ☒ *£11.* ☉ *Mar.–Oct., Mon.–Sat. 9–5, Sun. 10–5; Nov.–Feb., Tues.–Sat. 9–4, Sun.–Mon. 10–4 (Tower closes 1 hr after last admission and all internal buildings close 30 mins after last admission, but to see all the attractions, allow at least 3 hrs). Yeoman Warder guides conduct tours daily from Middle Tower; no charge. Subject to weather and availability of guides, tours are conducted about every 30 mins until 3:30 in summer, 2:30 in winter.*

Hampstead

Hampstead is a quaint village within the city, where many famous poets and writers have lived. Today it is a fashionable residential area, with a main shopping street and some rows of elegant 18th-century houses. The heath is one of London's largest and most attractive open spaces.

㉛ Abbey Road Studios. Here, outside the legendary Abbey Road Studios (the facility is closed to the public), is the most famous zebra crossing in the world. Immortalized on the cover of the Beatles' *Abbey Road* album of 1969, this pedestrian crosswalk is a spot beloved to countless Beatlemaniacs and baby boomers, many of whom venture here to leave their signature on the white stucco fence that fronts the adjacent studio facility. Abbey Road is not in Hampstead but in adjacent St. John's Wood, an elegant residential suburb a 10-minute ride on the tube from central London. ⊠ *3 Abbey Rd., NW8,* WEB *www.abbeyroad.co.uk. Tube: St. John's Wood.*

㉜ Kenwood House. On the north side of the heath is Kenwood House, built in the 17th century and remodeled by Robert Adam at the end of the 18th century. The house contains a collection of superb paintings by Rembrandt, Turner, Reynolds, Van Dyck, and Gainsborough—and *The Guitar Player,* probably the most beautiful Vermeer in England. Unfortunately, only one grand Adam interior remains. The house's lovely landscaped grounds provide the setting for symphony concerts in summer. ⊠ *Hampstead La., NW3,* ☎ *020/8348–1286.* ☺ *Easter–Aug., Sat.–Mon., Tues., and Thurs. 10–6, Wed. and Fri. 10:30–6; Dec.–Easter, Sat.–Mon., Tues., and Thurs. 10–4, Wed. and Fri. 10:30–5; Sept.–Nov. Sat.–Mon., Tues., and Thurs. 10–4, Wed. and Fri. 10:30–4. Tube: Golder's Green, then Bus 210.*

Greenwich

Home to a number of historical and maritime attractions, Greenwich—situated on the Thames some 8 km (5 mi) east of central London—is an ideal destination for a day out. You can get to Greenwich by Underground, by riverboat from Westminster and Tower Bridge piers, and by Thames Line's high-speed river buses.

Cutty Sark. Now in dry dock is the glorious 19th-century clipper ship *Cutty Sark.* ⊠ *King William Walk, SE10,* ☎ *020/8858–3445,* WEB *www.cuttysark.org.uk.* ☺ *Daily 10–5. DLR: Cutty Sark.*

National Maritime Museum. A treasure house of paintings, maps, models, and, best of all, ships from all ages, this is a fascinating museum. Don't miss the ornate royal barges.⊠ *Romney Rd., SE10,* ☎ *020/8858–4422.* ☺ *Mon.–Sat. 10–6, Sun. noon–6. DLR: Greenwich.*

Old Royal Observatory. Stand astride both hemispheres in the courtyard of the Old Royal Observatory, where the prime meridian—0° longitude—is set. The observatory is at the top of the hill, behind the National Maritime Museum and Royal Naval College, in the attractive **Greenwich Park,** which was originally a royal hunting ground. Founded in 1675, the observatory has original telescopes and other astronomical instruments on display. ⊠ *Greenwich Park, SE10,* ☎ *020/8858–4422,* WEB *www.rog.nmm.ac.uk.* ☺ *Daily 10–5. DLR: Greenwich.*

DINING

CATEGORY	COST*
$$$$	over £22
$$$	£16–£22
$$	£9–£15
$	under £9

per person for a main course at dinner

Bloomsbury

$$–$$$ ✗ **Chez Gérard.** This purveyor of steak-*frites* (with french fries) and similarly simple Gallic offerings is reliable, relaxed, and usefully located near Oxford Street (10 more are dotted around London). ⊠ *8 Charlotte St.,* ☎ *020/7636–4975. AE, DC, MC, V. Tube: Goodge St.*

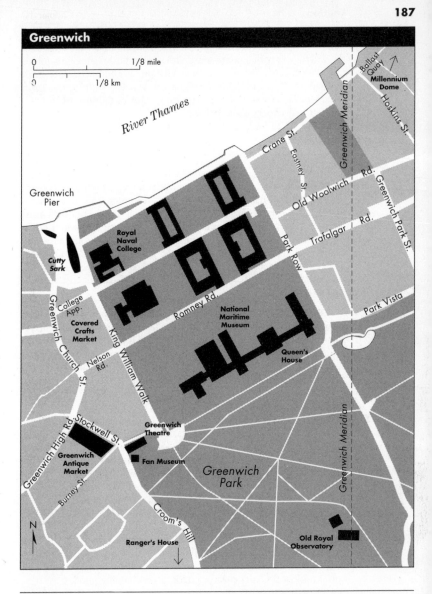

Greenwich

Chelsea

$$$$ ✗ **Gordon Ramsay.** A table at Ramsay's restaurant has been London's
★ toughest reservation to score for almost as long as it's been open, because the soccer star turned chef has every table gasping in awe at his
famous cappuccino of white beans with sautéed *girolles* (mushrooms)
and truffles, followed by—well, anything at all. Reserve months ahead;
go for lunch (£30) if money is an object. ⊠ *68–69 Royal Hospital Rd.,*
☎ *020/7352–4441 or 020/7352–3334. Reservations essential. AE,
DC, MC, V. Closed weekends. Tube: Sloane Sq.*

$$–$$$ ✗ **Bluebird.** Here's Sir Terence Conran's great "gastrodome"—food
market, brasserie, fruit stand, butcher shop, kitchen shop, and café-
restaurant, all housed in a snappy King's Road former garage. The menu
has more than a nod in the Asia-Pacific direction. Go for the synergy
and visual excitement—Conran's chefs share a tendency to promise more
than they deliver. ⊠ *350 King's Rd.,* ☎ *020/7559–1000. Reservations
essential. AE, DC, MC, V. Tube: Sloane Sq.*

$$ ✕ **Zaika.** Zaika has zoomed in from nowhere to become one of London's finest Indian restaurants. The chef/patron, Vineet Bhatia, mixes age-old flavors with modern sensibilities and is pushing the boundaries of Indian cuisine. The restaurant is dark (muds and browns), refined, and subtle. You can't top the signature starter of *dhungar machli tikka*—tandoor home-smoked salmon with drips of mustard and dill. Sign off with cheeky chocolate samosas—"chocomosas"—and Indian ice cream. ✉ *257–259 Fulham Rd.,* ☎ *020/7351–7823. Reservations essential. AE, MC, V. Tube: South Kensington.*

The City

$$ ✕ **St. John.** Resembling a stark monks' refectory crossed with an art gallery, this modern British innovator has equally uncompromising menus. Some loathe bone marrow and parsley salad, huge servings of braised pheasant with "black cabbage," or organ meats any which way, with English puddings and Malmsey wine to follow, but newspaper journalists and swank architects really love it. ✉ *26 St. John St.,* ☎ *020/7251–0848. Reservations essential. AE, DC, MC, V. Closed Sun. Tube: Farringdon.*

Covent Garden

$$$ ✕ **Asia de Cuba.** Ian Schrager's Philippe Starck–designed hotel brings Cool Britannia to its apogee. AdeC, the lead restaurant at St. Martins Lane Hotel, feels like a dreamscape. The food is fusion, and you're supposed to share. The Thai beef salad with Asian greens and roasted coconut is delicious, as is the lobster Mai Tai with rum and red curry. Schrager is right: hotels (and their restaurants) are the new disco. ✉ *St. Martins Lane Hotel, 45 St. Martin's La.,* ☎ *020/7300–5588. AE, DC, MC, V. Tube: Leicester Sq.*

$$$ ✕ **Rules.** This is probably the city's most beautiful restaurant—daffodil-
★   yellow walls, Victorian oil paintings, and hundreds of framed engravings make up the history-rich setting—and certainly one of the oldest (it has been here since 1798). Rules is traditional from soup to nuts or, rather, from venison and Dover sole to trifle and Stilton. There's the odd nod to newer cuisines, but the clientele of expense accounters and tourists who want to feast where Dickens and Lillie Langtry once did remains. ✉ *35 Maiden La.,* ☎ *020/7836–5314. AE, DC, MC, V. Tube: Covent Garden.*

$$–$$$ ✕ **The Ivy.** The epitome of style without pretentiousness, this restau-
★   rant beguiles everybody, including media, literary, and theatrical movers and shakers. The menu's got it all—fish-and-chips, sausage-and-mash, squid-ink risotto, sticky toffee pudding—and all are good. ✉ *1 West St.,* ☎ *020/7836–4751. Reservations essential. AE, DC, MC, V. Tube: Covent Garden.*

$–$$ ✕ **Joe Allen.** Long hours (thespians flock here after the curtains fall in
★   Theatreland) and a welcoming, brick-walled interior mean New York Joe's London branch is still swinging after more than two decades. The Modern American menu helps, with barbecued ribs with black-eyed peas, London's only available corn muffins, and roast monkfish with sun-dried-tomato salsa usually on tap. ✉ *13 Exeter St.,* ☎ *020/7836–0651. Reservations essential. AE, MC, V. Tube: Covent Garden.*

$ ✕ **busabe eathai.** You can't do better than this in Soho for £11. It's designed as a superior Thai canteen: diners sit at communal tables, but somehow it's still seductive. All around are deep bronzes, rattans, wooden benches, hardwood tables, low lights and watercolor paper lampshades. Good things include stir-fry chicken butternut squash, green chicken curry with pea aubergine, and seafood vermicelli. ✉ *106–110 Wardour St.,* ☎ *020/7255–8686. Reservations not accepted. AE, MC, V. Tube: Leicester Sq.*

Kensington

$$–$$$ ✕ **Bibendum.** Upstairs in the renovated 1911 Michelin Building, this
★   Art Deco dining extravaganza continues to entice with a menu as Gallic and gorgeous as ever. From the scallops in citrus sauce to the herring in sour cream, all the dishes are unpretentious but admirably
done. The separate Oyster Bar, downstairs, is another way to go. ⊠
81 Fulham Rd., ☎ *020/7581–5817. Reservations essential. AE, DC,
MC, V. Tube: South Kensington.*

$$–$$$ ✕ **La Poule au Pot.** One of London's most romantic restaurants, La
★   Poule au Pot is superb for proposals (or assignations). Gallic and rustic, this is a corner of France in darkest Belgravia. The "Chelsea Set"
love it; Americans do, too. It is candlelit at night—you could be in a
rambling French country house. The *poule au pot* (stewed chicken) with
uncut vegetables is strong and hearty. The service comes with *bonhomie.*
⊠ *231 Ebury St.,* ☎ *020/7730–7763. Reservations essential. AE, DC,
MC, V. Tube: Sloane Sq.*

Knightsbridge

$$$$ ✕ **La Tante Claire.** One of London's best restaurants has successfully
★   upped its pots and pans from Chelsea and moved to the Berkeley
Hotel. Chef Pierre Koffmann still holds the reins over the kitchen, so
you can expect his haute-cuisine fireworks, such as his signature dish
of pigs' feet stuffed with mousse of white meat with sweetbreads and
wild mushrooms. The set lunch menu (£28) is a genuine bargain.
Lunch reservations must be made three or four days in advance, dinner reservations three to four weeks in advance. ⊠ *Berkeley Hotel,
Wilton Pl.,* ☎ *020/7823–2003. Reservations essential. Jacket and tie.
AE, DC, MC, V. Closed Sun. No lunch Sat. Tube: Knightsbridge.*

$$$$ ✕ **Zafferano.** Princess Margaret, Eric Clapton, Joan Collins (she asked
★   that the lights be turned down), and any number of stylish folk have
flocked to this Belgravia place, London's best exponent of *cucina
nuova.* The fireworks are in the kitchen, not in the brick-wall-and-saf-
fron-hue decor: pheasant with rosemary and black truffle, venison medal-
lions with mash and roast cod, lentils and parsley sauce. The desserts
are also *delizioso,* especially the Sardinian pecorino pastries served with
undersweetened vanilla ice cream. The menus are prix fixe. Be sure to
book early. ⊠ *15 Lowndes St.,* ☎ *020/7235–5800. Reservations essential. AE, DC, MC, V. Tube: Knightsbridge.*

$$$ ✕ **Isola.** Isola guns to be the coolest restaurant in London, so don't be
surprised to see Joseph Fiennes mooching in a corner. It is grown-up
osteria fare cooked by a Frenchman, Bruno Loubet. Upstairs is ban-
quette-and-booth power dining; downstairs is more glam—diners sit
at leather "compromise sofas" amid chrome, mirrors, and molecular
lighting. Head for the *zuppa di fagiano e farro* (pheasant soup with
cabbage and farro) and the *faraona al forno* (wood-roasted guinea fowl
with liver and mascarpone). ⊠ *145 Knightbridge,* ☎ *020/7838–1044.
Reservations essential. AE, DC, MC, V. Tube: Knightsbridge.*

$–$$ ✕ **The Enterprise.** One of the new luxury breed of gastro-pubs, this is
perhaps the chicest of the lot—near Harrods and Brompton Cross, it's
filled with decorative types. The menu isn't overly pretty—seared tuna
and char-grilled asparagus, timbale of aubergine, salmon with artichoke
hearts—but the ambience certainly is. ⊠ *35 Walton St.,* ☎ *020/7584–
3148. AE, MC, V. Tube: South Kensington.*

Mayfair

$$$$ ✕ **Oak Room.** Marco Pierre White used to enjoy Jagger-like fame from
★   his TV appearances and gossip column reports of his eruptions of fury.

Sadly, things are duller, now that he has hung up his pans for good and concentrates on expanding his empire. However, his charges are superbly trained here at his most spectacular setting yet—all Belle Epoque soaring ceilings and gilded bits, and palms and paintings. Menus are prix fixe. ⊠ *Le Meridien, 21 Piccadilly,* ☎ *020/7437-0202. Reservations essential. AE, DC, MC, V. Tube: Piccadilly Circus.*

$$$–$$$$ ✕ **Nobu.** Nobuyaki Matsuhisa already has New York, Tokyo, Malabu, and Los Angeles, and now he's taken London, with the same formula of new-style sashimi with a Peruvian influence (such as salmon, ever so slightly seared in sesame-seed oil), plus the famous *omakase* (chef's choice) meals. Nobu is in the Metropolitan, one of London's hippest hotels, with staff, attitude, clientele, and prices to match. Ubon (backwards for Nobu) has opened in Canary Wharf. ⊠ *Metropolitan hotel, 19 Old Park La.,* ☎ *020/7447-4747. Reservations essential. AE, DC, MC, V. No lunch weekends. Tube: Hyde Park.*

$$ ✕ **Momo.** Momo is one of the hottest tickets in town. Algerian-born Mourad Mazouz—Momo to his friends—has stormed beau London with his casbah-like, Moroccan-inspired North African restaurant. The seats are low and placed close together, and there's often live music. Downstairs is the souk-like members-only Kemia Bar, and next door is Mô—a Moroccan tearoom, open to all. The lamb merguez is recommended. ⊠ *25 Heddon St.,* ☎ *020/7434-4040. Reservations essential. AE, DC, MC, V. Tube: Piccadilly Circus.*

Notting Hill

$$–$$$ ✕ **The Cow.** Tucked away in the backwaters of trendy Portobelloland, this is the nicest of a trio of foodie pubs that feed the neighborhood arty hipsters and media stars. It pretends to be a pub in County Derry, serving oysters, crab salad, and other seafood with the beer and heartier food in the cozy restaurant upstairs. ⊠ *89 Westbourne Park Rd.,* ☎ *020/7221-5400. Reservations essential (restaurant). AE, MC, V. Tube: Westbourne Park.*

$$–$$$ ✕ **Kensington Place.** Trendy and loud, this ever-popular place features enormous plate-glass windows through which to be seen and plenty of fashionable food—grilled foie gras with sweet-corn pancake and baked tamarillo with vanilla ice cream are perennials—but it's the fun buzz that draws the crowds. ⊠ *201 Kensington Church St.,* ☎ *020/7727-3184. DC, MC, V. Tube: Notting Hill Gate.*

$$ ✕ **192.** A noisy wine bar/restaurant just off Portobello Road, this is
★   as much a social hangout for the local media mafia as a restaurant, especially on weekends, when you'll feel like you've gate-crashed a party—if you manage to get a table, that is. The appetizer list is best—many people order two of these instead of an entrée. Try the pastas, the fish (cod, clams, chorizo, and saffron broth), or whatever sounds unusual. ⊠ *192 Kensington Park Rd.,* ☎ *020/7229-0482. Reservations essential. AE, DC, MC, V. Tube: Notting Hill Gate.*

$ ✕ **Tootsies.** A useful burger joint characterized by loudish rock and vintage advertisements on the walls, Tootsies serves some of London's better burgers, as well as chili, chicken, BLTs, taco salad, apple pie, fudge cake, and ice cream. There are seven other branches. ⊠ *120 Holland Park Ave.,* ☎ *020/7229-8567. Reservations not accepted. AE, MC, V. Tube: Holland Park.*

St. James's

$$–$$$ ✕ **Le Caprice.** Fabulously dark and glamorous, with black walls and
★   stark white tablecloths, Le Caprice does nothing wrong, from its efficient, nonpartisan (famous folk eat here often) service to its Pan-European menu (salmon fish cake with sorrel sauce; confit of goose

with prunes). ⊠ *Arlington House, Arlington St.,* ☎ *020/7629–2239. Reservations essential. AE, DC, MC, V. Tube: Green Park.*

Soho

$$$–$$$$ ✕ **Spoon +.** This is London's current top groovy destination. Set in Ian Schrager's Sanderson hotel, the Frenchman Alain Ducasse's first London foray has become the place to see and be seen. The menu is a complicated DIY system where the diner has to pick 'n' mix the ingredients. Ask for help, or go for the chef-decides "Sexy Spoon" option (£95 a head, with wine.) The adjacent 80-ft Long Bar is definitely the London bar to be. ⊠ *Sanderson Hotel, 50 Berners St.,* ☎ *020/7300– 1444. Reservations essential. AE, DC, MC, V. Tube: Oxford Circus.*

$$–$$$ ✕ **Titanic.** Marco Pierre White, the noted chef who opened this—the splashiest in the tide of trend-driven dining spots—claims it was not inspired by the blockbuster film. But like the movie, this place has pulled in the crowds, plus a clientele of the young, loud, and fashionable. Decor is Art Deco ocean liner; dinner is fun and casual, ranging from fish-and-chips to squid-ink risotto to sticky toffee pudding. ⊠ *81 Brewer St.,* ☎ *020/7437–1912. Reservations essential. AE, DC, MC, V. Tube: Piccadilly Circus.*

South Bank

$$–$$$ ✕ **OXO Tower Brasserie and Restaurant.** London finally has a room
★ with a view, and *such* a view. On the eighth floor of the beautifully revived OXO Tower Wharf building, this elegant space has Euro food with this year's trendy ingredients (acorn-fed black pig charcuterie with tomato and pear chutney is one example). The ceiling slats turn and change from white to midnight blue, but who notices, with the London Eye and St. Paul's dazzling you across the water? ⊠ *Barge House St., Southbank,* ☎ *020/7803–3888. AE, DC, MC, V. Tube: Waterloo.*

LODGING

Note that although British hotels have traditionally included breakfast in their nightly tariff, many of London's most expensive establishments charge extra for breakfast.

CATEGORY	COST*
$$$$	over £230
$$$	£160–£230
$$	£100–£160
$	under £100

Prices are for two people in a double room and include all taxes.

Bayswater

$$ ▥ **Commodore.** This peaceful hotel of three converted Victorian town
★ houses has some amazing (especially for the price) rooms—as superior to the regular ones (which usually go to package tour groups) as Harrods is to Kmart. Twenty are miniduplexes, with sleeping gallery. One (No. 11) is a real duplex, entered through a secret mirrored door, with a thick-carpeted, *very* quiet bedroom upstairs and its toilet below. ⊠ *50 Lancaster Gate, W2 3NA,* ☎ *020/7402–5291,* 𝖥𝖠𝖷 *020/7262–1088,* 𝖶𝖤𝖡 *www.commodore-hotel.com. 90 rooms. AE, MC, V. Tube: Lancaster Gate.*

$$ ▥ **London Elizabeth.** Steps from Hyde Park and the Lancaster Gate tube, this family-owned gem has one of the prettiest hotel facades in London. The charm continues inside—foyer and lounge are crammed with coffee tables and chintz drapery, lace antimacassars, and little chandeliers. ⊠ *Lancaster Terr., W2 3PF,* ☎ *020/7402–6641,* FAX *020/7224–8900,* WEB *www.londonelizabethhotel.co.uk. 55 rooms. Restaurant. AE, DC, MC, V. Tube: Lancaster Gate.*

$ 🏨 **Columbia.** The public rooms in these five joined Victorians are as big as museum halls, painted in icy hues of powder blue and buttermilk, or paneled in dark wood. At one end of the day they contain the hippest band in town drinking pints; at the other, there are sightseers sipping coffee. Rooms are clean, high-ceilinged, and sometimes very large—it's just a shame that teak veneer and avocado bathroom suites haven't made it back into the style bible yet. ⊠ *95–99 Lancaster Gate, W2 3NS,* ☎ *020/7402–0021,* FAX *020/7706–4691,* WEB *www.columbia-hotel.co.uk. 103 rooms. Restaurant. AE, MC, V. Tube: Lancaster Gate.*

Bloomsbury

$ 🏨 **Morgan.** This family-run hotel in an 18th-century terrace house has rooms that are small but comfortably furnished and look friendly and cheerful. The tiny paneled breakfast room is straight out of a dollhouse. The back rooms overlook the British Museum. ⊠ *24 Bloomsbury St., WC1B 3QJ,* ☎ *020/7636–3735,* FAX *020/7636–3045. 15 rooms with shower, 5 apartments. MC, V. Tube: Russell Sq.*

$ 🏨 **Ridgemount.** The kindly owners, Mr. and Mrs. Rees, make you feel at home in this tiny hotel by the British Museum. There's a homey, cluttered feel in the public areas, and some bedrooms overlook a leafy garden. ⊠ *65 Gower St., WC1E 6HJ,* ☎ *020/7636–1141. 34 rooms, 9 with bath. MC, V. Tube: Goodge St.*

Chelsea, Kensington, and Holland Park

$$$$ 🏨 **Blakes.** Patronized by musicians and film stars, this hotel is one of
★   the most exotic in town. Its Victorian exterior contrasts with the 1980s ultrachic interior, an arty mix of Biedermeier and bamboo, four-poster beds, and chinoiserie, all dramatically lit in film noir style. The bedrooms have individual designs ranging from swaths of black moiré silk to blood-red and lily-white in the 007 suite. ⊠ *33 Roland Gardens, SW7 3PF,* ☎ *020/7370–6701,* FAX *020/7373–0442. 52 rooms. Restaurant. AE, DC, MC, V. Tube: South Kensington.*

$$$$ 🏨 **Halcyon.** Discretion and decadent decor make this expensive, enor-
★   mous, wedding-cake Edwardian desperately desirable. The Blue Room has moons and stars, the Egyptian Suite is canopied like a bedouin tent, and on and on. All guest rooms are different but large, with the high ceilings and big windows. ⊠ *81 Holland Park, W11 3RZ,* ☎ *020/7727–7288,* FAX *020/7229–8516,* WEB *www.halcyon-hotel.co.uk. 42 rooms. Restaurant. AE, DC, MC, V. Tube: Holland Park.*

$$$ 🏨 **The Gore.** Every wall of every room in this friendly and quiet hotel
★   near the Albert Hall is smothered in prints and etchings, and antiques pepper the rooms. Some are spectacular follies—such as Tudor-style Room 101, with its minstrel gallery and four-poster. The crowd here is elegant and arty. ⊠ *189 Queen's Gate, SW7 5EX,* ☎ *020/7584–6601,* FAX *020/7589–8127,* WEB *www.gorehotel.com. 54 rooms. Restaurant. AE, DC, MC, V. Tube: Gloucester Rd.*

$$$ 🏨 **Portobello.** A faithful core of chic visitors returns again and again to this eccentric hotel in a Victorian terrace near the Portobello Road antiques market. Some rooms are tiny, but the ambience of '60s swinging London, the ecclesiastical antiques, and the peaceful vista of the gardens in back make up for it. ⊠ *22 Stanley Gardens, W11 2NG,* ☎ *020/7727–2777,* FAX *020/7792–9641. 22 rooms. Restaurant. AE, DC, MC, V. Closed 10 days at Christmas. Tube: Notting Hill.*

$ 🏨 **Abbey House.** Standards are high and the rooms unusually spacious in this hotel in a fine residential block near Kensington Palace and Gardens. ✉ *11 Vicarage Gate, W8,* ☎ *020/7727–2594. 16 rooms with shared bath. No credit cards. Tube: High Street Kensington.*

$ ⊞ **The Vicarage.** This has long been a favorite for the budget-minded. Family-owned, set on a leaf-shaded street just off Kensington Church Street, the Vicarage is set in a large, white Victorian house. Bedrooms are traditional and comfortable, with solid English furniture. Definitely a charmer—but it is beginning to fray around the edges. ✉ *10 Vicarage Gate, W8 4AG,* ☎ *020/7229–4030,* WEB *www.londonvicaragehotel.com. 19 rooms. No credit cards. Tube: High Street Kensington.*

Knightsbridge, Belgravia, and Victoria

$$$$ ⊞ **The Lanesborough.** Brocades and Regency stripes, moiré silks and fleurs-de-lis, antiques, oils, and reproductions in gilded splendor—everything undulates with richness in this upscale conversion of the old St. George's Hospital at Hyde Park Corner. To register you just sign the book, then retire to your room to find a personal butler, business cards with your in-room fax and phone numbers, VCR and CD player, umbrella, robe, huge flacons of unguents for bath time, and a drinks tray. ✉ *1 Lanesborough Pl., SW1X 7TA,* ☎ *020/7259–5599,* FAX *020/ 7259–5606,* WEB *www.lanesborough.com. 95 rooms. 2 restaurants. AE, DC, MC, V. Tube: Hyde Park Corner.*

$$$$ ⊞ **The Rubens.** The Rubens hotel claims to treat its guests like royalty—after all, you're only a stone's throw from the real thing, with Buckingham Palace just across the road. And if this is how Her Majesty lives, then we've all got reason to be jealous. With well-appointed rooms and a location that could not be more truly central, this elegant hotel provides the sort of deep comfort needed to soothe away a hard day's sightseeing. ✉ *39 Buckingham Palace Rd., SW1W 0PS,* ☎ *020/7834–6600,* FAX *020/7233–6037,* WEB *www.redcarnationhotels.com. 180 rooms. Restaurant. AE, DC, MC, V. Tube: Victoria.*

$$$–$$$$ ⊞ **Basil Street.** Family-run for some 80 years, this is a gracious Edwardian hotel on a quiet street. The rooms are filled with antiques, as are the various lounges, hushed like libraries with polished wooden floors and Oriental rugs. It sounds swanky, but Basil Street is more like home. ✉ *Basil St., SW3 1AH,* ☎ *020/7581–3311,* FAX *020/7581–3693,* WEB *www. thebasil.com. 80 rooms. Restaurant. AE, DC, MC, V. Tube: Knightsbridge.*

$$$–$$$$ ⊞ **The Pelham.** Magnificent 18th-century pine paneling in the draw-
★   ing room, glazed chintz and antique lace, four-posters in some rooms, fireplaces in others—all make this hotel feel more like an elegant home. It's near the big museums, and 24-hour room service and business services are available. ✉ *15 Cromwell Pl., SW7 2LA,* ☎ *020/7589–8288,* FAX *020/7584–8444,* WEB *www.firmdale.com. 50 rooms. Restaurant. AE, MC, V. Tube: South Kensington.*

$ ⊞ **London County Hall Travel Inn Capital.** Don't get too excited—this neighbor of the luxurious new Marriott in the County Hall complex lacks the fabled river view (it's at the back of the grand former seat of local government, on the south side of the Thames). Still, you get an incredible value, with the standard facilities of the cookie-cutter rooms of this chain: TV, tea/coffeemaker, en suite bath-shower, and foldout beds that let you accommodate two children at no extra charge. You're looking at £50 a night for a family of four, in the shadow of Big Ben. *That's* a bargain. ✉ *Belvedere Rd., SE1 7PB,* ☎ *020/7902–1600,* FAX *020/7902–1619,* WEB *www.travelinn.co.uk. 312 rooms. Restaurant. AE, MC, V. Tube: Westminster.*

West End

$$$$ ⊞ **Brown's.** Close to Bond Street, Brown's is like a country house in the middle of town, with wood paneling, grandfather clocks, and large

fireplaces. Founded in 1837 by Lord Byron's "gentleman's gentleman," James Brown, it has attracted Anglophilic Americans ever since. Both Theodore and Franklin Delano Roosevelt stayed here. ⊠ *34 Albemarle St., W1X 4BT,* ☎ *020/7493–6020,* FAX *020/7493–9381,* WEB *www.brownshotel.com. 118 rooms. Restaurant. AE, DC, MC, V. Tube: Green Park.*

$$$$ 🏨 **Claridge's.** This hotel has one of the world's classiest guest lists. The
★ liveried staff is friendly, and the rooms are luxurious. The hotel was founded in 1812, but the present decor is either 1930s Art Deco or country-house style. Have a drink or afternoon tea in the Foyer and hear the Hungarian mini-orchestra. It's worth a visit if you are the sort that hankers after personal butler service, and you don't mind paying for it. ⊠ *Brook St., W1A 2JQ,* ☎ *020/7629–8860 or 800/223–6800,* FAX *020/7499–2210,* WEB *www.savoy-group.co.uk. 200 rooms. Restaurant. AE, DC, MC, V. Tube: Bond St.*

$$$$ 🏨 **Covent Garden Hotel.** Clearly London's most relentlessly chic,
★ extrastylish hotel, this former 1880s-vintage hospital is in the midst of the artsy Covent Garden district and is now the London home-away-from-home for a mélange of off-duty celebrities, actors, and style mavens. Theatrically baronial, the public rooms will keep even the most picky atmosphere-hunter happy. ⊠ *10 Monmouth St., WC2H 9HB,* ☎ *020/7806–1000,* FAX *020/7806–1100,* WEB *www. firmdale.com. 46 rooms, 4 suites. Restaurant. AE, MC, V. Tube: Covent Garden.*

$$$$ 🏨 **Dukes.** This small Edwardian hotel in a cul-de-sac in St. James's is perennially popular, an oasis of peace and elegant comfort in the heart of London. The top-floor suites are real finds for their views, antiques, and homey comfort. ⊠ *35 St. James's Pl., SW1A 1NY,* ☎ *020/7491–4840,* FAX *020/7493–1264,* WEB *www.dukeshotel.co.uk. 80 rooms. Restaurant. AE, DC, MC, V. Tube: Green Park.*

$$$$ 🏨 **Savoy.** This grand, historic, late-Victorian hotel has been the by-
★ word for luxury for just over a century. Hemingway loved its American Bar, and Elizabeth Taylor spent her first honeymoon here. Spacious bedrooms have antiques and cream plasterwork, and the best ones overlook the Thames. More than a hint of dazzling 1920s style remains. ⊠ *Strand, WC2R 0EU,* ☎ *020/7836–4343,* FAX *020/7240–6040,* WEB *www.savoy-group.co.uk. 224 rooms. 3 restaurants, indoor pool. AE, DC, MC, V. Tube: Aldwych.*

$$$ 🏨 **Hazlitt's.** Still Soho's only hotel, this, the last home of William Hazlitt, the essayist (1778–1830), is crammed with prints on every wall, Victorian claw-foot baths, assorted antiques, plants, and bits of art. There's no elevator, the sitting room is minuscule, floors can be creaky and bedrooms tiny, but Hazlitt's legion of devotees doesn't mind. And who needs room service when you stay on Restaurant Row? ⊠ *6 Frith St., W1V 5TZ,* ☎ *020/7434–1771,* FAX *020/7439–1524,* WEB *www.gorehotel.com. 23 rooms. AE, DC, MC, V. Tube: Piccadilly.*

$$ 🏨 **Bryanston Court.** Three 18th-century houses have been converted into a traditional family-run hotel with open fires and comfortable armchairs. The bedrooms are contemporary. ⊠ *56–60 Great Cumberland Pl., W1H 7FD,* ☎ *020/7262–3141,* FAX *020/7262–7248,* WEB *www.bryanston-hotel.com. 56 rooms. AE, DC, MC, V. Tube: Marble Arch.*

$$ 🏨 **The Fielding.** Tucked away in a quiet alley, steps from the Royal Opera House, this cozy place is so adored by its regulars that you must book ahead. It's shabby-homey in decor and attitude—there's no elevator, only one room has a bathtub (most have showers), and there's no room service or restaurant, but it's cute and handy for the theater. ⊠ *4 Broad Ct., Bow St., WC2B 5QZ,* ☎ *020/7836–8305,* FAX *020/7497–0064. 24 rooms. AE, DC, MC, V. Tube: Covent Garden.*

NIGHTLIFE AND THE ARTS

The Arts

The most comprehensive list of events in the London arts scene can be found in *Time Out,* a weekly magazine available at most newsstands and bookstores. The city's evening paper, the *Evening Standard,* carries listings, as do the major Sunday papers, the daily *Independent* and *Guardian,* and, on Friday, the *Times.*

Ballet
The Royal Opera House is the traditional home of the world-famous **Royal Ballet.** As well as favorites like *The Nutcracker,* there are revivals of such productions as *Coppélia* which was originally presented by Dame Ninette de Valois, the founder of the company. Prices start at £2 (for ballet matinees). Bookings should be made well in advance. The **English National Ballet** and visiting companies perform at the Coliseum (☎ 020/7632–8300). In addition, the City Ballet of London performs at the **Peacock Theatre** (☎ 020/7863–8222). **Sadler's Wells Theatre** (☎ 020/7863–8000) hosts regional ballet and international modern dance troupes. Prices are reasonable. A popular venue for modern and experimental dance is **The Place** (☎ 020/7380–1268).

Concerts
Ticket prices for symphony orchestra concerts are still relatively moderate—between £5 and £35, although you can expect to pay more to hear big-name artists on tour. If you can't book in advance, arrive half an hour before the performance for a chance at returns.

The London Symphony Orchestra is in residence at the **Barbican Arts Centre** (☎ 020/7638–8891), although other top symphony and chamber orchestras also perform here. The **South Bank Centre** (☎ 020/7960–4242), which includes the **Royal Festival Hall** and the **Queen Elizabeth Hall,** is another major venue for choral, symphonic, and chamber concerts. For less expensive concert going, try the **Royal Albert Hall** (☎ 020/7589–8212) during the summer Promenade season; special tickets for standing room are available at the hall on the night of performance. Note, too, that the concerts are jumbo-screen broadcast in Hyde Park, but even a seat on the grass here requires a paid ticket. The **Wigmore Hall** (☎ 020/7935–2141) is a small auditorium, ideal for recitals. Inexpensive lunchtime concerts take place all over the city in smaller halls and churches, often featuring string quartets, vocalists, jazz ensembles, and gospel choirs. **St. John's, Smith Square** (☎ 020/7222–1061), a converted Queen Anne church, has a popular schedule of concerts.

Film
Most West End cinemas are in the area around Leicester Square and Piccadilly Circus. Tickets average £8.50. Matinees and Monday evenings are cheaper, and some theaters offer student discounts. Cinema clubs screen a wide range of films: classics, Continental, underground, rare, or underestimated masterpieces. A temporary membership fee is usually about £1. One of the best cinema clubs is the **National Film Theatre** (☎ 020/7928–3232), part of the South Bank Centre.

Opera
The **Royal Opera** presides over the main venue for opera in London, the fabled Royal Opera House (✉ Covent Garden, WC2E 9DD, ☎ 020/7304–4000), which ranks with the Metropolitan Opera House in New York in every way except, surprisingly, expense. Ballet matinees can cost as little as £2, although prices escalate to £150 for a top-price opera. Conditions of purchase vary—call for information.

The **Coliseum** (☎ 020/7632–8300) is the home of the English National Opera Company (ENO), whose productions are staged in English and are often innovative and exciting. Prices are lower than for the Royal Opera, ranging from £5 to £55.

Theater

London's theater life can more or less be divided into three categories: the government-subsidized national companies; the commercial, or "West End," theaters; and the fringe. The **Royal National Theatre Company** (NT) shares the laurels as the top national repertory troupe with the Royal Shakespeare Company. In similar fashion to the latter troupe, the NT presents a variety of plays by writers of all nationalities, ranging from the classics of Shakespeare to specially commissioned modern works. The NT is based at the South Bank Centre (☎ 020/7452–3000 box office). The **Royal Shakespeare Company** (RSC) is based at the Barbican Centre (☎ 020/7638–8891 or 01789/403–403 box office). The RSC has terminated their summer season in London, although their winter season remains. For general inquiries, phone the central box office in Stratford-Upon-Avon (☎ 020/7638–8891 or 01789/403–403). If you're visiting London in the summer, you can make up for the absence of the RSC by booking tickets at the spectacular new reconstruction of the famed Elizabethan-era **Shakespeare's Globe Theatre** (☎ 020/7401–9919 box office) on the South Bank, which offers open-air, late-afternoon performances from June through September.

The **West End theaters** stage musicals, comedies, whodunits, and revivals of lighter plays of the 19th and 20th centuries, often starring TV celebrities. Occasionally there are more serious productions, including successful productions transferred from the subsidized theaters, such as RSC's *Les Liaisons Dangereuses* and *Les Misérables*. The two dozen or so established **fringe theaters,** scattered around central London and the immediate outskirts, frequently present some of London's most intriguing productions, if you're prepared to overlook occasional rough staging and uncomfortable seating.

Most theaters have an evening performance at 7:30 or 8 Monday–Saturday, and a matinee twice a week (Wednesday or Thursday, and Saturday). Expect to pay from £10 for a seat in the upper balcony and at least £25 for a good seat in the stalls (orchestra) or dress circle (mezzanine)—more for musicals. Tickets may be booked in person at the theater box office, over the phone by credit card, or through ticket agents, such as **Ticketmaster** (☎ 020/7344–0055). The **SOLT Kiosk** in Leicester Square sells half-price tickets on the day of performance for about 25 theaters; there is a small service charge. It's open Monday–Saturday 2–6:30, Sunday noon–3. Beware of scalpers!

Nightlife

London's nightspots are legion; here are some of the best known. For up-to-the-minute listings, buy *Time Out* magazine.

Cabaret

The best comedy in town can be found in the big, bright **Comedy Store** (✉ Haymarket House, Oxendon St., near Piccadilly Circus, ☎ 020/7344–0234).

Jazz Clubs

Pizza Express (✉ 10 Dean St., W1, ☎ 020/7437–9595 or 020/7439–8722) is the capital's best-loved chain of pizza houses, but it is also one of London's principal jazz venues, with music every night except Monday in the basement restaurant. Eight other branches also have live music; check the listings for details. **Ronnie Scott's** (✉ 47 Frith St.,

W1, ☎ 020/7439–0747) is the legendary Soho jazz club where international performers regularly take the stage.

Nightclubs

Café de Paris (⊠ 3–4 Coventry St., W1V 7FL, ☎ 020/7734–7700) opened in 1914 and is one of London's most glamour-puss settings, once the haunt of royals and stars such as Noël Coward, Marlene Dietrich, Fred Astaire, and Frank Sinatra. **Hanover Grand** (⊠ 6 Hanover Sq., W1, ☎ 020/7499–7977) is a swank and opulent big West End club that attracts TV stars and others in the entertainment business for funky U.S. garage on Fridays and glam disco on Saturdays. The lines outside get long, so dress up to impress the bouncers. **Ministry of Sound** (⊠ 103 Gaunt St. SE1, ☎ 020/7378–6528) is more of an industry than a club, with its own record label, line of apparel, and, of course, DJs. Inside, there are chill-out rooms, dance floors, promotional Sony Playstations, Absolut shot bars—all the club kid's favorite things. If you are one, and you only have time for one night out, make it here.

Rock

The **Forum** (⊠ 9–17 Highgate Rd., Kentish Town, ☎ 020/7344–0044), a little out of the way, is a premier venue for medium-to-big acts. **100 Club** (⊠ 100 Oxford St., W1, ☎ 020/7636–0933) is a basement dive that's always been there for R&B, rock, jazz, and beer. The **Shepherds Bush Empire** (⊠ Shepherds Bush Green, W12, ☎ 020/7771–2000) is a major venue for largish acts in West London. The **Borderline** (⊠ Otange Yard, off Manette St., W1V, ☎ 020/7734–2095) is a central subterranean room with fake southwestern decor that puts on a surprisingly good array of Americana, blues and indie rock.

SHOPPING

Shopping is one of London's great pleasures. Different areas retain their traditional specialties, and it's fun to seek out the small crafts, antiques, and gift stores, designer-clothing resale outlets, and national department-store chains.

Shopping Districts

Centering on the King's Road, **Chelsea** was once synonymous with ultrafashion; it still harbors some designer boutiques, plus antiques and home furnishings stores. A something-for-everyone neighborhood, **Covent Garden** has numerous clothing chain stores, stalls selling crafts, and shops selling gifts of every type—bikes, kites, herbs, beads, hats, you name it. **Kensington**'s main drag, Kensington High Street, is a smaller, classier version of Oxford Street, with Barkers department store, and a branch of Marks & Spencer at the eastern end. Try Kensington Church Street for expensive antiques, plus a little fashion. Venture out to the W11 and W2 neighborhoods around the Holland Park–Westbourne Grove end of **Notting Hill,** and you'll find specialty shops for clothes, accessories, and home living, with must-have status, plus lots of fashionable bistros for sustenance. Kensington's neighbor, **Knightsbridge** has Harrods, of course, but also Harvey Nichols, the chicest clothes shop in London, and many expensive designers' boutiques along Sloane Street, Walton Street, and Beauchamp Place. Adjacent Belgravia is also a burgeoning area for posh designer stores.

Bond Street, Old and New, is the elegant lure in **Mayfair,** with the *hautest* of haute couture and jewelry outposts, plus fine art. South Molton Street offers high-price, high-style fashion—especially at Browns—and the tailors of Savile Row are of worldwide repute. Crowded and a bit past its prime, **Oxford Street** is lined with tawdry discount shops. However, Selfridges, John Lewis, and Marks & Spencer are wonderful department stores, and there are interesting boutiques secreted off Oxford Street, just north of the Bond Street tube stop, in little St. Christopher's Place and Gees Court. Check out the cobbled streets in West Soho, behind Liberty in Regent Street, for handcrafted jewelry, designer gear, and stylish cafés. Perpendicular to Oxford Street lies **Regent Street**—famous for its curving path—with possibly London's most pleasant department store, Liberty's, as well as Hamley's, the capital's toy mecca. Shops around once-famous **Carnaby Street** stock designer youth paraphernalia and at least 57 varieties of T-shirts. The fabled English gentleman buys much of his gear at stores in **St. James's**: handmade hats, shirts, and shoes; silver shaving kits; and hip flasks. Here is also the world's best cheese shop, Paxton & Whitfield. Don't expect any bargains in this neighborhood.

Street Markets

Street markets are one aspect of London life not to be missed. Here are some of the more interesting markets:

Bermondsey. Arrive as early as possible for the best treasure. ⊠ *Tower Bridge Rd., SE1. ۞ Fri. 4 AM–1 PM. Tube to London Bridge or Bus 15 or 25 to Aldgate and then Bus 42 over Tower Bridge to Bermondsey Sq.*

Camden Lock. The youth center of the world, apparently, it's good for cheap clothes and boots. The canalside antiques, crafts, and junk markets are also picturesque and very crowded. ⊠ *Chalk Farm Rd., NW1. ۞ Shops Tues.–Sun. 9:30–5:30, stalls weekends 8–6. Tube or Bus 24 or 29 to Camden Town.*

Camden Passage. The rows of little antiques stalls are a good hunting ground for silverware and jewelry. Stalls open Wednesday and Saturday, but there is also a books and prints market on Thursday. Surrounding shops are open the rest of the week. ⊠ *Islington, off Upper St., N1. ۞ Wed. and Sat. 8:30–3. Tube or Bus 19 or 38 to Angel.*

Petticoat Lane. Look for budget-priced leather goods, gaudy knitwear, and fashions, plus cameras, videos, stereos, antiques, books, and bric-a-brac. ⊠ *Middlesex St., E1. ۞ Sun. 9–2. Tube: Liverpool St., Aldgate, Aldgate East.*

Portobello Market. Saturday is the best day for antiques, though this neighborhood is London's melting pot, becoming more vibrant every year. Find fabulous small shops, the city's trendiest restaurants, and a Friday and Saturday flea market at the far end at Ladbroke Grove. ⊠ *Portobello Rd., W11. ۞ Fri. 5 AM–3 PM, Sat. 6 AM–5 PM. Tube or Bus 52 to Notting Hill Gate or Ladbroke Grove, or Bus 15 to Kensington Park Rd.*

LONDON A TO Z

To research prices, get advice from other travelers, and book travel arrangements, visit www.fodors.com.

AIR TRAVEL TO AND FROM LONDON

International flights to London arrive at either Heathrow Airport, 24 km (15 mi) west of London, or Gatwick Airport, 43 km (27 mi) south of the capital. Most flights from the United States go to Heathrow, although Gatwick has grown from a European airport into one that serves 21 scheduled U.S. destinations. A third airport, Stansted, is to the east of the city. It handles mainly European and domestic traffic, although there is a scheduled service from New York.

British Airways is the national flag carrier and offers mostly nonstop flights from 18 U.S. cities to Heathrow and Gatwick airports. Other major carriers serving Heathrow and Gatwick airports in Great Britain include American Airlines and Virgin Atlantic, which serve Heathrow and Gatwick; Continental, Delta, Northwest, and TWA, which serve Gatwick; and United, which serves Heathrow.

➤ AIRLINES AND CONTACTS: **American Airlines** (☎ 800/433–7300; 020/8572–5555 in London). **British Airways** (☎ 800/AIRWAYS; 0845/7222–1111 in London). **Continental** (☎ 800/231–0856; 0800/776464 in London). **Delta** (☎ 800/241–4141; 0800/414767 in London). **Northwest Airlines** (☎ 800/447–4747; 0870/507–4074 in London). **TWA** (☎ 800/892–4141; 0345/333333 in London). **United** (☎ 800/241–6522; 0845/844–4777 in London). **Virgin Atlantic** (☎ 800/862–8621; 01293/747747 serves London).

AIRPORT TRANSFERS

Airport Travel Line gives information and takes advance bookings on transfers to town and between airports, including National Express as listed below. The Heathrow Express train links the airport with Paddington Station in only 15 minutes. It costs £12, and service departs every 15 minutes from 5:10 AM to 11:40 PM. The Piccadilly Line serves Heathrow (all terminals) with a direct Underground (subway) link, costing £3.50. Airbus A2 costs £7 and leaves every 30 minutes 6 AM–9:30 PM to Euston and King's Cross stations among other stops, but the trip can be lengthy, as there are around 14 other stops en route. National Express Jetlink 777 coaches leave every 30 minutes to Victoria Coach Station direct and are the same price, from 5:40 AM–9:30 PM. Cars and taxis drive into London from Heathrow, often through heavy traffic, and cost £30–£40. Add a tip of 10%–15% to the basic fare.

From Gatwick the quickest way to London is the nonstop rail Gatwick Express, costing £10.20 one-way and taking 30 minutes to reach Victoria Station. Trains run every 15 minutes 5:20 AM–midnight, then hourly 1:35 AM–5:20 AM. The hourly bus service by National Express Jetlink 777 takes about 90 minutes, hourly, 4:15 AM–9:15 PM, and costs £7 one-way. Stops include Marble Arch, Hyde Park Corner, Baker Street, Finchley Road, and Hendon Central, but there are sometimes delays. From Gatwick taxi fare is at least £50, plus tip; traffic can be very heavy.

➤ INFORMATION: **Airport Travel Line** (☎ 0870/574–7777). **Heathrow Express** (☎ 0845/600–1515). **Airbus A2** (☎ 0870/574–7777). **National Express** (☎ 0870/580–8080).

BUS TRAVEL TO AND FROM LONDON

The National Express coach service has routes to more than 1,200 major towns and cities in the United Kingdom. It's considerably cheaper than the train, although the trips usually take longer. National Express offers two types of service: ordinary service makes frequent stops for refreshment breaks (although all coaches have toilet and washroom facilities and reclining seats); Rapide and Flightlink services have stewardess and refreshment facilities on board. Day returns are available on both, but booking is advised on the Rapide service.

➤ BUS INFORMATION: **National Express** (✉ Victoria Coach Station, Buckingham Palace Rd., SW1, ☎ 0870/580–8080).

BUS TRAVEL WITHIN LONDON

London's bus system consists of bright red double- and single-deckers, plus other buses of various colors. Destinations are displayed on the front and back, with the bus number on the front, back, and side. Not all buses run the full length of their route at all times. Some buses are still operated with a conductor whom you pay after finding a seat, but these days you will more often find one-person buses, in which you pay the driver upon boarding.

Buses stop only at clearly indicated stops. Main stops—at which the bus should stop automatically—have a plain white background with a red LT symbol on it. There are also request stops with red signs, a white symbol, and the word REQUEST added; at these you must hail the bus to make it stop. Smoking is not allowed on any bus. Although you can see much of the town from a bus, *don't* take one if you want to get anywhere in a hurry; traffic often slows travel to a crawl, and during peak times you may find yourself waiting at least 20 minutes for a bus and not being able to get on it once it arrives. If you intend to go by bus, ask at a Travel Information Centre for a free bus map.

All journeys within the central zone are £1, and all others outside are 70p. Travel from the outer to the central zone costs £1. Travelcards are good for tube, bus, and British Rail trains in the Greater London zones. There are also a number of bus passes available for daily, weekly, and monthly use, and prices vary according to zones. A photograph is required for monthly bus passes.

CAR TRAVEL

The best advice is to avoid driving in London because of the ancient street patterns and the chronic parking restrictions. One-way streets also add to the confusion.

EMERGENCIES

Bliss Chemist is the only pharmacy in the center of London which is open round the clock. The leading chain drugstore, Boots at Piccadilly Circus, is open until 8 PM seven days, while Boots at 151 Oxford Street is open until 8 PM Thursdays. (Note: a prescription can only be filled if issued by a British registered doctor.)

➤ EMERGENCY SERVICES: **Police, fire brigade, or ambulance** (☎ 999).
➤ 24-HOUR PHARMACIES: **Bliss Chemist** (✉ 5 Marble Arch, W1, ☎ 020/7723–6116). **Boots** (✉ 44 Piccadilly Circus, W1, ☎ 020/7734–6126, or (✉ 151 Oxford St., W1, ☎ 020/7409–2857).

TAXIS

London's black taxis are famous for their comfort and for the ability of their drivers to remember the city's mazelike streets. Hotels and main tourist areas have ranks (stands) where you wait your turn to take one of the taxis that drive up. You can also hail a taxi if the flag is up or the yellow FOR HIRE sign is lighted. Fares start at £1.40 and increase by units of 20p per 281 yards or 55.5 seconds until the fare exceeds £8.60. After that, it's 20p for each 188 yards or 37 seconds. Surcharges are a tricky extra, which range from 40p for additional passengers or bulky luggage to 60p for evenings 8 PM–midnight, and until 6 AM on weekends and public holidays—at Christmas it zooms to £2 and there's 40p extra for each additional passenger. Fares are occasionally raised from year to year. Tip taxi drivers 10%–15% of the tab.

TOURS

BOAT TOURS

In summer, narrow boats and barges cruise London's two canals, the Grand Union and Regent's Canal; most vessels operate on the latter, which runs between Little Venice in the west (the nearest tube is Warwick Ave. on the Bakerloo Line) and Camden Lock (about 200 yards north of Camden Town tube station). Canal Cruises offers three or four cruises daily March–October on the *Jenny Wren* and all year on the cruising restaurant *My Fair Lady*. Jason's Trip operates one-way and round-trip narrow-boat cruises on this route. Trips last 1½ hours. The

London Waterbus Company operates this route year-round with a stop at London Zoo: trips run daily April–October and weekends only November–March.

All year boats cruise up and down the Thames, offering a different view of the London skyline. In summer (April–October) boats run more frequently than in winter—call to check schedules and routes. Following is a selection of the main routes. For trips down river from Charing Cross to Greenwich Pier and historic Greenwich, call Catamaran Cruisers, or Westminster Passenger Boat Services which runs the same route from Westminster Pier. Thames Cruises goes to Greenwich and onwards to the Thames Barrier. Westminster Passenger Service Upriver runs through summer to Kew and Hampton Court from Westminster Pier. A Sail and Rail ticket combines the modern wonders of Canary Wharf and Docklands development with the history of the riverside by boat. Tickets are available year-round from Westminster Pier or Tower Gateway. Most of the launches have a public-address system and provide a running commentary on passing points of interest. Depending upon the destination, river trips may last from one to four hours.

➤ FEES AND SCHEDULES: **Canal Cruises** (☎ 020/7485–4433). **Catamaran Cruisers** (☎ 020/7839–3572). **Jason's Trip** (☎ 020/7286–3428). **London River Services** (☎ 020/7941–2400). **London Waterbus Company** (☎ 020/7482–2660). **Sail and Rail** (☎ 020/7363–9700). **Thames Cruises** (☎ 020/7930–3373). **Westminster Passenger Boat Services** (☎ 020/7930–4097). **Westminster Passenger Service Upriver** (☎ 020/7930–2062).

BUS TOURS

There is a choice of companies, each providing daily tours, departing (8:30–9 AM) from central points, such as Haymarket (check with the individual company). You may board or alight at any of the numerous stops to view the sights, and re-board on the next bus. Tickets are bought from the driver, good for all day, and prices vary according to the type of tour, although around £12 is the benchmark. The specialist in hop on–hop off tours is London Pride with friendly, informative staff on easily recognizable double-decker buses. The Original London Sightseeing Tour also offers frequent daily tours, departing from 8:30 AM from Baker Street (Madame Tussaud's), Marble Arch (Speakers' Corner), Piccadilly (Haymarket), or Victoria (Victoria Street) around every 12 minutes (less often out of peak summer season). The Big Bus Company runs a similar operation with a Red and Blue tour. The Red is a two-hour tour with 18 stops, and the Blue, one hour with 13. Both start from Marble Arch, Speakers' Corner. Evan Evans offers good bus tours which also visit major sights just outside the city. Another reputable agency that operates bus tours is Frames Rickards.

➤ FEES AND SCHEDULES: **The Big Bus Company** (☎ 020/8944–7810). **Evan Evans** (☎ 020/8332–2222). **Frames Rickards** (☎ 020/7837–3111). **London Pride** (☎ 020/7520–2050). **Original London Sightseeing Tour** (☎ 020/8877–1722).

EXCURSIONS

London Transport, Evan Evans, and Frames Rickards all offer day excursions (some combine bus and boat) to places of interest within easy reach of London, such as Windsor, Hampton Court, Oxford, Stratford-upon-Avon, and Bath. Prices vary and may include lunch and admission prices or admission only. Alternatively, make your own way, cheaply, to many of England's attractions on Green Line Coaches.

➤ FEES AND SCHEDULES: **Green Line Coaches** (☎ 020/8668–7261 or 0870/574–7777).

WALKING TOURS

One of the best ways to get to know London is on foot, and there are many guided and themed walking tours from which to choose. Two of the London-on-foot sightseeing experts are the Original London Walks and, for a more historical accent, Historical Walks, but your best bet is to peruse the variety of leaflets at a London Tourist Information Centre. The duration of the walks varies (usually one–three hours), and you can generally find one to suit even the most specific of interests.

If you'd rather explore on your own, then the City of London Corporation has laid out a Heritage Walk that leads through Bank, Leadenhall, and Monument; follow the trail by the directional stars set into the sidewalks. A map of this walk can be found in *A Visitor's Guide to the City of London,* available from the City Information Centre across from St. Paul's Cathedral. The Silver Jubilee Walkway covers 16 km (10 mi) and is marked by a series of silver crowns set into the sidewalks; Parliament Square makes a good starting point. For the Golden Jubilee year of 2002, there are some new sidewalk plaques and diversions along the way. The Thames Path is a National Trail that has been revamped along the modernized Docklands and south bank city route, and covers some 291 km (180 mi) from the river's source in Gloucestershire to the Thames Barrier; for information, call London Docklands Visitor Centre. Several guides offering further walks are available in bookshops. One of the most fascinating is *Secret London,* by Andrew Duncan (New Holland).

➤ FEES AND SCHEDULES: **Original London Walks** (☎ 020/7624–3978). **Historical Walks** (☎ 020/8668–4019). **London Docklands Visitor Centre** (☎ 020/7512–1111). **London Walking Forum** (WEB www. londonwalking.com).

TRAIN TRAVEL

London is served by no fewer than 15 main-line train stations, so be absolutely certain of the station for your departure or arrival. All have Underground stops either in the train station or within a few minutes' walk from it, and most are served by several bus routes. The principal routes that connect London to other major towns and cities are on an InterCity network. Seats can be reserved by phone only with a credit card. You can, of course, apply in person to any British Rail Travel Centre or directly to the station from which you depart.

Charing Cross Station serves southeast England, including Canterbury, Margate, Dover/Folkestone, and ferry ports. Euston/St. Pancras serves East Anglia, Essex, the Northeast, the Northwest, and North Wales, including Coventry, Stratford-upon-Avon, Birmingham, Manchester, Liverpool, Windermere, Glasgow, and Inverness, northwest Scotland. King's Cross serves the east Midlands; the Northeast, including York, Leeds, and Newcastle; and north and east Scotland, including Edinburgh and Aberdeen. Liverpool Street serves Essex and East Anglia. Paddington serves the south Midlands, west and south Wales, and the west country, including Oxford. Victoria serves southern England, including Gatwick Airport, Brighton, Dover/Folkestone and ferry ports, and the south coast. Waterloo serves the southwestern United Kingdom, including Salisbury, Portsmouth, Southampton, and Isle of Wight. Waterloo International is for the Eurostar to Europe.

If you're combining a trip to Great Britain with stops on the Continent, you can either drive your car onto a *Le Shuttle* train through the Channel Tunnel (35 minutes from Folkestone to Calais) or book a seat on the Eurostar high-speed train service to Paris or Brussels).

Fare structures are slowly changing as the formerly nationalized British Rail is now run by various independent operators. Generally speaking, it is less expensive to buy a return (round-trip) ticket, especially for day trips not far from London, and you should always inquire at the information office about discount fares. You can hear a recorded summary of timetable and fare information to many destinations by calling the appropriate "dial and listen" numbers listed under Rail in the telephone book. The telephone information number listed below gets you through to any of the stations.

➤ TRAIN INFORMATION: (☎ 0845/748–4950).

TRAVEL AGENCIES
➤ LOCAL AGENT REFERRALS: **American Express** (✉ 6 Haymarket, WC2, ☎ 020/7930–4411; 89 Mount St., W1, ☎ 020/7499–4436). **Thomas Cook** (✉ 1 Marble Arch, W1, ☎ 020/7530–7100; 184 Kensington High St., W8, ☎ 020/7707–2300; and other branches).

UNDERGROUND TRAVEL
Known as "the tube," London's extensive Underground system is by far the most widely used form of city transportation. Trains run both beneath and aboveground out into the suburbs, and all stations are clearly marked with the London Underground circular symbol. (A SUBWAY sign refers to an under-the-street crossing.) Trains are all one class; smoking is *not* allowed on board or in the stations.

There are 10 basic lines—all named. The Central, District, Northern, Metropolitan, and Piccadilly lines all have branches, usually taking you to the outlying sections of the city, so be sure to note which branch is needed for your particular destination. Electronic platform signs tell you the final stop and route of the next train, and some signs indicate how many minutes you'll have to wait for the train to arrive. Begun in the Victorian era, the Underground is still being expanded and improved. The supermodern Jubilee line extension sweeps from Green Park to south of the river, with connections to Canary Wharf and the Docklands, and east to Stratford. The zippy Docklands Light Railway (DLR) runs through the Docklands with a new extension to the *Cutty Sark* and maritime Greenwich.

From Monday through Saturday, trains begin running just after 5 AM; the last services leave central London between midnight and 12:30 AM. On Sunday, trains start two hours later and finish about an hour earlier. The frequency of trains depends on the route and the time of day, but normally you should not have to wait more than 10 minutes. A pocket map of the entire tube network is available free from most Underground ticket counters.

For both buses and tube fares, London is divided into six concentric zones; the fare goes up the farther afield you travel. Ask at Underground ticket counters for the LT booklet "Fares and Tickets," which gives all details. You must buy a ticket before you travel. Many types of travel cards can be bought from Pass Agents that display the sign: tobacconists, confectioners, newsagents, and mainline overground rail stations.

For one trip between any two stations, you can buy an ordinary single (one-way ticket) for travel anytime on the day of issue; if you're coming back on the same route the same day, then an ordinary return (round-trip ticket) costs twice the single fare. Singles vary in price from £1.40 to £3.40 for a six-zone journey—not a good option for the sightseer who wants to make several journeys. A Carnet (£10) is a convenient book of 10 single tickets to use in central zone 1 only. Note that these prices are subject to increases.

Travelcards allow unrestricted travel on the tube, most buses, and British Rail trains in the Greater London zones and are valid weekdays after 9:30 AM, weekends, and all public holidays. They cannot be used on airbuses, night buses, or for certain special services. There are different options available: a One Day Travelcard costs £3.80–£4.50; Weekend Travelcards, for the two days of the weekend and on any two consecutive days during public holidays, run £5.70–£6.70. Family Travelcards are one-day tickets for one or two adults with one to four children and cost £3–£3.60 with one child; extra children cost 60p each. Adults do not have to be related to the children or even to each other.

Visitor's Travelcards are the best bet for visitors, but they must be bought before leaving home (they're available in both the United States and Canada). They are valid for periods of three, four, or seven days ($25, $32, $49, respectively) and can be used on the tube and virtually all buses and British Rail services in London.

➤ UNDERGROUND INFORMATION: (☎ 020/7222–1234, 24 hours). Travelers with disabilities should call for the free leaflet "Access to the Underground" (☎ 020/7918–3312).

VISITOR INFORMATION
Visitorcall is the London Tourist Board's 24-hour phone service—a premium-rate (60p per minute) recorded information line, with different numbers for theater, events, museums, sports, transportation around town, and so on. Call to access the list of options, or see the separate categories in the telephone directory.

➤ TOURIST INFORMATION: **London Tourist Information Centre** (⊠ Victoria Station Forecourt). **Britain Visitor Centre** (⊠ 1 Regent St., Piccadilly Circus, SW1Y 4NX; ⊙ Weekdays 9–6:30, weekends 10–4, WEB www.visitbritain.com). **London Tourist Board** (☎ 09068/663344 Visitorcall, WEB www.londontown.com).

Great Britain Basics

BUSINESS HOURS
Banks are open weekdays 9:30–4:30. Some have extended hours on Thursday evening, and a few are open on Saturday morning. Museum hours vary considerably from one part of the country to another. In large cities most are open Tuesday–Saturday 10–5; many are also open on Sunday afternoon. The majority close one day a week. Be sure to double-check the opening times of historic houses, especially if the visit involves a special trip; most stately houses in the countryside are closed November–March. Shops are open Monday–Saturday 9–5:30, and many are open Sunday. Outside the main centers most shops close at 1 PM once a week, often Wednesday or Thursday. In small villages many also close for lunch. In large cities—especially London—department stores stay open for late-night shopping (usually until 7:30 or 8) one day midweek.

CUSTOMS AND DUTIES
For details on imports and duty-free limits, *see* Customs and Duties *in* Smart Travel Tips A to Z.

EMBASSIES
➤ CANADIAN HIGH COMMISSION: (⊠ McDonald House, 1 Grosvenor Sq., London W1X 0AB, ☎ 020/7258–6600).
➤ UNITED STATES: (⊠ 24 Grosvenor Sq., London W1A 1AE, ☎ 020/7499–9000).

HOLIDAYS

Parliament isn't the only institution to decide which days are national holidays: some holidays are actually subject to royal proclamation. England and Wales: New Year's Day; Good Friday and Easter Monday; May Day (first Monday in May); Spring Bank Holiday (last Monday in May); August Bank Holiday (last Monday in August); Christmas Day and Boxing Day (day after Christmas). A national holiday is also to be announced for the Queen's Golden Jubilee celebrations.

MONEY MATTERS

In general, transportation in Britain is expensive in comparison to other countries. You should take advantage of the many reductions and special fares available on trains, buses, and subways. Always ask about these when buying your ticket.

London now ranks with Tokyo as one of the world's most expensive hotel capitals. Finding budget accommodations—especially during July and August—can be difficult; you should try to book well ahead if you are visiting during these months. Dining out at top-of-the-line restaurants can be prohibitively expensive, but there are new chains of French-Italian–style café-brasseries, along with a large number of pubs and ethnic restaurants that offer excellent food at reasonable prices.

The gulf between prices in the capital and outside is wide. Be prepared to pay a value-added tax (VAT) of 17½% on almost everything you buy; in nearly all cases it is included in the advertised price.

Costs: in London, cup of coffee, £1–£2; pint of beer, £1.80–£2.20; glass of wine, £2–£4; soda, 80p–£1.50; 2-km (1-mi) taxi ride, £3; ham sandwich, £1.75–£3.50.

CURRENCY

The British unit of currency is the pound sterling (£), divided into 100 pence (p). Bills are issued in denominations of £5, £10, £20, and £50. Coins are £2, £1, 50p, 20p, 10p, 5p, 2p, and 1p. Scottish banks issue Scottish currency, of which all coins and notes—with the exception of the £1 notes—are accepted in England. At press time (summer 2001) the pound stood at £.68 to the U.S. dollar, £.44 to the Canadian dollar, £.81 to the Irish punt, £.35 to the Australian dollar, £.29 to the New Zealand dollar, and £.09 to the South African rand.

Traveler's checks are widely accepted in Britain, and many banks, hotels, and shops offer currency-exchange facilities. You will have to pay a £2 commission fee wherever you change them; banks offer the best rates, yet even these fees vary. If you are changing currency, you will have to pay (on top of commission) based on the amount you are changing. In London and other big cities, *bureaux de change* abound, but it definitely pays to shop around: they charge a flat fee and it's often a great deal more than that at other establishments, such as banks. American Express foreign exchange desks do not charge a commission fee on AmEx traveler's checks. Credit cards are universally accepted, and the most commonly used are MasterCard and Visa.

SALES TAX

Foreign visitors from outside Europe can avoid Britain's 17½% value-added tax (VAT) by taking advantage of the following two methods. By the Direct Export method, the shopkeeper arranges the export of the goods and does not charge VAT at the point of sale. This means that the purchases are sent on to your home separately. If you prefer to take your purchase with you, try the Retail Export scheme, run by most large stores: the special Form 407 (provided only by the retailer) is attached to your invoice. You must present the goods, form, and invoice to the customs officer at the last port of departure from the EU. Allow plenty of time to do this at the airport, as there are often long lines. The form is then returned to the store and the refund forwarded to you, minus a small service charge. For inquiries call the local Customs & Excise office listed in the telephone directory.

TELEPHONES
COUNTRY AND AREA CODES
The United Kingdom's country code is 44. When dialing a number in Britain from abroad, drop the initial 0 from the local area code.

DIRECTORY AND OPERATOR ASSISTANCE
For information anywhere in Britain, dial ☎ 192. For the operator, dial ☎ 100. For assistance with international calls, dial ☎ 155.

INTERNATIONAL CALLS
The cheapest way to make an overseas call is to dial it yourself. But be sure to have plenty of coins or phone cards close at hand (newsagents sell budget-rate international phone cards, such as First National and America First, which can be used from any phone by dialing an access number, then a personal identification number). After you have inserted the coins or card, dial 00 (the international code), then the country code— 1 for the United States—followed by the area code and local number. You call also make calls through AT&T, MCI, Worldphone, or Sprint Global One long-distance operators. To make a collect or other operator-assisted call, dial ☎ 155.
➤ ACCESS CODES: **AT&T** (☎ 0800/0130011). **MCI, Worldphone** (☎ 0800/890222). **Sprint Global One** (☎ 0800/890877 or 0500/890877).

LOCAL CALLS
Public telephones are plentiful in London. British Telecom is gradually replacing the distinctive red phone booths with generic glass and steel cubicles, but the traditional boxes still remain in the countryside. The workings of coin-operated telephones vary, but there are usually instructions in each unit. Most take 10p, 20p, 50p, and £1 coins. A phone card is also available; it comes in denominations of 10, 20, 50, and 100 units and can be bought in a number of retail outlets. You can often use your credit card, although this is a more expensive option.

A local call before 6 PM costs 15p for three minutes; this doubles to 30p for the same from a pay phone. A daytime call to the United States will cost 24p a minute on a regular phone (weekends are cheaper), 80p on a pay phone. Each large city or region in Britain has its own numerical prefix, which is used only when you are dialing from outside the city. In provincial areas the dialing codes for nearby towns are often posted in the booth.

AREA CODES
Some area codes and local numbers in the U.K. changed in 2000. There is one area code for London—020—followed by a prefix, either 7 (for inner London) or 8 (for outer London), before the 7-digit phone number. So, for example, for a phone call to inner London, you would dial 020/7242–4444; for outer London, 020/8242–4444.

11 MADRID

Dead center in the heart of Spain at 2,120 ft above sea level, Madrid is the highest capital in Europe and one of the continent's most exciting cities. Madrid's famous museum mile boasts more masterpieces per foot than anywhere else in the world. Home of Spain's royal court for the last 500 years, the city's regal palaces and gardens conceal a village-like medieval Madrid with narrow lanes and red-tiled roofs. This is all in contrast to the rowdy Madrid one finds after midnight, when the action really begins; Madrileños are vigorous, joyful people, famous for their defiance of the need for sleep.

EXPLORING MADRID

Numbers in the margin correspond to points of interest on the Madrid map.

You can see important parts of the city in one day if you stop only to visit the Prado and Royal Palace. Two days should give you time for browsing. You can begin in the Plaza Atocha (Glorieta del Emperador Carlos V), at the bottom of the Paseo del Prado.

★ ❶ **Centro de Arte Reina Sofía** (Queen Sofía Arts Center). Spain's Queen Sofía opened this center in 1986, and it quickly became one of Europe's most dynamic venues—a Spanish rival to Paris's Pompidou Center. A converted hospital, the center houses painting and sculpture, including works by Joan Miró and Salvador Dalí as well as Picasso's *Guernica,* the painting depicting the horrific April 1937 carpet bombing of the Basque country's traditional capital by Nazi warplanes aiding Franco in the Spanish Civil War. ⊠ *Main entrance, C. de Santa Isabel 52,* ☎ *91/467–5062.* ☼ *Mon. and Wed.–Sat. 10–9, Sun. 10–2:30.*

❿ **Convento de las Descalzas Reales** (Convent of the Royal Barefoot Nuns). This convent, founded by Juana de Austria, daughter of Charles

208

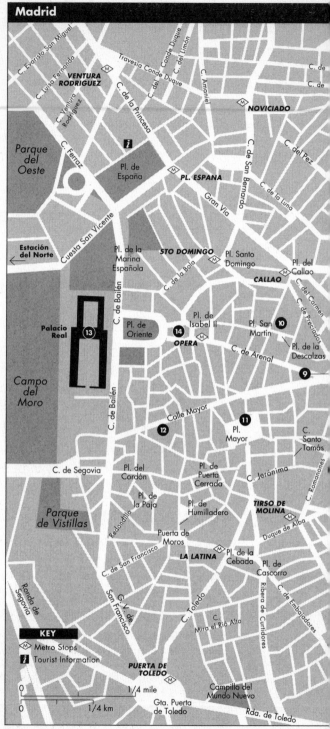

Madrid

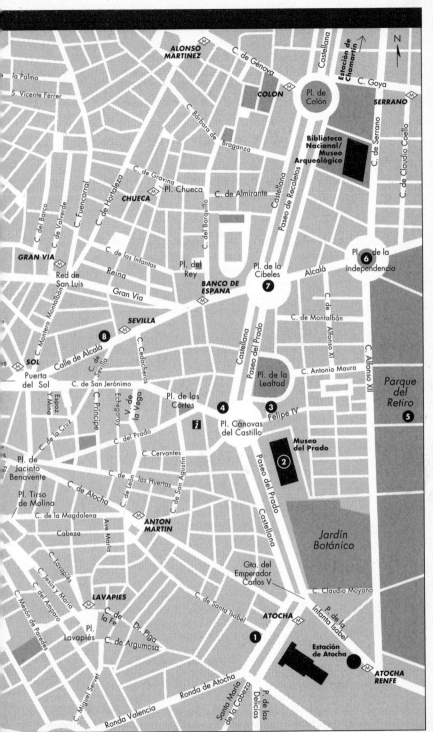

V, is still in use. Over the centuries, the nuns—daughters of royalty and nobility—have endowed it with an enormous wealth of jewels, religious ornaments, superb Flemish tapestries, and the works of such master painters as Titian and Rubens. A bit off the main track, it's one of Madrid's better-kept secrets. Your ticket includes admission to the nearby, but less interesting, **Convento de la Encarnación.** ⊠ *Plaza de las Descalzas 3,* ☎ *91/542–0059.* ⊙ *Tues.–Thurs. and Sat. 10:30–12:45 and 4–5:45, Fri. 10:30–12:45, Sun. 11–1:45.*

❼ Fuente de la Cibeles (Fountain of Cybele). Cybele, the Greek goddess of fertility and unofficial emblem of Madrid, languidly rides her lion-drawn chariot here, watched over by the mighty Palacio de Comunicaciónes, a splendidly pompous, cathedral-like post office. Fans of the home football team, Real Madrid, used to celebrate major victories by splashing in the fountain, but police now blockade it during big games. The fountain stands in the center of **Plaza de la Cibeles,** one of Madrid's great landmarks. ⊠ *C. de Alcalá.*

★ **❷ Museo del Prado** (Prado Museum). On the old cobblestone section of the Paseo del Prado you'll find Madrid's number one cultural site, one of the world's most important art museums. Plan to spend at least a day here; it takes at least two days to view the museum's treasures properly. Brace yourself for crowds. The greatest treasures—the Velázquez, Murillo, Zurbarán, El Greco, and Goya galleries—are all on the upper floor. Two of the best works are Velázquez's *La Rendición de Breda* and his most famous work, *Las Meninas,* awarded a room of its own. The Goya galleries contain the artist's none-too-flattering royal portraits, his exquisitely beautiful *Marquesa de Santa Cruz,* and his famous *La Maja Desnuda* and *La Maja Vestida,* for which the 13th duchess of Alba was said to have posed. Goya's most moving works, the *Second of May* and the *Fusillade of Moncloa,* or *Third of May,* vividly depict the sufferings of Madrid patriots at the hands of Napoléon's invading troops in 1808. Before you leave, feast your eyes on Hieronymus Bosch's flights of fancy, *Garden of Earthly Delights,* and the triptych the *Hay Wagon,* both on the ground floor. The museum is adding a new wing, designed by Rafael Moneo, much of which will be occupied by long-forgotten masterpieces by Zurbarán and Pereda. ⊠ *Paseo del Prado s/n,* ☎ *91/420–3768.* ⊙ *Tues.–Sat. 9–7, Sun. 9–2.*

❹ Museo Thyssen-Bornemisza. This museum, in the elegant Villahermosa Palace, has plenty of airy spaces and natural light. The ambitious collection—800 paintings—traces the history of Western art through examples from each important movement, beginning with 13th-century Italy. Among the museum's gems are the *Portrait of Henry VIII,* by Hans Holbein. Two halls are devoted to the Impressionists and post-Impressionists, with works by Pissarro as well as Renoir, Monet, Degas, van Gogh, and Cézanne. The more recent paintings include some terror-filled examples of German expressionism, but these are complemented by some soothing Georgia O'Keeffes and Andrew Wyeths. ⊠ *Paseo del Prado 8,* ☎ *91/369–0151.* ⊙ *Tues.–Sun. 10–7.*

★ **⓭ Palacio Real** (Royal Palace). This magnificent granite-and-limestone pile was begun by Philip V, the first Bourbon king of Spain, who was always homesick for his beloved Versailles and did his best to re-create its opulence and splendor. Judging by the palace's 2,800 rooms, with their lavish rococo decorations, precious carpets, porcelain, timepieces, mirrors, and chandeliers, his efforts were successful. From 1764, when Charles III first moved in, until the coming of the Second Republic and the abdication of Alfonso XIII in 1931, the Royal Palace proved a very stylish abode for Spanish monarchs; today,

King Juan Carlos, who lives in the far less ostentatious Zarzuela Palace outside Madrid, uses it only for official state functions. ✉ *Bailén s/n,* ☎ *91/542–0059.* ◷ *Mon.–Sat. 9–6, Sun. 9–3. Closed during official receptions.*

★ ✋ ❺ **Parque del Retiro** (Retiro Park). Once a royal retreat, Retiro is Madrid's prettiest park. Visit the beautiful rose garden, **La Rosaleda**; enjoy street musicians and magicians; row a boat around El Estanque; and wander past the park's many statues and fountains. Look particularly at the monumental **statue of Alfonso XII,** one of Spain's least notable kings (though you wouldn't think so from the statue's size), or wonder at the **Monument to the Fallen Angel**—Madrid claims the dubious honor of being the only capital to have a statue dedicated to the Devil. The **Palacio de Velázquez** and the beautiful, glass-and-steel **Palacio de Cristal,** built as a tropical plant house during the 19th century, now host occasional art exhibits. ✉ *Between C. Alfonso XII and Avda. de Menéndez Pelayo below C. de Alcalá.*

⑫ **Plaza de la Villa** (City Square). This plaza's notable cluster of buildings includes some of the oldest houses in Madrid. The **Casa de la Villa,** Madrid's city hall, was built in 1644 and has also served as the city prison and the mayor's home. Its sumptuous salons are occasionally open to the public; ask about guided tours, which are sometimes given in English. An archway joins the Casa de la Villa to the **Casa Cisneros,** a palace built in 1537 for the nephew of Cardinal Cisneros, primate of Spain and infamous inquisitor general. Across the square is the **Torre de Lujanes,** one of the oldest buildings in Madrid; it once imprisoned Francis I of France, archenemy of the emperor Charles V. ✉ *C. Mayor between C. Santiago and C. San Nicholas.*

★ ⑪ **Plaza Mayor** (Great Square). Without a doubt the capital's architectural showpiece, the Plaza Mayor was built in 1617–19 for Philip III—the figure astride the horse in the middle. The plaza has witnessed the canonization of saints, the burning of heretics, fireworks, and bullfights, and is still one of Madrid's great gathering places. ✉ *South of C. Mayor, west of Cava San Miguel.*

❻ **Puerta de Alcalá** (Alcalá Gate). Built in 1779 for Charles III, the grandiose gateway dominates the Plaza de la Independencia. A customs post once stood beside the gate, as did the old bullring until it was moved to its present site, Las Ventas, in the 1920s. At the beginning of the 20th century, the Puerta de Alcalá more or less marked the eastern edge of Madrid. ✉ *Plaza de la Independencia.*

❾ **Puerta del Sol** (Gate of the Sun). The old gate disappeared long ago, but you're still at the very heart of Madrid here, and indeed the very heart of Spain: kilometer distances for the whole nation are measured from the zero marker, a brass plaque on the south sidewalk. The square was expertly revamped in 1986 and now accommodates a copy of **La Mariblanca** (a statue that adorned a fountain here 250 years ago), a statue of Carlos III on horseback and, at the bottom of Calle Carmen, the much-loved statue of the **bear and strawberry tree.** The Puerta del Sol is inextricably linked with the history of Madrid and of Spain; a half century ago, a generation of literati gathered in Sol's long-gone cafés to thrash out the burning issues of the day. Nearly 200 years ago, the square witnessed the patriots' uprising immortalized by Goya in his painting *The Second of May.* ✉ *Meeting of C. Mayor and C. Alcalá.*

❽ **Real Academia de Bellas Artes de San Fernando** (St. Fernando Royal Academy of Fine Arts). Often overlooked in favor of the Prado, the Reina Sofia, and the Thyssen, this surprisingly comprehensive collection covers the masters (Murillo, Zurbarán, Ribera, El Greco, Velázquez, and Goya) with some 19th and 20th-century work (Zuloaga, Sorolla) as well. ⊠ *Alcalá 13*, ☏ *91/522–0046.* ⊙ *Tues.–Fri. 9:30–7, Sat.–Mon. 9:30–2.*

❸ **Ritz.** Alfonso II built Madrid's grande dame in 1910, when he realized that his capital had no hotels elegant enough to accommodate his wedding guests. The garden is a wonderfully aristocratic—if wildly overpriced—place to lunch in summer. ⊠ *Plaza de Lealtad 5.*

⓮ **Teatro Real** (Royal Theater). This neoclassical theater was built in 1850 and has long been a cultural center. Replete with golden balconies, plush seats, and state-of-the-art stage equipment for operas and ballets, the theater is a modern showpiece with its vintage appeal intact. ⊠ *Plaza de Isabel II,* ☏ *91/516–0600.*

BULLFIGHTING

Madrid's bullfighting season runs from March through October. Corridas are held on Sunday and sometimes also on Thursday; starting times vary between 4:30 and 7 PM. The height of the taurine spectacle comes with the San Isidro festival in May, with five weeks of daily bullfights. The bullring is at **Las Ventas,** formally known as the Plaza de Toros Monumental (⊠ Alcalá 237, ☏ 91/356–2200, metro: Ventas). You can buy tickets here before the fight or, for a 20% surcharge, at the agencies that line Calle Victoria, off Carrera de San Jerónimo near Puerta del Sol.

DINING

Spanish restaurants are officially classified from five forks down to one fork, with most places earning two or three forks. In our rating system, prices are for one dinner entrée. Sales tax (IVA) is usually included in the menu price; check the menu for *IVA incluído* or *IVA no incluído.* When it's not included, an additional 7% will be added to your bill. Most restaurants have a prix-fixe menu called a *menú del día;* however, this is often offered only at lunch and at dinner tends to be a reheated version of the same. *Menús* are usually the cheapest way to eat; à la carte dining is more expensive. Service charges are never added to your bill; leave around 10%, less in cheaper (one $) restaurants and bars. Note that some restaurants close for Holy Week.

CATEGORY	COST*
$$$$	over 3,000 ptas. (€18.03)
$$$	2,400 ptas.–3,000 ptas. (€14.42–€18.03)
$$	1,500 ptas.–2,400 ptas. (€7.510–€14.42)
$	under 1,500 ptas. (€7.51)

per person for a main course at dinner

$$$$ ✕ **La Broche.** Sergi Arola, who trained with celebrity chef Ferran Adriá,
★   has added his own twists and innovations to those of the Catalan master and vaulted directly to the top of Madrid's dining charts. The minimalist dining room clears the decks for maximum taste bud protagonism—a lucky thing as you'll want to concentrate on the hot-cold counterpoints of your codfish soup with bacon ice cream or the marinated sardine with herring roe. The wine list is superb; try a peppery Priorat (Miserere, for example). A full meal with appetizers and wine will run you about 12,000 ptas./€75.12. ⊠ *Miguel Angel 29,* ☏ *91/399–3778. Reservations essential. AE, DC, MC, V. Closed Sun. and Easter week. No lunch Sat.*

$$$$ ✕ **Lhardy.** Lhardy looks pretty much the same as it must have on day one (Sept. 16, 1839) with its dark-wood paneling, brass chandeliers, and red-velvet chairs. Most diners come for the traditional *cocido a la madrileña* (garbanzo-bean stew) and *callos a la madrileña* (tripe in spicy sauce). The dining rooms are upstairs; the ground-floor entry doubles as a delicatessen and stand-up coffee bar that fills up on chilly winter mornings with shivering souls sipping steaming-hot *caldo* (chicken broth) from silver urns. ⊠ *Carrera de San Jerónimo 8,* ☎ *91/522–2207. AE, DC, MC, V. No dinner Sun.*

$$$$ ✕ **Viridiana.** Viridiana, decorated in black and white, achieves the relaxed atmosphere of a bistro. Iconoclast chef Abraham García creates a new menu every two weeks, dreaming up such varied fare as red onions stuffed with *morcilla* (black pudding), soft flour tortillas wrapped around marinated fresh tuna, and filet mignon in white-truffle sauce. The tangy grapefruit sherbet for dessert is a marvel. ⊠ *Juan de Mena 14,* ☎ *91/531–5222. Reservations essential. AE, DC, MC, V. Closed Sun. and Aug.*

$$$$ ✕ **Zalacaín.** A deep-apricot color scheme, set off by dark wood and gleaming silver, makes this restaurant look like an exclusive villa. Zalacaín introduced nouvelle cuisine to Spain and continues to set the pace after 20 years at the top—splurge on such dishes as prawn salad in avocado vinaigrette, scallops and leeks in Albariño wine, and roast pheasant with truffles. A prix-fixe tasting menu allows you to sample the restaurant's best for about 6,500 ptas./€39.07. Service is somewhat stuffy, and jackets are required. ⊠ *Alvarez de Baena 4,* ☎ *91/561–5935. Reservations essential. AE, DC, V. Closed Sun. and Aug. No lunch Sat.*

$$$–$$$$ ✕ **Asador Fronton 1.** Long established in Tirso de Molina and now with two branches in northern Madrid, this popular Basque restaurant serves some of the most outstanding meat and fish in the city. Starters include fresh grilled anchovies, *anchos frescas,* and peppers stuffed with cod. The huge chunks of delicious steak, seared on a charcoal grill and then lightly sprinkled with sea salt, are for two or more. Order lettuce hearts or a vegetable to accompany. The *cocochas de merluza,* tender hake morsels in green parsley sauce, are deliciously light. ⊠ *Tirso de Molina 7 (rear, upstairs),* ☎ *91/369–1617. Reservations essential. AE, DC, MC, V. Closed Sun.*

$$$–$$$$ ✕ **El Cenador del Prado.** The Cenador's innovative menu has French
★ and Asian touches, as well as exotic Spanish dishes that rarely appear in restaurants. The house specialty is *patatas a la importancia* (sliced potatoes fried in a sauce of garlic, parsley, and clams); other possibilities are shellfish consommé with ginger ravioli, veal and eggplant in béchamel, and venison with prunes. For dessert try the *bartolillos,* custard-filled pastry. Settings are a Baroque salon and a plant-filled conservatory. ⊠ *C. del Prado 4,* ☎ *91/429–1561. AE, DC, MC, V. Closed Sun. and Aug. 1–15. No lunch Sat.*

$$$–$$$$ ✕ **Pedro Larumbe.** This excellent restaurant is atop the ABC shopping center between the Castellana and Calle Serrano. It has a lovely summer roof terrace, which is glassed in for the winter, and an Andalusian patio. Owner-chef Pedro Larumbe is famous for the presentation of his modern dishes, such as lobster salad. At lunch there is a salad bar; the dessert buffet is an art show; and the wine list is good. ⊠ *Serrano 61/Castellana 34,* ☎ *91/575–1112. AE, DC, MC, V. Closed Sun. and 15 days in Aug. No lunch Sat.*

$$–$$$ ✕ **Casa Botín.** Just off the Plaza Mayor, this is Madrid's oldest (1725)
★ and most famous restaurant. Its decor and food are traditionally Castilian, as are the wood-fire ovens used for cooking. *Cochinillo asado* (roast suckling pig) and *cordero asado* (roast lamb) are the specialties. The restaurant was a favorite of Hemingway's and is somewhat touristy, but it's still fun. Try to get a table in the basement or the upstairs din-

ing room. ⊠ *Cuchilleros 17,* ☎ *91/366–4217. Reservations essential. AE, DC, MC, V.*

$$–$$$ ✕ **La Cava Real.** Wine connoisseurs love the intimate atmosphere of this small, elegant restaurant and bar, which was Madrid's first true wine bar when it opened in 1983. There are a staggering 350 wines from which to choose, including 50 by the glass. The charming, experienced maître d', Chema Gómez, can help you select. Chef Javier Collar designs good-value set menus around wines, and the à la carte selection is also plentiful, mainly *nueva cocina* with game in season as well as fancy desserts and cheeses. ⊠ *Espronceda 34,* ☎ *91/442–5432. Reservation essential. AE, DC, MC, V. Closed Sun. and Aug.*

$$–$$$ ✕ **La Trainera.** La Trainera is all about fresh seafood. With nautical decor and a maze of little dining rooms, this informal restaurant has reigned as the queen of Madrid's fish houses for decades. Crab, lobster, shrimp, mussels, and a dozen other types of shellfish are served by weight and while Spaniards often share several plates of these delicacies as their entire meal, the grilled hake, sole, or turbot makes an unbeatable second course. Skip the house wine and go for a bottle of Albariño from the cellar. ⊠ *Lagasca 60,* ☎ *91/576–8035. AE, MC, V. Closed Sun. and Aug.*

$$ ✕ **La Gamella.** American-born chef Dick Stephens has created a rea-
★ sonably priced menu at this hugely popular spot. The sophisticated rust-red dining room, batik tablecloths, oversize plates, and attentive service remain the same, but much of the nouvelle cuisine has been replaced by more traditional fare, such as chicken in garlic, beef bourguignonne, and steak tartare à la Jack Daniels. A few signature dishes—such as sausage-and-red-pepper quiche and, for dessert, bittersweet chocolate pâté—remain, and the lunchtime menú del día is a great value. ⊠ *Alfonso XII 4,* ☎ *91/532–4509. AE, DC, MC, V. Closed Sun., Mon., and Aug. 15–31. No lunch Sat.*

$–$$ ✕ **Casa Mingo.** This Asturian cider tavern is built into a stone wall be-
★ neath the Norte train station. The nearby Ermita de San Antonio de la Florida with its famous Goya frescoes and Casa Mingo are a classic Madrid combination, especially in springtime. Succulent roast chicken, sausages, and salad are the only offerings, along with *sidra* (hard cider). The long plank tables are shared with other diners, while in summer, tables are set out on the sidewalk. ⊠ *Paseo de la Florida 2,* ☎ *91/547–7918. No credit cards.*

$–$$ ✕ **La Trucha.** This Andalusian deep-fry specialist is one of the happiest places in Madrid. The staff is perennially jovial and the house specialty, the *trucha a la truchana* (crisped trout stuffed with ample garlic and diced jabugo ham) is a work of art that deserves to be included in one of the nearby national museums. *Chopitos* (baby squid), *pollo al ajillo* (chunks of chicken in crisped garlic), and *espárragos trigueros* (wild asparagus) are among the star entrées here, while the *jarras* (pitchers) of chilled Valdepeñas, a beaujolais-like young claret, seem to act as laughing gas in this magic little bistro. The Nuñez de Arce branch, just down the street from the Hotel Reina Victoria, is usually less crowded, though no less jolly. ⊠ *Manuel Fernandez y Gonzalez 3 and Nuñez de Arce 6,* ☎ *91/429–3778. AE, MC, V. Closed Sun. and (at Nunez de Arce only) Aug.*

$–$$ ✕ **Nabucco.** With pastel-washed walls and subtle lighting from gigantic, wrought-iron candelabras, this pizzeria and trattoria is a trendy but elegant haven in gritty Chueca. Fresh bread sticks and garlic olive oil show up within minutes of your arrival. The spinach, ricotta, and walnut ravioli is heavenly, and this may be the only Italian restaurant in Madrid where you can order barbecued-chicken pizza. Considering the ambience and quality, the bill is a pleasant surprise. ⊠ *Hortaleza 108,* ☎ *91/310–0611. AE, MC, V.*

LODGING

CATEGORY	COST*
$$$$	over 28,000 ptas. (€168.28)
$$$	18,000 ptas.–28,000 ptas. (€108.18–€168.28)
$$	11,000 ptas.–18,000 ptas. (€66.11–€108.18)
$	under 11,000 ptas. (€66.11)

Prices are for two people in a double room, not including breakfast.

$$$$ ⊞ **Ritz.** Once Spain's most exclusive hotel, it is still elegant and aristocratic, with beautiful rooms, spacious suites, and sumptuous public salons furnished with antiques and handwoven carpets. The restaurant is justly famous, and the garden terrace is the perfect setting for summer dining. Weekend brunch is accompanied by harp music, and weekend tea or supper by chamber music from February through May. Near the Parque del Retiro and overlooking the Prado, the Ritz offers unadulterated luxury. ⊠ *Plaza Lealtad 5, 28014,* ☎ *91/701-6767,* FAX *91/701-6776,* WEB *www.ritz.es. 158 rooms. Restaurant. AE, DC, MC, V.*

$$$$ ⊞ **Santo Mauro.** Once the Canadian embassy, this turn-of-the-20th-cen-
★ tury neoclassical mansion is now an intimate luxury hotel. The architecture is accented by contemporary furniture (such as suede armchairs) in such hues as mustard, teal, and eggplant. The best rooms are in the main building, which also has a popular gourmet restaurant with garden terrace; the others are in a new annex and are split-level, with stereos and VCRs. Request a room with a terrace overlooking the gardens. ⊠ *Zurbano 36, 28010,* ☎ *91/319-6900,* FAX *91/308-5477,* WEB *www. ac-hotels.com. 37 rooms. Restaurant, pool. AE, DC, MC, V.*

$$$$ ⊞ **Villa Magna.** Renowned in the early '90s as the favorite of visiting financiers and reclusive rock stars, the Villa Magna has been humbled by competition. Still, it's one of Madrid's top luxury hotels, its modern facade belying an exquisite interior furnished with 18th-century antiques. With a champagne bar and a top Chinese restaurant, it offers all the amenities you'd expect from an internationally known hotel. All rooms have large desks and VCRs, and all bathrooms have fresh flowers. ⊠ *Paseo de la Castellana 22, 28046,* ☎ *91/587-1234,* FAX *91/575-3158,* WEB *www.madrid.hyatt.com. 164 rooms, 18 suites. Restaurant. AE, DC, MC, V.*

$$$$ ⊞ **Villa Real.** English antiques and 19th-century Aubusson tapestries set the tone in the lobby of this very personal hotel. The emphasis is on service and luxurious details. Decor in the rooms is somewhat clubby, with leather sofas and dark-red floral fabrics. The hotel overlooks the Plaza de las Cortes and is convenient to almost all major sights. ⊠ *Plaza de las Cortes 10, 28014,* ☎ *91/420-3767,* FAX *91/420-2547,* WEB *www.derbyhotels.es. 94 rooms, 20 suites. Restaurant. AE, DC, MC, V.*

$$$$ ⊞ **Westin Palace.** Built in 1912, Madrid's most famous grand hotel is
★ a Belle Epoque creation of Alfonso XIII. The guest rooms meet today's highest standards; banquet halls and lobbies have been lovingly beautified; and the facade has been finely restored. The Palace is more charming and stylish than ever—and while the glass dome over the lounge remains exquisitely original, the windows in the guest rooms are now double-glazed. ⊠ *Plaza de las Cortes 7, 28014,* ☎ *91/360-8000,* FAX *91/360-8100,* WEB *www.westin.com. 465 rooms, 45 suites. Restaurant. AE, DC, MC, V.*

$$$–$$$$ ⊞ **Reina Victoria.** Madrid's longtime favorite among bullfighters, this gleaming white Victorian building across the square from the Teatro Español has been transformed over the last decade into an upscale and modern establishment. The pervasive taurine theme is most concentrated in the bar where stuffed bulls' heads peer curiously over your shoulder. The best rooms are on the top floors, providing the most insulation from noise and great views over the rooftops and the theater. ⊠ *Plaza Santa Ana 14, 28012,* ☎ *91/531–4500,* FAX *91/522–0307. 195 rooms. Bar. AE, DC, MC, V.*

$$$ 🏠 **El Prado.** Wedged in among the classic buildings of Old Madrid, this slim hotel is within stumbling distance of Madrid's best bars and nightclubs. Rooms are soundproof, with double-pane glass, and are surprisingly spacious. Appointments include pastel floral prints and gleaming marble baths. ⊠ *Prado 11, 28014,* ☎ *91/369–0234,* FAX *91/429–2829,* WEB *www.hotelgreenprado.com. 47 rooms. AE, DC, MC, V.*

$$$ 🏠 **Liabeny.** A large, paneled lobby leads to bars, a restaurant, and a café in this 1960s hotel, centrally located near an airy plaza (and several department stores) between Gran Vía and Puerta del Sol. The large, comfortable rooms have floral fabrics and big windows; interior and top-floor rooms are the quietest. ⊠ *Salud 3, 28013,* ☎ *91/531–9000,* FAX *91/532–5306,* WEB *www.liabeny.es. 222 rooms. Restaurant. AE, DC, MC, V.*

$$–$$$ 🏠 **Carlos V.** If you like to be right in the center of things, hang your hat at this classic hotel on a pedestrian street: it's just a few steps away from the Puerta del Sol, Plaza Mayor, and Descalzas Reales convent. A suit of armor guards the tiny lobby, and crystal chandeliers add elegance to the second-floor lounge. All rooms are bright and carpeted, and the doubles with large terraces are a bargain. ⊠ *Maestro Victoria 5, 28013,* ☎ *91/531–4100,* FAX *91/531–3761,* WEB *www.carlosv.com. 67 rooms. AE, DC, MC, V.*

$–$$ 🏠 **Inglés.** This hotel was once a favorite with writers and artists, including Virginia Woolf. Though dreary, the rooms are comfortable enough, and the location is key: a short walk from the Puerta del Sol in one direction, the Prado in the other. Inexpensive restaurants and distinctive bars are close at hand. ⊠ *Echegaray 8, 28014,* ☎ *91/429–6551,* FAX *91/420–2423. 58 rooms. AE, DC, MC, V.*

$ 🏠 **Mora.** Right across the Paseo del Prado from the Botanical Garden, the Mora rewards your journey with a sparkling, faux-marble lobby and bright, carpeted hallways. Rooms are simple but large and comfortable. Those on the street have great views of the garden and Prado through soundproof, double-pane windows. For breakfast and lunch, the attached café is excellent, affordable, and popular with locals. ⊠ *Paseo del Prado 32, 28014,* ☎ *91/420–1569,* FAX *91/420–0564. 61 rooms. AE, DC, MC, V.*

NIGHTLIFE AND THE ARTS

The Arts

Details of all cultural events are listed in the daily newspaper *El País* and in the weekly *Guía del Ocio.* Two English-language publications, *The Broadsheet* and *In Spain,* are available free in Irish pubs and other expat hangouts and detail mainly expat activities.

Concerts and Opera

Madrid's main concert hall is the **Auditorio Nacional de Madrid** (⊠ Principe de Vergara 146, ☎ 91/337–0100). Beneath the Plaza de Colón, the underground **Centro Cultural de la Villa** (⊠ Plaza de Colon s/n, ☎ 91/575–6080 tickets; 91/553–2526 information) hosts an eclectic variety of performances, from gospel, spiritual, and blues festivals to Celtic dance. For ballet or opera, catch a performance at the legendary **Teatro Real** (⊠ Plaza de Isabel II, ☎ 91/516–0660), whose splendid facade dominates the Plaza de Oriente.

Film

Foreign films are mostly dubbed into Spanish, but movies in English are listed in *El País* or *Guía del Ocio* under "VO" (*versión original*). A dozen or so theaters now show films in English. **Alphaville** (✉ Martín de los Héros 14, off Plaza España, ☎ 91/548–4524) shows films in English. **Cines Renoir** (✉ Martín de los Héros 12, off Plaza España, ☎ 91/559–5760) is an old favorite, and shows films in VO. The **Filmoteca Cine Doré** (✉ Santa Isabel 3, ☎ 91/369–1125) is a city-run institution showing different classic English-language films every day. Your best bet for first-run films in the original language is the **Multicines Ideal** (✉ Doctor Cortezo 6, ☎ 91/369–2518).

Theater

Most theaters have two curtains, at 7 PM and 10:30 PM, and close on Monday. Tickets are inexpensive and often easy to come by on the night of the performance. The **Centro Cultural de la Villa** (☎ 91/575–6080), beneath the Plaza Colón, stages an eclectic range of theater and musical events. In summer, check listings for open-air events in Retiro Park. The **Círculo de Bellas Artes** (✉ Marqués de Casa Riera 2, off Alcalá 42, ☎ 91/360–5400) houses a leading theater. **Sala Triángulo** (✉ Zurita 20, ☎ 91/530–6891) is one of the many fringe theaters in Lavapiés, and is definitely worth a detour if you understand Spanish. The **Teatro Español** (✉ Príncipe 25 on Plaza Santa Ana, ☎ 91/429–6297) stages Spanish classics. The **Teatro María Guerrero** (✉ Tamayo y Baus 4, ☎ 91/319–4769), the home of the Centro Dramático Nacional, stages plays from García Lorca to Els Joglars.

Zarzuela

Zarzuela, a combination of light opera and dance that's ideal for non-Spanish speakers, is performed at the **Teatro Nacional Lírico de la Zarzuela** (✉ Jovellanos 4, ☎ 902/488–488) October–July.

Nightlife

Bars and Cafés

MESÓNES

The most traditional and colorful taverns are on Cuchilleros and Cava San Miguel, just west of Plaza Mayor, where you'll find a whole array of *mesónes* with such names as Tortilla, Champiñón, and Boqueron. These are the places to start your evening out in Madrid; many serve tapas and raciónes and close around midnight, when crowds move on to bars and nightclubs.

OLD MADRID

Wander the narrow streets between Puerta del Sol and Plaza Santa Ana—most are packed with traditional tapas bars. The **Cervecería Alemana** (✉ Plaza Santa Ana 6, ☎ 91/429–7033) is a beer hall founded more than 100 years ago by Germans and patronized, inevitably, by Ernest Hemingway. **El Abuelo** (✉ Victoria 6, ☎ 91/532–1219), or "Grandpa," serves only two tapas but does them better than anyone else: grilled shrimp and shrimp sautéed in garlic. For a more tranquil atmosphere try the lovely, old tiled bar **Viva Madrid** (✉ Fernández y González 7, ☎ 91/429–3640) early in the evening.

CALLE HUERTAS

Once lined with turn-of-the-20th-century bars playing guitar or chamber music, Calle Huertas now has more nightclubs than any other street in Madrid. **Casa Alberto** (✉ C. Huertas 18, ☎ 91/429–9356), a quiet restaurant-tavern with brick walls, has a good selection of draft beers, and tapas. **La Fídula** (✉ C. Huertas 57, ☎ 91/429–2947) often has live classical music. For zest, try the disco **La Fontanería** (✉ Huertas 38, ☎ 91/369–4904), where the action lasts until 4 AM.

PLAZA SANTA BÁRBARA
Just off Alonso Martínez, this area is packed with fashionable bars and beer halls. Stroll along Santa Teresa, Orellana, Campoamor, or Fernando VI and take your pick. The **Cervecería Santa Bárbara** (☎ 91/319–0449), in the plaza itself, is one of the most colorful, a popular beer hall with a good range of tapas.

CAFÉS
Madrid has no lack of old-fashioned cafés, with dark-wood counters, brass pumps, marble-top tables, and plenty of atmosphere. **Café Comercial** (✉ Glorieta de Bilbao 7, ☎ 91/521–5655) is a classic. **Café Gijón** (✉ Paseo de Recoletos 21, ☎ 91/521–5425) is a former literary hangout that offers a cheery set lunch; it's now one of many cafés with summer terraces that dot the Castellana and Paseo de Recoletos. **El Espejo** (✉ Paseo de Recoletos 31, ☎ 91/308–2347) has Art Nouveau decor and an outdoor terrace in summer. For a late-night coffee, or something stronger, stop into the Baroque **Palacio de Gaviria** (✉ Arenal 9, ☎ 91/526–6069), a restored 19th-century palace that often has live jazz. "International" parties are held every Thursday night.

Discos and Nightclubs

Nightlife—or *la marcha,* as the Spanish fondly call it—reaches legendary heights in Spain's capital. Smart, trendy dance clubs filled with well-heeled Madrileños are everywhere. For adventure, try the scruffy bar district in Malasaña, around the Plaza Dos de Mayo, where smoky hangouts line Calle San Vicente Ferrer. The often seedy haunts of Chueca, a popular gay area, can be exciting (watch your purse), but classy cafés and trendy live music venues occasionally break up the alleys of tattoo parlors, boutiques, techno discos, and after-hours clubs.

Amadis (✉ Covarrubias 42, under Luchana Cinema, ☎ 91/446–0036) has concerts, dancing, and telephones on every table, encouraging people to call each other with invitations to dance. You must be over 25 to enter. Salsa is a fixture in Madrid; check out the most spectacular moves at **Azucar** (✉ Paseo Reina Cristina 7, ☎ 91/501–6107). **El Clandestino** (✉ Barquillo 34, ☎ 91/521–5563) is a low-key bar-café with impromptu jam sessions. Madrid's hippest club for wild, all-night dancing to an international music mix is **El Sol** (✉ C. Jardines 3, ☎ 91/532–6490). **Fortuny** (✉ Fortuny 34, ☎ 91/319–0588) attracts a celebrity crowd, especially in summer, when the lush outdoor patio is open. The door is ultraselective. **Joy Eslava** (✉ Arenal 11, ☎ 91/366–3733), a downtown disco in a converted theater, is an old standby. **Pacha** (✉ Barceló 11, ☎ 91/447–0128), one of Spain's infamous chain discos, is always energetic. **Torero** (✉ Cruz 26, ☎ 91/523–1129) is for the beautiful people—quite literally: a bouncer allows only those judged *gente guapa* (beautiful people) to enter.

Flamenco

Madrid has an array of flamenco shows. Some are good, but many are aimed at the tourist trade. Dinner tends to be mediocre and overpriced, though it ensures the best seats; otherwise, opt for the show and a *consumición* (drink) only, usually starting around 11 PM and costing 3,000 ptas./€18.03–3,500 ptas./€21.04. **Arco de Cuchilleros** (✉ Cuchilleros 7, ☎ 91/364–0263) is one of the better and cheaper venues in the city to view flamenco. **Café de Chinitas** (✉ Torija 7, ☎ 91/559–5135) is expensive, but offers the best flamenco dancing in Madrid. **Casa Patas** (✉ Cañizares 10, ☎ 91/369–0496) is a major showplace; it offers good, if somewhat touristy, flamenco and tapas all at reasonable prices. **Corral de la Morería** (⊠ Morería 17, ☎ 91/365–8446) invites well-known flamenco stars to perform with the resident group.

Jazz Clubs

The city's best-known jazz venue is **Café Central** (⊠ Plaza de Angel 10, ☎ 91/369–4143). **Café del Foro** (⊠ San Andrés 38, ☎ 91/445–3752) is a friendly club with live music nightly. **Clamores** (⊠ Albuquerque 14, ☎ 91/445–7938) is known for its great champagne list. **Populart** (⊠ Huertas 22, ☎ 91/429–8407) features blues, Brazilian music, and salsa. Seasonal citywide festivals also present excellent artists; check the local press for listings and venues.

SHOPPING

The main shopping area in central Madrid surrounds the pedestrian streets Preciados and Montera, off the Gran Vía between Puerta del Sol and Plaza Callao. The Salamanca district, just off the Plaza de Colón, bordered roughly by Serrano, Goya, and Conde de Peñalver, is more elegant and expensive; just west of Salamanca, the shops on and around Calle Argensola, just south of Calle Génova, are on their way upscale. Calle Mayor and the streets to the east of Plaza Mayor are lined with fascinating old-fashioned stores straight out of the 19th century.

Antiques

The main areas for antiques are the Plaza de las Cortes, Calle Prado, the Carrera San Jerónimo, and the Rastro flea market, along the Ribera de Curtidores and the courtyards just off it.

Boutiques

Calle Serrano has the widest selection of smart boutiques and designer fashions—think Prada, Armani, and DKNY, as well as renowned Spanish designers such as Josep Font-Luz Diaz. **Adolfo Dóminguez** (⊠ Serrano 96, ☎ 91/576–7053; ⊠ C. Ortega y Gasset 4, ☎ 91/576–0084), one of Spain's top designers, has several boutiques in Madrid. **Jesús del Pozo** (⊠ Almirante 9, ☎ 91/531–3646) is one of Spain's premier young fashion designers, a scion of Spanish style for both men and women. **Loewe** (⊠ Serrano 26 and 34, ☎ 91/577–6056; ⊠ Gran Vía 8, ☎ 91/532–7024) is Spain's most prestigious leather store. **Seseña** (⊠ De la Cruz 23, ☎ 91/531–6840) has outfitted Hollywood stars with capes since the turn of the 20th century. **Sybilla** (⊠ Jorge Juan 12, ☎ 91/578–1322) is the studio of Spain's best-known woman designer, who designs fluid dresses and hand-knit sweaters in natural colors and fabrics.

Upscale shopping centers group a variety of exclusive shops stocked with unusual clothes and gifts. **Centro Comercial ABC** (⊠ Paseo de la Castellana 34) is a four-decker mall with a large café. **Galerías del Prado** (⊠ Plaza de las Cortes 7, on the lower level of the Palace Hotel) has fine books, gourmet foods, clothing, leather goods, art, and more. **Los Jardines de Serrano** (⊠ C. Goya and Claudio Coello) has smart boutiques. For street-chic fashion closer to medieval Madrid, check out the **Madrid Fusion Centro de Moda** (⊠ Plaza Tirso de Molina 15, ☎ 91/369–0018), where up-and-coming Spanish labels like Instinto, Kika, and Extart fill five floors with faux furs, funky jewelry, and the city's most eccentric selection of shoes. **Zara** (⊠ ABC, Serrano 61, ☎ 91/575–6334; ⊠ Gran Vía 32, ☎ 91/522–9727; ⊠ Princesa 63, ☎ 91/543–2415) is for men, women, and children with trendy taste and slim pocketbooks.

Department Stores

El Corte Inglés (⊠ Preciados 3, ☎ 91/531–9619; ⊠ Goya 76 and 87, ☎ 91/432–9300; ⊠ Princesa 56, ☎ 91/454–6000; ⊠ Serrano 47, ☎ 91/432–5490; ⊠ Raimundo Fernández Villaverde 79, ☎ 91/418–8800; ⊠ La Vaguada Mall, ☎ 91/387–4000) is Spain's largest chain department store, with everything from auto parts to groceries to fashions. The British chain **Marks & Spencer** (⊠ Serrano 52, ☎ 91/520–0000; ⊠ La Vaguarda Mall, ☎ 91/378–2234) is best known for its woolens and underwear, but most shoppers head straight for the gourmet-food shop in the basement. **FNAC** (⊠ Preciados 28, ☎ 91/595–6100) is filled with books, music, and magazines from all over the world.

Food and Flea Markets

The **Rastro,** Madrid's most famous flea market, operates on Sunday from 9 to 2 around the Plaza de Cascorro and the Ribera de Curtidores. A **stamp and coin market** is held on Sunday morning in the Plaza Mayor. Mornings, take a look at the colorful food stalls inside the 19th-century glass-and-steel **San Miguel** market, also near the Plaza Mayor. There's a **secondhand-book market** most days on the Cuesta Claudio Moyano, near Atocha Station.

Gift Ideas

Madrid is famous for handmade leather boots, guitars, fans, and capes. **Seseña** (⊠ Calle de la Cruz 23, ☎ 91/531–6840) has outfitted international celebrities in wool and velvet capes. **Tenorio** (⊠ Plaza de la Provincia 6, ☎ 91/366–4440) is where you'll find those fine old boots of Spanish leather, made to order with workmanship that should last a lifetime.

Department stores stock good displays of fans, but for superb examples, try the **Casa de Diego** (⊠ Puerta del Sol 12, ☎ 91/522–6643), established in 1853, for fans, umbrellas, and classic Spanish walking sticks with ornamented silver handles. The British royal family buys autograph fans here—white kid-skin fans for signing on special occasions. **José Ramirez** (⊠ C. La Paz 8, ☎ 91/531–4229) has provided Spain and the rest of the world with guitars since 1882, and his store includes a museum of antique instruments. Two stores opposite the Prado on Plaza Cánovas del Castillo, **Artesanía Toledana** and **El Escudo de Toledo,** have a wide selection of **souvenirs,** especially Toledo swords, marquetry ware, and pottery. Carefully selected handicrafts from all over Spain—ceramics, furniture, glassware, rugs, embroidery, and more—are sold at **Artespaña** (⊠ Hermosilla 14, ☎ 91/435–0221). **Casa Julia** (⊠ Almirante 1, ☎ 91/522–0270, ℻ 91/521–3137) is an artistic showcase, with two floors of tasteful antiques, paintings by up-and-coming artists, and furniture in experimental designs.

MADRID A TO Z

To research prices, get advice from other travelers, and book travel arrangements, visit www.fodors.com.

AIRPORTS AND TRANSFERS

Barajas Airport, 16 km (10 mi) northeast of town just off the NII Barcelona highway, receives international and domestic flights. Info-Iberia, at the airport, dispenses information on arrivals and departures. ➤ AIRPORT INFORMATION: **Barajas Airport** (☎ 91/305–8343 or 91/393–6000). **Info-Iberia** (☎ 91/329–5767).

TRANSFERS

For a mere 475 ptas./€2.85, there's a convenient bus to the central Plaza Colón, where you can catch a taxi to your hotel. Buses leave every 15 minutes between 5:40 AM and 2 AM (slightly less often very early or late in the day). Watch your belongings, as the underground Plaza Colón bus station is a favorite haunt of purse snatchers and con artists.

The metro is a bargain at 150 ptas./€0.90 per ticket (or 850 ptas./€5.11 for a 10-trip ticket that can also be used on city buses), but you have to change trains twice to get downtown, and the trip takes 45 minutes.

The fastest and most expensive route into town is by taxi (usually about 2,000 ptas./€12.02, but up to 2,500 ptas./€15.02, plus tip in traffic). Pay the metered amount plus the 350-pta./€2.10 surcharge and 150 ptas./€0.90 for each suitcase. By car take the NII (which becomes Avenida de América) into town, head straight into Calle María de Molina, then turn left on either Calle Serrano or the Castellana.

BUS TRAVEL TO AND FROM MADRID

Madrid has no central bus station. Check with the tourist office for departure points for your destination. The Estación del Sur serves Toledo, La Mancha, Alicante, and Andalucía. Auto-Rés serves Extremadura, Cuenca, Salamanca, Valladolid, Valencia, and Zamora; Auto-Rés has a central ticket and information office, just off Gran Vía, near the Hotel Arosa. The Basque country and most of north-central Spain are served by Continental Auto. For Àvila, Segovia, and La Granja, use Empresa La Sepulvedana. Empresa Herranz serves El Escorial and the Valley of the Fallen. La Veloz serves Chinchón.
➤ BUS INFORMATION: **Auto-Rés** (✉ Plaza Conde de Casal 6, ☎ 91/551–7200, metro: Conde de Casal; central ticket office: ✉ Salud 19, ☎ 91/551–7200). **Continental Auto** (✉ Alenza 20, ☎ 91/530–4800, metro: Ríos Rosas). **Empresa Herranz** (✉ 3 Moncloa Bus Terminal, ☎ 91/890–4100, metro: Moncloa). **Empresa La Sepulvedana** (✉ Paseo de la Florida 11, ☎ 91/530–4800, metro: Norte). **Estación del Sur** (✉ Méndez Álvaro s/n, ☎ 91/468–4200, metro: Palos de la Frontera). **La Veloz** (✉ Avda. Mediterraneo 49, ☎ 91/409–7602, metro: Conde de Casal).

BUS TRAVEL WITHIN MADRID

Red city buses run between 6 AM and midnight and cost 150 ptas./€0.90 per ride. After midnight, buses called *buyos* (night owls) run out to the suburbs from Plaza de Cibeles for the same price. Signs at every stop list all other stops by street name, but they're hard to comprehend if you don't know the city well. Pick up a free route map from EMT kiosks on the Plaza de Cibeles or the Puerta del Sol, where you can also buy a 10-ride ticket called a Metrobus (850 ptas./€5.11) that's equally valid for the metro. Drivers will generally make change for anything up to a 2,000-pta./€12.02 note. If you've bought a 10-ride ticket, step just behind the driver and insert it in the ticket-punching machine until the mechanism rings. If you speak Spanish, call the information line listed below.
➤ BUS INFORMATION: **General Information** (☎ 91/406–8810).

CAR TRAVEL

The main roads are as follows: north–south, the Paseo de la Castellana and Paseo del Prado; east–west, Calle de Alcalá, Gran Vía, and Calle de la Princesa. The M30 circles Madrid, and the M40 is an outer ring road about 12 km (7 mi) farther out. For Burgos and France, drive north up the Castellana and follow the signs for the NI. For Barcelona and Barajas Airport, head up the Castellana to Plaza Dr. Marañón, then right onto María de Molina and the NII; for Andalusia and Toledo,

head south down Paseo del Prado, and then follow the signs to the NIV
and N401, respectively. For Segovia, Ávila, and El Escorial, head west
along Princesa to Avenida Puerta de Hierro and onto the NVI–La
Coruña.

EMERGENCIES
The general emergency number in all EU nations (akin to 911 in the
United States) is 112. A list of pharmacies open 24 hours (*farmacias
de guardia*) is published daily in *El País*.
➤ EMERGENCY SERVICES: **Ambulance** (☎ 061, 91/522–2222, or 91/588–
4400). **Police** (☎ 091 emergencies; 092 Municipal Police [for towed
cars and traffic accidents]).
➤ HOSPITALS: **Hospital 12 de Octubre** (✉ Carretera de Andalucía, Km
5.4, ☎ 91/390–8000). **La Paz Ciudad Sanitaria** (✉ Paseo de la Castellana 261, ☎ 91/358–2600).

ENGLISH-LANGUAGE MEDIA
The International Bookshop carries secondhand books only.
➤ BOOKSTORES: **Booksellers** (✉ José Abascal 48, ☎ 91/442–8104). **Casa
del Libro** (✉ Gran Vía 29, ☎ 91/521–2113). **International Bookshop**
(✉ Campomanes 13, ☎ 91/541–7291).

SUBWAY TRAVEL
The metro offers the simplest and quickest means of transport and operates from 6 AM to 1:30 AM. Metro maps are available from ticket offices, hotels, and tourist offices. The flat fare is 150 ptas. a ride; a 10-ride
ticket, 850 ptas., is also valid for buses. Carry some change (5, 25, 50,
and 100 ptas.) for the ticket machines, especially after 10 PM; the machines make change and allow you to skip long ticket lines.

TAXIS
Taxis are one of Madrid's few truly good deals. Meters start at 200
ptas. and add 130 ptas. per km (½ mi) thereafter (150 ptas. per km at
night, on weekends and holidays, and beyond city limits). Numerous
supplemental charges, however, mean that your total cost often bears
little resemblance to what you see on the meter. Supplemental charges—
over and above your fare—include 150 ptas. on Sundays and holidays
and between 11 PM and 6 AM, 150 ptas. to sports stadiums or the bullring, and 450 ptas. (plus 50 ptas. per suitcase) to or from the airport.

Taxi stands are numerous, and taxis are easily hailed in the street—
except when it rains, at which point they're exceedingly hard to come
by. Available cabs display a LIBRE sign during the day, a green light at
night. No tip is expected, but if you're inspired to give one, 25 ptas.
is about right for shorter rides; you may want to go as high as 10%
for a trip to the airport. You can call a cab through Tele-Taxi, Ra-
dioteléfono Taxi, or Radio Taxi Gremial.
➤ TAXIS & SHUTTLES: **Radio Taxi Gremial** (☎ 91/447–5180). **Ra-
dioteléfono Taxi** (☎ 91/547–8200). **Tele-Taxi** (☎ 91/371–2131).

TOURS
Julià Tours, Pullmantur, and Trapsatur all run the same city orientation tours, conducted in Spanish and English. Reserve directly with their
offices, through any travel agent, or through your hotel. Departure points
are the addresses listed below, though you can often arrange to be picked
up at your hotel. Tours leave in morning, afternoon, and evening and
cover various selections of sites and activities.
➤ FEES AND SCHEDULES: **Julià Tours** (✉ Gran Vía 68, ☎ 91/559–
9605). **Pullmantur** (✉ Plaza de Oriente 8, ☎ 91/541–1807). **Trapsatur**
(✉ San Bernardo 23, ☎ 91/302–6039).

BUS TOURS

Trapsatur runs the Madridvision bus, which makes a one-hour tour of the city with recorded commentary in English. No reservation is necessary; catch the bus in front of the Prado every 1½ hours beginning at 10 AM, Tuesday–Sunday. There are no buses on Sunday afternoon. A round-trip ticket costs 1,750 ptas./€10.52, and a two-day pass, 2,500 ptas./€15.03. A similar service with an open-top double decker, is run by Sol Pentours.

➤ FEES AND SCHEDULES: **Sol Pentours** (⊠ Gran Vía 26, ☎ 902/303–903).

SINGLE- AND MULTIPLE-DAY TOURS

Julià Tours, Pullmantur, and Trapsatur run full- or half-day trips to El Escorial, Ávila, Segovia, Toledo, and Aranjuez, and in summer to Cuenca and Salamanca. Summer weekends, the popular *Tren de la Fresa* (Strawberry Train) takes passengers from the old Delicias Station to Aranjuez (known for its production of strawberries and asparagus) on a 19th-century train. Tickets can be obtained from RENFE offices, travel agents, and the Delicias Station (⊠ Paseo de las Delicias 61). Other one- or two-day excursions by train are available on summer weekends. Contact RENFE for details.

WALKING TOURS

The Municipal Tourist Office leads English-language tours of Madrid's Old Quarter every Saturday morning at 10. The *ayuntamiento* (city hall) has a popular selection of Spanish bus and walking tours under the name Descubre Madrid. Walking tours depart most mornings and visit many hidden corners as well as major sights; options include Madrid's Railroads, Medicine in Madrid, Goya's Madrid, and Commerce and Finance in Madrid. Schedules are listed in the "Descubre Madrid" leaflet available from the municipal tourist office. Tickets can be purchased at the Patronato de Turismo. If you want a personal tour with a local guide, contact the Asociación Profesional de Informadores.

➤ FEES AND SCHEDULES: **Asociación Profesional de Informadores** (⊠ Ferraz 82, ☎ 91/542–1214 or 91/541–1221). **Municipal Tourist Office** (⊠ Plaza Mayor 3). **Patronato de Turismo** (⊠ C. Mayor 69, ☎ 91/588–2900).

TRAIN TRAVEL

Madrid has two railroad stations. Chamartín, in the northern suburbs beyond the Plaza de Castilla, is the main station, with trains to France and the north (including Barcelona, Ávila, Salamanca, Santiago, and La Coruña). Most trains to Valencia, Alicante, and Andalusia leave from Chamartín but stop at the Atocha station as well. Atocha sends trains to Segovia, Toledo, Granada, Extremadura, and Lisbon. A convenient metro stop (Atocha RENFE) connects the Atocha rail station to the city subway system. The old Atocha station, designed by Eiffel, is Madrid's terminal for high-speed AVE service to Córdoba and Seville.

For all train information call or visit the RENFE offices, open weekdays 9:30–8. Ask for an English operator. There's another RENFE office in the international arrivals hall at Barajas Airport, or you can purchase tickets at any of the three main stations or from travel agents displaying the blue and yellow RENFE sign.

➤ TRAIN INFORMATION: **Atocha** (⊠ Glorieta del Emperador Carlos V, southern end of Paseo del Prado, ☎ 91/328–9020). **Chamartín** (⊠ Avda. Pío XII, ☎ 91/315–9976). **RENFE** (⊠ Alcalá 44, ☎ 902/240202, WEB www.renfe.es/ingles).

TRANSPORTATION AROUND MADRID

Madrid is a fairly compact city, and most of the main sights can be visited on foot. If you're staying in one of the modern hotels in northern

Madrid, however, off the Castellana, you may need to use the bus or subway.

TRAVEL AGENCIES

➤ LOCAL AGENTS: **American Express** (✉ Plaza de las Cortes 2, ☎ 91/322–5500). **Carlson Wagons-Lits** (✉ Condesa de Venadito 1, ☎ 91/724–9900). **Pullmantur** (✉ Plaza de Oriente 8, ☎ 91/541–1807).

VISITOR INFORMATION

Madrid Provincial Tourist Office is the best place for comprehensive information. The municipal tourist office is centrally located, but hordes of tourists tend to deplete its stock of brochures. Other tourist offices are located at the International Arrivals Hall in Barajas Airport and at Chamartín train station.

➤ TOURIST INFORMATION: **Madrid Provincial Tourist Office** (✉ Duque de Medinaceli 2, ☎ 91/429–4951). **Municipal Tourist Offices** (✉ Plaza Mayor 3, ☎ 91/588–1636; ✉ International Arrivals Hall, Barajas Airport, ☎ 91/305–8656; ✉ Chamartín train station, ☎ 91/315–9976, ⓦⒺⒷ www.munimadrid.es).

Spain Basics

BUSINESS HOURS

Banks are open Monday–Saturday 8:30 or 9 to 2 or 2:30 from October through June; in summer they are closed on Saturday. Hours for museums and churches vary; most are open in the morning, but most museums close one day a week, often Monday. Stores are open weekdays from 9 or 10 until 1:30 or 2, then in the afternoon from around 5 to 8. Larger department stores and supermarkets do not close at midday. In some cities, especially in summer, stores close on Saturday afternoon.

CUSTOMS AND DUTIES

For details on imports and duty-free limits, *see* Customs and Duties *in* Smart Travel Tips A to Z.

EMBASSIES

The following countries also maintain consular offices in Barcelona.

➤ AUSTRALIA: (✉ Plaza del Descubridor Diego de Ordás 3, Madrid, ☎ 91/441–9300).

➤ CANADA: (✉ Núñez de Balboa 35, Madrid, ☎ 91/431–4300).

➤ NEW ZEALAND: (✉ Plaza de La Lealtad 2, Madrid, ☎ 91/523–0226).

➤ UNITED KINGDOM: (✉ Fernando el Santo 16, Madrid, ☎ 91/700–8200).

➤ UNITED STATES: (✉ Serrano 75, Madrid, ☎ 91/577–4000).

HOLIDAYS

New Year's; Epiphany (January 6); Good Friday; Easter; May Day (May 1); St. James's Day (July 25); Assumption (August 15); National Day (October 12); All Saints' Day (November 1); Constitution (December 6); Immaculate Conception (December 8); Christmas.

LANGUAGE

Spanish (called Castellano, or Castilian) is spoken and understood throughout Spain. However, the Basques speak Euskera; in Catalonia, you'll hear Catalan; and in Galicia, Gallego. If you don't speak Spanish, you should have no trouble finding people who speak English in major cities and coastal resorts, but you won't necessarily be able to count on the bus driver or the passerby on the street. Fortunately, Spanish is fairly easy to pick up, and your efforts to speak the local tongue are bound to be graciously received.

MONEY MATTERS

The cost of living in Spain is on a par with that of most other European nations. In recent years, however, currency fluctuations have increased the buying power of those visiting from North America and the United Kingdom. A cup of coffee costs between 125 ptas./€0.75 and 166 ptas./€1; a glass of wine in a bar, 100 ptas./€0.60–135 ptas./€0.80; a sandwich 300 ptas./€1.80–416 ptas./€2.50; a local bus or subway ride 125 ptas./€0.75–200 ptas./€1.20; a 2-km (1-mi) taxi ride, about 500 ptas./€3.

CREDIT CARDS

Most hotels, restaurants, and stores accept credit cards. Visa is the most widely accepted card, followed by MasterCard (also called EuroCard in Spain).

CURRENCY

Spain, as one of the euro zone currency countries, will introduce euro (€) notes and coins on January 1, 2002. The euro and the Spanish peseta (ptas.) will circulate simultaneously through March 2002. Banks and ATMs will give all money in euros. Shops and restaurants are encouraged to give change in euros whenever possible. Prices are marked in both euros and Spanish pesetas. Pesetas come in bills of 1,000, 2,000, 5,000, and 10,000, and coins of 1, 5, 10, 25, 50, 100, 200, and 500 pesetas. At press time (summer 2001), the exchange rate was 186.52 ptas. to the U.S. dollar, 119.48 ptas. to the Canadian dollar, 268.29 ptas. to the pound sterling, 211.27 ptas. to the Irish punt, 94.87 ptas. to the Australian dollar, 76.08 ptas. to the New Zealand dollar, 23.27 ptas. to the South African rand, and 166.39 ptas. to the euro.

Visitors may take any amount of foreign currency in bills or traveler's checks into Spain, as well as any amount of euros. When leaving Spain you may take out only €3,000 or the equivalent in foreign currency, unless you can prove you declared the excess at customs on entering the country.

CURRENCY EXCHANGE

The word to look for is CAMBIO (exchange). Most Spanish banks take a 1½% commission, though some less scrupulous places charge more; always check, as rates can vary widely. To change money in a bank, you need your passport and plenty of patience, because filling out the forms takes time. Hotels offer rates lower than banks, but they rarely charge a commission, so you may well break even. Restaurants and stores, with the exception of those catering to the tour-bus trade, generally do not accept payment in dollars or traveler's checks. If you have a credit card with a personal identification number, you'll have no trouble drawing cash from automated teller machines.

TAXES
VALUE-ADDED TAX (VAT)

Value-added tax, called IVA, is levied on most goods and services. It's 7% at hotels and restaurants and 16% on goods and car rentals.

A number of shops, particularly large stores and boutiques in holiday resorts, participate in Global Refund (formerly Europe Tax-Free Shopping), an VAT refund service that makes getting your money back relatively hassle-free. On purchases of more than 14,975 ptas./€90, you're entitled to a refund of the 16% tax (there is no refund for the 7% tax). Ask for the Global Refund form (called a Shopping Cheque) in participating stores. You show your passport and fill out the form; the vendor then mails you the refund, or—often more convenient— you present your original receipt to the VAT office at the airport when you leave Spain. (In both Madrid and Barcelona, the office is near the duty-free shops. Save time for this process, as lines can be long.) Customs signs the original and refunds your money on the spot in cash (pesetas), or sends it to their central office to process a credit-card refund. Credit-card refunds take a few weeks.

TELEPHONES
COUNTRY AND AREA CODES
The country code for Spain is 34.

DIRECTORY AND OPERATOR ASSISTANCE
For the operator and directory information for any part of Spain, dial 1003. The international information and assistance operator is at 025 (some operators speak English). If you're in Madrid, dial 1008 to make collect calls to countries in Europe; 1005 for the rest of the world.

INTERNATIONAL CALLS
You can call abroad from any pay phone marked TELÉFONO INTERNACIONAL. Some are coin-operated, but it is best to purchase a *tarjeta telefónica* (telephone card), available at most newsagents and many shops. A few public phones also accept credit cards. Dial 00, then dial 1 for the United States, 0101 for Canada, or 44 for the United Kingdom, followed by the area code and number. For lengthy calls, go to the *telefónica,* a phone office found in all sizable towns: here an operator assigns you a private booth and collects payment at the end of the call. This is the cheapest and by far the easiest way to call overseas, and you can charge calls costing more than €3 to Visa or MasterCard. Private long-distance companies, such as AT&T, MCI, and Sprint, have special access numbers.
➤ ACCESS CODES: **AT&T** (☎ 900/990011). **MCI** (☎ 900/990014). **Sprint** (☎ 900/990013).

LOCAL CALLS
Note that to call anywhere within Spain—even locally—you need to dial the area code first. All provincial codes begin with a 9.

PUBLIC PHONES
Most pay phones have a digital readout, so you can see your money ticking away. You need at least 25 ptas./€0.15 for a local call, 75 ptas./€0.45 to call another province, and at least 100 pts./€0.60 if you are calling a Spanish cell phone. Some pay phones take only phone cards, which can be purchased at any tobacco shop in various denominations.

12 PARIS

If there's a problem with a trip to Paris, it's the embarrassment of riches that faces you. No matter which Paris you choose—touristy Paris, historic Paris, fashion-conscious Paris, pretentious bourgeois Paris, thrifty Paris, the legendary bohemian arty Paris of undying attraction—one thing is certain: you will find your own Paris, one that is vivid, exciting, often unforgettable. Paris is a city of vast, noble perspectives and intimate, ramshackle streets, of formal *espaces vertes* (green open spaces) and quiet squares—and this combination of the pompous and the private is one of the secrets of its perennial pull.

EXPLORING PARIS

Numbers in the margin correspond to points of interest on the Paris map.

As world capitals go, Paris is surprisingly compact. With the exceptions of the Bois de Boulogne and Montmartre, you can easily walk from one major sight to the next. The city is divided in two by the River Seine, with two islands (Ile de la Cité and Ile St-Louis) in the middle. The Left—or south—Bank has a more intimate, bohemian flavor than the haughtier Right Bank. The east–west axis from Châtelet to the Arc de Triomphe, via the rue de Rivoli and the Champs-Élysées, is the principal thoroughfare for sightseeing and shopping on the Right Bank.

The **Carte Musées–Monuments** pass, which allows you access to most Paris museums and monuments, can be obtained from museums or major métro stations (one-day pass, 80 frs/€12; three days, 160 frs/€24; five days, 240 frs/€36). Note, however, that this pass may only be useful to you if you plan to see *a lot* of museums in the allotted days.

The perfect introduction to Paris? Begin at the beginning—Notre-Dame and the little island of Ile de la Cité, where Paris was first settled more than 2,000 years ago. After visiting the nearby Gothic jewel of the Sainte-Chapelle, head over to the Louvre—home to the *Venus de Milo*, the *Winged Victory*, and the ironic, haunting smile of the *Mona Lisa*—then wander through the gardens of the Tuileries to the city's heart, Place de la Concorde. Take a boat along the Seine for a waterside rendezvous with the Eiffel Tower, and consider finishing off with dinner in Montmartre. Papa Hemingway was right: Paris is truly a moveable feast.

From Notre-Dame to the Latin Quarter

No matter how you first approach Paris—historically, geographically, emotionally—it is the river Seine that summons us, the Seine which harbors two islands, the Ile de la Cité and the Ile St-Louis, within the very center of Paris. Of them, it is the Ile de la Cité that forms the historic ground zero of the city. It was here that the earliest inhabitants of Paris, the Gaulish tribe of the Parisii, settled in about 250 BC). Here you'll find the great, brooding cathedral of Notre-Dame, the jewel-like Sainte-Chapelle, and the Conciergerie, last haunt of Queen Marie-Antoinette. To the east lies the smaller island of the Ile St-Louis—one of Paris's most romantic nooks—while across the river on the Left Bank of the Seine is the bohemian Quartier Latin, with its warren of steep sloping streets, populated largely by Sorbonne students and academics.

㉙ Conciergerie. Bringing a tear to the eyes of Ancien Régime devotées, this is the famous prison in which dukes and duchesses, lords and ladies, and, most famously, Queen Marie-Antoinette were imprisoned during the French Revolution before being bundled off for their date with the guillotine. You can still see the queen's cell and chapel and the superb vaulted 14th-century hall, the **Salles des Gens d'Armes** (Hall of the Men-at-Arms). The **Tour de l'Horloge** (Clock Tower) near the entrance on quai de l'Horloge has a clock that has been ticking off time since 1370. ⊠ *1 quai de l'Horloge,* ☏ *01–53–73–78–50.* ☉ *Apr.–Sept., daily 9:30–6:30; Oct.–Mar., daily 10–5. Métro: Cité.*

㉜ Ile St-Louis. Of the two islands in the Seine—the Ile de la Cité is located just to the west—it is the Ile St-Louis that best retains the loveliness of *le Paris traditionnel*. A tiny universe unto itself, shaded by trees, bordered by Seine-side quais, and overhung with ancient stone houses, the island has long been a coveted address for Parisians—Voltaire, Daumier, Cézanne, Baudelaire, Chagall, Helena Rubenstein, and the Rothschilds are just some of the lucky people who have called the St-Louis home. In summer, crowds line up for a scoop from Berthillon's ice-cream shop—savor your cone of *glace de Grande Marnier* by strolling along the isle's Seine-side streets. *Métro: Pont-Marie.*

★ ㉛ Notre-Dame. The cathedral of Notre-Dame remains Paris's historic and geographic heart, a place of worship for more than 2,000 years (the present building is the fourth on this site). Victor Hugo's Quasimodo sought sanctuary in its towers, kings and princes married before its great altar, and Napoléon crowned his empress here. The magnificent structure was begun in 1163, making it one of the earliest Gothic cathedrals, but wasn't finished until 1345. The interior is at its lightest and least crowded in the early morning. Window space is limited and filled with shimmering stained glass; the circular rose windows in the transept are particularly delicate. The 387-step climb up the towers is worth the effort for a perfect view of the gargoyles and Paris. ⊠ *Pl. du Parvis.* ☉ *Cathedral daily 8–7, treasury (religious and vestmental relics) weekdays 9:30–6:30. Métro: Cité.*

㉚ Panthéon. This Temple to the Famous started life as a church (1758–89). Since the Revolution, the crypt has harbored the remains of such national heroes as Voltaire, Rousseau, and Zola. The austere interior is ringed with Puvis de Chavannes's late-19th-century frescoes, relating the life of Geneviève, patron saint of Paris, and contains a swinging model of the giant pendulum used here by Léon Foucault in 1851 to prove the earth's rotation. ⊠ *Pl. du Panthéon*, ☎ *01–44–32–18–00.* ⊙ *Daily 10–6:15. Métro: Cardinal-Lemoine.*

㉘ **Place Dauphine.** At the western tail end of the Ile de la Cité, this charming plaza was built by Henri IV. The triangular place is lined with some 17th-century houses which the writer André Maurois felt represented the very quintessence of Paris and France; take a seat on the park bench and see if you agree. *Métro: Cité.*

★ ㉚ **Sainte-Chapelle** (Holy Chapel). One of the most beauteous achievements of the Middle Ages and home to the most ancient stained-glass windows in Paris, this chapel was built by Louis IX in the 1240s to house the Crown of Thorns he had bought from Emperor Baldwin. A lower chapel leads to the dazzling upper chapel, whose walls—if you can call them that—are almost completely made of stained glass. Like an enormous magic lantern, the scenes illuminate more than a thousand figures from stories of the Bible. Try to attend a candlelit concert here. ⊠ *4 bd. du Palais*, ☎ *01–53–73–78–51.* ⊙ *Apr.–Sept., daily 9:30–6:30; Oct.–Mar., daily 10–5. Métro: Cité.*

㉝ **Sorbonne.** Students at Paris's ancient university—one of the oldest in Europe—used to listen to lectures in Latin, which explains why the surrounding area is known as the Latin Quarter. You can visit the main courtyard and peek into the lecture halls if they're not in use. The Baroque chapel is open only during exhibitions. ⊠ *Rue de la Sorbonne. Métro: Cluny–La Sorbonne.*

From the Louvre to the Arc de Triomphe

From the gleaming glass pyramid entrance of the Louvre, the world's greatest museum, you can see the Arc de Triomphe standing foursquare at the top of the city's most famous avenue, the Champs-Élysées. Between the Louvre and the Arc lies the city's spiritual heart—the elegant Place de la Concorde.

❺ **Arc de Triomphe** (Triumphal Arch). This 164-ft arch was planned by Napoléon to celebrate his military successes. Yet when Empress Marie-Louise entered Paris in 1810, it was barely off the ground. Napoléon had been dead for 15 years when the Arc de Triomphe was finished in 1836. The arch looms over Place Charles-de-Gaulle, referred to by Parisians as L'Étoile (The Star), one of Europe's most chaotic traffic circles. Short of attempting a death-defying dash, your only way to get over to the Arc de Triomphe is to take the pedestrian underpass. France's Unknown Soldier is buried beneath the archway; the flame is rekindled every evening at 6:30. ⊠ *Pl. Charles-de-Gaulle*, ☎ *01–55–37–73–77.* ⊙ *Easter–Oct., daily 9:30 AM–11 PM; Nov.–Easter, daily 10 AM–10:30 PM. Métro, RER: Charles-de-Gaulle-Étoile.*

❻ **Champs-Élysées.** The cosmopolitan pulse of Paris beats strongest along this gracefully sloping, 2-km (1-mi) avenue, originally laid out in the 1660s by André Le Nôtre as parkland sweeping away from the Tuileries. There isn't much sign of that pastoral past these days, as you stroll by the cafés, restaurants, airline offices, car showrooms, movie theaters, and chic arcades that occupy its upper half. For a look at its more regal past, note the two 19th-century garden pavilion restaurants, Laurent and Ledoyen. *Métro: George-V, Franklin-D.-Roosevelt, Champs-Élysées–Clemenceau.*

Paris

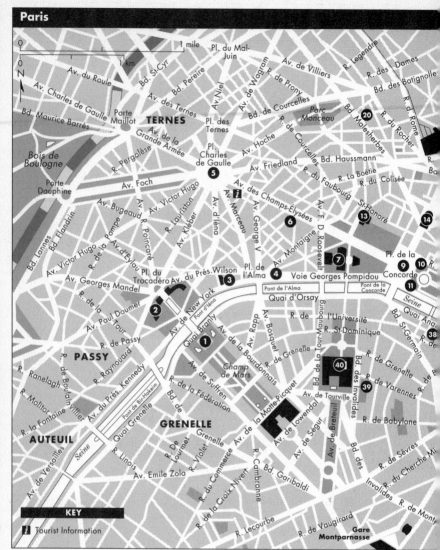

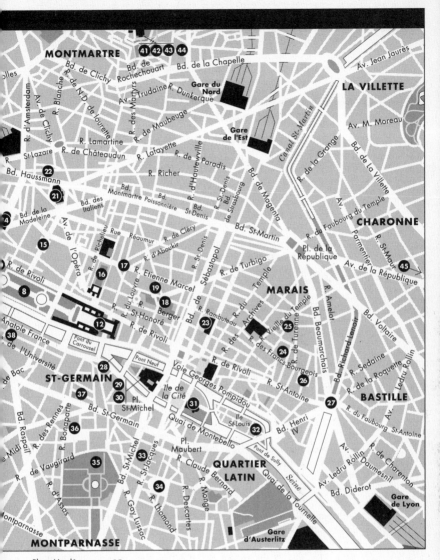

❼ Grand Palais (Grand Palace). This so-called palace built for the World Exhibition of 1900 is closed for renovation; but you can still visit the **Palais de la Découverte** (Palace of Discovery), with scientific and mechanical exhibits and a **planetarium.** ⊠ *Av. Winston-Churchill,* ☎ *01–56–43–20–21.* ☉ *Palais de la Découverte Tues.–Sat. 9:30–6, Sun. 10–7. Métro: Franklin-D.-Roosevelt.*

❽ Jardin des Tuileries (Tuileries Gardens). Immortalized in many Impressionist masterpieces by Renoir, Pissarro, and Monet, these enormous formal gardens are lined with trees, ponds, and statues. At the far end of the Tuileries, leading toward the Louvre, is the **Arc du Carrousel,** a dainty triumphal arch erected more quickly (1806–08) than its big brother at the far end of the Champs-Élysées. *Métro: Concorde, Tuileries.*

★ ⓬ Louvre. Leonardo da Vinci's *Mona Lisa* and *Virgin and Saint Anne,* Van Eyck's *Madonna of Chancellor Rolin,* Giorgione's *Concert Champêtre,* and Delacroix's *Liberty Guiding the People* . . . you get the picture. Once a royal palace, now the world's largest and most famous museum, the Louvre has been given fresh purpose by over a decade of expansion, renovation, and reorganization, symbolized by I. M. Pei's daring glass pyramid that now serves as the entrance to both the museum and an underground shopping arcade, the **Carrousel du Louvre.** Many thousands of treasures are newly cleaned and lit, so plan on seeing it all—from the red-brocaded Napoléon III salons to the fabled Egyptian collection, from the 186-carat Regent Diamond to the rooms crowded with Botticellis, Caravaggios, Poussins, and Géricaults. After all the renovations, the Louvre is now a coherent, unified structure and search parties no longer need to be sent in to find you and bring you out. In fact, Pei's new Louvre has emerged less cramped and more rationally organized.

The main attraction for some is a portrait of the wife of a certain Florentine millionaire, Francesco da Gioconda, better known as Leonardo da Vinci's *Mona Lisa* (in French, *La Joconde*), painted in 1503. It's smaller than you might have imagined, kept behind glass, and invariably encircled by a mob of tourists intent on studying her (or she is studying them?). Turn your attention instead to some less-crowded rooms and galleries nearby, where Leonardo's fellow Italians are strongly represented: Fra Angelico, Giotto, Mantegna, Raphael, Titian, and Veronese. El Greco, Murillo, and Velázquez lead the Spanish; Van Eyck, Rembrandt, Frans Hals, Brueghel, Holbein, and Rubens underline the achievements of northern European art. The English collection is highlighted by works of Lawrence, Reynolds, Gainsborough, and Turner. French frontrunners include works by Poussin, Fragonard, Chardin, Boucher, and Watteau—together with David's *Oath of the Horatii,* Géricault's *Raft of the Medusa,* and Delacroix's *Liberty Guiding the People.* Famous statues include the soaring *Victory of Samothrace*—remember Audrey Hepburn's fine-boned take on this work in *Funny Face?*—the celebrated *Venus de Milo,* and the realistic Egyptian *Seated Scribe.* New rooms for ancient Persian, Arab, and Greek art opened in 1997. ⊠ *Palais du Louvre (it's faster to enter through the Carrousel du Louvre mall on rue de Rivoli than through the pyramid),* ☎ *01–40–20–51–51 information,* 🕸 *www.louvre.com.* ☉ *Mon. and Wed. 9 AM–9:45 PM, Thurs.–Sun. 9–6. Métro: Palais-Royal.*

⓫ Musée du Jeu de Paume. Renovations transformed this museum, at the entrance to the Tuileries Gardens, into an ultramodern, white-walled showcase for excellent temporary exhibits of bold contemporary art. The building was once the spot of *jeu de paume* games (literally, palm game—a forerunner of tennis). ⊠ *1 pl. de la Concorde,* ☎ *01–42–60–69–69.* ☉ *Tues. noon–9:30, Wed.–Fri. noon–7, weekends 10–7. Métro: Concorde.*

➓ **Musée de l'Orangerie** (Orangery Museum). This museum in the Tuileries Gardens contains fine early 20th-century French works by many artists, most famously Monet (on view here are his largest paintings of *Water Lilies*); it should reopen in 2002 after renovation. ⊠ *Pl. de la Concorde,* ☎ 01–42–97–48–16. ⊘ *Wed.–Mon. 9:45–5:15. Métro: Concorde.*

➒ **Place de la Concorde.** Flanked by elegant neoclassical buildings, this huge square is often choked with traffic and perhaps at its most scenic come nightfall, when its floridly beautiful fountains are illuminated. More than 1,000 people, including Louis XVI and Marie-Antoinette, were guillotined here in the early 1790s. The obelisk, a gift from the viceroy of Egypt, originally stood at Luxor and was erected here in 1833; the top was gilded in 1998. *Métro: Concorde.*

The Faubourg St-Honoré

Fashions change, but the Faubourg St-Honoré—the area just north of the Champs-Élysées and the Tuileries—firmly maintains its tradition of high style. As you progress from the President's Palace, past a wealth of art galleries and the Neoclassic Madeleine Church to the stately place Vendôme, you will see that all is luxury and refinement here. On the ritzy square, famous boutiques sit side by side with famous banks—after all, elegance and finance has never been an unusual combination. Leading names in modern fashion are found farther east on Place des Victoires. Sublimely Parisian is the Palais-Royal and its elegant gardens.

➓ **Église de la Madeleine.** With its uncompromising array of columns, this church, known simply as La Madeleine, looks more like a Greek temple. Inside, the walls are richly decorated, with plenty of gold glinting through the murk. The church was designed in 1814 but not consecrated until 1842, after futile efforts to turn the site into a train station. ⊠ *Pl. de la Madeleine.* ⊘ *Mon.–Sat. 7:30–7, Sun. 8–7. Métro: Madeleine.*

➓ **Forum des Halles.** Since the city's much-lamented central glass-and-iron market halls were torn down during the late 1960s, the area has been transformed into a trendy—albeit slightly seedy—shopping complex, the Forum des Halles. A topiary garden basks in the shadow of the nearby **Bourse du Commerce** (Commercial Exchange) and bulky church of **St-Eustache.** *Métro: Les Halles; RER: Châtelet–Les Halles.*

➓ **Palais de l'Élysée** (Élysée Palace). This "palace," known to the French simply as L'Élysée, where the French president lives, works, and receives official visitors, was originally constructed as a private mansion in 1718 and has housed presidents only since 1873. ⊠ *55 rue du Faubourg St-Honoré. Not open to the public. Métro: Miromesnil.*

➓ **Palais-Royal.** This erstwhile Royal Palace, built in the 1630s and now partly occupied by the Ministry of Culture, has a beautiful garden bordered by arcades and boutiques, and an adjacent courtyard with modern, candy-stripe columns by Daniel Buren. Once home to the Bourbon kings, it is still a coveted residential address (Colette was one resident) and is home to the famous Le Grand Véfour restaurant. ⊠ *Pl. André-Malraux. Métro: Palais-Royal.*

➓ **Place Vendôme.** Mansart's rhythmically proportioned example of 17th-century urban architecture is one of the world's most opulent squares. Top jewelers compete for attention with the limousines that draw up outside the Ritz hotel. The square's central pillar was made from the melted bronze of 1,200 cannons captured by Napoléon at the Battle of Austerlitz in 1805. That's Napoléon at the top, disguised as a Roman emperor. *Métro: Tuileries.*

⑰ **Place des Victoires.** This circular square, home to many of the city's top fashion boutiques, was laid out in 1685 by Jules-Hardouin Mansart in honor of the military victories (*victoires*) of Louis XIV. The Sun King gallops along on a bronze horse in the middle. *Métro: Sentier.*

⑲ **St-Eustache.** This colossal church, also known as the Cathedral of Les Halles, was erected between 1532 and 1637 and testifies to the stylistic transition between Gothic and classical architecture. ✉ *2 rue du Jour. Métro: Les Halles; RER: Châtelet–Les Halles.*

From the Eiffel Tower to Pont de l'Alma

The Eiffel Tower lords it over this southwest area of Paris. Across the way, in the Palais de Chaillot on Place du Trocadéro, are a number of museums. In this area, too, is where you get the Bateaux Mouches, the boats that ply the Seine on their tours of Paris by water.

❹ **Bateaux Mouches.** These popular motorboats set off on their hour-long tours of Paris waters regularly (every half hour in summer). ✉ *Pl. de l'Alma,* ☎ *01–40–76–99–99,* 🕸 *www.bateaux-mouches.fr. Métro: Alma-Marceau.*

❶ **Eiffel Tower** (Tour Eiffel). What is now the worldwide symbol of Paris nearly became 7,000 tons of scrap iron when its concession expired in 1909—now much loved, it was once widely derided by Parisians as too big and too modern. Only its potential use as a radio antenna saved the day. Architect Gustave Eiffel, whose skill as an engineer earned him renown as a builder of iron bridges, created his tower for the World Exhibition of 1889. Restoration in the 1980s didn't make the elevators any faster—long lines are inevitable unless you come in the evening (when every girder is lit in glorious detail, with a special eye-popping display that goes off on the hour)—but decent shops and two good restaurants were added. The view from 1,000 ft up will enable you to appreciate the city's layout and proportions. ✉ *Quai Branly,* ☎ *01–44–11–23–23,* 🕸 *www.tour-eiffel.fr.* 🕙 *July–Aug., daily 9 AM–midnight; Sept.–June, Sun.–Thurs. 9 AM–11 PM, Fri.–Sat. 9 AM–midnight. Métro: Bir-Hakeim; RER: Champ-de-Mars.*

❸ **Musée d'Art Moderne de la Ville de Paris** (City of Paris Museum of Modern Art). Both temporary exhibits and a permanent collection of top-quality 20th-century art can be found at this modern art museum. It takes over, chronologically speaking, where the Musée d'Orsay leaves off. ✉ *11 av. du Président-Wilson,* ☎ *01–53–67–40–00.* 🕙 *Tues.–Sun. 10–5:30, Wed. 10–8:30. Métro: Iéna.*

❷ **Palais de Chaillot** (Chaillot Palace). This honey-color, Art Deco culture center facing the Seine, perched atop tumbling gardens with sculpture and fountains, was built in the 1930s. It houses three museums: the **Musée de la Marine** (Maritime Museum), with a salty collection of seafaring paraphernalia; the **Musée de l'Homme** (Museum of Mankind), an anthropology museum with an array of prehistoric artifacts; and the **Musée des Monuments Français** (French Monuments Museum), whose painstaking replicas of statues and archways is under restoration after a fire (this museum is set to reopen—as the "Cité de l'Architecture"—by 2003). ✉ *Pl. du Trocadéro.* 🕙 *Wed.–Mon. 10–5. Métro: Trocadéro.*

The Grand Boulevards

The focal point of this walk is the uninterrupted avenue that runs in almost a straight line from St-Augustin, the city's grandest Second Empire church, to Place de la République, whose very name symbolizes the ultimate downfall of the imperial regime. The avenue's name changes six times along the way, which is why Parisians refer to it as the *Grands Boulevards*.

㉒ Grands Magasins (Department Stores). Paris's most venerable department stores can be found behind the Opéra: **Galeries Lafayette** has an elegant turn-of-the-20th-century glass dome, **Au Printemps** an excellent view from its rooftop cafeteria. ⊠ *Bd. Haussmann. Métro: Havre-Caumartin.*

★ **㉒ Musée Nissim de Camondo.** The French perfected the *art de vivre*— the art of living—in the 18th century in elegant, luxurious salons. In today's Paris, it's hard to experience that fabled age for yourself, so thank Dieu for this *hôtel particulier* (private mansion), magnificently furnished with beautiful furniture, *boiseries* (carved wood panels), and bibelots of the rococo and neoclassical periods. ⊠ *63 rue de Monceau,* ☎ *01–53–89–06–40.* ☉ *Wed.–Sun. 10–5. Métro: Villiers.*

★ **㉑ Opéra Garnier.** Still the world's most glamorous theater, "home" to the infamous Phantom, and setting for some of Degas's most famous ballet paintings, the original Paris opera house was the flagship building of the Second Empire (1851–70). Architect Charles Garnier fused elements of neoclassical architecture—like the bas-reliefs on the newly cleaned facade—in an exaggerated combination imbued with as much subtlety as a Wagnerian cymbal crash. If you can't catch one of the ballet or opera performances, just visit the museum here, which allows you to walk through the Grand Foyer, whose staircase is so spectacular it makes even a count feel like a mouse, and to also view the lavishly upholstered auditorium, a monument of the super-opulent Napoléon III style, though now adorned with a ceiling painted by Marc Chagall in 1964. ⊠ *Pl. de l'Opéra,* ☎ *01–40–01–22–63.* ☉ *Daily 10–5. Métro: Opéra.*

The Marais and the Bastille

The Marais is one of the city's most historic, picturesque, and sought-after residential districts. The gracious architecture of the 17th and early 18th centuries sets the tone. Today, most of the Marais's *hôtels particuliers*—loosely, "mansions," onetime residences of aristocratic families—have been restored by rich, with-it couples, and many of the buildings are now museums. There are trendy boutiques and cafés among the kosher shops of the traditionally Jewish neighborhood around rue des Rosiers. On the eastern side of the neighborhood is Place de la Bastille, site of the infamous prison stormed on July 14, 1789, an event that came to symbolize the beginning of the French Revolution. The surrounding Bastille quarter is filled with galleries, shops, theaters, cafés, restaurants, and bars.

㉓ Centre Pompidou (Pompidou Center). The futuristic, funnel-top Pompidou Center was built in the mid-1970s and named in honor of former French president Georges Pompidou (1911–74). The center soon attracted more than 8 million visitors a year—five times more than intended—and was closed from 1997 to January 2000 for top-to-bottom renovation. The center is most famous for its **Musée National d'Art Moderne** (Modern Art Museum), covering 20th-century art from Fauvism and Cubism to postwar abstraction and video constructions. Other highlights include the new and chic Georges rooftop restaurant and the glass-tubed elevator that snakes up the side of the building. On the sloping piazza below is the **Atelier Brancusi** (Brancusi's Studio), four reconstituted rooms crammed with works by Romanian-born sculptor Constantin Brancusi. ⊠ *Pl. Georges-Pompidou,* ☎ *01–44–78–12–33,* WEB *www.centrepompidou.fr.* ☉ *Wed.–Mon. noon–10. Métro: Rambuteau.*

★ ㉔ **Musée Carnavalet.** Once the home of 17th-century Madame de Sévigné, this is now a museum devoted to the decorative arts and the history of Paris. Along with riveting objects of the French kings, there are also magnificent 17th- and 18th-century period salons on view, including recreations of Marcel Proust's cork-lined bedroom and the late 19th-century Fouquet jewelry shop. ⊠ *23 rue de Sévigné,* ☎ *01–44–59–58–58.* ☉ *Tues.–Sun. 10–5:40. Métro: St-Paul.*

㉕ **Musée Picasso** (Picasso Museum). The Hôtel Salé, an elegant mansion, is home to an extensive collection of little-known paintings, drawings, and engravings donated to the state by Picasso's heirs in lieu of death duties. Picasso, who loved to play the bohemian, actually loved the aristocratic lifestyle, so he would have been happy to have seen his paintings in this luxurious house. ⊠ *5 rue de Thorigny,* ☎ *01–42–71–25–21.* ☉ *Wed.–Mon. 9:30–5:30. Métro: St-Sébastien.*

㉗ **Place de la Bastille.** Nothing remains of the fortress stormed at the outbreak of the French Revolution; the soaring gilt-edge column, topped by the figure of Liberty, commemorates Parisians killed in the long-forgotten uprising of 1830. Also on the square is the modern, glass-fronted **Opéra de la Bastille** (Bastille Opera), opened in 1989 in commemoration of the Revolution's bicentennial. Rather more appealing is the **Viaduc des Arts** (Arts Viaduct), which leads off down avenue Daumesnil: a disused railway viaduct converted into boutiques below and a planted walkway on top. *Métro: Bastille.*

★ ㉖ **Place des Vosges.** The oldest monumental square in Paris—and probably still its most nobly proportioned—the place des Vosges was laid out by Henri IV at the start of the 17th century. Originally known as place Royale, it has kept its Renaissance beauty nearly intact, although its buildings have been softened by time, their pale pink brick crumbling slightly in the harsh Parisian air and the darker stone facings pitted with age. In the far corner is the **Maison de Victor Hugo** (Victor Hugo Museum), containing souvenirs of the great poet's life and many of his surprisingly able paintings and ink drawings. ⊠ *Maison de Victor Hugo: 6 pl. des Vosges,* ☎ *01–42–72–10–16.* ☉ *Tues.–Sun. 10–5:45. Métro: St-Paul.*

From St-Germain to Les Invalides

This area of the Left Bank extends from the lively St-Germain neighborhood (named for the oldest church in Paris and still one of Paris's richest residential quarters) to the stately area around the Musée d'Orsay and Les Invalides. Other highlights are the city's most colorful park, the Jardin du Luxembourg; the Palais Bourbon, home to the National Assembly; and the Musée Rodin. South of St-Germain is Montparnasse, which had its cultural heyday in the first part of the 20th century, when it was *the* place for painters and poets to live.

★ ㊵ **Hôtel des Invalides.** Soaring above expansive if hardly manicured lawns, Les Invalides was founded by Louis XIV in 1674 to house wounded (*invalid*) war veterans. Les Invalides itself remains an outstanding Baroque ensemble, designed by Libéral Bruant and Jules Hardouin-Mansart. Its second church, the Église du Dôme, is graced by the city's most elegant dome and is home to **Napoléon's Tomb,** where you can breathe the fumes of hubris amidst all the marble columns and onyx trim. The adjacent **Musée de l'Armée** is a museum with a collection of arms, armor, and uniforms, while the **Musée des Plans-Reliefs** contains a fascinating collection of scale models of French towns dating from the 17th century. ⊠ *Pl. des Invalides,* ☎ *01–44–42–37–72.* ☉ *Apr.–Sept., daily 10–6; Oct.–Mar., daily 10–4:30. Métro: La Tour–Maubourg.*

③⑤ **Jardin du Luxembourg** (Luxembourg Gardens). A favorite subject for 19th-century painters, Paris's most famous Left Bank park has tennis courts, flower beds, tree-lined alleys, and a large pond (with toy boats for rent alongside). The **Palais du Luxembourg** (Luxembourg Palace), built by Queen Maria de' Medici at the beginning of the 17th century in answer to Florence's Pitti Palace, houses the French Senate and is not open to the public. *Métro: Odéon; RER: Luxembourg.*

★ ③⑧ **Musée d'Orsay** (Orsay Museum). This museum, in a spectacularly renovated former train station, is one of Paris's star attractions, thanks to its imaginatively housed collections of the arts (mainly French) spanning the period 1848–1914. The chief artistic attraction is its Impressionist collection, which includes some of the most celebrated paintings in the world, including Manet's *Déjeuner sur l'Herbe* (*Lunch on the Grass*) and Renoir's depiction of a famous dancehall called *Le Moulin de la Galette,* to name just two among hundreds. Other highlights include Art Nouveau furniture, a faithfully restored Belle Epoque restaurant, and a model of the Opéra quarter beneath a glass floor. The restaurant here is set in a dazzling 19th-century foyer. ⊠ *1 rue de la Légion d'Honneur,* ☎ *01–40–49–48–14,* WEB *www.musee-orsay.fr.* ⊙ *Tues.–Wed., Fri.–Sat. 10–6, Thurs. 10–9:45, Sun. 9–6. Métro: Solférino; RER: Musée d'Orsay.*

★ ③⑨ **Musée Rodin** (Rodin Museum). The Faubourg St-Germain, studded with private mansions owned by the aristocracy and the rich, remains for the most part behind closed gates but get a peek at this fabled neighborhood by visiting the 18th-century Hôtel Biron, onetime home of the sculptor Auguste Rodin (1840–1917) and today a gracious setting for his work. In back is a pretty garden with Rodin works and hundreds of rosebushes. ⊠ *77 rue de Varenne,* ☎ *01–44–18–61–10.* ⊙ *Tues.–Sun. 9:30–5:45. Métro: Varenne.*

③⑦ **St-Germain-des-Prés.** The oldest church in Paris was first built to shelter a relic of the true cross, brought back from Spain in AD 542. The chancel was enlarged and the church consecrated by Pope Alexander III in 1163 (the church tower dates from this period). ⊠ *Pl. St-Germain-des-Prés.* ⊙ *Weekdays 8–7:30, weekends 8 AM–9 PM. Métro: St-Germain-des-Prés.*

③⑥ **St-Sulpice.** Stand back and admire the impressive 18th-century facade of this enormous 17th-century church. The unequal, unfinished towers strike a quirky, fallible note at odds with the chillingly impersonal interior, embellished only by the masterly wall paintings by Delacroix—notably *Jacob and the Angel*—in the first chapel on the right. ⊠ *Pl. St-Sulpice. Métro: St-Sulpice.*

Montmartre

On a dramatic rise above the city is Montmartre, site of the Sacré-Coeur Basilica (try to catch a sunset or sunrise over Paris from its terrace) and home to a once-thriving artistic community. Visiting Montmartre means negotiating a lot of steep streets and flights of steps. Some of the streets are now totally given over to the tourist trade, but if you wander and follow your nose, you can still find quiet corners that retain the poetry that once allured Toulouse-Lautrec and other great artists.

★ ④④ **Au Lapin Agile.** One of the most picturesque spots in Paris, this legendary bar-cabaret (open nights only) is a miraculous survivor from the 19th century. Founded in 1860, its adorable maison-cottage was a favorite subject of painter Maurice Utrillo, and it soon became the home-away-from-home for Braque, Modigliani, Apollinaire, Vlaminck, and most famously, Picasso. ⊠ *22 rue des Saules,* ☎ *01–46–06–85–87.* ⊙ *Tues.–Sun. 9 PM–2 AM. Métro: Lamarck-Caulaincourt.*

❹❸ Musée de Montmartre (Montmartre Museum). In its turn-of-the-20th-century heyday, Montmartre's historical museum was home to an illustrious group of painters, writers, and assorted cabaret artists. ⊠ *12 rue Cortot,* ☎ *01–46–06–61–11.* ⊘ *Tues.–Sun. 11–6. Métro: Lamarck-Caulaincourt.*

❹❷ Place des Abbesses. This triangular square is typical of the picturesque, slightly countrified style that has made Montmartre famous. The entrance to the Abbesses métro station, a curving, sensuous mass of delicate iron, is one of Guimard's two original Art Nouveau entrance canopies left in Paris. The innovative brick and concrete Art Nouveau church of St-Jean de Montmartre overlooks the square. *Métro: Abbesses.*

❹❶ Sacré-Coeur. If you start at Anvers métro station and head up rue de Steinkerque (full of budget clothing shops), you'll be greeted by the most familiar and spectacular view of the Sacré-Coeur, perched proudly atop the Butte Montmartre. The basilica was built in a bizarre, mock-Byzantine style between 1876 and 1910; although no favorite with aesthetes, it has become a major Paris landmark. It was constructed as an act of national penitence after the disastrous Franco-Prussian War of 1870—a Catholic show of strength at a time of bitter church-state conflict. ⊠ *Pl. du Parvis-du-Sacré-Coeur. Métro: Anvers.*

❹❺ Cimetière du Père-Lachaise (Father Lachaise Cemetery). This cemetery forms a veritable necropolis with cobbled avenues and tombs competing in pomposity and originality. Leading incumbents include Frédéric Chopin, Marcel Proust, Jim Morrison, Edith Piaf, and Gertrude Stein. Get a map at the entrance and track them down. ⊠ *Entrances on rue des Rondeaux, bd. de Ménilmontant, and rue de la Réunion.* ⊘ *Apr.–Sept., daily 8–6; Oct.–Mar., daily 8–5. Métro: Père-Lachaise, Gambetta, Philippe-Auguste.*

DINING

Forget the Louvre, the Tour Eiffel, and the Bateaux Mouches—the real reason for a visit to Paris is to dine at its famous temples of gastronomy. Whether you get knee-deep in white truffles at Alain Ducasse or merely discover pistacchioed sausage (the poor man's caviar) at a classic corner bistro, you'll discover that food here is an obsession, an art, a subject of endless debate. And if the lobster soufflé is delicious, the historic ambience is often more so. Just request Empress Josephine's table at Le Grand Véfour and find out.

Note that when prices are quoted for a restaurant which only offers prix fixe (set-price) complete dinners, it is given a price category that reflects this prix-fixe price. Tax (19.6%) and service are included in these prices, but not wine.

CATEGORY	COST*
$$$$	over 250 frs (€38)
$$$	150 frs–250 frs (€23–€38)
$$	80 frs–150 frs (€12–€23)
$	under 80 frs (€12)

per person for a main course at dinner

Right Bank

$$$$ ✕ **Alain Ducasse.** Mega-star chef Alain Ducasse took over the restaurant of the Hotel Plaza-Athénée (beloved of yankee glitterati) in mid-
★ 2000. The rosy rococo salons have been updated with metallic organza over the chandeliers and, in a symbolic move, Ducasse has made time

stand still by stopping the clock. Overlooking the prettiest courtyard in Paris, this makes for a setting as delicious as Ducasse's roast lamb garnished with "crumbs" of dried fruit or duckling roasted with fig leaves. ⊠ *Hotel Plaza-Athénée, 27 av. Montaigne,* ☎ *01–53–67–66– 65. Reservations essential. AE, DC, MC, V. Closed Sat. and Sun. No lunch Mon.–Wed. Métro: Alma-Marceau.*

$$$$ ✕ **Le Grand Véfour.** Originally built in 1784, set in the arcades of the
★ Palais-Royal, everyone from Napoléon to Jean Cocteau has dined beneath the golden *boiseries* (wainscoting) here—nearly every seat bears a plaque commemorating a famous patron and you can request to be seated at your idol's table. Chef Guy Martin pleases all with his foie gras–stuffed ravioli and truffled veal sweetbreads. Book way in advance. ⊠ *17 rue Beaujolais, 1ᵉʳ,* ☎ *01–42–96–56–27. Reservations essential several wks in advance. Jacket and tie. AE, DC, MC, V. Closed Fri. dinner, weekends and Aug. Métro: Palais-Royal.*

$$$–$$$$ ✕ **Les Ambassadeurs.** Les Ambassadeurs offers a setting right out of
★ Versailles—not surprisingly, since this 18th-century mansion was built by Louis XV. Honey-hued marble walls and gleaming chandeliers make a sumptuous setting for chef Dominique Bouche, who likes to mix luxe with more down-to-earth flavors: potato pancakes topped with smoked salmon, caviar-flecked scallops wrapped in bacon with tomato and basil, duck with rutabaga, turbot with cauliflower. ⊠ *10 pl. de la Concorde,* ☎ *01–44–71–16–16. Reservations essential. Jacket and tie at dinner. AE, DC, MC, V. Métro: Concorde.*

$$$–$$$$ ✕ **Taillevent.** Once the most traditional of all Paris luxury restaurants,
★ this grande dame is suddenly the object of a certain uncharacteristic buzz, since new chef Michel Del Burgo arrived. He's jazzed up the classic menu with such creations as cod on white Paimpol beans in an emulsion of olive oil and meat juice garnished with red pepper. The well-priced wine list is probably one of the top 10 in the world. ⊠ *15 rue Lamennais,* ☎ *01–45–63–39–94. Reservations essential 3–4 wks in advance. Jacket and tie. AE, MC, V. Closed weekends and Aug. Métro: Charles-de-Gaulle–Étoile.*

$$–$$$ ✕ **Bofinger.** Settle in to one of the tables dressed in crisp white linens, under the gorgeous Art Nouveau glass cupola, and enjoy fine classic brasserie fare, such as oysters, grilled sole, or fillet of lamb. Note that the no-smoking section here is not only enforced but is also in the prettiest part of the restaurant. ⊠ *5–7 rue de la Bastille,* ☎ *01–42–72– 87–82. AE, DC, MC, V. Métro: Bastille.*

$$–$$$ ✕ **Chez Georges.** When you ask sophisticated aristocrats and antiques dealers to name their favorite bistro, many choose Georges. The traditional bistro cooking is good—herring, sole, kidneys, steak, and *frîtes* (fries)—but the atmosphere is better. ⊠ *1 rue du Mail, 2ᵉ,* ☎ *01– 42–60–07–11. AE, DC, MC, V. Closed Sun. and Aug. Métro: Sentier.*

$$–$$$ ✕ **La Fermette Marbeuf.** Why have a blow-out at (sometimes disappointing) Maxim's when you can enjoy this magically beautiful Belle Epoque room, a favorite haunt of French TV and movie stars who adore the Art Nouveau mosaic and stained-glass mise-en-scène. The menu features solid, updated classic cuisine. ⊠ *5 rue Marbeuf,* ☎ *01–53– 23–08–00. AE, DC, MC, V. Métro: Franklin-D.-Roosevelt.*

$$–$$$ ✕ **Macéo.** If you want to enjoy classic French food with a modern spin,
★ then Macéo delivers. Contemporary lamps add a bold touch to the otherwise classic dining room, painted brick-red and cream. With its reasonably priced set menus (220 frs/€34 at lunch and 250 frs/€38 in the evening), this is an ideal spot for an elegant yet relaxed meal after a day at the Louvre and Palais Royal gardens. ⊠ *15 rue des Petits-Champs,* ☎ *01–42–97–53–85. MC, V. Closed Sun. No lunch Sat. Métro: Palais-Royal.*

$$–$$$ ✕ **Spoon, Food and Wine.** Star chef Alain Ducasse's blueprint of a bistro
★ for the 21st century has a do-it-yourself fusion-food menu that allows
you to mix and match dishes diversely American, Asian, and Italian in
origin. Sign of the future? There are many salads and vegetable and grain
dishes on the menu. Reservations are difficult—call a month ahead—but
you can drop in for a snack at the bar. Come late for the models and movie
stars. ⊠ *14 rue de Marignan,* ☎ *01–40–76–34–44. Reservations essential several wks in advance. AE, MC, V. Métro: Franklin-D.-Roosevelt.*

$$ ✕ **Café Runtz.** Next to the noted theater of Salle Favart, this friendly
bistro has old brass gas lamps on each table and rich *boiseries* (wood-
work) create a cozy and Flaubertian atmosphere. The fare is tasty, hearty,
and, in the main, Alsatian. ⊠ *16 rue Favart,* ☎ *01–42–96–69–86. AE,
MC, V. Closed Sun. and Aug. No lunch Sat. Métro: Richelieu-Drouot.*

$$ ✕ **La Grande Armée.** The Costes brothers' brasserie near the Arc de
★ Triomphe has knockout decor designed by Jacques Garcia. Here he's
unleashed an exotic Napoléon-III bordello decor—think black lacquered tables, leopard upholstery, Bordeaux velvet—for a carefully tou-
sled clientele picking at those dishes that chic Parisians like best these
days. ⊠ *3 av. de la Grande Armée,* ☎ *01–45–00–24–77. AE, DC, MC,
V. Métro: Charles-de-Gaulle–Étoile.*

$$ ✕ **Le Poquelin.** The theaterlike scenery gives this welcoming little
restaurant an atmosphere that's both elegant and relaxed. Classic
French cooking is served with a twist, such as duck breast topped with
foie gras. The popular, regularly changing "Menu Molière" is excel-
lent value. ⊠ *17 rue Molière,* ☎ *01–42–96–22–19. AE, DC, MC, V.
Closed Sun. No lunch Sat or Mon. Métro: Palais-Royal.*

$$ ✕ **Le Repaire de Cartouche.** Near the Cirque d'Hiver in the Bastille,
this split-level, 1950s-style bistro with dark-wood decor is the latest
good-value sensation in Paris. Rodolphe Paquin is a creative and impeccably trained chef who does a stylish take on earthy French regional
dishes. ⊠ *99 rue Amelot, 11ᵉ,* ☎ *01–47–00–25–86. Reservations essential. MC, V. Closed Sun., Mon. and Aug. Métro: Filles du Calvaire.*

$$ ✕ **Le Safran.** Le Safran almost exclusively offers food that is prepared
★ with organic produce—red mullet stuffed with cèpe mushrooms and
gigot de sept heures (leg of lamb cooked for seven hours) are two sig-
nature dishes. The little room is pretty, intimate, and painted in sunny
saffron. ⊠ *29 rue d'Argenteuil,* ☎ *01–42–61–25–30. MC, V. Closed
Sun. Métro: Tuileries, Pyramides.*

$ ✕ **Chartier.** This cavernous 1896 restaurant enjoys a huge following
among budget-minded students, solitary bachelors, and tourists. You
may find yourself sharing a table with strangers as you study the long,
old-fashioned menu of such favorites as hard-boiled eggs with may-
onnaise, steak tartare, and roast chicken with fries. ⊠ *7 rue du
Faubourg-Montmartre,* ☎ *01–47–70–86–29. Reservations not ac-
cepted. AE, DC, MC, V. Métro: Montmartre.*

$ ✕ **Le Kitsch.** Fighting the good fight against ennui, this fun place is a
favorite in the arty Bastille neighborhood. There's more than a touch
of Pee-Wee's Playhouse here, thanks to the faux-stucco walls, plastic
children's furniture, and naif paintings of cats. ⊠ *10 rue Oberkampf,*
☎ *01–40–21–94–14. No credit cards. Métro: Oberkampf.*

$ ✕ **Ladurée.** Pretty enough to bring a tear to Proust's eye, this ravish-
ing *salon de thé* (tea salon) looks barely changed from 1862. The fa-
mous lemon and caramel macaroons, little tea sandwiches, and a slew
of teas are on tap here. A new branch—one that also boasts a time-
burnished ambience—is at 75 av. des Champs-Élysées. ⊠ *16 rue
Royale,* ☎ *01–42–60–21–79. AE, MC, V. Métro: Madeleine.*

Left Bank

$$$ ✗ **59 Poincaré.** Famed chef Alain Ducasse's luxe bistro was originally intended to be a variant of his Monaco restaurant Bar et Boeuf ("Sea Bass and Beef")—but, always the businessman, he quickly adapted to the "mad cow" scare with a menu featuring vegetables, lamb, lobster, and fruit. Downstairs is a sleek modern brasserie where you can drop in for a quick meal, while the upstairs Belle Epoque dining room is now adorned with photos of farmers, gadgets on the tables, and a hip soundtrack. ⊠ *59 av. Raymond-Poincaré,* ☎ *01–44–05–66–10. Reservations essential. AE, DC, MC, V. Closed Sun. and Mon. Métro: Victor-Hugo.*

$$$ ✗ **Hélène Darroze.** Hélène Darroze has been crowned the newest female
★ culinary star in Paris, thanks to the creative flair she has given the tried-and-true classics of southwestern French cooking, from the lands around Albi and Toulouse. You know it's not going to be *la même chanson,* or the same old thing, when you spot the resolutely contemporary Tse & Tse tableware and red-and-purple color scheme. The downside? High prices, dainty servings, and often unprofessional service, so you might opt for the downstairs bistro, which offers the same dishes but in even smaller, tapas-style portions. ⊠ *4 rue d'Assas,* ☎ *01–42–22–00–11. AE, DC, MC, V. Closed Sun. No lunch Sat. Métro: Sèvres-Babylone.*

$$–$$$ ✗ **Alcazar.** Englishman Sir Terence Conran's stunning, large new brasserie—a remake of a famed 19th-century spot—is one of the chicest spots in town. It has a regularly changing, appealingly innovative menu. Recently revamped to satisfy cool Parisians' evolving tastes, the menu now even features "so British" fish-and-chips. For 115 frs/€18 you can snack on a main dish with a glass of wine at the funky bar. ⊠ *62 rue Mazarine,* ☎ *01–53–10–19–99. Reservations essential. AE, DC, MC, V. Métro: Odéon.*

$$ ✗ **Le Bouillon Racine.** Originally a *bouillon,* a Parisian soup restaurant popular at the turn of the 20th century, this two-story place is now a delightfully renovated Belle Epoque oasis with a good Franco-Belgian menu. ⊠ *3 rue Racine, 6ᵉ,* ☎ *01–44–32–15–60. Reservations essential. AE, MC, V. Métro: Odéon.*

$$ ✗ **La Coupole.** This world-renowned, cavernous spot in Montparnasse practically defines the term brasserie. La Coupole has been popular since the days when Jean-Paul Sartre and Simone de Beauvoir were regulars and is still great fun. Expect the usual brasserie menu—including perhaps the largest shellfish platter in Paris—choucroute, and a wide range of over-the-top desserts. ⊠ *102 bd. du Montparnasse,* ☎ *01–43–20–14–20. AE, DC, MC, V. Métro: Vavin.*

$$ ✗ **Thoumieux.** Delightfully Parisian, this place charms with red velour banquettes, yellow walls, and bustling waiters in white aprons. Budget prices for rillettes, duck confit, and cassoulet make Thoumieux—owned by the same family for three generations—popular. Don't come with gourmet expectations but for a solid, gently priced meal. ⊠ *79 rue St-Dominique,* ☎ *01–47–05–49–75. AE, MC, V. Métro: Invalides.*

$–$$ ✗ **Bistro Mazarin.** Leave the tourists on boulevard St-Germain and join local gallery owners and students at this casual bistro for bags of atmosphere and sturdy, satisfying food made to order with fresh ingredients. Lentil salad, steak with Roquefort sauce or one of two daily fish specials, and a pitcher of the house wine make for a decent meal. In good weather, the terrace offers great people-watching potential. ⊠ *42 rue Mazarine,* ☎ *01–43–29–99–01. AE, MC, V. Métro: Mabillon.*

$–$$ ✗ **Brasserie de l'Ile St-Louis.** In one of the most picturesque parts of the city, this brasserie serves good food on a great terrace. ⊠ *55 quai de Bourbon,* ☎ *01–43–54–02–59. No credit cards. Métro: Pont Marie.*

$–$$ ✗ **Les Pipos.** The tourist-trap restaurants along the romantic rue de la
★ Montagne Ste-Genevieve are enough to make you despair—and then

you stumble across this corner bistro. Slang for students of the famous Ecole Polytechnique nearby, Les Pipos is everything you could ask of a Latin Quarter bistro: the space is cramped, the food substantial (the cheese comes from the Lyon market), and conversation flows as freely as the wine. ⊠ *2 rue de L'Ecole Polytechnique,* ☎ *01–43–54–11–40. No credit cards. Closed Sun. Métro: Maubert-Mutualité.*

LODGING

CATEGORY	COST*
$$$$	over 1,200 frs (€184)
$$$	750 frs–1,200 frs (€115–€184)
$$	450 frs–750 frs (€68.70–€115)
$	under 450 frs (€68.70)

Prices are for standard double rooms and include tax (19.6%) and service charges.

Right Bank

$$$$ ⊞ **Costes.** Baron de Rothschild hasn't invited you this time? No mat-
★   ter—just stay here at Jean-Louis and Gilbert Costes's sumptuous hotel and you won't know the difference. The darling of the fashion and media set, the place conjures up the palaces of Napoléon III, with stunning rooms swathed in rich garnet and bronze tones and luxurious fabrics. ⊠ *239 rue St-Honoré, 75001,* ☎ *01–42–44–50–50,* FAX *01–42–44–50– 01. 85 rooms. Restaurant, bar. AE, DC, MC, V. Métro: Tuileries.*

$$$$ ⊞ **Crillon.** You can't spend the night at Versailles but the next best thing
★   may be the Crillon. Built by Louis XV and one of Paris's grandest 18th-century palaces, this famed hotel has welcomed royal guests from Marie-Antoinette (who took music lessons here) to Hollywood heavyweights. Most rooms are lavishly decorated with rococo and Directoire antiques, crystal and gilt wall sconces, and gold-leaf fittings. ⊠ *10 pl. de la Concorde, 75008,* ☎ *01–44–71–15–00; 800/888–4747 in the U.S.,* FAX *01–44–71–15–02. 115 rooms, 45 suites. 2 restaurants, 2 bars. AE, DC, MC, V. Métro: Concorde.*

$$$$ ⊞ **Meurice.** One of the finest hotels in the world is now even finer, thanks
★   to the multi-million-dollar face-lift given this treasure by the Sultan of Brunei. Few salons are as splendorous as the famous dining room here—all gilt boseries, pink roses, and Edwardian crystal—while guest rooms, furnished with Persian carpets, marble mantelpieces, and or-molu clocks, are now more soigné than ever. ⊠ *228 rue de Rivoli, 75001,* ☎ *01–44–58–10–10,* FAX *01–44–58–10–15. 160 rooms, 36 suites. 2 restaurants, bar. AE, DC, MC, V. Métro: Tuileries, Concorde.*

$$$$ ⊞ **Pavillon de la Reine.** This magnificent hotel, filled with Louis XIII–style fireplaces and antiques, is in a mansion reconstructed from original plans. Ask for a duplex with French windows overlooking the first of two flower-filled courtyards behind the historic Queen's Pavilion. ⊠ *28 pl. des Vosges, 75003,* ☎ *01–40–29–19–19; 800/447–7462 in the U.S.,* FAX *01–40–29–19–20. 30 rooms, 25 suites. Bar, breakfast room, free parking. AE, DC, MC, V. Métro: Bastille, St-Paul.*

$$–$$$ ⊞ **Louvre Forum.** This friendly hotel is a find: smack in the center of town, it has clean, comfortable, well-equipped rooms (with satellite TV) at extremely reasonable prices. ⊠ *25 rue du Bouloi, 75001,* ☎ *01–42–36–54–19,* FAX *01–42–33–66–31. 27 rooms, 16 with shower. AE, DC, MC, V. Métro: Louvre.*

$$ ⊞ **Axial Beaubourg.** A solid bet in the Marais, this hotel in a 16th-century building has beamed ceilings in the lobby and in the six first-floor rooms. Most guest rooms have pleasant decor, and all have satellite TV. The Centre Pompidou and the Picasso Museum are five minutes away. ✉ *11 rue du Temple, 75004,* ☎ *01–42–72–72–22,* FAX *01–42–72–03–53. 39 rooms with bath. AE, DC, MC, V. Métro: Hôtel-de-Ville.*

$$ 🏨 **Caron de Beaumarchais.** The theme of this intimate jewel is the
★ work of Caron de Beaumarchais, who wrote *The Marriage of Figaro* in 1778. Rooms are faithfully decorated to reflect the taste of 18th-century French nobility. The second- and fifth-floor rooms with balconies are the largest; those on the sixth floor have views across Right Bank rooftops. ✉ *12 rue Vieille-du-Temple, 75004,* ☎ *01–42–72–34–12,* FAX *01–42–72–34–63. 19 rooms, 2 with shower. AE, DC, MC, V. Métro: Hôtel-de-Ville.*

$$ 🏨 **Deux-Iles.** This converted 17th-century mansion on the picturesque Ile St-Louis has long won plaudits for charm and comfort. Flowers and plants are scattered throughout the stunning main hall and tapestries cover the exposed stone walls. The delightfully old-fashioned rooms, blessed with exposed beams, are small but airy and sunny. ✉ *59 rue St-Louis-en-l'Ile, 75004,* ☎ *01–43–26–13–35,* FAX *01–43–29–60–25. 17 rooms. AE, MC, V. Métro: Pont-Marie.*

$$ 🏨 **Place des Vosges.** A loyal, eclectic clientele swears by this small, historic Marais hotel on a delightful street just off place des Vosges. The Louis XIII–style reception area and rooms with oak-beamed ceilings and a mix of rustic finds from secondhand shops evoke the old Marais. ✉ *12 rue de Birague, 75004,* ☎ *01–42–72–60–46,* FAX *01–42–72–02–64. 16 rooms with bath. AE, DC, MC, V. Métro: Bastille.*

$$ 🏨 **St-Louis.** Louis XIII–style furniture and oil paintings set the tone in the public areas in this 17th-century town house on the romantic Ile St-Louis. Rooms are much simpler, but exposed beams and stone walls make them appealing. Breakfast is served in the atmospheric cellar. ✉ *75 rue St-Louis-en-l'Ile, 75004,* ☎ *01–46–34–04–80,* FAX *01–46–34–02–13. 21 rooms with bath. MC, V. Métro: Pont-Marie.*

$ 🏨 **Castex.** In a Revolution-era building in the Marais, this hotel is a bargain hunter's dream. Rooms are low on frills but squeaky clean, the owners are friendly, and the prices are rock-bottom, which ensures that the hotel is often booked months ahead by a largely young, American clientele. There's no elevator, and the only TV is on the ground floor. ✉ *5 rue Castex, 75004,* ☎ *01–42–72–31–52,* FAX *01–42–72–57–91. 27 rooms, 23 with shower. MC, V. Métro: Bastille.*

$ 🏨 **Grand Hôtel Jeanne-d'Arc.** If you're on a budget, you're sure to get your money's worth at this hotel near place des Vosges in the Marais. Though rooms are on the spartan side, they are clean, well-maintained, and fairly spacious. The staff is welcoming and friendly. ✉ *3 rue de Jarente, 75004,* ☎ *01–48–87–62–11,* FAX *01–48–87–37–31. 36 rooms with bath. MC, V. Métro: St-Paul.*

Left Bank

$$$$ 🏨 **Montalembert.** Whether appointed with traditional or contemporary furnishings, rooms at the Montalembert are all about simple lines and chic luxury. Ask about special packages if you're staying for more than three nights. ✉ *3 rue de Montalembert, 75007,* ☎ *01–45–49–68–68; 800/628–8929 in the U.S.,* FAX *01–45–49–69–49. 50 rooms, 6 suites. Restaurant, bar. AE, DC, MC, V. Métro: Rue du Bac.*

$$$$ 🏨 **Relais St-Germain.** The interior-designer owners of this hotel have
★ exquisite taste and a superb respect for tradition and detail. Moreover, rooms are at least twice the size of those at other area hotels. Much of the furniture was selected with a knowledgeable eye from the city's *brocantes* (secondhand dealers). Breakfast is included. ✉ *9 carrefour de l'Odéon, 75006,* ☎ *01–43–29–12–05,* FAX *01–46–33–45–30. 21 rooms, 1 suite. AE, DC, MC, V. Métro: Odéon.*

$$$–$$$$ 🏨 **Hôtel d'Aubusson.** Set in an historic house and now one of the finest
★   *petite hôtels de luxe* in the city, this place has original Aubusson
           tapestries, Versailles-style parquet floors, a chiseled stone fireplace, and
           restored antiques. Even the smallest rooms are a good size by Paris stan-
           dards. The 10 best rooms have canopied beds and ceiling beams. In
           summer, you can have your breakfast or predinner drink in the paved
           courtyard. ✉ *33 rue Dauphine, 75006,* ☎ *01–43–29–43–43,* 𝖥𝖠𝖷 *01–*
           43–29–12–62. 49 rooms with bath. AE, MC, V. Métro: Odéon.

$$$ 🏨 **Jardin du Luxembourg.** Blessed with a charming staff and a stylish
           look, this hotel is one of the most sought-after in the Latin Quarter.
           Rooms are a bit small (common for this neighborhood) but intelli-
           gently furnished to save space, and warmly decorated *à la provençale.*
           Ask for one with a balcony overlooking the street. ✉ *5 impasse*
           Royer-Collard, 75005, ☎ *01–40–46–08–88,* 𝖥𝖠𝖷 *01–40–46–02–28. 27*
           rooms. AE, DC, MC, V. Métro: Luxembourg.

$$–$$$ 🏨 **Le Tourville.** Here is a rare find: an intimate, upscale hotel at affordable
★   prices. Each room has crisp, virgin-white damask upholstery set against
           pastel or ocher walls, a smattering of antiques, original artwork, and
           fabulous old mirrors. ✉ *16 av. de Tourville, 75007,* ☎ *01–47–05–62–*
           62; 800/528–3549 in the U.S., 𝖥𝖠𝖷 *01–47–05–43–90. 27 rooms, 3 ju-*
           nior suites. Bar. AE, DC, MC, V. Métro: École Militaire.

$$ 🏨 **Bonaparte.** The congeniality of the staff only makes a stay in this in-
           timate place more of a treat. Old-fashioned upholsteries, 19th-century
           furnishings, and paintings create a quaint feel in the relatively spacious
           rooms. And the location in the heart of St-Germain is nothing short of
           fabulous. ✉ *61 rue Bonaparte, 75006,* ☎ *01–43–26–97–37,* 𝖥𝖠𝖷 *01–46–*
           33–57–67. 29 rooms with bath. MC, V. Métro: St-Germain-des-Prés.

$$ 🏨 **Hôtel de l'Université.** Staying at this hotel in a 17th-century town
           house between boulevard St-Germain and the Seine feels like going back
           in time. Guest rooms have English and French antiques and original
           fireplaces. Ask for one with a terrace on the fifth floor. ✉ *22 rue de*
           l'Université, 75007, ☎ *01–42–61–09–39,* 𝖥𝖠𝖷 *01–42–60–40–84. 27*
           rooms with bath. AE, MC, V. Métro: Rue-du-Bac.

$$ 🏨 **Latour Maubourg.** In the residential heart of the 7ᵉ arrondissement,
           a stone's throw from Les Invalides, this hotel is homey and unpreten-
           tious. With just 10 rooms, the accent is on intimacy and personalized
           service. ✉ *150 rue de Grenelle, 75007,* ☎ *01–47–05–16–16,* 𝖥𝖠𝖷 *01–*
           47–05–16–14. 9 rooms, 1 suite. MC, V. Métro: La Tour–Maubourg.

$–$$ 🏨 **Aramis–St-Germain.** Get great value for your money at this hotel,
           which, surprisingly, is part of the Best Western chain. It is understated
           yet classically French. Rooms have damask bedspreads and sturdy
           cherry-wood armoires. ✉ *124 rue de Rennes, 75006,* ☎ *01–45–48–*
           03–75; 800/528–1234 in the U.S., 𝖥𝖠𝖷 *01–45–44–99–29. 42 rooms. Bar.*
           AE, DC, MC, V. Métro: St-Placide.

$ 🏨 **Familia.** The hospitable Gaucheron family bends over backward for
           you. About half the rooms feature romantic sepia frescoes of celebrated
           Paris scenes; others have exquisite Louis XV–style furnishings or nice
           mahogany pieces. Book a month ahead for one with a walk-out bal-
           cony on the second or fifth floor. ✉ *11 rue des Écoles, 75005,* ☎ *01–*
           43–54–55–27, 𝖥𝖠𝖷 *01–43–29–61–77. 30 rooms, 16 with shower. AE,*
           MC, V. Métro: Cardinal-Lemoine.

$ 🏨 **Grandes Écoles.** This delightfully intimate hotel looks and feels like
           a country cottage dropped smack in the middle of the Latin Quarter.
           It is off the street and occupies three buildings on a beautiful, leafy
           garden, where breakfast is served in summer. Parquet floors, Louis-
           Philippe furnishings, lace bedspreads, and the absence of TV all add
           to the rustic ambience. ✉ *75 rue du Cardinal Lemoine, 75005,* ☎
           01–43–26–79–23, 𝖥𝖠𝖷 *01–43–25–28–15. 51 rooms with bath. MC, V.*
           Métro: Cardinal-Lemoine.

NIGHTLIFE AND THE ARTS

For detailed entertainment listings, look for the weekly magazines *Pariscope, L'Officiel des Spectacles, Zurban,* and *Figaroscope.* The **Paris Tourist Office**'s 24-hour English-language hot line (☎ 08–36–68–31–12) and Web site (WEB www.paris-touristoffice.com/index_va.html) are also good sources of information about weekly events.

Tickets can be purchased at the place of performance (beware of scalpers: counterfeit tickets have been sold); otherwise, try your hotel or a travel agency such as **Opéra Théâtre** (⊠ 7 rue de Clichy, 9ᵉ, ☎ 01–40–06–01–00, métro: Trinité). For most concerts, tickets can be bought at the music store **FNAC** (⊠ 1–5 rue Pierre Lescot, Forum des Halles, 1ᵉʳ, ☎ 01–49–87–50–50, métro: Châtelet–Les Halles). **Virgin Megastore** (⊠ 52 av. des Champs-Élysées, 8ᵉ, ☎ 08–03–02–30–24, métro: Franklin-D.-Roosevelt) has a particularly convenient ticket booth. Half-price tickets for same-day theater performances are available at the **Kiosques Théâtre** (⊠ across from 15 Pl. de la Madeleine, métro: Madeleine), and in front of the Gare Montparnasse (⊠ Pl. Raoul Dautry, 14ᵉ, métro: Montparnasse-Bienvenüe). Both are open Tuesday–Saturday 12:30–8, Sunday 12:30–4. Expect to pay a 16-fr/€2.44 commission per ticket and to wait in line.

The Arts

Classical Music and Opera

Inexpensive organ or chamber music concerts take place in many churches throughout the city. Following are other venues for opera, orchestral concerts and recitals. **Cité de la Musique** (⊠ in the Parc de La Villette, 221 av. Jean-Jaurès, 19ᵉ, ☎ 01–44–84–44–84, métro: Porte de Pantin) presents a varied program of classical, experimental, and world music concerts in a postmodern setting. **Opéra de la Bastille** (⊠ Pl. de la Bastille, 12ᵉ, ☎ 08–36–69–78–68, WEB www.opera-de-paris.fr, métro: Bastille) is the main venue for opera; however, grand opera deserves a grand house (not the modern Bastille one), so you might plan your trip around dates when the troupe presents an opera at the spectacular and historic Opéra Garnier, about twice a year. The Orchestre de Paris and other leading international orchestras play regularly at the **Salle Pleyel** (⊠ 252 rue du Faubourg-St-Honoré, 8ᵉ, ☎ 08–25–00–02–52, métro: Ternes). **Théâtre des Champs-Élysées** (⊠ 15 av. Montaigne, 8ᵉ, ☎ 01–49–52–50–50, métro: Alma-Marceau) is worth seeing just for its elegantly restored, plush art deco decor.

Dance

Opéra Garnier (⊠ Pl. de l'Opéra, 9ᵉ, ☎ 08–36–69–78–68, WEB www.opera-de-paris.fr, métro: Opéra), the "old Opéra," now concentrates on dance: in addition to being the home of the well-reputed Paris Ballet, it also bills a number of major foreign troupes. The **Théâtre de la Ville** (⊠ 2 pl. du Châtelet, 4ᵉ, métro: Châtelet; ⊠ 31 rue des Abbesses, 18ᵉ, métro: Abbesses, ☎ 01–42–74–22–77 for both) is the place for contemporary dance.

Film

Paris has hundreds of cinemas. Admission is generally 40 frs/€6–55 frs/€8.4, with reduced rates at some theaters on Monday. In principal tourist areas such as the Champs-Élysées and Les Halles, and on the boulevard des Italiens near the Opéra, theaters show English films marked *"version originale"* (v.o., i.e., not dubbed). Classics and independent films often play in Latin Quarter theaters. **Cinémathèque Française** (⊠ 42 bd. de Bonne-Nouvelle, 10ᵉ, ☎ 01–56–26–01–01, métro: Bonne-Nouvelle; ⊠ Palais de Chaillot, 7 av. Albert de Mun, ☎ 01–56–26–

01–01, métro: Trocadéro) shows classic French and international films Wednesday–Sunday.

Theater

There is no Parisian equivalent to Broadway or the West End, although a number of theaters line the Grands Boulevards between the Opéra and République. Shows are mostly in French. The **Comédie Française** (⊠ Pl. Colette, 1ᵉʳ, ☎ 01–44–58–15–15, métro: Palais-Royal) performs distinguished classical drama by the likes of Racine, Molière, and Corneille. The **Théâtre de la Huchette** (⊠ 23 rue de la Huchette, 5ᵉ, ☎ 01–43–26–38–99, métro: St-Michel) is a tiny venue where Ionesco's short plays make a deliberately ridiculous mess of the French language. The **Théâtre de l'Odéon** (⊠ Pl. de l'Odéon, 6ᵉ, ☎ 01–44–41–36–36, métro Odéon) has made pan-European theater its primary focus.

Nightlife

Bars and Clubs

The hottest area at the moment is around Ménilmontant and Parmentier, and the nightlife is still hopping in and around the Bastille. The Left Bank tends to be more subdued. The Champs-Élysées is making a strong comeback, though the crowd remains predominantly foreign. Gay and lesbian bars are mostly concentrated in the Marais (especially around rue Ste-Croix-de-la-Bretonnerie) and include some of the most happening addresses in the city.

If you want to dance the night away, some of the best clubs are the following: **Les Bains** (⊠ 7 rue du Bourg-l'Abbé, 3ᵉ, ☎ 01–48–87–01–80, métro: Étienne-Marcel) opened in 1978 and back in the disco era was often featured in French *Vogue*—believe it or not, this is still a hot ticket and difficult to get past the velvet rope. **Le Gibus** (⊠ 18 rue du Faubourg du Temple, 11ᵉ, ☎ 01–47–00–78–88, métro: République) hosts big concerts in its theater, but its cellars are *the* place for trance, techno and jungle. **Queen** (⊠ 102 av. des Champs-Élysées, 8ᵉ, ☎ 01–53–89–08–90, métro: George-V) is one of the most talked-about nightclubs in Paris: everyone lines up to get in. Monday is disco night.

Paris has many bars; following is a sampling: **Amnésia Café** (⊠ 42 rue Vieille-du-Temple, 4ᵉ, ☎ 01–42–72–16–94, métro: St-Paul) attracts a young, professional gay and lesbian crowd. **Barramundi** (⊠ 3 rue Taitbout, 9ᵉ, ☎ 01–47–70–21–21, métro: Richelieu-Drouot) is one of Paris's hubs of nouveau-riche chic; the lighting is dim, the copper bar long. **Buddha Bar** (⊠ 8 rue Boissy d'Anglas, 8ᵉ, ☎ 01–53–05–90–00, métro: Concorde) offers one of the most glittery settings in Paris—a bar overlooks the main restaurant, with its towering gold-painted Buddha contemplating enough Dragon Empress chinoiserie for five MGM movies. **Café Charbon** (⊠ 109 rue Oberkampf, 11ᵉ, ☎ 01–43–57–55–13, métro: St-Maur/Parmentier) is set in a beautifully restored 19th-century café. **Le Fumoir** (⊠ 6 rue Amiral de Coligny, 1ᵉʳ, ☎ 01–42–92–00–24, métro: Louvre) is a fashionable spot for cocktails, with comfy leather sofas and a library. **Polo Room** (⊠ 3 rue Lord Byron, 8ᵉ, ☎ 01–40–74–07–78, métro: George-V) is the very first Martini bar in Paris; there are polo photos on the walls, regular live jazz concerts, and DJs every Friday and Saturday night. **Wax** (⊠ 15 rue Daval, 11ᵉ, ☎ 01–40–21–16–16, métro: Bastille) is worth a trip simply for its decor—orange and pink walls, multicolored squiggles on the columns, and moulded plastic banquettes by the window; this is one of the most happening places in the city music-wise, with DJs spinning techno and house every evening.

Cabarets

Paris's cabarets are household names, shunned by Parisians and beloved of foreign tourists, who flock to the shows. Prices range from 200 frs (simple admission plus one drink) to more than 800 frs (dinner plus show). **Crazy Horse** (⊠ 12 av. George-V, 8ᵉ, ☎ 01–47–23–32–32, métro: Alma-Marceau) shows more bare skin than anyone else. **Lido** (⊠ 116 bis av. des Champs-Élysées, 8ᵉ, ☎ 01–40–76–56–10, métro: George-V) shows are oceans of feathers and sequins. **Moulin Rouge** (⊠ 82 bd. de Clichy, 18ᵉ, ☎ 01–53–09–82–82, métro: Blanche) has come a long way since the days of the cancan.

Jazz Clubs

Paris is one of the great jazz cities of the world. For nightly schedules consult the magazines *Jazz Hot, Jazzman,* or *Jazz Magazine.* Nothing gets going till 10 or 11 PM, and entry prices vary widely from about 40 frs to more than 100 frs. **New Morning** (⊠ 7 rue des Petites-Écuries, 10ᵉ, ☎ 01–45–23–51–41, métro: Château-d'Eau) is a premier spot for serious fans of avant-garde jazz, folk, and world music. The greatest names in French and international jazz play at **Le Petit Journal** (⊠ 71 bd. St-Michel, 5ᵉ, ☎ 01–43–26–28–59, RER: Luxembourg); it's closed Sunday. **Le Petit Opportun** (⊠ 15 rue des Lavandières–Ste-Opportune, 1ᵉʳ, ☎ 01–42–36–01–36, métro: Châtelet), in a converted bistro, often has top-flight American soloists with French backup.

Rock Clubs

Lists of upcoming concerts are posted on boards in the FNAC stores. Following are the best places to catch big French and international stars: **L'Olympia** (⊠ 28 bd. des Capucines, 9ᵉ, ☎ 01–47–42–25–49, métro: Opéra) once hosted legendary concerts by Jacques Brel and Edith Piaf, but the theater has since been completely rebuilt. **Palais Omnisports de Paris-Bercy** (⊠ 8 bd. de Bercy, 12ᵉ, ☎ 08–25–03–00–31, métro: Bercy) is the largest venue in Paris and is where English and American pop stars perform. **L'Élysée Montmartre** (⊠ 72 bd. Rochechouart, 18ᵉ, ☎ 01–55–07–06–00, métro: Anvers) dates from Gustave Eiffel, its builder, who, it is hoped, liked a good concert; emerging French and international rock groups appear here.

SHOPPING

Boutiques

Only Milan can compete with Paris for the title of Capital of European Chic. The top designer shops are found on **avenue Montaigne, rue du Faubourg-St-Honoré,** and **place des Victoires.** The area around **St-Germain-des-Prés** on the Left Bank is a mecca for small specialty shops and boutiques and has recently seen an influx of the elite names in haute couture. The top names in jewelry are grouped around the **place Vendôme,** and scores of trendy boutiques can be found around **Les Halles.** Between the pre-Revolution mansions and tiny kosher food stores that characterize the **Marais** are numerous gift shops and clothing stores. Search for bargains on the streets around the foot of Montmartre, or in the designer discount shops (Cacharel, Rykiel, Chevignon) along **rue d'Alésia** in Montparnasse.

Department Stores

Au Bon Marché (⊠ 24 rue de Sèvres, 7ᵉ, métro: Sèvres-Babylone). **Au Printemps** (⊠ 64 bd. Haussmann, 9ᵉ, métro: Havre-Caumartin). **Galeries Lafayette** (⊠ 40 bd. Haussmann, 9ᵉ, métro: Chaussée-d'Antin). **La Samaritaine** (⊠ 19 rue de la Monnaie, 1ᵉʳ, métro: Pont-Neuf).

Marks & Spencer (⊠ 35 bd. Haussmann, 9ᵉ, ☎ 01–47–42–42–91, métro: Havre-Caumartin, Auber, or Opéra).

Food and Flea Markets

Every *quartier* (neighborhood) has at least one open-air food market. Some of the best are on rue de Buci, rue Mouffetard, rue Montorgueuil, rue Mouffetard, and rue Lepic. Sunday morning till 1 PM is usually a good time to go; they are likely to be closed Monday.

The **Marché aux Puces de St-Ouen** (métro Porte de Clignancourt), just north of Paris, is one of Europe's largest flea markets; it's open Saturday–Monday. Best bargains are to be had early in the morning. Smaller flea markets also take place at **Porte de Vanves** and **Porte de Montreuil** (weekends only).

Gifts

Old prints are sold by ***bouquinistes*** (secondhand booksellers) in stalls along the banks of the Seine. **Les Caves Augé** (⊠ 116 bd. Haussmann, 8ᵉ, métro: St-Augustin) is one of the best wine shops in Paris. **Fauchon** (⊠ 30 pl. de la Madeleine, 8ᵉ, métro: Madeleine) is perhaps the world's most famous gourmet food shop. **Hédiard** (⊠ 21 pl. de la Madeleine, 8ᵉ, métro: Madeleine) is a foodie mecca with a seductive array of comestibles. **Guerlain** (⊠ 47 rue Bonaparte, 6ᵉ, métro: Mabillon) carries legendary French perfumes. The **Maison du Chocolat** (⊠ 56 rue Pierre-Charron, 8ᵉ, ☎ 01–47–23–38–25, métro: Franklin-D.-Roosevelt; ⊠ 8 bd. de la Madeleine, 9ᵉ, ☎ 01–47–42–86–52, métro: Madeleine; ⊠ 225 rue du Faubourg St-Honoré, 8ᵉ, ☎ 01–42–27–39–44, métro: Ternes) is the place for chocolate. The **Musée des Arts Décoratifs** (⊠ 107 rue de Rivoli, 1ᵉʳ, métro: Palais-Royal) has super chic home decorations.

PARIS A TO Z

To research prices, get advice from other travelers, and book travel arrangements, visit www.fodors.com.

AIRPORTS AND TRANSFERS

International flights arrive at either Charles de Gaulle Airport (known as Roissy to the French), 24 km (15 mi) northeast of Paris, or at Orly Airport, 16 km (10 mi) south of the city. Both airports have two terminals.

TRANSFERS

Both airports have train stations from which you can take the RER, the local commuter train, to Paris. The advantages of this are speed, price (49 frs/€7.50 to Paris from Roissy, 57 frs/€8.70 from Orly via the shuttle-train Orlyval with a change to the RER at Antony), and the RER's direct link with the métro system. The disadvantage is having to lug your bags around. Taxi fares between the airports and Paris are about 160 frs/€24.42 (Orly) and 230 frs/€35.11 (Roissy), with a 6-fr/€.92 surcharge per bag. The Paris Airports Service takes you by eight-passenger van to your destination in Paris from Roissy: 140 frs/€21.50 (one person) or 170 frs/€26 (two); Orly: 110 frs/€16.90 (one), 130 frs/€20 (two), less for groups. You need to book at least two days in advance (there are English-speaking clerks).

From Roissy, Air France Buses (open to all) leave every 15 minutes from 5:40 AM to 11 PM. The fare is 60 frs/€9.20 and the trip takes from 40 minutes to 1½ hours during rush hour. You arrive at the Arc de Triomphe or Porte Maillot, on the Right Bank by the Hôtel Concorde-Lafayette. From Orly, buses operated by Air France leave every 12 minutes from 6 AM to 11 PM and arrive at the Air France terminal near Les Invalides on the Left Bank. The fare is 45 frs/€6.90, and the trip takes between 30 and 60 minutes, depending on traffic. Alternatively, the Roissybus, operated by Paris Transport Authority (RATP), runs directly to and from rue Scribe, by the Opéra, every 15 minutes and costs 48 frs/€7.32. RATP also runs the Orlybus to and from Denfert-Rochereau and Orly every 15 minutes for 35 frs/€5.34; the trip takes around 35 minutes.

➤ TAXIS AND SHUTTLES: **Paris Airports Service** (☏ 01–49–62–78–78, FAX 01–49–62–78–79).

BUS TRAVEL TO AND FROM PARIS
Because of the excellent train service, long-distance buses are rare; they're found mainly where train service is scarce. Bus tours are organized by SNCF. Long-distance routes to many European cities are covered by Eurolines.

➤ BUS INFORMATION: **Eurolines** (✉ 28 av. Général-de-Gaulle, 93170 Bagnolet, ☏ 01–49–72–51–51, métro: Galliéni).

BUS TRAVEL WITHIN PARIS
Most buses run from around 6 AM to 8:30 PM; some continue until midnight. Routes are posted on the sides of buses. *Noctambus* (night buses) operate from 1 AM to 6 AM between Châtelet and nearby suburbs. They can be stopped by hailing them at any point on their route. You can use your métro tickets on the buses, or you can buy a one-ride ticket on board. You need to show weekly/monthly/special tickets to the driver; if you have individual tickets, state your destination and be prepared to punch one or more tickets in the red and gray machines on board the bus.

CAR TRAVEL
Expressways converge on the capital from every direction: A1 from the north (225 km/140 mi to Lille); A13 from Normandy (225 km/140 mi to Caen); A4 from the east (500 km/310 mi to Strasbourg); A10 from the southwest (580 km/360 mi to Bordeaux); and A7 from the Alps and Côte d'Azur (465 km/290 mi to Lyon). Each connects with the *périphérique*, the beltway, around Paris. Exits are named by *porte* (gateway), not numbered. The "Périphe" can be fast—but gets very busy; try to avoid it between 7:30 and 10 AM and between 4:30 and 7:30 PM.

EMERGENCIES
Automatic phone booths can be found at various main crossroads for use in police emergencies (Police-Secours) or for medical help (Services Médicaux).

➤ DOCTORS AND DENTISTS: **Dentist** (☏ 01–43–37–51–00), open 24 hrs. **Doctor** (☏ 01–47–07–77–77).

➤ EMERGENCY SERVICES: **Ambulance** (☏ 15 for emergencies; 01–45–67–50–50). **Police** (☏ 17).

➤ HOSPITALS: **American Hospital** (✉ 63 bd. Victor-Hugo, Neuilly, ☏ 01–46–41–25–25). **British Hospital** (✉ 3 rue Barbès, Levallois-Perret, ☏ 01–47–58–13–12).

➤ 24-HOUR PHARMACIES: **Pharmacie Dérhy** (✉ 84 av. des Champs-Élysées, ☏ 01–45–62–02–41), open 24 hrs. **Pharmacie Première** (✉ 204 bd. de Sébastopol, 4ᵉ, ☏ 01–48–87–62–30), open until 2 AM.

ENGLISH-LANGUAGE MEDIA
Most newsstands in central Paris sell *Time, Newsweek,* and the *International Herald Tribune,* as well as the English dailies. Some English-language bookstores include the ones listed below.

➤ BOOKSTORES: **Brentano's** (✉ 37 av. de l'Opéra). **Galignani** (✉ 224 rue de Rivoli). **Shakespeare & Co.** (✉ 37 rue de la Bûcherie). **W. H. Smith** (✉ 248 rue de Rivoli).

MÉTRO TRAVEL

Fourteen métro lines crisscross Paris and the nearby suburbs, and you are seldom more than a five-minute walk from the nearest station. It's essential to know the name of the last station on the line you take, since this name appears on all signs within the system. A connection (you can make as many as you please on one ticket) is called a *correspondance*. At junction stations illuminated orange signs bearing the names of each line terminus appear over the corridors that lead to the various correspondences.

The métro connects at several points in Paris with RER trains that race across Paris from suburb to suburb: RER trains are a sort of supersonic métro and can be great time-savers. All métro tickets and passes are valid for RER and bus travel within Paris.

Some lines and stations in the seedier parts of Paris are a bit risky at night—in particular, Line 2 (Porte-Dauphine–Nation) and the northern section of Line 13 from St-Lazare to St-Denis/Asnières. The long, bleak corridors at Jaurès and Stalingrad are a haven for pickpockets and purse snatchers. But the Paris métro is relatively safe, as long as you don't walk around with your wallet in your back pocket or travel alone (especially women) late at night.

Access to métro and RER platforms is through an automatic ticket barrier. Slide your ticket in flat and pick it up as it pops up farther along. Keep your ticket; you'll need it again to leave the RER system. Sometimes green-clad métro authorities will ask to see it when you enter or leave the station: be prepared—they aren't very friendly, and they will impose a large fine if you can't produce your ticket.

FARES AND SCHEDULES

The métro runs from 5:30 AM to 1:15 AM. Métro tickets cost 8 frs/€1.22 each, though a *carnet* (10 tickets for 58 frs/€8.90) is a far better value. If you're staying for a week or more, the best deal is the *coupon jaune* (weekly) or *carte orange* (monthly) ticket, sold according to zone. Zones 1 and 2 cover the entire métro network (85 frs/€13 per week or 285 frs/€43.51 per month). If you plan to take a suburban train to visit monuments in the Ile-de-France, you should consider a four-zone ticket (Versailles, St-Germain-en-Laye; 142 frs/€21.67 per week) or a six-zone ticket (Rambouillet, Fontainebleau; 194 frs/€29.61 per week). For these weekly or monthly tickets, you need a pass (available from train and major métro stations), and you must provide a passport-size photograph.

Alternatively, there are one-day (*Mobilis*) and two-, three-, and five-day (*Paris Visite*) unlimited travel tickets for the métro, bus, and RER. Unlike the coupon jaune, which is good from Monday morning to Sunday evening, the latter are valid starting any day of the week and give you admission discounts to a number of museums and tourist attractions. Prices are 32, 90, 120, and 175 frs (4.90, 13.80, 18.40, €26.90) for Paris only; 94, 175, 245, and 300 frs (14.40, 26.90, 37.60, €46) for the suburbs, including Versailles, St-Germain-en-Laye, and Disneyland Paris.

TAXIS

Taxis in Paris aren't a standard vehicle type or color. Daytime rates (7 to 7) within Paris are about 3.50 frs/€.53 per km (½ mi), and night-time rates are around 5.80 frs/€.89, plus a basic charge of 13 frs/€2. Rates outside the city limits are about 30% higher. Ask your hotel or restaurant to call for a taxi, since cruising cabs can be hard to find. There are numerous taxi stands, but you have to know where to look. Taxis seldom take more than three people at a time.

TOURS

BICYCLE TOURS

Paris à Vélo organizes three-hour cycling tours around Paris and rents bikes for 80 frs a day.

➤ FEES AND SCHEDULES: **Paris à Vélo** (✉ 37 bd. Bourdon, 4ᵉ, ☎ 01–48–87–60–01).

BOAT TOURS

Boat rides along the Seine are a must if it's your first time in Paris. The price for a 60-minute trip is 45–50 frs (€6.87–7.63). Boats depart in season every half hour from 10:30 to 5 (less frequently in winter). The *Bateaux Mouches* leave from the Pont de l'Alma, at the bottom of avenue George-V. The *Bateaux Parisiens* leave from the Pont d'Iéna, by the Eiffel Tower. The *Vedettes du Pont-Neuf* set off from beneath square du Vert-Galant on the western edge of the Ile de la Cité.

BUS TOURS

Bus tours of Paris provide a good introduction to the city. Tours usually start from the tour company's office and are generally given in double-decker buses with either a live guide or tape-recorded commentary. They last two to three hours and cost about 150 frs/€23. Tour operators also have a variety of theme tours (historic Paris, modern Paris, Paris by night) that last from 2½ hours to all day and cost up to 390 frs/€60, as well as excursions to Chartres, Versailles, Fontainebleau, the Loire Valley, and Mont-St-Michel (for a cost of 195–970 frs, or €30–149). Cityrama is one of the largest bus operators in Paris; it also runs minibus excursions that pick you up and drop you off at your hotel. Paris Vision is another large bus tour operator.

➤ FEES AND SCHEDULES: **Cityrama** (✉ 4 pl. des Pyramides, 1ᵉʳ, ☎ 01–44–55–60–00). **Paris Vision** (✉ 214 rue de Rivoli, 1ᵉʳ, ☎ 08–00–03–02–14).

PRIVATE GUIDES

Tours of Paris or the surrounding areas by limousine or minibus for up to seven passengers for a minimum of three hours can be organized. The cost starts at about 300 frs/€46 per hour. Contact Paris Major Limousines, Paris Bus, or Cityscope.

➤ CONTACTS: **Cityscope** (✉ 11 bis bd. Haussmann, 9ᵉ, ☎ 01–53–34–11–91). **Paris Bus** (✉ 22 rue de la Prévoyance, Vincennes, ☎ 01–43–65–55–55). **Paris Major Limousines** (✉ 14 rue Atlas, 19ᵉ, ☎ 01–44–52–50–00).

WALKING TOURS

Numerous special-interest tours concentrate on historical or architectural topics. Most are in French and cost between 40 and 60 frs (€6 and €9.2). Details are published in the weekly magazines *Pariscope* and *L'Officiel des Spectacles* under the heading "Conférences."

TRAIN TRAVEL

Paris has five international stations: Gare du Nord (for northern France, northern Europe, and England via Calais or the Channel Tunnel); Gare de l'Est (for Strasbourg, Luxembourg, Basel, and central Europe); Gare de Lyon (for Lyon, Marseille, the Côte d'Azur, Geneva, and Italy); Gare d'Austerlitz (for the southwest France and Spain); and Gare St-Lazare (for Normandy and England via Dieppe). The Gare Montparnasse serves western France (Nantes, Rennes, and Brittany) and is the terminal for the TGV Atlantic service from Paris to Tours, Poitiers, and Bordeaux. Call SNCF for information. You can reserve tickets at any Paris station regardless of the destination. Go to the Grandes Lignes counter for travel within France or to the Billets Internationaux desk if you're heading out of France.

➤ TRAIN INFORMATION: **SNCF** (☎ 08–36–35–35–35, 🌐 www.sncf.com).

TRANSPORTATION AROUND PARIS

Paris is relatively small as capital cities go, and most of its prize monuments and museums are within walking distance of one another. A river cruise is a pleasant way to get an overview. The most convenient form of public transportation is the métro; buses are a slower alternative, though they do allow you to see more of the city. Taxis are not that expensive but are not always so easy to find. Car travel within Paris is best avoided because finding parking is difficult and there is often a lot of traffic.

TRAVEL AGENCIES

➤ LOCAL AGENTS: **American Express** (✉ 11 rue Scribe, 9ᵉ, ☎ 01–47–77–77–07). **Wagons-Lits** (✉ 32 rue du Quatre-Septembre, 2ᵉ, ☎ 01–42–66–15–80).

VISITOR INFORMATION

The Paris Tourist Office is open daily 9–8. It has branches at all mainline train stations except Gare St-Lazare.

➤ TOURIST INFORMATION: **Paris Tourist Office** (✉ 127 av. des Champs-Élysées, ☎ 01–49–52–53–54; 01–49–52–53–56 for recorded information in English, 🌐 www.paris-touristoffice.com).

France Basics

BUSINESS HOURS

BANKS AND OFFICES

Banks are open weekdays 9:30–5, with variations; most close for at least an hour at lunch.

MUSEUMS AND SIGHTS

Museums are closed one day a week (often Monday or Tuesday) and on national holidays. Usual hours are from 9 or 10 to 5 or 6. Many museums close for lunch (noon–2); on Sunday many are open afternoons only.

SHOPS

Shops in big towns are open from 9 or 9:30 to 7 or 8 without a lunch break; though it's still rare, an increasing number are now open on Sunday. Smaller shops often open earlier and close later but take a lengthy lunch break (12:30–3 or 4). This siesta-type schedule is more typical in the south of France. Corner grocery stores frequently stay open until around 10 PM.

CUSTOMS AND DUTIES

For details on imports and duty-free limits, *see* Customs and Duties *in* Smart Travel Tips A to Z.

EMBASSIES

➤ AUSTRALIA: (✉ 4 rue Jean-Rey, 15ᵉ, ☎ 01–40–59–33–00, métro: Bir-Hakeim).

➤ CANADA: (✉ 35 av. Montaigne, 8ᵉ, ☎ 01–44–43–29–00, métro: Franklin-D.-Roosevelt).

➤ NEW ZEALAND: (✉ 7 ter rue Léonardo-da-Vinci, 16ᵉ, ☎ 01–45–00–24–11, métro: Victor-Hugo).

➤ UNITED KINGDOM: **United Kingdom** (✉ 35 rue du Faubourg–St-Honoré, 8ᵉ, ☎ 01–44–51–31–00, métro: Concorde).
➤ UNITED STATES: **United States** (✉ 2 av. Gabriel, 8ᵉ, ☎ 01–43–12–22–22, métro: Concorde).

HOLIDAYS

January 1; Easter Monday (usually late March or early April); May 1 (Labor Day); May 8 (VE Day); Ascension (usually early May); Pentecost Monday (usually mid-May); July 14 (Bastille Day); August 15 (Assumption); November 1 (All Saints' Day); November 11 (Armistice); December 25.

LANGUAGE

The French study English for a minimum of four years at school and, although few are fluent, their English is probably better than the French of most Americans. English is widely understood in major tourist areas, and in most hotels there is likely to be at least one person who can converse with you. Even if your own French is rusty, try to master a few words: people will greatly appreciate your efforts.

MONEY MATTERS

There's no way around it: Paris is expensive. But many travel basics—hotels, restaurants, plane, and train tickets—can be made more affordable by planning ahead, taking advantage of prix-fixe menus, and staying in smaller, family-run places. Prices are highest in Paris and on the Côte d'Azur, though even in these areas you can find reasonable accommodations and food.

Prices vary greatly depending on the region, proximity to tourist sights, and—believe it or not—whether you're sitting down (and where—inside or on the terrace) or standing up in a café! Here are a few samples: cup of coffee, 6–12 frs/€.92–1.84; glass of beer, 10–25 frs/€1.53–3.84; soft drink, 10–20 frs/€1.53–3; ham sandwich, 15–25 frs/€2.30–3.84; 1½-km (1-mi) taxi ride, 35 frs/€5.38.

CURRENCY

January 1, 2002, sees the French franc replaced by the new European Union (EU) currency, the euro, worth precisely 6.55957 francs. Coins and notes in French francs (subdivided into 100 centimes) will be gradually withdrawn from circulation over the first few months of 2002. International credit cards and traveler's checks are widely accepted throughout France, except in some rural areas.

In France, the long-awaited physical debut of the much touted euro will begin in a rather confusing manner; all banks, businesses, and money machines will be stocked in euros as of January 1, but French francs will *also* be valid until midnight February 17, a six-week period when you can still buy that newspaper with francs but receive your change in euros. Your best bet is to change your remaining francs into euros the minute you arrive in France, and for once it doesn't really matter where because the rate between the franc and the euro was irrevocably fixed in late 1999 (1 euro = 6.55957 frs), thus eliminating any fluctuations in the market and any need for commission. If anyone tries to charge you a commission when you are changing French francs into euros, stop the transaction immediately.

However, there is a big difference between exchanging old francs (set rate, with no commissions, and no worries) and exchanging dollars (competition, plus fluctuation and diverse commissions), or, in fact, any other non-European Union currencies, such as Japanese yen and British pounds. For these monies, which still fluctuate in value against the euro, you still need to follow the old guidelines, such as shopping around for the best exchange rates and checking the rates before leaving home. At press time (summer 2001), the U.S. dollar bought 7.1 francs, the Canadian dollar 4.7 francs, the pound sterling 10.4 francs, the Irish punt 8.3 francs, the Australian dollar 3.9 francs, the New Zealand dollar 3.1 francs, and the South African rand 0.9 francs. The U.S. dollar brought €1.11, the Canadian dollar €.71, the Irish punt €1.26, the Australian dollar €.57, the New Zealand dollar €.45, and the South American rand €.13.

TELEPHONES
French phone numbers have 10 digits. All phone numbers have a two-digit prefix determined by zone: Paris and the Ile-de-France, 01; the northwest, 02; the northeast, 03; the southeast, 04; and the southwest, 05.

COUNTRY AND AREA CODES
The country code for France is 33 and for Monaco 377. To call France from the United States, dial 011 (for all international calls), then dial 33 (the country code), and the number in France, minus any initial 0. To dial France from the United Kingdom, dial 00–33, then the number in France, minus any initial 0.

INTERNATIONAL CALLS
To call a foreign country from France, dial 00 and wait for the tone, then dial the country code, area code, and number. You can also contact your long distance carrier directly and charge your call to your calling card or make a collect call.
➤ ACCESS CODES: **AT&T** (☎ 08–00–99–00–11). **MCI** (☎ 08–00–99–00–19). **Sprint** (☎ 08–00–99–00–87).

LOCAL CALLS
To make calls within a region or to another region in France, simply dial the full, 10-digit number. A local call in France costs 60 centimes for the first minute and 22 centimes for every minute after that; cheaper rates apply between 7 PM and 8 AM and between noon Saturday and 8 AM Monday. Dial ☎ 12 for local operators.

PUBLIC PHONES
Telephone booths can almost always be found at post offices, cafés, and métro stations. Some French pay phones take 1-, 2-, and 5-fr coins (1-fr minimum), but most phones are now operated by *télécartes* (phone cards), sold in post offices, métro stations, and cafés with red TABAC signs by unit (cost: 48.60 frs/€7 for 50 units, 96.70 frs/€14.87 for 120 units).

VISAS
A valid passport is required for citizens of the United States, Canada, New Zealand, and Australia, but no visa for visits to France of less than three months. A valid passport is all that is required for British nationals.

13 PRAGUE

Poets, philosophers, and the Czech-in-the-street have long sung the praises of Praha (Prague), also referred to as the Golden City of a Hundred Spires. Like Rome, Prague is built on seven hills, which slope gently or tilt precipitously down to the Vltava (Moldau) River. The riverside location, enhanced by a series of graceful bridges, makes a great setting for two of the city's most notable features: its extravagant, fairy-tale architecture and its memorable music. Mozart claimed that no one understood him better than the citizens of Prague, and he was only one of several great masters who lived or lingered here.

It was under Karel IV (Chárles IV), in the 14th century, that Prague first became the seat of the Holy Roman Empire—virtually the capital of Western Europe—and acquired its distinctive Gothic imprint. The medieval inheritance is still here under the overlays of graceful Renaissance and exuberant Baroque. Prague escaped serious wartime damage, but it didn't escape neglect. During the 1990s, however, artisans and their workers have restored dozens of the city's historic buildings with care and sensitivity.

EXPLORING PRAGUE

Numbers in the margin correspond to points of interest on the Prague map.

Shades of the five medieval towns that combined to form Prague linger in the divisions of its historic districts. On the flat eastern shore of the Vltava River are three areas arranged like nesting boxes: **Josefov** (the old Jewish Quarter) within **Staré Město** (Old Town) bordered by **Nové Město** (New Town). **Malá Strana** (Lesser Quarter) and **Hradčany** (Castle District) perch along the river's hillier west bank. Spanning the Vltava is **Karlův most** (Charles Bridge), which links the Old Town to the

Lesser Quarter; everything within the historic center can be reached on foot in a half hour or less from here.

Nové Město and Staré Město (New Town and Old Town)

New Town is over 500 years old, and only new when compared to Old Town, which dates back to the 12th century. Both neighborhoods have a mix of Renaissance, Baroque, and modern architecture. Old Town has the slight advantage in historic sites, with its world famous Astronomical Clock Tower and Old Town Square. New Town, with its store-packed Wenceslas Square and multiple department stores, has the lead in shopping. Almost every street in this area has a building or monument worth checking out.

⓫ **Betlémská kaple** (Bethlehem Chapel). The martyr and national hero Jan Hus thundered his reform teachings from the chapel pulpit during the early 15th century. The structure was rebuilt in the 1950s, but the little door through which Hus came to the pulpit is original, as are some of the inscriptions on the wall. ⊠ *Betlémské nám.* ⊘ *Apr.–Sept., daily 9–6; Oct.–Mar., daily 9–5.*

❸ **Celetná ulice.** Medieval kings took this street on their way to their coronation at Prague Castle. The **Royal Route** continues past the Gothic spires of the Týn Church in Old Town Square; it then crosses Charles Bridge and goes up to the castle. Along the route stands every variety of Romanesque, Gothic, Renaissance, and Baroque architecture.

❿ **Clam-Gallas palác** (Clam-Gallas Palace). Squatting on a constricted site in the heart of the Old Town, this pompous Baroque palace was designed by the great Viennese architect J. B. Fischer von Erlach. All the sculptures, including the titans that struggle to support the two doorways, are the work of one of the great Bohemian Baroque artists, Matthias Braun. Peek inside at the superb staircase or attend an evening concert. ⊠ *Husova 20,* WEB *www.ahmp.cz.*

❹ **Dům U černé Matky Boží** (House of the Black Madonna). This Cubist building adds a jolt to the architectural styles along Celetná ulice. In the second decade of the 20th century, several leading Czech architects boldly applied Cubism's radical reworking of visual space to structures. The Black Madonna, designed by Josef Gočár, is unflinchingly modern yet topped with an almost Baroque tile roof. ⊠ *Celetná ul. (at Ovocný trh),* ☎ *2421–1732,* WEB *www.ecn.cz/cmvu/DCMB_a.htm.* ⊘ *Tues.–Sun. 10–6.*

❻ **Expozice Franze Kafky** (Franz Kafka's Birthplace). A museum in the house displays photos, editions of Kafka's books, and other memorabilia from the author's life. The corner that the building stands on was renamed in his honor in 2000. (Kafka's grave lies in the New Jewish Cemetery at the Želivského Metro stop.) ⊠ *Nám. Franze Kafky 5.* ⊘ *Tues.–Fri. 10–6, Sat. 10–5.*

❷ **Na Příkopě.** Once part of the moat surrounding the Old Town, this street is now an elegant (in places) pedestrian mall. It leads from the bottom of Wenceslas Square to the **Obecní dům** (Municipal House), Prague's most lavish Art Nouveau building, which reopened in 1997 after a controversial two-year refurbishment. A bridge links it to the **Prašná brána** (Powder Tower), a 19th-century neo-Gothic restoration of the medieval original. ⊠ *Nám. Republiky.*

★ ❺ **Staroměstské náměstí** (Old Town Square). The commercial center of the Old Town is now a remarkably harmonious hub—architecturally beautiful and relatively car-free and quiet. Looming over the center, the twin towers of **Kostel Panny Marie před Týnem** (Church of the Virgin

Mary before Týn) look forbidding despite Disneyesque lighting. The large Secession-style **sculptural group** in the square's center commemorates the martyr Jan Hus, whose followers completed the Týn Church during the 15th century. The white Baroque **Kostel svatého Mikuláše** (Church of St. Nicholas) is tucked into the square's northwest angle. It was built by Kilian Ignatz Dientzenhofer, co-architect also of the Lesser Quarter's church of the same name. Every hour, mobs converge on the Astronomical Clock Tower of the **Staroměstská radnice** (Old Town Hall) as the clock's 15th-century mechanism activates a procession that includes the 12 Apostles. A skeleton figure of Death tolls the bell. ⊠ *Pařížská, Dlouhá, Celetná, Železná, Melantrichova, and Kaprova.*

❽ Staronová synagóga (Old-New Synagogue). A small congregation still attends the little Gothic Old-New Synagogue, one of Europe's oldest surviving houses of Jewish prayer. Men are required to cover their heads upon entering; skull caps are sold for a small fee at the door. ⊠ *Červená 3 at Pařížská,* ☎ *02/2481– 0099,* WEB *www.jewishmuseum.cz.* ☉ *Sun.–Thurs. 9–5, Fri. 9–2.*

★ ❾ Starý židovský hřbitov (Old Jewish Cemetery). The crowded cemetery is part of **Josefov**, the former Jewish quarter, and is one of Europe's most unforgettable sights. Here, ancient tombstones lean into one another; below them, piled layer upon layer, are thousands of graves. Many gravestones—they date from the mid-14th to the late 18th centuries—are carved with symbols indicating the name, profession, and attributes of the deceased. If you visit the tomb of the 16th-century scholar Rabbi Löw, you may see scraps of paper covered with prayers or requests stuffed into the cracks. In legend, the rabbi protected Prague's Jews with the help of a *golem,* or artificial man; today he still receives appeals for assistance. ⊠ *Entrance at Pinkas Synagogue, Široká 3,* ☎ *02/2481–0099,* WEB *www.jewishmuseum.cz.*

❶ Václavské náměstí (Wenceslas Square). In the Times Square of Prague hundreds of thousands voiced their disgust for the Communist regime in November 1989 at the outset of the "Velvet Revolution." The "square" is actually a broad boulevard that slopes down from the **Národní muzeum** (National Museum) and the equestrian **statue of St. Václav** (Wenceslas). ⊠ *Between Wilsonova and jct. Na příkopě and 26 Října.*

❼ Židovské muzeum (Jewish Museum). The rich exhibits in Josefov's Pinkas Synagogue, Maisel Synagogue, Klaus Synagogue, Ceremonial Hall, and the newly renovated Spanish Synagogue, along with the Old Jewish Cemetery, make up the museum. Jews, forced to fulfill Adolf Hitler's plan to document the lives of the people he was trying to exterminate, gathered the collections. They include ceremonial objects, textiles, and displays covering the history of Bohemia's and Moravia's Jews. The interior of the Pinkas Synagogue is especially poignant, as it is painted with the names of 77,297 Jewish Czechs killed during World War II. Pinkas Synagogue also contains a permanent exhibition of drawings by children who were interned at the Terezín (Theresienstadt) concentration camp from 1942 to 1944. ⊠ *Museum ticket offices: U starého hřbitova 3a and Široká 3.* ☉ *Apr.–Oct., Sun.–Fri. 9–6; Nov.– Mar., Sun.–Fri. 9–4:30; closed Sat. and Jewish holidays. Old-New Synagogue closes 2–3 hrs early on Fri.*

Karlův most and Malá Strana (Charles Bridge and the Lesser Quarter)

Many of the houses in the charmingly quaint Lesser Side have large signs above the door with symbols such as animals or religious figures. These date to the time before houses were numbered, when each house

Prague (Praha)

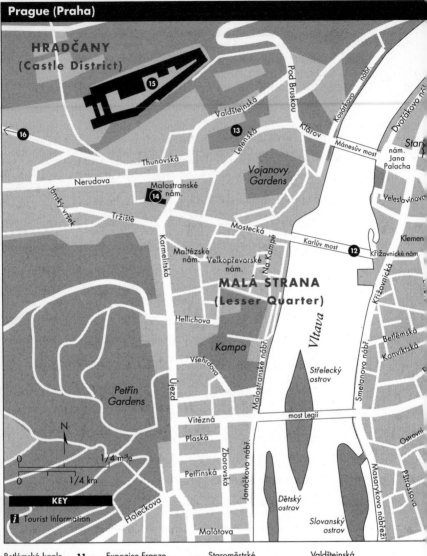

HRADČANY
(Castle District)

MALÁ STRANA
(Lesser Quarter)

KEY

Tourist Information

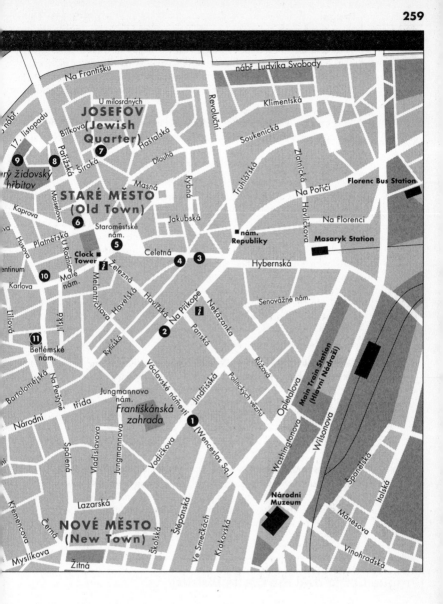

Na Františku

nábř. Ludvíka Svobody

U milosrdných

JOSEFOV
(Jewish
Quarter)

Bílkova

Klimentská

Revoluční

Soukenická

Haštalská

Dlouhá

Truhlářská

Zlatnická

Na Poříčí

Florenc Bus Station

Na Florenci

Na Havlíčkova

Masaryk Station

17. listopadu

nábř.

Pařížská

Široká

Masná

Rybná

Jakubská

STARÉ MĚSTO
(Old Town)

Maiselova

Kaprova

Platnéřská

Staroměstské
nám.

Celetná

Clock
Tower

Železná

i

Husova

Centinum

Karlova

Malé
nám.

Havelská

Na Příkopě

i

Nekázanka

nám.
Republiky

Hybernská

Senovážné nám.

Růžová

Lilová

Betlémské
nám.

Rytířská

Panská

Jindřišská

Politických vězňů

Opletalova

Main Train Station
(Hlavní Nádraží)

Bartolomějská

Na Perštýně

Melantrichová

U Radnice

Jilská

Jungmannovo
nám.

Františkánská
zahrada

Václavské náměstí
[Wenceslas Sq.]

Washingtonova

Wilsonova

Národní

třída

Spálená

Vladislavova

Jungmannova

Vodičkova

Španělská

Italská

Lazarská

Kremencova

Černá

Myslíkova

NOVÉ MĚSTO
(New Town)

Žitná

Štěpánská

Školská

Ve Smečkách

Krakovská

Národní
Muzeum

Mánesova

Vinohradská

② Na Příkopě

③

④

⑤

⑥

⑦

⑧

⑨

⑩

⑪

①

rý židovský
hřbitov

Maiselova

was referred to by name. Aristocrats built palaces here during the 17th century to be close to Prague Castle. Many of their private gardens have evolved into pleasant public parks with strutting peacocks. Some of the former palaces have become embassies, but increased security makes it hard to have more than a quick glance at the exterior.

⑭ **Chrám svatého Mikuláše** (Church of St. Nicholas). Designed by the late-17th-century Dientzenhofer architects, father and son, this is among the most beautiful examples of the Bohemian Baroque, an architectural style that flowered in Prague after the Counter-Reformation. On clear days you can enjoy great views from the tower. ✉ *Malostranské nám.* ⊙ *Sept.–May, daily 9–4; June–Aug., daily 9–6.*

★ ⑫ **Karlův most** (Charles Bridge). As you stand on this statue-lined stone bridge, unsurpassed in grace and setting, you see views of Prague that would be familiar to its 14th-century builder Peter Parler and to the artists who started adding the 30 sculptures in the 17th century. Today, nearly all the sculptures on the bridge are skillful copies of the originals, which have been taken indoors to be protected from the polluted air. The 12th on the left (starting from the Old Town side of the bridge) depicts St. Luitgarde (Matthias Braun sculpted the original, circa 1710). In the 14th on the left, a Turk guards suffering saints. (F. M. Brokoff sculpted the original, circa 1714.) The bridge itself is a gift to Prague from the Holy Roman emperor Charles IV. ✉ *Between Mostecká ul. on Malá Strana side and Karlova ul. on Old Town side.*

⑬ **Valdštejnská zahrada** (Wallenstein Gardens). This is one of the most elegant of the many sumptuous Lesser Quarter gardens. In the 1620s the Habsburgs' victorious commander, Czech nobleman Albrecht of Wallenstein, demolished a wide swath of existing structures in order to build his oversize palace with its charming walled garden. A covered outdoor stage of late-Renaissance style dominates the western end. ✉ *Entrance, Letenská 10.* ⊙ *May–Sept., daily 9–7.*

OFF THE
BEATEN PATH

VILLA BERTRAMKA – While in Prague, Mozart liked to stay at the secluded estate of his friends the Dušeks. The house is now a small museum packed with Mozart memorabilia. From Karmelitská ulice in Malá Strana, take Tram 12 south to the Anděl Metro station; walk down Plzeňská ulice a few hundred yards, and take a left at Mozartova ulice. ✉ *Mozartova ul. 169, Smíchov,* ☎ *02/543893.* ⊙ *Daily 9:30–6.*

Pražský hrad and Hradčany (Prague Castle and the Castle District)

No feature dominates the city more than Prague Castle, which, due to its hilltop location, can be seen from most of the city. The neighborhood in front of the castle once housed astronomers, alchemists, counts, and clergy hoping to obtain royal favors. Some of the palaces near the castle have become museums, others are used by government ministries. A large number of churches can be found here as well. Some offer tours, others can only be viewed after early-morning religious services.

⑯ **Loreta.** This Baroque church and shrine are named for the Italian town to which angels supposedly transported the Virgin Mary's house from Nazareth to save it from the infidel. The glory of its fabulous treasury is the monstrance *The Sun of Prague,* with its 6,222 diamonds. Arrive on the hour to hear the 27-bell carillon. ✉ *Loretánské nám. 7.* ⊙ *Tues.– Sun. 9–noon and 1–4:30.*

★ ⑮ **Pražský hrad** (Prague Castle). From its narrow hilltop, the monumental castle complex has witnessed the changing fortunes of the city for more than 1,000 years. The castle's physical and spiritual core, **Chrám svatého Víta** (St. Vitus Cathedral), took from 1344 to 1929 to build, so you can trace in its lines architectural styles from high Gothic to Art Nouveau. The eastern end, mostly the work of Peter Parler, builder of the Charles Bridge, is a triumph of Bohemian Gothic. "Good King" Wenceslas (in reality a mere prince, later canonized) has his own chapel in the south transept, dimly lit and decorated with fine medieval wall paintings. Note the fine 17th-century carved wooden panels on either side of the chancel. The left-hand panel shows a view of the castle and town in November 1620 as the defeated Czech Protestants flee into exile. The three easternmost chapels house tombs of Czech princes and kings of the 11th to the 13th centuries, although Charles IV and Rudolf II lie in the crypt, the former in a bizarre modern sarcophagus. On the southern facade of the cathedral, the 14th-century glass and quartz mosaic of the Last Judgment, long clouded over, has been restored to its original, brightly colored appearance.

Behind St. Vitus's, don't miss the miniature houses of **Zlatá ulička** (Golden Lane). Its name, and the apocryphal tale of how Holy Roman emperor Rudolf II used to lock up alchemists here until they transmuted lead into gold, may come from the gold-beaters who once lived here. Knightly tournaments often accompanied coronation ceremonies in the **Královský palác** (Royal Palace), next to the cathedral, hence the broad Riders' Staircase leading up to the grandiose Vladislavský sál (Vladislav Hall), with its splendid late-Gothic vaulting and Renaissance windows. Oldest of all the castle's buildings, though much restored, is the complex of **Bazilika svatého Jiří** (St. George's Basilica and Convent). The basilica's cool Romanesque lines hide behind a glowing salmon-color Baroque facade. The ex-convent houses a superb collection of Bohemian art from medieval religious sculptures to Baroque paintings. The castle ramparts afford glorious vistas of Prague's fabled hundred spires rising above the rooftops. ⊠ *Approach via Nerudova, Staré zámecké schody, or Keplerova. Main castle ticket office in Second Courtyard,* ☎ *02/2437–3368,* WEB *www.hrad.cz/index_uk.html.* ⌖ *100 Kč; tickets valid 3 days; admits visitors to cathedral, Royal Palace, and St. George's Basilica (but not convent gallery), and Powder Tower.* ☉ *Oct.–Mar., daily 9–4; Apr.–Sept., daily 9–5. Castle gardens Apr.–Oct., daily 9–5.*

DINING

Eating out is important to Prague residents; make reservations whenever possible. Prices are reasonable, even in some of the more expensive restaurants.

CATEGORY	COST*
$$$$	over 360 Kč
$$$	230 Kč–360 Kč
$$	120 Kč–230 Kč
$	under 120 Kč

per person for a main course at dinner

$$$$ ✕ **Circle Line Brasserie.** Elegant yet decidedly unstuffy, this dining spot tucked into a restored Baroque palace in Malá Strana offers delicious nouvelle cuisine specialties. Appetizers and main courses may include hare terrine with sun-dried plums and apricots; roasted lamb sweetbreads with truffle sauce; and grilled veal ribs with mustard-seed sauce. A pianist plays unintrusively each evening; service is gracious and discreet. ⊠ *Malostranské nám. 12, Malá Strana,* ☎ *02/5753–0021. Reservations essential. AE, DC, MC, V.*

$$$$ ✕ **Peklo.** This subterranean chamber beneath a former monastery was once a favorite drinking spot of the highly temperamental King Wenceslas IV. The old wine cellar has been replaced by a restaurant that serves meals such as fillet of devil's hoof and offers a good selection of Czech and French wines. The atmosphere is unbeatable and the service is attentive. ⊠ *Strahovské nádvoří 1/132, Prague 1,* ☎ *02/2051–6652. AE, MC, V.*

$$$$ ✕ **U Zlaté Hrušky.** Careful restoration has returned this restaurant to its original 18th-century style. It specializes in Moravian wines, which are well matched with fillet steaks and goose liver. ⊠ *Nový Svět 3, Hradčany,* ☎ *02/2051–5356. Reservations essential. AE, V.*

$$$$ ✕ **Vinárna V Zatiší.** Impeccably gracious service and serene surround-★   ings make an evening at the "Still Life" one of Prague's most memorable dining experiences. Continental cuisine is exquisitely prepared and presented—fish and game specialties are outstanding. The wine list is extensive, with special emphasis on French vintages. ⊠ *Liliová 1, Staré Město,* ☎ *02/2222–1155. Reservations essential. AE, MC, V.*

$$$–$$$$ ✕ **U Modré Kachničky.** The exuberant, eclectic decor is as attractive ★   as the Czech and international dishes, which include steaks, duck, and game in autumn, and Bohemian trout and carp. ⊠ *Nebovidská 6, Malá Strana,* ☎ *02/5732–0308. Reservations essential. AE, V.*

$$$ ✕ **Palffy palác.** The faded charm of an Old World palace makes this ★   a lovely, romantic spot for a meal. Very good Continental cuisine is served with elegance that befits the surroundings. Try the potatoes au gratin or chicken stuffed with goat cheese. Surprisingly, brunches here are not worth the price. Dining is also possible on the terrace in summer. ⊠ *Valdštejnská 14, Malá Strana,* ☎ *02/5731–2243. MC, V.*

$$$ ✕ **U Mecenáše.** This wine restaurant manages to be both medieval and elegant despite the presence of swords and battle axes. Try to get a table in the back room. The chef specializes in thick, juicy steaks served with a variety of sauces. ⊠ *Malostranské nám. 10, Malá Strana,* ☎ *02/5753–1631. Reservations essential. AE, MC, V.*

$$ ✕ **Chez Marcel.** This authentic French bistro on a quiet, picturesque street offers a little taste of Paris in the center of Prague's Old Town. French owned and operated, Chez Marcel has an extensive menu suitable for lingering over a three-course meal (French cheeses, salads, pâtés, rabbit, and some of the best steaks in Prague) or just a quick espresso. ⊠ *Haštalská 12, Staré Město,* ☎ *02/231–5676. No credit cards.*

$$ ✕ **Dynamo.** With a consistent clientele of beautiful people, this little green diner is one of the trendiest spots on what is fast becoming a veritable restaurant row. Dynamo's quirky menu offers tasty variations on Continental themes, such as liver and apples on toast, and succulent eggplant filled with grilled vegetables. ⊠ *Pštrossova 221/29, Nové Město,* ☎ *02/294224. AE, MC, V.*

$$ ✕ **Kavárna Slavia.** This legendary hangout for the best and brightest ★   of the Czech arts world—from composer Bedřich Smetana and poet Jaroslav Seifert to then-dissident Václav Havel offers a spectacular view both inside and out. Its Art Deco decor is a perfect backdrop for people-watching, and the vistas (the river and Prague Castle or the National Theater) are a compelling reason to linger over an espresso. ⊠ *Smetanovo nábřeží 1012/2, Nové Město,* ☎ *02/2422–0957. No credit cards.*

$$ ✕ **U Sedmi Švábů.** A medieval theme accents the truly old-fashioned Bohemian fare that includes millet pudding and mead. The less adventuresome can opt for the roast meat and poultry dishes. A special knight's feast requires 24 hours' advance notice. At the bottom of the stairs you can find a dungeon. ⊠ *Janský vršek 14, Malá Strana, Prague 1,* ☎ *02/5753–1455.*

$–$$ ✕ **Novoměstský pivovar.** Always packed with out-of-towners and locals alike, this microbrewery-restaurant is a maze of rooms, some painted in mock-medieval style, others decorated with murals of Prague street scenes. Pork knee (*vepřové koleno*) is a favorite dish. The beer is the cloudy, fruity, fermented style exclusive to this venue. ⊠ *Vodičkova 20, Prague 1,* ☎ *02/2223–2448. AE, MC, V.*

$ ✕ **Bohemia Bagel.** The casual, American-owned and child-friendly Bohemia Bagel serves a good assortment of fresh bagels from raisin-walnut to "supreme," with all kinds of spreads and toppings. The thick soups are among the best in Prague for the price, and the bottomless cups of coffee (from gourmet blends) are a further draw. ⊠ *Újezd 16, Malá Strana,* ☎ *02/531002. No credit cards.*

$ ✕ **Česká hospoda v Krakovské.** Right off Wenceslas Square, this clean pub noted for its excellent traditional fare is the place to try Bohemian duck. Pair it with cold Krušovice beer. ⊠ *Krakovská 20, Nové Město,* ☎ *02/2221–0204. No credit cards.*

$ ✕ **Country Life.** A godsend for Praguers and travelers, this health-food cafeteria offers a bounteous (and fresh) salad bar and daily rotating meat-free specials. The dining area has that rare Prague luxury for a low-end eating establishment: no blaring techno music. There's table service evenings after 6:30. It's off the courtyard connecting Melantrichova and Michalská streets. ⊠ *Melantrichova 15, Staré Město,* ☎ *02/ 2421–3366. No credit cards. Closed Sat.*

$ ✕ **Pivovarský dům.** Beer made on the premises is the main attraction here. They make not only traditional Pilsner-style but also a rotating choice of coffee, cherry, or even eucalyptus beer. The menu offers well-made traditional pub fare such as *guláš* with dumplings. Peek at the vats behind the glass to see beer fermenting. ⊠ *Lipová 20, Prague 2,* ☎ *02/9621–6666. No credit cards.*

$ ✕ **U Zlatého Tygra.** This crowded hangout is the last of a breed of authentic Czech pivnice. The smoke and stares preclude a long stay, but it's worth a visit for such pub staples as ham and cheese plates or roast pork. The service is surly, but the beer is good. ⊠ *Husova 17, Staré Město,* ☎ *02/2422–9020. Reservations not accepted. No credit cards.*

LODGING

Many of Prague's older hotels have been renovated, and new establishments in old buildings ornament the Old Town and Lesser Quarter. Very few hotel rooms in the more desirable districts go for less than $100 per double room in high season; most less-expensive hotels are far from the center of Prague. Private rooms and pensions remain the best budget deal.

Prices are for double rooms, generally including breakfast. Prices at the lower end of the scale apply to low season. Expect a 15%–25% rate increase at certain periods, such as Christmas, New Year's, Easter, or during festivals.

CATEGORY	COST*
$$$$	over 5,300 Kč
$$$	2,700 Kč–5,300 Kč
$$	1,400 Kč–2,700 Kč
$	under 1,400 Kč

Prices are for two persons sharing a double room.

$$$$ 🏨 **Diplomat.** Completed in 1990, the Diplomat fuses style with Western efficiency. A 10-minute taxi or subway ride from the Old Town, it's convenient to the airport. The hotel is modern and tasteful, with a huge, sunny lobby and comfortable rooms. ⊠ *Evropská 15, 160 00 Prague 6,* ☎ *02/2439–4111,* 🖷 *02/2439–4215,* 🌐 *www.diplomat-hotel.cz. 369 rooms, 13 suites. 2 restaurants. AE, DC, MC, V.*

$$$$ ⊞ **Dům U Červeného Lva.** In Malá Strana, a five-minute walk from
★   Prague Castle's front gates, the Baroque House at the Red Lion is an
intimate, immaculately kept hotel. The spare but comfortable guest rooms
have parquet floors, 17th-century painted-beam ceilings, superb antiques, and all-white bathrooms with brass fixtures. The two top-floor
rooms can double as a suite. There is no elevator, and stairs are steep.
⊠ *Nerudova 41, 118 00 Prague 1,* ☎ *02/537–239 or 02/538–192,* ⅆⅇⅹ
02/538–193. 8 rooms. 2 restaurants. AE, DC, MC, V.

$$$$ ⊞ **Hoffmeister.** On a picturesque (if a bit busy) corner near the Mal-
★   ostranská Metro station, this is one of the most stylish small hotels in
the city. Rooms have finely crafted wood built-ins and luxuriously appointed bathrooms. Museum-quality prints by the proprietor's father
hang throughout the hotel. ⊠ *Pod Bruskou 7, 118 00 Prague 1,* ☎
02/5101–7111, ⅆⅇⅹ *02/5101–7120,* ⅦⅇⅯ *www.hoffmeister.cz. 38 rooms.
Restaurant. AE, DC, MC, V.*

$$$$ ⊞ **Kampa.** An early Baroque armory turned hotel, the Kampa is tucked
away in a residential corner of the Lesser Quarter. The rooms are
clean, if spare, but the bucolic setting one block from the river as well
as a lovely park compensate for its relative remoteness. ⊠ *Všehrdova
16, 118 00 Prague 1,* ☎ *02/5732–0508 or 02/732–0404,* ⅆⅇⅹ *02/5732–
0262. 84 rooms. Restaurant. AE, DC, MC, V.*

$$$$ ⊞ **Palace Praha.** The Art Nouveau–style Palace is Prague's most elegant
★   and luxurious hotel, though it now faces competition from other luxury hotels. Rooms have high ceilings, marble baths with phones, and mini-
bars with complimentary snacks and beverages. Its central location just
off Wenceslas Square offers more convenience than local character. ⊠
Panská 12, 110 00 Prague 1, ☎ *02/2409–3111,* ⅆⅇⅹ *02/2422–1240,* ⅦⅇⅯ
www.palacehotel.cz. 125 rooms. Restaurant. AE, DC, MC, V.

$$$ ⊞ **Hotel U staré paní.** "The Old Lady" is a delightfully cozy hotel only
a five-minute walk from Old Town Square, in a renovated building on
one of Prague's most atmospheric Old Town lanes. Comfortable rooms
are decorated in soft tones with simple Scandinavian-style furnishings.
One of Prague's best jazz clubs has concerts nightly here in the base-
ment. (Yes, it is soundproofed.) ⊠ *Michalská 9, 110 00 Prague 1,* ☎
02/267267, 02/264920, or 02/261655, ⅆⅇⅹ *02/267–9841, 02/267267,
or 02/264920. 18 rooms. Restaurant. AE, MC, V.*

$$$ ⊞ **Opera.** Once the lodging of choice for divas performing at the
nearby State Theater, the Opera greatly declined under the Commu-
nists. The mid-'90s saw the grand fin-de-siècle facade rejuvenated with
a perky pink-and-white paint job and the installation of bathrooms and
TVs in all rooms. Comfy wing chairs add to the rooms, which are decorated in tan and white. ⊠ *Těšnov 13, 110 00 Prague 1,* ☎ *02/231–
5609,* ⅆⅇⅹ *02/231–1477,* ⅦⅇⅯ *www.hotel-opera.cz. 64 rooms, plus 4 suites.
Restaurant, bar. AE, DC, MC, V.*

$$ ⊞ **Balkán.** The hotel is a spiffy yellow building on an otherwise drab
street not far from the Lesser Quarter. Rooms are small, simple, clean:
white spreads and walls, tan paneling, lacy curtains. Request a room
at the back, as the hotel is on a major street, one block from the tram
stop. ⊠ *Svornosti 28, 150 00 Prague 5,* ☎ ⅆⅇⅹ *02/5732–7180. 24
rooms. Breakfast not included. Restaurant. AE.*

$$ ⊞ **Central.** Quite conveniently, this hotel lives up to its name, with a
site near Celetná ulice and Náměstí Republiky. Rooms are sparely fur-
nished, but all have baths. The Baroque glories of the Old Town are
steps away. ⊠ *Rybná 8, 110 00 Prague 1,* ☎ *02/2481–2041,* ⅆⅇⅹ *02/
232–8404. 62 rooms, 4 suites. Restaurant, bar. AE, MC, V.*

$ ⊞ **Pension Unitas.** Operated by the Christian charity Unitas in an Old
Town convent, this well-run establishment has sparely furnished rooms,
all of which are no-smoking. Note that an adjacent 3-star hotel, Cloister Inn, shares the same address and phone number. ⊠ *Bartolomějská*

9, 110 00 Prague 1, ☎ *02/232–7700,* FAX *02/232–7709. 34 rooms without bath. Reserve well in advance, even for off-season. Restaurant. No credit cards.*

$ 📺 **Penzion Sprint.** Basic, clean, no-frills rooms, most of which have their own tiny bathrooms, make the Sprint a fine budget choice. The rustic-looking pension is on a quiet residential street in the outskirts of Prague about 20 minutes from the airport; tram 18 rumbles directly to Old Town. ✉ *Cukrovarnická 64, 160 00 Prague 6,* ☎ *02/312–3338,* FAX *02/3335–1837,* WEB *web.telecom.cz/penzionsprint. 21 rooms. AE, MC, V.*

NIGHTLIFE AND THE ARTS

The Arts

Prague's cultural life is one of its top attractions—and its citizens like to dress up and participate; performances can be booked far ahead. Monthly programs of events are available at the PIS, Čedok, or hotels. The English-language newspaper *Prague Post* carries detailed entertainment listings. The main ticket agency for classical music is **Bohemia Ticket International** (✉ Na Příkopě 16, ☎ 02/2421–5031). **Ticketpro** (✉ Salvátorská 10, ☎ 02/2481–4020, FAX 02/2481–4021) sells tickets for most rock and jazz events, as well as theatrical performances and some tours. For major concerts, opera, and theater, it's much cheaper to buy tickets at the box office.

Concerts

Performances are held in many palaces and churches. Too often, programs lack originality (how many different ensembles can play the *Four Seasons* at once?), but the settings are lovely and the acoustics can be superb. Concerts at the **churches of St. Nicholas** in both the Old Town Square and the Lesser Quarter are especially enjoyable. At **St. James's Church** on Malá Štupartská (Old Town) cantatas are performed amid a flourish of Baroque statuary.

The excellent Czech Philharmonic plays in the intimate, lavish Dvořák Hall in the **Rudolfinum** (✉ Nám. Jana Palacha, ☎ 02/2489–3111). The lush home of the Prague Symphony, **Smetana Hall,** reopened in 1997 along with the rest of the Obecní dům building (✉ Nám. Republiky 5, ☎ 02/2200–2100 or 02/2200–2101).

Opera and Ballet

Opera is of an especially high standard in the Czech Republic. One of the main venues in the grand style of the 19th century is the beautifully restored **Národní divadlo** (National Theater: ✉ Národní třída 2, ☎ 02/2490–1448). The **Statni opera Praha** (State Opera of Prague: ✉ Wilsonova 4, ☎ 02/265353), formerly the Smetana Theater, is another historic site for opera lovers. The **Stavovské divadlo** (Estates Theater: ✉ Ovocný trh 1, ☎ 02/2421–5001) hosts opera, ballet, and theater performances by the National Theater ensembles. Mozart conducted the premiere of *Don Giovanni* here.

Puppet Shows

This traditional form of Czech entertainment, generally adaptations of operas performed to recorded music, has been given new life at the **Národní divadlo marionet** (National Marionette Theater: ✉ Žatecká 1, ☎ 02/232–3429).

Theater

A dozen or so professional companies play in Prague to packed houses. Nonverbal theater abounds as well, notably "black theater," a melding of live acting, mime, video, and stage trickery that, despite signs of fatigue, continues to draw crowds. The popular **Archa Theater** (⊠ Na Poříčí 26, ☎ 02/232–8800) offers avant-garde and experimental theater, music, and dance and hosts world-class visiting ensembles, including the Royal Shakespeare Company. **Laterna Magika** (Magic Lantern; ⊠ Národní třída 4, ☎ 02/2491–4129) is one of the more established producers of black-theater extravaganzas.

Nightlife

Discos and Cabaret

Discos catering to a young crowd blast sound onto lower Wenceslas Square. The newest dance music plays at the ever-popular **Radost FX** (⊠ Bělehradská 120, Prague 2, ☎ 02/251210).

Four clubs in one can be found at the renovated spa building near the Charles Bridge **Karlový lázně** (⊠ Novotného lávka), which has several live acts or DJs nightly and a café with Internet access in the daytime.

Jazz and Rock Clubs

Jazz clubs are a Prague institution, although foreign customers keep them in business. Excellent Czech groups play the tiny **AghaRTA** (⊠ Krakovská 5, ☎ 02/2221–1275); arrive well before the 9 PM show time to get a seat with a sight line. Top jazz groups (and the odd world-music touring ensemble) play **Jazz Club U staré paní** (⊠ Michalská 9, ☎ 02/264920) in Old Town. **Malostranská Beseda** (⊠ Malostranské nám. 21, ☎ 02/5753–2092) is a funky hall for rock, jazz, and folk. At **Palác Akropolis** (⊠ Kubelíkova 27, ☎ 02/2271–2287) you can hear world music, well-known folk, rock, and jazz acts, plus DJs. **Reduta** (⊠ Národní třída 20, ☎ 02/2491–2246), the city's best-known jazz club for three decades, stars mostly local talent. Hip locals congregate at **Roxy** (⊠ Dlouhá 33, ☎ 02/2481–0951) for everything from punk to funk to New Age tunes.

SHOPPING

Many of the main shops are in and around Old Town Square and Na Příkopě, as well as along Celetná ulice and Pařížská. On the Lesser Quarter side, Nerudova has the densest concentration of shops.

Department Stores

The biggest downtown department store is **Kotva** (⊠ Nám. Republiky 8), which grows flashier and more expensive every year. **Bílá Labuť'** (⊠ Na Poříčí 23) is a good-value option. The basement supermarket at **Tesco** (⊠ Národní třída 26) is the best and biggest in the center of the city.

Specialty Shops

Shops specializing in Bohemian crystal, porcelain, ceramics, and antiques abound in Old Town and Malá Strana and on Golden Lane at Prague Castle. Look for the name **Dílo** (⊠ Staroměstské nám. 15, Old Town; ⊠ U Lužického semináře 14, Malá Strana) for glass and ceramic sculptures, prints, and paintings by local artists. **Lidová Řemesla** (⊠ Jilská 22, Old Town; ⊠ Mostecká 17, Malá Strana) shops stock wooden toys, elegant blue-and-white textiles, and charming Christmas ornaments made from straw or pastry. **Moser** (⊠ Na Příkopě 12, ☎ 02/2421–1293) is the source for glass and porcelain.

PRAGUE A TO Z

To research prices, get advice from other travelers, and book travel arrangements, visit www.fodors.com.

AIRPORTS AND TRANSFERS

All international flights arrive at Prague's Ruzyně Airport, about 20 km (12 mi) from downtown.

➤ AIRPORT INFORMATION: **Ruzyně Airport,** ☎ 02/367760 or 02/2011–3314.

TRANSFERS

The private Cedaz minibus shuttle links the airport and Náměstí Republiky. Shuttles run every 30–60 minutes between 5:30 AM and 9 PM daily. The trip costs 90 Kč one-way and takes about 30 minutes. On regular Bus 119 the cost is 12 Kč, but you'll need to change to the subway at the Dejvická station to reach the center. By taxi, expect to pay 600 Kč to the center. Only one city-authorized firm, FIX, is permitted to pick up customers at the airport. (You may take any taxi *to* the airport, however.)

BUS TRAVEL TO AND FROM PRAGUE

The Czech bus network (ČSAD) operates from a station near Prague's main train station. Take Metro B or C to the Florenc stop.

➤ BUS INFORMATION: **ČSAD** (✉ Křižíkova 4, ☎ 02/121999).

BUS AND TRAM TRAVEL WITHIN PRAGUE

Trams are often more convenient than the Metro for short hops. Most bus lines connect outlying suburbs with the nearest Metro station. Trams 50–59 and buses numbered 500 and above run all night—at, however, intervals of up to an hour—after the Metro stops.

CAR TRAVEL

In the center of the city, meters with green stripes let you park up to six hours; an orange stripe indicates a two-hour limit. Blue-marked spaces are reserved for local residents. (Parking boots may be attached to offending vehicles.) There is an underground parking lot near Old Town Square.

➤ PARKING: **Underground parking lot** (✉ Alšovo nábřeží).

EMERGENCIES

Be prepared to pay in cash for medical treatment, whether you are insured or not. The Lékárna U Andělais 24-hour pharmacy is near the Anděl metro station, and the Lékárna Palackého 24-hour pharmacy is located downtown.

➤ EMERGENCY SERVICES: **Police** (☎ 158). **Ambulance** (☎ 155).

➤ HOSPITALS: **Foreigners' Department of Na Homolce Hospital** (☎ 02/5727–2146 and 02/5727–1111 weekdays; 02/5292–2403 and 02/807756 evenings and weekends). **American Medical Center** (☎ 02/807756; 02/807757; 02/807758 weekdays).

➤ 24-HOUR PHARMACIES: **Lékárna U Anděla** (✉ Štefánikova 6, Prague 1, ☎ 02/537039). **Lékárna Palackého** (✉ Palackého 5, Prague 1, ☎ 02/2494–6982).

ENGLISH-LANGUAGE MEDIA

The Knihkupectví U černé Matky Boží is good for hiking maps and atlases; go downstairs).

➤ BOOKSTORES: **Anagram Bookshop** (✉ Týn 4, Prague 1). **Big Ben Bookshop** (✉ Malá Štupartská 5, Prague 1). **Globe Bookstore and Coffeehouse** (✉ Pštrossova 6, Prague 1). **Knihkupectví U černé Matky Boží** (✉ Celetná ul. 34 at Ovocný trh, Prague 1). **U Knihomola** (✉ Mánesova 79, Prague 2).

SUBWAY TRAVEL

Prague's three modern Metro lines are easy to use and relatively safe. They provide the simplest and fastest means of transportation, and most new maps of Prague mark the routes. The Metro runs from 5 AM to midnight, seven days a week.

TAXIS

Regulations have set taxi rates at 25 Kč initial fee and 17 Kč per kilometer plus 4 Kč per minute waiting time. Drivers must also display a small license, although this has not stopped fare-related problems. It is still advisable to order a taxi in advance by telephone. Try AAA for quick, reliable service. Profitaxi is also fast and efficient. Some larger hotels have their own fleets, which are a little more expensive.

Note: Do not pick up cabs waiting at taxi stands in the tourist areas: many of these drivers have doctored their meters and have other tricks to rip you off.

➤ TAXI COMPANIES: **AAA** (☎ 02/14014). **Profitaxi** (☎ 02/14035).

TOURS

BUS TOURS

Čedok offers a daily three-hour tour of the city, starting at 10 AM from two offices. Martin-Tour offers a tour departing from Náměstí Republiky and three other Old Town points four times daily. PIS arranges guided tours at its Na Příkopě and Old Town Square locations.

Čedok's one-day tours out of Prague include excursions to the lovely medieval town of Kutná Hora, the unusual sandstone formations of the "Bohemian Paradise" region, famous spa towns and castles, wineries, and the Terezín ghetto.

➤ FEES AND SCHEDULES: **Čedok** (✉ Na Příkopě 18; Pařížská 6, ☎ 02/2419–7111). **Martin-Tour** (☎ 02/7122–2227). **PIS** (☎ 02/2448–2569).

PRIVATE GUIDES

Contact Čedok or PIS to arrange a personal walking tour of the city. Prices start at around 400 Kč per hour.

SPECIAL-INTEREST TOURS

For cultural tours call Čedok. These include visits to the Jewish quarter, performances of folk troupes, Laterna Magika, opera, and concerts.

TRAIN TRAVEL

The main station is Hlavní Nádraží, not far from Wenceslas Square. Some international trains use Nádraží Holešovice, on the same Metro line (C) as the main station.

➤ TRAIN INFORMATION: **Hlavní Nádraží** (✉ Wilsonova ul.). **Nádraží Holešovice** (✉ Vrbenského ul.). **Domestic and international schedules** (for both stations; ☎ 02/2422–4200, 02/2461–4030, or 02/2461–4031).

TRANSPORTATION AROUND PRAGUE

Public transportation is a bargain. *Jízdenky* (tickets) can be bought at hotels, newsstands, and dispensing machines in Metro stations. Transport passes for unlimited use of the system for 1 day (70 Kč) up to 15 days (280 Kč) are sold at some newsstands and at the windows marked DP or JÍZDENKY in the main Metro stations. Be sure to validate your pass by signing it where indicated. A basic 12-Kč ticket allows one hour's travel, with unlimited transfers (90 minutes on weekends and between 8 PM and 5 AM weekdays) on the Metro, tram, and bus network within the city limits. Cheaper 8-Kč tickets are good for a tram or bus ride up to 15 minutes without transferring, or 30 minutes on the Metro including transfers between lines; on the Metro, though, you cannot travel more than four stops from your starting point. For the Metro punch the ticket in the station before getting onto the escalators; for buses and trams punch the ticket inside the vehicle. (Enter the tram or bus through any door and stick the tickets horizontally—and gently—into the little yellow machines, which should "stamp" them with the date and time; it's an acquired trick of hand-eye coordination; ask for help from another passenger if your machine is not cooperating, which is often the case.) If you fail to validate your ticket you may be fined 400 Kč by a ticket inspector.

Note: Prague has quite a pickpocketing racket, to which the police apparently turn a blind eye. Be very wary of raucous groups of people making a commotion as they get on and off trams and metros; generally they are working the passengers. Keep close watch on your belongings and purses on crowded streets and in crowded sites.

TRAVEL AGENCIES
➤ LOCAL AGENT REFERRALS: **American Express** (✉ Václavské nám. 56, ☎ 02/2280–0223; 02/2280–0222 lost/stolen credit cards, FAX 02/2221–1131). **Thomas Cook** (✉ Národní třída 28, ☎ 02/2110–5371).

VISITOR INFORMATION
The English-language weekly *Prague Post* lists current events and entertainment programs.
➤ TOURIST INFORMATION: **Čedok** (main office; ✉ Na Příkopě 18, near Wenceslas Sq., ☎ 02/2419–7111; other branches, ✉ Rytířská 16 and ✉ Pařížská 6). **Prague Information Service** (PIS; ✉ Na Příkopě 20 and Staroměstské nám. 22, ☎ 02/2448–2569).
➤ TOURIST BUREAUS OUTSIDE PRAGUE: **Český Krumlov** (Infocentrum; ✉ Nám. Svornosti 1, ☎ 0337/711183). **Karlovy Vary** (✉ Ul. Dr. Bechera 21–23, ☎ 017/22281). **Mariánské Lázně** (Infocentrum; ✉ Hlavní 47, ☎ 0165/622474 or 0165/5892). **Mikulov** (Regional Tourist Center; ✉ Nám. 32, ☎ FAX 0625/2855). **Olomouc** (✉ Horní nám., ☎ 068/551–3385). **Tábor** (✉ Žižkovo nám., ☎ 0361/252385). **Telč** (✉ Town hall; Nám. Zachariáše z Hradce 10, ☎ 066/962233).

Czech Republic Basics

BUSINESS HOURS
Banks are open weekdays 8–5. Museums are usually open Tuesday–Sunday 10–5. Shops are generally open weekdays 9–6; some close for lunch between noon and 2. Many larger ones are also open Saturday and Sunday.

CUSTOMS AND DUTIES
You may import duty-free 200 cigarettes, 50 cigars, 1 liter of spirits, 2 liters of wine, and gifts with a total value of 1,000 Kč. Goods worth up to 3,000 Kč (approximately US$90) are not liable for duty upon arrival. Declare items of greater value (jewelry, computers, and so on) on arrival to avoid problems with customs officials on departure. You may only export antiques that are certified as not of historical value. Reputable dealers will advise. Play safe, and also save your receipts.

EMBASSIES
➤ AUSTRALIA: The Honorary Consulate and Trade Commission of Australia (✉ Na Ořechovce 38, ☎ 02/2431–0071 or 02/2431–0743).
➤ CANADA: (✉ Mickiewiczova 6, Hradčany, ☎ 02/7210–1800).
➤ IRELAND: (✉ Tržiště 13, ☎ 02/5753–0061).
➤ NEW ZEALAND: (Consulate: ✉ Dykova 19, ☎ 02/5753–0061).
➤ SOUTH AFRICA: (✉ Ruska 65, Vršovice, ☎ 02/6731–1114).
➤ UNITED KINGDOM: (✉ Thunovská 14, Malá Strana, ☎ 02/5753–0278).
➤ UNITED STATES: (✉ Tržiště 15, Malá Strana, ☎ 02/5753–0663, WEB www.usis.cz).

HOLIDAYS

January 1; Easter Sunday and Monday; May 1 (Labor Day); May 8 (Liberation Day); July 5 (Sts. Cyril and Methodius); July 6 (Jan Hus); October 28 (Czech National Day); November 17 (Uprising of Student for Freedom and Democracy); December 24–26.

LANGUAGE

Czech, which belongs to the Slavic family of languages along with Russian, Polish, and Slovak, uses the Latin alphabet like English but adds special diacritical marks to make certain sounds: č is written for the "ch" sound, for instance. Unlike words in many other languages, Czech words are spelled phonetically, and the emphasis is almost always on the first syllable. You'll find a growing number of English-speakers, especially among young people and in the tourist industry. German is generally understood throughout the country.

MONEY MATTERS

Costs are highest in Prague and only slightly lower in the main Bohemian resorts and spas, though even in these places you can now find inexpensive accommodations in private homes. The least expensive area is southern Moravia. Note that many public venues in Prague and the Czech Republic continue the odious practice of adhering to a separate pricing system for Czechs and for foreigners. (Foreigners may be charged double or more on museum admission, for example.)

Cup of coffee, 30 Kč; beer (½ liter), 16 Kč–30 Kč; Coca-Cola, 20 Kč; ham sandwich, 30 Kč; 1½-km (1-mi) taxi ride, 50 Kč–70 Kč; museum and castle admission, 20 Kč–300 Kč.

CURRENCY

The unit of currency in the Czech Republic is the crown, or koruna (plural koruny), written as Kč, and divided into 100 haléřů (hellers). There are bills of 50, 100, 200, 500, 1,000, and 5,000 koruny and coins of 10, 20, and 50 hellers and 1, 2, 5, 10, 20, and 50 koruny. At press time (summer 2001), the rate of exchange was 36.75 Kč to the U.S. dollar, 24.53 Kč to the Canadian dollar, 55.19 Kč to the pound sterling, 44.48 Kč to the Irish punt, 21.01 Kč to the Australian dollar, 16.62 Kč to the New Zealand dollar, and 4.86 Kč to the South African rand. Banks and ATMs give the best rates. Banks and private exchange outlets, which litter Prague's tourist routes, charge either a set fee or a percentage of the transaction or both. It's wise to compare. The koruna is fully convertible and can be purchased outside the country and changed into other currencies, but you should keep your receipts and convert your koruny before you leave the country just to be sure.

PASSPORTS AND VISAS

ENTERING THE CZECH REPUBLIC

United States, Canadian, and British citizens need only a valid passport to visit the Czech Republic as tourists. United States citizens may stay for 30 days without a visa; British and Canadian citizens, six months. Australians need tourist visas to enter the Czech Republic; the visa is less expensive if obtained at a Czech embassy or consulate outside the Czech Republic; at the Czech Republic border, it costs 1,600 Kč.

TELEPHONES

To use a public phone, buy a phone card at a newsstand or tobacconist. Cards cost 175 Kč for 50 units or 320 Kč for 100 units. CzechMate cards worth 500 or 750 Kč of telephoning—ideal for long-distance calls—are also sold at post offices. To place a call, lift the receiver, insert the card, and dial.

COUNTRY AND AREA CODES

The Czech Republic's country code is 420.

INTERNATIONAL CALLS

Some special international pay-phone booths in central Prague will take 5 Kč coins or accept phone cards that allow automatic dialing. You will also find coin and card booths at the main post office (✉ Jindřišská 14, near Václavské náměstí [Wenceslas Square]); the entrance for telephone service is in this building but around the corner on Politických vězňů. The international dialing code is 00. Dial 0132 for international inquiries to the United States, Canada, or the United Kingdom. Calls can be placed using AT&T USA Direct, MCI, and Sprint international operators. International rates vary according to destination.

➤ ACCESS CODES: **AT&T USA Direct** (☎ 0042–000101). **MCI** (☎ 0042–000112). **Sprint** (☎ 0042–087187).

LOCAL CALLS

Local calls cost one unit.

14 ROME

For 2,500 years, emperors, popes, and the citizens of the ages have left their mark on Rome, and the result is like nothing so much as a hustling, bustling open-air museum. Most of the city's major sights are in the *centro storico* (historic center), which lies between the long, straight Via del Corso and the Tiber River, and the adjacent area of *Roma antica* (ancient Rome), site of the Roman Forum and Colosseum. The best way to discover the city is to wander, taking time to notice the layers of history that make Rome unique. On your way between monuments and museums you'll walk into the past: medieval Rome, which covered the horn of land that pushes the Tiber toward the Vatican and extended across the river into Trastevere, and Renaissance Rome, which was erected upon medieval foundations and extended as far as the Vatican, with beautiful villas created in what were then the outskirts of the city.

EXPLORING ROME

Numbers in the margin correspond to points of interest on the Rome map.

The layout of the centro storico is irregular, but several landmarks serve as orientation points to identify the areas that most visitors come to see: the Colosseum, Pantheon, Piazza Navona, St. Peter's Basilica, the Spanish Steps, and the Baths of Caracalla. You'll need a good map to find your way around; newsstands offer a wide choice. Energetic sightseers will walk a lot, a much more pleasant way to see the city since traffic is barred from the center of town during the day; others might choose to take taxis, buses, or the Metro. If you are in Rome during a hot spell, do as the Romans do: start out early in the morning, have a light lunch and a long siesta during the hottest hours, then resume sightseeing in the late afternoon and end your evening with a leisurely meal outdoors, refreshed by cold Frascati wine and the *ponentino,* the cool evening breeze.

Ancient Rome

The geographic center of the city is at Piazza Venezia, site of the late-19th-century monument to the first king of a united Italy, Vittorio Emanuele. The most evocative ruins of the ancient city extend from the Campidoglio across the Foro Romano to the Colosseo and the Terme di Caracalla and include the Palatino and Circo Massimo. This is one of the world's most striking and significant concentrations of historic remains; stand at the back of the Campidoglio overlooking the Roman Forum and take in 2½ thousand years of history at a glance.

❽ Arco di Costantino (Arch of Constantine). The best preserved of Rome's triumphal arches, this 4th-century monument commemorates Constantine's victory over Maxentius at the Milvian Bridge. Just before this battle in AD 312, Constantine had a vision of a cross in the heavens and heard the words: "In this sign thou shalt conquer." The victory led not only to the construction of this majestic marble arch but also to a turning point in the history of Christianity: soon afterward a grateful—and converted—Constantine decreed that it was a lawful religion and should be tolerated throughout the empire. His newfound faith didn't seem to cure his imperial sticky fingers, however; the arch's decorations were pilfered from monuments to earlier emperors. ✉ *Piazza del Colosseo.*

❷ Campidoglio (Capitoline Hill). The majestic ramp and beautifully proportioned piazza are the handiwork of Michelangelo (1475–1564), who also designed the facades of the three palaces that face this square on Capitoline Hill. Palazzo Senatorio, at the center, is still the ceremonial seat of Rome's City Hall; it was built over the Tabularium, where ancient Rome's state archives were kept. The statue at the center of the square is a copy of an ancient Roman bronze of Marcus Aurelius (AD 120–180). The Capitoline Museums, the two palaces flanking the Senatorio, house the original. ✉ *Piazza del Campidoglio.*

★ ❻ Colosseo (Colosseum). Massive and majestic, this ruin is ancient Rome's hallmark monument, inaugurated in AD 80 with a program of games and shows that lasted 100 days. Before the imperial box, gladiators would salute the emperor and cry, "*Ave, imperator, morituri te salutant*" ("Hail, emperor, men soon to die salute thee"); it is said that when one day they heard the emperor Claudius respond, "Or maybe not," they became so offended that they called a strike. The Colosseum could hold more than 50,000 spectators; it was faced with marble, decorated with stuccos, and had an ingenious system of awnings to provide shade. It was built in just eight years. The Colosseum takes its name from a colossal, 118-ft statue of Nero that once stood nearby. ✉ *Piazza del Colosseo,* ☎ 06/7004261, WEB *www. archeorm.arti.beniculturali.it.* ☼ *Daily 9–2 hrs before sunset.*

❼ Domus Aurea. Nero's "Golden House" is a spectacular example of the excesses of Imperial Rome. After fire destroyed much of the city in AD 64, Nero took advantage of the resultant open space to construct a palace so large that contemporary accounts complained his house was bigger than the rest of the city. One wing of the building was given over to public functions, while the other served as the emperor's private residence. More than 150 rooms have been excavated, revealing a subterranean trove of ancient Roman architecture and some well-preserved Roman

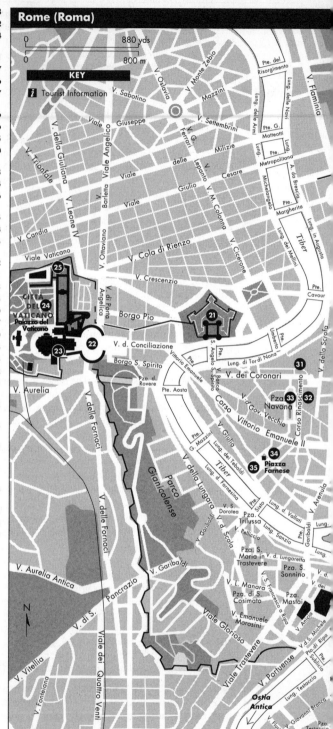

Rome (Roma)

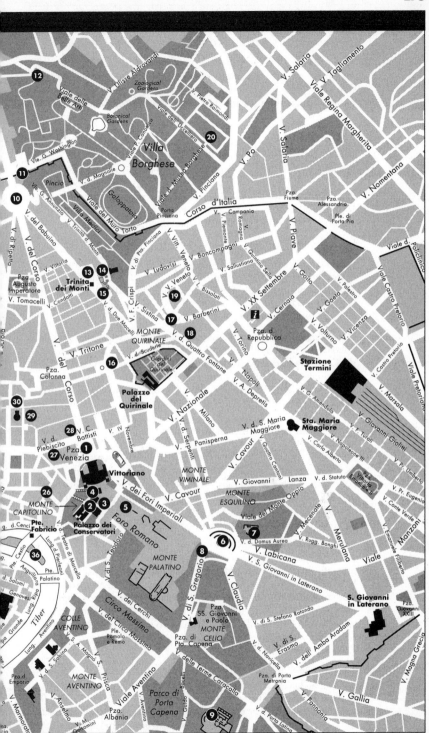

paintings decorating the walls. ⊠ *Via della Domus Aurea,* ☎ *06/ 6990110 information; 06/39967700 reservations,* WEB *www. archeorm.arti.beniculturali.it.* ☾ *Wed.–Mon. 9–7:45. Closed Tues.*

❺ **Foro Romano** (Roman Forum). Rome's foundations as a world capital and crossroads of culture are to be found here—literally. Excavations have shown that this site was in use as a burial ground as far back as the 10th century BC, hundreds of years before Rome's legendary founding by Romulus. But the Forum gained importance (and the name in use today) during Roman and Imperial times, when this marshy hollow was the political, commercial, and social center of Rome, and by extension, of the ancient world. The majestic ruins of temples and palaces visible today are fragments of the massive complex of markets, civic buildings, and houses of worship that dominated the city in its heyday. Wander down the **Via Sacra,** which runs the length of the Roman Forum, and take in the timeless view; then climb the **Colle Palatino** (Palatine Hill), where the emperors had their palaces and where 16th-century cardinals strolled in elaborate Italian gardens. From the *belvedere* (overlook) you have a good view of the **Circo Massimo** (Circus Maximus). Audio guides are available at the bookshop-ticket office at the Via dei Fori Imperiali entrance. ⊠ *Entrances at Via dei Fori Imperiali and Piazza del Colosseo,* ☎ *06/6990110 or 06/39967700,* WEB *www.archeorm.arti.beniculturali.it.* ☾ *Mon.–Sat. 9–2 hrs before sunset; Sun. and holidays 9–2.*

❸ **Musei Capitolini** (Capitoline Museums). The **Museo Capitolino** and **Palazzo dei Conservatori,** the palaces flanking Palazzo Senatorio on the Campidoglio, form a single museum holding some fine classical sculptures, including the gilded bronze equestrian statue of Marcus Aurelius that once stood on the pedestal in the piazza, as well as the *Dying Gaul,* the *Capitoline Venus,* and a series of portrait busts of ancient philosophers and emperors. In the courtyard of Palazzo dei Conservatori on the right of the piazza are mammoth fragments of a colossal statue of the emperor Constantine (circa 280–336). Inside are splendidly frescoed salons still used for municipal ceremonies, as well as sculptures and paintings. Don't miss the superb Baroque painting collection in the Pinacoteca, which holds masterpieces by Caravaggio and Rubens, among other stars. ⊠ *Piazza del Campidoglio, off Piazza Venezia,* ☎ *06/39967800,* WEB *www.comune.roma.it.* ☾ *Tues.–Sun. 9:30–7:30, Sat. open until 11 PM.*

❶ **Piazza Venezia.** Considered the geographical heart of the city, the square is dominated by the enormous marble monument (1911) honoring the first king of unified Italy, Vittorio Emanuele II (1820–78). Climb to the top of the "Vittoriano" for a stunning panorama over Rome. The piazza takes its name from the smaller but more historically important Palazzo Venezia, once Mussolini's headquarters. His most famous speeches were delivered from its balcony to the roaring crowds below. ⊠ *Square at intersection of Via del Corso, Via del Plebiscito, and Via del Fori Imperiali.* ☾ *Tues.–Sun. 10:30–1 hr before sunset.*

❹ **Santa Maria d'Aracoeli.** The 13th-century church on the Campidoglio can be reached by a long flight of steep stairs or, more easily, by way of the stairs on the far side of the Museo Capitolino. Stop in to see the medieval pavement, the Renaissance gilded ceiling that commemorates the victory of Lepanto, and the Pinturicchio (1454–1513) frescoes. ⊠ *Piazza Aracoeli,* ☎ *06/6798155.* ☾ *Oct.–May, daily 7–noon and 4– 6; June–Sept., daily 7–noon and 4–6:30.*

❾ **Terme di Caracalla** (Baths of Caracalla). The scale of the towering ruins of ancient Rome's most beautiful and luxurious public baths hint at their past splendor. Inaugurated by Caracalla in AD 217, the baths were used until the 6th century. An ancient version of a swank athletic club, the baths were open to all, though men and women used them separately; citizens could bathe, socialize, and exercise in huge pools and richly decorated halls and libraries. ⊠ *Via delle Terme di Caracalla 52*, ☎ *06/39967700*, WEB *www.archeorm.arti.beniculturali.it*. ⊘ *Oct.–Mar., Mon. 9–1, Tues.–Sun. 9–3:30; Apr.–Sept., Mon. 9–1, Tues.–Sun. 9–6.*

Piazzas and Fountains

The lush park of Villa Borghese is dotted with pines and fountains and neoclassical "ruins." It is a happy conjunction of the pleasure gardens and palaces of Renaissance prelates on the site of ancient Roman villas. It also holds the world-class museums of the Galleria Borghese and Villa Giulia, both with histories of their own. The Pincio, the ancient Pincian Hill, is a belvedere over the city and a vantage point over elegantly planned Piazza del Popolo, below. Crossing the piazza are dedicated shoppers heading for Via del Corso's emporia and the boutiques of Via Condotti, towards the bustle of the Piazza di Spagna. The scene around the Fontana di Trevi is equally crowded, forcing the wishful to toss their coins into the fountain from center field.

★ ⑯ **Fontana di Trevi** (Trevi Fountain). A spectacular fantasy of mythical sea creatures and cascades of splashing water, this fountain is one of Rome's Baroque greats. The fountain as you see it was completed in the mid-1700s, but there had been a drinking fountain on the site for centuries. Pope Urban VIII (1568–1644) almost sparked a revolt when he slapped a tax on wine to cover the expenses of having the fountain repaired. Legend has it that a coin tossed into the fountain ensures a return trip to Rome. ⊠ *Piazza di Trevi.*

⑳ **Galleria Borghese.** At the southeast corner of Villa Borghese, a park studded with pines and classical statuary, is this gallery created by Cardinal Scipione Borghese in the early 17th century as a showcase for his fabulous collection of ancient sculpture and Baroque painting. Highlights of the collection are the seductive reclining statue of Pauline Borghese by Canova (1757–1822) and some extraordinary works by Bernini (1598–1680), including the virtuoso *Apollo and Daphne*. The painting collection is no less impressive, with works by Caravaggio (1573–1610), Raphael (1483–1520), and Titian (circa 1488–1576), but the palace's restored magnificence is such that it would be a must-see even if it were empty. ⊠ *Piazza Scipione Borghese, in Villa Borghese*, ☎ *06/8548577 for information; 06/32810 for reservations (press 2 for English)*, WEB *www.galleriaborghese.it*. ⊘ *Winter, Tues.–Sun. 9–7; summer, Tues.–Fri. 9–9, Sat. 9–midnight, Sun. 9–8 reservations required.*

⑮ **Keats–Shelley Memorial House.** To the right of the Spanish Steps is the house where Keats (1795–1821) died; the building is now a museum dedicated to English Romanticism and Keats and Shelley memorabilia. It also houses a library of works by Romantic authors. ⊠ *Piazza di Spagna 26, next to the Spanish Steps*, ☎ *06/6784235*, WEB *www.Keats-Shelley-House.org*. ⊘ *Mon.–Fri. 9–1 and 3–6, Sat. 11–2 and 3–6.*

⑫ **Museo Etrusco di Villa Giulia** (Etruscan Museum of Villa Giulia). Pope Julius III (1487–1555) built this gracious Renaissance villa as a summer retreat. It's been turned into a fine museum dedicated to the Etruscans, central Italy's pre-Roman inhabitants. The collection, a well-explained cross-section of Etruscan statuary and sculpture, provides an introduction to this complex and ancient culture that is an interesting counterpoint to the city's usual emphasis on Imperial and Papal Rome. ⊠ *Piazzale di Villa Giulia 9*, ☎ *06/3226571*. ⊘ *Tues.–Sat. 9–7, Sun. 9–2.*

⓲ **Palazzo Barberini** (Barberini Palace). Rome's most splendid 17th-century palace houses the **Galleria Nazionale di Arte Antica.** Its gems include Raphael's *La Fornarina* and many other fine paintings, some lavishly frescoed ceilings, and a suite of rooms decorated in 1782 on the occasion of the marriage of a Barberini heiress. ⊠ *Via Barberini 18,* ☎ *06/4824184,* WEB *www.galleriaborghese.it.* ⊙ *Tues.–Sat. 9–7:30, Sun. 9–1.*

⓱ **Piazza Barberini.** This busy crossroads is marked by two Bernini fountains: the saucy **Fontana del Tritone** (Triton Fountain) in the middle of the square and the **Fontana delle Api** (Fountain of the Bees) at the corner of Via Veneto. Decorated with the heraldic Barberini bees, this latter shell-shaped fountain bears an inscription that was immediately seen as an unlucky omen by the superstitious Romans: it proclaimed that the fountain had been erected in the 22nd year of the reign of Pope Urban VIII, who commissioned it, whereas in fact the 21st anniversary of his election was still some weeks away. The incorrect numeral was hurriedly erased, but to no avail: Urban died eight days before the beginning of his 22nd year as pontiff. ⊠ *Square at intersection of Via del Tritone, Via Vittorio Veneto, and Via Barberini.*

⓾ **Piazza del Popolo.** Designed by neoclassical architect Giuseppe Valadier in the early 1800s, this circular square is one of the largest and airiest in Rome. It's a pleasant spot for an afternoon stroll. The 3,000-year-old obelisk in the middle of the square, brought to Rome from Egypt by the emperor Augustus, once stood in the Circus Maximus. ⊠ *Southern end of Via Flaminia and northern end of Via del Corso.*

⓭ **Piazza di Spagna.** The square is the heart of Rome's chic shopping district and a popular rendezvous spot, especially for the young people who throng the **Spanish Steps** on evenings and weekend afternoons. In the center of the elongated square, at the foot of the Spanish Steps, is the **Fontana della Barcaccia** (Old Boat Fountain) by Pietro Bernini (Gian Lorenzo's father). ⊠ *Southern end of Via del Babuino and northern end of Via Due Macelli.*

⓳ **Santa Maria della Concezione.** In the crypt under the main Capuchin church, skeletons and scattered bones of some 4,000 dead Capuchin monks are arranged in odd decorative designs, intended as a macabre reminder of the impermanence of earthly life. ⊠ *Via Veneto 27,* ☎ *06/4871185.* ⊙ *Fri.–Wed. 9–noon and 3–6.*

⓫ **Santa Maria del Popolo.** This medieval church rebuilt by Gian Lorenzo Bernini in Baroque style is rich in art; the pièces de résistance are two stunning Caravaggios in the chapel to the left of the main altar. ⊠ *Piazza del Popolo,* ☎ *06/3610836.* ⊙ *Mon.–Sat. 7–7, Sun. 8–2 and 4:30–7:30.*

★ ⓮ **Scalinata di Trinità dei Monti** (Spanish Steps). The 200-year-old stairway got its nickname from the nearby Spanish Embassy to the Holy See (the Vatican), though it was built with French funds in 1723, as the approach to the French church of **Trinità dei Monti** at the top of the steps. Rome's classic picture-postcard view is even more lovely when the steps are banked with blooming azaleas, from mid-April to mid-May. ⊠ *Piazza di Spagna and Piazza Trinità dei Monti.*

Castel Sant'Angelo and the Vatican

Given that the Vatican is home to many of Rome's (and the world's) greatest art treasures, as well as being the spiritual home of a billion Catholics, this area of the city is full of tourists and pilgrims almost year-round. Between the Vatican and the once-moated bulk of Castel Sant'Angelo, the pope's covered passageway flanks an enclave of workers and craftspeople, the old Borgo neighborhood, whose workaday charm is beginning to succumb to gentrification.

㉑ Castel Sant'Angelo (Sant'Angelo Castle). Transformed into a formidable fortress, this castle was originally built as the tomb of Emperor Hadrian (AD 76–138) in the 2nd century AD. In its early days it looked much like the Augusteo (Tomb of Augustus), which still stands in more or less its original form across the river. Hadrian's Tomb was incorporated into the city's walls and served as a military stronghold during the barbarian invasions. According to legend it got its present name in the 6th century, when Pope Gregory the Great, passing by in a religious procession, saw an angel with a sword appear above the ramparts to signal the end of the plague that was raging. Enlarged and fortified, the castle became a refuge for the popes, who fled to it along the Passetto, an arcaded passageway that links it with the Vatican.

Inside the castle are ancient corridors, medieval cells, and Renaissance salons, a museum of antique weapons, courtyards piled with stone cannonballs, and terraces with great views of the city. The highest terrace of all, under the bronze statue of the legendary angel, is the one from which Puccini's heroine Tosca threw herself to her death. **Ponte Sant'Angelo**, the ancient bridge spanning the Tiber in front of the castle, is decorated with lovely Baroque angels designed by Bernini. ✉ *Lungotevere Castello 50*, ☎ *06/6819111*, WEB *www.vatican.va*. ☉ *Tues.–Sun. 9–8 (ticket office 9–7); longer hrs in summer.*

㉔ Giardini Vaticani (Vatican Gardens). The attractively landscaped gardens can be seen in a two-hour tour that shows you a few historical monuments, fountains, and the lovely 16th-century house of Pius IV (1499–1565), designed by Pirro Ligorio (1500–83), as well as the Vatican's mosaic school. Vistas from within the gardens give you a different perspective on the basilica itself. Reserve two or three days in advance. ✉ *Tickets: Piazza San Pietro*, ☎ *06/69884466.* 🗃 *20,000 lire/€10.35.* ☉ *Tours Apr.–Oct., Mon.–Tues. and Thurs.–Sat. at 10; Nov.–Mar., Sat. at 10, weekdays by request for groups.*

★ ㉕ Musei Vaticani (Vatican Museums). One of the world's greatest collections of Western art, the holdings of the Vatican Museum are an embarrassment of riches that include Ancient Egyptian sarcophagi, Greek and Roman statuary, paintings by Giotto, Leonardo, and Raphael, and Michelangelo's magnificent frescoes in the Sistine Chapel. The nearly 8 km (5 mi) of displays are said to represent only a small part of the Vatican's holdings. The museums are almost unavoidably overwhelming, but four color-coded itineraries marked at the entrance and throughout the galleries help you make sense of it all. The shortest takes 90 minutes, the longest more than four hours, depending on your rate of progress. All routes include the famed **Cappella Sistina** (Sistine Chapel). In 1508 Pope Julius II (1443–1513) commissioned Michelangelo to paint the more than 10,000 square ft of the chapel's ceiling. For four years Michelangelo dedicated himself to painting in the fresco technique, over wet plaster, and the result is one of the Renaissance's masterworks. Cleaning has removed centuries of soot and revealed the original and surprisingly brilliant colors of the ceiling and the *Last Judgment*. The chapel is almost always unpleasantly crowded—try to avoid the tour groups by going early or late. This is one instance in which a pair of binoculars and an illustrated or audio guide will contribute greatly to understanding and appreciating the work.

A complete list of the great works on display would go on for pages; don't-miss highlights, however, certainly include the Egyptian collection, the Roman mosaics and wall paintings, and the great classical- and Hellenistic-style statuary in the Belvedere Courtyard, including the *Laocoön,* the *Belvedere Torso* (which inspired Michelangelo), and the *Apollo Belvedere.* The **Stanze di Raffaello** (Raphael Rooms) are decorated with masterful frescoes, and there are more of Raphael's works in the **Pinacoteca** (Picture Gallery). Bored children may perk up in the whimsical **Sala degli Animali,** a seemingly forgotten room full of animal statuary. ⊠ *Viale Vaticano,* ☎ *06/69884947,* WEB *www.vatican.va.* ۞ *Easter wk and mid-Mar.– Oct., weekdays 8:45–3:45, Sat. 8:45–12:45; Nov.–mid-Mar. (except Easter), Mon.–Sat. 8:45–12:45; last Sun. of every month 8:45–12:45. Closed religious holidays (Jan. 1 and 6, Feb. 11, Mar. 19, Easter Sun. and Mon., May 1, Ascension Thurs., Corpus Christi, June 29, Aug. 15 and 16, Nov. 1, Dec. 8, Dec. 25 and 26) and Sun., excepting last Sun. of month. Note: Ushers at the entrance of St. Peter's Basilica and the Vatican Museums will not allow entry to persons with inappropriate clothing (no bare knees, shoulders, or low-cut shirts).*

㉒ Piazza San Pietro (St. Peter's Square). Gian Lorenzo Bernini designed this vast, circular piazza in the 17th century with an eye to the dramatic contrast between the dark, narrow medieval streets of the area and the wide open space of the piazza, presided over by the magnificence of St. Peter's Basilica. Unfortunately for art history, Mussolini had his own ideas about dramatic effect, which led him to raze much of the medieval neighborhood around the square to create Via della Conciliazione, the broad avenue that leads to the square today. Other aspects of Bernini's vision of architectural harmony remain, however: look for the stone disks in the pavement halfway between the fountains and the obelisk. From these points the colonnades seem to be formed of a single row of columns all the way around. The square was designed to accommodate crowds, and it has held up to 400,000 people at one time. At noon on Sunday when he is in Rome, the pope appears at his third-floor study window in the **Palazzo Vaticano,** to the right of the basilica, to bless the crowd in the square, and in warm months he blesses visitors from a podium on the basilica steps on Wednesday mornings. ⊠ *End of Via Conciliazione.*

Since the Lateran Treaty of 1929, Vatican City has been an independent and sovereign state, which covers about 108 acres and is surrounded by thick, high walls. Its gates are watched over by the Swiss Guards, who still wear the colorful dress uniforms based on a Michelangelo design. Sovereign of this little state is the Pope of the Roman Catholic Church. For many visitors a **papal audience** is the highlight of a trip to Rome. Mass audiences take place on Wednesday morning in the square or in a modern audience hall (capacity 7,000) off the left-hand colonnade. Tickets are necessary. For audience tickets write or fax well in advance indicating the date you prefer, language you speak, and hotel in which you will stay. Or, apply for tickets in person on the Monday or Tuesday before the Wednesday audience. ⊠ *Tickets: Prefettura della Casa Pontificia, 00120 Vatican City,* ☎ *06/69883273,* FAX *06/ 69885863.* ۞ *Mon.–Tues. 9–1.*

★ **㉓ St. Peter's Basilica** (Basilica di San Pietro). In all of its staggering grandeur and magnificence, St. Peter's Basilica is best appreciated as the lustrous background for ecclesiastical ceremonies thronged with the faithful. The original basilica was built in the early 4th century AD by the emperor Constantine, above an earlier shrine that supposedly marked the burial place of St. Peter. After more than 1,000 years, the decrepit old basilica had to be torn down. The task of building a new, much larger one took almost 200 years and employed the genius of many of the Renaissance's greatest architects, including Alberti (1404–72), Bramante (1444–1514), Raphael, Peruzzi (1481–1536), Antonio Sangallo the Younger (1483–

1546), and Michelangelo, who died before the dome he had planned could be completed. The structure was finally finished in 1626.

The most famous work of art inside is Michelangelo's *Pietà* (1498), in the first chapel on the right as you enter the basilica. Michelangelo carved four statues of the Pietà, or Mary cradling her dead son; this one is the earliest and best known, two others are in Florence, and the fourth, the *Rondanini Pietà,* is in Milan. At the end of the central aisle is the bronze statue of St. Peter, its foot worn by centuries of reverent kisses. The bronze throne above the altar in the apse was created by Bernini to contain a simple wood-and-ivory chair believed to have once belonged to St. Peter. Bernini's baldachin over the papal altar was made with bronze stripped from the dome of the Pantheon at the order of Pope Urban VIII, one of the powerful Roman Barberini family. His practice of plundering ancient monuments for material with which to carry out his grandiose decorating schemes inspired the famous quip "*Quod non fecerunt barbari, fecerunt Barberini*" ("What the barbarians didn't do, the Barberinis did").

As you stroll up and down the aisles and transepts, notice the fine mosaic copies of famous paintings above the altars, the monumental tombs and statues, and the fine stuccowork. Stop at the **Museo Storico** (Historical Museum), which contains some priceless liturgical objects. ☉ *Apr.–Sept., daily 9–6; Oct.–Mar., daily 9–5.*

The entrance to the so-called **Grotte Vaticane** (Vatican Grottoes), crypts containing chapels and the tombs of various popes, is in one of the huge piers under the dome, next to the central altar. It's best to leave this visit for last, as the crypt's only exit takes you outside the church. It occupies the area of the original basilica, over the necropolis, the ancient burial ground where evidence of what may be St. Peter's burial place has been found. ☉ *Apr.–Sept., daily 7–6; Oct.–Mar., daily 7–5.*

To see the **roof and dome** of the basilica, take the elevator or climb the stairs in the courtyard near the exit from the Vatican Grottoes. From the roof you can climb a short interior staircase to the base of the dome for an overhead view of the basilica's interior. Then, and only if you are in good shape, you should attempt the very long, strenuous, and claustrophobic climb up the narrow stairs to the balcony of the lantern atop the dome, where you can look down on the Giardini Vaticani (Vatican Gardens) and out across all of Rome. ⊠ *Entrance in courtyard to the left as you leave the basilica.* ☉ *Apr.–Sept., daily 8–6; Oct.–Mar., daily 8–5.*

Free 60-minute tours of St. Peter's Basilica are offered in English daily (Monday–Saturday usually starting about 10 AM and 3 PM, Sunday at 2:30 PM) by volunteer guides. They start at the information desk under the basilica portico. At the Ufficio Scavi you can book special tours of the necropolis. Note that entry to St. Peter's, the Musei Vaticani, and the Gardens is barred to those wearing shorts, miniskirts, sleeveless T-shirts, and otherwise revealing clothing. Women can cover bare shoulders and upper arms with scarves; men should wear full-length pants or jeans. ⊠ *Piazza San Pietro,* ☎ *06/69884466,* WEB *www.vatican.va.* ☉ *Apr.–Sept., daily 7–7; Oct.–Mar., daily 7–6. Closed during ceremonies in the piazza. Necropolis (left beyond Arco delle Campane entrance to Vatican):* ☎ *06/69885318. Apply a few days in advance to Ufficio Scavi, or try in morning for the same day. Office Mon.–Sat. 9–5.*

Old Rome

The land between the Corso and the Tiber bend is packed with churches, patrician palaces, Baroque piazzas, and picturesque courtyards, with Piazza Navona as a magnificent central point. In between are narrow streets and intriguing little shops, interspersed with eating places and cafés that are a focus of Rome's easygoing, itinerant nightlife.

★ **㉞ Campo dei Fiori** (Field of Flowers). This wide square is the site of Rome's best-loved morning market, a crowded and colorful circus of fruits, flowers, and fish, raucously peddled daily 9–2. If you'd rather watch than participate in the genial chaos, sit at one of the pleasant cafés that line the square. The hooded bronze figure brooding over the piazza is philosopher Giordano Bruno (1548–1600), who was burned at the stake here for heresy in 1600. ⊠ *Piazza Campo dei Fiori.*

㉗ Chiesa del Gesù. This huge 16th-century church is a paragon of the Baroque style and the tangible symbol of the power of the Jesuits, who were a major force in the Counter-Reformation in Europe. Its interior gleams with gold and precious marbles, and it has a fantastically painted ceiling that flows down over the pillars, merging with painted stucco figures to complete the three-dimensional illusion. ⊠ *Piazza del Gesù,* ☎ *06/697001.* ✆ *Daily 7–noon and 4–7.*

㉖ Fontana delle Tartarughe (Turtle Fountain). The winsome turtles that are this 16th-century fountain's hallmark are thought to have been added around 1658 by Bernini as a low-budget way to bring the Renaissance fountain into the Baroque. Visit it on a stroll through Rome's former Jewish Ghetto, an atmospheric old neighborhood with medieval inscriptions and friezes on the old buildings on Via Portico d'Ottavia, and the remains of the Teatro di Marcello (Theater of Marcello), a theater built by Julius Caesar to hold 20,000 spectators. ⊠ *Piazza Mattei.*

㉘ Galleria Doria Pamphili. You can visit this rambling palazzo, still the residence of a princely family, to view the gallery housing the family's art collection and also some of the magnificently furnished private apartments. ⊠ *Piazza del Collegio Romano 2,* ☎ *06/6797323,* 𝚆𝙴𝙱 *www.doriapamphilj.it.* ✆ *Fri.–Wed. 10–5; private-apartments tours 10:30, 11, 11:30, noon. Closed May 1, Aug. 15, Nov. 1.*

㊱ Isola Tiberina. Built in 62 BC, Rome's oldest bridge, the **Ponte Fabricio,** links the Ghetto neighborhood on the Tiber's left bank to this little island, home to a hospital and the church of San Bartolomeo. The island has been dedicated to healing ever since a temple to Aesculapius was erected here in 291 BC. **Ponte Cestio** links the island with the Trastevere neighborhood on the right bank.

....

OFF THE   **Ostia Antica** (Ancient Ostia) – The well-preserved Roman port city of
BEATEN PATH Ostia Antica, near the sea, is now a vast archaeological park just outside
             Rome, a lovely day trip into the ancient past. Wander through ancient
             markets and ruined houses, or bring a picnic and enjoy the sea breeze.
             There's regular train service from the Ostiense Station (Piramide Metro
             Bstop). ⊠ *Via dei Romagnoli, Ostia Antica, not far from Fiumicino Air-*
             port, ☎ *06/56358099,* 𝚆𝙴𝙱 *www.itnw.roma.it/ostia/scavi.* ✆ *Excava-*
             tions: Tues.–Sun. 9 AM–1 hr before sunset. Museum: Tues.–Sun. 9–1:30.

....

㉛ Palazzo Altemps. A 15th-century patrician dwelling, the palace is a showcase for the sculpture collection of the **Museo Nazionale Romano** (National Museum of Rome). Informative labels in English make it easy to appreciate such famous sculptures as the intricate carved reliefs on the *Ludovisi Sarcophagus* and the *Galata,* representing the heroic death of a barbarian warrior. ⊠ *Piazza Sant'Apollinare 46,* ☎ *06/6833566,* 𝚆𝙴𝙱 *www.archeorm.arti.beniculturali.it.* ✆ *Tues.–Sun. 9–7:45.*

㉟ Palazzo Farnese. Now the French Embassy, one of the most beautiful of Rome's many Renaissance palaces dominates Piazza Farnese, where Egyptian marble basins from the Terme di Caracalla have been transformed into fountains. Note the unique brickwork patterns on the palace's facade. ✉ *Piazza Farnese.*

★ ③⓪ **Pantheon.** Lauded for millennia for its architectural harmony, the Pantheon is no less impressive in the 21st century. Built in 27 BC by Augustus's general Agrippa and totally rebuilt by Hadrian in the 2nd century AD, this unique temple (consecrated as a church in the Middle Ages) is a must-see. Notice the equal proportions of the height of the dome and the circular interior—unlike most angular buildings, the Pantheon is designed after a globe. The oculus, or opening in the ceiling, is meant to symbolize the all-seeing eye of heaven; in practice, it illuminates the building and lightens the heavy stone ceiling. In earlier times the dome was covered in bronze, later pilfered to construct the baldachin over the altar in St. Peter's. ✉ *Piazza della Rotonda,* ☎ 06/68300230. ⊙ *Mon.–Sat. 9–6:30, Sun. 9–1.*

★ ③③ **Piazza Navona.** This elongated 17th-century piazza traces the oval form of the underlying Circus of Diocletian. At the center, Bernini's lively **Fontana dei Quattro Fiumi** (Four Rivers Fountain) is a showpiece. The four statues represent rivers in the four corners of the world: the Nile, with its face covered in allusion to its then-unknown source; the Ganges; the Danube; and the River Plata, with its hand raised. You may hear the legend that this was Bernini's mischievous dig at Borromini's design of the facade of the church of **Sant'Agnese in Agone,** from which the statue seems to be shrinking in horror. In point of fact, the fountain was created in 1651; work on the church's facade began a year or two later. ✉ *North of Corso Vittorio Emanuele and west of Corso Rinascimento.*

③② **San Luigi dei Francesi.** The clergy of San Luigi considered Caravaggio's roistering and unruly lifestyle scandalous enough, but his realistic treatment of sacred subjects—seen in three paintings here—was just too much for them. They rejected his first version of the altarpiece and weren't particularly happy with the other two works either. Thanks to the intercession of Caravaggio's patron, an influential cardinal, they were persuaded to keep them—a lucky thing, since they are now recognized to be among the artist's finest paintings. Have a few 500-lire coins handy for the light machine. ✉ *Piazza San Luigi dei Francesi,* ☎ 06/688271. ⊙ *Fri.–Wed. 7:30–12:30 and 3:30–7, Thurs. 7:30–12:30.*

②⑨ **Santa Maria sopra Minerva.** Rome's only major Gothic church takes its name from the temple of Minerva over which it was built. Inside are some beautiful frescoes by Filippino Lippi (circa 1457–1504); outside in the square is a charming elephant by Bernini carrying an obelisk on its back. ✉ *Piazza della Minerva,* ☎ 06/6791217. ⊙ *Daily 7–noon and 4–7.*

DINING

Rome has no shortage of restaurants, and what the city lacks in variety of fare is made up for by overall quality. Don't make the mistake of assuming that expensive restaurants serve better or more authentic food; in Rome, you may pay top dollar for nothing more than a flourish of linen and silver. Some of Rome's prime restaurants are worth the expense, but you'll often do better at a more unassuming trattoria or osteria. Romans eat out a lot, and there's a wide variety of Italian fast food that caters to workers on lunch breaks. These places serve anything from a fruit salad and fresh spinach to lasagna and deep-fried cod fillets. Unfortunately, non-Italian cuisines haven't really caught on in Rome, although there are a few excellent Eritrean and Ethiopian places near Termini and some less appealing Chinese restaurants throughout the center. That old Roman standby, the paper-thin, crispy wood-oven pizza, is a low-budget favorite among locals and travelers alike, as is its to-go cousin, the heartier *pizza al taglio*. During August and over Christmas many restaurants close for vacation.

CATEGORY	COST*
$$$$	over 45,000 lire (€23)
$$$	35,000 lire–45,000 lire (€18–€23)
$$	25,000 lire–35,000 lire (€13–€18)
$	under 25,000 lire (€13)

*per person for a main course at dinner

$$$$ ✕ **La Rosetta.** The city's most elegant seafood restaurant, La Rosetta is still the place to go in Rome for artful presentations of first-rate fish. The space is elegant in its simplicity, with warm woods, fresh flowers, and a stunning display of fish at the entrance. Particularly good are the *vongole veraci* (sautéed clams), *tonnarelli ai frutti di mare* (poached fish on artichokes or potatoes), and sea bass with black truffles. Home-made desserts are worth saving room for. ⊠ *Via della Rosetta 9,* ☎ *06/6861002. Dinner reservations essential. AE, DC, MC, V.* ☺ *Closed Sun. and 2–3 weeks in Aug. No lunch Thurs. and Fri.*

$$$ ✕ **Sangallo.** Small and intimate, this is an old-fashioned restaurant where
★   the owner buys the fish himself, and where dinner is meant to last all night. The traditional menu leans heavily toward the gourmet, with dishes like oysters *tartare*, snapper with *foie gras*, Texas steaks and a fixed-price menu based on truffles. There are few tables in the tiny dining room, so make sure to book ahead. ⊠ *Vicolo della Vaccarella 11/a,* ☎ *06/6865549. AE, DC, MC, V. Closed Sun., 1 wk in Jan., and 2 wks in Aug. No lunch Mon.*

$$–$$$ ✕ **Checchino dal 1887.** Carved out of a hillside made of potsherds from Roman times, Checchino serves the most traditional Roman cuisine—carefully prepared and served without fanfare—in a clean, sober environment. You can try the variety of meats that make up the soul of Roman cooking, including *trippa* (tripe) and *coratella* (sweetbreads). There's also plenty to choose from for those uninterested in innards. ⊠ *Via di Monte Testaccio 30,* ☎ *06/5746318. AE, DC, MC, V. Closed Mon., Aug., and during Christmas. No dinner Sun.*

$$–$$$ ✕ **Dal Bolognese.** This classic restaurant is a trendy choice for a
★   leisurely lunch between sightseeing and shopping. An array of contemporary paintings decorates the dining room, but the real attraction is the lovely piazza—prime people-watching real estate. As the name of the restaurant promises, the cooking here adheres to the hearty tradition of Bologna, with delicious homemade *tortellini in brodo* (tortellini in broth), fresh pastas in creamy sauces, and *bollito misto* (steaming trays of boiled meats). ⊠ *Piazza del Popolo 1,* ☎ *06/3611426. AE, DC, MC, V. Closed Mon. and Aug.*

$$–$$$ ✕ **Papà Baccus.** Italo Cipriani, owner of Rome's best Tuscan restaurant, takes his meat as seriously as any Tuscan, using real Chianina beef for the house special, *bistecca alla fiorentina* (grilled, thick bone-in steak). If you're avoiding beef, you can sample such dishes as Tuscan bean soup, and the sweet and delicate prosciutto from Pratomagno. The welcome here is warm, the service excellent, and the decor has the feel of an upscale trattoria. ⊠ *Via Toscana 36,* ☎ *06/42742808. AE, DC, MC, V. Closed Sun., Aug., and during Christmas. No lunch Sat.*

$$ ✕ **Colline Emiliane.** Behind an opaque glass facade not far from Piazza Barberini lies this quiet, family-run restaurant reputed to serve the city's best classic Emilian cuisine: light homemade pastas, *tortelli di zucca* (pumpkin-filled ravioli), and meats ranging from *giambonetto di vitello* (roast veal) to *cotoletta alla bolognese* (fried veal cutlet with cheese and prosciutto). ⊠ *Via degli Avignonesi 22,* ☎ *06/4818564. Reservations essential. MC, V. Closed Fri. and Aug.*

$$ ✕ **Il Simposio di Costantini.** At the classiest wine bar in town—done out in wrought-iron vines, wood paneling, and velvet—choose from about 30 wines in *degustazione* (available by the glass) or order a bottle from a list of more than 1,000 Italian and foreign labels sold in the shop next door. Food is appropriately fancy: marinated and smoked fish, designer salads, fine cured meats, terrines and pâtés, and stellar cheeses. ✉ *Piazza Cavour 16, near the Vatican,* ☎ *06/3211502. AE, DC, MC, V. Closed Sun. and Aug. No lunch Sat.*

$$ ✕ **Myosotis.** The menu here rides a delicate line between tradition and
★ innovation, focusing more on the freshness and quality of the ingredients than on elaborate presentation. Fresh pasta gets special attention on the extensive menu: it's rolled out by hand to order for the *stracci alla delizia di mare* (pasta with seafood). The wine list is ample, and the prices are honest. ✉ *Vicolo della Vaccarella 3/5,* ☎ *06/6865554. AE, DC, MC, V. Closed Sun. and 2 wks in Aug.*

$–$$ ✕ **Dal Toscano.** The hallmarks of this great family-run Tuscan trattoria near the Vatican are friendly and speedy service, an open wood-fired grill, and such classic dishes as *ribollita* (a dense bread and vegetable soup) and the prized bistecca alla fiorentina. Wash it all down with a strong Chianti. All desserts are homemade and delicious. ✉ *Via Germanico 58,* ☎ *06/39725717. AE, DC, MC, V. Closed Mon., Aug., and 2 wks in Dec.*

$ ✕ **Alfredo e Ada.** There's no place like home, and you'll feel like you're back there from the moment you squeeze into a table at this hole in the wall just across the river from Castel Sant'Angelo. There's no menu, just plate after plate of whatever Ada thinks you should try, from hearty, classic pastas to *involtini di vitello* (savory veal rolls with tomato) and homemade sausage. Sit back and enjoy—it's all good. ✉ *Via dei Banchi Nuovi 14,* ☎ *06/6878842. No credit cards. Closed weekends.*

$ ✕ **Da Gino.** Trastevere's most elegant pizzeria serves all the classics but with a style that sets it apart from its more rough-and-tumble neighbors. Delectably thin wood-oven pizza shares menu space with treats like *fritto di moscardini* (fried baby squid); the wine list shows a sommelier's touch. Outdoor tables on a bustling pedestrian street are refreshing in summer. ✉ *Via della Lungaretta 85,* ☎ *06/5803403. AE, MC, V. Closed Wed. Lunch Sun. only.*

$ ✕ **Perilli.** A bastion of authentic Roman cooking and trattoria charm since 1911 (the decor has changed very little), this is the place to go to try rigatoni *con pajata* (with veal's intestines)—if you're into that sort of thing. Otherwise the carbonara and *all'amatriciana* (spicy tomato sauce with pancetta) are classics. The house wine is a golden nectar from the Castelli Romani. ✉ *Via Marmorata 39,* ☎ *06/5742415. AE, DC, MC, V. Closed Wed.*

LODGING

Hotels listed are within walking distance of at least some sights and handy to public transportation. Those in the $$ and $ categories do not have restaurants but serve Continental breakfast. Rooms facing the street may get traffic noise throughout the night, and few hotels in the lower price categories have double-glazed windows. Ask for a quiet room—or bring earplugs. Always make reservations, even if only a few days in advance. Always inquire about discounts. Should you find yourself in the city without reservations, however, contact **HR** (✉ Termini Station; Aeroporto Fiumicino, ☎ 06/6991000), a hotel reservation service, or **EPT** (✉ Via Parigi 5, ☎ 06/48899253, FAX 06/4819316; ✉ near Piazza della Repubblica; ✉ Aeroporto Fiumicino, ☎ 06/65956074; ✉ Stazione Termini, ☎ 06/4871270). The Rome municipal tourist information booths will also help you find a room.

CATEGORY	COST*
$$$$	over 500,000 lire (€258)
$$$	350,000 lire–500,000 lire (€180–€258)
$$	200,000 lire–350,000 lire (€103–€180)
$	under 200,000 lire (€103)

Prices are based on two people sharing a double room.

$$$$ 🏨 **Dei Borgognoni.** This quietly chic hotel near Piazza Colonna is as central as you could want, yet the winding byway stage set gives you a sense of being off the beaten track. The centuries-old building provides spacious lounges, a glassed-in garden, and rooms well arranged to create an illusion of space, though they are actually compact. The hotel has a garage (fee), a rarity in such a central location. ⊠ *Via del Bufalo 126, 00187,* ☎ *06/69941505,* FAX *06/69941501,* WEB *www. borgognoni.it. 51 rooms. AE, DC, MC, V.*

$$$$ 🏨 **Eden.** The historic Eden, a haunt of Hemingway, Ingrid Bergman,
★   and Fellini, merits superlatives for dashing elegance and stunning vistas of Rome from the rooftop restaurant and bar (also from some of the most expensive rooms). Precious but discreet antique furnishings, fine linen sheets, and marble baths whisper understated opulence. ⊠ *Via Ludovisi 49, 00187,* ☎ *06/478121,* FAX *06/4821584,* WEB *www.hotel-eden.it. 101 rooms, 12 suites. Restaurant. AE, DC, MC, V.*

$$$$ 🏨 **Hassler.** You can expect a cordial atmosphere and superb service at this hotel at the top of the Spanish Steps. The public rooms have an extravagant, somewhat dated decor, especially the clubby winter bar, garden bar, and the glass-roofed lounge, with gold marble walls and hand-painted tile floors. Elegant bedrooms are decorated in a variety of classic styles (the best feature is the frescoed walls). ⊠ *Piazza Trinità dei Monti 6, 00187,* ☎ *06/699340,* FAX *06/6789991,* WEB *www. hotelhasslerroma.com. 85 rooms, 15 suites. Restaurant. AE, DC, MC, V.*

$$$ 🏨 **Britannia.** A quiet locale off Via Nazionale is only one of the attractions
★   of this small, special hotel, where you will be coddled with luxury touches such as English-language dailies and local weather reports delivered to your room each morning. The well-furnished rooms (two with a rooftop terrace), frescoed halls, and lounge (where a rich breakfast buffet is served) attest the management really cares about superior service and value. ⊠ *Via Napoli 64, 00184,* ☎ *06/4883153,* FAX *06/ 4882343,* WEB *www.italyhotel.com. 32 rooms, 1 suite. AE, DC, MC, V.*

$$$ 🏨 **Farnese.** An early 20th-century mansion, the Farnese is in a quiet but
★   central residential district. Art Deco–style furniture is mixed with enchanting fresco decorations amid its compact rooms, plenty of lounge space, and a roof garden. ⊠ *Via Alessandro Farnese 30, 00193,* ☎ *06/3212553,* FAX *06/3215129,* WEB *www.travel.it. 24 rooms. AE, DC, MC, V.*

$$$ 🏨 **La Residenza.** A converted town house near Via Veneto, this hotel offers good value and first-class comfort at reasonable rates. Public areas are spacious and guest rooms are comfortable and have large closets and TVs. The hotel's clientele is mainly from the United States. Rates include a generous buffet breakfast. ⊠ *Via Emilia 22, 00187,* ☎ *06/ 4880789,* FAX *06/485721,* WEB *www.venere.it. 21 rooms, 6 suites. V.*

$$–$$$ 🏨 **Scalinata di Spagna.** An old-fashioned pensione loved by generations of romantics, this tiny hotel is booked solid for months ahead. Its location at the top of the Spanish Steps, inconspicuous little entrance, quaint hodgepodge of old furniture, and view from the terrace where you breakfast make it seem like your own special, exclusive inn. ⊠ *Piazza Trinità dei Monti 17, 00187,* ☎ *06/6793006,* FAX *06/69940598. 15 rooms. MC, V.*

$$ 🏨 **Amalia.** Handy to St. Peter's, the Vatican, and the Cola di Rienzo shopping district, this small hotel is owned and operated by the Consoli family—Amalia and her brothers. On several floors of a 19th-century building, it has large rooms with functional furnishings, TVs, mini-bars, pictures of angels on the walls, and gleaming marble bathrooms (hair dryers included). The Ottaviano stop of Metro A is a block away. ✉ *Via Germanico 66, 00192,* ☎ *06/39723356,* FAX *06/39723365,* WEB *www.hotelamalia.com. 30 rooms, 23 with bath. AE, MC, V.*

$ 🛏 **Margutta.** This small hotel near the Spanish Steps and Piazza del
★ Popolo has an unassuming lobby but bright, attractive bedrooms with wrought-iron bedsteads and modern baths. ✉ *Via Laurina 34, 00187,* ☎ *06/3223674,* FAX *06/3200395. 24 rooms. AE, DC, MC, V.*

$ 🛏 **Romae.** Near Termini Station, this mid-size hotel has clean, spacious rooms with light-wood furniture and small but bright bathrooms. The congenial, helpful management offers special winter rates and welcomes families. Low rates that include breakfast and free Internet access make this a good deal. ✉ *Via Palestro 49, 00185,* ☎ *06/4463554,* FAX *06/4463914,* WEB *www.hotelromae.com. 38 rooms. AE, MC, V.*

NIGHTLIFE AND THE ARTS

You will find information on scheduled events and shows at EPT and municipal tourist offices or booths. The biweekly booklet *Un Ospite a Roma,* free from concierges at some hotels, is another source of information, as is *Wanted in Rome,* published on Wednesday, available at newsstands. There are listings in English in the back of the weekly *Roma C'è* booklet, with handy bus information for each listing; it is published on Thursday and sold at newsstands. If you want to go to the opera, the ballet, or a concert, it's best to ask your concierge to get tickets for you. They are sold at box offices only, just a few days before performances.

The Arts

Concerts

The main concert hall is the **Accademia di Santa Cecilia** (✉ Via della Conciliazione 4, ☎ 06/68801044). Concerts are held year-round; look for posters or for schedules in the publications mentioned above.

Film

There are two original-language movie theaters in Rome, **Pasquino** (✉ Piazza Sant'Egidio, near Piazza Santa Maria in Trastevere, ☎ 06/5803622) and **Quirinetta** (✉ Via Minghetti 4, off Via del Corso near Piazza Venezia, ☎ 06/6790012). Programs are listed in Rome's daily newspapers, as well as the *Italy Daily* supplement to the *International Herald Tribune.* Several other movie theaters show films in English on certain days of the week; the listings in *Roma C'è* are reliable.

Opera

The opera season runs from November or December through May, and performances are staged in the **Teatro dell'Opera** (✉ Piazza Beniamino Gigli, ☎ 06/48160255 or 06/481601). From May through August, the spectacular performances are held in the open air at one end of the Stadio Olimpico, Rome's soccer stadium. Smaller opera companies put up their own low-budget, high-quality productions in various venues. Look for posters advertising performances.

Nightlife

Rome's "in" nightspots change frequently, and many fade into oblivion after a brief moment of glory. The best places to find an up-to-date list are the weekly entertainment guide "Trovaroma," published each Thursday in the Italian daily *La Repubblica,* and *Roma C'è,* the weekly guide sold at newsstands.

Bars

More and more American-style bars are lining Rome's streets these days. Try Trastevere or the area west of Piazza Navona for a bit of bar-hopping. One of the grandest places for a drink in well-dressed company is **Le Bar** (⊠ Via Vittorio Emanuele Orlando 3, ☎ 06/47091) of Le Grand Hotel. **Jazz Cafè** (⊠ Via Zanardelli 12, ☎ 06/6861990), near Piazza Navona, is an upscale watering hole with good live music downstairs. **Flann O'Brien** (⊠ Via Napoli 29, ☎ 06/4880418), one of a plethora of pubs that now monopolize the bar scene in Rome, has the feel of a good Irish pub. **Trinity College** (⊠ Via del Collegio Romano 6, near Piazza Venezia, ☎ 06/6786472) has two floors of Irish pub trappings, with happy chatter and background music until 3 AM.

Discos and Nightclubs

Testaccio's three-floor **Saint** (⊠ Via Galvani 46, ☎ 06/5747945) has two discos designated "Paradiso" and "Inferno" (Heaven and Hell). You might spot an American celeb at **Gilda** (⊠ Via Mario de' Fiori 97, ☎ 06/6784838), with a disco, piano bar, and live music. It's closed Monday and jackets are required. Just as exclusive is **Bella Blu** (⊠ Via Luciani 21, ☎ 06/3230490), a club in Parioli that caters to Rome's thirtysomething elite.

Music Clubs

For the best live music, including jazz, blues, rhythm and blues, African, and rock, go to **Big Mama** (⊠ Vicolo San Francesco a Ripa 18, ☎ 06/5812551). A membership card required for entry will set you back 20,000 lire/€10.35. Live performances of jazz, soul, and funk by leading musicians draw celebrities to **Alexanderplatz** (⊠ Via Ostia 9, in the Vatican area, ☎ 06/39742171). The music starts about 10 PM, and you can have supper while you wait.

SHOPPING

Via Condotti, directly across from the Spanish Steps, and the streets running parallel to Via Condotti, as well as its cross streets, form the most elegant and expensive shopping area for clothes and accessories in Rome—head here first for top Italian and European designer shops. Lower-price fashions are on display at shops on **Via Frattina** and **Via del Corso.** Romans in the know do much of their shopping along **Via Cola di Rienzo** and **Via Nazionale.** For prints, browse among the stalls at **Piazza Fontanella Borghese** or stop in at the shops in the Pantheon area. For minor antiques **Via dei Coronari** and other streets in the Piazza Navona area are good. High-end antiques dealers are situated in **Via del Babuino** and its environs. The open-air markets near **Campo dei Fiori** and in other neighborhoods throughout the city provide an eyeful of local color.

ROME A TO Z

To research prices, get advice from other travelers, and book travel arrangements, visit www.fodors.com.

AIRPORTS AND TRANSFERS

Rome's principal airport is Aeroporto Leonardo da Vinci, usually known as Fiumicino. The smaller Ciampino, on the edge of Rome, is used as an alternative by international and domestic lines, especially for charter flights.

➤ AIRPORT INFORMATION: **Aeroporto Leonardo da Vinci** (⊠ 29 km/18 mi southeast of Rome, ☎ 06/65953640 flight information). **Ciampino** (☎ 06/794941 flight information, WEB www.adr.it).

TRANSFERS

To get to downtown Rome from Fiumicino you have a choice of two trains. Ask at the airport (at EPT or train information counters) which one takes you closest to your hotel. The nonstop Airport–Termini express takes you directly to Track 22 at Termini Station, Rome's main train terminal, well served by taxis and the hub of Metro (subway) and bus lines. The ride to Termini takes 30 minutes; departures are hourly, beginning at 7:50 AM, with the final departure at 10:05 PM. Tickets cost 13,000 lire/€6.70. The other airport train (FM1) runs to Tiburtina station in Rome and beyond to Monterotondo, a suburban town to the east. The main stops in Rome are at the Trastevere, Ostiense, and Tiburtina stations. At each of these you can find taxis and bus and/or Metro connections to various parts of Rome. This train runs from 6:35 AM to 12:15 AM, with departures every 20 minutes. The ride to Tiburtina takes 40 minutes. Tickets cost 8,000 lire/€4.15. For either train, buy your ticket at an automated vending machine (you need Italian currency) or the ticket office just before the train platforms. There are ticket counters at some stations (Termini Track 22, Trastevere, Tiburtina). Remember to date-stamp your ticket in one of the yellow machines near the track.

A taxi to or from Fiumicino costs 70,000 lire/€36.15–80,000 lire/€41.30, including extra charges for baggage and off-hours. At a booth inside the terminal you can hire a four- or five-passenger car with driver for a little more. If you decide to take a taxi, use only the yellow or the newer white cabs, in line at the official stand outside the terminal; make sure the meter is running. Gypsy cab drivers solicit your business as you come out of customs; they're not reliable, and their rates may be higher. Ciampino is connected with the Anagnina station of the Metro A by bus (runs every half hour). A taxi between Ciampino and downtown Rome costs about 35,000 lire/€18.

BIKE AND MOPED TRAVEL

Pedaling through Villa Borghese, along the Tiber, and through the city center when traffic is light is a pleasant way to see the sights, but remember: Rome is hilly. Rental concessions are at the Piazza di Spagna and Piazza del Popolo Metro stops, and at Piazza San Silvestro and Largo Argentina. You will also find rentals at Viale della Pineta and Viale del Bambino on the Pincio, inside Villa Borghese. Collalti, just off Campo de' Fiori, leases and repairs bikes. St. Peter's Motor Rent rents bikes and mopeds. You can also rent a moped or scooter and mandatory helmet at Scoot-a-Long.
➤ BIKE AND MOPED RENTALS: **Collalti** (✉ Via del Pellegrino 82, ☎ 06/68801084). **Scoot-a-Long** (✉ Via Cavour 302, ☎ 06/6780206). **St. Peter's Motor Rent** (✉ Via di Porta Castello 43, near St. Peter's, ☎ 06/6875714).

BUS TRAVEL WITHIN ROME

Orange ATAC city buses (and a few streetcar lines) run from about 6 AM to midnight, with night buses (indicated N) on some lines. Bus lines 117 and 119, with compact electric vehicles, make a circuit of limited but scenic routes in downtown Rome. They can save you from a lot of walking, and you can get on and off as you please. The orange-and-blue J-Line buses are a handy alternative way to get across town; route information and tickets (1,900 lire/€1) are available at newsstands and tobacconists.
➤ BUS INFORMATION: **ATAC** (☎ 800/431784).

CAR TRAVEL

If you come by car, put it in a parking space (and note that parking in central Rome is generally either metered or prohibited) or a garage, and use public transportation. If you must park in a metered (blue-outlined) space, buy credits at the blue machines near parking areas, scratch off the time you've paid for, and display them on your dashboard. If you plan to drive into or out of the city, take time to study your route, especially on the GRA (Grande Raccordo Anulare, a beltway that encircles Rome and funnels traffic into the city, not always successfully). The main access routes to Rome from the north are the A1 autostrada from Florence and Milan and the Aurelia highway (SS 1) from Genoa. The principal route to or from points south, such as Naples, is the A2 autostrada.

EMBASSIES

➤ CANADA: (✉ Via Zara 30, ☎ 06/445981).

➤ UNITED KINGDOM: (✉ Via XX [pronounced "Venti"] Settembre 80a, ☎ 06/48903708).

➤ UNITED STATES: (✉ Via Veneto 121, ☎ 06/46741).

EMERGENCIES

Pharmacies are open 8:30–1 and 4–8. Some stay open all night, and all open Sunday on a rotation system; a listing of the neighborhood pharmacies open all night is posted at each pharmacy. The number below gives an automated list of three open pharmacies closest to the telephone from which you call. When calling for ambulance service, say *Pronto Soccorso* ("emergency room") and be prepared to give your address.

➤ EMERGENCY SERVICES: **Ambulance** (☎ 1188 or 06/5510). **Police** (☎ 113).

➤ HOSPITALS: **Salvator Mundi Hospital** (☎ 06/588961, WEB www.smih.pcn.net). **Rome American Hospital** (☎ 06/22551, WEB www.rah.it).

➤ 24-HOUR PHARMACIES: (☎ 1100).

ENGLISH-LANGUAGE MEDIA

➤ BOOKSTORES: **Anglo-American Bookstore** (✉ Via della Vite 102, ☎ 06/6795222, WEB www.aab.it). **Corner Bookstore** (✉ Via del Moro 48, Trastevere, ☎ 06/5836942). **Economy Book and Video Center** (✉ Via Torino 136, ☎ 06/4746877, WEB www.booksitaly.com). **Feltrinelli International** (✉ Via Emanuele Orlando 84, ☎ 06/4827878). **Open Door Bookshop** (Secondhand books, ✉ Via Lungaretta 25, ☎ 06/5896478).

METRO TRAVEL

The Metro (subway) is a fast and easy way to get around, but it doesn't serve many of the areas you'll probably want to visit, particularly Old Rome. It opens at 5:30 AM, and the last train leaves each terminal at 11:30 PM. Metro A runs from the eastern part of the city to Termini station and past Piazza di Spagna and Piazzale Flaminio to Ottaviano-S. Pietro, near St. Peter's and the Vatican museums. Metro B serves Termini, the Colosseum, and Tiburtina station (where the FM1 Fiumicino Airport train stops).

TAXIS

Taxis wait at stands and, for a small extra charge, can also be called by telephone. They're very difficult to hail, but you can try to flag down taxis whose roof lights are illuminated. The meter starts at 4,500 lire/€2.65; there are extra charges for night service (5,000 lire/2.50 extra from 10 PM to 7 AM) and on Sunday and holidays, as well as for each piece of baggage. Use the yellow or the newer white cabs only, and be very sure to check the meter. To call a cab, dial one of the numbers listed below; the operator will give you a medallion number and arrival time.

➤ TAXI COMPANIES: (☎ 06/3570, 06/5551, 06/4994, or 06/88177).

TOURS

Most operators offer half-day excursions to Tivoli to see the Villa d'Este's fountains and gardens; Appian Line and CIT run half-day tours to Tivoli that also include Hadrian's Villa and its impressive ancient ruins. Operators also offer all-day excursions to Assisi, to Pompeii and/or Capri, and to Florence. For do-it-yourself excursions to Ostia Antica and other destinations, pick up information at the APT information offices. American Express, Appian Line, ATAC, and CIT all offer orientation tours of Rome.

➤ FEES AND SCHEDULES: **American Express** (⊠ Piazza di Spagna 38, ☎ 06/67641). **Appian Line** (⊠ P. Esquilino 6, ☎ 06/487861, WEB www. appianline.it). **ATAC** (⊠ Information booth, Termini Station). **CIT** (⊠ Piazza della Repubblica 65, ☎ 06/4620311, WEB www.citonline.it).

WALKING TOURS

Enjoy Rome offers a variety of walking and bicycling tours in English, including a nighttime tour of Old Rome. Scala Reale also has English-language tours. For more information contact city tourist offices.

➤ FEES AND SCHEDULES: **Enjoy Rome** (⊠ Via Varese 39, ☎ 06/4451843, WEB www.enjoyrome.com). **Scala Reale** (⊠ Via dell'Olmata 30, 00184 Rome, ☎ 06/4745673; 800/732–2863 Ext. 4052 in the U.S., WEB www.scalareale.org).

TRAIN TRAVEL

Termini Station is Rome's main train terminal, although the Tiburtina, Ostiense, and Trastevere stations serve some long-distance trains, many commuter trains, and the FM1 line to Fiumicino Airport. For train information call the toll-free number below, or try the English-speaking personnel at the information office in Termini, or at any travel agency. Tickets and seats can be reserved and purchased at travel agencies bearing the FS (Ferrovie dello Stato) emblem. Tickets are sold up to two months in advance. Short-distance tickets are also sold at tobacconists and ticket machines in the stations.

➤ TRAIN INFORMATION: **FS** (☎ 848/888088).

TRANSPORTATION AROUND ROME

Rome's integrated Metrebus transportation system includes buses and trams (ATAC), Metro and suburban trains and buses (COTRAL), and some other suburban trains (FS) run by the state railways. A ticket valid for 75 minutes on any combination of buses and trams and one admission to the Metro costs 1,500 lire/€.75 (time-stamp your ticket when boarding the first vehicle; you're supposed to stamp it again if you board another vehicle just before the ticket runs out, but few do). Tickets are sold at tobacconists, newsstands, some coffee bars, automated ticket machines in Metro stations, some bus stops, and at ATAC and CO-TRAL ticket booths. A BIG tourist ticket, valid for one day on all public transport, costs 6,000 lire/€3.10. A weekly ticket (Settimanale, also known as CIS) costs 24,000 lire/€12.40 and can be purchased only at ATAC and Metro booths.

TRAVEL AGENCIES

➤ LOCAL AGENTS: **American Express** (⊠ Piazza di Spagna 38, ☎ 06/67641). **CIT** (⊠ Piazza della Repubblica 65, ☎ 06/4620311, WEB www.citonline.it). **CTS** (youth and budget travel, discount fares; ⊠ Via Genova 16, ☎ 06/4620431, WEB www.cts.it).

VISITOR INFORMATION

➤ TOURIST INFORMATION: **APT** (Rome Provincial Tourist Agency, main office; ⊠ Via Parigi 5, 00185, ☎ 06/48899253; Termini Station, ☎ 06/4871270; Fiumicino Airport, ☎ 06/65956074). **City tourist infor-**

mation booths (⊠ Largo Goldoni, corner of Via Condotti; Via del Corso in the Spanish Steps area; Via dei Fori Imperiali, opposite the entrance to the Roman Forum; Via Nazionale, at Palazzo delle Esposizioni; Piazza Cinque Lune, off the north end of Piazza Navona; Piazza Sonnino, in Trastevere, 🆆🅴🅱 www.romaturismo.it).

Italy Basics

BUSINESS HOURS

Banks are open weekdays 8:30–1:30 and 2:45–3:45. Churches are usually open from early morning to noon or 12:30, when they close for about two hours or more, opening again in the afternoon until about 7 PM. National museums (*musei statali*) are usually open from 9 AM until 2 and are often closed on Monday, but there are many exceptions, especially at major museums. Non-national museums have entirely different hours, which may vary according to season. Most major archaeological sites are open every day from early morning to dusk, except some holidays. At all museums and sites, ticket offices close an hour or so before official closing time. Always check with the local tourist office for current hours and holiday closings. Shops are open, with individual variations, from 9 to 1 and from 3:30 or 4 to 7:30 or 8. They are open Monday–Saturday but close for a half day during the week; for example, in Rome most shops are closed on Monday morning, although food shops close on Thursday afternoon in fall–spring. All shops, including food shops, close Saturday afternoon in July and August, though a 1995 ordinance allows greater freedom. Some tourist-oriented shops and department stores—in downtown Rome, Florence, and Venice—are open all day, every day.

CUSTOMS AND DUTIES

For details on imports and duty-free limits in Italy, *see* Customs and Duties *in* Smart Travel Tips A to Z.

HOLIDAYS

January 1; January 6 (Epiphany); Easter Sunday and Monday; April 25 (Liberation Day); May 1 (May Day); August 15 (Assumption, known as Ferragosto); November 1 (All Saints' Day); December 8 (Immaculate Conception); December 25–26.

The feast days of patron saints are observed locally. Many businesses and shops may be closed in Florence, Genoa, and Turin on June 24 (St. John the Baptist); in Rome on June 29 (Sts. Peter and Paul); in Palermo on July 15 (Santa Rosalia); in Naples on September 19 (San Gennaro); in Bologna on October 4 (San Petronio); in Trieste on November 3 (San Giusto); and in Milan on December 7 (St. Ambrose). Venice's feast of St. Mark is April 25, the same as Liberation Day, and the city also celebrates November 21 (Madonna della Salute).

LANGUAGE

Italy is accustomed to English-speaking tourists, and in major cities you will find that many people speak at least a little English. In smaller hotels and restaurants and on public transportation, knowing a few phrases of Italian comes in handy.

MONEY MATTERS

Venice, Milan, Florence, and Rome are the more expensive Italian cities to visit. Taxes are usually included in hotel bills; there is a 20% tax on car rentals, usually included in the rates. A cup of espresso enjoyed while standing at a bar costs from 1,000 lire/€0.50 to 1,500 lire/€0.75, the same cup served at a table, triple that. At a bar, beer costs from 4,000 lire/€2.05 to 6,000 lire/€3.10, a soft drink about 3,000 lire/€1.55. A *tramezzino* (small sandwich) costs about 2,500 lire/€1.30, a more substantial one about 3,500 lire/€1.80–5,000 lire/€2.60. You will pay about 15,000 lire/€7.75 for a short taxi ride. Admission to a major museum is about 12,000 lire/€6.20.

CREDIT CARDS
Credit cards are generally accepted in shops and hotels but may not always be welcome in restaurants. When you wish to leave a tip beyond the 15% service charge that is usually included with your bill, leave it in cash rather than adding it to the credit card slip.

CURRENCY
The unit of currency in Italy is the lira (plural, lire). There are bills of 1,000, 2,000, 5,000, 10,000, 50,000, 100,000, and 500,000 lire (impossible to change, except in banks); coins are worth 50, 100, 200, 500, and 1,000 lire. In 1999 the new single currency of the European Union, the euro, was introduced as a banking currency. Euro coins and notes will be issued in January of 2002, and in a few months lire will be withdrawn from circulation. At press time (summer 2001) the exchange rate was 2,171 lire/€1.12 to the U.S. dollar, 1,376 lire/€.71 to the Canadian dollar, 3,108 lire/€1.60 to the pound sterling, 2,458 lire/€1.27 to the Irish punt, 1,054 lire/€.54 to the Australian dollar, 876 lire/€.45 to the New Zealand dollar, and 267 lire/€.14 to the South African rand.

When your purchases run into hundreds of thousands of lire, beware of being shortchanged, a dodge that is practiced at ticket windows, toll booths, and cashiers' desks, as well as in shops and even in banks. *Always count your change before you leave the counter.* Always carry some smaller-denomination bills for sundry purchases.

SALES TAX
Foreign tourists who have spent more than 300,000 lire/€155 (before tax) in one store can obtain a refund of Italy's value-added tax (IVA). At the time of purchase, with passport or ID in hand, ask the store for an invoice describing the article or articles and the total lire amount. If your destination when you leave Italy is a non-EU country, you must have the invoice stamped at customs upon departure from Italy; if your destination is another EU country, you must obtain the customs stamp upon departure from that country. Once back home—and within 90 days of the date of purchase—you must send the stamped invoice back to the store, which should forward the IVA rebate directly to you. If the store participates in the Europe Tax-Free Shopping System (those that do display a sign to the effect), things are simpler. Note that, to calculate the price without IVA, you don't subtract 20% from the price on the label, which already includes IVA. Instead, you need to subtract roughly 16.5%. Transaction fees which go to the companies providing the tax-free service are 3%–4%, so in this case you should expect to get only about 13% of the purchase price back.

TELEPHONES
COUNTRY AND AREA CODES
The country code for Italy is 39. Do not drop the 0 in the regional code when calling Italy.

INTERNATIONAL CALLS
To place an international call, insert a phone card, dial 00, then the country code, area code, and phone number. The cheaper and easier option, however, is to use your AT&T, MCI, or Sprint calling card. To make collect calls, dial the AT&T USADirect number below. For information and operators in Europe and the Mediterranean area, dial 15; for intercontinental service, dial 170.

➤ ACCESS CODES: **AT&T USADirect** (☎ 172–1011). **MCI Call USA** (☎ 172–1022). **Sprint Express** (☎ 172–1877).

LOCAL CALLS

For all local calls, you must dial the regional area codes, even in cities. Most local calls cost 200 lire/€.10 for two minutes. Pay phones take either 100-, 200-, or 500-lire coins or *schede telefoniche* (phone cards), purchased in bars, tobacconists, and post offices in either 5,000-10,000-, or 15,000-lire denominations. The phone card called Time Europa (50,000 lire/€25.80) is a good-value card for calling Europe and the United States, at only 540 lire/€.30 per minute. For directory information in Italy, dial 12.

15 VENICE

It was called La Serenissima Repubblica, a name suggesting the monstrous power and majesty of the city that was for centuries the unrivaled mistress of trade between Europe and the Far East, and the staunch bulwark of Christendom against the tides of Turkish expansion. Venice is a labyrinth of narrow streets and waterways, opening now and again onto an airy square or broad canal. Many of its magnificent palazzi are slowly crumbling; but far from making it a down-at-the-heels slum, somehow in Venice the shabby, derelict effect is magically transformed into one of beauty and charm. The place is romantic, especially at night when the lights from the vaporetti and the stars overhead pick out the gargoyles and arches of the centuries-old facades. Though the power and glory of its days as a wealthy city-republic are gone, the art and exotic aura remain.

EXPLORING VENICE

Numbers in the margin correspond to points of interest on the Venice map.

To enjoy the city you will have to come to terms with the crowds of day-trippers, who take over the center around San Marco from May through September and during Carnival. Venice is cooler and more welcoming in early spring and late fall. Romantics like it in the winter, when prices are much lower, the streets are often deserted, and the sea mists impart a haunting melancholy to the *campi* (squares) and canals. Piazza San Marco is the pulse of Venice, but after joining with the crowds to visit the Basilica di San Marco and the Doge's Palace, strike out on your own and just follow where your feet take you—you won't be disappointed.

Piazza San Marco and the San Polo Neighborhood

Piazza San Marco alone would be worth a trip to Venice: an estimated 35,000 visitors a day come here to admire the sights that made Venice world famous well before the days of mass tourism; no wonder that the streets north and west of the square are clustered with fashion boutiques and expensive shops. The less crowded (and more affordable) San Polo district, with its lively alleys, is fun to explore on foot.

★ ❸ **Basilica di San Marco** (St. Mark's Basilica). Half Christian church, half Middle Eastern mosque, this building was conceived during the 11th century to hold the relics of St. Mark the Evangelist, the city's patron saint. Inside are more than 43,055 square ft of golden mosaics, lending an extraordinarily exotic aura. Be sure to see the **Pala d'Oro,** a dazzling gilded silver screen encrusted with 1,927 precious gems and 255 enameled panels. The richly decorated facade is surmounted by copies of four famous gilded bronze horses; the originals are in the **museum** (☎ 041/5225205) upstairs. ⊠ *Piazza San Marco,* ☎ *041/5225205.* ✆ *Basilica Nov.–Apr., Mon.–Sat. 9:45–4:30, Sun. 1–4:30; May–Oct., Mon.–Sat. 9:45–5:30, Sun. 1–5:30 (last entry 30 mins before closing); tours June–Aug., Mon.–Sat.*

★ ❺ **Campanile di San Marco.** Venice's famous brick bell tower (325 ft tall, plus the angel) stood here for 1,000 years before it collapsed without warning one morning in 1912. It was swiftly rebuilt according to the old plan. In the 15th century, clerics found guilty of immoral behavior were suspended in wooden cages from the tower, sometimes forced to subsist on bread and water for as long as a year, other times left to starve. The stunning view from the tower on a clear day includes the Lido, the lagoon, and the mainland as far as the Alps, but, strangely enough, none of the myriad canals that snake through the city. ⊠ *Piazza San Marco,* ☎ *041/5224064.* ✆ *June–Sept., daily 9:30–9:30; Oct.–May, daily 9:30– sunset (last entry 30 mins before closing). Closed 2 wks in Jan.*

❷ **Museo Correr.** Exhibits here range from the absurdly high-soled shoes worn by 16th-century Venetian ladies (who walked with the aid of a servant on either side) to fine Venetian paintings and 11 rooms illustrating the period from the Napoleonic and Austrian occupation through the unification of Italy. Map buffs should not miss the huge, exceptionally detailed *Grande Pianta Prospettica* by Jacopo de' Barberi (circa 1440–1515), which faithfully portrays every inch of 16th-century Venice. The Quadreria (Picture Gallery) on the second floor features Gothic works by the *madoneri,* a group of Greek-Venetian artists who specialized in the painting of glittering gold Madonnas. ⊠ *Piazza San Marco, Ala Napoleonica,* ☎ *041/5225625.* ✆ *Apr.–Oct., daily 9– 7; Nov.–Mar., daily 9–5 (last entry 1 hr before closing).*

★ ❹ **Palazzo Ducale** (Doge's Palace). During Venice's heyday, this was the epicenter of its great empire. More than just a palace, it was a combination White House, Senate, Supreme Court, torture chamber, and prison. The building's facade is a Gothic-Renaissance fantasia of pink-and-white marble. It is filled with frescoes, paintings, and a few examples of statuary by some of the Renaissance's greatest artists. Don't miss the famous view from the balcony, overlooking the piazza, St. Mark's Basin, and the church of San Giorgio Maggiore across the lagoon. ⊠ *Piazzetta di San Marco,* ☎ *041/5224951.* ⌑ *24,000 lire/€12.40* ✆ *Apr.– Oct., daily 9–7; Nov.–Mar., daily 9–5 (last entry 1½ hrs before closing). English tours daily 10:30; reservations essential.*

★ ❶ **Piazza San Marco.** In the most famous square in Venice—the only one called a *piazza;* the rest are called *campi* (fields)—pedestrian traffic jams clog the surrounding byways and even pigeons have to fight for space. The short side of the square opposite the Basilica of San Marco is known as the **Ala Napoleonica,** a wing built by order of Napoléon, enclosing it to form what he called "the most beautiful drawing room in all of Europe."

❻ Santa Maria Gloriosa dei Frari. This soaring Gothic brick church known simply as I Frari contains a number of the most important pictures in Venice. Paradoxically, as the principal church of the Franciscans it is austere in design, suitably reflecting the order's vows of poverty. Chief among the works is the magnificent Titian altarpiece, the immense *Assumption of the Virgin,* over the main altar. Titian is buried here, the only one of 70,000 plague victims to be given a personal church burial. ✉ *Campo dei Frari,* ☎ *041/5222637.* ☉ *Mon.–Sat. 9–6, Sun. 1–6.*

❼ Scuola Grande di San Rocco (School of St. Rocco). In the 1500s Tintoretto embellished the school with more than 50 canvases. The *Crucifixion* in the Albergo (the room just off the great hall) is held to be his masterpiece. ✉ *Campo di San Rocco, San Polo,* ☎ *041/5234864.* ☉ *Nov. 3–Mar., daily 10–4; Apr.–Nov. 2, daily 9–5:30 (last entry 30 mins before closing).*

The Grand Canal

Set off on a boat tour along the Grand Canal, which serves as Venice's main thoroughfare. The canal winds in the shape of a backwards "S" for more than 3½ km (2 mi) through the heart of the city, past some 200 Gothic and Renaissance palaces. The vaporetto tour gives you an idea of the opulent beauty of the palaces and a peek into the side streets and tiny canals where the Venetians go about their daily business.

★ ⑫ Ca' d'Oro. This exquisite Gothic palace was once literally a "Golden House," when its marble traceries and ornaments were embellished with pure gold. It was created in 1434 by the rich and enamored patrician Marino Contarini for his wife. It holds the **Galleria Franchetti,** a fine collection of antiquities, sculptures, paintings, and the only surviving example of frescoes that adorned the exterior of a Venetian building (commissioned by those who could not afford a marble facade). ✉ *Calle della Ca' d'Oro, 3933 Cannaregio,* ☎ *041/5238790.* ☉ *Tue.–Sun. 8:15–7:15, Mon. 8:15–2.*

★ ⑩ Ca' Rezzonico. Considered by many to be Venice's most beautiful building, Ca' Rezzonico was begun in the 1660s and completed by Giorgio Massari (1686–1766) a century later. It is embellished with stuccowork, colored marble fixtures, and valuable frescoes and furnished with brocade tapestry, fine furniture, and Murano glass chandeliers. It houses the **Museo del Settecento Veneziano** (Museum of 18th-century Venice). A worthwhile art gallery includes delightful genre pictures by Pietro Longhi (1702–85). ✉ *Fondamenta Pedrocco, 3136 Dorsoduro,* ☎ *041/2410100.* ☉ *Due to open in June 2001.*

❽ Collezione Peggy Guggenheim. Peggy Guggenheim (1898–1979) was among the 20th century's greatest collectors of modern art. Her collection includes pieces from the most important artists of the 20th century: Picasso and Braque; Balla, Severini, and Boccioni; De Chirico; Kandinsky; Magritte; and Rothko, Motherwell, Pollock, and Bacon. ✉ *Palazzo Venier dei Leoni, entrance on Calle San Cristoforo, 701 Dorsoduro,* ☎ *041/5206288.* ☉ *Wed.–Mon. 10–6.*

★ ❾ Gallerie dell'Accademia (Accademia Gallery). Unquestionably the largest collection of Venetian art in the world, the Accademie Galleries include

Venice (Venezia)

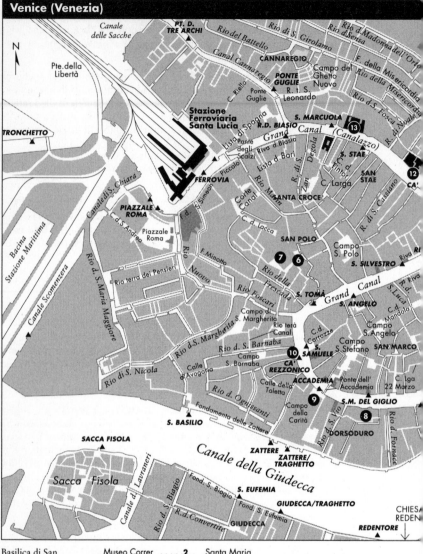

Sacca
della
Misericordia

Canale delle Navi

CIMITERO ▲

Cimitero
San
Michele

0   440 yards
0   400 meters

Racchetta

Fondamente

Rio S. Caterina

R. d. Gesuiti Nuove

C. d. della Panada

C.d Testa

dei Mendicanti

C. d. Squero

Strada
Nuova

FOND. NUOVE ▲

D'ORO ▲

Campo d.
Pescheria

Rio d. Santi Apostoli

Erberia

R. d. Vin

Campo
S. Marina

16

R. d. Barbaria

Campo
Santi
Giovanni e
Paolo
delle Tole

15

OSPEDALE
CIVILE ▲

R. d. S.
Giustina

CELESTIA ▲

11

RIALTO ▲

del Carbon

R. di Fava

Mercena

Campo
S. Maria
Formosa

Campo
Manin

C. dei Fabbri

Sal. di S. Lio

C. d Bande

14

Ruga Giuffa

R. S. Severo

R. d. S. Lorenzo

C. Lion

C. d
Furlani

R. d. S.
Francesco

R. di Scudi

R. d. Greci

R. l. Pietà

Canale d. Galeazze

Darsena
Grande

Rio d. Vergini

Rio di S. Daniele

Can. di S. Pietro

Frezzeria

R. d. Fabbri

2 **1** **5** **3** **4**

SAN
ZACCARIA

Fond.
Osmarin

R. d. Palazzo

Ponte dei
Sospiri

Riva degli

Molo

CASTELLO

Schiavoni

Campo dell'
Arsenale

R. d. Arsenale

CAMPO
DELLA
TANA

Rio della Tana

S. MOISÈ

R. d.

i

i

Piazza
San Marco

S. ZACCARIA ▲

RIVA DEGLI
SCHIAVONI ▲

ARSENALE ▲

V. Garibaldi

Riva dei Sette Martiri

Rio d. S. Anna

R. d. S. Giuseppe

Rio dei Giardini

S. MARCO
VALLARESSA

S. MARCO
GIARDINETTI

Canale di S. Marco

GIARDINI ▲

Riva dei Partigiani

SALUTE ▲

DEL
ORE

ZITELLE ▲

S. GIORGIO ▲

S. Giorgio
Maggiore

Fond.
delle Zitelle

Calle
Michelangelo

Ci

LIDO
↓

oils by Giovanni Bellini (1430–1516), Giorgione (1477–1511), Titian, and Tintoretto (1518–94) and superb later works by Veronese (1528–88) and Tiepolo (1696–1770). ✉ *Campo della Carità, Accademia, Dorsoduro,* ☎ *041/5222247.* ⊙ *Tues.–Sat. 8:15–7:15, Mon. 8:15–2.*

⑬ Palazzo Vendramin Calergi. This Renaissance gem dates from the 1480s. The German composer Wagner died in a room here in 1883 following the success of his *Parsifal.* Today the palace houses Venice's casino. ✉ *2040 Cannaregio, San Marcuola vaporetto stop.* ⊙ *Casino daily 11 AM–2:30 AM.* ☎ *041/5297111.*

★ ⑪ Ponte di Rialto (Rialto Bridge). The first permanent stone bridge across the Grand Canal, the Rialto was built in the late 1500s after a competition that attracted the best architects of the period, including Michelangelo, Palladio, and Sansovino. The job went to Antonio da Ponte, whose plan focused on structure rather than elaborate decoration and kept costs down at a time when the Republic's coffers were low due to continual wars against the Turks and the opening of oceanic trade routes. A single arcade, more than 91 ft in length, supports two rows of shops, with windows that open onto the often crowded central passage. The side paths offer a prime look at one of the city's most captured views: the Grand Canal full of gondolas and boats in the background. Make a point of seeing the adjacent Rialto food market and the fish market beyond it (Tuesday–Saturday mornings; fish market closed Monday). Ruga San Giovanni and Ruga del Ravano, beside the market, will bring you face to face with scores of shops. Start from the Salizzada San Giovanni side of the bridge.

North of San Marco

Fold the map away and it's easy to get lost in the picturesque neighborhoods north of San Marco: here low-key shops, bakeries, and tiny watering holes have not been replaced by tourist-oriented places and humble houses are festooned with laundry hung from lines stretched across the dark-green canals.

⑯ Santa Maria dei Miracoli. Perfectly proportioned and sheathed in marble, the late-15th-century church embodies the classical serenity of the early Renaissance. The interior is decorated with marble reliefs by the church's architect, Pietro Lombardo, and his son Tullio. ✉ *Campo Santa Maria Nova,* ☎ *041/5235293.* ⊙ *Mon.–Sat. 10–5, Sun. 1–5.*

⑭ Santa Maria Formosa. This graceful white marble church, built by Mauro Coducci in 1492, was grafted onto 11th-century foundations. Inside is a hodgepodge of Renaissance and Baroque styles. A small vegetable market bustles in the square weekday mornings. ✉ *Campo Santa Maria Formosa,* ☎ *041/5234645.* ⊙ *Mon.–Sat. 10–5, Sun. 1–5.*

⑮ Santi Giovanni e Paolo. This massive Dominican church is the twin (and rival) of the Franciscan Santa Maria Gloriosa dei Frari and contains a wealth of artwork. Twenty-five doges are buried here. Outside in the campo stands Verrocchio's magnificent equestrian monument of **Bartolomeo Colleoni** (1400–75), who fought for the Venetian cause during the mid-1400s. ✉ *Campo Santi Giovanni e Paolo,* ☎ *041/5237510.* ⊙ *Mon.–Sat. 8–12:30 and 3:30–6, Sun. 3:30–6.*

Venetian Lagoon

A vaporetto excursion to the main islands of the lagoon makes for a perfect escape from the busy streets of Venice. Start with Murano, famous for its glass furnaces; then continue to Burano, where fishermen painted their toy-like houses with the brightest colors possible to make them visible even in the thickest of the lagoon's fog; the further-flung Torcello has a dream-like atmosphere of its own, which makes it one of the most romantic places in the region.

⑰ Torcello. This is where the first Venetians landed in their flight from the barbarians 1,500 years ago. Even after many settlers left to found the city of Venice on the island of Rivo Alto (Rialto), Torcello continued to grow and prosper until its main source of income, wool manufacturing, was priced out of the marketplace. It's hard to believe now, looking at this almost deserted island, that in the 16th century it had 20,000 inhabitants and 10 churches.

The island's cathedral, **Santa Maria Assunta,** dates from the 11th century. The ornate Byzantine mosaics are testimony to the importance and wealth of an island that could attract the best artists and craftsmen of its day. The vast mosaic on the inside of the facade depicts the *Last Judgment* as artists of the 11th and 12th centuries imagined it: figures writhe in vividly depicted contortions of pain. Facing it, as if in mitigation, is the calm mosaic figure of the Madonna, alone in a field of gold above the staunch array of Apostles. ⊠ *Torcello,* ☏ 041/730084. ⊙ *June–Sept., daily 10:30–6; Oct.–May, daily 10–4.*

DINING

Venetians love seafood, and it figures prominently on most restaurant menus, sometimes to the exclusion of meat dishes. Fish is generally expensive, and you should remember when ordering that the price given on menus for fish as a main course is often per 100 grams, not the total cost of what you are served, which could be two or three times that amount. However, *sarde in saor* (fried sardines marinated with onions, vinegar, pine nuts and raisins) is a tasty traditional dish that can cost as little as a pizza. City specialties also include *pasta e fagioli* (pasta and bean soup), risotto, and the delicious *fegato alla veneziana* (liver with onions) served with grilled polenta.

CATEGORY	COST*
$$$$	over 45,000 lire (€23)
$$$	35,000 lire–45,000 lire (€18–€23)
$$	25,000 lire–35,000 lire (€13–€18)
$	under 25,000 lire (€13)

*per person for a main course at dinner

$$$-$$$$ ✕ **Da Arturo.** The tiny Da Arturo is a refreshing change from the numerous seafood restaurants of which Venetians are so fond. The cordial proprietor prefers, instead, to offer varied and delicious seasonal vegetable and salad dishes, or tasty, generous meat courses such as *braciola alla veneziana* (pork chop schnitzel with vinegar). ⊠ *Calle degli Assassini, 3656 San Marco,* ☏ 041/5286974. *Reservations essential. No credit cards. Closed Sun., 10 days after Carnival, and Aug.*

$$$-$$$$ ✕ **Osteria Da Fiore.** Long a favorite with Venetians, Da Fiore has been
★ discovered by tourists, so reservations are imperative. It's known for its excellent seafood dinners, which might include such specialties as *pasticcio di pesce* (fish pie) and *seppioline* (little cuttlefish). Not easy to find, it's just off Campo San Polo. ⊠ *Calle dello Scaleter, 2202/A San Polo,* ☏ 041/721308. *Reservations essential. AE, DC, MC, V. Closed Sun.–Mon., Aug. 10–early Sept., and Dec. 25–Jan. 15.*

$$$ ✕ **Fiaschetteria Toscana.** Once the storehouse of a 19th-century wine merchant from Tuscany, this popular restaurant has long been a favorite of Venetians and visitors. Courteous, cheerful waiters serve such specialties as *rombo* (turbot) with capers, an exceptionally good *pasta alla buranella* (pasta with shrimp, au gratin), and zabaglione. ⊠ *Campo*

San Giovanni Crisostomo, 5719 Cannaregio, ☏ 041/5285281. AE, DC, MC, V. Closed Mon. lunch, Tues. and 4 wks in July–Aug.

$$–$$$ ✕ **Al Covo.** This small osteria changes its menu according to the day's
★ bounty—mostly local seafood caught just hours before. Cesare Benelli and his American wife, Diane, insist on only the freshest ingredients and claim to not use butter or animal fats. Try the *zuppa di pesce* (fish broth) followed by the fish of the day either grilled, baked, or steamed. The flexible tasting menu at lunch is a good deal. ⊠ *Campiello della Pescaria, 3968 Castello, ☏ 041/5223812. No credit cards. Closed Wed. and Thurs., 2 wks in Aug., and 1 month between Dec. and Jan.*

$$ ✕ **Alle Testiere.** A strong local following can make it tough to get one
★ of the five tables at this tiny trattoria near Campo Santa Maria Formosa. Chef Bruno Gavagnin's dishes stand out for lightness and balance. Try the *gnocchetti con moscardini* (little gnocchi with tender baby octopus), or the baked turbot with radicchio di Treviso. A short but well-assembled wine list allows for some interesting combinations. Save room for a slice of homemade pear tart. ⊠ *Calle del Mondo Novo, 5081 Castello, ☏ 041/5227220. Reservations essential. MC, V. Closed Sun., 3 wks in Aug., and 3 wks in Dec.–Jan.*

$$ ✕ **Vini da Gigio.** An attractive, family-run establishment, this trattoria is on the quayside of a canal, just off the Strada Nuova. The service is affable and the food tasty, with homemade pasta, fish, and meat dishes and good draft wine. The barroom is pleasant and casual for lunch. ⊠ *Fondamenta de la Chiesa, 3628A Cannaregio, ☏ 041/5285140. AE, DC, MC, V. Closed Mon., 3 wks between Jan. and Feb., 1 wk in June, and 3 wks between Aug. and Sept.*

$ ✕ **Ae Oche.** But for the clientele, there's not much Venetian about this
★ saloon-like pizzeria with rows of imported stouts on the shelves and a no-smoking room. Eighty pizza combinations include the popular Campagnola, lavishly sprinkled with a mix of tomato, mozzarella, mushroom, Brie, and *speck* (smoked prosciutto), but purists should stick to the *margherita* with tomato, mozzarella, and basil. A selection of 16 salads plus a few pasta dishes make the Oche an ideal stop for a light meal between sights. ⊠ *Calle delle Oche, 1552/a–b Santa Croce, ☏ 041/5241161. AE, DC, MC, V. Closed Mon., Nov.–Dec.*

$ ✕ **L'Incontro.** This trattoria between San Barnaba and Campo Santa Margherita has a faithful clientele drawn by good food (excellent meat, but no fish) at reasonable prices. Menu choices include freshly made Sardinian pastas, juicy steaks, wild duck, boar, and (with advance notice) roast suckling pig. ⊠ *Rio Terrá Canal, 3062A Dorsoduro, ☏ 041/5222404. AE, D, MC, V. Closed Mon., Jan., and 2 wks in Aug. No lunch Tues.*

LODGING

Space in the time-worn but renovated palaces-cum-hotels is at a premium in this city, and even in the best hotel, rooms can be small and offer little natural light. Preservation restrictions on buildings often preclude the installation of such things as elevators and air-conditioning. On the other hand, Venice's luxury hotels can offer rooms of fabulous opulence and elegance, and even in the more modest hotels you can find comfortable rooms of great charm and character, sometimes with stunning views. Venice attracts visitors year-round, although the winter months, with the exception of Carnival time, are generally much quieter, and most hotels offer lower rates during this period. It is always worth booking in advance, but if you haven't, AVA (Venetian Hoteliers Association) booths will help you find a room after your arrival in the city.

CATEGORY	COST*
$$$$	over 500,000 lire (€258)
$$$	350,000 lire–500,000 lire (€180–€258)
$$	200,000 lire–350,000 lire (€103–€180)
$	under 200,000 lire (€103)

Price categories are determined by the cost of two people in a double room.

$$$$ ⊞ **Danieli.** Parts of this rather large hotel are built around a 15th-century palazzo bathed in sumptuous Venetian colors. The downside is that the Danieli also has several modern annexes that some find bland and impersonal, and the lower-price rooms can be exceedingly drab. Still, celebrities and English-speaking patrons crowd its sumptuous four-story-high lobby, chic salons, and dining terrace with a fantastic view of St. Mark's Basin. ⊠ *Riva degli Schiavoni, 4196 Castello, 30122,* ☎ *041/5226480,* FAX *041/5200208,* WEB *www.luxurycollection.com. 219 rooms, 11 suites. Restaurant. AE, DC, MC, V.*

$$$$ ⊞ **Gritti Palace.** This haven of pampering luxury is like an aristocratic
★ private home, with fresh flowers, fine antiques, lavish appointments, and Old World service. The dining terrace overlooking the Grand Canal is best in the evening when boat traffic dies down. ⊠ *Campo Santa Maria del Giglio, 2467 San Marco, 30124,* ☎ *041/794611,* FAX *041/5200942,* WEB *www.luxurycollection.com. 87 rooms, 6 suites. Restaurant. AE, DC, MC, V.*

$$$–$$$$ ⊞ **Metropole.** Guests can step from their water taxi or gondola into the
★ lobby of this small, very well-run hotel, rich in precious antiques and just five minutes from Piazza San Marco. Many rooms have a view of the lagoon and others overlook the garden at the back. ⊠ *Riva degli Schiavoni, 4149 Castello, 30122,* ☎ *041/5205044,* FAX *041/5223679,* WEB *www. hotelmetropole.com. 67 rooms, 7 suites. Restaurant. AE, DC, MC, V.*

$$$ ⊞ **Londra Palace.** Fine views of the lagoon and the church of San Giorgio offer a soothing alternative to the concoction of plush carpets and costly tapestries that fill the over-the-top interiors of the Londra Palace, one of the grand hotels of Venice. Handsome Biedermeier tables, couches, and writing desks stand out against the numerous marble columns planted all around to support such heavy luxury. Rooms overlooking the Riva cost 10% more than the smaller, top-floor rooms with mansard ceilings. ⊠ *Riva degli Schiavoni, 4171 Castello, 30122,* ☎ *041/5200533,* FAX *041/5225032,* WEB *www.hotelondra.it. 36 rooms, 17 suites. Restaurant. AE, DC, MC, V.*

$$ ⊞ **Accademia.** Hidden within the heart of Venice, this miniature Pal-
★ ladian villa—complete with canal-side garden—is one of the city's most enchanting hotels. It has plenty of atmosphere, with a touch of romance. Many rooms overlook the gardens. ⊠ *Fondamenta Bollani, 1058 Dorsoduro, 30123,* ☎ *041/5210188,* FAX *041/5239152,* WEB *www.pensioneaccademia.it. 27 rooms, 25 with bath. AE, DC, MC, V.*

$$ ⊞ **Ala.** The Ala is between San Marco and Santo Stefano, a few steps from the Santa Maria del Giglio vaporetto stop. Some rooms are large with coffered ceilings and old-style furnishings; smaller ones have more modern decor and orthopedic beds. Breakfast is served in a beautiful room overlooking a small canal. ⊠ *2494 San Marco, 30124,* ☎ *041/5208333,* FAX *041/5206390,* WEB *www.hotelala.it. 85 rooms. AE, DC, MC, V.*

$$ ⊞ **La Calcina.** The Calcina sits in an enviable position along the sunny
★ Zattere with views across the wide Giudecca Canal. You can sunbathe on the *altana* (wooden-roof terrace), or enjoy an afternoon tea in one of the reading corners of the shadowy, intimate hall with flickering candlelight and soft classical music. A stone staircase leads to the rooms upstairs (no elevator), with shiny wooden floors, Art Deco furnishings, and firm beds; some suffer from a lack of storage space. The annex nearby offers lower-priced rooms without a view. ⊠ *780 Dorsoduro,*

30123, ☎ *041/5206466,* FAX *041/5227045,* WEB *www.veniceinfo.it. 42 rooms. AE, DC, MC, V.*

$$ 🏠 **Wildner.** Rooms in this pleasant family-run, unpretentious pensione are spread over four floors (no elevator), half with a view of San Giorgio; the others (cooler and quieter in summer) overlook Campo San Zaccaria. ⊠ *Riva degli Schiavoni, 4161 Castello, 30122,* ☎ *041/ 5227463,* FAX *041/5265615,* WEB *www.veneziahotels.com. 16 rooms. AE, DC, MC, V.*

$–$$ 🏠 **Paganelli.** The lagoon views here so impressed Henry James that he wrote the Paganelli up in the preface to his *Portrait of a Lady.* This charming, small hotel on the waterfront has an annex on the quiet square of Campo San Zaccaria and is tastefully decorated in Venetian style. ⊠ *Riva degli Schiavoni, 4687 Castello, 30122,* ☎ *041/5224324,* FAX *041/ 5239267,* WEB *www.gpnet.it. 22 rooms, 19 with bath. AE, MC, V.*

$ 🏠 **Bucintoro.** Whistler once stayed here, and today the Bucintoro is still favored by artists, drawn by the lagoon views from every room. Slightly off the tourist track, this friendly, family-run hotel has clean and simple rooms. The price is unbeatable for such spectacular vistas. ⊠ *Riva San Biagio, 2135 Castello, 30122,* ☎ *041/5223240,* FAX *041/5235224. 28 rooms, 25 with bath. Restaurant. No credit cards. Closed mid-Dec.– early Feb.*

$ 🏠 **Dalla Mora.** Tucked into the end of a quiet calle beyond the main
★ flow of traffic, this hotel occupies two simple, well-maintained houses, both with a view. The cheerful, tiny entry hall leads upstairs to a delightful terrace. Rooms are spacious, with basic wooden furniture and tile floors. The annex across the calle has rooms without private bathrooms and others with only showers and sinks. Excellent quality for the price makes this a particularly good place to stay. ⊠ *Off Salizzada San Pantalon, 42 Santa Croce, 30123,* ☎ *041/710703,* FAX *041/723006. 14 rooms, 6 with bath. AE, DC, MC, V.*

NIGHTLIFE AND THE ARTS

For a detailed listing of what's going on, pick up the monthly *Venezia News* from a newsstand. It has plenty of information in English about concerts, opera, ballet, theater, exhibitions, movies, sports, sightseeing, and a useful "Servizi" section with late-night pharmacies, operating hours for the busiest vaporetto and bus lines, and a listing of the main trains and flights from Venice.

The Arts

Venice is a stop for major traveling exhibits, from Maya art to contemporary art retrospectives. In odd years, usually from late June to early November, the **Biennale dell'Arte** exhibition draws the work of hundreds of contemporary international artists and holds events throughout the season, including the yearly Mostra Internazionale del Cinema (International Film Festival), which begins at the end of August.

Concerts

Although there are occasional jazz and Italian pop concerts in clubs around town, the vast majority of music played in Venice is classical. Vivaldi (Venice's most famous composer) is usually on the playbill; the churches of the Pietà, San Stae, Santo Stefano, and San Bartolomeo are frequent venues. For information on these often impromptu events, ask at the APT office and look for posters on walls and in restaurants and shops. **Kele e Teo Agency** (⊠ Ponte dei Bareteri, 4930 San Marco, ☎ 041/5208722, FAX 041/5208913) and **Nalesso** (⊠ Calle dello Spezier off Campo Santo Stefano, 2765 San Marco, ☎ 041/5203329) handle tickets for several musical events.

Opera

The Teatro La Fenice is one of Italy's oldest opera houses, a pilgrimage site for all opera lovers and the scene of many memorable operatic premieres, including, in 1853, the dismal first-night flop of Verdi's *La Traviata*. The great opera house was badly damaged by fire in January 1996, and the meticulous restoration work—helped in large part by donations from opera lovers around the world—is expected to continue for several years. Until the Fenice reopens, opera, symphony, and ballet performances are held year-round at the **Palafenice** (⊠ Cassa di Risparmio bank, Campo San Luca, ☎ 041/5210161; 041/786511 ticket information, WEB www.teatrolafenice.it), near the Tronchetto parking area.

Nightlife

For dancing, try the tiny **Disco Club Piccolo Mondo** (⊠ 1056/A Dorsoduro, ☎ 041/5200371), near the Accademia Gallery. The large **Casanova** (⊠ Lista di Spagna, 158/a Cannaregio, ☎ 041/2750199) is a restaurant-cabaret-disco with big projection screens, metallic walls, and red leather couches. **Fiddler's Elbow** (⊠ Strada Nuova, 3847 Cannaregio, ☎ 041/5239930) offers all the typical trappings of an Irish pub: gab, grub, and frothy Guinness. The **Martini Scala Club** (⊠ Calle del Cafetier, 1077 San Marco, ☎ 041/5224121) is an elegant piano bar with a restaurant. Tunes start at 10 PM and go until the wee hours.

SHOPPING

At **Gilberto Penzo** (⊠ Calle Seconda dei Saoneri, 2681 San Polo, ☎ 041/719372) you'll find small-scale models of gondolas and their graceful oar locks known as *forcole*. **Norelene** (⊠ Calle della Chiesa, 727 Dorsoduro, near the Guggenheim, ☎ 041/5237605) has hand-painted fabrics that make wonderful wall hangings or elegant jackets and chic scarves. **Venetia Studium** (⊠ Calle Larga XXII Marzo, 2430 San Marco, ☎ 041/5229281) is famous for Fortuny-inspired lamps and elegant scarves.

Glass

There's a lot of cheap, low-quality Venetian glass for sale around town; if you want something better, try **l'Isola** (⊠ Campo San Moisè, 1468 San Marco, ☎ 041/5231973), where Carlo Moretti's contemporary designs are on display. **Domus** (⊠ Fondamenta dei Vetrai, Murano, ☎ 041/739215), on Murano, has a good selection of glass objects.

Shopping Districts

Le Mercerie, the **Frezzeria,** and **Calle dei Fabbri** are some of Venice's busiest shopping streets and lead off of Piazza San Marco.

VENICE A TO Z

To research prices, get advice from other travelers, and book travel arrangements, visit www.fodors.com.

AIRPORTS AND TRANSFERS

➤ AIRPORT INFORMATION: **Aeroporto Marco Polo** (⊠ 10 km/6 mi northeast of Venice on the mainland, ☎ 041/2609260 flight information).

TRANSFERS

The most direct way between the airport and downtown is by the Alilaguna launch, with regularly scheduled service until midnight; it takes about an hour to get to the landing (just off Piazza San Marco), stopping at

the Lido on the way, and the fare is 17,000 lire/€8.80 per person, including bags. Blue ATVO buses make the 25-minute trip in to Piazzale Roma, where the road to Venice terminates; the cost is 5,000 lire/€2.60. From Piazzale Roma visitors will most likely have to take a vaporetto to their hotel. Water taxis (slick high-power motorboats called *motoscafi*) should cost about 140,000 lire/€72.30. Land taxis are available, running the same route as the buses; the cost is about 55,000 lire/€28.40.
➤ INFORMATION: **Alilaguna** (☎ 041/5235775). **Land Taxis** (☎ 041/5237774). **Water Taxis** (☎ 041/5235775).

BOAT AND FERRY TRAVEL
BY GONDOLA
If you mustn't leave Venice without treating yourself to a gondola ride, take it in the quiet of the evening, when the churning traffic on the canals has died down, the palace windows are illuminated, and the only sounds are the muted splashes of the gondolier's oar. Make sure he understands that you want to see the *rii*, or smaller canals, as well as the Grand Canal. There's supposed to be a fixed minimum rate of about 120,000 lire/€61.95 for 50 minutes and a nighttime supplement of 30,000 lire/€15.50. Set the terms with your gondolier *before* stepping into his boat.

BY TRAGHETTO
Few tourists know about the two-man gondolas that ferry people across the Grand Canal at various fixed points. It's the cheapest and shortest gondola ride in Venice, and it can save a lot of walking. The fare is 700 lire/€0.35, which you hand to one of the gondoliers when you get on. Look for TRAGHETTO signs.

BY VAPORETTO
ACTV water buses run the length of the Grand Canal and circle the city. There are several lines, some of which connect Venice with the major and minor islands in the lagoon. The fare is 6,000 lire/€3.10 on all lines. A 24-hour tourist ticket costs 18,000 lire/€9.30, a three-day ticket 35,000 lire/€18.10, and a seven-day ticket 60,000 lire/€31; these are especially worthwhile if you are planning to visit the islands. Free timetables are available at the ticket office at Piazzale Roma. Timetables are posted at every landing stage, but there is not always a ticket booth operating. After 9 PM, tickets are available on the boats, but you must immediately inform the controller that you need a ticket. For this reason it may be useful to buy a *blocchetto* (book of tickets) in advance. Landing stages are clearly marked with name and line number, but check before boarding, particularly with the 52 and 82, to make sure the boat is going in your direction.

Line 1 is the Grand Canal local, calling at every stop, and continuing via San Marco to the Lido. (The trip takes about 45 minutes from the station to San Marco.) Other major lines are 41 and 42 (between San Zaccaria and Murano), 51 and 52 (between the railway station and the Lido), 61 and 62 (between the Lido and Murano), and 82 (a loop beginning and ending at San Zaccaria), all of which make stops at key locations along the way. At night, there is only line N, with boats every 30 minutes making stops at the Lido, San Zaccaria, Rialto, Piazzale Roma, Giudecca, and Zattere.

BY WATER TAXI
Motoscafi, or taxis, are excessively expensive, and the fare system is as complex as Venice's layout. A minimum fare of about 50,000 lire/€25.82 gets you nowhere, and you'll pay three times as much to get from one end of the Grand Canal to the other. *Always agree on the fare before starting out.* It's probably worth considering taking a water taxi only if you are traveling in a small group. Contact the Cooperativa San Marco.

➤ BOAT AND FERRY INFORMATION: **ACTV** (Daily 7:30 AM–8 PM, ☎ 041/ 5287886, WEB www.actv.it). **Cooperativa San Marco** (☎ 041/5222303).

CAR TRAVEL

PARKING

If you bring a car to Venice, you will have to pay for a garage or parking space during your stay. Do not be waylaid by illegal con artists often wearing fake uniforms who may try to flag you down and offer to arrange parking and hotels. Continue on until you reach the automated ticket machines.

Parking at Autorimessa Comunale costs 36,000 lire/€18.60 for 24 hours. The private Garage San Marco costs 35,000 lire/€18.10 for 12 hours and 48,000 lire/€24.80 for 24 hours. To reach the privately run Tronchetto parking area, follow the signs to turn right before Piazzale Roma. Parking costs 30,000 lire/€15.50 for 24 hours. Do not leave valuables in the car. There is a left-luggage office, open daily 8–8, next to the Pullman Bar on the ground floor of the municipal garage at Piazzale Roma. The AVA has arranged a discount of about 20% per day for hotel guests who use the Garage San Marco or Tronchetto parking facility. Ask for a voucher when you check into your hotel. Present the voucher when you pay the parking fee. A vaporetto (No. 82) runs from Tronchetto to Piazzale Roma and Piazza San Marco (also to the Lido in summer). In thick fog or when tides are extreme, a bus runs instead to Piazzale Roma, where you can pick up a vaporetto.
➤ CONTACTS: **Autorimessa Comunale** (✉ Piazzale Roma, end of S11 road, ☎ 041/2727301). **Garage San Marco** (✉ Piazzale Roma 467/f, end of S11 road, ☎ 041/5232213). **Tronchetto** (☎ 041/5207555).

CONSULATES

➤ UNITED KINGDOM: (✉ Campo della Carità, 1051 Dorsoduro, ☎ 041/ 5227207).

EMERGENCIES

Pharmacies are open weekdays 9–12:30 and 3:45–7:30, Saturday 9– 12:45; a notice telling where to get late-night and Sunday service is posted outside every pharmacy.
➤ DOCTORS AND DENTISTS: **Doctor** (emergency room, Venice's hospital, ☎ 041/5230000).
➤ EMERGENCY SERVICES: **Ambulance** (☎ 118). **Carabinieri** (military police; ☎ 112). **General emergencies** (☎ 113).

TOURS

SINGLE-DAY TOURS

The Cooperativa San Marco organizes tours of the islands of Murano, Burano, and Torcello departing April–September, daily at 9:30 and 2:30, and October–March 1, daily at 2 PM, from the landing stage in front of Giardini Reali near Piazza San Marco. Tours last about 3½ hours and cost about 30,000 lire/€15.50. They do tend to be annoyingly commercial, however, and emphasize glass factory showrooms where you are pressured to buy, often at higher than standard prices.

American Express books a day trip to Padova by boat along the Brenta River, with stops at three Palladian villas. The tours run three days a week from March to October; the cost is about 120,000 lire/€61.95 per person; bookings need to be made the day before. Alternatively, the Palladio Villa Tour (by mini-bus, max. 8 people), besides a visit to the Palladian villas, includes a walking tour of Vicenza (190,000 lire/€98.15 per person). Other full-day excursions which can be booked at American Express focus on the hills of the Veneto, with stops in the towns of Marostica, Bassano del Grappa, Asolo, at Villa Barbaro at

Maser, and at a vineyard along the Strada del Prosecco for a Prosecco wine tasting (175,000 lire/€90.38), and on the Dolomite mountains, with stops at the lake of Misurina and in Cortina d'Ampezzo (180,000 lire/€92.95 per person includes packet lunch). For these last three tours it is essential to make reservations a couple of weeks in advance.

➤ FEES AND SCHEDULES: **American Express** (⊠ Salizzada San Moisè, 1471 San Marco, ☎ 041/5200844, FAX 041/5229937). **Cooperativa San Marco** (⊠ just off Piazza San Marco, ☎ 041/2406736 or 041/5235775).

PRIVATE GUIDES

American Express can provide guides for walking or gondola tours of Venice, or cars with driver and guide for excursions on the mainland. Pick up a list of licensed guides and their rates from the main IAT office or directly contact the Guides' Association.

➤ CONTACTS: **Guides' Association** (⊠ 750 San Marco, near San Zulian, ☎ 041/5209038, FAX 041/5210762). **IAT** (⊠ San Marco 71/F, near the Museo Correr).

WALKING TOURS

American Express and other operators offer two-hour walking tours of the San Marco area, taking in the basilica and the Doge's Palace. The cost is about 45,000 lire/€23.25, including admission. From April 25 through November 15, American Express offers an afternoon walking tour that ends with a short gondola ride (about 50,000 lire/€25.80). Some tour operators offer group gondola rides with a serenade. The cost is about 50,000 lire/€25.80. From June through August, free guided tours of the Basilica di San Marco are offered by the Procuratoria; information is available at a desk in the atrium of the church (no tours on Sun.).

TRAIN TRAVEL

Make sure your train goes all the way to the Stazione Ferroviaria Santa Lucia. Some trains leave passengers at the Stazione Ferroviaria Venezia-Mestre. All trains traveling to and from Santa Lucia stop at Mestre, so to get from Mestre to Santa Lucia, or vice versa (a 10-minute trip), take the first available train, remembering there is a *supplemento* (extra charge) for traveling on Intercity, Eurocity, and Eurostar trains and that if you board one of these trains without having paid in advance for this part of the trip, you are subject to a hefty fine. Since most tourists arrive in Venice by train, tourist services are conveniently located at Santa Lucia, including an APT information booth and baggage depot. Directly outside the train station are the main vaporetto landing stages; from here, vaporetti can transport you to your hotel's neighborhood. Be prepared with advance directions from the hotel and a good map.

➤ TRAIN INFORMATION: **APT** (☎ 041/5298727). **Stazione Ferroviaria Santa Lucia** (⊠ Venice's northwest corner, ☎ 8488/88088 toll-free). **Stazione Ferroviaria Venezia-Mestre** (⊠ on the mainland, ☎ 8488/880880 toll-free).

TRANSPORTATION AROUND VENICE

First-time visitors find that getting around Venice presents some unusual problems: the complexity of its layout (the city is made up of more than 100 islands, all linked by bridges); the bewildering unfamiliarity of waterborne transportation; the apparently illogical house numbering system and duplication of street names in its six districts; and the necessity of walking whether you enjoy it or not. This is the only way to reach many parts of Venice, so wear comfortable shoes and count on getting lost more than once. It's essential to have a good map showing all street names and water-bus routes; buy one at any newsstand.

TRAVEL AGENCIES

➤ LOCAL AGENTS: **American Express** (✉ Salizzada San Moisè, 1471 San Marco, ☎ 041/5200844, ℻ 041/5229937). **Albatravel** (✉ Calle dei Fabbri 4538, San Marco, ☎ 041/5210123, ℻ 041/5200781).

VISITOR INFORMATION

The Venetian Hoteliers Association (AVA) will make free same-day reservations for those who come in person to their booths at the Piazzale Roma (open daily 9 AM–10 PM), at the Santa Lucia train station (open daily 8 AM–9 PM), and at the Marco Polo airport (open daily 9 AM–10 PM); a deposit, which will be deducted from your hotel bill, is required to hold the room. Alternatively, Venezia Sì's offers free reservations over the phone (Mon.–Sat. 9 AM–7 PM).

➤ TOURIST INFORMATION: **AVA** (☎ 041/5228004; ✉ Piazzale Roma, ☎ 041/5231397; ✉ inside the Santa Lucia train station, ☎ 041/715288; ✉ Marco Polo airport, ☎ 041/5415133). **IAT Information booths** (✉ Santa Lucia train station, ☎ 041/5298727; ✉ 71/f San Marco, near the Museo Correr; Lido in summer, ✉ Gran Viale S. Maria Elisabetta 6A, ☎ 041/5265721, ℻ 041/5298720, Tourist information over phone ☎ 041/5298711; weekdays 8:30–5). **Venezia Sì's** (☎ 800/843006; 0039/0415222264 outside Italy; ℻ 0039/0415221242).

Italy Basics

BUSINESS HOURS

Banks are open weekdays 8:30–1:30 and 2:45–3:45. Churches are usually open from early morning to noon or 12:30, when they close for about two hours or more, opening again in the afternoon until about 7 PM. National museums (*musei statali*) are usually open from 9 AM until 2 and are often closed on Monday, but there are many exceptions, especially at major museums. Non-national museums have entirely different hours, which may vary according to season. Most major archaeological sites are open every day from early morning to dusk, except some holidays. At all museums and sites, ticket offices close an hour or so before official closing time. Always check with the local tourist office for current hours and holiday closings. Shops are open, with individual variations, from 9 to 1 and from 3:30 or 4 to 7:30 or 8. They are open Monday–Saturday but close for a half day during the week; for example, in Rome most shops are closed on Monday morning, although food shops close on Thursday afternoon in fall–spring. All shops, including food shops, close Saturday afternoon in July and August, though a 1995 ordinance allows greater freedom. Some tourist-oriented shops and department stores—in downtown Rome, Florence, and Venice—are open all day, every day.

CUSTOMS AND DUTIES

For details on imports and duty-free limits in Italy, *see* Customs and Duties *in* Smart Travel Tips A to Z.

HOLIDAYS

January 1; January 6 (Epiphany); Easter Sunday and Monday; April 25 (Liberation Day); May 1 (May Day); August 15 (Assumption, known as Ferragosto); November 1 (All Saints' Day); December 8 (Immaculate Conception); December 25–26.

The feast days of patron saints are observed locally. Many businesses and shops may be closed in Florence, Genoa, and Turin on June 24 (St. John the Baptist); in Rome on June 29 (Sts. Peter and Paul); in Palermo on July 15 (Santa Rosalia); in Naples on September 19 (San Gennaro); in Bologna on October 4 (San Petronio); in Trieste on

November 3 (San Giusto); and in Milan on December 7 (St. Ambrose). Venice's feast of St. Mark is April 25, the same as Liberation Day, and the city also celebrates November 21 (Madonna della Salute).

LANGUAGE
Italy is accustomed to English-speaking tourists, and in major cities you will find that many people speak at least a little English. In smaller hotels and restaurants and on public transportation, knowing a few phrases of Italian comes in handy.

MONEY MATTERS
Venice, Milan, Florence, and Rome are the more expensive Italian cities to visit. Taxes are usually included in hotel bills; there is a 20% tax on car rentals, usually included in the rates.

A cup of espresso enjoyed while standing at a bar costs from 1,000 lire/€0.50 to 1,500 lire/€0.75, the same cup served at a table, triple that. At a bar, beer costs from 4,000 lire/€2.05 to 6,000 lire/€3.10, a soft drink about 3,000 lire/€1.55. A *tramezzino* (small sandwich) costs about 2,500 lire/€1.30, a more substantial one about 3,500 lire/€1.80–5,000 lire/€2.60. You will pay about 15,000 lire/€7.75 for a short taxi ride. Admission to a major museum is about 12,000 lire/€6.20.

CREDIT CARDS
Credit cards are generally accepted in shops and hotels but may not always be welcome in restaurants. When you wish to leave a tip beyond the 15% service charge that is usually included with your bill, leave it in cash rather than adding it to the credit card slip.

CURRENCY
The unit of currency in Italy is the lira (plural, lire). There are bills of 1,000, 2,000, 5,000, 10,000, 50,000, 100,000, and 500,000 lire (impossible to change, except in banks); coins are worth 50, 100, 200, 500, and 1,000 lire. In 1999 the new single currency of the European Union, the euro, was introduced as a banking currency. Euro coins and notes will be issued in January 2002, and in a few months lire will be withdrawn from circulation. At press time (summer 2001) the exchange rate was 2,171 lire/€1.12 to the U.S. dollar, 1,376 lire/€.71 to the Canadian dollar, 3,108 lire/€1.60 to the pound sterling, 2,458 lire/€1.27 to the Irish punt, 1,054 lire/€.54 to the Australian dollar, 876 lire/€.45 to the New Zealand dollar, and 267 lire/€.14 to the South African rand.

When your purchases run into hundreds of thousands of lire, beware of being shortchanged, a dodge that is practiced at ticket windows, toll booths, and cashiers' desks, as well as in shops and even in banks. *Always count your change before you leave the counter.* Always carry some smaller-denomination bills for sundry purchases.

SALES TAX
Foreign tourists who have spent more than 300,000 lire/€155 (before tax) in one store can obtain a refund of Italy's value-added tax (IVA). At the time of purchase, with passport or ID in hand, ask the store for an invoice describing the article or articles and the total lire amount. If your destination when you leave Italy is a non-EU country, you must have the invoice stamped at customs upon departure from Italy; if your destination is another EU country, you must obtain the customs stamp upon departure from that country. Once back home—and within 90 days of the date of purchase—you must send the stamped invoice back to the store, which should forward the IVA rebate directly to you. If the store participates in the Europe Tax-Free Shopping System (those that do display a sign to the effect), things are simpler. Note that, to calculate the price without IVA, you don't subtract 20% from the price

on the label, which already includes IVA. Instead, you need to subtract roughly 16.5%. Transaction fees which go to the companies providing the tax-free service are 3%–4%, so in this case you should expect to get only about 13% of the purchase price back.

TELEPHONES
COUNTRY AND AREA CODES
The country code for Italy is 39. Do not drop the 0 in the regional code when calling Italy.

INTERNATIONAL CALLS
To place an international call, insert a phone card, dial 00, then the country code, area code, and phone number. The cheaper and easier option, however, is to use your AT&T, MCI, or Sprint calling card. To make collect calls, dial the AT&T USADirect number below. For information and operators in Europe and the Mediterranean area, dial 15; for intercontinental service, dial 170.

➤ ACCESS CODES: **AT&T USADirect** (☎ 172–1011). **MCI Call USA** (☎ 172–1022). **Sprint Express** (☎ 172–1877).

LOCAL CALLS
For all local calls, you must dial the regional area codes, even in cities. Most local calls cost 200 lire/€.10 for two minutes. Pay phones take either 100-, 200-, or 500-lire coins or *schede telefoniche* (phone cards), purchased in bars, tobacconists, and post offices in either 5,000-10,000-, or 15,000-lire denominations. The phone card called Time Europa (50,000 lire/€25.80) is a good-value card for calling Europe and the United States, at only 540 lire/€.30 per minute. For directory information in Italy, dial 12.

16 VIENNA

Vienna has been characterized as an "old dowager of a town"—an Austro-Hungarian empress widowed in 1918 by the Great War. It's not just the aristocratic and courtly atmosphere, with monumental doorways and facades of former palaces at every turn. Nor is it just that Vienna (Wien in German) has a higher proportion of middle-aged and older citizens than any other city in Europe, with a concomitant air of stability, quiet, and respectability. Rather, it's these factors—combined with a love of music; a discreet weakness for rich food (especially cakes); an adherence to old-fashioned and formal forms of address; a high regard for the arts; and a gentle mourning for lost glories—that preserve the enchanting elegance of Old World dignity.

EXPLORING VIENNA

Numbers in the margin correspond to points of interest on the Vienna map.

Most main sights are in the inner zone, the oldest part of the city, encircled by the Ring, once the course of the city walls and today a broad, tree-lined boulevard. Carry a ready supply of AS10 coins; many places of interest have coin-operated tape-recording machines that provide English commentaries. As you wander around, train yourself to look upward; some of the most memorable architectural delights are found on upper stories and along roof lines. Note that addresses throughout the chapter ending with "-strasse" or "-gasse" (both meaning "street") are abbreviated "str." or "g." respectively (Augustinerstrasse will be "Augustinerstr."; Dorotheergasse will be "Dorotheerg.").

The Heart of Vienna

The Innere Stadt (Inner City), or First District, comprised the entire city of Vienna in medieval times, and for more than eight centuries the enormous bulk of the Stephansdom (St. Stephen's Cathedral) has remained the nucleus around which the city grew. Beginning in the 1870s, when Vienna reached the zenith of its imperial prosperity, the medieval walls were replaced by the Ringstrasse (Ring), along which a series of magnificent buildings were erected: the Staatsoper (opera house), the Hofburg Palace, the KunsthistorischesMuseum, the Parliament building, and the Rathaus (city hall). The pedestrian zone around the Stephansdom is lined with designer boutiques, cafes and upscale restaurants.

❶ Albertina. Some of the greatest Old Master drawings—including Dürer's *Praying Hands*—are housed in this unassuming building, home to the world's largest collection of drawings, sketches, engravings, and etchings. Other highlights include works by Rembrandt, Michelangelo, and Correggio. The building is undergoing restoration and is scheduled to reopen in September 2002. ⊠ *Augustinerstr. 1,* ☎ *01/581–3060–21.* ⊙ *Tues.–Sun. 10–5.*

❸ Augustinerkirche (St. Augustine's Church). The interior of this 14th-century church has undergone restoration; while much of the earlier Baroque ornamentation was removed in the 1780s, the gilt organ decoration and main altar remain as visual sensations. This was the court church; the Habsburg rulers' hearts are preserved in a chamber here. On Sunday, the 11 AM mass is sung in Latin. ⊠ *Josefspl.*

㉓ Figarohaus (Mozart Memorial Rooms). A commemorative museum occupies the small apartment in the house on a narrow street just east of St. Stephen's Cathedral where Mozart lived from 1784 to 1787. It was here that the composer wrote *The Marriage of Figaro* (hence the nickname Figaro House) and, some claim, spent the happiest years of his life. Fascinating Mozart memorabilia are on view, unfortunately displayed in an inappropriately modern fashion. ⊠ *Domg. 5,* ☎ *01/513–6294.* ⊙ *Tues.–Sun. 9–6.*

㉕ Freud Museum. The original famous couch is gone (there's a replica), but the apartment in which Sigmund Freud developed modern psychiatry and treated his first patients is otherwise generally intact. Other rooms include a reference library. ⊠ *Bergg. 19,* ☎ *01/319–1596.* ⊙ *July–Sept., daily 9–6; Oct.–June, daily 9–4.*

🖐 ⑱ Haus der Musik (House of Music). It would be easy to spend an entire day at this new, ultra high-tech museum housed on several floors of an early 19th-century palace near Schwarzenbergplatz. There are special rooms dedicated to each of the great Viennese composers—Haydn, Mozart, Beethoven, Strauss, and Mahler—complete with music samples and manuscripts. There are also dozens of interactive computer games. You can even record your own CD with a variety of everyday sounds. ⊠ *Seilerstätte 30,* ☎ *01/51648,* WEB *haus-der-musik-wien.at.* ⊙ *Daily 10–10. Restaurant, café. U-Bahn: U1, U2, U4 Karlsplatz, then Streetcar D to Schwarzenbergpl.*

🖐 ㉜ Heeresgeschichtliches Museum (Museum of Military History). Designed by Theophil Hansen, this impressive neo-Gothic building houses war artifacts ranging from armor and Turkish tents confiscated from the Turks during the 16th-century siege of Vienna to fighter planes and tanks. Also on display is the bullet-riddled car that Archduke Franz Ferdinand and his wife were riding in when they were assassinated in Sarajevo in 1914. ⊠ *Arsenal 3, Bldg. 18,* ☎ *01/795–610.* ⊙ *Sat.–Thurs. 9–5. Tram 18/Ghegastr., near the Belvedere.*

314

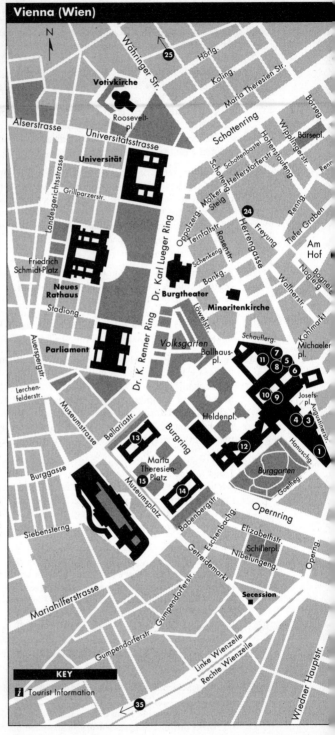

Vienna (Wien)

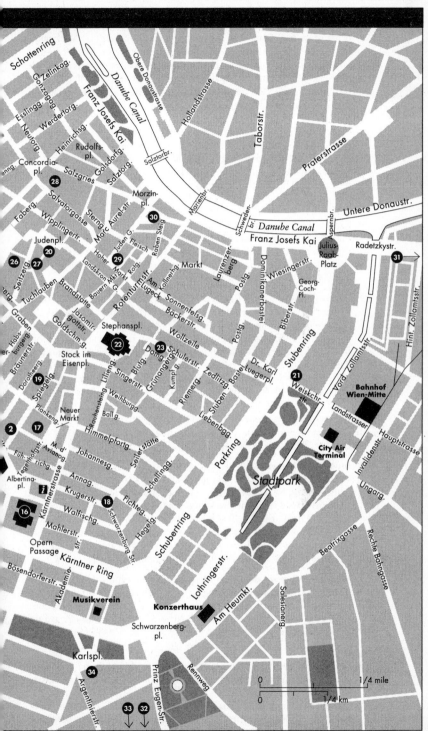

★ ❼ **Hofburg** (Imperial Palace). This centerpiece of Imperial Vienna is actually a vast complex comprising numerous buildings, courtyards, and
other must-sees. Start with the magnificent domed entry—**Michaelertor** (St. Michael's Gate), the principal gateway to the Hofburg—and
go through the courtyards to the vast, grassy Heldenplatz (Hero's
Square), on the front. The palace complex, with sections dating from
the 13th through 18th centuries, includes the **Augustinerkirche**, the **Nationalbibliothek**—its central room is one of the most spectacular
Baroque showpieces anywhere—and the **Hofburgkapelle,** home to the
Vienna Boys Choir. Here, too, are the famous **Spanische Reitschule**—
where the Lipizzaners go through their paces—and three fascinating
museums: the **Silberkammer,** the **Schauräume in der Hofburg,** and the
Schatzkammer, as well as the **Schmetterlinghaus** (Butterfly House), alive
with unusual butterflies. The complex also houses the office of the federal presidency, a glittering chandelier-lit convention center, an elegant
multipurpose hall (Redoutensaal), and private apartments as well as
lesser government offices. The complex of the Hofburg is centered on
the ☞ **Neue Burg** palace. ⊠ *Hofburg: main streets circling complex—
Opernring, Augustinerstr., Schauflerg., and Dr. Karl Renner-Ring,
Schmetterlinghaus: entrance in Burggarten,* ☎ *01/533–7570.* ☉ *Apr.–
Oct., daily 10–5; Nov.–Mar., daily 10–4.*

❿ **Hofburgkapelle** (Court Chapel). Home to the renowned Vienna Boys
Choir, this Gothic chapel dates from 1449. You'll need tickets to hear
the angelic boys sing mass (only 10 side balcony seats afford views) at
9:15 AM on Sunday, mid-September through June; tickets are available
from travel agencies at a substantial markup, at the chapel itself (open
daily 11:30–1 and 3–5), or by writing two months in advance to the
Hofmusikkapelle (⊠ Hofburg, Schweizerhof, A-1010 Vienna). General seating costs AS70; prime seats in the front of the church, AS380.
The City Tourist Office can sometimes help with ticket applications.
Limited standing room is available for free; get to the chapel by at least
8:30 AM on Sunday for a shot at a spot. ⊠ *Hofburg, Schweizer Hof,*
☎ *01/533–9927–71,* ℻ *01/533–9927–75.*

⓴ **Judenplatz Museum.** In what was once the old Jewish ghetto, construction workers discovered the remains of a 13th-century synagogue
while digging for a new parking garage. Simon Wiesenthal (a Vienna
resident) helped to turn it into a museum dedicated to the Austrian Jews
who died in World War II. Outside is a concrete cube resembling library shelves, designed by Rachel Whiteread. Downstairs are three exhibition rooms on medieval Jewish life and the synagogue excavations.
⊠ *Judenpl. 8,* ☎ *01/535–0431.* ☉ *Sun.–Thurs. 10–6, Fri. 10–2.*

⓳ **Jüdisches Museum der Stadt Wien** (Jewish Museum). Housed in the
former Eskeles town palace, the city's Jewish Museum offers exhibits
that portray the richness of the Jewish culture and heritage that con-
tributed so much to Vienna and Austria. On the top floor is a staggering collection of Judaica. ⊠ *Dorotheerg. 11,* ☎ *01/535–0431,* 🕸
www.jmw.at. ☉ *Sun.–Wed. and Fri. 10–6, Thurs. 10–8.*

⓱ **Kapuzinerkirche** (Capuchin Church). The ground-level church is nothing
unusual, but the basement crypt holds the imperial vault, the **Kaisergruft,**
the final resting place of many sarcophagi of long-dead Habsburgs. The
oldest tomb is that of Ferdinand II; it dates from 1633. The most recent
one is that of Empress Zita, widow of the last of the kaisers, who died
in 1989. ⊠ *Neuer Markt 1,* ☎ *01/512–6853–12.* ☉ *Daily 9:30–4.*

★ ㉞ **Karlskirche** (St. Charles's Church). The classical Baroque facade and
dome flanked by vast twin columns instantly identify the Karlskirche,
one of the city's best-known landmarks. The church was built around

1715 by Fischer von Erlach. In the surprisingly small oval interior, the ceiling has airy frescoes, while the Baroque altar is adorned with a magnificent sunburstlike array of gilded shafts. ⊠ *Karlspl.*

★ ⑭ **Kunsthistorisches Museum** (Art History Museum). One of the finest art collections in the world, housed in palatial splendor, this is the crown jewel of Vienna's museums. Its glories are the Italian and Flemish collections, assembled by the Habsburgs over many centuries. The group of paintings by Pieter Brueghel the Elder is the largest in existence. The large-scale works concentrated in the main galleries shouldn't distract you from the masterworks in the more intimate side wings. One level down is the remarkable Kunstkammer (Art Cabinet) displaying priceless objects created for the Habsburg emperors. These include curiosities made of gold, silver, and crystal (including Cellini's salt cellar). ⊠ *Maria-Theresien-Pl.,* ☎ *01/525–240.* ⊙ *Tues.–Wed. and Fri.–Sun. 10–6, Thurs. 10–9.*

↺ ⑥ **Lipizzaner Museum.** To learn more about the extraordinary Lipizzan horses of the Spanish Riding School, visit the adjacent museum set in what used to be the imperial pharmacy. Exhibits document the history of the Lipizzaners through paintings, photographs, and videos giving an overview from the 16th century to the present. A visit to the nearby stables—part of the Spanish Riding School complex—allows you to see the horses up close through a window. ⊠ *Reitschulg. 2,* ☎ *01/533–7811,* FAX *01/533–3853.* ▣ *Combination ticket with morning training session at the Spanish Riding School AS140/€10.17.* ⊙ *Daily 9–6.*

↺ ⑮ **Museumsquartier** (Museum Quarter). Scheduled to open in the summer of 2001, this vast culture center, which claims to be the largest of its kind in the world, will be housed in what was once the Imperial Court Stables. The 250-year-old Baroque complex is ideally situated near the Hofburg Palace in the heart of the city. Four museums are planned, the **Leopold Museum** (⊙ Wed.–Thurs., Sat.–Mon. 11–7, Fri. 11–9), to contain the Egon Schiele collection, the **Museum moderner Kunst Stiftung Ludwig** (⊙ Tues.–Wed., Fri.–Sun. 10–6, Thurs. 10–9), or modern art museum, the **Kunsthalle** (⊙ Fri.–Wed. 10–7, Thurs. 10–10), an art hall to be used for special exhibits, and a children's museum, the **ZOOM Kinder Museum** (⊙ Mon.–Fri. 8–5, Sat.–Sun. 10–5:30). The annual Wiener Festwochen (theater arts festival) and the International Tanzwochen (dance festival) will be held in the former winter riding hall. In addition to all this, there will be an architecture center for contemporary design, a theater where the annual Viennale Film Festival will be held, and shops, cafés, and art galleries. ⊠ *Museumspl. 1–5,* ☎ *01/523–5881,* WEB *www. museumsquartier.at. U-Bahn: U2 Babenbergerstr./U2, U3 Volkstheater.*

㉑ **Museum für angewandte Kunst (MAK)** (Museum of Applied Arts). This fascinating museum contains a large collection of Austrian furniture, porcelain, art objects, and priceless Oriental carpets. The museum puts on changing exhibitions of contemporary art, with artists ranging from Chris Burden to Nam June Paik. The museum also houses the popular MAK Cafe. ⊠ *Stubenring 5,* ☎ *01/711–36–0.* ⊙ *Tues.–Wed., Fri.–Sun. 10–6, Thurs. 10–9. U-bahn: U3 Stubentor.*

★ ④ **Nationalbibliothek** (National Library). The focus here is on the stunning Baroque central hall—one of Europe's most magnificently decorated spaces. Look for the fascinating collection of globes on the third floor. ⊠ *Josefspl. 1,* ☎ *01/534–100 library; 01/534–10–297 globe museum.* ⊙ *Library: hrs vary, generally May 7–Oct. 26, Mon.–Wed., Fri.–Sat. 10–4, Thurs. 10–7, Sun. 10–2; Oct. 27–May 6, Mon.–Sat. 10–2. Globe museum: Mon.–Wed. and Fri. 11–noon, Thurs. 2–3.*

⑬ **Naturhistorisches Museum** (Natural History Museum). The twin building opposite the art-filled Kunsthistorisches Museum houses ranks of assorted showcases filled with stuffed animals, but such special collections as butterflies are better presented. There are dinosaur skeletons, of course. Here also is the Venus of Willendorf, a 25,000-year-old statuette discovered in Lower Austria. ⊠ *Maria-Theresien-Pl.,* ☎ *01/ 521–77–0.* ☉ *Thurs.–Mon. 9–6:30, Wed. 9–9.*

⑫ **Neue Burg** (New Wing of the Imperial Palace). This 19th-century edifice—Hitler announced the annexation of Austria from its balcony in 1938—now houses a series of museums whose exhibits range from musical instruments (Beethoven's piano) to weapons to the collections of the **Völkerkunde** (Ethnological) and **Ephesus** (Classical Antiquity) museums. ⊠ *Heldenpl. 1,* ☎ *01/525–240.* ☉ *Ethnological museum: Tues.–Sun. 10–6. Ephesus museum: Wed.–Mon. 10–6.*

★ ⑨ **Schatzkammer** (Imperial Treasury). An almost overpowering display includes the magnificent crown jewels, the imperial crowns, the treasure of the Order of the Golden Fleece, regal robes, and other secular and ecclesiastical treasures. The imperial crown of the Holy Roman Empire is more than 1,000 years old. ⊠ *Hofburg, Schweizer Hof,* ☎ *01/533–7931.* ☉ *Wed.–Mon. 10–6.*

⑧ **Schauräume in der Hofburg** (Imperial Apartments). The long, repetitive suite of conventionally luxurious rooms has a poignant feel. The decoration (19th-century imitation of 18th-century rococo) tries to look regal but ends up looking merely official. Among the few signs of genuine life are Emperor Franz Josef's spartan, iron field bed, and Empress Elizabeth's wooden gymnastics equipment. Obsessed with her looks, she suffered from anorexia and was fanatically devoted to exercise. ⊠ *Michaelerpl. 1; entrance under Michaelertor dome,* ☎ *01/533–7570.* ☉ *Daily 9–4:30.*

★ ⑪ **Silberkammer** (Court Silver and Tableware Museum). See how royalty dined in this brilliant showcase of imperial table settings. Little wonder Marie-Antoinette—who, as a child of Maria Theresa, grew up in Schloss Schönbrunn—had a taste for extreme luxury. You can buy a combination ticket, which includes the imperial apartments around the corner. ⊠ *Burghof inner court, Michaelertrakt,* ☎ *01/533–7570.* ☉ *Daily 9–4:30.*

★ ⑤ **Spanische Reitschule** (Spanish Riding School). Probably the most famous interior in Vienna, the riding arena of the Spanish Riding School—wedding-cake white and crystal-chandeliered—is where the beloved white Lipizzaner horses train and perform dressage when they are not stabled in stalls across the Reitschulgasse to the east side of the school. For performance schedules and tickets, write to the Spanische Reitschule (⊠ *Hofburg, A-1010 Vienna) at least* three months in advance. The AmEx office sometimes has a few last-minute tickets, but expect a 22% service charge. You can watch the 10 AM–noon training sessions Tuesday–Friday during much of the performance season (tickets only at the door) but the full-scale rehearsal session on Saturday requires advance booking for tickets through travel agencies, as does, needless to say, the main dressage performance offered on Sunday. ⊠ *Michaelerpl. 1, Hofburg,* ☎ *01/533–9031–0,* 𝔽𝔸𝕏 *01/535–0186.* 💷 *AS250/€18.17–AS900/€65.40, standing room AS200/€14.53, morning training sessions AS100/€7.27; classical dressage sessions with music AS250/€18.17, available only through travel agencies.* ☉ *Tues.– Sun., Mar.–June and Sept.–mid-Dec.; closed tour wks.*

⑯ **Staatsoper** (State Opera House). Considered one of the best opera houses in the world, the Staatsoper is a focus of Viennese social life as well. Almost totally destroyed in the last days of World War II (only the walls and front foyers were saved), it was rebuilt in its present, simpler elegance and reopened in 1955. Tickets for seats can be expensive and scarce, but among the very best bargains in Vienna are the Staatsoper standing-room tickets, available for each performance at delightfully affordable prices—as low as AS50 (€3.70). Backstage tours are also available. ✉ *Opernring 2,* ☎ *01/514–4426–13.*

★ ㉒ **Stephansdom** (St. Stephen's Cathedral). The towering Gothic spires and gaudy 19th-century tile roof of the city's central landmark still dominate the skyline. The oldest parts of the structure are the 13th-century entrance, the soaring **Riesentor** (Great Entry), and the **Heidentürme** (Heathens' Towers). Inside, the church is mysteriously shadowy, filled with an array of monuments, tombs, sculptures, paintings, and pulpits. Despite numerous Baroque additions—and extensive wartime damage—the atmosphere seems authentically medieval. Climb the 343 steps of the south tower— der alte Steffl (Old Stephen) as the Viennese call it—for a stupendous view over the city. If you take a 30-minute tour of the crypt, you can see the copper jars in which the entrails of the Habsburgs are carefully preserved. ✉ *Stephanspl.,* ☎ *01/515–520.* ⊙ *Guided tour Mon.–Sat. at 10:30 and 3, Sun. at 3; evening tour Jun.–Sept., Sat. at 7; catacombs tour Mon.–Sat. from 10–11:30 and 1:30–4:30 every half hr, Sun. from 1:30– 4:30 every half hr. North Tower elevator to Pummerin bell Apr.–Jun. and Sept., daily 9–6; Jul.–Aug., daily 9–6:30; Nov.–Mar., daily 8:30–5.*

☝ ❷ **Theater Museum.** Housed in the noted 18th-century Palais Lobkowitz— Beethoven was a regular visitor here—this museum covers the history of theater in Vienna and the rest of Austria. A children's museum in the basement—alas, open only by appointment—is reached, appropriately, by a slide. ✉ *Lobkowitzpl. 2,* ☎ *01/512–8800–0.* ⊙ *Tues., Thurs.–Sun. 10–5, Wed. 10–8.*

Other Corners of Vienna

City planning in the late 1800s and early 1900s was essential to manage the growth of the burgeoning imperial capital. Within a short walk of the Stephansdom are other sights that give a sense of the history of old Vienna, with colorful cobblestone squares, statues and Baroque churches. A little further out, the glories of imperial Austria are nowhere shown off more opulently than in Schönbrunn Palace, the summer residence of the court, and Belvedere Palace. Both palaces with their extensive gardens were in what was once the countryside, but are now incorporated into the city proper.

㉖ **Am Hof.** The name of this remarkable square translates simply as "at court." On the east side of Am Hof, most of the Baroque overlay both inside and out on the massive **Kirche am Hof** (also known as the Church of the Nine Choirs of Angels) dates from the 1600s. In style, the somewhat dreary interior is reminiscent of those of many Dutch churches. In the northeast corner of the square check out what is possibly the most ornate fire station in the world. You'll find an open-air antiques market in the square on Thursday and Friday in summer and frequent seasonal markets at other times. ✉ *Bounded by Tiefer Graben on west, Naglerg. on south, and Seitzerg. on east.*

㉙ **Hoher Markt.** This ancient cobblestone square with its imposing central monument celebrating the betrothal of Mary and Joseph sits atop **Roman ruins** (✉ Hoher Markt 3, ☎ 01/535–5606), remains of the 2nd-century Roman legion encampment. On the north side of Hoher Markt is the amusing **Anker-Uhr**, a clock that marks the hour with a parade of moving figures. The figures are identified on a plaque at the lower left of the clock. ✉ *Judeng. and Fisch-hof Str.*

㉛ **Hundertwasserhaus** (Hundertwasser House). This structure is an eccentric modern masterpiece envisioned by the late Austrian avant-garde artist Friedensreich Hundertwasser—an astonishing apartment complex marked by turrets, towers, unusual windows, and uneven floors. The nearby **KunstHaus Wien** (Vienna House of Art; ⊠ Untere Weissgerberstr. 13, ☎ 01/712–0491) is an art museum designed by the artist; it offers a floor of his work plus changing exhibits of other modern art. ⊠ *Kegelg. and Löweng.* ☉ *Daily 10–7.*

㉘ Maria am Gestade (St. Mary's on the Bank). When built around 1400, this was a church for fishermen from the nearby canal, hence the name. Note the arched stone doorway and the ornate carved-stone-latticework "folded hands" spire. ⊠ *Salvatorg. and Passauer Pl.*

㉚ Ruprechtskirche (St. Rupert's Church). Vienna's oldest church, dating from the 11th century, is usually closed but sometimes opens for local art shows and summer evening classical concerts. ⊠ *Ruprechtspl.*

★ **㉝ Schloss Belvedere** (Belvedere Palace). On a rise overlooking the city, this Baroque-era palace is one of the showpieces of Vienna. It was commissioned by Prince Eugene of Savoy and built by Johann Lukas von Hildebrandt in 1721–22. The palace consists of two separate buildings, one at the foot of the hill and the other at the top. The Upper Belvedere houses a gallery of 19th- and 20th-century Viennese art, featuring works by Klimt (including his world-famous painting *The Kiss*), Schiele, Waldmüller, and Makart; the Lower Belvedere has a Baroque museum together with exhibits of Austrian art of the Middle Ages. Take Streetcar D toward the Südbahnhof to reach the Belvedere. ⊠ *Prinz-Eugen-Str. 27,* ☎ *01/79557–100.* ☉ *Tues.–Sun. 10–5.*

★ **㉟ Schloss Schönbrunn** (Schönbrunn Palace). The Versailles of Vienna, this magnificent Baroque residence with grandly formal gardens was built for the Habsburgs between 1696 and 1713. The complex has been a summer residence for such personages as Maria Theresa and Napoléon. Kaiser Franz Josef I was born and died here. His "office" (kept as he left it in 1916) is a touching reminder of his spartan life. In contrast, other rooms are filled with truly spectacular imperial elegance. The ornate reception areas are still used for state occasions. A guided tour leading through more than 40 of the palace's 1,441 rooms is the best way to see inside the palace (the most dazzling salons start at No. 21). Ask to see the **Berglzimmer,** ornately decorated ground-floor rooms generally not included in tours. To get to the palace, take the U4 subway line from Karlsplatz in the city center to Schönbrunn. ⊠ *Schönbrunner Schloss-Str.,* ☎ *01/81113–239.* 🎫 *AS145/€10.54 with guided tour; AS120/€8.72 without tour (40 rooms).* ☉ *Apr.–Oct., daily 8:30–5; Nov.–Mar., daily 8:30–4:30.*

☾ On the grounds of the Schönbrunn Palace is the **Tiergarten** (zoo), Europe's oldest menagerie, established in 1752 to amuse and educate the court. It houses an extensive assortment of animals; the original Baroque enclosures now serve as viewing pavilions, with the animals housed in effective, modern settings. ☎ *01/877–9294–0.* ☉ *Nov.–Jan., daily 9–4:30; Feb., daily 9–5; Mar. and Oct., daily 9–5:30; Apr., daily 9–6; May–Sept., daily 9–6:30.*

Pathways lead up through the formal gardens to the **Gloriette,** an 18th-century Baroque folly on the rise behind Schloss Schönbrunn built to afford superb views of the city. A café is inside. ☉ *Daily 9–5.*

☾ The **Wagenburg** (Imperial Coach Collection), near the entrance to the palace grounds, displays splendid examples of bygone conveyances, from ornate children's sleighs to the grand carriages built to carry the coffins of deceased emperors in state funerals. ☎ *01/877–3244.* ☉ *Nov.–Mar., Tues.–Sun. 10–4; Apr.–Oct., daily 9–6.*

Wander the grounds to discover the **Schöner Brunnen** (Beautiful Fountain) for which the Schönbrunn Palace is named; the re-created but convincing massive **Römische Ruinen** (Roman Ruins); and the great glass **Palmenhaus** (Palm House), with its orchids and exotic plants. ⊠ *Palm House: nearest entrance Hietzing,* ☎ *01/877–5087–406.* ⊙ *Nov.– Mar., daily 8:30–4:30; Apr. and Oct., daily 9:30–4:30 May–Sept., daily 9:30–5:30.*

㉔ Schottenkirche, Museum im Schottenstift (Scottish Church and Museum). Despite its name, the monks who founded this church around 1177 were actually Irish, not Scots. The present imposing building dates from the mid-1600s. In contrast to the plain exterior, the interior bubbles with cherubs and angels. The Benedictines have set up a small but worthwhile museum of mainly religious art, including a late-Gothic winged altarpiece removed from the church when the interior was given a Baroque overlay. The museum entrance is in the courtyard. ⊠ *Freyung 6,* ☎ *01/534–98–600.* ⊙ *Thurs.–Sat. 10–5, Sun. noon–5.*

㉗ Uhrenmuseum (Clock Museum). Tucked away on several floors of a lovely Renaissance structure is an amazing collection of clocks and watches. Try to be here when the hundreds of clocks strike the noon hour. ⊠ *Schulhof 2,* ☎ *01/533–2265.* ⊙ *Tues.–Sun. 9–4:30.*

Vienna Environs

Wienerwald (Vienna Woods). You can reach a small corner of the historic Vienna Woods by streetcar and bus: take a streetcar or the U-2 subway line to Schottentor/University and, from there, Streetcar 38 (Grinzing) to the end of the line. To get into the woods, change in Grinzing to Bus 38A. This will take you to the Kahlenberg, which provides a superb view out over the Danube and the city. You can take the bus or hike to the Leopoldsberg, the promontory over the Danube from which Turkish invading forces were repulsed during the 16th and 17th centuries. Grinzing itself is a village out of a picture book. Unfortunately, it is sometimes a tour-bus mecca. For less touristy wine villages, try Sievering (Bus 39A), Neustift am Walde (U-4, U-6 subway to Spittelau, then Bus 35A), or the suburb of Nussdorf (Streetcar D).

DINING

In the mid-1990s Vienna, once a culinary backwater, produced a new generation of chefs willing to slaughter sacred cows and create a *Neue Küche,* a new Vienna cuisine. This trend relies on lighter versions of the old standbys and clever combinations of such traditional ingredients as *Kürbiskernöl* (pumpkin-seed oil) and fruit sauces instead of butter and cream. Austria also claims the distinction of having more organic farms than any other country in Europe, so restaurants feature some of the healthiest, freshest foods around.

In a first-class restaurant you will pay as much as in most other Western European capitals. But you can still find good food at refreshingly low prices in the simpler restaurants, particularly at neighborhood Gasthäuser (rustic inns) in the suburbs. Remember if you eat your main meal at noon (as the Viennese do), you can take advantage of the luncheon specials available at most restaurants and in cafés.

CATEGORY	COST*
$$$$	over AS325 (€23.61)
$$$	AS200–AS325 (€14.53–€23.61)
$$	AS125–AS200 (€9.08–€14.53)
$	Under AS125 (€9.08)

*per person for a main course at dinner

\$\$\$–\$\$\$\$ ✕ **Steirereck.** Generally conceded to be the most famous restaurant in
★ Austria, Steirereck consistently ranks high on critics' lists. You can choose
from three elegant settings: the intimate Kaminstüberl with its Renaissance-style fireplace and decorative columns; the sunny, plant-
filled Winter Garden; or the light, spacious room filled with French
Impressionist reproductions. Fish choices are plentiful and may include
delicate smoked catfish or turbot in an avocado crust. Also good is the
lamb with crepes and spinach cooked simply with garlic and olive oil.
⊠ *Rasumofskyg. 2, A-1030,* ☎ *01/713–3168. Reservations essential.
Jacket and tie. AE, DC, MC, V. Closed Sat.–Sun.*

\$\$–\$\$\$ ✕ **Artner.** This modern, pleasantly lit spot has one of the most inno-
★ vative menus in the city and is unique in showcasing superb wines and
goat cheeses from its own 350-year-old winery and farm in the Car-
nuntum region east of Vienna. Signature dishes include free-range
chicken with basil risotto, or pike perch in a zucchini crust, and homemade pasta topped with fresh basil and diced ruby-red tomatoes. ⊠
Florag. 6 (entrance on Neumanng.), ☎ *01/503–5033. AE, DC, MC,
V. No lunch weekends.*

\$\$–\$\$\$ ✕ **Bauer.** As soon as you're seated in this pretty 17th-century house
with its bay window and dusky-rose walls, you know you're in for a
treat. A variety of freshly baked breads and a light herbed spread are
brought to your table while you're perusing the seasonal menu, which
might include the unusual but delicious light cream of chestnut soup
with truffles, fillet of *Zander* (pike perch) in a sesame crust, or a big,
tender steak with homemade potato chips. ⊠ *Sonnenfelsg. 17,* ☎ *01/
512–9871. Reservations essential. AE. Closed Sun.–Mon. No lunch.*

\$\$–\$\$\$ ✕ **Palmenhaus.** Twenty-ft-high palm trees and exotic plants decorate
this airy restaurant, in the old Hofburg Palace conservatory at the back
of the Burggarten. There's a blackboard that lists daily fresh-fish specials, and several vegetarian dishes are also offered, such as pumpkin
gnocchi. It's also worth a stop for coffee and a pastry. In fine weather,
tables are set outside on the terrace overlooking the park. Service can
be slow. ⊠ *Burggarten (or through Goetheg. gate after 8 PM),* ☎ *01/
533–1033. Reservations essential. DC, MC, V.*

\$\$–\$\$\$ ✕ **Vincent.** Across the Danube canal from Schwedenplatz, Vincent
★ has several dining rooms. The offerings change every few days, and
it's possible to order à la carte from the two set menus. You might start
with baby shrimp and smoked salmon in a dill cream sauce, followed
by little crispy pike perch with a salad of field greens. Main courses
could include a big tender filet mignon or game hen with black truffles and polenta. Serving until midnight, it's a perfect choice for dining after the opera or theater. ⊠ *Grosse Pfarrg. 7,* ☎ *01/214–1516.
Reservations essential. AE, D, MC, V. Closed Sun. No lunch.*

\$–\$\$\$ ✕ **Frank's.** A cavernous cellar-like restaurant with aged brick walls,
★ arches, and candlelight is not exactly what you'd expect to find inside
the ultramodern central post office building. Choose from the vast selection of pizzas, burgers, salads, and pastas. There are also plenty of
vegetarian and fresh-fish items. From October to April, Frank's offers
a popular Sunday brunch, featuring, among other American-style sta-
ples, bagels and Bloody Marys. ⊠ *Laurenzerberg 2/entrance Postpassage
Schwedenpl.,* ☎ *01/533–7805. Reservations essential. D, MC, V.
Closed Sun. May–Sept. No lunch Sat.*

\$–\$\$\$ ✕ **MAK Cafe.** In the Museum of Applied Arts, also known as MAK,
this is one of the "scene" places in Vienna. The menu changes frequently
and includes lots of vegetarian items. One staple is the delicious pierogi
stuffed with either potatoes or minced beef. In summer sit outside in
the shaded inner courtyard. ⊠ *Stubenring 3–5,* ☎ *01/714–0121. No
credit cards. Closed Mon.*

$–$$$ ✕ **Neu Wien.** As the name says, this is a taste of the new Vienna. The vaulted interior is enlivened by cheeky modern art. The eclectic menu changes frequently, but look for the herbed goat-cheese salad with basil oil dressing or veal with tagliatelle in a truffle sauce. ✉ *Bäckerstr. 5, near St. Stephen's,* ☎ *01/512–0999. Reservations essential. MC, V. Closed weekends in summer. No lunch.*

$–$$ ✕ **Brezl Gwölb.** Housed in a medieval pretzel factory between Am Hof and Judenplatz, this snug restaurant fills up fast at night. Try the scrumptious *Tyroler G'röstl,* home-fried potatoes with slivered ham and onions served in a blackened skillet. Best tables are downstairs in the authentic medieval cellar, which looks like a set from *Phantom of the Opera.* ✉ *Ledererhof 9,* ☎ *01/533–8811. AE, DC, MC, V.*

$–$$ ✕ **Figlmüller.** Known for its gargantuan Wiener schnitzel—so large it usually overflows the plate—Figlmüller is always packed with diners sharing benches and long tables. Food choices are limited, and everything is à la carte. Try to get a table in the "greenhouse" passageway area. ✉ *Wollzeile 5 (passageway from Stephansdom),* ☎ *01/512–6177. No credit cards. Closed Aug.*

$–$$ ✕ **Hansen.** Housed downstairs in the Börse (Vienna Stock Exchange), ★ this unique restaurant is also an exotic, upscale flower market. The decor is modern and elegant, with close-set tables covered in white linen. The menu highlights Mediterranean-inspired dishes such as scampi risotto or spaghettini with oven-dried tomatoes in a black-olive cream sauce. There are also Austrian dishes done with a fresh, light slant. Lunch is the main event here, though you can also come for breakfast or a pretheater dinner. ✉ *Wipplingerstr. 34,* ☎ *01/532–0542. Reservations essential. AE, DC, MC, V. Closed Sun. and after 8 PM.*

$–$$ ✕ **Lebenbauer.** Vienna's premier vegetarian restaurant even has a no-smoking room, rare in this part of Europe. Specialties include spinach tortelloni in a Gorgonzola sauce, or tender flying duck breast in a marsala sauce with roasted chestnuts and pumpkin polenta. ✉ *Teinfaltstr. 3, near Freyung,* ☎ *01/533–5556–0. AE, DC, MC, V. Closed Sat.–Sun. and first 2 wks in Aug.*

LODGING

Vienna's first district (A-1010) is the best base for visitors because it's so close to most of the major sights, restaurants, and shops. This accessibility translates, of course, into higher prices. Try asking for discounts at the larger international chain hotels during the off-season.

Although exact rates vary, a single room generally costs more than half the price of a comparable double. Breakfast at the roll-and-coffee level is often included in the room rate; full and sumptuous breakfast buffets, however, can involve a supplementary charge. Keep in mind that hotels outside Vienna may offer comprehensive rates that include breakfast *and* dinner; these are often excellent deals.

CATEGORY	COST*
$$$$	over AS4,000 (€290.70)
$$$	AS1,750–AS2,500 (€127.18–€181.69)
$$	AS1,000–AS1,750 (€72.67–€127.18)
$	under AS1,000 (€72.67)

All prices are for two persons in a standard double room, including local taxes (usually 10%), service (15%), and breakfast (except in most $$$$ hotels).

$$$$ ▥ **Bristol.** Opposite the Staatsoper (State Opera House), the Bristol has one of the finest locations in the city. The accent here is on tradition, from the brocaded walls to the Biedermeier period furnishings in the public rooms and some bedrooms. The building dates from 1892,

and during the 1945–55 occupation it was the U.S. military headquarters. ⊠ *Kärntner Ring 1, A-1010,* ☎ *01/515–16–0,* FAX *01/515–
16–550,* WEB *www.westin.com/bristol. 141 rooms. 2 restaurants, café.
AE, DC, MC, V.*

$$$$ 🏨 **Imperial.** The hotel is as much a palace today as when it was formally
opened in 1873 by Emperor Franz Josef. The emphasis is on Old Vienna
elegance and privacy; the guest list is littered with famous names, from
heads of state to Michael Jackson. The beautiful rooms are furnished in
antique style, though only the first three floors are part of the original
house and have high ceilings. Included in the room price is limousine
transfer from the airport or train station. ⊠ *Kärntner Ring 16, A-1010,*
☎ *01/501–10–0,* FAX *01/501–10–410,* WEB *www.luxurycollection.com/
imperial. 128 rooms. Restaurant, café. AE, DC, MC, V.*

$$$$ 🏨 **Palais Schwarzenberg.** Set against a vast formal park, the palace,
★   built in the early 1700s, seems like a country estate (though just a few
minutes' walk from the heart of the city). The public salons are grand
and each guest room is individual and luxuriously appointed. A renovated wing has ultramodern suites by Italian designer Paolo Piva. You
don't have to be a guest here to come for a drink, coffee, or light lunch,
served outside on the terrace in summer or beside a roaring fireplace in
the main sitting room in winter. ⊠ *Schwarzenbergpl. 9, A–1030,* ☎ *01/
798–4515–0,* FAX *01/798–4714,* WEB *www.palais-schwarzenberg.com. 44
rooms. Restaurant, bar, pool. AE, DC, MC, V.*

$$$$ 🏨 **Sacher.** The grand old Sacher dates from 1876, and it has retained
★   its sense of history over the years while providing luxurious, modern-
day comfort. The corridors are a veritable art gallery, and the exquisitely
furnished bedrooms also contain original artwork. Meals in the Red
Room or Anna Sacher Room are first-rate; the Café Sacher, of course,
is legendary. ⊠ *Philharmonikerstr. 4, A-1010,* ☎ *01/514–56–0,* FAX *01/
514–57–810,* WEB *www.sacher.com. 108 rooms. Restaurant, bar. AE,
DC, MC, V.*

$$$ 🏨 **Altstadt.** A real gem, this small hotel was once a patrician home.
★   Rooms are large, with all the modern comforts, though they retain an
antique feel. The English-style lounge has a fireplace and plump flo-
ral sofas. The breakfast room is bright. You're one streetcar stop or a
pleasant walk from the main museums. ⊠ *Kircheng. 41, A-1070,* ☎
01/526–3399–0, FAX *01/523–4901. 25 rooms. AE, DC, MC, V.*

$$$ 🏨 **König von Ungarn.** This utterly charming hotel is tucked away in
the shadow of St. Stephen's. Rooms are furnished with country antiques
(some have Styrian wood-paneled walls) and come with walk-in clos-
ets and double sinks in the sparkling bathrooms. The two suites are
two-storied. ⊠ *Schulerstr. 10, A-1010,* ☎ *01/515–84–0,* FAX *01/515–
848. 33 rooms. Restaurant. DC, MC, V.*

$$–$$$ 🏨 **Austria.** Tucked away on a tiny cul-de-sac, this older house offers
the ultimate in quiet only five minutes' walk from the heart of the city.
The high-ceilinged rooms are pleasing in their combination of dark wood
and lighter walls; the decor is mixed, with Oriental carpets on many
floors. The nice courtyard terrace is a perfect place to sip coffee. ⊠
Wolfeng. 3/Fleischmarkt 20, A-1010, ☎ *01/515–23–0,* FAX *01/515–23–
506. 46 rooms, 40 with shower, 6 with bath. AE, DC, MC, V.*

$$–$$$ 🏨 **Regina.** This dignified old hotel sits regally on the edge of the Altstadt,
★   commanding a view of Sigmund Freud Park. The high-ceilinged rooms
are quiet, spacious, and attractively decorated, and most have charming
sitting areas. Freud, who lived nearby, used to eat breakfast in the hotel's
café every morning. Buffet breakfast is included. ⊠ *Rooseveltpl. 15,
A-1090,* ☎ *01/404–460,* FAX *01/408–8392,* WEB *www.kremslehner.
hotels.or.at. 125 rooms. Restaurant. AE, DC, MC, V.*

$$ 🏨 **Kärntnerhof.** Behind the "Schönbrunn yellow" facade of this ele-
gant 100-year-old house, set on a quiet cul-de-sac, lies one of the

friendliest small hotels in the city center. The dated lobby is cheered by a gorgeously restored Biedermeier elevator. Guest rooms are functionally decorated but clean and serviceable. Pets are welcome. ⊠ *Grashofg. 4, A-1010,* ☎ *01/512–1923–0,* FAX *01/513–2228–33. 43 rooms, 35 with shower, 8 with bath. AE, DC, MC, V.*

$$ ⊞ **Museum.** Located in a beautiful Belle Époque mansion just a five-★ minute walk from the Art History and Natural History museums, this elegant pension offers large, comfortable rooms with TV. There is also a pretty, sunny sitting room with deep, stuffed sofas and wing-back chairs, perfect for curling up in with a good book. This is a popular place, so book ahead. ⊠ *Museumstr. 3, A-1070,* ☎ *01/523–44–260,* FAX *01/523–44–2630. 15 rooms. AE, DC, MC, V.*

$$ ⊞ **Zur Wiener Staatsoper.** A great deal of loving care has gone into this family-owned hotel near the State Opera, reputed to be one of the Viennese settings in John Irving's *The Hotel New Hampshire.* Rooms are small but have high ceilings and are charmingly decorated with pretty fabrics. ⊠ *Krugerstr. 11, A-1010,* ☎ *01/513–1274,* FAX *01/513–1274–15. 22 rooms with shower. AE, MC, V.*

$ ⊞ **Pension Riedl.** Across the square from the Postsparkasse—the famous 19th-century postal savings bank designed by Otto Wagner—this small establishment offers pleasant rooms with cable TV. As an added touch, breakfast is delivered in your room. Friendly owner Maria Felser is happy to arrange concert tickets and tours. ⊠ *Georg-Coch-Pl. 3/4/10 (near Julius-Raab Pl.), A-1010,* ☎ *01/512–7919,* FAX *01/512–7919–8. 7 rooms with bath, 1 with shower. DC, MC, V. Closed last wk in Jan. and first 2 wks in Feb.*

$ ⊞ **Reimer.** The cheery, comfortable Reimer is in a prime location just off the Mariahilferstrasse. Rooms have high ceilings and large windows. Breakfast is included. ⊠ *Kircheng. 18, A-1070,* ☎ *01/523–6162,* FAX *01/524–3782. 14 rooms, 8 with shower, 6 with bath. MC, V.*

NIGHTLIFE AND THE ARTS

The Arts

Music

Classical concerts are held in the **Konzerthaus** (⊠ Lothringerstr. 20, ☎ 01/712–1211), featuring the Vienna Symphonic Orchestra, which also occasionally plays modern and jazz pieces. The **Musikverein** (⊠ Bösendorferstr. 12, ☎ 01/505–8190–0) is the home of the acclaimed Vienna Philharmonic Orchestra. Tickets can be bought at their box offices or ordered by phone. Tickets to various musical events are sold through the **Vienna Ticket Service** (☎ 01/534–1775, FAX 01/534–1328 or 01/534–1726).

Theater and Opera

Check the monthly program published by the city; posters also show opera and theater schedules. The **Staatsoper,** one of world's great opera houses, presents major stars in its almost-nightly original-language performances. The **Volksoper** offers operas, operettas, and musicals, also in original-language performances. Performances at the **Akadamietheater** and **Burgtheater** are in German. Tickets for the Staatsoper, the Volksoper, and the Burg and Akademie theaters are available at the **central ticket office** (⊠ Bundestheaterkassen, Hanuschg. 3, ☎ 01/514–44–2959), open weekdays 8–6, weekends and holidays 9–noon, to the left rear of the Staatsoper. Tickets go on sale a month before performances. Unsold tickets can be obtained at the evening box office. Tickets can be ordered three weeks or more in advance in writing, by fax (FAX 01/514–44–2969), or a month in advance by phone (☎ 01/513–1513). Standing-room tickets for the Staatsoper are a great bargain.

Theater is offered in English at **Vienna's English Theater** (✉ Josefsg. 12, ☎ 01/402–1260–0). The **International Theater** (✉ Porzellang. 8, ☎ 01/319–6272) is also a popular choice for seeing plays in English.

Nightlife

The central district for nightlife in Vienna is nicknamed the **Bermuda-Dreieck** (Bermuda Triangle). Centered on Judengasse/Seitenstettengasse, next to St. Ruprecht's, a small Romanesque church, the area is jammed with everything from good bistros to jazz clubs.

Cabarets

Most cabarets are expensive and unmemorable. One leading option is **Casanova** (✉ Dorotheerg. 6, ☎ 01/512–9845), which emphasizes striptease. A popular cabaret-nightclub is **Moulin Rouge** (✉ Walfischg. 11, ☎ 01/512–2130), where there are floor shows and some striptease.

Cafés

A quintessential Viennese institution, the coffeehouse, or café, is club, pub, and bistro all rolled into one. To savor the atmosphere of the coffeehouses you must take your time: set aside an afternoon, a morning, or at least a couple of hours, and settle down in one of your choice. There is no need to worry about overstaying your welcome, even over a single small cup of Mokka—although in some of the more opulent coffeehouses this cup of coffee and a pastry can cost as much as a meal.

Alte Backstube (✉ Langeg. 34, ☎ 01/406–1101), in a gorgeous Baroque house—with a café in front and restaurant in back—was once a bakery and is now a museum as well. **Café Central** (✉ Herreng. 14, ☎ 01/533–3763–26) is where Trotsky played chess; in the Palais Ferstel, it's one of Vienna's most beautiful cafés. **Cafe Landtmann** (✉ Dr. Karl Leuger Str. 4, ☎ 01/532–0621), next to the dignified Burgtheater, with front-row views of the Ringstrasse, was reputedly Freud's favorite café. A 200-year-old institution, **Demel** (✉ Kohlmarkt 14, ☎ 01/535–1717–0) is the grande dame of Viennese cafés. The elegant front rooms have more atmosphere than the airy modern atrium, while the first room is reserved for nonsmokers. Order the famous coffee and compare the Sacher torte with the one served up at the Sacher—for more than a hundred years there has been an ongoing feud over who owns the original recipe. **Gerstner** (✉ Kärntnerstr. 11–15, ☎ 01/512–496377) is in the heart of the bustling Kärntnerstrasse, and one of the more modern Viennese cafés. Popular here is the Bruegel torte, a marzipan and chocolate pastry. **Museum** (✉ Friedrichstr. 6, ☎ 01/586–5202), with its original interior by the architect Adolf Loos, draws a mixed crowd and has an ample supply of newspapers. The **Sacher** (✉ Philharmonikerstr. 4, ☎ 01/512–1487) is hardly a typical Vienna café; more a shrine to plush gilt and marzipan, it's both a must-see and a must-eat, despite the crowds of tourists here to order the world's ultimate chocolate cake.

Discos

Atrium (✉ Schwarzenbergpl. 10, A-1040, ☎ 01/505–3594) is open Monday through Saturday and draws a lively young crowd. **Eden Bar** (✉ Lilieng. 2, ☎ 01/512–7450) is the leading spot for the well-heeled, mature crowd with a live band offered most nights. **Havana** (✉ Mahlerstr. 11, ☎ 01/513–2075) is great for salsa dancing and draws the twentysomething crowd. The **U-4** (✉ Schönbrunnerstr. 222, ☎ 01/815–8307) ranks high among the young set who like their music loud.

Nightclubs

A former 1950s cinema just off the Kärntnerstrasse, **Kruger** (✉ Krugerstr. 5, ☎ 01/512–2455) now draws the crowds with its deep leather sofas and English gentleman's club atmosphere. **First Floor** (✉ corner of Seitenstetteng. and Rabensteig., ☎ 01/533–7866) is actually one floor up from ground level and garners the attractive thirtysomething crowd. An outdoor glass elevator whisks you up to the **Skybar** (✉ Kärntnerstr. 19, ☎ 01/513–1712–25) at the top of the Steffl department store, where dramatic views and piano music set the mood.

Wine Taverns

Some of the city's atmospheric *Heurige,* or wine taverns, date from as far back as the 12th century. Open at lunchtime as well as evenings, the **Augustinerkeller** (✉ Augustinerstr. 1, ☎ 01/533–1026), in the Albertina building, is a cheery wine tavern with live, schmaltzy music after 6 PM. The **Esterházykeller** (✉ Haarhof 1, ☎ 01/533–3482), in a particularly mazelike network of rooms, has good wines. The **Zwölf Apostelkeller** (✉ Sonnenfelsg. 3, ☎ 01/512–6777), near St. Stephen's, has rooms that are down, down, down underground.

SHOPPING

Boutiques

Famous names line the **Kohlmarkt** and **Graben** and their respective side streets, as well as the side streets off **Kärntnerstrasse.**

Folk Costumes

The main resource for exquisite Austrian *Trachten* (native dress) is **Loden-Plankl** (✉ Michaelerpl. 6, ☎ 01/533–8032).

Food and Flea Markets

The **Naschmarkt** (foodstuffs market; ✉ between Rechte and Linke Wienzeile) is a sensational open-air market offering specialties from around the world. The fascinating **Flohmarkt** (flea market; subway U-4 to Kettenbrückeng.), open Saturday 8–4, operates year-round beyond the Naschmarkt. An **Arts and Antiques Market** (✉ beside Danube Canal near Salztorbrücke) has a mixed selection, including some high-quality offerings. It's open May–September, Saturday 2–6 and Sunday 10–6. Check Am Hof square for antiques and collectibles on Thursday and Friday from late spring to early fall. Also look for the seasonal markets in Freyung Square.

Shopping Districts

Kärntnerstrasse is lined with luxury boutiques and large emporiums. The Viennese do much of their in-town shopping in the many department and specialty stores of **Mariahilferstrasse.**

VIENNA A TO Z

To research prices, get advice from other travelers, and book travel arrangements, visit www.fodors.com.

AIRPORTS AND TRANSFERS

All flights use Schwechat Airport, about 16 km (10 mi) southwest of Vienna.

➤ AIRPORT INFORMATION: **Schwechat Airport** (☎ 01/7007–0).

TRANSFERS

Buses leave the airport for the city air terminal, Wien-Mitte Landstrasse Hauptstrasse (✉ Am Stadtpark, ☎ 01/5800–33369), by the Hilton, on every half hour from 5 to 6:30 AM and every 20 minutes from 6:50 AM to 11:30 PM; after that, buses depart every hour until 5 AM. Buses also run every hour (Apr.–Sept., weekends every ½ hr) from the airport to the Westbahnhof (West Train Station) and the Südbahnhof (South Train Station). The one-way fare for all buses is AS70/€5.09. The S7 train (called the *Schnellbahn*) shuttles every half hour between the airport and the Landstrasse/Wien-Mitte (city center) and Wien-Nord (north Vienna) stations; the fare is AS34/€2.47 and it takes about 35 minutes. Follow the signs picturing a train to the basement of the airport. A taxi from the airport to downtown Vienna costs about AS400/€29.07–AS500/€36.34; agree on a price in advance. Cabs (legally) do not meter this drive, as airport fares are more or less fixed (legally again) at about double the meter fare. The cheapest cab service is C+K Airport Service, charging a set price of AS290/€22, though you should give another AS30/€2.18 as tip. C+K will also meet your plane at no extra charge if you let them know in advance.

➤ CONTACTS: C+K Airport Service (☎ 01/44444).

BIKE TRAVEL
Vienna has hundreds of miles of marked cycle routes, including reserved routes through the center of the city. Paved cycling routes parallel the Danube. For details, get the city brochure on cycling. Bicycles can be rented at a number of locations and can be taken on the Vienna subway (with the exception of the U-6 line) year-round all day Sunday and holidays from 9 to 3, after 6:30 on weekdays, and, from May through September, after 9 AM Saturday. You'll need a half-fare ticket for the bike.

BUS TRAVEL WITHIN VIENNA
Inner-city buses are numbered 1A through 3A and operate weekdays until about 7:40 PM, Saturday until 7 PM. Reduced fares are available for these routes (buy a *Kurzstreckenkarte*; it allows you four trips for AS38/€2.76) as well as designated shorter stretches (roughly two to four stops) on all other bus and streetcar lines. Streetcars and buses are numbered or lettered according to route, and they run until about midnight. Night buses marked *N* follow 22 special routes every half hour between 12:30 AM and 4:30 AM. Get a route plan from any of the public transport or VORVERKAUF offices. The fare is AS25/€1.82, payable on the bus unless you have a 24-hour, three-day, or eight-day ticket; then you need only pay an AS10/€.73 supplement. The central terminus is Schwedenplatz. Streetcars 1 and 2 run the circular route around the Ring clockwise and counterclockwise, respectively.

CAR TRAVEL
The main access routes are the expressways to the west and south (Westautobahn A1, Südautobahn A2). Routes leading to the downtown area are marked ZENTRUM.

Unless you know your way around the city, a car is more of a nuisance than a help. The center of the city is a pedestrian zone, and city on-street parking is a problem. Observe signs; tow-away is expensive. In winter, overnight parking is forbidden on city streets with streetcar lines. Overnight street parking in districts I, VI, VII, VIII, and IX is restricted to residents with stickers; check before you leave a car on the street, even for a brief period. However, you can park in the inner city for free on Saturday, Sunday, and holidays and at night from 7 PM until midnight, but check street signs first.

CONSULATES
➤ UNITED KINGDOM: (✉ Jauresg. 10, near Schloss Belvedere, ☎ 01/71613–5151).
➤ UNITED STATES: (✉ Gartenbaupromenade, Parkring 12A, in Marriott building, ☎ 01/313–39).

EMERGENCIES

If you need a doctor, ask your hotel, or in an emergency, phone your embassy or consulate. In each neighborhood, one pharmacy (*Apotheke*) in rotation is open all night and weekends; the address is posted on each area pharmacy.

➤ EMERGENCY SERVICES: **Ambulance** (☎ 144). **Police** (☎ 133).

ENGLISH-LANGUAGE MEDIA

➤ BOOKSTORES: **Big Ben Bookshop** (✉ Alserstr. 4, Courtyard 1, No. 17, ☎ 01/409–3567). **British Bookshop** (✉ Weihburgg. 24–26, ☎ 01/ 512–1945–0; ✉ Mariahilferstr. 4, ☎ 01/522–6730). **Shakespeare & Co.** (✉ Sterng. 2, ☎ 01/535–5053).

SUBWAY TRAVEL

Subway (U-bahn) lines—stations are marked with a huge blue "U"— are designated U-1, U-2, U-3, U-4, and U-6, and are clearly marked and color-coded. Trains run daily until about 12:30 AM. Additional services are provided by fast suburban trains, the S-bahn, indicated by a stylized blue "S" symbol. Both are tied into the general city fare system.

TAXIS

Cabs can be flagged on the street if the FREI (free) sign is lit. You can also dial ☎ 60160, 31300, or 40100 to request one. All rides around town are metered. The initial fare is AS35/€2.54, but expect to pay AS80/€5.81–AS100/€7.27 for an average city ride. There are additional charges for luggage, and a surcharge of AS16/€1.16 is added at night, on Sunday, and for telephone orders. Tip the driver AS5/€.36– AS8/€.58 by rounding up the fare.

TOURS

BUS TOURS

Tours will take you to cultural events and nightclubs, and there are daytime bus trips to the Danube Valley, Salzburg, and Budapest, among other spots. Check with the City Tourist Office or your hotel.

The following are city orientation tours. Prices are similar, but find out whether you will visit or just drive past Schönbrunn and Belvedere palaces and whether admission fees are included. Cityrama provides city tours with hotel pickup. Vienna Sightseeing Tours offers a short highlights tour or a lengthier one to the Vienna Woods, Mayerling, and other sights near Vienna. Tours start in front of or beside the Staatsoper on the Operngasse.

➤ FEES AND SCHEDULES: **Cityrama** (☎ 01/534–130). **Vienna Sightseeing Tours** (☎ 01/712–4683–0).

WALKING TOURS

Guided walking tours in English are available almost daily and include such topics as "Jewish Vienna." Check with the City Tourist Office or your hotel.

TRAIN TRAVEL

Vienna has four train stations. The Westbahnhof is for trains to and from Linz, Salzburg, and Innsbruck and to and from Germany, France, and Switzerland. The Südbahnhof is for trains to and from Graz, Klagenfurt, Villach, and Italy. The Franz-Josefs-Bahnhof, or Nordbahnhof, is for trains to and from Prague, Berlin, and Warsaw. Go to the Wien-Mitte/Landstrasse Hauptstrasse station for local trains to and from the north of the city. Budapest trains use both the Westbahnhof and Südbahnhof, and Bratislava trains both Wien-Mitte and the Südbahnhof, so check.

TRANSPORTATION AROUND VIENNA

Vienna addresses include a roman numeral that designates in which of the city's 23 districts the address is located. The first district (I, the inner city) is bounded by the Ringstrasse and the Danube Canal. The 2nd through 9th (II–IX) districts surround the inner city, starting with the 2nd district across the Danube Canal and running clockwise; the 10th through the 23rd (X–XXIII) districts form a second concentric ring of suburbs.

Vienna is fairly easy to explore on foot; much of the heart of the city—the area within the Ringstrasse—is a pedestrian zone. Public transportation is comfortable, convenient, and frequent, though not cheap. Tickets for buses, subways, and streetcars are available in subway stations and from dispensers on buses and streetcars. Tickets in multiples of five are sold at cigarette shops—look for the sign TABAK-TRAFIK—or at the window marked VORVERKAUF at such central stations as Karlsplatz or Stephansplatz. A block of five tickets costs AS95/€6.90, a single ticket AS19/€1.38, a 24-hour ticket AS60/€4.36, a three-day tourist ticket AS150/€10.90, and an eight-day ticket AS300/€21.80. Maps and information in English are available at the Stephansplatz, Karlsplatz, and Praterstern U-bahn stations.

The Vienna Card, available for AS210/€15.26 at tourist and transportation information offices and most hotels, gives you unlimited travel for 72 hours on city buses, streetcars, and the subway; reductions on selected museum entry fees; plus tips and discounts on various attractions and selected shopping throughout the city.

TRAVEL AGENCIES
➤ LOCAL AGENTS: **American Express** (✉ Kärntnerstr. 21–23, ☎ 01/515–40–0). **Ökista** (✉ Garnisong. 7, A-1090, ☎ 01/401–480). **Österreichisches Verkehrsbüro** (Austrian Travel Agency; ✉ Friedrichstr. 7, A-1010, ☎ 01/588–000, FAX 01/58800–280).

VISITOR INFORMATION
➤ TOURIST INFORMATION: **City Tourist Office** (✉ Am Albertinapl. 1, A-1010, ☎ 01/211–14–222).

Austria Basics

BUSINESS HOURS
BANKS AND OFFICES

Banks are open weekdays 8–noon or 12:30 and 1:30–3; until 5 on Thursday; closed Saturday. Hours vary from one city to another. Principal offices in cities stay open during lunch.

MUSEUMS AND SIGHTS

Museum opening days and times vary considerably from one city to another and depend on the season and other factors. Monday is often a closing day. Your hotel or the local tourist office will have current details.

SHOPS

Shops are open weekdays from 8 or 9 until 6, in shopping centers until 7:30, and Saturday until 5, although some may still close at noon or 1. Many smaller shops close for one or two hours at midday. Larger food markets are open weekdays from 7:30 to 7:30, Saturday to 5.

CUSTOMS AND DUTIES
Austria's duty-free allowances are as follows: 200 cigarettes or 50 cigars or 250 grams of tobacco; 2 liters of wine and 1 liter of spirits; 1 bottle of toilet water (about 250-milliliter size); and 50 milliliters of perfume for those age 17 and over arriving from non–European Union

countries. Tourists also do not have to pay duty on personal articles brought into Austria temporarily for their own use.

EMBASSIES
For consulates, *see* Vienna A to Z.
➤ CANADA: (✉ Laurenzerberg 2, 3rd floor of Hauptpost building complex, ☎ 01/531–38–3000).
➤ UNITED KINGDOM: (✉ Jauresg. 10, near Schloss Belvedere, ☎ 01/71613–5151).
➤ UNITED STATES: (✉ Boltzmanng. 16, ☎ 01/313–39).

HOLIDAYS
All banks and shops are closed on national holidays: January 1 (New Year's Day); January 6 (Epiphany); Easter Sunday and Monday; May 1 (May Day); Ascension Day; Pentecost Sunday and Monday; Corpus Christi; August 15 (Assumption); October 26 (National Day); November 1 (All Saints' Day); December 8 (Immaculate Conception); December 25–26. On the December 8 holiday, banks and offices are closed but most shops are open.

LANGUAGE
German is the official national language. In larger cities and most resort areas you will have no problem finding English speakers; hotel and restaurant employees, in particular, speak English reasonably well. Most younger Austrians speak at least passable English.

MONEY MATTERS
Austria has become expensive, but as inflation is relatively low, the currency has remained fairly stable. Vienna and Salzburg are the most expensive cities, along with fashionable resorts at Kitzbühel, Seefeld, Badgastein, Velden, Zell am See, Pörtschach, St. Anton, Zürs, and Lech. Many smaller towns near these resorts offer virtually identical facilities at half the price. Drinks in bars and clubs cost considerably more than in cafés or restaurants. Austrian prices include service and tax.

Sample prices include: cup of coffee in a café or restaurant, AS35/€2.54–AS58/€4.21; half a glass of draft beer, AS34/€2.47–AS48/€3.49; small glass of wine, AS28/€2.03–AS80/€5.81; Coca-Cola, AS28/€2.03; open sandwich, AS25/€1.82; theater ticket, AS200/€14.53–AS300/€21.80; concert ticket, AS250/€18.17–AS500/€36.34; opera ticket, AS600/€43.60 and up; 2-km (1.6-mi) taxi ride, AS60/€4.36.

CREDIT CARDS
Credit cards are not as widely used in Austria as they are in other European countries, and not all establishments that accept plastic take all cards. Some may require a minimum purchase if payment is to be made by card. Many restaurants take cash only. American Express has money machines in Vienna at its main office and at the airport. Many of the Bankomat money dispensers will also accept Visa cards if you have an encoded international PIN (Personal Identification Number).
➤ CONTACTS: **American Express** (main office; ✉ Kärntnerstr. 21–23).

CURRENCY
The unit of currency is the Austrian schilling (AS), divided into 100 groschen. There are AS20, AS50, AS100, AS500, AS1,000, and AS5,000 bills; AS1, AS5, AS10, and AS20 coins; and 10- and 50-groschen coins. At press time (summer 2001), the exchange rate was AS14.75 to the U.S. dollar, AS9.7 to the Canadian dollar, AS21.50 to the pound sterling, AS17.20 to the Irish punt, AS6.4 to the New Zealand dollar, AS8.4 to the Australian dollar, and AS1.95 to the South African rand. You

may bring in any amount of either foreign currency or schillings and take out any amount with you.

The year 2002 spells the end of the schilling: January 1, 2002 sees the long-awaited introduction of coins and notes in the new European Union (EU) currency, the euro. Until 2002, consumers will be able to make payments in both schillings and euros, though this could change. One euro is equivalent to 13.76 schillings, which is a fixed, irrevocable rate.

Exchange traveler's checks at a bank, a post office, or the American Express office to get the best rate. All charge a small commission; some smaller banks or "change" offices may give a poorer rate *and* charge a higher fee. All change offices at airports and at main train stations in major cities cash traveler's checks. In Vienna, bank-operated change offices with extended hours are found on Stephansplatz and at the main rail stations. Bank Austria machines on Stephansplatz, at Kärntnerstrasse 51 (to the right of the Opera), and at the Raiffeisenbank on Kohlmarkt (at Michaelerplatz) change bills from other currencies into schillings, but rates are poor and the commission hefty.

TELEPHONES
COUNTRY AND AREA CODES
The country code for Austria is 43. When dialing an Austrian number from abroad, drop the initial 0 from the local area code.

INTERNATIONAL CALLS
It costs considerably more to telephone *from* Austria than it does *to* Austria. Calls from post offices are least expensive. To avoid hotel charges, call overseas and ask to be called back; use an international credit card, available from AT&T and MCI. Use the AT&T access code to reach an operator. Another option for long-distance access is MCI WorldPhone. To make a collect call—you can't do this from pay phones—dial the operator and ask for an *R*-Gespräch (pronounced "air-ga-*shprayk*"). For international information dial 11812 for numbers in Germany, 11813 for numbers in other European countries, and 11814 for overseas numbers. Most operators speak English; if yours doesn't, you'll be passed along to one who does.
➤ ACCESS CODES: **AT&T** (☎ 0800-200-288). **MCI WorldPhone** (☎ 022/903–012).

LOCAL CALLS
Pay telephones take AS1, AS5, AS10, and AS20 coins. Emergency calls are free. Instructions are in English in most booths. The initial connection for a local call costs AS2. Insert AS1 or more to continue the connection when you hear the tone warning that your time is up. Phone cards, available at post offices, work in all phones marked WERTKARTENTELEFON. The cost of the call will be deducted from the card automatically. Phone numbers throughout Austria are currently being changed. A sharp tone indicates either no connection or that the number has been changed. Dial 11811 for numbers in Austria.

17 ZÜRICH

Stroll around on a fine spring day and you'll ask yourself if this city, with its glistening lake, swans on the river, sidewalk cafés, and hushed old squares of medieval guild houses, can really be one of the great business centers of the world. There's not a gnome—a mocking nickname for a Swiss banker—in sight. For all its economic importance, this is a place where people enjoy life.

Zürich started in 15 BC as a Roman customs post on the Lindenhof overlooking the River Limmat, but its growth really began around the 10th century AD. It became a free imperial city in 1336, a center of the Reformation in 1519, and gradually assumed commercial importance during the 1800s. Today the Zürich stock exchange is fourth in the world, and the city's extraordinary museums and galleries and luxurious shops along the Bahnhofstrasse, Zürich's 5th Avenue, attest to its position as Switzerland's cultural—if not political—capital.

EXPLORING ZÜRICH

Numbers in the margin correspond to points of interest on the Zürich map.

Although Zürich is Switzerland's largest city, it has a population of only 360,000 and is small enough to be explored comfortably on foot. The Limmat River, crisscrossed with lovely low bridges, bisects the city. On the left bank are the Altstadt (Old Town), the polished section of the old medieval center; the Hauptbahnhof, the main train station; and the Bahnhofplatz, a major urban crossroads and the beginning of the world-famous luxury shopping street, Bahnhofstrasse. The right bank, divided into the Oberdorf (Upper Village), toward Bellevueplatz, and the Niederdorf (Lower Village), around the Central, is young and lively and buzzes on weekends. The latest addition to the city's profile is Zürich West, an industrial neighborhood that's quickly being reinvented. Amid the cluster of cranes, former factories are being turned into spaces for restaurants, bars, art galleries, and dance clubs. Construction and restoration will most likely be ongoing well into 2006.

334

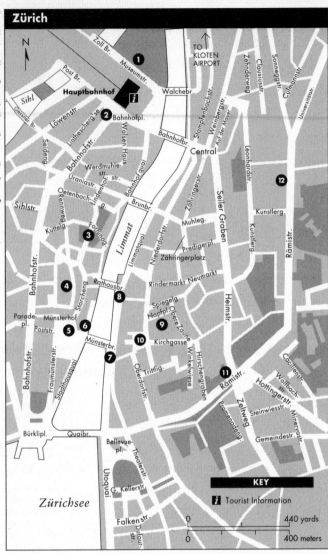

Zürich

KEY

 Tourist Information

0   440 yards

0   400 meters

---

❾ **Altstadt.** Zürich's medieval core is a maze of well-preserved streets and buildings easily explored on foot in a few hours. The area stretches from Bahnhofplatz to Bürkliplatz on the left bank. On the right bank of the city's historic center is a livelier section known as the **Niederdorf**, which reaches from Central to Bellevueplatz.

❷ **Bahnhofstrasse.** Zürich's principal boulevard offers concentrated luxury shopping, while much shifting and hoarding of the world's wealth takes place discreetly behind the upstairs windows of the banking institutions. ✉ *Runs north–south, west of Limmat.*

★ **❺** **Fraumünster.** Of the church spires that are Zürich's signature, the Fraumünster's is the most delicate, a graceful sweep to a narrow spire. The Romanesque, or pre-Gothic, choir has stained-glass windows by Chagall. ✉ *Stadthausquai.* ☉ *May–Sept., Mon.–Sat. 9–6; Mar.–Apr. and Oct., Mon.–Sat. 10–5; Nov.–Feb., Mon.–Sat. 10–4.*

⑫ **Graphische Sammlung** (Graphic Collection). This impressive collection of the Federal Institute of Technology displays portions of its vast holdings of woodcuts, etchings, and engravings by European masters such as Dürer, Rembrandt, Goya, and Picasso. ⊠ *Rämistr. 101,* ☎ *01/ 6324046.* ☉ *Mon.–Tues. and Thurs.–Fri. 10–5, Wed. 10–7.*

★ ❿ **Grossmünster** (Great Church). In the 3rd century AD, St. Felix and his sister Regula were martyred nearby by the Romans. Legend maintains that having been beheaded, they then walked up the hill carrying their heads and collapsed on the spot where the Grossmünster now stands. On the south tower of this 11th-century structure you can see a statue of Charlemagne (768–814), who is said to have founded the church when his horse stumbled on the same site. In the 16th century, the Zürich reformer Huldrych Zwingli preached sermons here that were so threatening in their promise of fire and brimstone that Martin Luther himself was frightened. ⊠ *Zwinglipl.,* ☎ *01/2513860.* ☉ *Late Mar.–Oct., daily 9–6; Nov.–Mar., daily 10–5.*

★ ⓫ **Kunsthaus.** With a varied, high-quality permanent collection of paintings—medieval, Dutch and Italian Baroque, and Impressionist—the Kunsthaus is Zürich's best art museum. There's a rich collection of works by Swiss artists, though some could be an acquired taste. Besides those of Ferdinand Hodler (1853–1918), there are darkly ethereal paintings by Johann Heinrich Füssli and a terrifying *Walpurgisnacht* by Albert Welti. Other European artists, including Picasso, Klee, Degas, Matisse, Kandinsky, Chagall, and Munch, are satisfyingly represented. ⊠ *Heimpl. 1,* ☎ *01/2538484,* WEB *www.kunsthaus.ch.* ☉ *Tues.–Thurs. 10–9, Fri.–Sun. 10–5.*

☝ ❸ **Lindenhof.** On this quiet square are the remains of the original Roman customs house and fortress, and the imperial medieval residence. A fountain commemorates the day in 1292 when Zürich's women saved the city from the Habsburgs. As the story goes, the town was on the brink of defeat when its women donned armor and marched to the Lindenhof. On seeing them, the enemy thought they were faced with another army and promptly beat a strategic retreat. ⊠ *Bordered by Fortunag. to west and intersected by Lindenhofstr.*

❽ **Rathaus** (Town Hall). Zürich's 17th-century town hall is strikingly Baroque, with its interior as well-preserved as its facade. There's a richly decorated stucco ceiling in the Banquet Hall and a fine ceramic stove in the government council room. ⊠ *Limmatquai 55.* ☉ *Tues. and Thurs.– Fri. 10–11:30 AM.*

❹ **St. Peters Kirche** (St. Peter's Church). Zürich's oldest parish church, dating from the early 13th century, has the largest clock face in Europe. ⊠ *St. Peterhofstatt.* ☉ *Weekdays 8–6, Sat. 8–4.*

★ ☝ ❶ **Schweizerisches Landesmuseum** (Swiss National Museum). In a gargantuan neo-Gothic building, this museum possesses an enormous collection of objects dating from the Stone Age to modern times, including costumes, furniture, early watches, and a great deal of military history, including thousands of toy soldiers reenacting battles. ⊠ *Museumstr. 2,* ☎ *01/2186511,* WEB *www.musee-suisse.ch.* ☉ *Tues.–Sun. 10:30–5.*

❼ **Wasserkirche** (Water Church). This is one of Switzerland's most delicate late-Gothic structures; its stained glass is by Augusto Giacometti. ⊠ *Limmatquai 31.* ☉ *Tues.–Wed. 2–5.*

❻ **Zunfthaus zur Meisen.** Erected for the city's wine merchants during the 18th century, this Baroque guildhall today houses the Landesmuseum's exquisite ceramics collection. ⊠ *Münsterhof 20,* ☎ *01/2212807,* WEB *www.musee-suisse.ch.* ☉ *Tues.–Sun. 10:30–5.*

Elsewhere in Zürich

Museum Rietberg. A wonderful representation of art from India, China, Africa, Japan, and Southeast Asia is displayed in the neoclassic Villa Wesendonck (as in *Wesendonck Songs*), where Richard Wagner once lived. ✉ *Gablerstr. 15 (take Tram 7 from city center)*, ☎ *01/2024528,* WEB *www.rietberg.ch.* ☉ *Tues., Thurs.–Sun. 10–5, Wed. 2–5.*

DINING

Over the past few years, new restaurants, both Swiss and international, have been sprouting up all over town. The newcomers tend to eschew the traditional, heavily curtained decor and meat-and-Rösti menus in favor of lighter cuisine and bright rooms, frequently open to the street. Prices are often steep; for savings, watch for posted Tagesteller lunches.

CATEGORY	COST*
$$$$	over 50 SF
$$$	30 SF–50 SF
$$	20 SF–30 SF
$	under 20 SF

per person for a main course at dinner

$$$$ ★ ✕ **Petermann's Kunststuben.** This is one of Switzerland's gastronomic meccas, and although it's south of the city center—in Küssnacht on the lake's eastern shore—it's more than worth the 8-km (5-mi) pilgrimage. The ever-evolving menu may include lobster with artichoke and almond oil or Tuscan dove with pine nuts and herbs. Come here for serious, world-class food—and prices to match. ✉ *Seestr. 160, Küssnacht,* ☎ *01/9100715. Reservations essential. AE, DC, MC, V. Closed Sun.–Mon., 2 wks in Feb., and 3 wks in late summer.*

$$$–$$$$ ✕ **La Rotonde.** Even when it's not illuminated by candlelight, the Dolder Grand Hotel's haute-cuisine restaurant is one of the city's most grandiose spots. Housed in a great arc of a room, La Rotonde provides sweeping lake views. The atmosphere is formal, the staff attentive to a fault, the culinary style traditional French with a fashionably light touch—sweetbreads on a bed of gnocchi with asparagus and truffles, for instance. ✉ *Kurhausstr. 65,* ☎ *01/2693000. Reservations essential. Jacket and tie. AE, DC, MC, V.*

$$$–$$$$ ★ ✕ **Kronenhalle.** From Stravinsky, Brecht, and Joyce to Nureyev, Deneuve, and Saint-Laurent, this beloved landmark has always drawn a stellar crowd for its genial, formal but relaxed atmosphere; hearty cooking; and astonishing collection of 20th-century art. Try the herring in double cream, tournedos with truffle sauce, or duck à l'orange with red cabbage and *Spätzli* (tiny dumplings). Have a cocktail in the adjoining bar: anyone who's anyone in Zürich drinks here. ✉ *Rämistr. 4,* ☎ *01/2516669. Reservations essential. AE, DC, MC, V.*

$$$–$$$$ ✕ **Veltliner Keller.** Though its rich, carved-wood decor borrows from Graubündner Alpine culture, this ancient dining spot is no tourist-trap transplant: the house, built in 1325, has functioned as a restaurant since 1551. There is a definite emphasis on the heavy and the meaty, but the kitchen is flexible and reasonably deft with more modern favorites as well: grilled salmon, veal steak with Gorgonzola, and dessert mousses. ✉ *Schlüsselg. 8,* ☎ *01/2254040. AE, DC, MC, V. Closed weekends.*

$$–$$$ ✕ **La Salle.** This is a favorite of theatergoers heading for the new Schiffbauhalle Theater, as it conveniently shares the same building. The glass, steel and concrete interior mixes well with the brick elements left from the original building. Elegantly dressed patrons enjoy delicate dishes such as sole medallions in saffron sauce and rack of lamb with herb fig sauce, beneath an enormous Murano glass chandelier. The hefty wine

list can also be enjoyed at the bar, where a smaller version of the menu is available. ⊠ *Schiffbaustr. 4,* ☏ *01/2587071. AE, DC, MC, V.*

$$–$$$ ✕ **Oepfelchammer.** This was once the haunt of Zürich's beloved writer
★   Gottfried Keller, and it still draws unpretentious literati. The bar is dark and riddled with graffiti, with sagging timbers and slanting floors; the welcoming little dining rooms have carved oak paneling, coffered ceilings, and damask linens. The traditional meats—calves' liver, veal, tripe in white wine sauce—come in generous portions; salads are fresh and seasonal. It's always packed and service can be slow. ⊠ *Rindermarkt 12,* ☏ *01/2512336. MC, V. Closed Sun.–Mon.*

$$–$$$ ✕ **Zunfthaus zur Zimmerleuten/Küferstube.** While the pricier Zunfthaus
★   upstairs is often overwhelmed with conference crowds, at basement level a cozy, candlelit haven dubbed "Coopers' Pub" serves intimate, atmospheric meals in a dark-beamed, Old Zürich setting. Standard dishes have enough novelty to stand apart: braised sole in saffron sauce, roast pork with smoked bacon, and homemade cinnamon ice cream with wine-poached pears. ⊠ *Limmatquai 40,* ☏ *01/2520834. AE, DC, MC, V.*

$–$$ ✕ **Adler's Swiss Chuchi.** Right on the Niederdorf's busy main square, Hirschenplatz, this squeaky-clean, Swiss-kitsch restaurant features an airy, modern decor, with carved fir, Alpine-rustic chairs, Big Boy–style plastic menus, and good home-cooked national specialties, particularly fondue. Excellent lunch menus are rock-bottom cheap and served double-quick. ⊠ *Roseng. 10,* ☏ *01/2669666. AE, DC, MC, V.*

$–$$ ✕ **Bierhalle Kropf.** Under the mounted boar's head and restored cen-
★   tury-old murals, businesspeople, workers, and shoppers share crowded tables to feast on generous hot dishes and a great selection of sausages. The *leberknödli* (liver dumplings) are tasty, *apfelküechli* (fried apple slices) tender and sweet, and the service as wisecracking-cranky as in a New York deli. ⊠ *In Gassen 16,* ☏ *01/2211805. AE, DC, MC, V. Closed Sun.*

$–$$ ✕ **Reithalle.** In a downtown theater complex behind the Bahnhofstrasse, this old military horse barn now serves as a noisy and popular restaurant, with candles perched on the mangers and beams and heat ducts exposed. Young locals share long tables arranged mess-hall style to sample French and Italian specialties, many vegetarian, and an excellent, international blackboard list of wines. ⊠ *Gessnerallee 8,* ☏ *01/ 2120766. AE, MC, V.*

$–$$ ✕ **Zeughauskeller.** Built as an arsenal in 1487, this enormous stone-
★   and-beam hall offers hearty meat platters and a variety of beers and wines amid comfortable, friendly chaos. The waitstaff is harried and brisk, especially at lunchtime, when crowds are thick with locals—don't worry, just roll up your sleeves and dig in. ⊠ *Bahnhofstr. 28, at Paradepl.,* ☏ *01/2112690. AE, DC, MC, V.*

$ ✕ **Les Halles.** This old warehouse space in Zürich West is less renovated than cleaned and enhanced with an eclectic mix of antiques and '50s collectibles. The fare is health-conscious, made from organic ingredients sold in the attached health food store; try the couscous with vegetables, chicken with peppers, tomatoes, and eggplant. ⊠ *Pfingstweidstr. 6,* ☏ *01/2731125. AE, DC, MC, V.*

LODGING

Zürich has an enormous range of hotels, from chic and prestigious to modest. Prices tend to be high, but you will get what you pay for: quality and good service are guaranteed. Deluxe hotels—the five-star landmarks—average between 450 SF and 600 SF per night for a double, and you'll be lucky to get a shower and toilet in your room for less than 140 SF.

CATEGORY	COST*
$$$$	over 350 SF
$$$	250 SF–350 SF
$$	150 SF–250 SF
$	under 150 SF

*Prices are for two people in a double room with bath or shower, including
taxes, service charges, and Continental breakfast.

$$$$ 🏨 **Baur au Lac.** This is the highbrow patrician of Swiss hotels, with
★ luxurious but low-key facilities—like the Rolls-Royce limousine service. Its broad back is turned to the commercial center, while its front
rooms overlook the lake, canal, and manicured lawns of the hotel's
private park. The decor is posh, discreet, and firmly fixed in the Age
of Reason. ⊠ *Talstr. 1, CH-8022,* ☎ *01/2205020,* 🖷 *01/2205044. 108
rooms, 17 suites. 2 restaurants. AE, DC, MC, V.*

$$$$ 🏨 **Dolder Grand.** A cross between Camp David and Maria Theresa's
★ summer palace, this sprawling Victorian fantasy-palace sits high on a
wooded hill over Zürich, quickly reached from Römerhof by funicular railway (free for guests). It's a picturesque hodgepodge of turrets,
cupolas, half-timbering, and mansards; the uncompromisingly modern wing was added in 1964. For the authentic grand-hotel experience,
a room in the old section is a must. Its restaurant, La Rotonde, excels
in traditional French cuisine. ⊠ *Kurhausstr. 65, CH-8032,* ☎ *01/
2693000,* 🖷 *01/2693001,* 🌐 *www.doldergrand.ch. 149 rooms, 34
suites. Restaurant, pool. AE, DC, MC, V.*

$$$$ 🏨 **Splügenschloss.** Befitting its age (built in 1897 in the Art Nouveau
style), this Relais & Châteaux property maintains its ornate, antiques-
filled decor. One room is completely paneled in Alpine-style pine;
others are decorated in fussy florals. Its location (a 10-minute walk from
Paradeplatz) may be a little out of the way for tourists, but atmosphere
buffs will find it worth the effort. ⊠ *Splügenstr. 2, CH-8002,* ☎ *01/
2899999,* 🖷 *01/2899998,* 🌐 *www.splugenschloss.ch. 50 rooms, 2
suites. Restaurant. AE, DC, MC, V.*

$$$$ 🏨 **Widder.** One of the city's most captivating hotels, the Widder rev-
★ els in the present while preserving the past. Ten adjacent medieval houses
were gutted and combined to create it. Behind every door is a fascinating mix of old and new—a guest room could pair restored 17th-
century frescoes with a leather bedspread and private fax. ⊠ *Rennweg.
7, CH-8001,* ☎ *01/2242526,* 🖷 *01/2242424,* 🌐 *www.widderhotel.ch.
42 rooms, 7 suites. 2 restaurants. AE, DC, MC, V.*

$$$$ 🏨 **Zum Storchen.** In a stunning central location, tucked between
★ Fraumünster and St. Peters Kirche, this 600-year-old structure has become an impeccable modern hotel. It has warmly appointed rooms,
some with French windows opening over the Limmat, and a lovely restaurant with riverfront terrace seating. ⊠ *Weinpl. 2, CH-8001,* ☎ *01/
2272727,* 🖷 *01/2272700,* 🌐 *www.storchen.ch. 73 rooms. Restaurant. AE, DC, MC, V.*

$$$ 🏨 **Florhof.** In a quiet residential area by the Kunstmuseum, this is an
★ anti-urban hotel—a gentle antidote to the bustle of downtown com-
merce. This Romantik property pampers guests with its polished wood,
blue-willow fabrics, and wisteria-sheltered garden. ⊠ *Florhofsg. 4, CH-
8001,* ☎ *01/2614470,* 🖷 *01/2614611,* 🌐 *www.romantikhotels.
com/zuerich. 33 rooms, 2 suites. Restaurant. AE, DC, MC, V.*

$$–$$$ 🏨 **Haus zum Kindli.** This charming little bijou hotel could pass for
a 3-D Laura Ashley catalog, with every cushion and bibelot as art-
fully styled as a magazine ad. The result is welcoming, intimate, and
a sight less contrived than most cookie-cutter hotels. At the Opus
restaurant downstairs, guests get 10% off menu prices, though you
may have to vie with crowds of locals for a table. ⊠ *Pfalzg. 1, CH-*

8001, ☏ 01/2115917, FAX 01/2116528. 21 rooms. Restaurant. AE, DC, MC, V.

$$–$$$ 🏨 **Rössli.** This ultrasmall but friendly hotel is set in the heart of Oberdorf. The chic white-on-white decor mixes stone and wood textures with bold textiles and mosaic bathrooms. Extras include safes and bathrobes—unusual in this price range. Some singles are tiny, but all have double beds. ✉ *Rösslig. 7, CH-8001,* ☏ *01/2567050,* FAX *01/2567051,* WEB *www.hotelroessli.ch. 16 rooms, 1 suite. AE, DC, MC, V.*

$–$$ 🏨 **Leoneck.** From the cowhide-covered front desk to the edelweiss-print curtains, this budget hotel wallows in its Swiss roots but balances this with no-nonsense conveniences: tile baths (with cow-print shower curtains) and built-in pine furniture. It's one stop from the Central tram stop, two from the Hauptbahnhof. ✉ *Leonhardst. 1, CH-8001,* ☏ *01/ 2542222,* FAX *01/2542200,* WEB *www.leoneck.ch. 65 rooms. AE, DC, MC, V.*

$ 🏨 **Limmathof.** This spare but welcoming city hotel inhabits a handsome historic shell and is ideally placed on the Limmatquai, minutes from the Hauptbahnhof. Rooms have tile bathrooms and plump down quilts. There's an old-fashioned *Weinstube* (wine bar), as well as a vegetarian restaurant that doubles as the breakfast room. ✉ *Limmatquai 142, CH-8023,* ☏ *01/2614220,* FAX *01/2620217. 62 rooms. Restaurant. AE, DC, MC, V.*

NIGHTLIFE AND THE ARTS

Zürich has a lively nightlife scene, largely centered in the Niederdorf area on the right bank of the Limmat. And despite its small population, Zürich is a big city when it comes to the arts; it supports a top-ranked orchestra, an opera company, and a theater. For information on goings-on, check *Zürich News,* published weekly in English and German. Also check "Züri-tipp," a German-language supplement to the Friday edition of the daily newspaper *Tages Anzeiger.* Tickets to opera, concert, and theater events can also be bought from the tourist office. **Ticketcorner** (☏ 0848/800800) allows you to purchase advance tickets by phone for almost any event. **Musik Hug** (✉ Limmatquai 28–30, ☏ 01/2694100) can make reservations for selected events. **Jecklin** (✉ Rämistr. 30, ☏ 01/2537676) sells tickets for all major concert events, plus its own productions, which showcase small classical concerts and independent artists.

The Arts

During July or August, the **Theaterspektakel** takes place, with circus tents housing avant-garde theater and experimental performances on the lawns by the lake at Mythenquai. The Zürich Tonhalle Orchestra, named for its concert hall **Tonhalle** (✉ Claridenstr. 7, ☏ 01/2063434), was inaugurated by Brahms in 1895 and enjoys international acclaim. Tickets sell out quickly, so book directly through the Tonhalle. The music event of the year is the **Züricher Festspiele** (Zürich International Festival), when, from late June to mid-July, orchestras and soloists from all over the world perform and plays and exhibitions are staged. Book well ahead. Details are available from Info- und Ticketoffice (✉ Postfach 6036, CH-8023, ☏ 01/2154030).

Nightlife

Bars and Lounges

Not just for intellectuals, **I.Q.** has a good selection of whiskies (✉ Hardstr. 316, ☏ no phone). The **Jules Verne Panorama Bar** (✉ Uraniastr. 9, ☏ 01/2111155) shakes up cocktails with a wraparound downtown view. The narrow bar at the **Kronenhalle** (⊠ Rämistr. 4, ☎ 01/2511597) draws mobs of well-heeled locals and internationals. Serving a young, arty set until 4 AM, **Odéon** (⊠ Am Bellevue, ☎ 01/2511650) is a cultural and historic landmark (Mata Hari danced here and James Joyce scrounged drinks).

Dancing

The medieval-theme **Adagio** (⊠ Gotthardstr. 5, ☎ 01/2063666) offers classic rock, jazz, and tango to well-dressed thirtysomethings. **Kaufleuten** (⊠ Pelikanstr. 18, ☎ 01/2253300) is a landmark dance club that draws a well-dressed, upwardly mobile crowd. **Paradise** (⊠ Theaterstr. 10, ☎ 01/2524481) draws all ages on week nights, and a young crowd on weekends, for funk and soul.

Jazz Clubs

Moods (⊠ Schiffbaustr. 6, ☎ 01/2768000) hosts international and local acts in the hip new Zürich West district. The **Widder Bar** (⊠ Widderg. 6, ☎ 01/2242411), in the Hotel Widder, attracts local celebrities with its 800-count "library of spirits" and international jazz groups.

SHOPPING

One of the broadest assortments of watches in all price ranges is available at **Bucherer** (⊠ Bahnhofstr. 50, ☎ 01/2112635). **Heimatwerk** (⊠ Rudolf-Brun Brücke, Rennweg 14 and Bahnhofstr. 2, ☎ 01/2178317) specializes in Swiss handicrafts, all of excellent quality. **Jelmoli** (⊠ Seideng. 1, ☎ 01/2204411), Switzerland's largest department store, carries a wide range of tasteful Swiss goods. You can snag some of last season's fashions at deep discounts at **Check Out** (⊠ Tödistr. 44, ☎ 01/2027226), which jumbles chichi brands on thrift-shop style racks. If you have a sweet tooth, stock up on truffles at **Sprüngli** (⊠ Paradepl., ☎ 01/2244711). The renowned chocolatier **Teuscher** (⊠ Storcheng. 9, ☎ 01/2115153) concocts a killer champagne truffle. For the latest couture, go to one of a dozen **Trois Pommes** (⊠ Weggengasse 1, ☎ 01/2124710) boutiques featuring top-name designers such as Versace and Armani.

ZÜRICH A TO Z

To research prices, get advice from other travelers, and book travel arrangements, visit www.fodors.com.

AIR TRAVEL TO AND FROM ZÜRICH

Swissair flies nonstop from major international cities. "Fly-Rail Baggage" allows Swissair passengers departing Switzerland to check their bags at any of 120 rail or postal bus stations throughout the country; luggage is automatically transferred to the airplane. At many Swiss railway stations, passengers may complete all check-in procedures for Swissair flights, including picking up their boarding pass and checking their bags.

AIRPORTS AND TRANSFERS

Zürich-Kloten is Switzerland's most important airport. Several airlines fly directly to Zürich from major cities in the United States, Canada, and the United Kingdom.

➤ AIRPORT INFORMATION: **Zürich-Kloten** (☎ 0900/571060).

BUS TRAVEL TO AND FROM ZÜRICH

All bus services to Zürich will drop you at the Hauptbahnhof (main train station), which is between Museumstrasse and Bahnhofplatz. There are also hotel bus services that charge 22 SF per person.

BUS TRAVEL WITHIN ZÜRICH

VBZ Züri-Linie (Zürich Public Transport) buses and trams run daily from 5:30 AM to midnight, every six minutes on all routes at peak hours, and about every 12 minutes at other times. Before you board the bus, you must buy your ticket from one of the automatic vending machines found at every stop. An all-day pass is a good buy at 7.20 SF. Free route plans are available from VBZ offices and larger kiosks.

CAR TRAVEL

Highways link Zürich to France, Germany, and Italy. The quickest approach is from Germany; the A5 autobahn reaches from Germany to Basel, and the A2 expressway leads from Basel to Zürich. The A3 expressway feeds into the city from the southeast.

CONSULATES

➤ NEW ZEALAND (CONSULATE): (✉ 2 chemin des Fins, Geneva, ☎ 022/9290350).
➤ UNITED KINGDOM: (✉ Minervastr. 117, Zürich, ☎ 01/3836560).

EMERGENCIES

➤ DOCTORS AND DENTISTS: **Doctor/Dentist Referral** (☎ 01/2616100).
➤ EMERGENCY SERVICES: **Ambulance** (☎ 144). **Police** (☎ 117).
➤ 24-HOUR PHARMACIES: **Bellevue** (✉ Theaterstr. 14, ☎ 01/2525600).

ENGLISH-LANGUAGE MEDIA

English-language magazines are available at most large kiosks, especially in the Hauptbahnhof.
➤ BOOKSTORES: The **Bookshop** (✉ Bahnhofstr. 70, ☎ 01/2110444). **Payot** (✉ Bahnhofstr. 9, ☎ 01/2115452).

TAXIS

Taxis are very expensive, with an 8 SF minimum.

TOURS

BUS TOURS

The daily "Trolley Zürich" tour (29 SF) gives a good general tour of the city in two hours. "Zürich's Surroundings" covers more ground and includes an aerial cableway trip to Felsenegg; it takes 3 hours and costs 39 SF for adults. The daily "Cityrama" tour hits the main sights, then visits Rapperswil, a nearby lakeside town; it costs 39 SF. All tours start from the Hauptbahnhof. Contact the tourist office for reservations. This tourist office service also offers day trips by coach to Luzern; up the Rigi, Titlis, or Pilatus mountains; and the Jungfrau.

WALKING TOURS

Two-hour conducted walking tours (18 SF) starting at the train station are given daily from May to October, and Wednesday to Saturday from November to March. You can join a group with English-language commentary, but the times for these tours vary, so call ahead.

TRAIN TRAVEL

Zürich is the northern crossroads of Switzerland, with swift and punctual trains arriving from Basel, Geneva, Bern, and Lugano. All routes lead to the Hauptbahnhof (main train station).
➤ TRAIN INFORMATION: **Hauptbahnhof** (✉ between Museumstr. and Bahnhofpl., ☎ 0900/300300).

TRAVEL AGENCIES

➤ LOCAL AGENTS: **American Express** (✉ Uraniastr. 14, ☎ 01/2287777). **Kuoni Travel** (✉ Bahnhofpl. 7, ☎ 01/2243333).

VISITOR INFORMATION
➤ TOURIST INFORMATION: **Zürich Tourist Information** (✉ Hauptbahnhof, ☎ 01/2154000). **Hotel reservations** (☎ 01/2154040, FAX 01/
2154044).

Switzerland Basics

BUSINESS HOURS
Banks are open weekdays 8:30–4:30 or 5 but are often closed at lunch.
Museum times vary considerably, though many close on Monday—
check locally. Shops are generally open 8–noon and 1:30–6:30, though
some may have late hours on Thursday or Friday evening. Some close
Monday morning and at 4 or 5 on Saturday. In cities, many large stores
do not close for lunch. All shops are closed on Sundays except those
in resort areas during high season and in the Geneva and Zürich airports and train stations.

CUSTOMS AND DUTIES
For details on imports and duty-free limits, *see* Customs and Duties *in*
Smart Travel Tips A to Z.

EMBASSIES
➤ AUSTRALIA: (✉ 56 rue de Moillebeau, Geneva, ☎ 022/9182900).
➤ CANADA: (✉ Kirchenfeldstr. 88, Bern, ☎ 031/3573200).
➤ IRELAND: (✉ Kirchenfeldstr. 68, Bern, ☎ 31/3521442).
➤ SOUTH AFRICA: (✉ Alpenstr. 29, Bern, ☎ 031/3501313).
➤ UNITED KINGDOM: (✉ Thunstr. 50, Bern, ☎ 031/3525021).
➤ UNITED STATES: (✉ Jubiläumsstr. 93, Bern, ☎ 031/3577011).

HOLIDAYS
New Year's (January 1–2); Good Friday; Easter Sunday and Monday;
Ascension; Whitsunday, Pentecost; National Day (August 1); Christmas (December 25–26). Note that May 1 (Labor Day) is celebrated in
most cantons, but not all.

LANGUAGE
French is spoken in the southwest, around Lake Geneva (Lac Léman),
and in the cantons of Fribourg, Neuchâtel, Jura, Vaud, and the western portion of Valais; Italian is spoken in the Ticino; and German is
spoken everywhere else—in more than 70% of the country, in fact. (Keep
in mind that the Swiss versions of these languages can sound very different from those spoken in France, Italy, and Germany.) The Ro-
mance language called Romansh has regained a firm foothold throughout
the Upper and Lower Engadine regions of the canton Graubünden, where
it takes the form of five different dialects. English, however, is spoken
widely. Many signs are in English as well as in the regional language,
and all hotels, restaurants, tourist offices, train stations, banks, and
shops have at least a few English-speaking employees.

MONEY MATTERS
Switzerland's high standard of living is reflected in its prices. You'll
pay more for luxury here than in almost any other European country.
Though annual inflation has been less than 2% for years, and the dollar has regained its strength against the Swiss franc, Switzerland's ex-
orbitant cost of living makes travel noticeably expensive. You'll find
plenty of reasonably priced digs and eats, however, if you look for them.

Zürich and Geneva are Switzerland's priciest cities, followed by Basel,
Bern, and Lugano. Price tags at resorts—especially the better-known

Alpine ski centers—rival those in the cities. Off the beaten track and in the northeast prices drop considerably.

Some sample prices (may be more at top resorts) include: cup of coffee, 3 SF; bottle of beer, 3.50 SF; soft drink, 3.50 SF; sausage and Rösti, 16 SF; 2-km (1-mi) taxi ride, 12 SF (more in Geneva, Lugano, Zürich).

CREDIT CARDS
Most major credit cards are generally, though not universally, accepted at hotels, restaurants, and shops. Traveler's checks are almost never accepted outside banks and railroad station change counters.

CURRENCY
The unit of currency is the Swiss franc (SF), divided into 100 centimes (in Suisse Romande) or rappen (in German Switzerland). There are coins of 5, 10, 20, and 50 rappen/centimes and of 1, 2, and 5 francs. Bills come in denominations of 10, 20, 50, 100, 200, and 1,000 francs. At press time (summer 2001), the Swiss franc stood at 1.65 SF to the U.S. dollar, 1.10 SF to the Canadian dollar, 2.40 SF to the pound sterling, 1.95 SF to the Irish punt, 0.89 SF to the Australian dollar, 0.73 SF to the New Zealand dollar, and 0.21 SF to the South African rand.

TELEPHONES
COUNTRY AND AREA CODES
The country code for Switzerland and Liechtenstein is 41. When dialing Switzerland from outside the country, drop the initial zero from the area code.

INTERNATIONAL CALLS
To dial international numbers directly from Switzerland, dial 00 before the country's code. If a number cannot be reached directly, dial 1141 for a connection. Dial 1159 for international numbers and information. International access codes for the major telephone companies will put you directly in touch with an operator who will place your call. Calls to the United States and Canada cost 0.12 SF per minute; calls to the United Kingdom, Australia, and New Zealand cost 0.25 SF per minute. International telephone rates are lower on weekends.
➤ ACCESS CODES: **AT&T** (☎ 0848/804343). **MCI Worldcom** (☎ 01/5808011). **Sprint** (☎ 155/9777).

PUBLIC PHONES
Calls from booths are far cheaper than those made from hotels. A phone card, available in 5 SF, 10 SF, and 20 SF units at the post office, kiosk, or train station, allows you to call from any adapted public phone. Note that very few public phones accept coins.

INDEX

Icons and Symbols

★ Our special recommendations

✕ Restaurant

🏨 Lodging establishment

✕🏨 Lodging establishment whose restaurant warrants a special trip

🦆 Good for kids (rubber duck)

☞ Sends you to another section of the guide for more information

✉ Address

☎ Telephone number

🕐 Opening and closing times

💵 Admission prices

Numbers in white and black circles ③ ❸ that appear on the maps, in the margins, and within the tours correspond to one another.

NOTES

NOTES